Bears' Guide to Earning Degrees by Distance Learning

14TH EDITION

John Bear, Ph.D.
Mariah Bear, M.A.

Additional writing and research by
Tom C. Head, M.A.

Ten Speed Press
Berkeley Toronto

Other Degree.net books:
Bears' Guide to the Best Computer Degrees by Distance Learning
Bears' Guide to the Best MBAs by Distance Learning
College Degrees by Mail and Internet

Degree.net
A division of Ten Speed Press
P.O. Box 7123
Berkeley, CA 94707
www.degree.net

Distributed in Australia by Simon & Schuster, in Canada by Ten Speed Press Canada, in New Zealand by Southern Publishers Group, in South Africa by Real Books, in Southeast Asia by Berkeley Books, and in the United Kingdom by Airlift Books.

Cover design by Cale Burr
Text design by Jeff Brandenburg, ImageComp

Disclaimer:
While the authors believe that the information in this book is correct as of the time of publication, it is possible we may have made errors, which we will correct at the first available opportunity. We, the publisher, are not responsible for any problems that may arise in readers' interactions with any schools described in the book.

Library of Congress Cataloging-in-Publication Data on file with publisher.

First printing this edition, 2001
Printed in Canada

2 3 4 5 6 7 8 9 10 — 05 04 03 02 01

Contents

Dedications

Mariah's

To Joe,
the best darn husband commercially available

John's

To Marina,
for the fourteenth consecutive time, with undiminished love,
thanks, and gratitude for all you have done

Acknowledgments

We do not have a staff. We do not have platoons of graduate students whom we can send to the library to do research for us. Like Blanche Dubois, we are dependent upon the kindness of strangers: those many hundreds of readers who regularly write, fax, and email to tell us of errors, changes, new schools, and new programs in old schools. Thank you, one and all.

For this 14th edition, we begin with very special thanks to our editor at Ten Speed Press/Degree.net Books, Justin Wells, for his splendid editing, writing, and research skills. Also in the Ten Speed orbit, we are grateful to Jeff Brandenburg for the internal design, Cale Burr for another fine cover, Katalin Galasi for research help, and Tom Southern for all-around support.

We have benefited greatly from the help of the group charmingly known as the Gang of Six. A diploma mill operator used to complain, on the Internet, about the "Gang of Six," six people who regularly pointed fingers at his illegal activities. We adopted the nomenclature for ourselves, and over the years, the "gang" has expanded to these helpful people, who regularly share information and opinions on the world of distance learning: Russ Blahetka, George Brown, Rich Douglas, Tom Head, Bill Gossett, Dennis Huber, Larry McQueary, Joseph Wang, Jonathan Whatley, and Chip White; member emeritus Steve Levicoff; and member-in-waiting Bill Sloane.

Finally, for reasons too complex to explain, we offer thanks to Freaky Tah.

About the Authors:
Their Lives, Their Biases, and a Request for Help

This book was once called *Bear's Guide*. A few years ago, the apostrophe moved one notch to the right. No longer *Bear's Guide*, it is now *Bears' Guide*, signifying more than one Bear involved. Here is some of the background of the two Bears who produced this 14th edition.

John Bear attended school at a time when nontraditional education was virtually nonexistent in the United States. Still, he was able to create his own alternative program within the traditional framework. He started working full-time during his junior year at Reed College, and continued to hold a variety of demanding off-campus jobs while earning his bachelor's and master's from Berkeley and Ph.D. from Michigan State University. He was generally able to integrate these jobs—which included working as a newspaper reporter, prison psychologist, advertising writer, and researcher at a school for the deaf—into his academic studies, but received little support or encouragement from faculty or administration.

Dr. Bear has taught at major universities (Iowa, Berkeley, Michigan State) and small schools (City College of San Francisco, College of the Redwoods), and been a business executive (research director for Bell & Howell's educational division, director of communications for the Midas Muffler Shop chain), director of the Center for the Gifted Child in San Francisco, and consultant to a wide range of organizations, including General Motors, Xerox, *Encyclopaedia Britannica*, and the Grateful Dead. Since 1974, he has devoted much of his time to investigating and writing about nontraditional higher education.

In 1977, he established Degree Consulting Services, to offer detailed consulting to people seeking more personal advice than a book can provide. While he no longer counsels individual clients, the service is still available (see Appendix C for further information).

John's daughter Mariah can honestly claim a lifelong involvement with nontraditional education, beginning around the age of seven when she earned allowance money working in her father's office. She took six years to get her bachelor's degree at Berkeley (Phi Beta Kappa), scheduling classes around a flex-time job with a major book publisher. (Well-intentioned admissions counselors discourage this sort of thing; they often seem to feel a challenging job is incompatible with academic success.) In graduate school, Mariah managed to schedule all but one of her required classes in the evenings, allowing her to freelance at *New York* magazine, the *Village Voice,* and other publications while earning a master's in journalism

from New York University. She is now executive editor at Lonely Planet Books, but still puts in a fair amount of time with *Bears' Guide.*

The rest of the family pursued similarly nontraditional paths to higher education. Twenty years after completing her traditional B.A., Marina (wife of John, mother of Mariah) earned the nonresident M.A. in humanities at California State University-Dominguez Hills, followed by a Ph.D. at Vanderbilt University. The other two children, twin daughters, both left high school at age 15, midway through tenth grade, and passed the state high school equivalency exam. Susannah went on to college at that early age; Tanya worked for three years, then entered college at the "traditional" age of 18.

Biases

As you read this book, you will note that it is biased. The authors have strong opinions about which schools and programs are good and which are not, and do not hesitate to say so. John has been sued three times for millions of dollars by people who operate what he called (and continues to call) illegal diploma mills. None has ever won a cent. While the research and experiences are largely John's, the opinions are shared by both authors.

Over the years, John has done consulting or advisory work for various schools in return for money, goods (generally the use of their mailing lists to help sell this book), and, in two cases, stock:

▶ In return for consulting work in the mid-1970s, Columbia Pacific University paid him with a small amount of its stock, which he sold nearly 20 years ago.

▶ Bear was one of four founders of Fairfax University, a not-for-profit nontraditional school. Once it was launched, he resigned, and had no further connection whatsoever.

▶ In 1987, eager to experience nontraditional education from the other side of the desk, as it were, he accepted the presidency of the International Institute for Advanced Studies, a small, older (in this field, being founded in 1972 makes one a true pioneer) nonprofit school. That school evolved into Greenwich University, where he served as full-time president in Hawaii for 18 months in 1990–1991.

► In 1991, John's company, IBE, Inc., was appointed the U.S. agents for the Heriot-Watt University (Edinburgh, Scotland) Distance Learning MBA, and a few years later, for the M.S. in training & human resource management of Leicester University, England. In 1998, the assets of IBE (including the copyright to this book) were purchased by Pearson PLC, a large British publisher (Penguin, Prentice Hall, Financial Times, etc.). Pearson subsequently decided *Bears' Guide* did not fit their plans after all, and sold the copyrights to Ten Speed Press, which had been the publisher of the 7th through 11th editions, and now, happily, is again for the 14th.

We are confident that these activities have had, and will continue to have, no bearing on the opinions expressed in this book. Hundreds of excellent schools have never even taken us to lunch, yet we recommend them highly. (We will probably accept if they ever do offer lunch.) On the other side of the ledger, there is no way in the world we can be persuaded to say good things about bad, or questionable, schools. While individual evaluations may change (schools do get better or worse, new information comes to light), the basic judgment criteria are not subject to outside influence. And contrary to what some operators of sleazy schools have claimed, no one has ever paid a cent to be listed in this book. (We were intrigued when, in mid-2000, three other publishers of school guides admitted that they did take paid listings, not identified as such, sometimes to the tune of several million dollars worth in a single edition. As Jack Benny used to say at such times, "Hmmmmmmmmmmmmm.")

Help

Over the years, readers have provided great amounts of immensely valuable feedback. If you are aware of schools or programs we have overlooked, please let us know. If your experience with a school is at odds with what we've written, please don't hesitate to tell us about it. This book may be biased, but the authors like to think they are open-minded, and many schools' evaluations have changed (both up and down) in the past quarter century. Please communicate in writing or by email, and if you'd like a reply (we can't guarantee it, but we'll do our best), please enclose a stamped self-addressed envelope or, outside the U.S., two international reply coupons, available at your post office. Our email address is *johnandmariah@degree.net*, and our postal address is *Bears' Guide*, P.O. Box 7123, Berkeley, CA 94707, U.S.A.

Thank you.

www.degree.net

Complementing our distance-learning books is our distance-learning Web site at *www.degree.net*. The Internet allows us to provide more timely coverage of nontraditional education than we're able to do in our books. On our site you'll find the latest distance-learning news and gossip, links to our favorite online resources, and bulletin boards for sharing questions and tips with the authors and other experts in the field. We're devoting a special page—*www.degree.net/updates/bearsguide14*—for posting updates and corrections to this book. Consider it the last chapter, an always up-to-date electronic appendix, of the 14th edition of *Bears' Guide*.

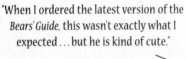

"When I ordered the latest version of the *Bears' Guide*, this wasn't exactly what I expected ... but he is kind of cute."

"Mmmm, so is she."

CHAPTER 1

What Nontraditional Education Is All About

In times of great change, learners inherit the earth, while the learned find themselves beautifully equipped for a world that no longer exists.

Michael Porter

The man on the telephone was so distraught, he was almost in tears. For more than 20 years, he had been in charge of sawing off dead tree branches for a large Midwestern city. But a new personnel policy in that city decreed that henceforth, all department heads would have to have bachelor's degrees. If this man could not earn a degree within two years, he would no longer be permitted to continue in the job he had been performing satisfactorily for over two decades.

It is an unfortunate but very real aspect of life today that a college or university degree is often more important (or at least more useful) than a good education or substantial knowledge in your field, whether that field involves nuclear physics or sawing off branches. It doesn't matter if you've been reading, studying, and learning all your life. It doesn't matter how good you are at what you do. In many situations, if you don't have a piece of (usually imitation) parchment that certifies you as a bachelor, master, or doctor, you are perceived as somehow less worthy, and are often denied the better jobs and higher salaries that go to degree holders.

In fact, as more and more degree holders, from space scientists to philosophers, are unable to find employment in their specific chosen fields and move elsewhere in the job market, degrees become more important than ever. Consider a job opening for a high school English teacher. Five applicants with comparable skills apply, but one has a doctorate while the other four have bachelor's degrees. Who do you think would probably get the job?

Never mind that you don't need a Ph.D. to teach high school English any more than you need a B.A. to chop down trees. The simple fact is that degrees are extremely valuable commodities in the job market.

Happily, as the need for degrees increases, availability has kept pace. Since the mid 1970s, there has been a virtual explosion in what is now commonly called "alternative" or "nontraditional" and "external" or "off-campus" education—ways and means of getting an education or a degree (or both, if you wish) without sitting in classrooms day after day, year after year.

The rallying cry was, in fact, sounded in 1973 by Ewald B. Nyquist, then president of the wonderfully innovative University of the State of New York (now called Excelsior College). He said:

There are thousands of people ... who contribute in important ways to the life of the communities in which they live, even though they do not have a college degree. Through native intelligence, hard work ,and sacrifice, many have gained in knowledge and understanding. And yet, the social and economic advancement of these people has been thwarted in part by the emphasis that is put on the possession of credentials ... As long as we remain a strongly credentialed society ... employers will not be disposed to hire people on the basis of what they know, rather than on what degrees and diplomas they hold. If attendance at a college is the only road to these credentials, those who cannot or have not availed themselves of this route but have acquired knowledge and skills through other sources will be denied the recognition and advancement to which they are entitled. Such inequity should not be tolerated.

Nontraditional education takes many forms, including the following:

► credit (and degrees) for life-experience learning, even if the learning took place before you entered school;

► credit (and degrees) for passing examinations;

► credit (and degrees) for independent study, even when not enrolled in a school at the time it was done;

► credit (and degrees) through intensive study (for instance, 10 hours a day for a month instead of one hour a day for a year);

► credit (and degrees) through guided private study at your own pace, from your own home or office, under the supervision of a faculty member with whom you communicate on a regular basis;

► credit (and degrees) for work done on your home or office computer, linked to your school's computer, wherever in the world it may be;

► credit (and degrees) from weekend schools, evening schools, and summer-only schools;

► credit (and degrees) entirely by correspondence;

► credit (and degrees) through the use of audio- and videotaped courses reviewed at your convenience.

This book endeavors to cover all these areas, and more, as completely as possible. Yet this is truly an impossible task. New programs are introduced literally every day. In recent years, an average of one new college or university has opened for business every week, while old, established universities are disappearing at the rate of two or three per month.

So, although this book is as current and correct as we can possibly make it, some recent changes probably won't be covered, and, inevitably, there will be errors and omissions. For all of these, we apologize now, and invite your suggestions and criticisms for the next edition. Thank you. Perhaps the best way to make clear, in a short space, the differences between the traditional (dare one say old-fashioned) approaches to education and degrees and the nontraditional (or modern) approach is to offer the following dozen comparisons:

Traditional education awards degrees on the basis of time served and credit earned.

Nontraditional education awards degrees on the basis of competencies and performance skills.

Traditional education bases degree requirements on a medieval formula that calls for some generalized education and some specialized education.

Nontraditional education bases degree requirements on an agreement between the student and the faculty, aimed at helping the student achieve his or her career, personal, or professional goals.

Traditional education awards the degree when the student has taken the required number of credits in the required order.

Nontraditional education awards the degree when the student's actual work and learning reach certain previously agreed-upon levels.

Traditional education considers the years from age 18 to age 22 the appropriate time to earn a first degree.

Nontraditional education assumes learning is desirable at any age, and that degrees should be available to people of all ages.

Traditional education considers the classroom to be the primary source of information and the campus the center of learning.

Nontraditional education believes that some sort of learning can and does occur in any part of the world.

Traditional education believes that printed texts should be the principal learning resource.

Nontraditional education believes the range of learning resources is limitless, from the daily newspaper to personal interviews, from videotapes to computers to world travel.

Traditional faculty must have appropriate credentials and degrees.

Nontraditional faculty are selected for competency and personal qualities in *addition* to credentials and degrees.

Traditional credits and degrees are based primarily on mastery of course content.

Nontraditional credits and degrees add a consideration of learning *how to learn*, and the integration of diverse fields of knowledge.

Traditional education cultivates dependence on authority through prescribed curricula, required campus residence, and required classes.

Nontraditional education cultivates self-direction and independence through planned independent study, both on and off campus.

Traditional curricula are generally oriented toward traditional disciplines and well-established professions.

Nontraditional curricula reflect a range of individual students' needs and goals, and are likely to be problem-oriented, issue-oriented, and world-oriented.

Traditional education aims at producing "finished products"—students who are done with their education and ready for the job market.

Nontraditional education aims at producing lifelong learners, capable of responding to their own evolving needs and those of society over an entire lifetime.

Traditional education, to adapt the old saying, gives you a fish and feeds you for a day.

Nontraditional education teaches you how to fish, and feeds you for life.

Traditional education had nothing to offer the dead-tree-limb expert.

Nontraditional education made it possible for him to complete a good bachelor's degree in less than a year, entirely by correspondence and at a modest cost. His job is now secure.

CHAPTER 2

What Are Colleges and Universities, and How Do They Work?

A college is a machine that transfers information from the notes of the professor to the notes of the student without it passing through the mind of either.

Traditional

The question posed by this chapter's title may sound trivial or inconsequential, but it turns out to be quite a complex issue-one for which there is no simple answer at all.

Many state legislatures have struggled with the problem of producing precise definitions of words like "college" and "university." (One school even tried to sue its state's department of education to force them to define "educational process." The state managed to evade the suit.)

Some states have simply given up the problem as unsolvable, which is why they either have virtually no laws governing higher education, or laws that are incredibly restrictive. Needless to say, the former policy encourages the proliferation of degree mills and other bad schools, and the latter policy discourages the establishment of any creative new nontraditional schools or programs.

Other states have, from time to time, produced rather ingenious definitions, such as Ohio's (later repealed), stating that a "university" was anything that (a) said it was a university and (b) had an endowment or facilities worth $1 million. The assumption, of course, was that no degree mill could be so well endowed. California once had a similar law under which the sum was only $50,000. In the 1980s, much tougher requirements were instituted and California soon lost its title as place to go to open an unaccredited (and often dreadful) university, first to Arizona, then Louisiana, then to Hawaii, and, most recently, South Dakota.

Many people remember a famous CBS *60 Minutes* episode in 1978 (rerun many times since), in which the proprietor of a flagrant diploma mill was actually arrested while being interviewed by Mike Wallace. At the time, his school, California Pacifica University, was licensed by the state of California. The owner had bought some used books and office furniture, declared this property to be worth $50,000, and consequently received state authorization to grant degrees, up to and including doctorates.

History repeated itself in 1990 when the proprietor of yet another degree mill, North American University, was enjoined from operating by the state of Utah on the very day that *Inside Edition*'s television crew arrived to film his nefarious operation.

The problem of definition is made even more complicated by the inconsistent way in which the words "college" and "university" are used.

In the United States, the two words are used almost interchangeably. Before long, they will probably mean exactly the same thing. Historically, a college has been a subdivision of a university. For instance, the University of California is divided into a College of Arts and Sciences, a College of Education, a College of Law, and so on. The University of Oxford is comprised of Balliol College, Exeter College, Magdalen College, and about three dozen others.

Today, however, many degree-granting colleges exist independent of any university, and many universities have no colleges. There is also an ever growing trend for colleges to rename themselves as universities, either to reflect their growth or enhance their image, or both. In recent years, dozens of colleges, from Antioch in Ohio to San Francisco State in California, have turned themselves into universities. While many British traditionalists sneered at the U.S. for doing this, the same thing happened in the United Kingdom in the early and mid 1990s: dozens of technical schools, colleges, and institutes became universities overnight, at least in name.

The situation outside the United States makes all this even more complex. In most countries, the word "college" rarely refers to a degree-granting institution and often is used for what Americans call a high school. American personnel managers and admissions officers have been fooled by this fact. An Englishman, for instance, who states on his job application, "Graduate of Eton College," means, simply, that he has completed the high school of that name.

Many readers have told us that they simply will not go to a "college," no matter how good it may be, because the word just doesn't sound real enough to them.

Finally, some degree-granting institutions choose a name other than "college" or "university." The most common are "school" (e.g., the New School for Social Research; California School of Professional Psychology, etc.) and "institute" (e.g., Fielding Institute, Union Institute, etc.).

How Colleges and Universities Work

The Calendar

In some countries, "calendar" refers to the school's catalogue or prospectus; in others, it refers to the scheduling of classes (which is the meaning we use here). There is no uniform pattern in calendars from one school to the next. However, most schools tend to follow one of four basic patterns:

1. **The semester plan.** A semester is 16 to 18 weeks long and there are usually two semesters per year, plus a shorter summer session. Many classes are one semester long, but some extend over two or more semesters (e.g., Algebra I in the fall semester and Algebra II in the spring). A class that meets three hours a week for one semester is likely to be worth 3 semester hours of credit. The *actual* amount of credit could be anywhere from 2 to 6 semester hours for such a class, depending on the amount of homework, additional reading, laboratory time, etc.

2. **The quarter plan.** Many universities divide the year into four quarters of equal length, usually 11 or 12 weeks each. Many courses require two or more quarters to complete. A course that meets three hours a week for a quarter will probably be worth three quarter hours, or quarter units, but can range from two to six. One semester unit is equal to one-and-a-half quarter units.

3. **The trimester plan.** A much smaller number of schools divide the year into three equal trimesters of 15 or 16 weeks each. A trimester unit is usually equal to one-and-a-quarter semester units.

4. **Weekend colleges.** This innovative and increasingly common system allows schools to make more efficient use of their facilities and helps working students to earn a conventional degree. All courses are taught intensively on Friday nights, Saturdays, and/or Sundays.

Hundreds of traditional residential schools in the U.S. offer some weekend programs, many of which are listed in chapters 20 and 23. For additional programs in your area, check with nearby community colleges, colleges, and universities.

Other alternatives: National University, University of Phoenix, and other relatively new schools have popularized a system in which students take one course per month and can begin their degree program on the first day of any month.

Many nonresident programs have no calendar at all. Students can begin their independent study as soon as they have been admitted.

How Credit Is Earned

In a traditional school, most credit is earned by taking classes. Nontraditional units may be earned in other ways. There are four common methods (all of which will be discussed in some detail in later chapters):

1. **Life experience learning.** Credit is given for what you have learned, regardless of how or where it was learned. For example, a given university might offer six courses in German worth 4 semester units each. If you can show them that you speak and write German just as well as someone who has taken and passed those six courses, they will award you 24 semester units of German, whether you learned the language from your grandmother, from living in Germany, or from Berlitz tapes. The same philosophy applies to business experience, learning to fly an airplane, military training, and dozens of other nonclassroom learning experiences.

2. **Equivalency examinations.** Many schools say that anyone who can pass an examination in a subject should get credit for knowing that subject, without having to sit in a classroom month after month to "learn" what they already know. More than 100 standard equivalency exams are offered, worth anywhere from 2 to 30 semester units each. In general, each hour of examination is worth from 2 to 6 semester units, but different schools may award significantly different amounts of credit for the same examinations. Some schools will design their own written or oral examinations in fields for which there are no standard exams.

3. **Correspondence courses.** Several hundred universities offer thousands of home-study courses, most of which can be taken by people living anywhere in the world. These courses are generally worth 2 to 6 semester units each and can take anywhere from a month or two to a year or more to complete.

4. **Learning contracts.** Quite a few schools negotiate learning contracts with their students. A learning contract is a formal, negotiated agreement between the student and the school, stating that if the student successfully completes certain tasks (for instance, reads these books, writes a paper of this length, does the following laboratory experiments, etc.), the school will

"Oh, no, not again, Louella. That's what you said after Anthro 101 and look where it got us. You have little Augustus, and I am relegated to teaching online students in rural Wyoming."

"Professor Halberstadt, if you'll only reconsider and give me a passing grade in Anthro 102, I'll do anything. Anything."

award an agreed-upon number of credits. Learning contracts can be written for a few units, an entire degree program, or anything in between. Often the school will provide a faculty member to guide the course of study.

Grading and Evaluation Systems

Most schools, traditional and nontraditional, use one of four common grading systems. Grades are generally given for each separate course taken. Some schools assign grades to equivalency examinations, learning-contract work, and correspondence courses as well. Life-experience credit is rarely graded; schools usually assign it a certain number of units without further evaluation. The four common systems are:

1. **Letter grades.** An "A" is the highest grade, "B" means "good," "C" means "average," "D" stands for "barely passing" (or, in some cases, "failing"), and "F" is a failing grade. ("E" is rarely used.) Some schools add pluses and minuses—a B+ is better than a B, but not quite as good as an A-. Some schools use "AB" instead of B+ or A-. And some give an "A+" for superior work.

2. **Number grades.** Many schools grade on a scale of 0 (worst grade) to 4 (highest grade). The best students receive grades of 3.9 or 4.0; other outstanding students might get a 3.7 or 3.8. To pass, students usually must score at

least 1.0 (or a 1.5). Just to make it even more confusing, some schools use a 0 to 3 or 0 to 5 scale, but 4 is the most common top grade. A small number of schools give the numerical equivalent of A+, a 4.5, which means that even on a four-point scale, it is possible to have a grade point average higher than four.

3. **Percentage grades.** A smaller number of schools follow the European system of grading each student in each class on a percentage score, from 0 to 100 percent. In most (but not all) schools, a grade of 90 to 100 percent is considered excellent, 80 to 90 is good, 70 to 80 is fair, 60 to 70 is either failure or barely passing, and below 60 percent is failing.

4. **Pass/fail.** Quite a few universities offer a pass/fail option, either for some classes or, more rarely, for all classes. In such a system, the teacher does not evaluate the student's performance beyond stating whether each student has passed or failed the course. At many schools students may choose the pass/fail option for one or two out of the four or five courses they are expected to take each semester or quarter. In some pass/fail situations, a numerical or letter grade is actually given, but not revealed to the student or used to calculate grade point average. And in a few schools, the actual grade will be revealed only if the student asks and, sometimes, pays an additional fee.

Grade Point Average

Most schools report a student's overall performance in terms of the G.P.A., or grade point average. This is the average of all grades received, weighted by the number of semester or quarter units each course is worth.

For example, if a student gets a 4.0 (or an A) in a course worth 3 semester units, and a 3.0 (or a B) in a course worth 2 semester units, his or her G.P.A. would be calculated like this: 3 x 4.0 = 12. And 2 x 3.0 = 6. So, 12 + 6 = 18, divided by a total of 5 semester units, results in a G.P.A. of 3.6.

Pass/fail courses are generally not taken into account when calculating a grade point average.

One's G.P.A. can be very important. Often it is necessary to maintain a certain average in order to earn a degree—typically a 2.0 (in a four-point system) for a bachelor's degree, and a 3.0 for a master's degree or doctorate. Honors degrees (*magna cum laude*, etc.), scholarships, and even permission to play on the football team are dependent on the G.P.A. (No, nonresident schools do not have football teams. Some of us are waiting for a chess-by-mail or computer-game league to spring up, however.)

CHAPTER 3

Degrees, Degree Requirements, and Transcripts

It is not titles that honor men, but men that honor titles.

Niccoló Machiavelli

A degree is a title conferred by a school to show that a certain course of study has been successfully completed. A diploma is the actual document or certificate that is given to the student as evidence that the degree has been awarded.

Diplomas are also awarded for courses of study that do *not* result in a degree such as, for example, on completion of a program in real-estate management, air-conditioning repair, or military leadership. This can lead to confusion, often intentionally, as in the case of someone who says, "I earned my diploma at Harvard," meaning that he or she attended a weekend seminar there, and received some sort of diploma of completion.

The following six kinds of degrees are awarded by colleges and universities in the United States:

The Associate's Degree

The associate's degree is a relatively recent development, reflecting the tremendous growth of two-year community colleges (which is the new and presumably more respectable name for what used to be known as junior colleges).

Since many of the students who attend these schools do not continue on to another school to complete a bachelor's degree, a need was felt for a degree to be awarded at the end of these two years of full-time study (or their equivalent by nontraditional means). More than 2,000 two-year schools now award the associate's degree, and a small but growing number of four-year schools award it to students who leave after two years.

The two most common associate's degrees are the A.A. (Associate of Arts) and the A.S. (Associate of Science), but more than 100 other titles have been devised, rang-

ing from the A.M.E. (Associate of Mechanical Engineering) to the A.D.T. (Associate of Dance Therapy).

An associate's degree typically requires 60 to 64 semester hours of credit (or 90 to 96 quarter hours), which, in a traditional program, normally takes two academic years (four semesters, or six quarters) to complete.

The Bachelor's Degree

The bachelor's degree has been around for hundreds of years. In virtually every nation worldwide, it is the first university degree earned. (The associate's is little used outside the United States.) In America, the bachelor's is traditionally considered to be a four-year degree (120 to 128 semester units, or 180 to 192 quarter units, of full-time study), although a rather surprising report in 1990 revealed that the average bachelor's takes closer to six years. In most of the rest of the world, it is expected to take three years. Through nontraditional approaches, some people with a good deal of prior learning and/or skill at taking examinations can earn their bachelor's degrees in as little six months.

The bachelor's degree is supposed to signify that the holder has accumulated a "batch" of knowledge; that he or she has learned a considerable amount in a particular field of study (the "major") and gained some broad general knowledge of the world as well (history, literature, art, social science, mathematics). This broad approach to the degree is peculiar to traditional American programs. In most other countries, and in nontraditional American programs, the bachelor's degree involves much more intensive study in a given field. When someone educated in England says, "I read history at Oxford," it means that for the better part of three years he or she did, in fact, read history and not much else. This is one reason traditional American degrees take longer to acquire than most foreign ones.

More than 300 different bachelor's degree titles have been used in the last hundred years, but the great majority of the million-plus bachelor's degrees awarded in the United States each year are either the B.A. (Bachelor of Arts) or the B.S. (Bachelor of Science), sometimes with additional letters to indicate the field (B.S.E.E. for electrical engineering, B.A.B.A. for business administration, and so on). Other common bachelor's degree titles include the B.B.A. (Bachelor of Business Administration), B.Mus. (Music), B.Ed. (Education), and B.Eng. (Engineering). Some nontraditional schools and programs award the B.G.S. (Bachelor of General Studies), B.I.S. (Independent Studies), or B.L.S. (Liberal Studies).

In the late 19th century, educators felt that the title of "Bachelor" was inappropriate for young ladies, so some schools awarded female graduates titles such as Mistress of Arts or Maid of Science.

The Master's Degree

Until the 20th century, the "Master" and "Doctor" titles were used somewhat interchangeably, and considered appropriate for anyone who had completed work of significance beyond the bachelor's degree. Today, however, the master's is almost always the first degree earned after the bachelor's, and is always considered to be a lower degree than the doctorate.

The traditional master's degree requires from one to two years of on-campus work after the bachelor's. Some nontraditional master's degrees may be earned entirely through nonresident study, while others require anywhere from a few days to a few weeks on campus.

There are several philosophical approaches to the master's degree. Some schools (or departments within schools) regard it as a sort of advanced bachelor's, requiring only the completion of one to two years of advanced-level studies and courses. Others see it as more of a junior doctorate, requiring at least *some* creative, original research, culminating in the writing of a thesis, or original research paper. Some programs let students choose their approach, requiring, for example, either 10 courses and a thesis or 13 courses with no thesis.

And in a few world-famous schools, including Oxford and Cambridge, the master's degree is an almost meaningless award, given automatically to all holders of the school's bachelor's degree who have managed, as the saying goes, to stay out of jail for four years, and can afford the small fee. (Most American schools had a similar practice at one time, but Harvard abolished it more than a century ago and the rest followed suit soon after. However, some Ivy League schools—Harvard, Yale, etc.—do maintain the quaint practice of awarding a master's degree to new professors who do not happen to have a degree from that school, even if they have a doctorate from one of equal renown. It is a sort of housewarming gift, so that all senior faculty will have at least one degree from the school at which they are teaching.)

Master's degree titles are very similar to bachelor's—the M.A. (Master of Arts) and M.S. (Master of Science) are by far the most common, along with that staple of American business, the M.B.A. (Master of Business Administration). Other common master's degrees include the M.Ed., M.Eng., M.L.S. (Library Science), and M.J. (either Journalism or Jurisprudence).

The Doctorate

The term "Doctor" has been a title of respect for a learned person since biblical times. Moses, in Deuteronomy 31:28 (Douay version), says, "Gather unto me all the ancients of your tribes and your doctors, and I will speak these words in their hearing."

About 800 years ago, in the mid 12th century, outstanding scholars at the University of Bologna and the University of Paris began to be called either "Doctor" or "Professor," the first recorded academic use of the term.

The first American use came in the late 17th century, under, as the story has it, rather amusing circumstances. There had long been a tradition (and, to a large extent, there still is) that "it takes a Doctor to make a Doctor." In other words, only a person with a doctorate can confer a doctorate on someone else.

But in all of America, no one had a doctorate, least of all Harvard's president, Increase Mather, who, as a Dissenter, was ineligible for a doctorate from any English university, all of which were controlled by the Church.

Still, Harvard was eager to get into the doctorate business, so their entire faculty (that is to say, a Mr. Leverett and a Mr. Brattle) got together and unanimously agreed to award an honorary doctorate to Mr. Mather, whereupon Mather was then able to confer doctorates upon his faculty who, subsequently, were able to doctor their students.

This, in essence, was the start of graduate education in America, and there are those who say things have gone downhill ever since.

America's next doctorate, incidentally, was also awarded under rather odd circumstances. In this case, a British physician named Daniel Turner was eager to get into the Royal Society of Physicians and Surgeons, but needed an M.D. to do so. In England, then as now, most doctors have a *Bachelor* of Medicine; the *Doctor* of Medicine is an advanced degree. No English university would give Turner a doctorate because he did not belong to the Church of England. Scottish universities turned him down because he had published some unkind remarks about the quality of Scottish education. And of course no European university would give a degree to an Englishman. So Mr. Turner made a deal with Yale University.

Yale agreed to award Turner the doctorate in absentia (he never set foot in America), and he, in turn, gave Yale a gift of 50 valuable medical books. Wags at the time remarked that the M.D. he got must stand for the Latin *multum donavit*, "he gave a lot."

Nowadays the academic title of "Doctor" (as distinguished from the professional and honorary titles, to be discussed shortly) has come to be awarded for completion of an advanced course of study, culminating in a piece of original research in one's field, known as the doctoral thesis or dissertation.

While traditional doctorates used to require at least two years of on-campus study after the master's degree, followed by a period of dissertation research and writing, the trend lately has been to require little more than the dissertation. More and more schools are letting people without a master's into their doctoral programs, and awarding the master's along the way, on completion of the coursework (and any qualifying exams). The total elapsed time can be anywhere from three years on up. Indeed, the trend in the 1980s and '90s has been for doctorates to take longer and longer. In his splendid book, *Winning the Ph.D. Game*, Richard Moore offers evidence that a typical Ph.D. now takes six or seven years, with a range from three to ten (not all of it necessarily spent in residence on campus, however).

Many nontraditional doctoral programs waive the on-campus study, on the assumption that a mature candidate already knows a great deal about his or her field. Such programs require little or no coursework, focusing instead on the dissertation, with the emphasis on demonstrating creativity.

Some nontraditional doctoral programs permit the use of work already done (books written, symphonies composed, business plans created, etc.) as partial (or, in a few cases, full) satisfaction of the dissertation requirement. But many schools insist on all, or almost all, new work.

The most frequently awarded (and, many people feel, the most prestigious) doctorate is the Doctor of Philosophy (known as the Ph.D. in North America, and the D.Phil. in many other countries). The Doctor of Philosophy does not necessarily have anything to do with the study of philosophy. It is awarded for studies in dozens of fields, ranging from chemistry to communication, from agriculture to aviation management.

Until well into the 20th century, the Ph.D. was also given as an honorary degree. But in the late 1930s, Gonzaga University in Spokane, Washington, spoiled the whole thing by handing out an honorary Ph.D. to one Harry Lillis "Bing" Crosby, to thank him for donating some equipment to the football team. Crosby made great sport about being a doctor on his popular radio program that week. The academic world rose in distressed anger and that, effectively, was the end of the honorary Ph.D.

More than 500 other types of doctorate have been identified in the English language alone. After the Ph.D., the most common include the Ed.D. (Education), D.B.A. (Business Administration), D.P.A. (Public Administration), D.A. (Art or Administration), Eng.D. (Engineering), Psy.D.

(Psychology), D.Sc. (Science), and D.Hum. (Humanities). The latter two are often, but not always, awarded as honorary degrees in the U.S.; in the rest of the world, they are earned like any other doctorate.

A bachelor's degree is almost always required for admission to a doctoral program, and many traditional schools require a master's as well. However, more and more doctoral programs are admitting otherwise qualified applicants without a master's degree. Most nontraditional programs will accept equivalent career experience in lieu of a master's, and, in rare instances, in lieu of a bachelor's as well.

In the late 1950s, someone submitted what was essentially Eleanor Roosevelt's resumé (changing the name and disguising some of her more obvious remarkable achievements) as part of an application to various doctoral programs. Mrs. Roosevelt had never attended college. All 12 schools turned her down, most suggesting that she reapply after completing a bachelor's and a master's, presumably six to eight years later.

In Europe, but very rarely in America, a so-called "higher doctorate" (typically the D.Litt., Doctor of Letters) is awarded solely on the basis of one's life work, with no further studies required. The great majority of those receiving a D.Litt. already have one doctorate, but it is not essential. In most quarters, the D.Litt. is considered to be an earned, not an honorary, degree, but there are those who disagree.

Finally, it should be mentioned that several American schools, concerned with what one called the "doctoral glut," are reported to be seriously considering instituting a new degree, *higher* than the doctorate, presumably requiring more years of study and a more extensive dissertation. The name "Chancellorate" has been bandied about. Indeed, the prestigious *Chronicle of Higher Education* devoted a major article to this possibility a few years ago. It may well be that holders of a Chancellorate (Ph.C.?) would not appreciably affect the job market, since most of them would be drawing their old age pensions by the time they completed this degree.

Professional Degrees

Professional degrees are earned by people who intend to enter what are often called "the professions"—medicine, dentistry, law, the ministry, and so forth. In the United States, these degrees are almost always earned after completing a bachelor's degree, and almost always carry the title of "Doctor" (e.g., Doctor of Medicine, Doctor of Divinity).

In many other countries, it is common to enter professional school directly from high school, in which case the first professional degree earned is a bachelor's. (For instance, there is the British Bachelor of Medicine, whose holders are invariably called "Doctor," unless they have earned the more advanced Doctor of Medicine degree, in which case they insist on being called "Mister." No one ever said the British were easy to understand.)

One exception in the United States is the D.C. (Doctor of Chiropractic), a program that students used to be able to enter right from high school. It now requires two years of college, but still no bachelor's degree. This may be one reason so many medical doctors look down their noses at chiropractors.

Another exception used to be the law degree which, until the mid 1960s, was an LL.B., or Bachelor of Laws. Many lawyers objected to working three or four years beyond their bachelor's degree simply to end up with yet another bachelor's degree, while optometrists, podiatrists, and others were becoming doctors in the same length of time.

Nowadays, virtually every American law school awards a doctorate as the first law degree, usually the J.D., which stands for either Doctor of Jurisprudence or Juris Doctor.

Almost all law schools offered their graduates with Bachelor of Law degrees the option of turning in their old LL.B. diplomas and, in effect, being retroactively doctored with a J.D. A fair number of lawyers accepted this unprecedented offer, although few actually call themselves "Doctor."

The LL.D., known as both Doctor of Law and Doctor of Laws, is now used almost exclusively as an honorary title in the U.S.; elsewhere in the world, it is an earned, advanced law degree.

The traditional law degree requires three years of study beyond the bachelor's degree. Some nontraditional approaches will be discussed in chapter 25.

The most widely accepted medical degree in America is the M.D. (Doctor of Medicine), which requires four years of study beyond the bachelor's degree, although some shorter approaches, and some alternative ones, will be discussed in chapter 26.

A number of other medical or health specialties have their own professional doctorates. These include, for instance, D.O. (Osteopathy), D.P. (Podiatry), and O.D. (Optometry).

There are no accelerated approaches to the dental degree, and few of us would really want to go to a dentist who had taken shortcuts. The traditional dental degree for many years has been the D.D.S. (Doctor of Dental Surgery), although there has recently been a strong trend toward the D.M.D. (Doctor of Medical Dentistry). Both programs require four years of study beyond the bachelor's degree.

More than 100 different professional degree titles have been awarded in the area of religion. None can be said to be the standard one. They include the S.T.D. (Sacred Theology), D.Min. (Ministry), Th.D. (Theology), D.D. (Divinity), D.Rel. (Religion), D.R.E. (Religious Education), D.S.R. (Science of Religion), and so forth, as well as the Ph.D. in religion.

The American Educational System, illustrated by Ms. Fannie Flange.

The Canadian mathematician and humorist Stephen Leacock writes that shortly after he received his Ph.D., he was on board a cruise ship. When a lovely young lady fainted, the call went out, "Is there a doctor on board?" Leacock says he rushed to the captain's cabin, but he was too late. Two D.D.'s and an S.T.D. had gotten there before him.

Quite a few other degrees are deemed honest professional titles by those who hold them, but are regarded with vigorously raised eyebrows by many others. These include the N.D. (Naturopathy, Naprapathy, or Napropathy), D.Hyp. (Hypnotism), H.M.D. or M.D.(H.) (Homeopathic Medicine), D.M.S. (Military Science), Met.D. (Metaphysics), Graph.D. (Graphoanalysis), and so forth.

Honorary Degrees

The honorary degree is truly the stepchild of the academic world, and a most curious one at that. In fact, it is a reflection of academic achievement to the same degree that former basketball star Doctor J's title reflected his medical skills. It is simply a title that some institutions (and some scoundrels) have chosen to bestow, from time to time, and for a wide variety of reasons, upon certain people. These reasons often have to do with the donation of money or with attracting celebrities to a commencement ceremony.

The honorary doctorate has no academic standing whatsoever, and yet, because it carries the same title, "Doctor," as the earned degree, it has become an extremely desirable commodity for those who covet titles and the prestige they bring. For respectable universities to award the title of "Doctor" via an honorary doctorate is as peculiar as if the Army awarded civilians the honorary title of "General"—a title the civilians could then use in their everyday life.

More than 1,000 traditional colleges and universities award honorary doctorates (anywhere from 1 to 50 per year each), and a great many Bible schools, spurious schools, and degree mills hand them out with wild abandon to almost anyone willing to pay the price. The situation is discussed in detail in chapter 28.

Transcripts

A transcript is, quite simply, an official record of all the work one has done at a given university. While the diploma is the piece of paper (or parchment) that shows that a given degree has been earned, the transcript is the detailed description of all the work done to earn that degree.

The traditional transcript is a computer printout listing all the courses taken, when they were taken, and the grade received. The overall G.P.A. (grade point average) is calculated as of the end of each semester or quarter.

Nearly all nontraditional schools and programs issue transcripts as well. Sometimes they try to make the transcripts look as traditional as possible, listing, for instance, life-experience learning credit for aviation as "Aviation 100, 4 units," "Aviation 101, 3 units," etc. Other programs offer a *narrative transcript*, which describes the procedures used by the school to evaluate various types of experience.

The original copy of a transcript is always kept by the school. Official copies, bearing an official raised seal or, sometimes, printed on special paper that cannot easily be tampered with, can be made for the student, other schools, or employers, at the student's request.

Unfortunately, there is a great deal of traffic in forged transcripts. Students have been known to change a few grades to improve the G.P.A., or even add entire classes. Of course such changes would normally only affect the copy, which is why most schools and many employers will only accept transcripts that are sent directly from the office of the school's registrar. Beginning in the late 1980s, however, and continuing into the 1990s, there have been more than a few fake transcript scandals. Some involved creative use of color copiers and laser printers. Others involved tampering with a university's computer, either by hackers having fun or by dishonest employees selling their services. Such unfortunate behaviors raise questions about the validity of *any* university-produced document.

CHAPTER 4

Is a Degree Worth the Effort?

Question: I'm 38 years old, and thinking about pursuing a bachelor's degree, but I'm not sure I should, because if I do, I'll be 42 years old when I'm done.

Answer: And how old will you be in four years if you don't do it?

Paraphrased from the Dear Abby column

The simple answer to the question in the chapter title is "yes" for nontraditional degrees; very likely "no" for traditional degrees. Let us first elaborate on why the nontraditional degree is worth the effort, and then offer arguments as to why the old-fashioned way may not be worth it.

Why the Nontraditional Degree Makes Sense

Much depends on the degree itself, and on the reasons for wanting it. If, for instance, you need to have a bachelor's degree to get a job, promotion, or salary increase, then an accredited degree from Excelsior College, earned entirely by correspondence courses, is exactly as good as any bachelor's degree earned by sitting in classrooms for four or five or six years at a state university, and it would be about 95 percent cheaper (not to mention that one can continue earning a living while pursuing the nontraditional degree).

As another example, a nonresident doctorate, earned through a combination of life-experience credit and new work from one of the better unaccredited state-licensed universities, is likely to be of little or no value in getting a faculty position at any properly accredited university. But such degrees have proved useful in some cases for advancement in business, government, and industry, not to mention doing wonders for self-image and gaining the respect of others. There is always, however, a potential for embarrassment or bad publicity,

Finally, a doctorate purchased for a hundred bucks from a no-questions-asked degree mill may ultimately bring shame, public embarrassment, loss of a job, and even a fine and imprisonment.

Many nontraditional degrees with recognized accreditation are good for most people in most situations. But there can be major exceptions, which is why it pays to check out any school that you are considering in advance (this book is a good place to start) and to make as sure as you can that the degree you seek will satisfy any gatekeepers who may appear in your path.

A word of warning: Please do not be misled by the results of a study on the acceptance of nontraditional degrees, sponsored by the National Institute of Education in the late 1970s. This study, by Sosdian and Sharp, has been misquoted and misinterpreted in the literature of dozens of nontraditional universities, in a most misleading effort to convince prospective students that their degrees will be accepted in the academic, professional, or business world.

Sosdian and Sharp did indeed determine that there was a high level of acceptance—but their research was based entirely on the acceptance level of associate's and bachelor's degrees that were either regionally accredited or, in a very few cases, state-run schools that were candidates for regional accreditation. It is totally misleading to imply, as many have done, that results would be comparable for unaccredited degrees, much less master's and doctorates. It just isn't so, and those schools should be ashamed of themselves.

The important issue of choosing an accredited or an unaccredited school is discussed at length in chapter 9.

Now, let's look at the six main reasons why people choose to pursue nontraditional degrees, and the kinds of degrees that may be most appropriate.

1. **Job or salary advancement in business, industry, or civil service.** Many job descriptions specify that a certain degree is required, or that additional salary will be paid, if a certain degree is held. In a small number of these situations, a good unaccredited degree will suffice.

   It is crucial to find out in advance, whenever possible, if a given degree will be accepted. While some businesses, large and small, may recognize good unaccredited degrees, most will not. We have heard dozens of tragic stories from people who spent many thousands of dollars on degree programs, only to find that the degree they earned was not acceptable to their employer or potential employer.

2. **Job or salary advancement in education.** The academic world has been more reluctant to accept unaccredited degrees than has the world of business or government. Even some excellent accredited, nontraditional degrees have caused problems. However, the situation remains extremely variable. It is almost impossible to draw general rules or conclusions. Many universities refuse to consider hiring a faculty member with an unaccredited degree or to admit people with such degrees into their graduate programs. The most enlightened schools will consider each case on its own merits.

   Once again, the watchword is to check in advance before spending any money with any school.

3. **Job or salary advancement in the professions.** When a profession must be licensed by the state or a trade organization, that body often has certain degree requirements. Depending on the state, this may apply to psychologists, marriage counselors, engineers, accountants, real-estate brokers, social workers, hypnotists, massage practitioners, and others. Each state has its own policy, and so does each field of endeavor.

   In one state, for example, a psychologist must have a traditionally accredited doctorate while a civil engineer with sufficient career experience could have an unaccredited degree or no degree at all. In another state, it may be just the opposite. Many regulations are exceedingly unclear on this subject, so a judgment is made in each individual case. Once again, it is crucial to determine in advance if a given degree will meet a given need, and, to the extent possible, to consider future developments. Many people have discovered, when wishing to move from one state or country to another, that the degree or credentials that had served them well will not be honored in the new location.

4. **Admission to traditional graduate schools.** In an earlier edition, we suggested a trend toward increased acceptance of nontraditional degrees "including the better unaccredited degrees" for admission to master's and doctoral programs at traditional universities. Extensive communications from readers over the past few years persuade us that if there is a trend, it is toward case-by-case determinations, rather than a blanket policy of any sort.

The key factor here is that while undergraduate admissions decisions are usually made by the admissions office of the school, at the master's and doctoral level these decisions are made, or heavily influenced, by the academic department itself. It is generally accepted that if the department (or a key faculty member in the department) really wants a certain applicant, that person is likely to be accepted, regardless of the nature of his or her specific academic credentials.

5. **Self-satisfaction.** This is a perfectly good reason for wanting a degree, and no one should ever feel embarrassed about it. Many clients of the degree consulting service (see appendix C) seek a degree (generally a doctorate) for self-satisfaction, to gain respect from others, to feel more comfortable with colleagues, or to "validate" a long and worthwhile career. Such people are more likely to be satisfied with a degree from one of the more respectable unaccredited schools. One of the main criteria to consider here is avoidance of potential embarrassment. More than one holder of a degree from a legitimate, but not especially good, nontraditional school has suffered extreme discomfort or embarrassment when newspaper articles or television stories on the school made big local waves.

One of John's favorite consulting clients wrote to him some years ago that his doctoral dissertation had been rejected by Columbia University in 1910, and now he'd like to finish the degree. John wrote back offering suggestions, and mentioned what he thought was an amusing typographical error in the letter; he'd said 1910. No, the man wrote back, that's correct. He was now 96 years old, and these events had happened 70 years earlier. He was accepted by a good nontraditional external program, and completed his Ph.D. shortly before his 100th birthday.

6. **Fooling people.** An alarming number of people want fake degrees for all manner of devious purposes. After CBS broadcast its degree-mill report on *60 Minutes*, they received a huge number of telephone calls from people wanting to know the addresses and phone numbers of the fake schools they had just seen exposed.

   Almost every week we hear from people who would like "a doctorate from Harvard University, please, with no work required, and can it be backdated to 1983, and I need it by next Tuesday." The best one can do is warn these people that they are endangering their reputations (and possibly their freedom) by considering such a course. Then we usually suggest that if they must have a degree by return mail, they consider a degree from a far-less-dangerous, second-rate Bible college. Nothing to be especially proud of, but less hazardous to one's health.

Why a Traditional Degree Makes Less Sense

People attend traditional colleges for a great many different reasons, as Caroline Bird writes in her fascinating book, *The Case Against College*:

> A great majority of our nine million post-secondary students who are "in college" are there because it has become the thing to do, or because college is a pleasant place to be … because it's the only way they can get parents or taxpayers to support them without working at a job they don't like; because Mother wanted them to go; or for some reasons utterly irrelevant to the course of studies for which the college is supposedly organized.

There seem to be two basic reasons people go to college: to get an education or to get a degree. The two can be quite independent. Some people only care about the training, others only want the degree, and some want or need both.

Sadly, there is a strong trend in America toward what David Hapgood calls "diplomaism" in his book of that title. He writes:

> We are well on our way to repealing the American dream of individual accomplishment and replacing it with a system in which the diploma is the measure of a man, a diploma which bears no relation to performance. The career market is closing its doors to those without degrees. … Diplomaism zones people into a set of categories that tends to eliminate the variety and surprise of human experience. In a system run by diplomas, all avenues to personal advancement are blocked except one: the school that gives the diploma. … When we leave the institution, like carcasses coming off a packing plant's assembly line, an anonymous hand affixes an indelible stamp … which thereafter determines what we can do, and how we shall be rewarded. And that stamp, unlike the imprint on a side of beef, reflects neither our personal value to the society, nor the needs of the economic system.

There are, in fact, three major problems with traditional schools and traditional degree programs:

1. There is often little connection between degrees earned traditionally and on-the-job performance.

2. There is much evidence that vast numbers of students are spending huge amounts of time being trained for jobs that simply do not exist.

3. The cash investment in a traditional college education is frequently an extremely poor investment indeed.

Let us consider each of these three problems in greater depth.

Traditional College Training and On-the-Job Performance

Many studies have found little or no relationship between college coursework and "real life" performance, and in some cases that relationship was a negative one. One extensive study, by Ivar Berg of Columbia University, published under the delightful title, "Education and Jobs: The Great Training Robbery," looked at various jobs in which people with degrees and people without were doing identical work. In many situations, there was no difference in performance between the two groups, and in a few jobs (including air traffic controllers and pants makers), the people without the degrees were doing a better job.

Sadly, Berg also found that many bosses either ignored or refused to believe the evidence that had been collected in their own offices and factories. For instance, in one big chemical firm where the laboratory workers without degrees were outperforming those with degrees, the management steadfastly maintained its policy of promoting only those employees with degrees.

Hapgood believes that personnel practices at such firms are not likely to be changed in the foreseeable future, because "employers made it clear they were demanding diplomas for reasons that had little to do with job performance." The real reasons, he thinks, had to do with conformity to the dominant culture and with the "ability" to stay in school for four or more years. "It proves that he was docile enough (or good or patient or stupid enough; choose your own adjective) to stay out of trouble for 13 or 17 or 20 years in a series of institutions that demand a high degree of unthinking conformity."

John was given similar responses when he surveyed the personnel managers of major airlines. Almost all require pilots to have an accredited bachelor's degree, but they don't care whether the degree is in aviation or Chinese history. The important thing, they say, is that an employee is disciplined enough to complete a degree program. You may have been flying for ten years for the navy or the air force, but that doesn't count. And if the hypocrisy needs to be underlined, consider the fact that when pilot trainees are in short supply, the degree requirement mysteriously disappears.

Whatever the reasons, the system is a confused and disarrayed one, with the one strongly positive note being the increasing acceptance of properly accredited nontraditional degrees, whose holders often have far more practical knowledge and experience through on-the-job training than those who learned about the subject in the college classroom.

There is an ever growing number of employers who will say, for instance, that you learn more about practical journalism in your first two weeks working on a daily newspaper than in four years of journalism school. (The same goes for law, advertising, and dozens of other fields.) And the person who has both the experience and the nontraditional degree based, at least in part, on that experience may be in the best situation of all.

It used to be the case that many employers denied jobs to people without degrees, even if the degree had nothing to do with the ability to perform the job. But following a key Supreme Court decision (*Griggs v. Duke Power Company, 1971*), employers must now prove that a degree is required to do a certain job, or they cannot discriminate against those without them. This is equally true for high school diplomas, doctorates, and everything in between.

Is a Traditional College Degree Useful in Today's Marketplace?

A certain large state prison used to take great pride in its vocational training program. It operated a large cotton mill, where the inmates learned how to run the equipment and, in fact, made their own prison uniforms. When they got out of prison, however, they learned that not only was the equipment they had learned to operate hopelessly out-of-date, but also the nearest large cotton mill was 2,000 miles away. No wonder many of them returned to a life of crime.

Much the same sort of thing goes on in traditional colleges and universities. As an example, throughout the 1960s hundreds of thousands of students were told about the great teacher shortages that were coming, so they graduated with degrees in education. But, as Alexander Mood wrote in a report for the Carnegie Commission:

It has been evident for some time to professors of education that they were training far more teachers than would ever find jobs teaching school, but few of them bothered to mention that fact to their students. That is understandable, of course, since their incomes depend on having students.

Much the same thing happened with the study of space science and astrophysics in the 1970s, and again with computer science in the 1980s and '90s, and the social sciences in the 2000s.

And so we find thousands of people with doctorates teaching high school, people with master's degrees teaching first grade, and an awful lot of people with bachelor's degrees in education waiting on tables and doing clerical work.

In virtually any field you look at, from psychology to civil engineering, you find lots of well-trained and unemployed practitioners. In one recent year, for instance, there were over 100,000 graduates in the field of communications, and about 14,000 new jobs in the communications industries. Five thousand anthropology graduates are finding about 400 job openings in their field. And so it goes. Or doesn't go.

The field of business is a reminder that things are constantly changing, in one direction or another. One survey by the *Wall Street Journal* found copious numbers of highly disillusioned MBA students and recent graduates. But only a few years later, MBA graduates were in such demand, some of them being offered ten or more high-paying jobs as their graduation day neared.

According to Bird, "Law schools are already graduating twice as many new lawyers every year as the Department of Labor thinks will be needed," and Mood says that

in the past, the investment in higher education did at least pay off for most students; that is, they did get access to higher-status jobs; now for the first time in history, a college degree is being judged by many parents and students as not worth the price. They see too many of last year's graduates unable to find work, or taking jobs ordinarily regarded as suitable for high school graduates....Moreover, this is not a temporary phenomenon.

The Bureau of Labor Statistics says that about 25 percent of college graduates entering the labor market are getting jobs previously held by people without degrees. That doesn't mean the degrees are needed to perform those jobs, of course, but only that there are millions of job-seekers with degrees who cannot find jobs requiring their degrees.

So the outlook for the traditional degree is rather bleak. People will continue to pursue them for the wrong reasons, and industry will continue to require them for the wrong reasons. And enlightened people of all ages will, more and more, come to realize that a nontraditional degree can do just about anything a traditional one can—with a much smaller expenditure of time, effort, and money.

Is a Traditional Degree Worth the Cost?

Just what is the cost? Anything we write today will be out of date tomorrow, because traditional college costs are escalating so fast. In 2000, two U.S. Senators (Fred Thompson and Joseph Lieberman) held hearings on this troublesome issue. They noted that over the past 20 years, tuition has more than doubled at both public and private schools, outpacing grants, loans, state appropriations and other subsidies to schools, as well as aid to students and their families. According to a report by the American Council on Education, 71 percent of Americans believe that "a four-year college education is not affordable." Two-thirds of Americans list the cost of a college education as a bigger concern than violent crimes against children, children's health-care, and quality of public schools.

According to a report from the American Council on Education, in the year 2000 the average cost of attending a private college for one year in the United States was $24,025, including tuition, room and board, books, etc. Allowing a conservative growth rate of 6 percent, the cost of four years would be $104,990. At public colleges, the average cost for four years would be "only" $67,400.

Based on a highly conservative 6 percent rate of academic inflation (most schools do try to hold the line, but there are limits to how much they can do), here is how things may look in years to come with regard to college costs

YEAR	4 YRS. PRIVATE COLLEGE	4 YRS. PUBLIC COLLEGE
2000	$104,990	$67,400
2005	$140,500	$90,155
2010	$188,000	$120,648

It seems more than likely that a child who was born in 2000, who will enter college in 2018, can expect to pay well over $200,000 for a traditional college education.

Even today, many people simply cannot afford to pursue a traditional degree. Yet a degree can almost always mean a higher salary, increased likelihood of getting better jobs, and personal satisfaction. For a while, the gap seemed to be narrowing. In the early 1980s, the average bachelor's degree–holder was earning about 35 percent more than the average high school graduate. In recent years, however, that trend has dramatically reversed. The most recent available census data (1996) show the average bachelor's degree–holder earning 53 percent more than a high school graduate.

Here, from those census data, are average lifetime earnings for males, based on levels of education. The amount shown is total lifetime earnings, from the year of entering the job market (at the age of 18 for high school graduates, 22 for bachelor's degree–holders, etc.) until age 65. The figures

for women are roughly 40 percent lower. (Who says that the Equal Rights Amendment is unnecessary?)

EDUCATIONAL LEVEL	LIFETIME EARNINGS
Attended high school, did not graduate	$962,000
High school graduate, did not go to college	$1,373,000
Attended college for 1 to 3 years	$1,616,000
Bachelor's degree	$2,113,000
Master's degree	$2,613,000
Doctorate	$3,007,000
Professional degree	$3,580,000

EDUCATIONAL LEVEL	ANNUAL EARNINGS, MEN	ANNUAL EARNINGS, WOMEN
No high school diploma	$20,464	$10,881
High school diploma/G.E.D.	$29,218	$15,848
Some college	$35,923	$19,828
Bachelor's	$49,147	$28,926
Master's	$63,748	$36,711
Doctorate	$81,271	$51,751
Law or medicine	$102,309	$68,326

From the above numbers, it may look, to an 18-year-old on the brink of either college or a job, as if taking four years off to earn a bachelor's degree is going to be worth more than $700,000 in the long run. However, author Caroline Bird thinks that if the only reason people go to college is to make more money, then higher education may be a dumb financial investment.

She argues this way (we have adapted her older figures to the reality of the different interest rates of the early 2000s): The average Princeton graduate will have spent about $200,000 to get a degree, including tuition, room and board, books, travel, etc. If such a person put that sum of money into certificates of deposit earning 6 percent interest, they would have over $2.5 million by the age of 65, without ever having done a day's work. That, needless to say, is about twenty percent more than the average bachelor's degree–holder makes in a lifetime of work.

Of course, most people wouldn't have the $200,000 to invest at age 18. But Bird argues that if one enters the job market at 18, the earnings over the next four years, plus, perhaps, some advance from parents on what they would otherwise have spent on college tuition, wisely invested, would produce a similar result.

A study by Doctors J. H. Hollomon of the Massachusetts Institute of Technology and Richard Freeman of Harvard University concluded that "in the brief span of about five

"My bonnie lad's a distance learner,
Learning far across the sea.
But my soul has great insistence,
Praying he'll give up the distance,
And sail home to me, to me,
And show me his degree."

years, the college job market has gone from a major boom to a major bust. Large numbers of young people, for the first time, are likely to obtain less schooling and potentially lower occupational status than their parents."

All very well and good, but none of these people takes nontraditional education and degrees into account. Bird and others have produced some powerful reasons not to pursue a traditional degree. But it is now possible, and will become increasingly easier, to earn degrees at a low cost while remaining fully employed, thereby having the best of both worlds.

Whether pursuing a degree for the learning, the diploma, or both, the alternative student seems far more likely:

► to be motivated to complete his or her program;

► to select courses and programs that are appropriate and relevant to his or her needs;

► to avoid cluttering up campuses and dormitories (which, in the words of former Columbia University president William McGill, are in danger of becoming "storage houses for bored young people");

► to save years over the time of traditional programs (or, alternatively, to pursue educational objectives

without giving up job or family) and, perhaps most importantly for most people, to save a tremendous amount of money compared to the costs of a traditional degree program.

Many nontraditional programs, in fact, come very close to John Holt's ideal educational system, which he describes by analogy with a public library: you go whenever you want something it has to offer, no one checks your credentials at the door, you leave when you have gotten what you wanted, and it is you, not the librarian, who decides if it has been a worthwhile experience.

Where, Then, Are Things Going?

One message of Charles Reich's fascinating book, *The Greening of America*, was that things are happening now that have never happened before; that for the first time, the standards and lessons of the past may have no relevance for the future.

Things are indeed changing almost amazingly fast in higher education. The direction in which they are changing is away from traditional education and degrees toward alternative higher education and nontraditional degrees.

It is always difficult—and challenging—to live in a time of great change. On one hand, we have universities that have refused (or were unable, by law) to invite people like Bill Gates, Eleanor Roosevelt, Buckminster Fuller, Andrew Wyeth, or Eric Hoffer to lecture, because they never earned a college degree. On the other hand, we have people earning higher degrees entirely by correspondence or use of the Internet, entering prestigious doctoral programs without even a high school diploma, and earning law degrees without ever seeing the inside of a law school.

In 1970, if you wanted to earn a degree without sitting in classrooms for three or four years, and wanted to remain in North America, you had exactly two legal alternatives: the University of London and the University of South Africa, both of which offered (and still offer) nonresident programs from the bachelor's level through the doctorate, as well as various professional degrees. Now you have this entire book with well over 1,000 splendid options

At the same time, predictably, many traditional universities and colleges are suffering the financial impact of decreased enrollments and rising costs. Unprecedented numbers of traditional schools are simply going out of business (an average of one accredited college or university in the United States every three weeks!), and many others are almost frantically implementing online and other distance programs as a last resort to stay afloat.

Distance education and degrees by distance learning seem, indeed, to be the wave of the educational future.

CHAPTER 5

Using Titles

Question: What do you call the person who finishes last in his or her medical school class?

Answer: Doctor.

Traditional

One question that arose regularly in the degree consulting practice John used to operate was this: "If I earn a degree, especially a degree by distance learning or other nontraditional means, in what way am I entitled to use the degree, and the title that comes with it (in the case of doctorates), in my life and career?"

There is no simple answer to this question, since rules and regulations vary from country to country, state to state, province to province, and from profession to profession. The basic philosophy behind these laws is essentially this: You can probably do almost anything you want in the way of titles, as long as you do not do it with the intent of deceiving anyone, and as long as it is not specifically forbidden by law. For instance, in the 1990s, Florida had a law that prohibited people with unaccredited degrees, even from long-established, state-approved schools, from even mentioning those degrees in any way, in writing or orally, whether on a business card, letterhead, advertisement, etc. That law was found to be unconstitutional, so now Billy Graham does not have to worry about being nabbed upon crossing the Florida border.

No one ever had Colonel Sanders arrested for pretending to be a military officer, nor is Doctor Demento or Doc Marten in danger of prosecution for impersonating a physician. However, when a man who has never earned a doctorate gets a job as a meteorologist for a New York television station using the title of "Doctor," there *is* a major problem, because it can be reasonably assumed that the title helped him get the job—even if he was performing his duties satisfactorily without benefit of doctoral training. (That meteorologist lost his job after his lack of a degree was exposed.)

In general, as long as the degree comes from an unquestionably legal and legitimate school, there is usually no problem in using that degree in public life, as long as all local and licensing requirements are met.

In some states, a "quickie" doctorate from a one-room Bible school is sufficient to set up practice as a marriage counselor and psychotherapist. In other states with stiffer licensing requirements, this same behavior could result in major legal problems.

The use of degree titles varies considerably from profession to profession, and from nation to nation. Most people in the United States do not append a bachelor's degree notation to their letterhead or signature, while in most of the rest of the world, it is quite common to see, for instance, "Maxwell Zeryck, B.A." The name or abbreviation of the school is often appended as well: "Kata Galasi, B.A. (Oxon)" or "B.A. (Cantab)," indicating that the degree is from Oxford or Cambridge.

Master's degrees are more commonly used in print in the United States, especially the M.B.A. (e.g., "Joseph Judd, M.B.A.").

Holders of a doctorate almost always use it in their public or professional lives—with the curious exception of politicians. (Most prominent politicians with earned doctorates, from Woodrow Wilson to George McGovern to Newt Gingrich, seem to have gone to great lengths to avoid public disclosure of the degree. Perhaps there is merit to columnist Herb Caen's belief that people will never vote for anyone they think is more intelligent than they are.)

There are, and probably always will be, educational conservatives who decry the use of nontraditional (and particularly unaccredited nontraditional) titles. A typical situation has occurred in the field of electrical engineering, where a gentleman in New York formed the "Committee of Concerned E.E.'s" for the purpose of carrying on a vigorous campaign against the right of electrical engineers with unaccredited doctorates to use the title of "Doctor." The journals in this field often carry articles and letters from people on various sides of this issue.

Thomas Carlyle's observation regarding the "peculiar ambition of Americans to hobble down to posterity on crutches of capital letters" notwithstanding, Americans are far less likely than Europeans and Asians to use all the letters at their command. Whereas a typical Englishman will list all his degrees, and perhaps a few fellowships besides (e.g., "Lowell James Hicks, B.A., M.A., Ph.D., F.R.S.,

L.C.P."), most Americans would only use their highest degree (e.g., "Heather Bourne, Ph.D."), unless they have more than one doctorate, in which case both would be listed (e.g., "Howard Siegel, M.D., Ph.D.").

Not everyone agrees with this. The former president of a California religious school, for instance, regularly used all nine of his claimed doctorates, with his civil-service rank (G.S.9) thrown in between doctorates number four and five for good measure. And then there was the chap who wrote to us from Massachusetts, using these letters after his name: L.R.A., M.N.G.S., B.S.A. When asked, he explained that the letters stood for Licensed Real Estate Agent, Member of the National Geographic Society, and Boy Scouts of America.

Holders of honorary doctorates are treading on far more dangerous ground when they use their degrees in public, especially if such degrees were purchased "over the counter," no matter how legally. Still, public figures from Billy Graham to the late Edward Land, founder of Polaroid, regularly use (or used) the title "Doctor" based on honorary degrees from major universities.

Nonetheless, if an insurance agent makes a sale, if a clergyman makes a convert, or if a teacher makes a salary increase that can be attributed, even in part, to the prestige of being called "Doctor," and if that doctorate is unearned, then the claim can always be made that that person is acting, at least in part, on false pretenses.

In 1994, the newly appointed secretary of education of a quite large western country proudly listed a doctorate from Harvard on his resume. Following an inquiry, his office later conceded that he had only a master's degree from Harvard. A month later, his office announced that, actually, he did not even have a bachelor's degree. In January of 1995, he resigned, admitting that, in fact, his academic career ended when he was expelled from the second grade for bad behavior.

There is also the matter of whether a doctorate-holder chooses to call himself, for example, Roger Williams, Ph.D. or Dr. Roger Williams. Although either form would appear to be acceptable in many circumstances, a New York audiologist (someone who fits hearing aids) suffered legal repercussions for calling himself Dr. So-and-so rather than So-and-so, Ph.D. The prosecution's claim was that the use of the word "Doctor" in such a near-medical field was done to deceive clients into thinking he was a medical doctor. (Incidentally, it is incorrect to use the title at both ends of the name simultaneously. "Dr. Albert Goldschmidt, Ph.D." is a no-no.)

Another category of title abusers are those people who use degrees they never earned, and there are a surprising number of them. When the head of a major motion picture studio got into legal troubles a few years back, a sidelight of the case was that the degree he said he had from Yale University turned out to be nonexistent. At the same time, Yale revealed that they keep files on all cases of publicly claimed Yale degrees that were never actually awarded, and that to date they had logged more than 7,000 such fraudulent claims.

It seems reasonable to hypothesize that these 7,000 are just the tip of the iceberg. Untold thousands of others are going about free, only because so few people ever bother to check up on anyone's degrees. Most exposures happen in connection with other events, often when something good happens to a person. Let us give a number of examples, in the hopes of dissuading some readers from considering this course of action.

- ▶ In 2000, a school psychologist for a major southwestern city not only lost his job but also his license when it was learned he had bought his Ph.D. from the fraudulent University of Palmers Green.

- ▶ In 1999, the Speaker of the Nigerian House of Representatives lost his job and was fined when it turned out he had faked his degree from the University of Toronto. "Pulling a Toronto" has become the euphemism for using a fake degree there.

- ▶ The Arizona "Teacher of the Year" for 1987, after he entered the public eye, was discovered to have falsified his claim to a doctorate. He forfeited the $10,000 prize that came with this honor, and his career was in jeopardy.

- ▶ Two of the 1988 presidential hopefuls, Biden and Robertson, got a lot of press coverage when it turned out their academic credentials were not as they had represented.

- ▶ The chairman of the board of a major university in the South resigned when it became known his doctorate was from a "school" whose founder was in federal prison for selling degrees.

- ▶ The young woman whose 1981 Pulitzer Prize was taken away when it turned out she had falsified her story about a young drug addict also turned out to have two fake degrees listed on her *Washington Post* job application.

- ▶ A finalist for fire chief in a major midwestern city in 1994 was found (by one of his opponents) to have a bachelor's degree that he purchased for $45 from a Texas degree mill.

- ▶ The chief engineer of San Francisco's transit system lost his $81,000-a-year job when his employer discovered that he did not have the degree he claimed.

- ▶ The President-elect of Poland turned out not to have the master's degree he listed on his official resume. This is a crime punishable by jail in Poland. "I passed all my exams," he said, "But never formally concluded my studies with a master's degree."

▶ The superintendent of one of California's largest school districts lost his $98,000-a-year job and faced criminal charges when a reporter learned he did not have the Stanford doctorate he claimed.

▶ A prominent Florida university professor of surgery resigned when someone checked up and found he didn't have the master's degree he had listed on his resume.

▶ A controversial member of the Canadian parliament got huge front-page headlines in Toronto when it was learned that he was signing letters "LL.B." even though he did not have a law degree.

▶ During the 1998 elections, candidates in five states were discovered to be claiming degrees they did not earn. After the ensuing publicity, four lost.

▶ The London *Daily Telegraph* revealed gleefully that Italian neo-fascist MP Alessandra Mussolini, granddaughter of Il Duce, had allegedly purchased her degree in history and moral philosophy from Rome's Sapienza University for about $500, utilizing professors' signatures forged by a porter. (The newspaper suggested that the porter might have been just as good a judge of moral philosophy as the professors.)

▶ A large midwestern county went to court to obtain a summary judgment to remove its health commissioner, after learning that the source of his graduate degree was less than reputable.

▶ The newly hired president of an Idaho college got bad publicity (and perhaps worse) when trustees realized his doctorate was from the unaccredited "University of Berkley" and not the University of California, Berkeley.

▶ The very same man also got in trouble at his previous job for listing a doctorate from the University of Idaho when, in fact, he had only a master's degree.

And so it goes. Do you know where your own doctor, lawyer, and accountant earned their degrees? Have you checked with the schools just to be sure? A diploma on the wall is not sufficient evidence. We know of three different places that have sold fake diplomas from any school, printed to order for a modest sum. John has two fake Harvard diplomas hanging on his wall, alongside his real ones. His medical degree cost $50 from a "lost diploma replacement service" in Oregon. What if your family doctor had their catalog? His Harvard law degree was purchased from another "service" in Florida. (No, we are not going to give out names and addresses; these businesses do enough damage in the world as it is.)

This topic moves very rapidly from the abstract to the concrete when something happens nearby. It was clearly brought home some years ago when a locally prominent "certified public accountant" who lived just down the road from us hurriedly packed his shingle and left town. One of his clients had decided to check, and found out that he simply did not have the credentials he said he had.

So then, common sense should be sufficient to make your decision on how to use a degree in almost any situation that may arise. Where there is any doubt at all about using a given degree or title, it may be wise to seek legal advice, or at the very least to check with the relevant state agencies—generally the state education department (see chapter 6) or the appropriate licensing agencies.

And, in general, it isn't a bad idea to worry just a little about other people's degrees and titles. A lot of fakes and frauds are out there right now, practicing medicine, teaching classes, practicing law, counseling troubled families, building bridges, pulling teeth, and keeping books, without benefit of a degree, a license, or proper training. If more people would ask a few more questions about the title before the name, or the document on the wall, these dangerous phonies would be stopped before they do more harm to us all.

Big companies are often not nearly as thorough as one might wish. When some of the sleaziest schools put out lists of corporations who pay for their employees to get those degrees, they are often telling the truth. Either the companies confuse the sleazy school with another of similar or identical name, they don't know that there are such things as fake accrediting agencies as well as fake schools, or they simply don't care.

Legitimate schools themselves, however, are getting better and better at detecting phonies. At the national registrars' conventions, for instance, there are always sessions on identifying fraud. Although some registrars grumble about having to become detectives, and lament the invention of the color laser copier and other tools of the scoundrels, they are doing good work on the front lines in the war against academic fraud.

Almost every school will confirm, either by mail or by telephone, whether or not a given person has indeed earned a degree from them. This is not an invasion of privacy, since the facts are known as "directory information," available to the public through printed directories or publicly accessible university information files.

(Glad you asked. John Bear's Ph.D. was awarded by Michigan State University, East Lansing, Michigan, on March 19, 1966, and you are most welcome to check it out with them.)

Nonacademic Titles

There are two kinds of things people do, other than earning (or buying) degrees, that result in letters after their names and/or titles before them. These "designations" and "titles" are not the main provenance of this book, but they are closely allied, which is why we address them briefly.

"Geoffrey, I don't need to go off to college.
I'm a distance learner."

Designations

Designations are, typically, titles or credentials awarded by various professional and trade organizations and associations upon completion of a course of study and, often, passage of an examination. Perhaps most common are the designations of C.P.A. (Certified Public Accountant) in the U.S. and C.A. (Chartered Accountant) in Canada.

Other popular designations are those of C.L.U. (Certified Life Underwriter), C.F.P. (Certified Financial Planner), and Realtor. But there are many hundreds of others, some easy to gain, others requiring arduous examinations, and most permitting the holder to add letters following his or her name.

Some organizations, especially those in Europe, have several levels of designation, depending on which series of examinations one has passed. For instance, one can be an M.A.B.E. (Member of the Association of Business Executives) or, following additional exams, an F.A.B.E. (Fellow of the [etc.]).

Some designations are clearly academic and are regarded as such by many institutions. For instance, an American C.P.A. will often not have to take either an accounting or a quantitative methods course if he or she enrolls in certain M.B.A. programs.

One thing the world has needed is a comprehensive guide to designations in all countries, making clear just what was done to earn them, and how each country regards other countries' designations. Happily, this information is now available from a series of books (including, for instance, *A Guide to Over 400 Organizations and Their Designations*, from LBA Publications, 18 Portsmouth Drive, Scarborough, Ontario M1C 5E1, Canada; phone: +1 (416) 283 4051; fax: +1 (416) 283 7497; email: *lbalkaran@attcanada.net*).

Titles

People often ask, "Well, if I can't become a Doctor overnight, what about becoming a baron or a knight or something?" Indeed, it has been suggested that one reason honorary doctorates are so popular in America is that we don't have titles of nobility. This topic is really not within the scope of the book, but if you have interest, there are plenty of books, articles, and Internet sites out there. Indeed, when we did an Internet search for "titles of nobility," a total of 19,177 sites were found, offering the opportunity to become a Baron of Bosnia, Knight of the Byzantine Empire, Knight of Malta (at least 19 competing organizations), Knight Templar, and Patriarch of Antioch.

According to some books, there are various European services that specialize in getting their clients either married into or adopted into the royal houses of Europe at fees ranging from $20,000 to more than $300,000. In this vein, *Parade Magazine* reported that Zsa Zsa Gabor's eighth husband, Prince Frederick von Anhalt, Duke of Saxony, Count of Ascania, is the son of a German policeman, who was adopted by an impoverished German princess, after which he sold 68 knighthoods at $50,000 each.

In earlier editions, we printed the addresses of some of these dispensers, but they seem to move often, sometimes without awarding the titles that had been ordered. So we've stopped doing that. Anyway, if truth be known, we worried that readers might be arrested for impersonating a baron, or be drafted into the Byzantine army.

If you simply must have a title, Burke's Peerage, a company that publishes books on European nobility, also brokers the purchase of Scottish and French titles (such as Baron, Marquis, Count) acquired through the purchase of land, often in the $50,000 to $100,000 range (6 Wells Court, Pevensey Garden, Worthing, West Sussex, United Kingdom; email: *burkestitles@aol.com*; Web site: *www.burkestitles.com*). Another source is a company called Noble Titles, located at "Whispers," Mouse Lane, Steyning, West Sussex BN44 3LP, United Kingdom; email: *titles@nobility.co.uk*; Web site: *www.nobility.co.uk*. A third source is the Council of Westphalia, The Roman Forum, 13 Oakleigh Road, Stratford-upon-Avon, Warwickshire CV37 0DW, United Kingdom, which is in the business of finding extinct British titles that are unlikely ever to be used again, and bestowing them on people who support their archaeological research.

CHAPTER 6

How to Evaluate a School

Some people spend more time deciding which soda to buy from a soft drink machine than they do in choosing the school where they will earn their degree.

Prosecutor at the trial of a state psychologist with a phony Ph.D.

An investigative reporter for a large newspaper once told John that he could go into any building on the street, "that office, that hospital, that laundromat, that factory—and given enough time and money, I would find a story there that would probably make page one."

The same is very likely true of virtually every school in this book, from Harvard on down. Some simply have a lot more skeletons in a lot more closets than others.

It would be wonderful to have an army of trained investigators and detectives at our disposal. With our very limited resources and manpower, we cannot do a detailed and intensive investigation of every single school. Happily, we have received a great deal of assistance from readers of this book, who have followed our advice on checking out schools and have reported their findings to us.

Here, then, is the four-step procedure we recommend for investigating schools that are not covered in this book, or looking further into those that are. And please, if you do this, share your research with us. Email us at *johnandmariah@degree.net* or write to us at *Bears' Guide*, P.O. Box 7123, Berkeley, California 94707. (Thank you.)

Step One: Check It Out in This Book

If a school isn't here, it may be because it is very new, or because we didn't consider it sufficiently nontraditional for inclusion—or quite possibly because we simply missed it. And even if it *is* listed here, don't take our opinions as the gospel truth. Hardly a day passes that we don't get a letter challenging our opinions. Sometimes they begin, "You idiot, don't you know that . . ." and sometimes they begin, "I beg to differ with you in regard to . . . " Whatever the tone, we are always glad to have these opinions. There have been quite a few instances where such a letter spurred us to look more closely at a school, resulting in a revised opinion, either upward or downward.

Step Two: Check It Out with Friends, Colleagues, or Employers

If you need the degree for a new job, a salary increase, or a state license, be sure to find out specifically if this degree will suffice before investing any money in any school. Many schools will gladly enter into correspondence with employers, state agencies, or others you may designate, to explain their programs and establish their credentials.

All too often, we hear horror stories about people who have lost thousands of dollars and wasted incredible amounts of time completing a degree that was useless to them. "But the school said it was accredited," they lament.

Step Three: Check It Out with the Proper Government Agency

Every state and every nation has an agency that oversees higher education. Check the school out with the agency in the state or country in which the school is located. A list of these agencies is given at the end of the chapter. Some correspondence schools are well known (positively or negatively) to the Better Business Bureau as well, but do not rely on this; some of the worst diploma mills have also been members of the BBB. And all nations have a department, bureau, or ministry of education that may be able to supply information on a school. They also all have embassies in Washington, D.C., and all national capitals, as well as United Nations delegations in New York to which questions may be addressed. You may get bogged down in voice mail, but it is at least worth trying.

We have gotten some criticism from readers for reporting, in some school listings, that we "are trying to learn more" from a relevant agency. People wonder how it is possible not to be able to learn something as simple as, well, what the process of accreditation involves in the sovereign nation of St. Kitts & Nevis, home to 35,000 people and at least six international universities. We spent more than four years writing, faxing, emailing, and trying to telephone the Ministry of Education and their embassy in Washington, with absolutely zero success. A colleague, a seasoned admissions officer, got intrigued and also took on this task. Finally, after more than a dozen inquiries, he was informed that "the Minister of Education has a great deal of authority when it comes to recognition of private schools." Thank you very much.

Step Four: Check Out the School Itself

Visit the campus or the offices if at all possible, especially if you have any doubts. If the school's literature does not make clear its precise legal or accreditation status, or if you still have any questions, check with the appropriate accrediting agency. They are all listed in chapter 8. If the accreditor is not listed in chapter 8, be careful. There are a lot of phony accrediting agencies in operation as well as phony schools.

Here are some of the questions you may wish to ask a school you are checking out. **Do not just make up a form letter and send it to 50 or more schools, as more than a few readers have done.** Being more selective, both about schools and questions, will save you and the schools time and money. Also, match the question to the school. If you are inquiring of an obscure unaccredited school, it may be appropriate to ask where the president earned his or her degrees, but there is no need to ask that of, say, a major state university.

▶ How many students are currently enrolled? (Curiously, quite a few schools seem reluctant to reveal these numbers. Sometimes it is because they are embarrassed about how large they are, as, for instance, in the case of one alternative school that at one time had more than 3,000 students and a faculty of five! Sometimes it is because they are embarrassed about how small they are, as is the case with one heavily advertised school that has impressive literature, extremely high tuition, and fewer than 50 students.)

▶ How many degrees have been awarded in the last year?

▶ What is the size of the faculty? How many of these are full-time and how many are part-time or adjunct faculty? If the catalog doesn't make it clear, from which schools did the faculty earn their degrees?

▶ From which school(s) did the president, the dean, and other administrators earn their own degrees? (There is nothing inherently wrong with staff members earning degrees from their own school, but when the number doing so is 25 percent or more, as is the case at some institutions, it starts sounding a little suspicious.)

▶ May I have the names and addresses of some recent graduates in my field of study, and/or in my geographical area?

▶ May I look at the work done by students? (Inspection of master's theses and doctoral dissertations can often give a good idea of the quality of work expected, and the caliber of the students. But you may either have to visit the school [not a bad idea] or offer to pay for making and sending copies.)

▶ Will your degree be acceptable for my intended needs (state licensing, certification, graduate school admission, salary advance, new job, whatever)?

▶ Which other universities or colleges have accepted your degrees or transfer credits? Was acceptance on a case-by-case basis, or is it a routine policy?

▶ What exactly is your legal status, with regard to state agencies and to accrediting associations? If accreditation (or candidacy for accreditation) is claimed, is it with an agency that is approved either by the U.S. Department of Education or the Council on Higher Education Accreditation? If not accredited, are there any plans to seek accreditation? Is the school listed in any of the major reference sources used by registrars and admissions officers worldwide, including the four that are associated with GAAP, Generally Accepted Accreditation Principles: *International Handbook of Universities* (UNESCO), *Commonwealth Universities Yearbook*, *AACRAO World Education Series*, or *NOOSR Countries Series* (Australia)?

No legitimate school should refuse to answer questions like these. Remember, you are shopping for something that may cost you thousands of dollars, that you will use for the rest of your life. It is definitely a buyer's market, and the schools all know this. If they see that you are an informed customer, they will know that they must satisfy you or you will take your business elsewhere.

Remember too that alternative education does not require all the trappings of a traditional school. Don't expect to find a big campus with spacious lawns, an extensive library, or a football team. Some outstanding nontraditional schools are run from relatively small suites of rented offices.

You definitely cannot go by the catalog or other school literature alone. Some really bad schools and some outrageous degree mills have hired good writers and designers, and produced very attractive catalogs that are full of lies and misleading statements. A common trick, for instance, is to show a photograph of a large and impressive building, which may or may not be the building in which the school rents a room or two. Another common device is to list a large number of names of faculty and staff, sometimes with photographs of their smiling faces. Our files are full of certified, deliver-to-addressee-only letters sent to these people that have been returned as undeliverable.

Next, just because a school advertises in a prestigious or popular publication does not mean they are legitimate. Indeed there are all too many major magazines and newspapers that regularly run ads from fake or nonwonderful schools. When the totally fraudulent Columbia State University was finally closed following an FBI raid, we heard from a lot of victims who said, "I trusted them because they advertised regularly in *The Economist*. I couldn't imagine *The Economist* would run fake ads." (When we earlier suggested to *The Economist* that they were not doing their readers a service by running such ads, they replied that "Our readers are smart enough to make their own decisions." We estimate that this policy cost *Economist* readers well over a million dollars.)

Next, there is the matter of an Internet address ending in *.edu*. The legend has arisen that this suffix is hard to get, and must signify a good school. No. It may be harder to get now than it was in the '90s, but we are aware of dozens of fraudulent, even nonexistent "schools" who have a *.edu* Web address.

Finally, be very suspicious of schools where you cannot reach anyone by telephone, where you have to leave a number and they'll call you. We once attempted to check out a new and heavily advertised school called North American University. The people who answered their toll free phone line were cheerful, but after many calls, we were never put through to anyone. It was always, "Dr. Peters will call you back." "Dr. Peters" turned out to be an alias for the school's owner, a convicted felon, who would return calls from his home in another state.

On the other side of the ledger, some good, sincere, legitimate schools have issued typewritten and photocopied catalogs, either to save money or to go along with their low-key images. One sincere, very low-budget school even operated without a telephone for a while.

Agencies for Higher Education

Most countries have some sort of government agency that oversees higher education. In the U.S. and Canada, there is such an agency for every state or province. If you have any concerns about the legality of an institution, or its right to award degrees, these are the places to ask.

(In earlier editions, we also listed the SPRE, or State Postsecondary Review Entity, an abortive attempt to bring some uniformity to the diverse systems, but Congress did away with this in the late '90s.)

Whom Do You Ask First?

No simple answer, so be prepared to spend a bit of time on the phone or writing letters if you wish to learn the exact status of a school in a given country, state, or province. Starting with the main higher education agency makes sense, although in some U.S. states a second agency (as with California) may be the best place.

We call various state agencies fairly often. We have found that once we get through the voice mail, the basic answers are generally correct, but often incomplete. A lot depends on who happens to answer the phone. For instance, one time when we called Alabama to check on an unaccredited school operating there, we were told, "Oh, we've been trying to close them down for years. At least we got them to agree not to accept students from the state of Alabama." But on another call to the same office, we were told, "The state of Alabama has no official position with regard to this school."

In another example, we called the proper California agency to ask about a school which we had heard had just lost its state approval. The helpful person on the phone confirmed this, and gave us the exact date it had happened. But then we found out, a few days later, that the school had gone to court and secured a Writ, which prohibited the state from enforcing its decision until further hearings were held, and thus the school continued legitimately in business.

The inconsistency from state to state, the level of knowledge of state personnel, and the volatile situation with regard to many schools and many laws, makes our job a harder one, and yours as well.

The following agencies are those that license, regulate, or are otherwise concerned with higher education in their state, province, or country. The contact information changes on almost a daily basis. If you discover errors or changes, please let us know; we will post updates on our Web site at *www.degree.net*.

United States

Alabama
Commission on Higher Education
100 North Union St.
Montgomery, AL 36130
Phone: (334) 242 1998
Fax: (334) 242 0268
Web site: www.ache.state.al.us

Another relevant agency
Department of Postsecondary Education
401 Adams Ave.
Montgomery, AL 36130
Phone: (334) 242 2900
Fax: (334) 242 2888

Alaska
Alaska Commission on Postsecondary Education
3030 Vintage Boulevard
Juneau, AK 99801
Phone: (907) 465 2962
Fax: (907) 465 5316
Web site: www.state.ak.us/acpe

"At St. Gabriel University, we eschew the Internet and postal system, and make our own arrangements to deliver your distance learning textbooks."

Arizona

Arizona Board of Regents
2020 North Central Ave., Suite 230
Phoenix, AZ 85004
Phone: (602) 229 2500
Fax: (602) 229 2555
Web site: www.abor.asu.edu

Another relevant agency

Arizona Commission for Postsecondary Education
2020 North Central Ave.,Suite 275
Phoenix, AZ 85004
Phone: (602) 229 2591
Fax: (602) 229 2599
Web site: www.acpe.asu.edu

Arkansas

Arkansas Department of Higher Education
114 East Capitol Ave.
Little Rock, AR 72201
Phone: (501) 371 2000
Fax: (501) 371 2003

California

California Postsecondary Education Commission
1303 J St., #500
Sacramento, CA 95814
Phone: (916) 445 7933
Fax: (916) 327 4417
Web site: www.cpec.ca.gov

Another relevant agency

Bureau for Private, Postsecondary and
    Vocational Education
1027 10th St., 4th Floor
Sacramento,CA 95814
Phone: (916) 445 3427
Fax: (916) 323 6571
Web site: www.dca.ca.gov/bppve

This is the former Council on Private, Postsecondary [etc.], which was moved from the Department of Education to the Department of Consumer Affairs in 1997. They are charged with evaluating the state's unaccredited schools, to determine if they should be granted State Approval.

Colorado

Colorado Commission on Higher Education
1300 Broadway, 2nd Floor
Denver, CO 80203
Phone: (303) 866 2723
Fax: (303) 860 9750

Connecticut

Board of Governors for Higher Education
61 Woodland St.
Hartford, CT 06105
Phone: (860) 947 1801
Fax: (860) 947 1310
Web site: ctdhe.commnet.edu

Delaware

Delaware Higher Education Commission
Carvel State Office Building
820 North French St.
Wilmington, DE 19801
Phone: (302) 577 3240
Fax: (302) 577 6765
Web site: www.doe.state.de.us

District of Columbia

Office of Postsecondary Education Research and
    Assistance
2100 Martin Luther King, Jr. Ave. SE
Suite 401
Washington, DC 20020
Phone: (202) 727 3688
Fax: (202) 727 2739

Florida

Florida Postsecondary Education Planning
    Commission
Turlington Building
Tallahassee, FL 32399
Phone: (904) 488 7894
Fax: (904) 922 5388

Georgia
Board of Regents
270 Washington St. SW
Atlanta, GA 30334
Phone: (404) 656 2202
Fax: (404) 657 6979
Web site: www.usg.edu

Hawaii
State Postsecondary Education Commission
2444 Dole St., Room 209
Honolulu, HI 96822
Phone: (808) 956 8207
Fax: (808) 956 5286

Idaho
Idaho Board of Education
P.O. Box 83720
Boise, ID 83720-0027
Phone: (208) 334 2270
Fax: (208) 334 2632
Web site: www.sde.state.id.us/Dept

Illinois
Board of Higher Education
431 East Adams, 2nd Floor
Springfield, IL 62701
Phone: (217) 782 2551
Fax: (217) 782 8548
Web site: www.ibhe.state.il.us

Indiana
Indiana Commission for Higher Education
101 West Ohio St., Suite 550
Indianapolis, IN 46204
Phone: (317) 464 4400
Fax: (317) 464 4410
Web site: www.che.state.in.us

Iowa
Board of Regents
100 Court Ave., Suite 203
Des Moines, IA 50319
Phone: (515) 281 3934
Fax: (515) 281 6420
Web site: www2.state.ia.us/regents

Kansas
Kansas Board of Regents
700 S.W. Harrison, Suite 1410
Topeka, KS 66603
Phone: (913) 296 3421
Fax: (913) 296 0983
Web site: www.kansasregents.org

Kentucky
Kentucky Council on Postsecondary Education
1024 Capital Center Dr., Suite 320
Frankfort, KY 40601
Phone: (502) 573 1555
Fax: (502) 573 1535
Web site: www.cpe.state.ky.us

Louisiana
Board of Regents
150 Third St., Suite 129
Baton Rouge, LA 70801
Phone: (504) 342 4253
Fax: (504) 342 9318
Web site: www.regents.state.la.us

Maine
Department of Education Office of Higher
    Education
23 State House Station
Augusta, ME 04333
Phone: (207) 287 5323
Fax: (207) 287 1344
Web site: janus.state.me.us/education

Maryland
Maryland Higher Education Commission
16 Francis St.
Annapolis, MD 21401
Phone: (410) 974 2971
Fax: (410) 974 3513
Web site: www.mhec.state.md.us

Massachusetts
Massachusetts Board of Higher Education
1 Ashburton Place, Room 1401
Boston, MA 02108
Phone: (617) 727 7785
Fax: (617) 727 6397
Web site: www.mass.edu

Michigan
Michigan Department of Career Development
Office of Postsecondary Services
P.O. Box 30714
Lansing, MI 48909
Phone: (517) 373 3820
Fax: (517) 373 2759
Web site: www.state.mi.us/career

Minnesota
Minnesota Higher Education Services Office
1450 Energy Park Dr., Suite 350
St. Paul, MN 55108
Phone: (651) 642 0502
Fax: (651) 642 0672
Web site: www.mheso.state.mn.us

Mississippi
Board of Trustees of State Institutions of
Higher Learning
3825 Ridgewood Road
Jackson, MS 39211
Phone: (601) 982 6623
Fax: (601) 987 4172
Web site: www.ihl.state.ms.us

Missouri
Coordinating Board for Higher Education
3515 Amazonas Dr.
Jefferson City, MO 65109
Phone: (573) 751 2361
Fax: (573) 751 6635
Web site: www.mocbhe.gov

Montana
Office of the Commissioner of Higher Education
Montana University System
2500 Broadway
Helena, MT 59620
Phone: (406) 444 6570
Fax: (406) 444 1469
Web site: www.montana.edu/wwwoche

Nebraska
Coordinating Commission for Postsecondary
Education
P.O. Box 95005
Lincoln, NE 68509
Phone: (402) 471 2847
Fax: (402) 471 2886
Web site: www.ccpe.state.ne.us

Nevada
University and Community College
System of Nevada
2601 Enterprise Road
Reno, NV 89512
Phone: (775) 784 4905
Fax: (775) 784 1127
Web site: www.nevada.edu

New Hampshire
New Hampshire Postsecondary Education
Commission
2 Industrial Park Dr.
Concord, NH 03301
Phone: (603) 271 2555
Fax: (603) 271 2696
Web site: www.state.nh.us/postsecondary

New Jersey
Commission on Higher Education
20 West State St.
P.O. Box 542
Trenton, NJ 08625
Phone: (609) 292 4310
Fax: (609) 292 7225
Web site: www.state.nj.us/highereducation

New Mexico
Commission on Higher Education
1068 Cerrillos Road
Santa Fe, NM 87501
Phone: (505) 827 7383
Fax: (505) 827 7392
Web site: www.nmche.org

New York
New York State Education Department
89 Washington Ave.
Albany, NY 12234
Phone: (518) 474 5844
Fax: (518) 473 4909
Web site: www.nysed.gov

North Carolina
Commission on Higher Education Facilities
UNC General Administration
910 Raleigh Rd., P.O. Box 2688
Chapel Hill, NC 27515
Phone: (919) 962 4611
Fax: (919) 962 0008

North Dakota
North Dakota University System
10th Floor, State Capitol
600 East Boulevard Ave, Dept. 215
Bismarck, ND 58505
Phone: (701) 328 2960
Fax: (701) 328 2961
Web site: www.ndus.nodak.edu

Ohio
Ohio Board of Regents
30 East Broad St., 36th Floor
Columbus, OH 43266
Phone: (614) 466 6000
Fax: (614) 466 5866
Web site: www.bor.state.oh.us

Oklahoma
Oklahoma State Regents for Higher Education
500 Education Building
State Capitol Complex
Oklahoma City, OK 73105
Phone: (405) 524 9100
Fax: (405) 524 9230
Web site: www.okhighered.org

Oregon
Governor's Office of Education and Workforce
Policy
Office of Degree Authorization
255 Capitol St. NE, Suite 126
Salem, OR 97310
Phone: (503) 378 3921
Fax: (503) 378 4789
Web site: www.ode.state.or.us

Pennsylvania

Pennsylvania Department of Education
Postsecondary and Higher Education
333 Market St., 12th Floor
Harrisburg, PA 17126
Phone: (717) 787 5041
Fax: (717) 783 0583
Web site: www.pde.psu.edu

Rhode Island

Office of Higher Education
301 Promenade Street
Providence, RI 02908
Phone: (401) 222 6560
Fax: (401) 222 6111
Web site: www.uri.edu/ribog

South Carolina

South Carolina Commission on Higher Education
1333 Main St., Suite 200
Columbia, SC 29201
Phone: (803) 737 2260
Fax: (803) 737 2297
Web site: www.che400.state.sc.us

South Dakota

South Dakota Board of Regents
306 E. Capital Ave.
Pierre, SD 57501
Phone: (605) 773 3455
Fax: (605) 773 5320
Web site: www.ris.sdbor.edu

Tennessee

Tennessee Higher Education Commission
Parkway Towers, Suite 1900
404 James Robertson Pkwy.
Nashville, TN 37243
Phone: (615) 741 3605
Fax: (615) 741 6230
Web site: www.state.tn.us/thec

Texas

Texas Higher Education Coordinating Board
P.O. Box 12788
Austin, TX 78711
Phone: (512) 427 6101
Fax: (512) 483 6127
Web site: www.thecb.state.tx.us

Utah

Utah State Board of Regents
3 Triad Center, Suite 550
Salt Lake City, UT 84180
Phone: (801) 321 7101
Fax: (801) 321 7199
Web site: www.utahsbr.edu

Vermont

State Department of Education
Career and Lifelong Learning
120 State St.
Montpelier, VT 05620
Phone: (802) 828 3147
Fax: (802) 828 3140
Web site: www.cit.state.vt.us/educ

Virginia

State Council of Higher Education for Virginia
James Monroe Building, 9th Floor
101 N. 14th St.
Richmond, VA 23219
Phone: (804) 225 2600
Fax: (804) 371 7911
Web site: www.schev.edu

Washington

Higher Education Coordinating Board
917 Lakeridge Way
P.O. Box 43430
Olympia, WA 98504
Phone: (360) 753 7800
Fax: (360) 753 7808
Web site: www.hecb.wa.gov

West Virginia

West Virginia Higher Education Policy Commission
1018 Kanawha Blvd., East, Suite 700
Charleston, WV 25301
Phone: (304) 558 2101
Fax: (304) 558 5719
Web site: www.hepc.wvnet.edu

Wisconsin

Higher Educational Aids Board
131 W. Wilson St., Room 902
Madison, WI 53703
Phone: (608) 267 2206
Fax: (608) 267 2808
Web site: heab.state.wi.us

Wyoming

Wyoming Community College Commission
2020 Carey Ave., 8th Floor
Cheyenne, WY 82002
Phone: (307) 777 7763
Fax: (307) 777 6567
Web site: commission.wcc.edu

American Samoa

Board of Higher Education
American Samoa Community College
P.O. Box 2609
Pago Pago, AS 96799
Phone: (684) 699 9155

Puerto Rico

Puerto Rico Council on Higher Education
P.O. Box 19900
San Juan, PR 00910
Phone: (787) 724 7100
Fax: (787) 725 1275

Canada

Alberta

Alberta Learning
7th Floor, Commerce Place
10155-102 St.
Edmonton, Alberta T5J IX4
Phone: +1 (780) 427 7219
Fax: +1 (780) 422 1263

British Columbia

Ministry of Education, Training, and Technology
P.O. Box 9880
Station Provincial Government
Victoria, BC V8W 9T6
Phone: +1 (250) 953 3585
Fax: +1 (250) 356 6063
Deals with public institutions.

Another relevant agency

Private Postsecondary Education Commission
960 Quayside Dr., Suite 405
New Westminster, BC V3M 6G2
Phone: +1 (604) 660 4400
Fax: +1 (604) 660 3312
Deals with private institutions.

Manitoba

Department of Education and Training
2nd floor, 800 Portage Ave.
Winnipeg, Manitoba R3C 0N4
Phone: +1 (204) 945 2211
Fax: +1 (204) 945 8692
Web site: www.gov.mb.ca/educate

New Brunswick

Department of Training and Employment
Development
P.O. Box 6000
470 York St.
Frederickton, NB E3B 5H1
Phone: +1 (506) 453 2597
Fax: +1 (506) 453 3038

Newfoundland

Newfoundland and Labrador Council on Higher
Education
3rd Floor, West Block, Confederation Building
P.O. Box 8700
St. John's, Newfoundland A1B 4J6
Phone: +1 (709) 729 2083
Fax: +1 (709) 729 3669
Web site: www.gov.nf.ca/edu

Nova Scotia

Department of Education
P.O. Box 578
2021 Brunswick St., Ste. 402
Halifax, NS B3J 2S9
Phone: +1 (902) 424 5168
Fax: +1 (902) 424 0511
Web site: www.ednet.ns.ca

Ontario

Ministry of Education
14th Floor, Mowat Block
900 Bay St.
Toronto, ON M7A 1L2
Phone: +1 (416) 325 2929
Fax: +1 (416) 325 2934
Web site: www.edu.gov.on.ca

Prince Edward Island

Department of Education
Second Fl., Sullivan Building
16 Fitzroy Street, P.O. Box 2000
Charlottetown, PEI C1A 7N8
Phone: +1 (902) 368 4600
Fax: +1 (902) 368 4663
Web site: www.gov.pe.ca

Quebec

Ministere de l'Education
1035, rue De La Chevrotière
Édifice Marie-Guyart, 28e étage
Québec G1R 5A5
Phone: +1 (418) 643 7095
Web site: www.meq.gouv.qc.ca

Saskatchewan

Saskatchewan Education
2220 College Ave.
Regina, SK S4P 3V7
Phone: +1 (306) 787 6030
Fax: +1 (306) 787 7392
Web site: www.sasked.gov.sk.ca

Agencies Outside the U.S. and Canada

Australia

Department of Education, Training, and Youth
   Affairs
Sydney
Phone: +61 (2) 9298 7200
Web site: www.deet.gov.a
At press time, DETYA is in process of establishing the
Australian University Quality Agency.

Belgium

Ministry of National Education
Centre Arts Lux, 4th & 5th Floors
58 Ave. des Arts, BP5
1040 Brussels
Phone: +32 (2) 512 66 60

Brazil

Ministry of Education and Culture
Esplanada dos Ministerios, Bloco L
74.047 Brasilia, DF
Phone: +55 (61) 214 8432

Bulgaria

Ministry of Education and Science
Blvd. A, Stamboliski 18
Sofia 1000

'Hold victim firmly, and...and...drat, I left my
fire safety textbook in there on the desk.'

Cuba

Ministry of Higher Education
Calle 23y F, Vedado
Havana

Denmark

The Danish Ministry of Education
Frederiksholms Kanal 21
DK-1220 Copenhagen
Phone: +45 3392 5000
Fax: +45 3392 5547
Web site: www.uvm.dk/eng

Egypt

Ministry of Education
12 El Falaki Street, Cairo
Phone: +20 (2) 516 9744
Fax: +20 (2) 516 9560

Finland

Ministry of Education
P.O. Box 293
FIN-00171 Helsinki
Phone: +358 (9) 1341 71
Fax: +358 (9) 135 9335
Web site: www.minedu.fi

France

Ministry of National Education
110 Rue de Grenelle
75700 Paris
Phone: +33 (1) 45 50 10 10

Germany

Ministry of Education and Science
Heinemannstr. 2
5300 Bonn 2

Greece

Ministry of Education and Science
Odo Mihalakopoulou 80, Athens
Phone: +30 (1) 21 3230461

Hungary

Ministry of Education
Szalay u. 10-14
1055 Budapest
Phone: +36 (1) 302 0600
Fax: +36 (1) 302 3002
Web site: www.om.hu

India

Department of Education
Ministry of Human Resource Development
Government of India
Shastri Bhawan, New Delhi-110001
Phone: +91 (11) 3387342
Fax: +91 (11) 3381355
Web site: education.nic.in

Indonesia

Ministry of National Education
Jalan Jenderal Sudirman
Senayan, Jakarta Pusat
Web site: www.pdk.go.id

Ireland

Department of Education and Science
Marlborough St.
Dublin 1
Phone: +353 (1) 8734700 ext.2162
Fax: +353 (1) 8786712
Web site: www.irlgov.ie/educ

Israel

Council for Higher Education
P.O. Box 4037
Jerusalem 91040
Phone: +972 (2) 5679911
Fax: +972 (2) 5660625
Web site: www.israel-mfa.gov.il

Italy

Ministry of Public Education
Viale Trastevere 76/A
00153 Rome
Phone: +39 (6) 58 49 1
Web site: www.istruzione.it

Japan

Ministry of Education, Science, Sports and Culture
Web site: www.monbu.go.jp

Mexico

Secretaria de Education Publica
Web site: www.sep.gob.mx

Netherlands

Ministry of Education, Culture and Science
Department of Foreign Information
P.O.B. 25000
2700 LZ Zoetermeer
Phone: +31 (79) 3232323
Fax: +31 (79) 3232320
Web site: www.minocw.nl

New Zealand

Ministry of Eduation
National Office
45-47 Pipitea St., P.O. Box 1666
Thorndon, Wellington
Phone: +64 (4) 473 5544
Fax: +64 (4) 499 1327

Norway

Ministry of Education, Research and Church Affairs
Akersgt. 44, P.O. Box 8119 Dep.
0032 Oslo
Phone: +47 (22) 24 77 01
Fax: +47 (22) 24 27 33
Web site: odin.dep.no/kuf/engelsk

Philippines

Department of Education, Culture and Sports
DECS Complex, Meralco Avenue
Pasig City
Phone: +63 (2) 633 7228
Fax: +63 (2) 632 0805
Web site: www.decs.gov.ph

Portugal

Ministry of Education
Av. 5 de Outubro 107
Lisbon
Phone: +351 (1) 21 793 16 03
Fax: +351 (1) 21 796 41 19
Web site: www.min-edu.pt

South Africa

Department of Education
Private Bag X895
Pretoria 0001
Phone: +27 (12) 312 5911
Fax: +27 (12) 325 6260
Web site: education.pwv.gov.za

South Korea

Ministry of Education
77, Sejong-ro, Chongro-ku
Seoul 110-760
Phone: +82 (2) 739 3345
Fax: +82 (2) 723 7691
Web site: www.moe.go.kr/english

Spain

Ministry of Education and Culture
Web site: www.mec.es

Sweden

Ministry of Education and Cultural Affairs
Mynttorget 1
Stockholm 103 33
Phone: +46 (8) 736 10 00

Turkey

Ministry of Education, Youth, and Sports
Milli Egitum, Genclik ve Spor
Bakanligi, Anakara

United Kingdom

Department of Education and Science
Elizabeth House, York Rd.
London SEI 7PH
Phone: +44 (171) 928 9222

CHAPTER 7

School Licensing Laws: State, Provincial, National, and International

Morality cannot be legislated, but behavior can be regulated.

Martin Luther King, Jr.

This chapter, more than any other, could benefit from almost a daily update, as both the laws themselves and the way they are interpreted are in constant flux. We start with the reminder that we are not lawyers (even if John did buy a $58 Harvard law degree by mail). If you have any question about whether a given school operates legally, whether its degree will meet your needs, or indeed how to start a school, you would be well advised to seek competent legal counsel.

Six Reasons Why This Chapter Is So Complicated

1. There are so many jurisdictions

Consider a university that uses a mailing address in a Caribbean country, actually operates from Europe, and has an office in the United States. And consider a potential student who seeks a degree in psychology, wishing to become a marriage counselor. Who's in charge here? The state or province where the student lives? (Each of the 50 U.S. states has its own school and licensing laws, as do the Canadian provinces and most other political subdivisions.) The psychology licensing board? (Again, each jurisdiction is different; some do not require any degree at all; others require a doctorate.) The accrediting agency? (But in the U.S. alone, there are a number of regional, national, and professional accreditors.) The national government? (But of which country? Or is it more than one?) Some international agency (or agencies)?

2. Laws change and interpretations change

What keeps many lawyers and judges in business is interpreting, reinterpreting, and challenging the law. And what keeps many politicians and bureaucrats occupied is writing, rewriting, and changing laws. Marijuana used to be legal. Birth control used to be illegal. In Florida, it was legal to use an unaccredited degree in public ways (as on a business card or in advertising). Then the court determined that it was illegal. Following a challenge, the state Supreme Court overturned the lower court ruling and made it legal. And now the legislature is considering new laws to make it illegal.

3. Legality varies from one location to another

People are more mobile than ever before. A child therapist with an unaccredited California degree can probably take the state licensing exam in Colorado but not in Wyoming. A practicing lawyer with an unaccredited Virginia law degree may be able to take the Bar exam in New York, but not in Ohio. What about engineers from Kazakhstan who want to be licensed in Ontario? Accountants from Hong Kong who want to practice in Oregon? Linguists from Illinois who want to teach in Korea?

There are hundreds of states, provinces, and countries, and dozens of fields of study that are regulated in some, most, or all places. The regulation can come from any number of governmental, quasi-governmental, independent, or trade organizations, which do not always agree with one another.

4. It's not clear who has jurisdiction

When the school itself has a presence (or an apparent presence) in more than one location, the issue grows even more complex, for both acceptance of a credential, and for regulation of the school itself. The fraudulent Columbia State University, for instance, managed to exist for more than ten years because the attorney general of Louisiana was saying, in effect, "We know they're really in California, so it's not my business," while the California attorney general was saying, "They're using a Louisiana mailing address and telephone number, so it's not my business." Such operations fall through the cracks, until finally some federal agency, which operates across state lines (typically the FBI, the Postal Service, the Federal Trade Commission, and/or the Internal Revenue Service) finally takes action.

5. It is not always easy to get information

In fact, sometimes it is downright impossible. It seems odd to us, still, that a reference book such as this one should have to say, "We aren't sure," or "We don't know." But when we have done all the library and Internet research we can, can't find certain information, and then dozens of letters and telephone calls and faxes to what may be the relevant agency go unanswered, short of staging a hunger strike in their lobby, what is one to do?

As one example out of many, we have been trying for more than seven years to get a copy of a U.S. Department of Education publication that lists all the schools that qualify for federal aid programs. We got a copy in 1991 when the person at a wrong number we reached in Washington took pity on us and sent us her personal copy. We write. We call. We fax. We spend hours in voice-mail hell. We even attempted to enlist the aid of our congressperson, all to no avail. Earlier, we described our years of fruitless efforts to learn something about the accreditation process in a Caribbean nation.

6. People in power don't know, won't tell, or get it wrong

On more than a few occasions, we discover that the "right person" (or office) either doesn't know, won't tell us, or tells us something wrong. Again, if this sort of thing happened rarely, and only at obscure ministries in tiny or remote countries, it might be predicted and acceptable. But it happens over and over, in California, in London, and in Ottawa as well as in St. Kitts, in Costa Rica, and in Liberia. Sometimes they don't know (as in the case of a state Department of Education official who wrote to us that a

20-year-old state-approved university "is not known to the State of California. Perhaps they went out of business years ago"). Sometimes it is the people who, in earlier years, probably admired the Emperor's new clothes. It was an officer in the Department of Education in Great Britain who wrote to us that "No unlicensed or unrecognized universities operate now from Britain." When we replied asking about twelve specific non-GAAP, unrecognized schools currently run from addresses in Britain, we received no answer, despite three requests.

There are, of course, many exceptions: caring, helpful, knowledgeable officials, who are helpful to us and to members of the general public who call, write, fax, or email for information.

• • • • •

Having said all that, here is the situation as best we can determine. Things used to be relatively stable. Some U.S. states militantly forbade any nontraditional schools or programs, others allowed anyone to do anything, and most were somewhere in between. When there was a change in a state law or its interpretation, one could almost see the flow of schools from Place 1 to Place 2, and the arising of new schools in Place 2. From California to Arizona, then Arizona to Louisiana, then Louisiana to Hawaii and Iowa, with lesser ventures into Idaho, New Mexico, Wyoming, Montana, and South Dakota.

We simply cannot cover the situation with regard to every country, state, and province and with respect to all the various fields of study requiring licensing or certification. (That would make a darn good master's or senior thesis for someone!) Here, then, are some comments on what we know (or believe) is the situation in the states with the greatest number of nontraditional schools, both good and bad, and in some of the countries where there exists other than 'official' state-run or state-funded institutions.

United States

Alabama

For many years, Alabama has had a school licensing law. It doesn't have much power. There is no evaluation; no visit by the state is required. The "campus" can be a post office box or secretarial service. Indeed, some Alabama universities are, in fact, run from Louisiana, Rhode Island, California, and other locations. The situation has been, for years, complicated by the fact that four universities operated by Dr. Lloyd Clayton from Birmingham (Chadwick, American Institute of Computer Science, and two health and nutrition schools) did not even have the most minimal state license, yet they clearly operated with the knowledge and, it seemed, permission of the state. They did not, however, accept students living in the state of Alabama. The schools' position was that not taking Alabama students was simply their policy. It took us nearly five years of writing letters, sending faxes, and making telephone calls before we finally learned the truth. It seems that in the 1980s, the then-attorney general of Alabama issued a ruling that schools that did not do business in the state of Alabama did not need to be licensed by the state.

In 1996, however, this all changed. In response to a request from the Department of Education, the current attorney general ruled that all institutions based in the state *must* be licensed by the state, regardless of their policy for accepting in-state students. Nearly two years later, Chadwick and the others finally got their license to operate, and one of Dr. Clayton's schools, the American Institute of Computer Science, even went on to get recognized accreditation.

But in 2000, the state still does not evaluate the schools that it allows to call themselves "state approved." Some may be quite good; others have a "campus" that is a mailbox rental store. The state doesn't care.

Arizona

Arizona went from being one of the worst states to one of the toughest, following publication of a four-day series called "Diploma Mills: a festering sore on the state of Arizona" in the Phoenix newspaper in the 1980s. But Arizona law does allow new degree-granting universities to be established, as long as it is done on a small scale: fewer than 100 students unless and until the school gains recognized accreditation.

California

Well, at least California is unfailingly interesting. For many years, until the late 1980s, California was the laughingstock of the nation (a mantle subsequently assumed by Louisiana, and then by Hawaii, and now the current holder, South Dakota—with Wyoming and Montana warming up in the bullpen). California authorization required little more than a short disclosure form, and evidence of $50,000 in assets. Shady operators were declaring that their homes were their universities, or buying a bundle of obsolete textbooks and declaring that they were worth $100 each. At the time diploma mill operator Ernest Sinclair went to federal prison for mail fraud (selling degrees), his California Pacifica University was still a state-authorized institution.

For a few years, the state had a three-tiered system: authorized (the $50,000 rule) for entire schools, state approved (for specific programs within schools), or accredited. The authorized category was dropped, and approval was extended to entire schools, resulting in the current two-tier system. At that time, dozens of schools closed down, and some of the big ones opened offices in other states: Kennedy-Western in Idaho (later Hawaii and Wyoming),

Century in New Mexico, Pacific Western in Louisiana (later Hawaii), Kensington in Hawaii (later Montana), etc.

State approval used to be granted by the Department of Education, through the Council on Private Postsecondary and Vocational Education. Then things got really silly.

In the early '90s, California's Superintendent of Public Instruction was indicted and convicted of several counts of felony conflict of interest and removed from office. For three years, the state had no superintendent, and things went somewhat adrift.

California has a "sunset" law, which decrees that state commissions automatically go out of business unless they are renewed by the legislature. Normally this is a routine rubber-stamp process. However in 1996, after the legislature had voted to continue the Council on Private Postsecondary and Vocational Education for another five years, Governor Pete Wilson surprised many people by vetoing the bill, declaring that the Council was not doing a good job, and should be replaced by something better. In the eight months between the veto and the expiration date, there was much bickering, but no solution. With a few days to go, it looked as if California would be without a school regulatory agency. The federal government suggested that such a situation could have a serious effect on student loans and other federal programs.

On the last possible day (June 30, 1997), the legislature extended the life of the Council for a generous 18 days, and then the politicians got serious. On the 18th day, a compromise was reached: the Council on Private Postsecondary and Vocational Education would die on the last day of 1997, to be replaced by the Bureau of Private Postsecondary and Vocational Education, which would move from the Department of Education to the Department of Consumer Affairs. And thus it came to pass that California has become the only state in the country, perhaps the only government in the world, in which school licensing and regulation does not take place in the Department of Education.

After a few years of operation, it seems that the Bureau differs little from the Council. They are still underfunded and understaffed, and they still seem unable to deal with the common situation of schools that are run from California but claim their legitimacy from licensing in an easier state: Kennedy-Western (run from California, license from Wyoming), Kensington (California/Montana), Pacific Western (California/Hawaii), Century (California/New Mexico), and so on.

Another confusion in California is that the state senate decreed that holders of approved degrees should be permitted to take relevant state licensing exams, such as those in marriage, family, and child counseling. But the state board of professional licensing refused to go along with this automatic permission, saying that the standards for approval and the standards for certain exams were not at all the same. They now permit degree-holders from some schools, but not others, to take the exams. And almost no other state will accept California-approved degrees for state licensing purposes. Be sure to check on these matters if state licensing is part of your goal.

Florida

Florida is a classic case of what can happen when legislation gets out of hand. A 1988 Florida statute (Sections 817.566 and .567, Florida Statutes, 1988 Supplement) made it a crime to use an unaccredited degree in any way in that state, even if it is from a school approved or licensed in another state. It was a "misdemeanor of the first degree" [*sic*] for a person with, say, a California-approved or a Minnesota-approved degree, to reveal, within the boundaries of Florida, that he or she has that degree.

This rather extraordinary statute was challenged in court, and in 1995, the state supreme court found it to be unconstitutional. However, the judges strongly suggested that if the legislature were to rewrite the law a bit more carefully, it could achieve the same intent and be within the bounds of the constitution. So at the present time, it would appear that holders of legitimate degrees from other states can use them in Florida, but it is clear the situation is far from over. Indeed the legislature is once again considering a strong school licensing law.

Hawaii

Until 1999, Hawaii did not regulate any institutions of higher education at all. In 1990, a law was passed requiring the state Department of Consumer Affairs to register all unaccredited schools in the state, but it was minimally enforced. (It also required unaccredited schools to state that fact in their literature in boldface type. Since the law doesn't specify the *size* of such type, you can imagine what some schools do.)

Small wonder that Hawaii now has more unaccredited and highly questionable "universities" than the other 49 states combined. An article in the *Pacific Business News* in 2000 listed more than 200 unaccredited colleges and universities with Hawaii addresses, along with the dozen-or-so properly accredited ones.

When Edward Reddeck, one of America's most notorious degree mill operators, moved his fake schools to the state of Hawaii, neither the state's attorney general nor the Department of Consumer Affairs showed any interest, nor did the education editor of Honolulu's major newspaper (who declined to run a story on this situation, stating, "Our job is to *report* news, not *make* news"). Fortunately, in this instance, federal authorities *did* care, and those phony schools were closed by the action of postal inspectors. *Then* the newspaper ran a big page-one story!

In the late 1990s, the state's Department of Consumer Affairs exercised a little muscle for the first time, with lawsuits for violation of the disclosure law, against American State University, Pacific Western University, Cambridge State University, Monticello University, and others.

Finally, in 1999, the legislature passed a law calling for the regulation of unaccredited schools. It says that any unaccredited schools claiming to operate from Hawaii must have at least one employee living in Hawaii, and at least 25 full-time students in the state of Hawaii. It is not yet clear how this law will be either defined or enforced, but some Hawaii schools are claiming they have been given three years to be in compliance.

Iowa

Iowa is another state in transition. Until 1995, it not only had a somewhat misleading school licensing law, but it also seemed extremely lax in enforcing what little law they had. Registration with the state was virtually automatic, but only gave schools permission to offer classes in Iowa. It did not authorize them to award degrees or to claim they were an Iowa-licensed school. Nonetheless, at least half a dozen schools did just that.

In 1995, the legislature attempted to address this situation by requiring all unaccredited schools to be on an approved "accreditation track," or leave the state: the so called "up or out" provision. But three years later, nothing seemed to have changed, with some of Iowa's wonders still operating without benefit of accreditation or any motion toward it.

We finally learned, thanks to a persistent reader of this book, that the Department of Education felt that it was too much to expect a school to get on an accreditation track quickly, and so they quietly gave the Iowa unaccredited schools three years to get on track. At least three of the many various unaccredited Iowa schools announced they would be applying for accreditation from the Distance Education and Training Council. But none of them seems actually to have done so, yet this may have bought more time from the state. Other schools with Iowa addresses have moved to more hospitable states like Alabama and Wyoming.

Louisiana

For many years, Louisiana has been the victim of what one highly-placed state regulator privately calls the "Woody Jenkins law." Jenkins is the prominent Republican politician who is so opposed to the state regulation of almost *anything* that even though he graduated from law school with highest honors, he has refused to take the Bar exam, believing that the state has no right to require such of lawyers.

Under Jenkins' influence, the legislature required that Louisiana's Board of Regents register any school that filled out a short form, with no evaluation whatsoever. This permitted some completely phony schools to advertise that they were "Appropriately registered with the Board of Regents," or even (improperly) that they were "Recognized by the Board of Regents."

"These correspondence poetry slams lack verve, don't you think?"

In 1991, Louisiana passed a new law, which gave the Board of Regents power to regulate proprietary (privately owned) schools, although nonprofit schools were still exempt. In 1992, the Board of Regents decided that only proprietary schools with an actual physical presence in the state could be registered. Since dozens of "Louisiana" schools operate either from mail forwarding services or "executive suite" office-rental-by-the-hour establishments, quite a few schools using Louisiana addresses moved their addresses elsewhere, mostly to Iowa, Hawaii, or South Dakota. More than 20 closed down.

Following Jenkins defeat in his try for the U.S. Senate, Louisiana legislators saw their chance, and in 1999 passed a law regulating not-for-profit schools that ostensibly operate from within Louisiana but, in fact, have nothing more than a convenience address and telephone answering service there. It took effect in early 2000 and, like the laws in Arizona and Iowa, requires unaccredited schools to be on an approved accreditation path. Unlike the other states, Louisiana inaugurated clear and specific requirements.

Louisiana unaccredited schools must now be accepted as an accreditation applicant by the Distance Education and Training Council (DETC), a recognized national accreditor. Schools rejected by DETC (as happened to Fairfax University, one of the first through the gate) either lose their Louisiana license or (as happened with Fairfax) can choose the one loophole in the new law: dropping all but purely religious degrees.

Schools whose applications are accepted by DETC must then pursue accreditation with all deliberate speed. If they get it, they remained licensed; if not, they lose their license to operate (and presumably look toward South Dakota, Montana, Wyoming, or oblivion).

The Louisiana religious loophole is now a tiny one, but it was not always this way. Previously, religious schools were exempt from licensing, but there was no requirement that they offer purely religious degrees. LaSalle University, which operated for years under the religious exemption, used to claim that even their Ph.D.'s in physics, psychology, and political science were religious, because God created everything, including atoms, minds, and politicians. No matter what you study, they argued, you are studying the work of God. Thankfully, the loophole has been redefined; religious schools can offer only religious degrees: divinity, theology, and so on.

Oregon

Hands down, Oregon has the strictest school laws of any state in the nation. In Oregon, it is *illegal* to use a degree from an institution not accredited by an accrediting agency recognized by the U.S. Department of Education or approved by Oregon's Office of Degree Authorization (ODA). In *Bears' Guide* terms, that roughly translates to any school listed in chapters 21, 22, 23, or 27.

Oregon takes the additional strong step of publishing, at *www.osac.state.or.us/oda*, a list of the most recently reported schools whose degrees are illegal in Oregon.

The list, as it appeared when we went to press:

Barrington University (Alabama/Florida)
Berne University (New Hampshire/St. Kitts)
California Coast University (California)
Canyon College (Idaho)
Columbia Pacific University (California)
Columbia Southern University (Alabama)
Columbia State University (Louisiana/Hawaii; now closed)
Frederick Taylor University (Hawaii, California)
Greenleaf University (Missouri)
Hamilton University (Wyoming)
Harrington University (Great Britain, Cyprus)
Kennedy-Western University (Wyoming, Idaho, California)
Kensington University (California/Montana/Hawaii)
LaSalle University (Louisiana)
Monticello University (Kansas; closed)
Oxford International University (Great Britain)
Preston University (Wyoming/Pakistan)
Rushmore University (South Dakota/Georgia)
University of Advanced Research (Hawaii)
University of Northern Washington (Hawaii)
University of San Moritz (Great Britain, Cyprus)
University of Santa Barbara (California)
University of Santa Monica (California)

South Dakota

There are times when we speculate that there must be some secret newsletter circulated among the owners of the dreadful schools of America, in which articles appear analyzing the various states and their tolerance for these kinds of operations. Either that, or just the 'herd' instinct. In any event, as laws and the enforcement thereof showed signs of getting tougher in former havens such as Hawaii, Louisiana, and Iowa, the dreadful schools suddenly began to advertise from addresses in South Dakota, typically in malls and business centers just across the border from some of the larger towns in Iowa. Clearly it had simply never occurred to the good folks who run South Dakota that they needed a bunch of rules on the books to deal with a sudden influx of universities. And so there are virtually none. In the year 2000, one can take out a business license, rent a mailbox in a Mail Boxes Etc. store, hire a telephone answering service, and in little more than 24 hours, this new legal "state-licensed" (i.e. that business license) university can place its first ads in *The Economist* and *USA Today*.

To their credit, the South Dakotans took notice of the situation much more rapidly than most other states have. The newspapers, radio and television stations, and the Better Business Bureau have all been heard from. Can the legislators be far behind?

Wyoming

Wyoming may be the only state that not only does not regulate "religious" schools but also does not question the fact that a school says it is religious. Thus it is the last refuge of that strategy that says, "Let's start a religious school with a non-religious name, not tell the public that we are religious, and off we go." This has led, for example, to a truly dreadful place called Hamilton University operating without benefit of any scrutiny or regulation. Because Hamilton advertises extensively, and doubtless people are regularly calling the Department of Education to ask about them, this has led to the piteous situation in which Hamilton is the *only* school mentioned on the official state education Web site:

> Question: Does the State of Wyoming exempt any post secondary school from licensing?
>
> Answer:…The following types of schools are…exempt: any parochial, church, or religious school under the control of a local church, or religious congregation or a denomination, such as Hamilton University…

Read it and weep at *www.k12.wy.us/higher_ed/faq.html*.

The Rest of the United States

Often, legislation arises in response to behavior. If legislators don't like the behavior, they pass laws against it. Commonly, it is only after unaccredited schools (good, bad, or in between) become so numerous or so visible they cannot be ignored that states consider and even pass legislation to restrict or regulate them. For instance, for some years, New Mexico had only one visible unaccredited school, Century University. But after the number reached two, then three, then four, with other schools looking in that direction and writing to the state agency in Santa Fe for information, New Mexico's Commission on Higher Education issued "Rule 730," a 21-page set of rules and guidelines for proprietary schools which either operate within the state, or recruit citizens of New Mexico from outside the state. This rule makes it a little harder to operate an unaccredited school in that state.

Unless and until there is more international cooperation, it may be that schools will continue to be run like puppets: operators in one country pulling the strings that make the school work in another country. As an example, there are at least six well-advertised universities actually run from England, but claiming their degree-granting authority from their registration in the U.S., Ireland, or a Caribbean nation. England apparently looks on them as "American" or "Irish" (etc.) schools and doesn't try to regulate them.

And the U.S., Ireland, etc., may consider them to be British schools, since it is from there that things are run.

The Rest of the World

This is an evolving section, which may, one day, include both the laws and the actual practices of school licensing in countries worldwide. This is no simple matter, in part because of the difficulty of getting information, and in part because some smaller countries are just not prepared to deal with the matter of newly appearing universities in their territory. A few years ago, no one would have predicted, for instance, that the tiny island nation of St. Kitts and Nevis, with no degree-granting institutions of its own, would be home to five or more international universities (which happen to be run from the U.S., England, and Australia). Surely not the Minister of Youth, Education, and Community Affairs, who issues Certificates of Accreditation with, it seems, little or no semblance of a traditional evaluation process. For instance, the totally fraudulent Eastern Caribbean University, run from Smithville, Texas, was duly accredited by St. Kitts a few years ago.

Thankfully, the United Nations and other agencies have addressed this issue, and make the process of determining the legitimacy of schools relatively straightforward, at least as far as many registrars, admissions officers, and other evaluators are concerned. The *International Handbook of Universities*, published regularly by UNESCO, is the generally accepted arbiter in most places. Other prime sources include the *World Education Series* published by PIER (Projects in International Education Research); the annual directory of the Association of Commonwealth Universities; and the *Countries Series* published by Australia's National Office on Overseas Skills Recognition. If a university in Singapore or St. Kitts, Barbados or Bangladesh, appears in any of these books, then it is safe to assume that it meets the standards of GAAP, Generally Accepted Accreditation Principles (which is discussed more at the start of chapter 8). If it is not in those books, it still might be OK, but more due diligence is suggested.

What about the notion of an international accrediting agency? One that was thorough and well-respected and internationally accepted in the academic, government, and business worlds would be a wonderful thing to have. The waters have been well-muddied by dozens of such agencies that have arisen in recent years, ranging, in our opinion, from dreadful to extremely dreadful. One bright light on the horizon is GATE, the Global Association for Transnational Education, funded by Glenn Jones, the same entrepreneur who founded the now-regionally-accredited Jones International University. GATE has done good things in the direction of putting on international conferences on many aspects of reconciling the different education systems of 200+ countries, and has, in fact, initiated a "certification" process for schools. Perhaps one day, they will let the other shoe, the one called "international accreditation," drop. GATE's Web site is found at *www.edugate.org*.

CHAPTER 8

Accreditation

The comfortable world of accreditation seems to be unraveling.

Opening sentence, Chronicle of Higher Education *article on the state of accreditation, 1993*

The accreditation community is in the early stages of addressing [the] challenge ... of distance learning.

Council on Higher Education Accreditation Quality Assurance and Distance Education Conference, 1998

Accreditation "Lite"

This is a complex chapter. If you read nothing else, read this small section.

1. Generally, you can't go wrong by choosing a school that meets GAAP, Generally Accepted Accreditation Principles. (See box on page 45.)

2. There are a small number of legitimate and useful unaccredited schools.

3. There is an even smaller number of legitimate but unrecognized accrediting agencies.

4. There are a great many phony or useless accrediting agencies.

5. The world of accreditation is slowly changing, generally in the direction of dealing more with outcomes: how schools teach or train their students and how well the students perform.

Accreditation "Regular"

Accreditation is perhaps the most complex, confusing, and important issue in higher education. It is surely the most misunderstood and the most misused concept—both intentionally and unintentionally.

In selecting a school, there are four important things to know about accreditation:

1. What it is;

2. Why it is important in certain situations;

3. What are the many kinds of accreditors, and

4. What's all the fuss and bother that led to those two quotations at the top of this chapter?

We will address these matters more or less in this order.

What is Accreditation?

Quite simply, it is a validation—a statement by a group of persons who are, theoretically, impartial experts in higher education, that a given school, or department within a school, has been thoroughly investigated and found worthy of approval.

Accreditation is a peculiarly American concept. In every other country in the world, all colleges and universities either are operated by the government, or gain the full right to grant degrees directly from the government, so there is no need for a separate, independent agency to say that a given school is OK. Countries such as Australia and England use the word "accreditation" but it has a very different meaning there, and does not relate to the widespread acceptance of a given school or degree program.

In the United States, accreditation is an *entirely voluntary process*, done by private, nongovernmental agencies. As a result of this lack of central control or authority, there have evolved good accrediting agencies and bad ones, recognized ones and unrecognized ones, legitimate ones and phony ones.

So when a school says, "we are accredited," that statement alone means nothing. You must always ask,

"Accredited by whom?" Unfortunately, many consumer-oriented articles and bulletins simply say that one is much safer dealing only with accredited schools, but they do not attempt to unravel the complex situation. We hear regularly from distressed people who say, about the degrees they have just learned are worthless, "But the school was accredited; I even checked with the accrediting agency." The agency, needless to say, turned out to be as phony as the school. The wrong kind of accreditation can be worse than none at all.

Normally, a school wishing to be accredited will make application to the appropriate accrediting agency. After a substantial preliminary investigation to determine that the school is probably operating legally and run legitimately, it may be granted correspondent or provisional status. Typically this step will take anywhere from several months to several years or more, and when completed does not imply any kind of endorsement or recommendation, but is merely an indication that the first steps on a long path have been taken.

Next, teams from the accrediting agency, often composed of faculty of already accredited institutions, will visit the school. These "visitations," conducted at regular intervals throughout the year, are to observe the school in action, and to study the copious amounts of information that the school must prepare, relating to its legal and academic structure, educational philosophy, curriculum, financial status, planning, and so forth.

After these investigations and, normally, following at least two years of successful operation (sometimes a great deal more), the school may be advanced to the status of "candidate for accreditation." Being a candidate means, in effect, "Yes, you are probably worthy of accreditation, but we want to watch your operation for a while longer."

This "while" can range from a year or two to six years or more. The great majority of schools that reach candidacy status eventually achieve full accreditation. Some accreditors do not have a candidacy status; with them it is an all-or-nothing situation. (The terms "accredited" and "fully accredited" are used interchangeably. There is no such thing as "partly accredited.")

Once a school is accredited, it is visited by inspection teams at infrequent intervals (every five to ten years is common) to see if it is still worthy of its accreditation. The status is always subject to review at any time, should new programs be developed or should there be any significant new developments, positive or negative.

Note: Everything in the foregoing section applies to accreditation as done by recognized agencies. Many of the other agencies, even those that are not illegal, will typically accredit a new school within days, even minutes, of its coming into existence.

The Importance of Accreditation

Although accreditation is undeniably important to both schools and students (and would-be students), this importance is undermined and confused by these three factors:

1. There are no significant national standards for accreditation. What is accreditable in New York may not be accreditable in California, and vice versa. The demands and standards of the group that accredits schools of chemistry may be very different from the people who accredit schools of forestry. And so on.

2. Some decent schools (or departments within schools) are not accredited, either by their own choice (since accreditation is a totally voluntary and often very expensive procedure), or because they are too new (all schools were unaccredited at one time in their lives) or too experimental (some would say too innovative) for the generally conservative accreditors.

3. Many very bad schools claim to be accredited—but it is always by unrecognized, sometimes nonexistent accrediting associations, often of their own creation.

Still, accreditation is the only widespread system of school evaluation that we have. A school's accreditation status can be helpful to the potential student in this way: while some good schools are not accredited, it is very unlikely that any very bad or illegal school is authentically accredited. (There have been exceptions, but they are quite rare.)

In other words, *authentic* accreditation is a pretty good sign that a given school is legitimate. But it is important to remember that *lack of accreditation need not mean that a school is either inferior or illegal.* Authentic accreditation is based on performance, not proposed performance.

We stress the term *authentic* accreditation, since there are very few laws or regulations anywhere governing the establishment of an accrediting association. Anyone can start a degree mill, then turn around and open an accrediting agency next door, give his school its blessing, and begin advertising "fully accredited degrees." Indeed, this has happened many times.

The crucial question, then, is this:

Who Accredits the Accreditors?

The situation is confusing, unsettled, and still undergoing change and redefinition for the third millennium. To get some sort of a handle on the situation, it will be helpful to have a bit of a historical perspective. In this instance, it makes some sense to begin in 1980, when the Republican party platform echoed Ronald Reagan's belief that the Department of Education should be closed down, since it was inappropriate for the federal government to meddle in matters better left to the states and to private enterprise.

At that time, there were two agencies, one private and one governmental, that had responsibility for evaluating and approving or recognizing accrediting agencies:

1. The U.S. Department of Education's Eligibility and Agency Evaluation Staff (EAES), which is required by law to "publish a list of nationally recognized accrediting agencies which [are determined] to be reliable ... as to the quality of training offered." This is done as one measure of eligibility for federal financial aid programs for students. EAES also had the job of deciding whether unaccredited schools could qualify for federal aid programs, or their students for veterans' benefits. This was done primarily by what was called the "three-by-three" rule: Proof that credits from at least three students were accepted by at least three accredited schools (nine total acceptances). If they were, then the unaccredited school was recognized by the Department of Education for that purpose. Schools qualifying under the three-by-three rule had to submit evidence of continued acceptance of their credits by accredited schools in order to maintain their status. ("Three-by-three" later became "four-by-four.")

2. COPA, the Council on Postsecondary Accreditation. COPA was a nationwide nonprofit corporation, formed in 1975 to evaluate accrediting associations and award recognition to those found worthy.

President Reagan was unable to dismantle the Department of Education during his administration, although key people in the department strongly suggested that they should get out of the business of recognizing accrediting agencies, and leave that to the states. "Education President" Bush apparently did not share this view; at least no significant changes were made during his administration.

One of the frequent complaints levied against the recognized accrediting agencies (and not just by Republicans) is that they have, in general, been slow to acknowledge the major trend toward alternative or nontraditional education.

Some years ago, the Carnegie Commission on Higher Education conducted research on the relationship between accreditation and nontraditional approaches. Their report, written by Alexander Mood, confirmed that a serious disadvantage of accreditation is "in the suppression of innovation. Schools cannot get far out of line without risking loss of their accreditation—a penalty which they cannot afford." "Also," the report continued, "loss of accreditation implies that the curriculum is somewhat inferior and hence that the degree is inferior. Such a large penalty . . . tends to prevent colleges from striking out in new directions. . . As we look toward the future, it appears likely that accrediting organizations will lose their usefulness and slowly disappear. Colleges will be judged not by what some educational bureaucracy declares but by what they can do for their students. Of much greater relevance would be statistics on student satisfaction, career advancement of graduates, and other such data."

Faced with high-powered criticism of this sort, some accrediting agencies sponsored (with a major grant from the Kellogg Foundation) a large-scale study of how the agencies should deal with nontraditional education.

The four-volume report of the findings of this investigation said very much what the Carnegie report had to say. The accreditors were advised, in effect, not to look at the easy quantitative factors (percentage of doctorate-holders on the faculty, books in the library, student-faculty ratio, acres of campus, etc.), but rather to evaluate the far more elusive qualitative factors, of which student satisfaction and student performance are the most crucial.

In other words, if the students at a nontraditional, nonresident university regularly produce research and dissertations that are as good as those produced at traditional schools, or if graduates of nontraditional schools are as likely to gain admission to graduate school or high-level employment and perform satisfactorily there—then the nontraditional school may be just as worthy of accreditation as the traditional school.

The response of the accrediting agencies was pretty much to say, "But we already are doing just those things. No changes are needed."

But, with the Carnegie and Kellogg reports, the handwriting was on the wall, if still in small and hard-to-read letters. Things would be changing, however.

In 1987, then Secretary of Education William Bennett (later to become "Drug Czar," and then a bestselling author–philosopher) voiced similar complaints about the failure of accrediting agencies to deal with matters such as student competency and satisfaction. "Historically," he said, "accrediting agencies have examined institutions in terms of the resources they have, such as the number of faculty with earned doctorates and the number of books in the library. Now [we] are considering the ways agencies take account of student achievement and development."

In 1990, Bennett's successor, Lauro F. Cavazos, while splitting an infinitive or two, said almost exactly the same thing: "Despite increasing evidence that many of our schools are failing to adequately prepare our children, either for further study or for productive careers, the accreditation process still focuses on inputs, such as the number of volumes in libraries or percentage of faculty with appropriate training. It does not examine outcomes—how much students learn."

Around the same time, John W. Harris, chairman of the National Advisory Committee on Accreditation, echoed these concerns: "It is not enough to know that teachers have certain degrees and that students have spent so much time in the classroom. The question is, can institutions document the achievement of students for the degrees awarded?"

The accrediting agencies continued to assure us that they *do* deal with such matters.

In 1992, Secretary of Education Lamar Alexander went further still, issuing an open invitation for new accrediting agencies to come forward and seek his department's blessing, strongly implying that the existing ones were not doing a satisfactory job. And around the same time, high administrators at at least three major universities seriously questioned whether accreditation was necessary for their school. "Why should we spend upwards of $100,000 in staff time and real money to prepare a self-study for the accreditors?" said one administrator. "It is quite likely that the University of Wisconsin would still be taken seriously even if it did not have accreditation."

In 1992, Secretary Alexander flung down an unignorable gauntlet by denying the usual "automatic" reapproval of the powerful Middle States Accrediting Association, because he maintained that their standards for accreditation did not meet the department's. (Middle States had previously denied reaccreditation to a major school because it did not meet certain standards of diversity, including "appropriate" numbers of minority students and faculty. Alexander suggested that Middle States was paying attention to the wrong things. Middle States finally backed down, and made its diversity standards optional.)

When Bill Clinton took office in 1993, the accreditation situation was no less murky, and his choice for Secretary of Education, Richard Riley of South Carolina, seemed more interested in primary and secondary education than in postsecondary. Into this already murky area came two bombshells.

Bombshell #1:

First, in 1993, the six regional accrediting associations, claiming that "the concept of self-regulation as embodied in regional accreditation is being seriously questioned and potentially threatened," announced that they planned to drop out of the Council on Postsecondary Accreditation, and start their own new group to represent them in Washington. The *Chronicle of Higher Education* reported that "some higher-education observers said they questioned the significance of the action [while] others called it disturbing." The president of the American Council on Education said that "Their pulling out is tantamount to the destruction of COPA."

Bombshell #2:

He was right. In April 1993, at their annual meeting in San Francisco, COPA voted itself out of existence as of year-end, by a vote of 14 to two, one abstention. One board member, C. Peter Magrath, president of the National Association of State Universities and Land-Grant Colleges, said that he thought COPA "focused too much on the minutiae of accreditation and not enough on the big issues of improving the quality of undergraduate education."

And so, in April 1993, things were indeed unsettled. The six regional associations were apparently planning to start a new organization to govern themselves, without the participation of the dozens of professional accreditors who were part of COPA. COPA was going about its business, but planning to turn off the lights and shut the door by the end of 1993. And the Clinton Department of Education was busily drawing up proposals that would turn the world of accreditation and school licensing on its ear.

The early thrust of the Clinton/Riley thinking echoed much that had been discussed during the Bush/Bennett/Cavazos/Alexander era: giving increased power to the states to decide what can and cannot be done in the way of higher education within their borders. The big stick wielded by the federal folks, of course, was student aid: loans and grants. The prospect of each state having different standards by which a student could get a Pell Grant, for instance, was daunting.

Around this time, Ralph A. Wolff, an executive with one of the regional accrediting associations, wrote an important 'think piece' for the influential *Chronicle of Higher Education*: "Restoring the Credibility of Accreditation" (June 9, 1993, page B1). Wolff wrote that

> We have constructed a Potemkin Village in which there is less behind the façade of accreditation than we might like to acknowledge....The accreditation process has not held colleges and universities accountable for issues such as the writing ability of graduates or the effectiveness of general-education requirements...If accreditation is to regain some of its lost credibility, everyone involved in the process needs to refocus on standards and criteria for demonstrating educational effectiveness. Even the most prestigious institutions will need to address how much students are learning and the quality of student life at the institution.

Right around the time Wolff was writing, the Department of Education was sending out a limited number of "secret" (not for publication or circulation) drafts of its proposed new regulations. And the six regional accreditors apparently rose up as one to say, in effect, "Hey, wait a minute. You, the feds, are telling us how to run our agencies, and we don't like that."

For instance, the draft regulations would have required accreditors to look at the length of various programs, and their cost vis-a-vis the subject being taught.

A response by James T. Rogers, head of the college division of the Southern Association (a regional accreditor) was typical:

> If final regulations follow the pattern in this latest draft, the Department of Education will have co-opted, in very profound ways, members of the private, voluntary accrediting community to serve as enforcement for the department. . . . This is an extremely disturbing abdication of the department's responsibility to police its own operation.

The *Chronicle* reported (August 4, 1993) that "many of the accrediting groups have sent notices to their member colleges urging them to be prepared to battle the department if the draft is not significantly altered."

And David Longanecker, Assistant Secretary for post-secondary education, was quoted in the *Chronicle* as saying "Many people in higher education say 'You can't measure what it is that we do, it's too valuable.' I don't buy that, and I don't think most people in America buy that today, either."

The battle lines were drawn or, as the more polite *Chronicle* put it on August 11, 1993, "Accreditors and the Education Department [are] locked in a philosophical disagreement over the role of accreditation." At this point, the six regional accreditors announced they would be joining with seven higher-education groups to form an organization to represent their interests in Washington. This lobbying group was to be called the National Policy Board on Higher Education Institutional Accreditation, or NPBHEIA. And various subsets of the by-now lame duck COPA were making plans to start as many as three replacement organizations to take over some or most or all of COPA's functions.

During the rest of 1993, the Department of Education was busily rewriting its accreditation guidelines, taking into account the unexpectedly fierce "leave us alone" response from the regional and professional accreditors. Meanwhile, Congress, not wishing to be left out of the mix entirely, passed, on November 23, 1993, the Higher Education Technical Amendments of 1993, which, among much, much else, decreed that the Department of Education was to cause each of the 50 states to establish a new State postsecondary review "entity" (SPRE) to evaluate schools within each state, both for compliance with various federal aid programs and, unexpectedly, to evaluate those colleges and universities that have "been subject to a pattern of complaints from students, faculty, or others, including...misleading or inappropriate advertising and promotion of the institution's educational programs...." If that wasn't an invitation for the states to go into the accreditation business, it was certainly in that direction.

Good-bye COPA, Hello CORPA

And while this was going on, the COPA-ending clock was ticking away. Ten days before COPA was to disappear forever, the formation of a single new entity to replace it was announced. COPA was to be replaced with (small fanfare, please) CORPA, the Commission on Recognition of Postsecondary Accreditation. All members of COPA were automatically recognized by CORPA. All COPA provisions for recognition of schools were adopted by CORPA, with the understanding that they might be refined and modified over time. And CORPA's initial Committee on Recognition was composed of the members of COPA's Committee on Recognition. All of this appears to be the academic equivalent of saying that *The Odyssey* was not

written by Homer, but by another Greek with the same name. The only apparent difference between COPA and CORPA is the addition of the "R" and the fact that the six regionals were no longer members.

The Department of Education's guidelines were finally published in the Federal Register on January 24, 1994: 24 small-type pages on accreditors, and 20 more on the establishing SPREs, the State Postsecondary Review Entities. Once the regulations were published, the public and the higher education establishment had 45 days in which to respond. And respond they did. The headline in the next week's *Chronicle of Higher Education* read: "Accreditors Fight Back."

It turned out that the six regional accreditors, the American Council on Education, and other groups had been meeting privately in Arizona to formulate a battle plan. They considered abandoning the regional approach entirely, in favor of a single national accreditor, but scrapped that in favor of four still-quite-radical ideas (among others):

1. Establishment of minimum uniform national standards for accreditation;

2. Setting of higher standards for schools, focusing on teaching and learning (what a novel concept!);

3. Making public their reports on individual colleges and schools; and

4. Moving toward ceasing to cooperate with the federal government in certifying the eligibility of colleges for federal financial aid.

During the 45-day response period following publishing of the draft guidelines, hundreds of long and serious responses were received from college and university presidents opposing some, most, or all of the regulations that had been proposed by the Department of Education.

The issue of diversity and political correctness in accreditation remained just as controversial as before. While the Western Association (a regional accreditor) for instance, believes that academic quality and ethnic diversity are "profoundly connected," many colleges, large and small, apparently agreed with Stanford president Gerhard Casper, who said, "No institution should be required to demonstrate its commitment to diversity to the satisfaction of an external review panel. The [Western Association] is attempting to insert itself in an area in which it has no legitimate standing." Other schools, including the University of California at Berkeley, defended the diversity policy.

By early May, 1994, the Department of Education backed away from some of the more controversial rules, both in terms of telling the accreditors what to look for, and in the powers given to the SPREs. They did this by continuing to say what things an accrediting agency must evaluate, but only suggesting, not demanding, the ways and means by which they might do it. In addition, SPREs would now be limited to dealing with matters of fraud and abuse, and could not initiate an inquiry for other reasons.

Under the then-final guidelines, accrediting agencies were required to evaluate these twelve matters, but the way they do it can be individually determined:

1. Curricula

2. Faculty

3. Facilities, equipment, and supplies

4. Fiscal and administrative capacity

5. Student support services

6. Program length, tuition, and fees in relation to academic objectives

7. Program length, tuition, and fees in relation to credit received

8. Student achievement (job placement, state licensing exams, etc.)

9. Student loan repayments

10. Student complaints received by or available to the accreditor

11. Compliance with student aid rules and regulations

12. Everything else, including recruiting, admissions practices, calendars, catalogues and other publications, grading practices, advertising and publicity, and so on

And that is where we had gotten to by 1996. Then, just when it seemed as things were calming down a bit, two more bombshells (shall we call them #3 and #4?) were dropped.

Bombshell #3: Good-bye CORPA, Hello CHEA

In late 1996, CORPA announced that it was closing down, in favor of a new organization, CHEA, the Council on Higher Education Accreditation, same address, but a new telephone number. So *The Odyssey* wasn't written by Homer or the other guy named Homer, but by yet a third Homer, this one apparently with closer ties to the administrators of the various accredited schools.

Bombshell #4: Good-bye AACSB, Hello Confusion

For years, the main guideline for determining the validity of an accrediting agency has been whether it is recognized by the U.S. Department of Education (with additional recognition by COPA, CORPA, or CHEA as an added niceness).

Then the U.S. Department of Education determined that the Higher Education Amendments to the laws required it only to recognize those accreditors who help to enable the schools or programs they accredit to establish eligibility to participate in certain federal aid and other federal programs. As a result of this determination, more than a dozen respectable, well regarded, and formerly recognized accrediting agencies lost their Department of Education

recognition, including the very prestigious AACSB, the American Assembly of Collegiate Schools of Business, which accredits Harvard, Yale, Stanford, and suchlike.

Does this mean that the accreditation of those nine agencies is no longer as useful? It is too soon to know, but unlikely, since the various professional fields still support that accreditation. The foresters, the social workers, the veterinarians, and so on, still regard accreditation by their professional associations as valuable and so, clearly, do the hundreds of schools that have or seek this accreditation. Finally, it seems more than likely that these nine agencies will retain their recognition by CHEA.

And in any event, virtually every college and university accredited by these nine *also* has regional accreditation as well.

In any event, after decades of minimal interest and attention, the always fascinating world of accreditation is clearly getting more than its fifteen minutes of fame.

The Approved Accrediting Agencies

Each of the six regional associations has responsibility for schools in one region of the United States and its territories. Each one has the authority to accredit an entire college or university. And there are also about 80 professional associations, each with authority to accredit either specialized schools or specific departments or programs within a school.

Thus, it may be the case, for instance, that the North Central Association (one of the six regional associations) will accredit Dolas University. When this happens, the entire school is accredited, and all its degrees may be called accredited degrees, or more accurately, degrees from an accredited institution.

Or it may be the case that just the art department of Dolas University has been accredited by the relevant professional association, in this case the National Association of Schools of Art. If this happens, then only the art majors at Dolas can claim to have accredited degrees.

So if an accredited degree is important for your needs, the first question to ask is, "Has the school been accredited by one of the six regional associations?" If the answer is no, then the next question is, "Has the department in which I am interested been accredited by its relevant professional association?" (There are very, very few schools that have professional accreditation but not regional accreditation.)

There are those jobs (psychology and nursing are two examples) in which professional accreditation is often at least as important as regional accreditation, sometimes more so. In other words, even if a school is accredited by its regional association, unless its psychology department is also accredited by the American Psychology Association, its degree will be less useful for psychology majors.

One of the legends about accreditation has arisen because of these matters: the widespread belief that Harvard is not accredited. Harvard University is duly accredited by its regional agency, but its psychology department, and many others, are not accredited by the relevant professional agencies.

In Great Britain, however, the similar legend that Oxford and Cambridge Universities are not accredited turns out to be partially true. While all the other British universities are accredited through the granting of a Royal Charter or by a special act of Parliament, it turns out that the two oldest universities have no Royal Charter of their own, although their constituent colleges do.

Totally unrecognized accrediting agencies may still be quite legitimate, or they may be quite phony. Some of the unrecognized ones will be discussed after the following listing of the recognized ones. Each of the approved accreditors will gladly supply lists of all the schools (or departments within schools) they have accredited, and those that are candidates for accreditation and in correspondent status. They will also answer any questions pertaining to any school's status (or lack of status) with them.

Accrediting Agencies Recognized Under GAAP

The Agencies That Recognize Accrediting Agencies

U.S. Department of Education
Accrediting Agency Evaluation Branch
Office of Postsecondary Education
Washington, DC 20202
Phone: (202) 401 2000 • (800) USA LEARN
Web site: www.ed.gov

Council For Higher Education Accreditation (CHEA)
One Dupont Circle NW, Suite 510
Washington DC, 20036-1136
Phone: (202) 955 6126
Fax: (202) 955 6129
Email: chea@chea.org
Web site: www.chea.org

Regional Accrediting Agencies

Middle States Association of Colleges and Schools
Commission on Higher Education
3624 Market St.
Philadelphia, PA 19104
Phone: (215) 662 5606
Fax: (215) 662 5501
Email: info@msache.org
Web site: www.msache.org
Delaware, District of Columbia, Maryland, New Jersey, New York, Pennsylvania, Puerto Rico, Virgin Islands.

What Is GAAP?

Any school can claim that it is accredited; the use of that word is not regulated in any way. This chapter distinguishes between those accrediting agencies that are recognized under GAAP, Generally Accepted Accrediting Principles, and those that are not. In the U.S., there is near-unanimous agreement on GAAP (although not everyone calls it this, the concept is the same) by the relevant key decision-makers: university registrars and admissions officers, corporate human resources officers, and government agencies.

Note that in some countries, the word *accredited* is not used, although that country's evaluation process (e.g., the British Royal Charter) is accepted as "accredited" under GAAP. Note too that accreditors that do not meet the standards of GAAP are not necessarily bad, illegal, or fake. They simply would not be generally accepted as recognized accreditors.

GAAP Criteria

To offer recognized accreditation under GAAP, an accrediting agency must meet at least one of the following four criteria:

▶ Recognized by the Council on Higher Education Accreditation (CHEA) in Washington, DC

▶ Recognized by the U.S. Department of Education

▶ If non-U.S., recognized by (or more commonly, a part of) the relevant national education agency (as listed in chapter 6)

▶ Schools the agency accredits are routinely listed in one or more of the following publications: the *International Handbook of Universities* (a UNESCO publication), the *Commonwealth Universities Yearbook*, the *World Education Series* (published by PIER), or the *Countries Series* (published by NOOSR in Australia)

New England Association of Schools and Colleges
209 Burlington Rd.
Bedford, MA 01730
Phone: (781) 271 0022
Fax: (781) 271 0950
Web site: www.neasc.org
Connecticut, Maine, Massachusetts, New Hampshire, Rhode Island, Vermont.

HI, THERE. THIS IS YOUR SURPRISE ACCREDITATION VISIT FROM THE NORTH CENTRAL ASSOCIATION.

Western Association of Schools and Colleges

985 Atlantic Ave., Suite 100
Alameda, CA 94501
Phone: (510) 748 9001
Fax: (510) 748 9797
Email: wascsr@wascsenior.org
Web site: www.wascweb.org
California, Hawaii, American Samoa, Guam, Trust Territory of the Pacific.

National Accrediting Agencies

Accrediting Council for Independent Colleges and Schools (ACICS)

750 First St. NE, Suite 980
Washington, DC 20002
Phone: (202) 336 6780
Fax: (202) 482 2593
Email: info@acics.org
Web site: www.acics.org

Distance Education and Training Council (DETC)

1601 18th St. NW
Washington, DC 20009
Phone: (202) 234 5100
Fax: (202) 332 1386
Email: detc@detc.org
Web site: www.detc.org

North Central Association of Colleges and Schools

30 North LaSalle St., Suite 2400
Chicago, IL 60602
Phone: (312) 263 0456 • (800) 621 7440
Fax: (312) 263 7462
Email: info@ncacihe.org
Web site: www.ncacihe.org
Arizona, Arkansas, Colorado, Illinois, Indiana, Iowa, Kansas, Michigan, Minnesota, Missouri, Nebraska, New Mexico, North Dakota, Ohio, Oklahoma, South Dakota, West Virginia, Wisconsin, Wyoming.

Northwest Association of Schools and Colleges

11300 NE 33rd Place, Suite 120
Bellevue, WA 98004
Phone: (425) 827 2005
Fax: (425) 827 3395
Web site: www.cocnasc.org
Alaska, Idaho, Montana, Nevada, Oregon, Utah, Washington.

Southern Association of Colleges and Schools

1866 Southern Lane
Decatur, GA 30033
Phone: (404) 679 4500 • (800) 248 7701
Fax: (404) 679 4558
Web site: www.sacs.org
Alabama, Florida, Georgia, Kentucky, Louisiana, Mississippi, North Carolina, South Carolina, Tennessee, Texas, Virginia.

Professional Accrediting Agencies

THE ARTS

Architecture

National Architectural Accrediting Board

1735 New York Ave. NW
Washington, DC 20006
Phone: (202) 783 2007
Email: info@naab.org
Web site: www.naab.org
Recognized by CHEA but not by the U.S. Department of Education.

Art

National Association of Schools of Art and Design

Commission on Accreditation
11250 Roger Bacon Dr., Suite 21
Reston, VA 20190
Phone: (703) 437 0700
Email: info@arts-accredit.org
Web site: www.arts-accredit.org/nasad

Dance

National Association of Schools of Dance
11250 Roger Bacon Dr., Suite 21
Reston, VA 20190
Phone: (703) 437 0700
Email: info@arts-accredit.org
Web site: www.arts-accredit.org/nasd

Landscape Architecture

American Society of Landscape Architects
636 Eye St. NW
Washington, DC 20001-3736
Phone: (202) 898 2444
Web site: www.asla.org
Recognized by CHEA but not by the U.S. Department of Education.

Music

National Association of Schools of Music
11250 Roger Bacon Dr., Suite 21
Reston, VA 20190
Phone: (703) 437 0700
Email: info@arts-accredit.org
Web site: www.arts-accredit.org/nasm

Theater

National Association of Schools of Theater
11250 Roger Bacon Dr., Suite 21
Reston, VA 20190
Phone: (703) 437 0700
Email: info@arts-accredit.org
Web site: www.arts-accredit.org/nast

BUSINESS

American Assembly of Collegiate Schools of Business
See: International Association for Management Education

Association of Collegiate Business Schools and Programs (ACBSP)
7007 College Blvd., Suite 420
Overland Park, KS 66211
Phone: (913) 339 9356
Web site: www.acbsp.org
CHEA recognition pending.

International Association for Management Education (AACSB)
600 Emerson Rd., Suite 300
St. Louis, MO 63141
Phone: (314) 872 8481
Web site: www.aacsb.edu
Formerly known as the American Assembly of Collegiate Schools of Business (and, confusingly, still referred to as the AACSB). Recognized by CHEA but not by the U.S. Department of Education.

EDUCATION

Continuing Education

Accrediting Council for Continuing Education and Training (ACCET)
1722 N St. NW
Washington, DC 20036
Phone: (202) 955 1113
Web site: www.accet.org

Liberal Education

American Academy for Liberal Education
1700 K St. NW, Suite 901
Washington, DC 20006
Phone: (202) 452 8611
Email: info@aale.org
Web site: www.aale.org

Montessori Education

Montessori Accreditation Council for Teacher Education
University of Wisconsin - Parkside
900 Wood Rd., Box 2000
Kenosha, WI 53141-2000
Phone: (262) 595 3335
Web site: www.macte.org

Occupational, Trade, and Technical Education

Accrediting Commission of Career Schools and Colleges of Technology
2101 Wilson Blvd., Suite 302
Arlington, VA 22201
Phone: (703) 247 4212
Email: info@accsct.org
Web site: www.accsct.org

Council on Occupational Education
41 Perimeter Center East, NE, Suite 640
Atlanta, GA 30346
Phone: (770) 396 3898 • (800) 917 2081
Email: info@council.org
Web site: www.council.org

Rehabilitation Education

Council on Rehabilitation Education
1835 Rohlwing Rd., Suite E
Rolling Meadows, IL 60008
Phone: (847) 394 1785
Web site: www.core-rehab.org
Recognized by CHEA but not by the U.S. Department of Education.

Teacher Education

National Council for Accreditation of Teacher Education

2010 Massachusetts Ave. NW
Washington, DC 20036
Phone: (202) 466 7496
Email: info@ncate.org
Web site: www.ncate.org

LAW

American Bar Association

Section of Legal Education and Admissions to the Bar
550 West North St., Suite 349
Indianapolis, IN 46202
Phone: (317) 264 8340
Email: legaled@abanet.org
Web site: www.abanet.org/legaled

MEDICINE AND HEALTH

Acupuncture and Oriental Medicine

Accreditation Commission for Acupuncture and Oriental Medicine

1010 Wayne Ave., Suite 1270
Silver Spring, MD 20910
Phone: (301) 608 9680
Web site: www.ccaom.org

Allied Health

Accrediting Bureau of Health Education Schools

803 West Broad St., Suite 730
Falls Church, VA 22046
Phone: (703) 533 2082
Web site: www.abhes.org

Accredits programs for medical laboratory technicians and medical assistants.

Commission on Accreditation of Allied Health Education Programs

35 East Wacker Dr., Suite 1970
Chicago, IL 60601-2208
Phone: (312) 553 9355
Email: caahep@caahep.org
Web site: www.caahep.org

Accredits programs in anesthesiologist assistant education, athletic training, blood bank technology, cardiovascular technology, cytotechnology, diagnostic medical sonography, electroneurodiagnostic technology, emergency medical services, kinesiotherapy, medical record education, opthalmic medical technology, orthotic and prosthetic technology, perfusion, physican assistant education, respiratory therapy, and surgical technology.

Chiropractic

Council on Chiropractic Education

8049 North 85th Way
Scottsdale, Arizona 85258-4321
Phone: (480) 443 8877
Email: cce@cce-usa.org
Web site: www.cce-usa.org

Dentistry

American Dental Association

211 East Chicago Ave.
Chicago, IL 60611
Phone: (312) 440 2500
Web site: www.ada.org

Dietetics

American Dietetic Association

Commission on Accreditation for Dietetics Education
216 West Jackson Blvd.
Chicago, IL 60606
Phone: (312) 899 4872 • (800) 877 1600
Email: education@eatright.org
Web site: www.eatright.com/cade

Health Services Administration

Accrediting Commission on Education for Health Services Administration

730 Eleventh St. NW, Suite 400
Washington, DC 20001
Phone: (202) 638 5131
Email: acehsa@acehsa.org
Web site: www.acehsa.org

National Accrediting Agency for Clinical Laboratory Sciences

8410 West Bryn Mawr Ave., Suite 670
Chicago, IL 60631
Phone: (773) 714 8880
Email: naaclsinfo@naacls.org
Web site: www.naacls.org

Accredits programs in histologic technology, medical laboratory technology, medical technology, and pathologist assistant education.

Medical Schools

American Medical Association

515 North State St.
Chicago, IL 60610
Phone: (312) 464 4933
Web site: www.ama-assn.org

The accreditor for medical schools in odd-numbered years, beginning on July 1.

Association of American Medical Colleges
> 2450 N St. NW
> Washington, DC 20037
> **Phone:** (202) 828 0596
> **Web site:** www.aamc.org

The accreditor for medical schools in even-numbered years, beginning on July 1.

Naturopathy

Council on Naturopathic Medical Education
> P.O. Box 11426
> Eugene, OR 97440
> **Phone:** (503) 484 6028
> **Email:** dir@cnme.org
> **Web site:** www.cnme.org

Nursing

American Association of Nurse Anesthetists
> 222 South Prospect Ave.
> Park Ridge, IL 60068-4001
> **Phone:** (847) 692 7050
> **Email:** info@aana.com
> **Web site:** www.aana.com

American College of Nurse-Midwives
> 818 Connecticut Ave. NW, Suite 900
> Washington, DC 20006
> **Phone:** (202) 728 9860
> **Email:** info@acnm.org
> **Web site:** www.midwife.org

National Association of Nurse Practitioners in Women's Health
> 503 Capital Court, NE, Suite 300
> Washington, DC 20002
> **Phone:** (202) 543 9693
> **Email:** info@npwh.org
> **Web site:** www.npwh.org

National League for Nursing
> 61 Broadway, 33rd Floor
> New York, NY 10006
> **Phone:** (212) 363 5555 • (800) 669 1656
> **Web site:** www.nlnac.org

Optometry and Opticianry

American Optometric Association
> 243 North Lindbergh Blvd.
> St. Louis, MO 63141
> **Phone:** (314) 991 4100
> **Web site:** www.aoanet.org

Commission on Opticianry Accreditation
> 7023 Little River Turnpike, Suite 207
> Annandale, VA 22003
> **Phone:** (703) 941 9110
> **Email:** coa@erols.com
> **Web site:** www.coaccreditation.com

Osteopathy

American Osteopathic Association
> 142 East Ontario St.
> Chicago, IL 60611
> **Phone:** (312) 202 8048
> **Email:** info@aoa-net.org
> **Web site:** www.aoa-net.org

Pharmacy

American Council on Pharmaceutical Education
> 311 West Superior St., Suite 512
> Chicago, IL 60610
> **Phone:** (312) 664 3575
> **Web site:** www.acpe-accredit.org

Physical Therapy

American Physical Therapy Association
> 1111 North Fairfax St.
> Alexandria, VA 22314
> **Phone:** (703) 684 2782
> **Email:** accreditation@apta.org
> **Web site:** www.apta.org

Podiatry

American Podiatric Medical Association
> 9312 Old Georgetown Rd.
> Bethesda, MD 20814-1698
> **Phone:** (301) 571 9200
> **Web site:** www.apma.org

Public Health

Council on Education for Public Health
> 800 Eye St. NW, Suite 202
> Washington, DC 20001-3710
> **Phone:** (202) 789 1050
> **Web site:** www.ceph.org

Radiologic Technology

Joint Review Committee on Education in Radiologic Technology
> 20 North Wacker Dr., Suite 900
> Chicago, IL 60606
> **Phone:** (312) 704 5300

Veterinary Medicine

American Veterinary Medical Association
> 1931 North Meacham Rd., Suite 100
> Schaumburg, IL 60173
> **Phone:** (847) 925 8070
> **Email:** avmainfo@avma.org
> **Web site:** www.avma.org

RELIGION

Bible College Education

Accrediting Association of Bible Colleges
P.O. Box 780339
Orlando, FL 32878-0339
Phone: (407) 207 0808
Email: exdir@aabc.org
Web site: www.aabc.org

Christian Studies Education

Transnational Association of Christian Colleges and Schools
P.O. Box 328
Forest, VA 24551
Phone: (804) 525 9539
Web site: www.tracs.org

Clinical Pastoral Education

Association for Clinical Pastoral Education
1549 Clairmont Rd., Suite 103
Decatur, GA 30033-4611
Phone: (404) 320 1472
Web site: www.acpe.edu

Rabbinical and Talmudic Education

Association of Advanced Rabbinical and Talmudic Schools
175 Fifth Ave., Room 711
New York, NY 10010
Phone: (212) 477 0950

Theology

Association of Theological Schools in the United States and Canada
10 Summit Park Dr.
Pittsburgh, PA 15275
Phone: (412) 788 6505
Email: ats@ats.edu
Web site: www.ats.edu

SCIENCE AND ENGINEERING

Computer Science

Computing Sciences Accreditation Board
184 North St.
Stamford, CT 06901
Phone: (203) 975 1117
Email: csab@csab.org
Web site: www.csab.org
Recognized by CHEA but not by the U.S. Department of Education.

Engineering

Accrediting Board for Engineering and Technology
111 Market Place, Suite 1050
Baltimore, MD 21202
Phone: (410) 347 7700
Email: accreditation@abet.org
Web site: www.abet.org

Environment

National Environmental Health Science and Protection Accreditation Council
720 S. Colorado Blvd., Suite 970-S
Denver, CO 80246-1925
Phone: (303) 756 9090
Web site: www.neha.org/AccredCouncil.html

Forestry

Society of American Foresters
5400 Grosvenor Lane
Bethesda, MD 20814
Phone: (301) 897 8720
Web site: www.safnet.org
Recognized by CHEA but not by the U.S. Department of Education.

SOCIAL SCIENCES

City Planning

Planning Accreditation Board
3800 Merle Hay Rd.
Merle Hay Tower, Suite 302
Des Moines, IA 50310
Phone: (515) 252 0729
Web site: www.netins.net/showcase/pab_fi66
Recognized by CHEA but not by the U.S. Department of Education.

Counseling

Council for Accreditation of Counseling and Related Educational Programs
5999 Stevenson Ave., 4th Floor
Alexandria, Virginia 22304
Phone: (703) 823 9800
Web site: www.counseling.org/cacrep
Recognized by CHEA but not by the U.S. Department of Education.

Family and Consumer Sciences

American Association of Family and Consumer Sciences
1555 King St.
Alexandria, VA 22314
Phone: (703) 706 4600
Email: info@aafcs.org
Web site: www.aafcs.org
Recognized by CHEA but not by the U.S. Department of Education.

Marriage and Family Therapy

American Association for Marriage and Family Therapy

    1133 15th St. NW, Suite 300
    Washington, DC 20005
    Phone: (202) 452 0109
    Web site: www.aamft.org

Occupational Therapy

American Occupational Therapy Association

    4720 Montgomery Lane
    P.O. Box 31220
    Bethesda, MD 20824
    Phone: (301) 652 2682
    Web site: www.aota.org

Psychology

American Psychological Association

    750 1st St. NE
    Washington, DC 20002
    Phone: (202) 336 5979
    Email: apaaccred@apa.org
    Web site: www.apa.org/ed/accred.html

Public Affairs and Administration

National Association of Schools of Public Affairs and Administration

    1120 G St. NW, Suite 730
    Washington, DC 20005
    Phone: (202) 628 8965
    Email: napaa@naspaa.org
    Web site: www.naspaa.org
Recognized by CHEA but not by the U.S. Department of Education.

Recreation, Park, and Leisure Studies

National Recreation and Park Association

    22377 Belmont Ridge Rd.
    Ashburn, VA 20148
    Phone: (703) 858 0784
    Web site: www.nrpa.org
Recognized by CHEA but not by the U.S. Department of Education.

Social Work

Council on Social Work Education

    1725 Duke St., Suite 500
    Alexandria, VA 22314
    Phone: (703) 683 8080
    Web site: www.cswe.org
Recognized by CHEA but not by the U.S. Department of Education.

The Spirit of Distance Learning begs recognition from the Traditional Accreditor.

Speech-Language Pathology and Audiology

American Speech-Language-Hearing Association

    10801 Rockville Pike
    Rockville, MD 20852
    Phone: (301) 897 5700
    Web site: www.asha.org

VOCATIONAL AND PRACTICAL FIELDS

Construction Education

American Council for Construction Education

    1300 Hudson Lane, Suite 3
    Monroe, LA 71201
    Phone: (318) 323 2816
    Web site: www.acce-hq.org
Recognized by CHEA but not by the U.S. Department of Education.

Cosmetology

National Accrediting Commission of Cosmetology Arts and Sciences

    901 North Stuart St., Suite 900
    Arlington, VA 22203
    Phone: (703) 527 7600
    Web site: www.naccas.org

Culinary Arts

American Culinary Federation

10 San Bartola Dr.
St Augustine, FL 32086
Phone: (904) 824 4468
Email: acf@acfchefs.net
Web site: www.acfchefs.org
Recognized by CHEA but not by the U.S. Department of Education.

Funeral Service Education

American Board of Funeral Service Education

38 Florida Ave.
Portland, ME 04103
Phone: (207) 878 6530
Web site: www.abfse.org

Interior Design

Foundation for Interior Design Education Research

60 Monroe Center NW, Suite 300
Grand Rapids, MI 49503
Phone: (616) 458 0400
Email: fider@fider.org
Web site: www.fider.org
Recognized by CHEA but not by the U.S. Department of Education.

Journalism and Mass Communications

Accrediting Council on Education in Journalism and Mass Communications

University of Kansas School of Journalism
Stauffer-Flint Hall
Lawrence, KS 66045
Phone: (785) 864 3986
Web site: www.ukans.edu/~acejmc

Librarianship

American Library Association

50 East Huron St.
Chicago, IL 60611
Phone: (312) 280 2432
Web site: www.ala.org
Recognized by CHEA but not by the U.S. Department of Education.

Recognized State-Run Accrediting Agencies

New York State Board of Regents

State Education Department
89 Washington Ave.
Albany, NY 12234
Phone: (518) 474 5844
Web site: www.regents.nysed.gov

Accrediting Agencies Not Recognized Under GAAP

There are quite a few accrediting agencies that are not recognized under GAAP, the Generally Accepted Accreditation Principles, as described earlier in this chapter. These agencies are not recognized by either the Council on Higher Education Accreditation (CHEA) or the U.S. Department of Education, nor by UNESCO or by the education departments or ministries of major countries. They range from a few sincere efforts which are working for recognition to many agencies started by less-than-wonderful schools in order to accredit themselves. Following is a listing of many such accreditors that we have noticed over the years. For updates to this ever changing list, visit our Web site at *www.degree.net*.

Academy for the Promotion of International Cultural and Scientific Exchange (APICS) Headquartered in Switzerland, with offices in Germany, Bulgaria, and Hawaii. Shares its Swiss address with one of its member schools, the University of Ecoforum For Peace. Most of its accredited members are European schools; American members include Honolulu University, Columbia Southern, and California Yuin University. In the past we had some disagreements with former APICS U.S. representative, Dr. Denis K. Muhilly, over the quality of this accreditor. Also known by the German name Akademie fuer Internationale Kultur und Wissenschaftsfoerderung.

Accreditation Association of Ametrican [sic] College [sic] and Universities (AAACU) Unrecognized agency from which the American University of Hawaii has claimed accreditation.

Accreditation Commission for International Internet Education (ACIIE) Deals primarily with Internet-based high schools, but also accredits the higher education programs of E-School! International. Les Carr and Richard Crews, of Columbia Pacific University, were on the original board of directors.

Accrediting Commission for Colleges and Universities (ACCU) One of the unrecognized accreditors claimed by the Intercultural Open University (based in the Netherlands), whose Web site is the only evidence we've found of ACCU's existence.

Accrediting Commission for Specialized Colleges (ACSC) Gas City, Indiana. Established by "Bishop" Gordon Da Costa and associates (one of whom was Dr. George Reuter, who left to help establish the International Accrediting Commission, described in this section) from the address of Da Costa's Indiana Northern Graduate School (a dairy farm in Gas City). According to their literature, the accrediting procedures of ACSC seem superficial at best. The only requirement for becoming a candidate for accreditation was to mail in a check for $110.

Accrediting Commission International for Schools, Colleges and Theological Seminaries (ACI) Beebe, Arkansas. See also: "International Accrediting Commission for Schools, Colleges and Theological Seminaries (IAC)" in this section. After the IAC was fined and closed down by authorities in Missouri in 1989, Dr. Reuter retired. A short time later, ACI opened in the adjoining state, and wrote a letter to the IAC schools offering them automatic accreditation by the ACI. We are not aware of any that turned it down. ACI refuses to make public a list of schools they have accredited. We have noted more than 130 schools that claim ACI accreditation, most of them apparently evangelical Bible schools, but more than a few nonreligious schools as well, including Century University, Columbia Southern University, Wisconsin International University, and Western States University.

Akademie fuer Internationale Kultur und Wissenschaftsfoerderung See: Academy for Promotion of International Cultural and Scientific Exchange

Alternative Institution Accrediting Association Allegedly in Washington, DC, and the accreditor of several phony schools.

American Association of Accredited Colleges and Universities Another unlocatable agency, the claimed accreditor of Ben Franklin Academy.

American Association of Drugless Practitioners Accreditor for the American Institute of Holistic Theology, Clayton College of Natural Health, the Southern College of Naturopathy, and the Academy of Natural Therapies.

American Association of Independent Collegiate Schools of Business Unlocatable accreditor mentioned by Rushmore University.

American Association of Nontraditional Collegiate Business Schools Another plausible-sounding but unlocatable accreditor mentioned by Rushmore University.

American Council of Private Colleges and Universities (ACPCU) A fake accrediting agency set up by the Wyoming-based diploma mill, Hamilton University.

American Education Association for the Accreditation of Schools, Colleges, and Universities The accreditor claimed at one time by the University of America. Could not be located.

American International Commission for Excellence in Higher Education, Inc. After Les Snell's fake Monticello University and its fake accreditor, the International Commission for Excellence in Higher Education, Inc., was shut down by the state of Kansas in 1999, he briefly reappeared on the scene in 2000 with a new fake school, Amherst University, and a new fake accreditor, the *American* International Commission for Excellence in Higher Education, Inc.

American Naprapathic Association Accredits the Chicago National College of Naprapathy.

American Naturopathic Medical Certification and Accreditation Board Its letter officially granting accreditation to Westbrook University was word-for-word identical to a letter from another of Westbrook's unrecognized accreditors, the National Board of Naturopathic Examiners.

American Psycotherapy [*sic*] Association Board of Psycotherapy [*sic*] Examiners, Katy, Texas; originally chartered in Florida, they say, while apologizing for but not correcting the misspellings.

APIX Institute Claimed by the probably phony Horizons University, whose campus is either a driving school or a hairdresser in Paris.

Arizona Commission of Non-Traditional Private Postsecondary Education Established in the late 1970s by the proprietors of Southland University, which claimed to be a candidate for their accreditation. The name was changed after a complaint by the real state agency, the Arizona Commission on Postsecondary Education. See also: Western Council on Non-Traditional Private Post Secondary Education

Association for Online Academic Excellence An unrecognized accrediting agency claimed by Trinity College & University (U.S.).

Association Internationale des Educateurs pour la Paix Mondiale Many schools, including Adam Smith University, Saint Clements University, and Stanton University, claim a "diploma of recognition" from this organization, supposedly affiliated with UNESCO. If you are also "interested in the promotion of international understanding and world peace through education, the protection of the environment from man-made pollution, and/or the safeguard of human rights everywhere," you can have one too!

Association of Accredited Private Schools This unrecognized agency wrote to many schools in 1997, inviting them to send a $1000 application fee. City University Los Angeles claims to be a "member in good standing."

Association of Career Training Schools A slick booklet sent to schools says, "Have your school accredited with the Association. Why? The Association Seal . . .

could be worth many $ $ $ to you! It lowers sales resistance, sales costs, [and] improves image." Nuff said.

Association of Christian Schools and Colleges Pickering University claims accreditation from an institution by this name. We found a Web site posted by an (if not *the*) Association of Christian Schools and Colleges, whose stated objective is to "promote by all legal means the aims and objectives of education in the Philippines."

Association of Private Colleges and Universities (APCU) According to its literature, the APCU's "primary objectives are to identify and annihilate illegal diploma mills wherever they are located and operating in the world." Wow! Arnold Schwarzenegger meets the world of higher education. Before a school can buy the APCU "seal of approval," it must provide three student email addresses, offer a 30-day, money-back guarantee, and show that it delivers the student's diploma within 30 days of graduation. The APCU says it is "not an accreditation agency, and makes no claims to be so"; considering such "tough" standards for gaining approval, we would have to agree. Founded by Gus Payne, who was a founder of Trinity College & University (U.S.).

Association of Virtual Universities, Colleges, and Schools No member schools are listed on this unrecognized accreditor's Web site, which shares its registration address in Fremont, CA, with the Web site of Julius Caesar University.

Association of World Universities and Colleges An unrecognized accreditor, allegedly from Switzerland, that has been claimed by the University of Asia. Web site, no longer working, is registered to Bilal Nasrullah, president of the University of Asia. Not to be confused (though perhaps that was intended) with the also-unrecognized World Association of Universities and Colleges (WAUC).

Australian Universities Association Unrecognized accreditor that has been claimed by the University of Asia. Web site (now defunct) registered to Bilal Nasrullah, owner of University of Asia.

Canadian National Accreditation [sic] Commission An apparently nonexistent organization, claimed as accreditor by Generale University (whose Vancouver campus is a mailbox rental store).

College for Professional Assessment Unlocatable accreditor claimed by the Thomas Jefferson Education Foundation and its quiver of schools.

Commission for the Accreditation of European Non-Traditional Universities The University de la Romande, in England, used to claim accreditation from this agency, which we could never locate.

Commonwealth Universities Association Another unrecognized accreditor claimed by University of Asia. Web site, *www.cwlthuniversitiesassoc.org.uk*, is registered to Bilal Nasrullah, owner and president of—yes, you guessed it—University of Asia.

Correspondence Accreditation Association Created by and the accreditor for Trinity College & University in the U.K.

Council for National Academic Accreditation In 1998, they wrote to schools from Cheyenne, Wyoming, offering the opportunity to be accredited on payment of a fee up to $1,850. No listed phone. Accreditor claimed by Universitas Mons Calpe, allegedly in Gibraltar.

Council for the Accreditation of Correspondence Colleges Several curious schools claimed their accreditation; the agency is supposed to be in Louisiana.

Council on Post Secondary Accreditation Claimed by the dubious South Atlantic University.

Council on Postsecondary Alternative Accreditation An accreditor claimed in the literature of Western States University. Western States never responded to requests for the address of their accreditor. The name seems to have been chosen to cause confusion with the reputable organization originally known as the Council on Postsecondary Accreditation.

Council on Postsecondary Christian Education Established by the people who operated LaSalle University and Kent College in Louisiana.

Distance Education Council of America Quite reminiscent in name and literature to the recognized Distance Education and Training Council, DECA arose in Delaware in 1998, offering schools the opportunity to pay $200 or more for accreditation and $150 more for an "Excellence" rating.

Distance Graduation Accrediting Association (DGAA) An unrecognized agency claimed by Capitol University and Concordia College & University.

Euro-American Accreditation Agency From the Web site of Northwestern International University: "The Euro-American Accreditation Agency was formed as a division of Northwestern International University by its trustees to ensure the highest possible standards of academic excellence in curriculum design and operational policies in all University programs. The agency is currently accepting applications from other reputable schools of higher learning for accreditation."

Global Accreditation Commission Unrecognized accreditor claimed by Adam Smith University and the International University of Graduate Studies.

Integra Accreditation Association We somehow intercepted an email from this agency, sent June 2000, offering its accrediting services to a who's who list of nonwonderful schools, including Kennedy-Western, Lacrosse, and SCUPS.

Inter-Collegiate Joint Committee on Academic Standards Its domain name, *jointcommittee.org*, is owned by a Robert Kerr, who also owns the domain name for Chapparal Western University (*yourdegreenow.com*).

InterAmerican Association of Postsecondary Colleges and Schools The agency from which the Universitas Sancti Martin claims accreditation. We have not been able to locate this agency.

International Accreditation and Recognition Council An unrecognized accreditor based in Australia.

International Accreditation Association The literature of the University of North America claimed accreditation from this association. No address was provided, nor could one be located.

International Accreditation Association of Nontraditional Colleges and Universities Unrecognized accreditor allegedly located in the British West Indies. Web site (*www.iaancu.nu*) does not list its accredited members.

International Accreditation Commission for Post Secondary Education Institutions The University of the United States and Nasson University claimed accreditation from this agency which, according to the schools' apparently shared Web site, had "not sought specific recognition from any single nation."

International Accrediting Agency for Private and Post Secondary Institutes Nonexistent agency claimed by the equally nonexistent CliffPort University and Glamount University, apparently in Pakistan.

International Accrediting Association The address in Modesto, California, is the same as that of the Universal Life Church, an organization that awards doctorates of all kinds, including the Ph.D., to anyone making a "donation" of $5 to $100.

International Accrediting Commission for Postsecondary Institutions Unrecognized agency from which Adam Smith University claims accreditation.

International Accrediting Commission for Schools, Colleges and Theological Seminaries (IAC) Holden, Missouri. More than 150 schools, many of them Bible schools, were accredited by this organization. In 1989, the attorney general of Missouri conducted a clever "sting" operation, in which he created a fictitious school, the "East Missouri Business College," which rented a one-room office in St. Louis and issued a typewritten catalog with such school executives as "Peelsburi Doughboy" and "Wonarmmd Mann." The Three Stooges were all on the faculty. Their marine biology text was *The Little Golden Book of Fishes*. The school's motto, translated from Latin, was "Education is for the birds." Nonetheless, Dr. George Reuter, Director of the IAC, visited the school, accepted their money, and duly accredited them. Soon after, the IAC was enjoined from operating and slapped with a substantial fine, and the good Dr. Reuter decided to retire. (But the almost identical "Accrediting Commission International" immediately arose in Arkansas, offering instant accreditation to all IAC members. See listing above.) Before he was apprehended, when someone wrote to Dr. Reuter to ask why this book had less-than-good things to say about his association, Dr. Reuter replied, "Some of us do not rate Dr. John Bear very high. We think he is really a traditionalist and really favors those colleges and universities, and, at the same time, strives to plant dissent with others." Oh dear, oh dear.

International Assembly for Collegiate Business Education (IACBE) The newest player in the confusing field of business school accreditation. Started by the same gentleman, Dr. John L. Green, who founded but is no longer associated with the Association of Collegiate Business Schools and Programs (ACBSP). The IACBE is applying for CHEA recognition.

International Association of Colleges and Universities Accreditor claimed by the dubious University of America, based in Georgia and licensed by St. Kitts and Nevis.

International Association of Educators for World Peace Accreditor claimed by European Union University. No listed telephone.

International Association of Monotheistic Schools Accreditor claimed by Allen Mitchell School of Psychology. No other evidence of its existence.

International Association of Non-Traditional Schools The claimed accreditor of several British degree mills and one now-defunct nonwonderful Mexican school; allegedly located in England.

International Association of Schools, Colleges, and Universities (IASCU) Antwerp, Belgium. The accreditor for Newport University International, who happens to own IASCU's email domain name. Other schools claiming accreditation from IASCU include Westbrook University, American Pacific University, and e Online University.

International Association of Universities and Schools (IAUS) Created by and accreditor for Barrington University.

International Commission for Excellence in Higher Education, Inc. According to Monticello University's online catalog, this commission "was formed by the Board of Trustees of Monticello University to ensure the highest possible standards of academic excellence in curriculum design and operational policies for member universities. Monticello University is the first distance learning institution to be accredited by this agency." We do not know of any other accredited members.

International Commission for the Accreditation of Colleges and Universities Established in Gaithersburg, Maryland, by a diploma mill called the United States University of America (now defunct) primarily for the purpose of accrediting themselves.

International Commission on Distance Education Accreditor claimed by European Union University. The accreditor and the university share the same president.

International Council of Colleges and Universities We have been unable to verify the existence of this institution whose last known address was in Lebanon, TN.

International University Accreditation Foundation London, England. The Web domain name for this accreditor—*iuaf.org*—is owned by St. George University International. And guess who is the accreditor for St. George University International?

International University Accrediting Association (IUAA) One of two unrecognized accrediting agencies (the other is the Virtual University Accrediting Association) founded and operated by Dr. Chief Swift Eagle of the Cherokee Western Federation Church and Tribe. The only accredited member we know of is International Theological University, also founded by Dr. Chief Swift Eagle.

Life Experience Accreditation Association (LEAF) Unrecognized agency claimed by Earlscroft University. No address or URL ever found.

Louisiana Capital Education Foundation Unrecognized accreditor claimed by Louisiana Capital College. The similarity in name is most likely not a coincidence.

Middle States Accrediting Board A nonexistent accreditor, made up by Thomas University and other degree mills, for the purpose of self-accreditation. The name was chosen, of course, to cause confusion with the Middle States Association of Colleges and Schools, in Philadelphia, one of the six regional associations.

Midwestern States Accreditation Agency One of two phony accreditors (the other was the National Association of Open-Campus Colleges) that was part of an elaborate diploma mill scheme in the early '80s that included such schools as American Western University, National College of Arts and Sciences, Northwestern College of Allied Science, Regency College, and Saint Paul's Seminary.

National Accreditation Association Established in Riverdale, Maryland, by Dr. Glenn Larsen, whose doctorate is from a diploma mill called the Sussex College of Technology. His associate is Dr. Clarence Franklin, former president and chancellor of American International University (described in the chapter on diploma mills). In a mailing to presidents of unaccredited schools, the NAA offered full accreditation by mail, with no on-site inspection required.

National Association for Schools and Colleges See: National Association of Private, Nontraditional Schools and Colleges

National Association of Alternative Schools and Colleges Western States University claimed in their literature that they had been accredited by this organization, which we have never been able to locate.

National Association of Open Campus Colleges
Southwestern University of Arizona and Utah (which closed after its proprietor was sent to prison as a result of the FBI's diploma mill investigations) claimed accreditation from this agency. The address in Springfield, Missouri, was the same as that of Disciples of Truth, an organization that has in the past operated a chain of diploma mills.

National Association of Private, Nontraditional Schools and Colleges (NAPNSC) A serious effort to establish an accrediting agency specifically concerned with alternative schools and programs. It was established in Grand Junction, Colorado, in the 1970s by a group of educators associated with Western Colorado University, a nontraditional school that has since gone out of business. Although NAPNSC's standards for accreditation have grown more rigorous over the years, their application for recognition has been turned down many times by the U.S. Department of Education, but they plan to keep trying. Formerly the National Association for Schools and Colleges.

National Board of Naturopathic Examiners One of the three unrecognized accreditors of Westbrook University. Shares its address with a store called Matts Health Foods, whose owner, Norbert Matts, is a faculty member at Westbrook as well as the chairman of this accrediting agency.

National Council for the Accreditation of Private Universities and Schools of Law Unrecognized agency from which the now-defunct degree mill, Monticello University, claimed accreditation.

National Council of Schools and Colleges Accreditation by this agency was claimed by International University, formerly of New Orleans, later of Pasadena, California, and now out of existence. Despite many inquiries, the proprietors of the school never provided information on their accreditor.

National Diet and Nutrition Association Unrecognized accreditor claimed by Universitas Sancti Martin.

North American Regional Accrediting Commission Accreditor of the fake International University of Louisiana.

Pacific Association of Schools and Colleges Established in 1993, this organization is operated by a man who had previously been a senior official in the California Department of Education (and who has a doctorate from an unaccredited school). PASC appeared to be a serious attempt to create an accreditor that would be better able

to deal with nontraditional schools, but as of 2000, they are no longer in business.

Society of Academic Recognition Associated with the fake University of Corpus Christi.

Southern Cross International Association of Colleges and Schools (SCIACS) The accreditor claimed by Cambridge Graduate School and its sister school, Emmanuel College of Christian Studies, but we can find no other evidence of its existence.

Transworld Accrediting Commission (TAC) Accreditor of Evangel Christian University. "The philosophy of TAC is to demonstrate accountability to the consuming public for education obtained in traditional and nontraditional evangelical educational institutions."

United Congress of Colleges Unrecognized agency claimed by Earlscroft University. No address or URL ever found.

Universal Accrediting Association The creation of and the accreditor for the Universal Life Church & University.

Universal Accrediting Commission for Schools, Colleges and Universities Athens, Greece. Accreditor of Romano Byzantine College.

Uniworld Association Incorporated This unrecognized accreditor's Web site, *www.uniworld.org*, is registered to Bilal Nasrullah, who is the president of the University of Asia, which happens to be this accreditor's only member school.

Virtual University Accrediting Association (VUAA) See: International University Accrediting Association

West European Accrediting Society Established from a mail-forwarding service in Liederbach, Germany, by the proprietors of a chain of diploma mills such as Loyola, Roosevelt, Lafayette, Southern California, and Cromwell universities, for the purpose of accrediting themselves.

Western Association of Private Alternative Schools One of several accrediting agencies claimed in the literature of Western States University. No address or phone number has ever been provided, despite many requests.

Western Association of Schools and Colleges This is the name of the legitimate regional accreditor for the West coast. However, it is also the name of a fake accreditor with a Los Angeles address set up by the proprietors of such diploma mills as Loyola, Roosevelt, Lafayette, Southern California, and Cromwell universities.

World Association of Universities and Colleges versus William Howard Taft University

It's always interesting (and a bit unusual) when a school sues its own accrediting agency. In August, 1999, Taft (a California-approved university that had joined WAUC in 1994) filed suit against WAUC, alleging, among other matters, that WAUC failed to make an on-site evaluation of Taft's facilities, and failed to follow its own published evaluation procedures for Taft and other member institutions. The matter was resolved in May, 2000, and described in a press release issued and posted on the Internet by Taft University. Here are a few of the highlights:

1. WAUC gave Taft its accreditation without a visit, and indeed renewed the accreditation automatically, without Taft having made an application to renew.

2. Taft pointed out that WAUC "has consistently promoted itself as a nonprofit organization," but then acknowledged to Taft in writing that "WAUC is a for-profit corporation."

3. In a matter that Taft's president David Boyd later called the "most disconcerting" matter, WAUC was "not able to provide any documented evidence they had *ever* conducted a site visit at *any* member institution."

4. Taft stated that they applied to WAUC because the accreditor told them it was exploring recognition by the U.S. Department of Education. In the discovery part of the suit, WAUC was unable to provide even "a single piece of correspondence with the Department of Education."

Western Council on Non-Traditional Private Post Secondary Education An accrediting agency started by the founders of Southland University, presumably for the purpose of accrediting themselves and others. See also: Arizona Commission of Non-Traditional Private Postsecondary Education

Western European Accrediting Society Phony accreditor that was claimed by Cromwell University, a diploma mill.

World Association of Universities and Colleges (WAUC) Established in 1992 by Dr. Maxine Asher, and run from a secretarial service in Nevada. Accredits a long list of nonwonderful institutions, including Lacrosse University, IOND University, Cambridge State, and Columbus University. Not surprisingly, also accredits American World University, which is also operated by Dr. Asher. In February 1995, the national investigative publication *Spy Magazine* ran a most unflattering article on WAUC. Dr. Asher also operates the Ancient Mediterranean Research Association which has produced a film that "clearly demonstrates the existence of Atlantis off the coast of Spain." When asked about John Bear, Dr. Asher has written to people that "almost no one in higher education takes John Bear seriously."

World Council of Excellence in Higher Education Shares all of its addresses—mail, email, and URL—with Intercultural Open University (based in the Netherlands), the only school we know of who claims this accreditor.

World Council of Global Education As part of the World Natural Health Organization, issues accreditation to institutions that provide an education in the natural health care field. Bernadean University is the only school we've come across that claims accreditation from these folks.

World Organization of Institutes, Colleges, and Universities Omega University "enjoys" their international accreditation, but a fairly thorough Internet search reveals that they must be the only ones doing so.

Worldwide Accrediting Commission Operated from a mail-forwarding service in Cannes, France, for the purpose of accrediting the fake Loyola University (Paris), Lafayette University, and other American-run degree mills.

Bible School Accreditors

There are six recognized accreditors of religious schools, listed earlier among the "Professional Accrediting Agencies," which cover everything from evangelical Christian schools to rabbinical seminaries. Religious schools often claim they have not sought accreditation since there are no relevant accreditors. They are not exactly accurate. There are also a great many unrecognized accreditors. Since many Bible schools readily acknowledge that their degrees are not academic in nature, accreditation of them has quite a different meaning. Some of these associations may well be quite legitimate, but their accreditation has no academic relevance. Some accreditors are apparently concerned primarily with doctrinal soundness; others may have other motivations. Among the Bible school accreditors are:

Accreditation Association of Christian Colleges and Seminaries Morgantown, KY

Accrediting Association of Christian Colleges and Seminaries Sarasota, FL

AF Sep We don't know what this means, but Beta International University claims it is the name of their accrediting association. Address unknown.

American Accrediting Association of Theological Institutions Rocky Mount, NC. They accredit Patriot University, among others, on payment of a $100 fee.

American Association of Accredited Colleges and Universities Address unknown.

American Educational Accrediting Association of Christian Schools See: American Educational Association of Non-Traditional Christian Schools

American Educational Association of Non-Traditional Christian Schools Dothan, Alabama. Formerly the American Educational Accrediting Association of Christian Schools.

American Federation of Christian Colleges and Schools Lakeland, FL

Association of Christian Colleges and Theological Schools Louisiana

Association of Christian Schools and Colleges Address unknown.

Association of Fundamental Institutes of Religious Education (AFIRE) Address unknown.

Eastern Christian Accrediting Association of Colleges, Universities, and Seminaries Address unknown.

International Accrediting Association of Church Colleges Address unknown.

International Accrediting Commission Kenosha, WI

National Accrediting Agency for Private Schools Atlanta, GA

National Educational Accrediting Association Columbus, OH

Southeast Accrediting Association of Christian Schools, Colleges and Seminaries Milton, FL

Southern Accrediting Association of Christian Schools Address unknown.

World-Wide Accreditation Commission of Christian Educational Instituations Address unknown.

Words That Do Not Mean "Accredited"

Some unaccredited schools use terminology in their catalogs or advertising that might have the effect of misleading unknowledgeable readers. Here are six common phrases:

1. **Pursuing accreditation.** A school may state that it is "pursuing accreditation," or that it "intends to pursue accreditation." But that says nothing whatever about its chances for achieving same. It's like saying that you are practicing your tennis game, with the intention of playing in the finals at Wimbledon. Don't hold your breath.

2. **Chartered.** In some places, a charter is the necessary document that a school needs to grant degrees. A common ploy by diploma mill operators is to form a corporation, and state in the articles of incorporation that one of the purposes of the corporation is to grant degrees. This is like forming a corporation whose charter says that it has the right to appoint the Pope. You can *say* it, but that doesn't make it so.

3. **Licensed or registered.** This usually refers to nothing more than a business license, granted by the city or county in which the school is located, but which has nothing to do with the legality of the school, or the usefulness of its degrees.

4. **Recognized.** This can have many possible meanings, ranging from some level of genuine official recognition at the state level, to having been listed in some directory often unrelated to education, perhaps published by the school itself. Two ambitious degree mills (Columbia State University and American International University) have published entire books that look at first glance like this one, solely for the purpose of being able to devote lengthy sections in them to describing their phony schools as "the best in America."

Apostille and Authentication

More than a few less-than-wonderful schools suggest in their literature that their diplomas are stamped, sealed, approved, and/or authenticated by the United States or other state or national governments. Sometimes they say this is by the process of "apostille," or "authentication." Here, for instance, is the catalog wording of one dreadful school:

> Our documents are prepared at your request and submitted to the U.S. Department of State for authentication for your final presentation to an Embassy for approval.

Quite a few university registrars and company human resources people have told us that they often see this process abused, often by well-meaning graduates who were told (improperly) by their university that the process of apostille or authentication somehow makes the diploma or transcript valid, official, or certified. *This is not the case.*

All that apostille or authentication does is confirm that the person (notary or school official) who signed the diploma or transcript is who he or she says they are, and they signed it with their own validated signature. It is a form of government notarization, nothing more or less. It says *nothing whatever* about the content of the document.

Let's say you sit down in your kitchen and start a fake school, Godzilla University. You sell me a medical degree for a thousand dollars. You take the diploma (and the phony transcript you just typed up) to your local Notary Public, who, for $10, will notarize your signature (that is, compare it with the one on your driver's license and say yes, it is the same). Then you take (or send) the phony diploma and notarized certificate to your state capital, where they will confirm that it is indeed a certificate signed by a licensed notary, relating to the diploma. And finally, you submit your packet—the fake diploma and transcript, the notarization, and the state confirmation—to the federal government (Department of State or an embassy) and they will issue the apostille or authentication.

At no point in the process does anyone know or care what the document itself is, or whether it is legitimate. Whether your diploma is issued by Oxford, Harvard, or Godzilla University, you can get the same authentication or apostille.

5. **Authorized.** In California, this has had a specific meaning (see chapter 7). Elsewhere, the term can be used to mean almost anything the school wants it to—sometimes legitimate, sometimes not. A Canadian degree mill once claimed to be "authorized to grant degrees." It turned out that the owner had authorized his wife to go ahead and print the diplomas.

6. **Approved.** In California, this has a specific meaning (see chapter 7). In other locations, it is important to know who is doing the approving. Some not-for-profit schools call themselves "approved by the U.S. Government," which means only that the Internal Revenue Service has approved their nonprofit status for income taxes—and nothing more. At one time, some British schools called themselves "Government Approved," when the approval related only to the school-lunch program.

7. **Member.** Swiss Business School, for example, advertises itself as a "member" of the accrediting agency, the Association of Collegiate Business Schools and Programs. That's not a lie, but it's not exactly being frank either. Some accrediting bodies also serve as trade associations for their respective fields, and in that capacity they offer industry representation, in the form of "membership," to any school that pays them annual dues, whether it's accredited by that body or not. Indeed, membership is often a prerequisite to accreditation candidacy.

The Second-to-Last Word on Accreditation

There have been quite an extraordinary number of new accrediting associations started in the last few years, and they are getting harder and harder to check out, either because they seem to exist only on the Internet, or because they exist in so many places: an address in Hawaii, another in Switzerland, a third in Germany, a fourth in Hong Kong, and so on. Some new ones have adopted the clever idea of bestowing their accreditation on some major universities, quite possibly unbeknownst to those schools. Then they can say truthfully, but misleadingly, that they accredit such well-known schools. This is the accreditation equivalent of those degree mills that send their diplomas to some famous people, and then list those people as graduates.

The Last Word on Accreditation

Don't believe everything anyone says. It seems extraordinary that any school would lie about something so easily checked as accreditation, but it is done. Degree mills have unabashedly claimed accreditation by a recognized agency. Such claims are totally untrue. They are counting on the fact that many people won't check up on these claims.

Salespeople trying to recruit students sometimes make accreditation claims that are patently false. Quite a few schools ballyhoo their "fully accredited" status but never mention that the accrediting agency is unrecognized, and so the accreditation is of little or (in most cases) no value.

One accrediting agency (the aforementioned International Accrediting Commission for Schools, Colleges and Theological Seminaries) boasted that two copies of every accreditation report they issue are "deposited in the Library of Congress." That sounds impressive, until you learn that for $20, anyone can copyright anything and be able to make the identical claim.

CHAPTER 9

Accredited versus Unaccredited: How Does One Decide?

Lord Brougham: Pray, Mr. Bickersteth, what is to prevent London University from awarding degrees now?

Mr. Bickersteth: The universal scorn and contempt of mankind.

1834 conversation, reported in the Grenville Diaries

There are hundreds of colleges and universities in the world that do not have recognized accreditation. They range from totally fraudulent degree mills run by ex-convicts who sell worthless degrees to anyone willing to pay, to major new academic endeavors, well-funded and run by experienced educators of good reputation, and extremely likely to become properly accredited before too long.

In almost every instance, the unaccredited schools cost less, and offer a faster path to a degree, often with more flexibility. It is a tempting consideration, and a common dilemma for many people in search of a school. As a result, it is probably the most common question we get: should I pursue an unaccredited degree? Since we cannot know each questioner's situation and needs, we typically reply by saying, "If you are absolutely confident that an unaccredited degree will meet your current and your predictable future needs, then it might well be appropriate to pursue such a degree."

Note: For the purpose of the following discussion, we include schools with accreditation claimed from an unrecognized accreditor as equivalent to unaccredited, for that is how such schools are almost certain to be treated by evaluators and decision makers.

There is no simple answer

There truly is no simple answer to the accredited vs. unaccredited issue, other than to say that one can rarely go wrong with a properly accredited degree. We hear from a moderate number of people who have made good use of an unaccredited (but totally legitimate) degree, but we hear from many more who have had significant problems with such degrees, in terms of acceptance by employers, admission to other schools, or simply bad publicity.

Acceptance of unaccredited degrees

Acceptance is very low in the academic world and the government world, somewhat higher in the business world. One large and decent unaccredited school, in operation for a quarter century, can only point to a dozen instances in which its degrees were accepted by other schools, most of those on a case-by-case basis. Some companies have no clear policy with regard to accreditation, and indeed may not even understand the concept, as was the case with the head of human resources for one of the ten largest companies on the planet, who got a copy of this book and then told us of her astonishment at learning that there were unaccredited schools and fake accrediting agencies.

Who can benefit from unaccredited degrees?

The largest group are those people who really don't *need* a degree, but they want one, either for self satisfaction ("validating my life's work" is a phrase we hear often) or to give themselves a marketing edge. One large subset of satisfied unaccredited degree-users, for instance, are therapists, who typically need only a master's degree for their state license. But they feel that if they have a Ph.D., and use that title in their advertising, yellow pages, etc., they will have an edge over competitors without the doctorate. The same is the case with owners or executives of small businesses. A real estate agent with an MBA or a business planner with a doctorate in finance may get more clients because of the higher degree, and indeed may have additional useful knowledge.

What problems can arise?

We get a lot of mail from people who were having major problems with a previously satisfactory unaccredited degree. This situation occurs after one of two events. One is a change in employer policy. A company that may have accepted or tolerated or unwittingly gone along with unaccredited degrees may have a change, either due to new personnel policies or new ownership, and previously acceptable degrees no longer are. Similarly, when an employee seeks work at a new company, he or she may learn that the degree held is no longer useful. The other is when there is bad publicity, and the light of public scrutiny is focused on the school or the degrees. In recent years, the media have devoted more and more attention to these matters. *American Journal*, *60 Minutes*, *Inside Edition*, *Extra*, and dozens of local television consumer reporters have addressed the matter of bad schools and degrees. When *American Journal* devoted a long segment to a popular unaccredited school, and when a large daily newspaper gave an eight-column front-page headline to the state's lawsuit against another large and popular unaccredited school, many students and alumni of those schools had some highly uncomfortable moments.

Does the level of the degree make a difference?

We think it does. We can find very few reasons why it would ever make sense to pursue an unaccredited associate's or bachelor's degree. There are two reasons for this. One is that there are so very many distance bachelor's programs with recognized accreditation, and those degrees can actually be faster and less expensive than some of the unaccredited ones. The other is that a person with at least one accredited degree, as the foundation, is seen to be someone clearly capable of doing university level work, and if they chose to pursue an unaccredited master's or doctorate, after earning the accredited bachelor's, they must have had a good reason. Alternatively, a person with only an unaccredited degree, or series of degrees, will often be under a cloud of suspicion, especially in a world where it is possible to get a not-illegal bachelor's degree in six months or less.

Will degrees with recognized accreditation always be accepted?

Most annoyingly, no. In the sometimes-snobbish world of higher education, schools without regional accreditation are sometimes seen to be inferior. As one simple but telling example, Excelsior College, one of the largest and best-respected distance-learning schools in the U.S., itself with regional accreditation, will not accept degrees or credits from schools accredited by the Distance Education and Training Council, a recognized accreditor, unless the individual courses have been independently evaluated by the American Council on Education. Quite a few regionally accredited schools *will* accept DETC accreditation, in our experience, but by no means all. This depressing fact is just one more reason to "shop around" to be sure any given degree will meet your needs.

Another factor in acceptance is regional accreditation versus professional accreditation. In some fields, such as psychology, architecture, and engineering, accreditation from the relevant professional association can be especially important. For example, there are job descriptions for therapists that require degrees accredited by the American Psychological Association, a professional accreditor, which accredits fewer than half the psychology programs in America.

What happens if my school becomes accredited after I earn my degree?

Theoretically one only has an accredited degree if it was earned after accreditation. For many practical purposes, however, it is unlikely that an employer will say, for instance, "Did you earn your degree from Capella University before or after November 17, 1997?" Once a school has been accredited, it is likely (but not certain) that all its degrees will be regarded as accredited, whenever earned. Some schools offer the option of going back and doing a modest amount of additional work, and earning a "replacement" degree after the accreditation is gained.

What happens if the accreditor is recognized after I earn my degree?

In this scenario, the student earns a degree from a school that is accredited by an unrecognized agency, and later the agency is recognized by the Department of Education. This is such a rare situation, we really don't know if there is a precedent. Common sense suggests that if the school or degree was accredited all along, and if the only change is that the accreditor becomes recognized, then the student would have a degree with recognized accreditation. But common sense does not always prevail in the world of higher education.

Is unrecognized accreditation worse than none at all?

In many cases, we think so, because it adds one more layer of possible irregularity to attract the attention of investigators, regulators, decision makers, and others. When, for instance, a national magazine did an extremely unflattering article on the unrecognized World Association of Universities and Colleges (*Spy*, February 1995), the caustic comments and the various revelations led readers to think less favorably of the schools this association had accredited. On the other hand, some of the larger distance-learning schools make no accreditation claims whatsoever (California Coast, California Pacific, Fairfax, Southwest, etc.), and still manage to attract students.

It is common for unrecognized accrediting agencies to talk or write about their intention to become recognized by the Department of Education. In our opinion, however, of the more-than-60 active unrecognized accreditors described in the "Accreditation" chapter, only one has even a remote chance of recognition, and that one, the National Association of Private, Nontraditional Schools and Colleges, has been turned down many times over the past twenty years. Some of these accreditors suggest that it is their choice not to be recognized, by writing things like, "This association has not sought recognition . . ." or ". . . does not choose to be listed by the Department of Education." And we have chosen not to be awarded the Nobel Prize in literature.

CHAPTER 10

Scholarships and Other Financial Aid

If you think education is expensive, try ignorance.

Derek Bok, former president of Harvard University

Financial assistance comes in four forms:

Outside scholarships. An outright gift of money paid to you or the school by an outside source (government, foundation, corporation, etc.).

Inside scholarships. The school itself reduces your tuition and/or other expenses. No money changes hands.

Fellowships. Money either from the school or an outside source, usually but not always in return for certain work or services to be performed at the school (generally teaching or research).

Loans. From outside lenders, or from the school itself, to be paid back over a period of anywhere from 1 to 10 years, generally at interest lower than the current prime rate.

Sadly, as college costs continue to rise substantially, the amount of money available for financial aid is diminishing dramatically. Many loan and scholarship programs were either funded or guaranteed by the federal government, and much of this money was eliminated as part of the Reagan administration's cutbacks and has not been restored. After all, 300,000 canceled full-tuition scholarships can buy one nuclear-powered aircraft carrier. And already have. (This remark in previous editions has resulted in three stern letters from veterans asking, in effect, if we would rather be protected from a commie invasion by a nuclear battleship or by 300,000 scholars. We're still not sure.)

Still, billions of dollars are available to help pay the college costs of people who need help. The vast majority of it goes to full-time students under age 25, pursuing residential degrees at traditional schools.

Tapping into that particular fount is outside the scope of this book. There are several very useful books on this subject, which are described in the reference section, including our own book, *Finding Money for College*, published by Ten Speed Press.

That book is the only one we know of that is specifically oriented to the nontraditional student, the older student, and the graduate student. It covers a wide range of nontraditional strategies, such as bartering skills (gardening, athletic coaching, etc.) for tuition, recruiting new students on a commission basis, and exploiting real estate and tax angles.

Some computerized services collect data on tens of thousands of individual scholarships, and can match their clients' needs and interests with donors for a modest fee. All but a few of these services are licensees, and tap into the same database, so there is no point in getting more than one report. If you'd like to see what they have to offer, you might wish to get the literature from the pioneer in this field, the National Scholarship Research Service, at 2280 Airport Road, Santa Rosa, CA 95403; phone: (800) 432 3782 or (707) 546 6777; fax: (707) 546 6785; email: *nsrs@msn.com*.

If you'd like to do your own research, a great place to start is on the Web at *www.finaid.org*. For folks who prefer to do their research off-line, Dan Cassidy, founder of National Scholarship Research Service, has made it easy for you. Their complete database of available scholarships has been published in a series of three books, for undergraduates, graduates, and people who wish to study abroad. Details are in the "Bibliography" chapter.

Some of the scholarships available are, admittedly, awfully peculiar: for rodeo riders with high grades, for Canadian petunia fanciers, for reformed prostitutes from Seattle, for people named Baxendale or Murphy, for people born on certain dates and/or in certain towns, and so on. And many are quite small and/or highly competitive. But many, too, are quite general, and a fair number do not depend on financial need or net worth.

Many colleges and universities subscribe to a service called CASHE (College Aid Sources for Higher Education), a database of nearly 200,000 scholarships, grants, loans, fellowships, and work study programs. Some schools offer the service free to students or potential students; others make a nominal charge.

Many students enrolled in nontraditional, even non-residential, programs have their expenses paid, all or in part, by their employer. Thousands of large corporations, including nearly all of the Fortune 500, have tuition plans for their employees, and so do a great many small ones. But *billions* of dollars in corporate funds go unclaimed each year, simply because people don't ask for them, or because neither employers nor employees realize that there are significant tax advantages to both in setting up an employee tuition-paying plan.

The tax laws governing such things are what drive the corporate funding. But the tax laws are not etched in stone. In some recent years, companies were allowed to deduct up to $5,500 per employee per year for educational expenses, and the employees didn't have to pay tax on the employers' donations. This law expired, then was reenacted and made retroactive to the expired time, but was then in jeopardy of expiring again. This is the sort of thing that keeps tax accountants solvent.

At times when the law is in place, it is quite a persuasive thing for an employee of any size company to go to his or her boss and say, in effect, "If you pay up to $5,500 of my school expenses, it is all tax deductible for you, and the benefit is not taxable to me."

Some, but not too many, corporations will pay for unaccredited programs. Some unaccredited schools list in their literature the names of hundreds of corporations as well as U.S. and foreign government agencies where their graduates are employed, but this does not necessarily mean the companies paid or reimbursed them.

Most nontraditional schools, accredited and unaccredited, offer inside scholarships to their students who need them. In other words, they will award a partial scholarship, in the form of tuition reduction (10 to 30 percent is the usual range), rather than lose a student altogether. Quite a few schools also offer an extended payment plan, in which the tuition can be paid in a series of smaller monthly installments, or even charged to a major credit card.

There are schools, traditional and nontraditional, that offer tuition reduction in the form of commissions, or finders' fees, for bringing in other students. This quite ethical procedure can result in a tuition reduction of from 50 dollars to several hundred dollars for each referral, when the referred student enrolls.

But the biggest factors, by far, in financial aid for students at nontraditional schools are the speed of their education and the possibility of remaining fully employed while pursuing the degree. If even one year can be cut from a traditional four-year bachelor's degree program, the savings (including revenue from a year of working for pay) are greater than 99 percent of all scholarship grants. And, as mentioned earlier, the average "four year" bachelor's degree now takes six years, which should be taken into account in figuring time lost from jobs.

So, while it is nice to "win" money from another source, it is surely the case that to be able to complete an entire degree program for an out-of-pocket cost of from $4,000 to $8,000 (a typical range at nontraditional schools) is one of the great financial bargains of these ever-more-expensive times.

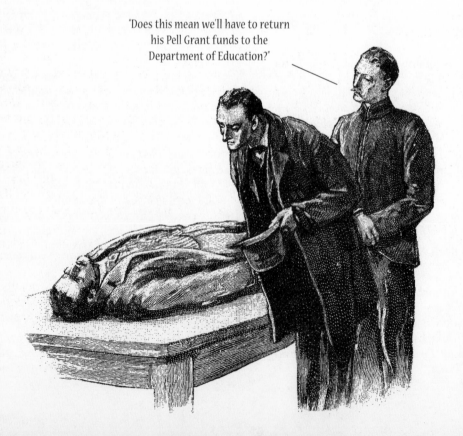

"Does this mean we'll have to return his Pell Grant funds to the Department of Education?"

CHAPTER 11

Applying to Schools

When any Scholar is able to read Tully or such like classical Latin Author ex tempore, and to make and speak true Latin in verse and prose, and shall have accepted Jesus Christ as his savior, and decline perfectly the paradigms of nouns and verbs in the Greek tongue, then may he be admitted into the College, nor shall any claim admission before such qualifications.

Admissions Standards, Harvard College, c.1650

How Many Schools Should You Apply To?

No single answer to this question is right for everyone. Each person will have to determine his or her own best answer. The decision should be based on the following four factors:

Likelihood of Admission

Some schools are extremely competitive or popular and admit fewer than 10 percent of qualified applicants. Some have an "open admissions" policy and admit literally everyone who applies. Most are somewhere in between.

If your goal is to be admitted to one of the highly competitive schools (for instance, Harvard, Yale, Princeton, or Stanford), where your chances of being accepted are not high, then it is wise to apply to at least four or five schools that would be among your top choices, and to at least one "safety valve"—an easier one, in case all else fails.

If your interest is in one of the good, but not world-famous, nonresident programs, your chances for acceptance are probably better than nine in ten, so you might decide to apply only to one or two.

Cost

There is a tremendous range of possible costs for any given degree. For instance, a respectable MBA could cost in the vicinity of $10,000 at a good nonresident school, or more than $50,000 at a well-known university—not even taking into account the lost salary. In general, we think it makes sense to apply to no more than two or three schools in any given price category.

What They Offer You

Shopping around for a school is a little like shopping for a new car. Many schools either have money problems, or operate as profit-making businesses, and in either case, they are most eager to enroll new students. Thus it is not unreasonable to ask the schools what they can do for you. Let them know that you are a knowledgeable "shopper" and that you have read this book. Do they have courses or faculty advisors in your specific field? If not, will they get one for you? How much credit will they give for prior life-experience learning? How long will it take to earn the degree? Are there any scholarships or tuition reduction plans available? Does tuition have to be paid all at once, or can it be spread out over time? If factors like these are important for you, then it could pay to shop around for the best deal.

You might consider investigating at least two or three schools that appear somewhat similar, because there will surely be differences.

Caution: Remember that academic quality and reputation are probably the most important factors—so don't let a small financial saving be a reason to switch from a good school to a less-good school.

Your Own Time and Money

Applying to a school can be a time-consuming process—and it costs money, too. Many schools have application fees ranging from $25 to $100. Some people get so carried away with the process of applying to school after school that they never get around to enrolling in one, let alone earning their degree.

Of course once you have prepared a good detailed resume, curriculum vita, or life-experience portfolio, you can use it to apply to more than one school.

Another time factor is how much of a hurry you are in. If you apply to several schools at once, the chances are good that at least one will admit you, and you can begin work promptly. If you apply to only one, and it turns you down, or you get into long delays, then it can take a month or two to go through the admissions process elsewhere.

Speeding Up the Admissions Process

The admissions process at most traditional schools is very slow; most people apply nearly a year in advance and do not learn if their application has been accepted for four to six months. Nontraditional programs vary immensely in their policies in this regard. Some will grant conditional acceptance within a few weeks after receiving the application. ("Conditional" means that they must later verify the prior learning experiences you claim.) Others take just as long as traditional programs.

The following three factors can result in a much faster admissions process:

Selecting Schools by Policy

A school's admissions policy should be stated in its catalog. Since you will find a range among schools of a few weeks to six months for a decision, the simple solution is to ask, and then apply to schools with a fast procedure.

Asking for Speedy Decisions

Some schools have formal procedures whereby you can request an early decision on your acceptance. Others do the same thing informally, for those who ask. In effect, what this does is put you at the top of the pile in the admissions office, so you will have the decision in, perhaps, half the usual time. Other schools use what they call a "rolling admissions" procedure, which means, in effect, that each application is considered soon after it is received instead of being held several months and considered with a large batch of others.

Applying Pressure

As previously indicated, many schools are eager to have new students. If you make it clear to a school that you are in a hurry and that you may consider going elsewhere if you don't hear from them promptly, they will usually speed up the process. It is not unreasonable to specify a time frame. If, for instance, you are mailing in your application on September 1, you might enclose a note saying that you would like to have their decision mailed or phoned to you by October 1. (Some schools routinely telephone their acceptances, others do so if asked, some will only do so by collect call, and others will not, no matter what.)

How to Apply to a School

The basic procedure is essentially the same at all schools, traditional or nontraditional:

1. You write (or telephone) for the school's catalog, bulletin, or other literature, and admissions forms.

2. You complete the admissions forms and return them to the school, with application fee, if any.

3. You complete or provide any other requirements the school may have (exams, transcripts, letters of recommendation, etc.).

4. The school notifies you of its decision.

It is step three that can vary tremendously from school to school. At some schools all that is required is the admissions application. Others will require various entrance examinations to test your aptitude or knowledge level, transcripts, three or more letters of reference, a statement of financial condition, and possibly a personal interview, either on the campus or with a local representative in your area.

Happily, the majority of nontraditional schools have relatively simple entrance requirements. And all schools supply the materials that tell you exactly what they expect you to do in order to apply. If it is not clear, ask. If the school does not supply prompt, helpful answers, then you probably don't want to deal with them anyway. It's a buyer's market.

It is advisable, in general, *not* to send a whole bunch of stuff to a school the very first time you write to them. A short note asking for their catalog should suffice. You may wish to indicate your field and degree goal ("I am interested in a master's and possibly a doctorate in psychology . . .") in case they have different sets of literature for different programs. It probably can do no harm to mention that you are a reader of this book; it might get you slightly prompter or more personal responses. (On the other hand, more than a few grouchy readers have written saying, "I told them I was a personal friend of yours, and it still took six months for an answer." Oh dear. Well, if they hadn't said that, it might have been even longer. Or perhaps shorter. Who knows?)

Entrance Examinations

Many nonresident degree programs, even at the master's and doctoral levels, do not require any entrance examinations. On the other hand, the majority of residential programs *do* require them. The main reason for this appears to be that nontraditional schools do not have to worry about overcrowding on the campus, so they can admit more students. A second reason is that they tend to deal with more mature students who have the ability to decide which program is best for them.

There are, needless to say, exceptions to both reasons. If you have particular feelings about examinations—positive or negative—you will be able to find schools that meet your requirements. Do not hesitate to ask any school about their exam requirements if it is not clear from the catalog.

Bachelor's Admission Examinations

Most residential universities require applicants to take the SAT or Scholastic Aptitude Test, run by a private agency, the College Entrance Examination Board (45 Columbus Avenue, New York, NY 10023-6992; (609) 771 7600; *www.collegeboard.org*). The general SAT measures verbal and mathematical abilities. There are also subject exams, testing knowledge levels in specific areas such as biology, U.S. history, Spanish, etc. These examinations are given at centers all over North America several times each year for modest fees, and by special arrangement in many foreign locations.

A competing private organization, ACT (2201 North Dodge Street, P.O. Box 168, Iowa City, IA 52243-0168; (319) 337 1000; *www.act.org*), offers a similar range of entrance examinations.

The important point is that very few schools have their own exams; virtually all rely on either the SAT or the ACT.

Graduate Degrees

Again, many nonresidential schools do not require any entrance examinations. Many, but by no means all, residential master's and doctoral programs ask their applicants to take the GRE, or Graduate Record Examination, administered by the Educational Testing Service (P.O. Box 6000, Princeton, NJ 08541; (609) 771 7670; *www.gre.org*). The basic GRE consists of a three-and-a-half-hour aptitude test (of verbal, quantitative, and analytical abilities). Some schools also require GRE subject-area exams, which are available in a variety of specific fields (chemistry, computer science, psychology, etc.).

Professional Schools

Most law, business, and medical schools also require a standard examination, rather than having one of their own. The MCAT (Medical College Admission Test) and LSAT (Law School Admission Test) are given several times a year by ACT; the GMAT (Graduate Management Admissions Test) is given by ETS.

There are many excellent books available at most libraries and larger bookstores on how to prepare for these various exams, complete with sample questions and answers. Some of these are listed in the bibliography of this book. Also, the testing agencies themselves sell literature on their tests as well as copies of previous years' examinations.

The testing agencies used to deny vigorously that either cramming or coaching could affect one's scores. In the face of overwhelming evidence to the contrary, they no longer make those claims. Some coaching services have documented score increases of 25 to 30 percent. Check the Yellow Pages or the bulletin boards on high school or college campuses for test-preparation workshops in your area.

CHAPTER 12

Equivalency Examinations

Do, or do not. There is no "try."

Yoda

The nontraditional approach to higher education says that if you have knowledge of an academic field, then you should get credit for that knowledge, regardless of how or where you acquired the knowledge. The simplest and fairest way of assessing that knowledge is through an examination.

About 3,000 colleges and universities in the United States and Canada, many of whom would deny vigorously that there is anything "nontraditional" about them, award students credit toward their bachelor's degrees (and, in a few cases, master's and doctorates) solely on the basis of passing examinations.

Many of the exams are designed to be equivalent to the final exam in a typical college class, and the assumption is that if you score high enough, you get the same amount of credit you would have gotten by taking the class—or, in some cases, a good deal more.

While there are many sources of equivalency exams, including a trend toward schools developing their own, two national testing agencies are dominant in this field: the College-Level Examination Program (CLEP) and Excelsior College Examinations. Together, they administer more than 70 equivalency exams that are given at hundreds of testing centers all over North America. By special arrangement, many of them can be administered almost anywhere in the world.

CLEP Tests

CLEP is offered by the College Entrance Examination Board, known as "the College Board" (45 Columbus Avenue, New York, NY 10023-6992; (212) 713 8064; fax: (212) 713 8063; email: *clep@info.collegeboard.org*; Web site: *www.collegeboard.org/clep*). Military personnel who want

to take CLEP exams should see their education officer or contact DANTES/CLEP at P.O. Box 6604, Princeton, NJ 08541; (609) 720 6740.

CLEP tests are given at more than 1,200 centers, most of them on college or university campuses. Each center sets its own schedule for frequency of testing, so it may pay to "shop around" for convenient dates. After July 1, 2001, the tests are only offered on computer.

The exams are designed to correspond to typical one-semester or full-year introductory-level courses offered at a university, and they are titled accordingly. Test takers are given 90 minutes to answer multiple-choice questions at a computer terminal. The Composition and Literature exams have an optional essay section (required by some

"The exam room is downstairs, but I don't know if they'll let you in, with that silly hat."

70

colleges). It costs about $50 to take any test in one of the following fields:

Business
Information Systems and Computer Applications
Principles of Management
Principles of Accounting
Introductory Business Law
Principles of Marketing

Composition and Literature
English Composition
Humanities
American Literature
Analyzing and Interpreting Literature
Freshman College Composition

Languages Other than English
College-Level French
College-Level German
College-Level Spanish

History and Social Sciences
Social Sciences and History
American Government
History of the U.S.: Early Colonizations to 1877
History of the U.S.: 1865 to the Present
Human Growth and Development
Introduction to Educational Psychology
Principles of Macroeconomics
Principles of Microeconomics
Introductory Psychology
Introductory Sociology
Western Civilization: Ancient Near East to 1648
Western Civilization: 1648 to the Present

Science and Mathematics
General Mathematics
Natural Sciences
Calculus with Elementary Functions
College Algebra
College Algebra—Trigonometry
General Biology
General Chemistry
Trigonometry

Note: Before 2001, CLEP made a distinction between "general" exams and "subject" exams. As we went to press, that distinction was in the process of being eliminated. What were the five general exams—English Composition, Humanities, Social Sciences & History, College Mathematics, and Natural Sciences—have been integrated into the subject exam categories you see in the list above.

Excelsior College Examinations

Excelsior College Examinations are developed by Excelsior College (Test Administration Office, 7 Columbia Circle, Albany, NY 12203-5159; (888) 723 9267; Web site: *www.excelsiorcollege.edu*).

Please note: Excelsior College was formerly known as Regents College, and the exam program, respectively, was known as Regents College Examinations. It was, in fact, just before this book went to press that the name change from Regents to Excelsior had been announced. Officials at Regents/Excelsior told us that their exam program would change its name accordingly, although it hadn't yet happened before we went to the printer. In anticipation of when you'll be reading this, we're going ahead and calling them Excelsior College Examinations, but if the new name doesn't seem to be working for you in whatever context you're using it, swapping "Regents" for "Excelsior" will probably solve the problem.

(**Note also:** Before all this, and in the last edition of this book, it was called the Proficiency Examination Program, or PEP.)

Excelsior College Examinations are administered at Sylvan Technology Centers (*www.educate.com*) at more than 200 locations throughout the U.S. and Canada. Persons living more than 250 miles from a test center may make special arrangements for the test to be given nearer home.

While CLEP tests generally correspond to introductory-level college courses, Excelsior College Examinations are more geared toward the intermediate to advanced college-level. The tests are three hours long, but a few are four hours. Ranging in price from $70 to $370 per exam, they are offered in the following fields:

Art and Science
Abnormal Psychology
American Dream
Anatomy & Physiology
English Composition
Ethics: Theory & Practice
Foundations of Gerontology
History of Nazi Germany
Life Span Developmental Psychology
Microbiology
Pathophysiology
Psychology of Adulthood and Aging
Religions of the World
Research Methods in Psychology
Statistics
Structure & Change: Our Place in the World
Values & Responsibility: The Individual & Society
World Population

Education
Reading Instruction in the Elementary School

Business
Business Policy & Strategy
Human Resource Management
Labor Relations
Organizational Behavior
Production/Operations Management

Nursing
18 specialized exams, ranging from professional strategies in nursing to maternity nursing

How Exams Are Scored and Credited

Each college or university sets its own standards for passing grades, and also decides for itself how much credit to give for each exam. Both of these factors can vary substantially from school to school. Take, for example, the Excelsior exam in anatomy and physiology, a three-hour multiple-choice test that hundreds of schools give credit for passing. But the amount of credit given, as well as the score required to pass, is different for almost every school:

- ▶ Central Virginia Community College requires a score of 45 (out of 80), and awards nine credit hours for passing.

- ▶ Edinboro University in Pennsylvania requires a score of 50 to pass, and awards six credit hours for the same exam.

- ▶ Concordia College in New York requires a score of 47, but awards only three credit hours.

Similar situations prevail on most of the exams. There is no predictability or consistency, even within a given school. For instance, at the University of South Florida, a three-hour multiple-choice test in maternal nursing is worth 18 units while a three-hour multiple-choice test in psychiatric nursing is worth only nine.

So, with dozens of standard exams available, and with about 3,000 schools offering credit, it pays to shop around a little and select both the school and the exams that will give you the most credit.

How Hard Are These Exams?

This is, of course, an extremely subjective question. However, we have heard from a great many readers who have attempted CLEP and Excelsior exams, and the most common response is "Gee, that was a lot easier than I had expected." This is especially true with more mature students. The tests are designed for 18-to-20-year-olds, and there appears to be a certain amount of factual knowledge, as well as experience in dealing with testing situations, that people acquire in ordinary life situations as they grow older.

There is no stigma attached to poor performance on these tests. In fact, if you wish, you may have the scores reported only to you, so that no one but you and the computer will know how you did. Then, if your scores are high enough, you can have them sent on to the schools of your choice. CLEP allows exams to be taken every six months; you can take the same Excelsior College exam twice in any 12-month period.

Preparing (and Cramming) for Exams

Both testing agencies issue detailed syllabuses describing each test and the specific content area it covers. They both sell an "official study guide" that gives sample questions and answers from each examination. On its Web site, CLEP also offers practice tests with sample questions.

The testing agencies create their exam questions from college textbooks, so for studying they recommend that you go to the source. At the bookstore of a local college, browse the textbook selection for the course that corresponds to the test you'll be taking.

At least four educational publishers have produced series of books on how to prepare for such exams, often with full-length sample tests. These can be found in the education or reference section of any good bookstore or library.

For years, the testing agencies vigorously fought the idea of letting test-takers take copies of the test home with them. But consumer legislation in New York has made at least some of the tests available, and a good thing, too. Every so often, someone discovers an incorrect answer or a poorly-phrased question that can have more than one correct answer, necessitating a recalculation and reissuance of scores to all the thousands of people who took that test.

In recent years, there has been much controversy over the value of cramming for examinations. Many counseling clients report having been able to pass four or five CLEP exams in a row by spending an intensive few days (or weeks) cramming for them. Although the various testing agencies used to deny that cramming can be of any value, in the last few years there have been some extremely persuasive research studies that demonstrate the short-term effectiveness of intensive studying.

These data have vindicated the claims made by people and agencies that assist students in preparing for examinations. Such services are offered in a great many places, usually in the vicinity of college campuses, by graduate students and moonlighting faculty. The best place to find them is through the classified ads in campus newspapers, on bulletin boards around the campus, and through on-campus extension programs. Prices vary widely, so shop around.

But buyer beware: Test prep services are an unregulated industry and quality varies widely. Some make promises that that they simply cannot keep. We have heard reports of a growing number of fraudulent test prep services; many of them seem to be targeting members of the military and their families. Watch out for demands of large payments up front, strange-looking credit agreements, outdated preparation materials, book lists that include dictionaries or encyclopedias, or claims to be representing one of the testing agencies such as CLEP. The people who make the tests don't make sales calls.

Often the best strategy is to take a self-scoring test from one of the guidebooks. If you do well, you may wish to take the real exam right away. If you do badly, you may conclude that credit by examination is not your cup of hemlock. And if you score in between, consider studying (or cramming) on your own, or with the help of a paid tutor or tutoring service.

Other Examinations

Here are some other examinations that can be used to earn substantial credit toward many nontraditional degree programs:

Graduate Record Examination

The GRE is administered by the Educational Testing Service (P.O. Box 6000, Princeton, NJ 08541; (609) 771 7670; email: *gre-info@ets.org*; Web site: *www.gre.org*). There is a general test, which is more of an aptitude test, which is now given on demand at more than 600 computer centers throughout North America. On completing this exam by computer, the student is given the choice of either erasing the exam entirely and walking out (no harm, no foul), or pressing another button, and being given an instantaneous (but still unofficial) score.

The GRE Subject Tests are still given in written form, although this may change in the near future. It is a three-hour multiple-choice test, designed to test knowledge that would ordinarily be gained by a bachelor's degree–holder in that given field. The exams are available in the fields of:

Biochemistry	English literature
Biology	Mathematics
Chemistry	Physics
Computer science	Psychology

This menu changes often, so check GRE's Web site for the latest list.

Few schools give credit for the general GRE. Schools vary widely in how much credit they will give for each subject-area GRE; for some schools it even depends on your score. The range is from none at all to 30 semester units (in the case of Excelsior College).

A National Guard sergeant once crammed for, took, and passed three GRE exams in a row, thereby earning 90 semester units in ten and a half hours of testing. Then he took five CLEP exams in two days, and earned 30 more units, which was enough to earn an accredited bachelor's degree (from what is now Excelsior College), start to finish, in 18 hours, starting absolutely from scratch with no college credit.

DANTES

The Defense Activity for Non-Traditional Education Support tests, or DANTES, were developed for the Department of Defense, but are available to civilians as well. The tests were developed by the Educational Testing Service, and are offered by hundreds of colleges and universities nationwide. While there is some overlap with CLEP and Excelsior exams, there are also many unique subjects. DANTES information is available from the DANTES Program, P.O. Box 6604, Princeton, NJ 08541; (609) 720 6740; *www.chauncey.com/dantes*.

Tests include, among others:

Anthropology
Art of the Western World
Astronomy
Business Law
Civil War and Reconstruction
College Algebra
Criminal Justice
Drug & Alcohol Abuse
Ethics in America
Geography
History of the Vietnam War
Human Resource Management
Modern Middle East
Organizational Behavior
Physical Geology
Physical Science
Principles of Finance
Principles of Financial Accounting
Public Speaking
Rise & Fall of the Soviet Union
Statistics
Technical Writing
World Religions

University End-of-Course Exams

Several schools offer the opportunity to earn credit for a correspondence course solely by taking (and passing) the final exam for that course. One need not be enrolled as a student in the school to do this. Two schools with especially large programs of this kind are Ohio University (Independent Study, 302 Tupper Hall, Athens, OH 45701; *www.cats.ohiou.edu/independent*) and the University of North Carolina (UNC Division of Continuing Education, CB# 1020 The Friday Center, Chapel Hill, NC 27599-1020; *www.fridaycenter.unc.edu*).

Advanced Placement Examinations

The College Board (45 Columbus Avenue, New York, NY 10023-6992; (212) 713 8066; *ap@collegeboard.org*) offers subject-specific exams specifically for students who wish to earn college credit while still in high school. For a list of the available subjects, go to *www.collegeboard.org/ap/students*.

Special Assessments

For people whose knowledge is both extensive and in an obscure field (or at least one for which no exams have been developed), some schools are willing to develop special exams for a single student. Each school has its own policy in this regard, so once again it can pay to "shop around."

CHAPTER 13

Courses by Mail and Internet

The postman is the agent of impolite surprises. Every week, we ought to have an hour for receiving letters—and then go and take a bath.

Friedrich Nietzsche

In all previous editions of this book, this chapter was called "Correspondence Courses," and we dutifully listed over a hundred universities where you could take one or many courses. The focus here was not on degree programs, but on individual courses, which could be applied to any number of degree programs.

But the world is quite different now, even from a year or two ago. While there are more than 10,000 home study courses offered the "old fashioned" way—utilizing the postal system—there are many, many more courses available entirely or almost entirely over the Internet.

It no longer makes sense to us to devote twenty pages to a list of universities with "mail order" courses. Nor is it practical to produce a list of available online courses, for the following two good reasons:

1. There are far too many of them. When we did a search in our favorite Internet search engine (*www.google.com*) for "online courses," it found the astonishing (well, we were astonished) total of 808,984 locations. Even devoting one line to each of them would add approximately 13,000 pages to this book.

2. There have arisen, over the past few years, so-called higher education "portals": Internet companies in the business of helping you get where you're going, by offering sophisticated search engines that can take you exactly where you would like to go. An online astronomy course for beginners. A series of courses in management information systems, with online chat rooms and lectures. A cheap, fast, and easy course in home ice cream making. (The legendary one taken from Penn State University by Ben and Jerry cost them five bucks.)

We invite you, then, to do your own online searches. For starters, we give you the Internet addresses of what were seven of the leading portals at the time of this writing—with the warning, needless to say, that "dot.com" companies come and go with the morning dew, and there is no guarantee that these will be around when you read this. But others will, and search engines will be with us forever.

Some Portals to Online Courses

www.hungryminds.com
www.embark.com
www.mindedge.com
www.cyberu.com
www.lifelonglearning.com
www.edupoint.com
www.dlcoursefinder.com

Correspondence Courses

Perhaps for the last time in *Bears' Guide*, then, we will devote a few pages to the "old fashioned" correspondence courses, but with much less depth than in the last edition.

There are two kinds of correspondence study, or home-study, courses: vocational and academic. Vocational courses (meat-cutting, locksmithing, appliance repair, etc.) often offer useful training, but rarely lead to degrees, so they are not relevant for this book. The Distance Education and Training Council (1601 18th Street NW, Washington, DC 20009; *www.detc.org*) offers excellent free information on the sources of vocational home-study courses in many fields.

More than 100 major universities and teaching institutions in the United States and dozens more in other countries offer academic correspondence (or email) courses—more than 13,000 courses in hundreds of subjects, from accounting to zoology. Virtually all of these courses can be counted toward a degree at almost any college or university. However, most schools have a limit on the amount of correspondence credit they will apply to a degree. This limit is typically around 50 percent, but the range is from zero to 100 percent. Through such schools such as Excelsior

College, Thomas Edison State College of New Jersey, and Western Illinois University, it is possible to earn an accredited bachelor's degree entirely through correspondence study.

Each of the institutions publishes or offers online a catalog or bulletin listing their available courses—some offer just a few, others have hundreds. All of the schools accept students living anywhere in the United States, although some charge more for out-of-state students. About 80 percent accept foreign students, but all courses are offered in English only.

Our arch-rival, Peterson Publishing, used to publish an excellent compendium of all the 13,000+ correspondence courses in a book called *The Independent Study Catalog*. But there hasn't been a new edition for several years, and it may have fallen victim to the computer age. Still you will find much useful information on their Web site, *www.petersons.com*.

Correspondence courses range from one to six semester hours worth of credit, and can cost anywhere from less than $40 to more than $150 per semester hour. The average is just over $80, so that a typical three-unit course would cost about $250. Because of the wide range in costs, it pays to shop around.

A typical correspondence course will consist of from five to twenty lessons, each one requiring a short written paper, answers to questions, or an unsupervised test graded by the instructor. There is almost always a supervised final examination. These can usually be taken anywhere in the world that a suitable proctor can be found (usually a high school or college teacher).

People who cannot go to a testing center because, for instance, they are handicapped, live too far away, or are in prison, can usually arrange to have a test supervisor come to them. Schools can be extremely flexible. One correspondence program administrator told us he had two students—a husband and wife—working as missionaries on a remote island where they were the only people who could read and write. He allowed them to supervise each other.

Many schools set limits on how quickly and how slowly you can complete a correspondence course. The shortest time is generally three to six weeks, while the upper limit ranges from three months to two years. Some schools limit the number of courses you can take at one time, but most do not. Even those with limits are concerned only with courses taken from their own institution. There is no cross-checking, so in theory one could take simultaneous courses from all 100+ institutions.

A sidelight: We would have thought that correspondence programs would remain quite stable, since so much time and effort is required to establish one. However, in the three years between editions of *Peterson's Guides*, it's not unusual for up to 10 percent of the list to change—five or six schools will drop their programs, and a similar number start new ones.

Students who want an even wider range of correspondence courses might consider taking one or more from a foreign university (see list below). While these courses are generally intended for citizens who cannot, for whatever reason, attend residential classes, Americans, Canadians, (and others) are often welcome to enroll. Although there's greater potential for problems (with the mails, deadlines, etc.), it's worth it for students who are interested in unusual fields or specific countries (studying Kiswahili with the University of Nairobi as part of an African-American Studies program, for instance).

Instead of using many pages to list and describe all of the 100+ U.S. schools and dozens of non-U.S. schools, we will prime the pump for you by identifying a couple of dozen with the widest range of available courses, undergraduate and graduate. If you don't use the Internet, you should find just about anything you want in the "old fashioned" ink-on-paper format at these schools.

Brigham Young University

Independent Study
206 Harman Building, P.O. Box 21514
Provo, UT 84602
(801) 378 2868 • (800) 914 8931
ce.byu.edu/is

Charter Oak State College

55 Paul J. Manafort Dr.
New Britian, CT 06053-2142
(860) 832 3800
www.cosc.edu

Colorado State University

Division of Educational Outreach
Spruce Hall
Fort Collins, CO 80523-1040
(970) 491 5288 • (877) 491 4336
www.csu2learn.colostate.edu

Indiana University

School of Continuing Studies
Owen Hall 002
Bloomington, IN 47405
(812) 855 2292 • (800) 334 1011
scs.indiana.edu

Louisiana State University

Office of Independent Study
E106 Pleasant Hall
Baton Rouge, LA 70803
(225) 388 3171 • (800) 234 5046
www.is.lsu.edu

Ohio University

Office of Independent Study
302 Tupper Hall
Athens, OH 45701
(740) 593 2910 • (800) 444 2910
www.cats.ohiou.edu/independent

Pennsylvania State University
Department of Distance Education
207 Mitchell Building
University Park, PA 16802
(814) 865 5403 • (800) 252 3592
www.cde.psu.edu/de

Stephens College
School of Graduate and Continuing Education
Campus Box 2083
Columbia, MO 65215
(573) 876 7125 • (800) 388 7579
www.stephens.edu

University of California at Berkeley
UC Extension Online
2000 Center St., Suite 400
Berkeley, CA 94704
(510) 642 4124
learn.berkeley.edu

University of Iowa
Guided Correspondence Study
116 International Center
Iowa City, IA 52242
(319) 353 2575 • (800) 272 6430
www.uiowa.edu/~ccp

University of Minnesota
Independent and Distance Learning
150 Wesbrook Hall
77 Pleasant St. SE
Minneapolis, MN 55455
(612) 624 4000 • (800) 234 6564
www.uc.umn.edu/idl

University of Missouri
Center for Distance and Independent Study
136 Clark Hall
Columbia, MO 65211-4200
(572) 882 6431 • (800) 609 3727
cdis.missouri.edu

University of Wisconsin
Independent Learning
505 South Rosa Rd., Suite 200
Madison, WI 53719-1257
(800) 442 6460
learn.wisconsin.edu/il

**U.S. Department of Agriculture
Graduate School**
Correspondence and Online Program
Room 1112, South Building
1400 Independence Avenue, SW
Washington, DC 20250-9911
(202) 314 3670
www.grad.usda.gov

Some Non-U.S. Schools with Correspondence Courses

Australia

Curtin University of Technology
GPO Box U 1987
Perth, Western Australia 6845
www.curtin.edu.au

Deakin University
221 Burwood Highway
Burwood, Victoria 3125
www.deakin.edu.au

Edith Cowan University
Pearson St., Churchlands, Western Australia 6018
www.cowan.edu.au

James Cook University
Townsville, Queensland 4811
www.jcu.edu.au

University of South Australia
Underdale Campus, External Studies
Holbrooks Road
Underdale, South Australia 5032
www.unisa.edu.au

Canada

Acadia University
Division of Continuing and Distance Education
Wolfville, Nova Scotia B0P 1X0
www.acadiau.ca

Athabasca University
1 University Drive
Athabasca, Alberta T95 3A3
www.athabascau.ca

McGill University
Centre for Continuing Education
688 Sherbrooke Street West
Montreal, Quebec H3A 3R1
www.mcgill.ca

University of Manitoba
Distance Education Program
188 Continuing Education Complex
Winnipeg, Manitoba R3T 2N2
www.umanitoba.ca/coned

University of New Brunswick
P.O. Box 4400
Fredericton, New Brunswick E3B 5A3
www.unb.ca/coned

University of Toronto
School of Continuing Studies
158 St. George St.
Toronto, Ontario M5S 2V8
www.continuallyuoft.utoronto.ca

University of Waterloo
Continuing Education
Waterloo, Ontario N2L 3G1
dce.uwaterloo.ca

Costa Rica

Universidad Estatal a Distancia
Apartado 474-2050 de Montes de Oca
San Jose, Costa Rica
www.uned.ac.cr

Kenya

University of Nairobi
Institute of Adult and Distance Education
P.O. Box 30197
Nairobi, Kenya

Pakistan

Allama Iqbal Open University
Sector H-8
Islamabad, Pakistan
www.aiou.edu.pk

South Africa

University of South Africa
P. O. Box 392
Unisa 0003, South Africa
www.unisa.ac.za

University of Cape Town
Rondebosch 7701, South Africa
www.uct.ac.za

United Kingdom

Open University
Walton Hall, Milton Keynes MK7 6AA
www.open.ac.uk

Zimbabwe

Zimbabwe Distance Education College
Moffat Street/Albion Road
P.O. Box 316
Harare, Zimbabwe

The advent of night mail delivery gave a
real boost to the growth of correspondence
study in Minnesota.

A Graduate School Fable

One sunny day a rabbit came out of her hole in the ground to enjoy the fine weather. The day was so nice that she became careless and a fox snuck up behind her and caught her.

"I am going to eat you for lunch!" said the fox.

"Wait!" replied the rabbit, "You should at least wait a few days."

"Oh yeah? Why should I wait?"

"Well, I am just finishing my thesis on *The Superiority of Rabbits over Foxes and Wolves*."

"Are you crazy? I should eat you right now! Everybody knows that a fox will always win over a rabbit."

"Not really, not according to my research. If you like, you can come into my hole and read it for yourself. If you are not convinced, you can go ahead and have me for lunch."

"You really are crazy!" But since the fox was curious and had nothing to lose, it went with the rabbit. The fox never came out.

A few days later the rabbit was again taking a break from writing and sure enough, a wolf came out of the bushes and was ready to set upon her.

"Wait!" yelled the rabbit, "you can't eat me right now."

"And why might that be, my furry appetizer?"

"I am almost finished writing my thesis on *The Superiority of Rabbits over Foxes and Wolves*."

The wolf laughed so hard that it almost lost its grip on the rabbit.

"Maybe I shouldn't eat you. You really are sick … in the head. You might have something contagious."

"Come and read it for yourself. You can eat me afterward if you disagree with my conclusions."

So the wolf went down into the rabbit's hole … and never came out.

The rabbit finished her thesis and was out celebrating in the local lettuce patch. Another rabbit came along and asked, "What's up? You seem very happy."

"Yup, I just finished my thesis."

"Congratulations. What's it about?"

"*The Superiority of Rabbits over Foxes and Wolves*."

"Are you sure? That doesn't sound right."

"Oh yes. Come and read it for yourself."

So together they went down into the rabbit's hole. As they entered, the friend saw the typical graduate student abode, albeit a rather messy one after writing a thesis. The computer with the controversial work was in one corner. To the right there was a pile of fox bones, to the left a pile of wolf bones. And in the middle was a very large, well-fed lion.

The moral of the story:

The title of your thesis doesn't matter.

The subject doesn't matter.

The research doesn't matter.

All that matters is who your advisor is.

—one of those wonderful things that is circulated on the Internet, but without credit to the author. Thank you, whoever you are. (Let us know!)

CHAPTER 14

Credit for Life-Experience Learning

The engineering major asks, "How does it work?"

The physics major asks, "Why does it work?"

The liberal arts major asks, "Would you like fries with that?"

Traditional (since 1996, anyway)

The philosophy behind credit for life-experience learning can be expressed very simply: Academic credit is given for what you know, without regard for how, when, or where the learning was acquired.

Consider a simple example: Quite a few colleges and universities offer credit for courses in typewriting. For instance, at Western Illinois University, Business Education 261 is a basic typing class. Anyone who takes and passes that class is given three units of credit.

An advocate of credit for life-experience learning would say: "If you know how to type, regardless of how and where you learned, even if you taught yourself at the age of nine, you should still get those same three units of credit, once you demonstrate that you have the same skill level as a person who passes Business Education 261."

Of course not all learning can be converted into college credit. But many people are surprised to discover how much of what they already know is, in fact, creditworthy. With thousands of colleges offering hundreds of thousands of courses, it is a rare subject indeed that someone hasn't determined to be worthy of some credit. There is no guarantee that a given school will honor a given learning experience, or even accept another school's assessment for transfer purposes. Yale might not accept typing credit. But then again, the course title often sounds much more academic than the learning experience itself, as in "Business Education" for typing, "Cross-Cultural Communication" for a trip to China, or "Fundamentals of Applied Kinesiology" for golf lessons.

Here are eight major types of life experience that may be worth college credit, especially in nontraditional degree-granting programs:

1. **Work.** Many of the skills acquired in paid employment are also skills that are taught in colleges and universities. These include, for instance, typing, filing, shorthand, accounting, inventory control, financial management, map reading, military strategy, welding, computer programming or operating, editing, planning, sales, real estate appraisals, and literally thousands of other things.

2. **Homemaking.** Home maintenance, household planning and budgeting, child rearing, child psychology, education, interpersonal communication, meal planning and nutrition, gourmet cooking, and much more.

3. **Volunteer work.** Community activities, political campaigns, church activities, service organizations, volunteer work in social service agencies or hospitals, and so forth.

4. **Noncredit learning in formal settings.** Company training courses, in-service teacher training, workshops, clinics, conferences and conventions, lectures, courses on radio or television, noncredit correspondence courses, etc.

5. **Travel.** Study tours (organized or informal), significant vacation and business trips, living for periods in

other countries or cultures, participating in activities related to other cultures or subcultures.

6. **Recreational activities and hobbies.** Musical skills, aviation training and skills, acting or other work in a community theater, sports, arts and crafts, fiction and nonfiction writing, public speaking, gardening, visiting museums, designing and making clothing, attending plays and concerts, and many other leisure-time activities.

7. **Reading, viewing, listening.** This may cover any field in which a person has done extensive or intensive reading and study, and for which college credit has not been granted. This category has, for instance, included viewing various series on public television.

8. **Discussions with experts.** A great deal of learning can come from talking to, listening to, and working with experts, whether in ancient history, carpentry, or theology. Significant, extensive, or intensive meetings with such people may also be worth credit.

The Most Common Error Most People Make

The most common error most people make when thinking about getting credit for life experience is confusing *time spent* with *learning*. Being a regular churchgoer for 30 years is not worth any college credit in and of itself. But the regular churchgoer who can document that he or she has prepared for and taught Sunday school classes, worked with youth groups, participated in leadership programs, organized fund-raising drives, studied Latin or Greek, taken tours to the Holy Land, or even engaged in lengthy philosophical discussions with a clergyman, is likely to get credit for those experiences. Selling insurance for 20 years is worth no credit—unless you describe and document the learning that took place in areas of marketing, banking, risk management, entrepreneurial studies, etc.

It is crucial that the experiences can be documented to a school's satisfaction. Two people could work side by side in the same laboratory for five years. One might do little more than follow instructions—running routine experiments, setting up and dismantling apparatus, and then heading home. The other, with the same job title, might do extensive reading in the background of the work being done, get into discussions with supervisors, make plans and recommendations for other ways of doing the work, propose or design new kinds of apparatus, or develop hypotheses on why the results were turning out the way they were.

It is not enough just to say what you did, or to submit a short resumé. The details and specifics must be documented. The two most common ways this is done are by preparing a life-experience portfolio (essentially a long, well-documented, annotated resumé) or by taking an equivalency examination to demonstrate knowledge gained.

Presenting Your Learning

Most schools that give credit for life-experience learning require that the student make a formal presentation, usually in the form of a life-experience portfolio. Each school has its own standards for the form and content of such a portfolio, and many, in fact, offer either guidelines or courses (some for credit, some not) to help the nontraditional student prepare a portfolio.

Several books on this subject have been published by the Council for Adult and Experiential Learning. For a list of current publications, contact them at CAEL, 55 East Monroe Street, Suite 1930, Chicago, IL 60603; (312) 499 2600; *www.cael.org*.

CAEL offers for sale a number of books designed to help people prepare life-experience portfolios. These and some from other publishers are described in the "Bibliography" section. Sadly, CAEL no longer offers sample portfolios for sale; that was an excellent service, now discontinued.

The following list should help to get you thinking about the possibilities, by presenting a sampling of some 24 other means by which people have documented life-experience learning, sometimes as part of a portfolio, sometimes not:

▶ official commendations

▶ audiotapes

▶ slides

▶ course outlines

▶ bills of sale

▶ records or photographs of exhibitions

▶ programs of recitals and performances

▶ videotapes

▶ awards and honors

▶ mementos

▶ copies of speeches made

▶ licenses (pilot, real estate, etc.)

▶ certificates

▶ testimonials and endorsements

▶ interviews with others

▶ newspaper articles

▶ official job descriptions

▶ copies of exams taken

▶ military records

▶ samples of arts or crafts made

▶ samples of writing

▶ designs and blueprints

▶ works of art

▶ films and photographs

How Life-Experience Learning Is Turned into Academic Credit

It isn't easy. In a perfect world, there would be universally accepted standards, and it would be as easy to measure the credit value in a seminar on refrigeration engineering as it is to measure the temperature inside a refrigerator. Some schools and national organizations *are* striving to create extensive "menus" of nontraditional experiences, to ensure that anyone doing the same thing would get the same credit.

There continues to be progress in this direction. Many schools have come to agree, for instance, on aviation experience: a private pilot's license is worth four semester units, an instrument rating is worth six additional units, and so forth.

The American Council on Education, a private organization, regularly publishes a massive multivolume set of books, in two series: *The National Guide to Educational Credit for Training Programs* and *Guide to the Evaluation of Educational Experiences in the Armed Forces* (see Bibliography for details), which many schools use to assign credit directly; others use them as guidelines in doing their own evaluations. A few examples will demonstrate the sort of thing that is done:

▶ A nine-day Red Cross training course called The Art of Helping is evaluated as worth two semester hours of social work.

▶ The John Hancock Mutual Life Insurance Company's internal course in technical skills for managers is worth three semester hours of business administration.

▶ Portland Cement Company's five-day training program in kiln optimization, whatever that may be, is worth one semester hour.

▶ The Professional Insurance Agents' three-week course in basic insurance is worth six semester units: three in principles of insurance and three in property & liability contract analysis.

▶ The U.S. Army's 27-week course in ground surveillance radar repair is worth 15 semester hours: ten in electronics and five more in electrical laboratory.

▶ The Army's legal-clerk training course can be worth 24 semester hours, including three in English, three in business law, three in management, etc.

There are hundreds of additional business and military courses that have been evaluated already, and thousands more that will be worth credit for those who have taken them, whether or not they appear in these ACE volumes.

The Controversy Over Graduate Credit for Life-Experience Learning

As Norman Somers writes, "Powerful forces in graduate education have declared the granting of credit for pre-matriculation experiences anathema. Many professors and graduate deans have spoken out against the assessment of learning experiences which have occurred prior to a student's formal enrollment."

The policy of the Council of Graduate Schools is that "no graduate credit should be granted for experiential learning that occurs prior to the student's matriculation." It should, they insist, be given "only when a graduate faculty and dean of an accredited institution have had the opportunity to plan the experience, to establish its goals, and to monitor the time, effort, and the learning that has taken place."

In other words, if I enroll in a school and then study and master advanced statistical techniques, they should give me, say, nine units of credit. But if, say, I learned those techniques during 20 years on the job as chief statistician for the Bureau of the Census, no credit should be given.

Fortunately, many schools and organizations, including the influential American Council on Education, disagree with this policy. Their guidelines, described earlier, regularly include recommendations for graduate credit, based on "independent study, original research, critical analysis, and the scholarly and professional application of the specialized knowledge or discipline."

Some Inspiration

There are always some people who say, "Oh, I haven't ever done anything worthy of college credit." We have yet to meet anyone with an IQ higher than room temperature who has not done at least some creditworthy things. Often it's just a matter of presenting them properly, in a portfolio. Here are two sources of inspiration.

First, a list of 100 things that *could* be worth credit for life-experience learning. And second, a detailed description by an expert in portfolio preparation, detailing how he earned more than 80 percent of the credit for his bachelor's degree by creative portfolio management.

100 Things

This list could easily be 10 or 100 times as long. Please note the "could." Some reviewers in the past have made fun of this list, suggesting that we were saying you can earn a degree for buying Persian rugs. Not so. We *do* suggest, however, that a person who made a high-level study of Persian art and culture, preparatory to buying carpets, and who could document the reading, consultations, time spent, sources, etc., could probably earn some portfolio credit for this out-of-classroom endeavor. Here, then, is the list:

Playing tennis
Preparing for natural childbirth
Leading a church group
Taking a bodybuilding class
Speaking French
Selling real estate
Studying gourmet cooking
Reading *War and Peace*
Building model airplanes
Traveling through Belgium
Learning shorthand
Starting a small business
Navigating a small boat
Writing a book
Buying a Persian carpet
Watching public television
Decorating a home or office
Attending a convention
Being a summer-camp counselor
Studying Spanish
Bicycling across Greece
Interviewing senior citizens
Living in another culture
Writing advertisements
Throwing a pot
Repairing a car
Performing magic
Attending art films
Welding and soldering
Designing and weaving a rug
Negotiating a contract
Editing a manuscript
Planning a trip
Steering a ship
Appraising an antique
Writing a speech
Studying first aid or CPR
Organizing a Canadian union
Researching international laws
Listening to Shakespeare's plays on tape
Designing a playground
Planning a garden
Devising a marketing strategy
Reading the newspaper
Designing a home
Attending a seminar
Playing the piano
Studying a new religion
Reading about the Civil War
Taking ballet lessons
Helping a dyslexic child
Riding a horse

Pressing flowers
Keeping tropical fish
Writing press releases
Writing for the local newspaper
Running the PTA
Acting in little theater
Flying an airplane
Designing a quilt
Taking photographs
Building a table
Developing an inventory system
Programming a home computer
Helping in a political campaign
Playing a musical instrument
Painting a picture
Playing political board games
Serving on a jury
Volunteering at the hospital
Visiting a museum
Attending a "great books" group
Designing and sewing clothes
Playing golf
Having intensive talks with a doctor
Teaching the banjo
Reading the Bible
Leading a platoon
Learning Braille
Operating a printing press
Eating in an exotic restaurant
Running a store
Planning a balanced diet
Reading *All and Everything*
Learning sign language
Teaching Sunday school
Training an apprentice
Being an apprentice
Weaving a rug
Learning yoga
Laying bricks
Making a speech
Being Dungeonmaster
Negotiating a merger
Developing film
Learning calligraphy
Applying statistics to gambling
Doing circle dancing
Taking care of sick animals
Reading this book

The Levicoff Portfolio

That sounds like a Robert Ludlum novel, but this is, rather, an essay by Steve Levicoff, Ph.D. (Union Institute), who earned his bachelor's, master's, and Ph.D. from accredited nontraditional schools. In his bachelor's program, he made extensive use of the portfolio assessment approach. When we read this essay of his, explaining his approach to the process, we felt it would be of interest to our readers, and Dr. Levicoff kindly agreed to let us reproduce it here:

1. Choose a school that is flexible on portfolios (e.g., Edison is more flexible than Excelsior).

2. Go to a library that has a good selection of college catalogs—those from traditional colleges in general.

3. Leaf through the catalogs and make a photocopy of every course description (the course name plus the three- or four-line description of its content) that you feel you could challenge based on the description of the course. Make a note of the college, the year of the catalog, the department offering the course, and the catalog page number.

4. Next, go to your basement, closets, and any other place you store trivial papers, photographs, or other mementos that you thought would never do you any good and match whatever you find to the course description. Do the same for any significant papers in your filing cabinet(s).

5. Gather up any current documentation that you feel could be useful to challenging a course, especially work-related items if you are in a position that involves a lot of paperwork: memos, projects, etc. Match them up with the course descriptions.

6. Make a list of all relevant books you have read on the subjects you want to challenge. List any courses, professional workshops you have attended, and in-service training you have received. Start with your own bookshelf or any certificates you have in your file. Then relate them to the subjects you want to challenge.

7. Now just write up your rationale for earning credit for the courses you've chosen based on the "validating evidence" you can submit.

8. Seek out people with whom you work or have ever worked and ask them to write letters confirming your experience. Remember, these are not letters of recommendation, they are letters of validation. If your boss writes a letter saying "Bill Morrow is a nice guy," it won't get you anywhere. However, if he or she writes, "Bill Morrow coordinates administration, personnel, and purchasing for our firm and exhibits sound fiscal, legal, and negotiating skills," you've got enough to validate your submissions in three different courses: administrative management, personnel, and purchasing & negotiation. It also helps if you have written your company's administrative manual, employee handbook, or purchasing policies and procedures.

9. Make sure your course selection includes an adequate number of upper-level credits. At Edison, for instance, these are defined as any credits in a specific subject over six, which provides a tremendous amount of flexibility. For example, if you challenge three-credit courses in Trumpet I, French Horn I, and Piano I, one of them can be treated as upper level, even though they may all have lower-level course numbers in the college catalog from which you cut the descriptions. However, try to concentrate on four-year college catalogs, as some schools have a cap on the number of courses you can challenge from junior or community colleges.

10. Finally, learn how to "work the system." If, for example, you want to earn credit in "word processing," don't look for a four-year college that offers a course in word processing; look for a junior or community college that offers two or three courses in word processing and challenge them based on different levels (such as basic, advanced, and supervisory). Also, remember that when it comes to computer courses, a submission must have a significant math component in order to qualify for liberal arts; if it is practical in orientation, it does not qualify for liberal arts but can still fit in as a free elective. (For example, BASIC, COBOL, or Intro. to Computer Science could qualify as liberal arts courses under the math/natural science header; RPG, word processing, and database management do not have significant math components, so they would fit into the free elective area.) Last but not least, be careful not to "double-dip" with similar course titles; in other words, don't try to challenge "19th Century American History" and "United States History 1801–1900." They're the same course.

Remember that the more culturally literate you already are, the more courses you will be able to challenge. If you have spent years watching PBS and reading nonfiction, you'll have a much easier time than someone who has spent years reading comic books and watching soap operas. Even then, chances are that, with a little research, you'll still find courses to meet your needs. (Even Berkeley offers a course titled "The Films of Keanu Reeves.") I once challenged a two-credit course in folk guitar (for the curious, I found that one in the catalog of Kent State U.), earning credit in about five minutes by playing two songs for the evaluator.

Also remember that, if you are culturally literate and can challenge a degree largely by portfolio, you won't learn a lot at the bachelor's level (although you will certainly learn how to work the system). So start making plans to find a graduate program where you can actually learn something substantive and have some more fun.

Incidentally, if you don't have enough hard or written evidence for a portfolio challenge, don't let that stop you. Remember that you have the option of earning credit based on evidence alone, testing alone, or a combination of evidence and testing. If you opt for testing, try to do it in an oral exam format. Written exams tend to represent only the evaluator's perspective and do not allow the flexibility of the oral format. It's like dancing with your evaluator, with the difference being which party will lead and which will follow. Also remember that hard evidence can take many forms. It doesn't have to be a written work, but can be drawings or other art, musical compositions, playbills from acting experience, original recipes, sermons preached, talks given, ad infinitum. And the same evidence can be used for multiple submissions without being construed as "double dipping." For example, if you have written an employee handbook, it can be used as evidence in courses ranging from personnel administration to labor law to business writing.

Many schools, including Edison and Excelsior, have portfolio development manuals available; you should obtain copies of both so you have an idea of the language (or "jargon") they use.

Notarized photograph submitted for credit
in Performance Art 101.

For the curious, here's how I did my own B.A. in humanities from Thomas Edison, earning 98 credits by portfolio, testing out of an additional 16 credits through TECEP and DANTES exams, and carrying in only six credits by previous coursework. Incidentally, even though I entered with only six credits, the whole ball of wax took me only a year and a half. With administrative and graduation paperwork included, I was in and out in one year and ten months, and have never been turned down by any graduate program to which I've applied.

The broad area headers below represent Thomas Edison's "distribution requirement" for a bachelor's degree in a liberal arts area.

Written Expression (6)

Advanced Writing, Academic Forms, Portfolio, 3
Business English, Portfolio, 3

Humanities (12)

Solfeggio & Dictation I, Course, 2
Keyboard Harmony I, Course, 1
Performance Class, Course, 1
Chorus, Course, 2
Radio Production I, Portfolio, 3
Mass Media, Portfolio, 3

Social Sciences (13)

Alcohol Abuse—Fund. Facts, TECEP exam, 3
Substance Abuse—Fund. Facts, TECEP, 4
Society & Sexual Variations, Portfolio, 3
Arms Control & Disarmament, Portfolio, 3

Math/Natural Sciences (12)

BASIC, TECEP, 3
Intro. to Computers & Program Design, Portfolio, 3
Human Reproductive Biology & Behavior, Portfolio, 3
Astronomy, DANTES, 3

Liberal Arts Electives (18)

A Comprehensive Analysis of Abortion, Portfolio, 3
Advanced Radio Production, Portfolio, 3
Public Speaking I, Portfolio, 3
Broadcast Journalism I, Portfolio, 3
Rudiments of Music, Portfolio, 3
Folk Music in the United States, Portfolio, 3

Concentration Area (33)

Public Speaking II, Portfolio, 3
Intro. to News Reporting, TECEP, 3
Publicity Methods in Organizations, Portfolio, 3
Recording Studio, Portfolio, 2
Harmony I, Portfolio, 3
Applied Piano, Portfolio, 3
Elementary Voice, Portfolio, 3
Folk Guitar Class, Portfolio, 2
Theology of the Cults, Portfolio, 3
Christian Social Ethics, Portfolio, 3
Toward a Theology of Peace, Portfolio, 3
Roman Catholic Theology, Portfolio, 2

Free Electives (26)

Administrative Management & Supervision, Portfolio, 3
Word Processing I, Portfolio, 3
Word Processing II, Portfolio, 3
Word Processing III, Portfolio, 3
Intro. to Publishing, Portfolio, 3
Piano Service Playing, Portfolio, 1
Cardiopulmonary Resuscitation, Portfolio, 1
Technical Writing, Portfolio, 3
Purchasing & Contracting, Portfolio, 3
Personnel Management, Portfolio, 3

Summary by subject area

Written expression, 9
Humanities, 64
Communications, 29
Music, 24
Theology, 11
Social Sciences, 16
Math/science, 13
Business, 18

Summary by source of credit

Courses transferred, 6
Testing (TECEP/DANTES), 16
Portfolio, 98

Summary by evaluation method

Accepted on evidence, 78
Testing, 6
Evidence plus testing, 6

CHAPTER 15

Credit by Learning Contract

An oral agreement isn't worth the paper it's written on.

Samuel Goldwyn

A mainstay of many nontraditional degree programs is the learning contract, also known as a study plan, study contract, degree plan, etc. It is essentially a formal agreement between the student and the school, setting forth a plan of study the student intends to undertake, goals he or she wishes to reach, and the action to be taken by the school once the goals are reached—normally the granting either of a certain amount of credit or of a degree.

A well-written learning contract is good for both student and school, since it reduces greatly the chances of misunderstandings or problems after the student has done a great deal of work, and the inevitable distress that accompanies such an event.

We've heard from people who have been distressed to discover that some project on which they had been working for many months was really not what their faculty advisor or school had in mind, and so they would be getting little or no credit for it.

Indeed, one of the authors had a similar sort of experience. After John had worked for nearly two years on his doctorate at Michigan State University, one key member of his faculty guidance committee suddenly died, and a second transferred to another school. No one else on the faculty seemed interested in working with him, and without a binding agreement of any sort, there was no way he could make things happen. He simply dropped out. (Three years later, a new department head invited him back to finish the degree, and he did so. But a lot of anguish could have been avoided if he had had a contract with the school.)

A learning contract can be legally binding for both the student and the school. If the student does the work called for, then the school must award the predetermined number of credits. In case of disputes arising from such a contract, there are usually clauses calling for mediation, and, if necessary, binding arbitration by an impartial third party.

Looking at examples of a simple, and then a somewhat more complex, learning contract should make clear how this concept works.

A Simple Learning Contract

The Background

In the course of discussing the work to be done for a bachelor's degree, the student and her faculty advisor agree that it would be desirable for the student to learn to read in German. Rather than take formal courses, the student says that she prefers to study the language on her own, with the help of an uncle who speaks the language. If the student had taken four semesters of German at a traditional school, she would have earned 20 semester hours of credit. So the learning contract might consist of these eight simple clauses:

The Contract

1. Student intends to learn to read German at the level of a typical student who has completed four semesters of college-level German.

2. Student will demonstrate this knowledge by translating a 1000-word passage from one of the novels of Erich Maria Remarque.

3. The book and passage will be selected and the translation evaluated by a member of the German faculty of the college.

4. The student will have three hours to complete the translation, with the assistance of a standard German-English dictionary.

5. If the student achieves a score of 85% or higher in the evaluation, then the college will immediately award 20 semester hours of credit in German.

6. If the student scores below 85%, she may try again at 60-day intervals.

7. The fee for the first evaluation will be $200, and, if necessary, $100 for each additional evaluation.

8. If any dispute shall arise over the interpretation of this contract, an attempt will be made to resolve the dispute by mediation. If mediation fails, the dispute will be settled by binding arbitration. An arbitrator shall be chosen jointly by the student and the school. If they cannot agree in choosing an arbitrator, then each party will choose one. If the two arbitrators cannot agree, they shall jointly appoint a third, and the majority decision of this panel of three shall be final and binding. The costs of arbitration shall be shared equally by the two parties.

This contract has the four basic elements common to any learning contract:

1. The student's objectives or goals.

2. The methods by which these goals are to be reached.

3. The method of evaluation of the performance.

4. What to do in case of problems or disagreement.

The more precisely each of these items can be defined, the less likelihood of problems later. For instance, instead of simply saying, "The student will become proficient in German," the foregoing agreement defines clearly what "proficient" means.

A More Complex Learning Contract

What follows is an abridgement of a longer learning contract, freely adapted from some of the case histories provided in a catalog from the late, lamented Beacon College.

Goals

At the end of my master's program, I plan to have the skills, experience, and theoretical knowledge to work with an organization in the role of director or consultant, to help the organization set and reach its goals, and to work with individuals or small groups as a counselor, providing a supportive or therapeutic environment in which to grow and learn.

I want to acquire a good understanding of and grounding in group dynamics, how children learn, and why people come together to grow, learn, and work.

Hazelclaw University issues every online student a portable email device suitable for use in crowded elevators.

I am especially interested in alternative organizations. I want to have the skills to help organizations analyze their financial needs, and to locate and best utilize appropriate funding.

Methods

Theory and Skill Development (40% of work)

I shall take the following three courses at Vista Community College [courses listed and described] = 20% of program.

After reading the following four books [list of books], and others that may be suggested by my faculty advisor, I shall prepare statements of my personal philosophy of education and growth, as a demonstration of my understanding of the needs of a self-directed, responsible, caring human = 10% of program.

I shall attend a six-lesson workshop on power dynamics and assertiveness, given by [details of the workshop] = 10% of program.

Leadership and Management Practicum (30% of work)

I shall work with the Cooperative Nursery School to attempt to put into practice the things I have learned in the first phase of my studies, in the following way: [much detail here]. Documentation shall be through a journal of my work, a log of all meetings, a self-assessment of my performance, and commentary supplied by an outside evaluator = 15% of program.

I shall donate eight hours a week for 20 weeks to the Women's Crisis Center, again endeavoring to put into practice the ideas which I have learned. [much detail here on expectations and kinds of anticipated activities] = 15% of program.

Organizational Development, Analysis, and Design (30% of work)

I shall study one of the above two groups (nursery school or crisis center) in great detail, and prepare an analysis and projection for the future of this organization, including recommendations for funding, management, and development = 20% of program.

Documentation will be in the form of a 40- to 50-page paper detailing my findings and recommendations and relating them to my philosophy of growth and organization development. This paper will be read and evaluated by [name of persons or committee] = 10% of program.

Outcome

Upon completion of all of the above, the college will award the degree of Master of Arts in Organization Development. [Arbitration clause comparable to Simple Contract]

• • • • •

Learning contracts are truly negotiable. There is no right or wrong, no black or white. Someone who is good at negotiating might well get more credit for the same amount of work, or the same degree for a lesser amount of work, than a less skillful negotiator.

Some schools will enter into a learning contract that covers the entire degree program, as in the second example. Others prefer to have separate contracts, each one covering a small portion of the program: one for the language requirement, one for science, one for humanities, one for the thesis, and so forth.

It is uncommon, but not unheard of, to seek legal advice when preparing or evaluating a learning contract, especially for a long or complex one covering an entire master's or doctoral program. A lawyer will likely say, "It is better to invest a small amount of money in my time now, rather than get into an expensive and protracted battle later, because of an unclear agreement." Dozens of colleges and universities are sued every year by students who claim that credits or degrees were wrongfully withheld from them. Many of these suits could have been avoided by the use of well-drawn learning contracts.

CHAPTER 16

Credential and Transcript Evaluation Services

'Tis with our judgements as our watches, none go just alike, yet each believes his own.

Alexander Pope

There are many thousands of universities, colleges, technical schools, institutes, and vocational schools all over the world offering courses that are at least the equivalent of work at American universities. In principle, most universities are willing to give credit for work done at schools in other countries.

But can you imagine the task of an admissions officer faced with the student who presents an Advanced Diploma from the Wysza Szkola Inzynierska in Poland, or the degree of Gakushi from the Matsuyama Shoka Daigaku in Japan? Are these equivalent to a high school diploma, a doctorate, or something in between?

Until 1974, the U.S. Office of Education helped by evaluating educational credentials earned outside the United States and translating them into approximately comparable levels of U.S. achievement. This service is no longer available. There have arisen, to fill this gap, quite a few private, independent credential and transcript evaluation services. Some deal exclusively with credentials and transcripts earned outside the United States and/or Canada, while others also consider experiential learning wherever it took place (such as military courses, aviation credentials, company training programs, and the like).

It is important to note that these organizations are neither endorsed, licensed, nor recommended by the U.S. government, nor is there any regulation of them. The various organizations would appear to have very different ways of going about their work, often yielding quite different results. We know this, because we conducted an informal but quite revealing survey, as follows.

We have a friend who has a quite unusual education background: initially educated on one continent, further schooled on a second continent, and now living on a third, accumulating along this long path a variety of earned academic degrees and designations.

We invited this person to submit applications to ten credential evaluation services. The results varied wildly, both in terms of the quality and level of their service (fees, for instance, ranged from $50 to over $600) and in the nature of their evaluations. For instance, the external master's degree of a large old Royal Chartered British university was evaluated as the exact equivalent of a U.S. regionally accredited MBA by some of the agencies, the equivalent of an M.A. in business by several, and as not even at the level of an American bachelor's degree by another.

The message from this research, and from a considerable amount of communication from readers, is that it may well pay to shop around, especially if the evaluation from one agency doesn't meet your expectations.

We give this advice reluctantly, in part because it is annoying and expensive to have to do this sort of thing, and in part because of our concern that people with questionable credentials might still find validation. For instance, one traditional, regionally accredited university shared with us an application from a student whose bachelor's degree came from a school we regard as, for all intents and purposes, a diploma mill. But when the traditional school challenged his degree, he shopped around and found one of these services (but only one) who evaluated his miserable degree as equivalent to an accredited American school. On that basis, the university provisionally admitted him, but he proved incapable of doing even the most basic of assignments.

Some of these organizations are used mostly by the schools themselves, to evaluate applicants from abroad or with foreign credentials, but individuals may deal with them directly, at relatively low cost. Many schools accept the recommendations of these services, but others will not. Some schools do their own foreign evaluations, while others have a short list of those credential evaluators they will accept.

It may be wise, therefore, to determine whether a school or schools in which you have interest will accept the recommendations of such services before you invest in them. We have also noted that schools which appear to require the evaluation from a certain agency or group of agencies are still, sometimes, willing to accept the evaluation from an agency not on their list.

Depending on the complexity of the evaluation, the cost runs from $50 to $200 or more. One agency, which we have deleted from our list, provided our experimental subject with a one-sentence response to his initial paid $50 application, and said that the full report would cost $800. Some of the services are willing to deal with non-school-based experiential learning as well. The services operate quickly. Less than two weeks for an evaluation is not unusual.

Typical evaluation reports give the exact U.S. equivalents of non-U.S. work, both in terms of semester units earned, and of any degrees or certificates earned. For instance, we would expect all of them to report that the Japanese degree of Gakushi is almost exactly equivalent to the American bachelor's degree.

Given the significant differences in the opinions of these services, if one report seems inappropriate or incorrect, it might be wise to seek a second (and even third) opinion.

Here is a list of some of the organizations performing these services, in alphabetical order, first in the U.S., then Canada.

Those with a "†" are approved by the state of California's Commission on Teacher Credentialing (*www.ctc.ca.gov*).

Those with a "#" are members of the industry's trade association, the National Association of Credential Evaluation Services: (414) 289 3412; email: *margit@ece.org*; Web site: *voled.doded.mil/dantes/refpubs/ftr.htm*.

United States

AACRAO (American Association of Collegiate Registrars and Admissions Officers)
Foreign Education Evaluation Service
One Dupont Circle, NW, Suite 520
Washington, DC 20036-1135
Phone: (202) 293 9161
Fax: (202) 872 8857
Email: info@aacrao.org
Web site: www.aacrao.org
Their service is offered only to schools, but they sell a wide variety of publications for people interested in doing evaluations.

Academic Credentials Evaluation Institute†
P.O. Box 6908
Beverly Hills, CA 90212
Phone: (310) 275 3530 • (800) 234 1597
Fax: (310) 275 3528
Email: acei@acei1.com
Web site: www.acei1.com

Academic and Professional International Evaluations, Inc.†
P.O. Box 5787
Los Alamitos, CA 90721
Phone: (562) 594 6498
Email: apie@email.msn.com
Web site: www.apie.org

American Education Research Corporation†
P.O. Box 996
West Covina, CA 91793-0996
Phone: (626) 339 4404
Fax: (626) 339 9081
Email: aerc@cyberg8t.com
Web site: www.aerc-eval.com

Center for Applied Research, Evaluation & Education
P.O. Box 20348
Long Beach, CA 90801-3348
Phone: (562) 430 1105
Fax: (562) 430 8215
Email: evalcaree@earthlink.net

Educational Credential Evaluators, Inc.†#
P.O. Box 92970
Milwaukee, WI 53217
Phone: (414) 289 3400
Fax: (414) 289 3411
Email: eval@ece.org
Web site: www.ece.org

Education Evaluators International, Inc.
P.O. Box 5397
Los Alamitos, CA 90720
Phone: (562) 431 2187
Fax: (562) 493 5021
Email: garyeei@ix.netcom.com

Educational Records Evaluation Service†#
777 Campus Commons Road, #200
Sacramento, CA 95825
Phone: (916) 565 7475
Fax: (916) 565 7476
Email: edu@eres.com
Web site: www.eres.com

Evaluation Service, Inc.#
P.O. Box 85
Hopewell Junction, NY 12533
Phone: (845) 223 6455
Fax: (845) 223 6454
Email: esi@capital.net
Web site: www.evaluationservice.net

Globe Language Services
319 Broadway
New York, NY 10007
Phone: (212) 227 1994
Fax: (212) 693 1489

Foundation for International Services, Inc.#
19015 North Creek Parkway, #103
Bothell, WA 98011
Phone: (425) 487 2245
Fax: (425) 487 1989
Email: info@fis-web.com
Web site: www.fis-web.com

Foreign Academic Credential Service, Inc.#
P.O. Box 400
Glen Carbon, IL 62034
Phone: (618) 288 1661
Fax: (618) 288 1691
Email: facs@aol.com
Web site: www.facsusa.com

Foreign Educational Document Service#
P.O. Box 4091
Stockton, CA 95204
Phone: (209) 948 6589

Global Credential Evaluators, Inc.
P.O. Box 9203
College Station, TX 77842
Phone: (979) 690 8912
Fax: (979) 690 6342
Email: jringer@mail.myriad.net
Web site: www.gcevaluators.com

Global Education Group
407 Lincoln Rd., Suite 2H
Miami Beach, FL 33139
Phone: (305) 534 8745
Fax: (305) 534 3487
Email: global@globaledu.com
Web site: www.globaledu.com

Institute for International Credentials Evaluations†
5150 North Maple Avenue, M/S 56
Joyal Administration, Room 211
California State University, Fresno
Fresno, CA 93740-8026
Phone: (559) 278 7622
Fax: (559) 278 7879
Email: carolm@zimmer.csufresno.edu

International Consultants of Delaware, Inc.#
109 Barksdale Professional Center
Newark, DE 19711
Phone: (302) 737 8715
Fax: (302) 737 8756
Email: icd@icdel.com
Web site: www.icdel.com

International Credentialing Associates, Inc.
7245 Bryan Dairy Rd.
Largo, FL 33777
Phone: (727) 549 8555
Fax: (727) 549 8554
Email: info@icaworld.com
Web site: www.icaworld.com

International Education Research Foundation†#
P.O. Box 3665
Culver City, CA 90231-3655
Phone: (310) 258 9451
Fax: (310) 397 7686
Email: info@ierf.org
Web site: www.ierf.org

Joseph Silny & Associates, Inc.#
P.O. Box 248233
Coral Gables, FL 33124
Phone: (305) 666 0233
Fax: (305) 666 4133
Email: info@jsilny.com
Web site: www.jsilny.com

SpanTran Educational Services, Inc.#
7211 Regency Square Blvd., #205
Houston, TX 77036
Phone: (713) 266 8805
Fax: (713) 789 6022
Email: info@ spantran-edu.com
Web site: www.spantran-edu.com

World Education Services†#
P.O. Box 745
Old Chelsea Station
New York, NY 10013
Phone: (212) 966 6311 • (800) 937 3895
Fax: (212) 966 6395
Email: info@wes.org
Web site: www.wes.org

Canada

International Credential Evaluation Service
4355 Mathissi Place
Burnaby, BC V5G 4S8, Canada
Phone: +1 (604) 431 3402
Fax: +1 (604) 431 3382
Email: icesinfo@ola.bc.ca
Web site: www.ola.bc.ca/ices

International Qualifications Assessment Service
Department of Learning, Government of Alberta
4th Floor, Sterling Place, 9940 - 106 St.
Edmonton, Alberta T5K 2N2, Canada
Phone: +1 (780) 427 2655
Fax: +1 (780) 422 9734
Email: iqas@aecd.gov.ab.ca
Web site: www.aecd.gov.ab.ca/iqas

University of Toronto
Comparative Education Service
315 Bloor St. West
Toronto, ON M5S 1A3, Canada
Phone: +1 (416) 978 2185

For those interested in educational equivalents for one particular country, there is the World Education Series of books or monographs published by AACRAO, the American Association of Collegiate Registrars and Admissions Officers (One Dupont Circle, NW, Suite 520, Washington, DC 20036; *www.aacrao.org*). Each publication in this series describes the higher education system in a given country, and offers advice and recommendations on how to deal with their credits.

The problem with these AACRAO reports is that they are issued with such low frequency that many of them are way out of date and of minimal usefulness.

In the early 1990s, the Australians (whose higher education system is similar to that of the U.S. and Canada) attempted to deal with this problem by commissioning the researching and writing of comparative monographs on the educational equivalency of 87 countries, all at the same time. The monographs are published by the Australian Government Publishing Service, GPO Box 84, Canberra ACT 2601, Australia. (John did the initial research and writing for 15 of these monographs.)

Alumni of Burbridge University traditionally carry their MBA diplomas with them at all times.

CHAPTER 17

The Credit Bank Service

It is amazing what you can accomplish if you do not care who gets the credit.

Harry S. Truman

Alot of people have very complicated educational histories. They may have taken classes at several different universities and colleges, taken some evening or summer-school classes, perhaps some company-sponsored seminars, some military training classes, and possibly had a whole raft of other informal learning experiences. They may have credits or degrees from schools that have gone out of business, or whose records were destroyed by war or fire. When it comes time to present a cohesive educational past, it may mean assembling dozens of transcripts, certificates, diplomas, job descriptions, and the like, often into a rather large and unwieldy package.

There is, happily, an ideal solution to this problem: the Excelsior College Credit Bank, operated by the enlightened Excelsior College in New York, and available to people anywhere in the world.

Excelsior College Credit Bank

Excelsior College
7 Columbia Circle
Albany, NY 12203
Phone: (518) 464 8500
Web site: www.excelsiorcollege.edu

(*Please note: Excelsior College was formerly known as Regents College, and the credit bank service was known as the Regents College Credit Bank. It was, in fact, just before this book went to press that the name change from Regents to Excelsior had been announced. Officials at Regents/Excelsior told us the credit bank would change its name accordingly, although it hadn't yet happened before we went to the printer. In anticipation of when you'll be reading this, we're going ahead and calling it the Excelsior College Credit Bank, but if the new name doesn't seem to be working for you in whatever context you're using it, swapping "Regents" for "Excelsior" will probably solve the problem.*)

The Credit Bank is an evaluation and transcript service for people who wish to consolidate their academic records, perhaps adding credit for nonacademic career and learning experiences (primarily through equivalency examinations). The Credit Bank issues a single widely accepted transcript on which all credit is listed in a simple, straightforward, and comprehensible form.

The Credit Bank works like a money bank, except that you deposit academic credits, as they are earned, whether through local courses, correspondence courses, equivalency exams, or other methods. There are seven basic categories of learning experience that can qualify to be "deposited" in a Credit Bank account, and of course various elements of these seven can be combined as well:

1. College courses taken either in residence or by distance learning from regionally accredited schools in the U.S., or their equivalent in other countries

2. Scores earned on a wide range of equivalency tests, both civilian and military

3. Military service schools and military occupational specialties that have been evaluated for credit by the American Council on Education

4. Workplace-based learning experiences, such as company courses, seminars, or in-house training from many large and smaller corporations, evaluated by the American Council on Education or the New York National Program on Noncollegiate Sponsored Instruction

5. Pilot training licenses and certificates issued by the Federal Aviation Administration

6. Approved nursing performance examinations

7. Special assessment of knowledge gained from experience or independent study

The first six categories have predetermined amounts of credit. The CLEP basic science exam will always be worth 6 semester units. Fluency in Spanish will always be worth 24 semester units. Xerox Corporation's course in repairing the 9400 copier will always be worth 2 semester units. The army course in becoming a bandleader will always be worth 12 semester units. And so forth, for thousands of already evaluated nonschool learning experiences.

While the Credit Bank offers an excellent option for many clients, there are others who have two kinds of learning experiences which may suggest the Credit Bank is not for them.

One is the matter of having extensive learning in a field for which there does not exist a standard test. One may be the world's leading expert in Persian military history, or be fluent in five Asian languages, but since there are no readily available tests of these areas, credit may not be given. The Credit Bank used to offer a special assessment service, in which people with such specialized knowledge could come to New York for an oral examination by two or more experts in the field, at the end of which credit was awarded, but this option is not listed in current literature.

The other consists of credits and degrees earned at schools accredited by certain recognized accrediting agencies other than regional agencies, such as the Distance Education and Training Council. If, for instance, a student earns a bachelor's degree at American Military University or the California College for Health Sciences, those degrees

are not acceptable to Excelsior. Such degrees and credits are accepted by many other regionally accredited schools, so this nonacceptance by the Excelsior Credit Bank seems unusual and unfortunate to us.

One more caution. The Credit Bank literature states that foreign academic credentials must be evaluated by a company called Educational Credential Evaluators (ECE) in Wisconsin, except for Israeli credentials, which are to be evaluated by a company called Josef Silny and Associates. As is made clear in chapter 16, which covers credential and transcript evaluation services, the various agencies that do this often differ widely in evaluating the same credentials. When one of these anomalies was pointed out to Excelsior, they agreed to accept the evaluation of an agency other than the two they list.

There is a $200 fee to set up a Credit Bank account. There is a $25 fee each time a new "deposit" is made. (These rates are dramatically lower than those charged a few years ago.)

Work that is, for whatever reason, deemed not credit-worthy may still be listed on the transcript as "noncredit work." Further, the Credit Bank will only list those traditional courses from other schools that the depositor wishes included. Thus any previous academic failures, low grades, or other embarrassments may be omitted from the Credit Bank report.

Students who enroll in Excelsior College automatically get Credit Bank service, and do not need to enroll separately.

"Mother, I wish to begin amassing credits toward my B.S. Will you bankroll my course in preadolescent psychology for starters?"

CHAPTER 18

Accredited Schools
With Degrees Entirely
by Distance Learning

Education is hanging around until you've caught on.

Robert Frost

Any school can claim that it is accredited; the use of that word is (unfortunately) not regulated in any way. In the United States, there are many situations in which an accredited degree is required: admission to another school, transfer of credits, job applications, applying for permission to take various exams (law, psychology, accounting, engineering, etc.), and so on. In almost every case, these situations require not just "accreditation" but accreditation that is generally accepted.

In the world of accounting, there is the concept of GAAP: Generally Accepted Accounting Principles. Not absolutely, not always, not universally; but generally. The same concept makes just as much sense in the world of accreditation—GAAP: Generally Accepted Accreditation Principles.

We first heard the term used, informally, at the national convention of registrars and admissions officers (AACRAO) in Reno, a few years ago. It made good sense to us, and we have adopted it.

This chapter includes only those schools that are accepted as "accredited" under the education version of GAAP, Generally Accepted Accreditation Principles. In the U.S., there is near-unanimous agreement on this among the relevant key decision-makers, especially university registrars and admissions officers, corporate human resource officers, and government agencies. Not everyone calls it "GAAP," but the concept is the same: If a school meets certain criteria, they will probably accept its credits or degrees; if not, they probably won't.

Note, too, that schools that do not meet the standards of GAAP are not necessarily bad, illegal, or fake. They simply would not be generally accepted as accredited.

What are the criteria for GAAP?

▶ For schools based in the U.S., there is no disagreement: accreditation by an accrediting agency recognized either by the U.S. Department of Education, and/or by the Council on Higher Education Accreditation (CHEA).

▶ For schools in Great Britain and the British Commonwealth, it is membership in the Association of Commonwealth Universities and a listing in the *Commonwealth Universities Yearbook*.

▶ For schools in Australia, it is recognition by the Australian Qualifications Framework.

▶ For schools in other countries, it is an appropriate listing in the *International Handbook of Universities* (published by UNESCO); an appropriate description in the *World Education Series* (published by PIER, Projects in International Education Research, a joint venture of AACRAO, NAFSA [the Association of International Educators], and the College Board); or a listing in the *Countries Series*, published by NOOSR, the Australian National Office for Overseas Skills Recognition.

All the schools in this chapter meet the standards of GAAP. The degree programs listed do not require any campus attendance; they can be completed entirely through distance-learning methods.

The basic format for each listing is as follows:

Name of School   Associate's, Bachelor's, Master's, Doctorate, Law

Postal Address (United States if country not specified)

Fields of study **offered**

Year founded

Accreditation (Regional, National, Professional, or International; see chapter 8 for an explanation of these terms)

Phone ▪ Tollfree phone (If a U.S. number, country code (+1) not included)

Fax

Email address

Web site URL

Description of programs

Note: We have in the past given cost information, but this changes so quickly and is so subjective that we have decided to discontinue the practice. If a program is extremely inexpensive, or disproportionately expensive, we've mentioned this in the listing. In most cases, the best way to find out about the cost of any particular program is to contact the school directly.

Note also: It is the nature of reference book publishing that *Bears' Guide* starts going out of date the very day it comes off the press. Schools change their name, get a new area code, add new degree programs, shut down, etc., and in the world of distance learning, change seems to happen at a rate much faster than the rest of higher education.

Part of the reason we developed Degree.net, the *Bears' Guide* Web site, was to take advantage of the "real time" publishing capabilities of the Internet. Updates and corrections to the 14th edition of *Bears' Guide* can be found at *www.degree.net/updates/bearsguide14*. Consider it the last chapter of this book, an electronic appendix.

And remember, we count on *you* to help us keep this book up to date. Through 25 years and 14 editions (and counting), reader correspondence has played a huge role in our coverage of nontraditional education. Please, whether it's a defunct area code or a hot new distance-learning program, bring it to our attention.

You can email us at *johnandmariah@degree.net*, or write to us at *Bears' Guide*, P.O. Box 7123, Berkeley, CA 94707.

Advance Learning Network   B

14920 Westminster Way North, Suite 1B
Shoreline, WA 98133
Fields offered: General studies, management
Year founded: 1996
Accreditation: Regional
Phone: (206) 789 7326 ▪ (800) 246 5940
Fax: (206) 417 4830
Email: clugston@advancelearn.net

Web site: www.advancelearn.net
Offers courses with credit recommendations from the American Council on Education (ACE). A program in organizational management (51 semester credits) is offered by Internet delivery and can be transferred toward a bachelor's degree at Charter Oak State College (CT) and Thomas Edison State College (NJ). Classroom-based courses are offered at various corporate sites in the United States. Formerly called Internet Distance Education Associates.

American Bible College and Seminary   B, M, D

4300 Highline Rd.
Oklahoma City, OK 73108
Fields offered: Biblical studies, divinity, ministry
Accreditation: National (TRACS)
Phone: (405) 945 0100 ▪ (800) 488 2528
Fax: (405) 945 0311
Email: info@abcs.edu
Web site: www.abcs.edu
Offers B.A. and M.A. degrees in biblical studies, a Master of Divinity (M.Div.), and a Doctor of Ministry (D.Min.) through correspondence and online classes with no on-campus residency. Programs at all levels and in all fields have a decisively biblical focus. Accredited by the Transnational Association of Colleges and Schools (TRACS).

American College of Prehospital Medicine   B

7552 Navarre Parkway, Suite 1
Navarre, FL 32566-7312
Fields offered: Emergency medical services
Year founded: 1991
Accreditation: National (DETC)
Phone: (850) 939 0840 ▪ (800) 735 2276
Fax: (800) 350 3870
Email: admit@acpm.edu
Web site: www.acpm.edu
Bachelor of Science in emergency medical services, open to any licensed EMT professional at or above the level of EMT/Ambulance. Credit given for prior training and experience. Foreign students welcome. Accredited by the Distance Education and Training Council (DETC).

American Graduate University   M

733 N. Dodsworth Ave.
Covina, CA 91724
Fields offered: Project management, acquisition management
Year founded: 1975
Accreditation: National (DETC)
Phone: (626) 966 4576
Fax: (626) 915 1709
Email: info@agu.edu
Web site: www.agu.edu
Offers a Master of Project Management (M.P.M.) and a Master of Acquisition Management (M.A.M.). Courses may be taken entirely by correspondence, or by attending seminars given at various locations around the U.S. A bachelor's degree is required for admission. Accredited by the Distance Education and Training Council (DETC).

American Health Science University   M

1010 South Joliet St., #107
Aurora, CO 80012
Fields offered: Nutrition science
Year founded: 1980
Accreditation: National (DETC)
Phone: (303) 340 2054 ▧ (800) 530 8079
Fax: (303) 367 2577
Email: nuted@aol.com
Web site: www.ahsu.com

Offers a 12-course master's program in nutrition science, wholly through distance-learning methods. Support is available by phone and fax, and exams can be taken at a local library or other approved site. Formerly known as the National Institute of Nutritional Education.

American Institute for Computer Sciences   B, M

2101 Magnolia Ave., #200
Birmingham, AL 35205
Fields offered: Computer science, information systems
Year founded: 1989
Accreditation: National (DETC)
Phone: (205) 323 6191 ▧ (800) 729 2427
Fax: (205) 328 2229
Email: admiss@aics.com
Web site: www.aics.edu

B.S. and M.S. in computer science and a B.S. in information systems. Courses use standard college-level texts, along with supplemental CDs or Web-based instruction. Founded by Dr. Lloyd Clayton, who also established Chadwick University and two health-related universities. AICS has progressed from being unlicensed and unable to accept Alabama-based students, to becoming state licensed, to finally gaining recognized accreditation from the Distance Education and Training Council (DETC). Until the day of their DETC accreditation in 2000, they had claimed accreditation from the nonwonderful World Association of Universities and Colleges.

American Military University   B, M

9104-P Manassas Dr.
Manassas, VA 20111
Fields offered: See below
Year founded: 1994
Accreditation: National (DETC)
Phone: (703) 330 5398
Fax: (703) 330 5109
Email: amunet@amunet.edu
Web site: www.amunet.edu

Offers totally nonresident B.A. programs in criminal justice, intelligence studies, management, marketing, military history, and military management. An M.A. in military studies is also available with specialization in air warfare, civil war studies, defense management, intelligence, land warfare, management, naval warfare, transportation management (requiring some short residencies through the U.S. Merchant Marine Academy), or unconventional warfare. A maximum 15 (of the 36 required) credit hours can come from some combination of transfer credits, ACE-approved military training, and life experience eval-

uation. After enrolling in a course, the student contacts the instructor (four phone contacts are a requirement) to ask about focus and expectations for the course of study. Most courses involve some small writing assignments, an "open book" midterm exam, a research paper, and a proctored final exam (you nominate a proctor whom the university approves). Accredited by the Distance Education and Training Council (DETC).

Andrew Jackson University   B, M

10 Old Montgomery Highway
Birmingham, AL 35209
Fields offered: Business, business administration, communication, criminal justice, public administration
Year founded: 1994
Accreditation: National (DETC)
Phone: (205) 871 9288 ▧ (800) 429 9300
Fax: (800) 321 9694
Email: info@aju.edu
Web site: www.aju.edu

Degrees are offered exclusively by distance learning: B.A. in communication, B.S. in business or criminal justice, MBA, Master of Public Administration, and an M.S. in criminal justice. Accredited by the Distance Education and Training Council (DETC). AJU was incorporated by University Church, Inc., and maintained "that the foundation of all knowledge is God's truth and must be Christ-centered [which] was resulted in an integration of divine principles throughout the university's curriculum...." The "statement of faith" does not appear in the most recent catalog.

Anglia Polytechnic University   B, M

Radiography, School of Applied Sciences
East Rd.
Cambridge CB1 1PT, United Kingdom
Fields offered: Health sciences, medical imaging, radiography
Year founded: 1989
Accreditation: International (GAAP)
Phone: +44 (1223) 363 271
Fax: +44 (1223) 576 157
Email: jsvensson@bridge.anglia.ac.uk
Web site:
www.anglia.ac.uk/radiography/home.htm

Offers a B.Sc. in health sciences with optional specialization in diagnostic and therapeutic radiography. M.Sc. degrees in medical imaging (with optional specialization in MRI or ultrasound) and radiography (with optional specialization in diagnostic or therapeutic radiography) are also available. All programs are geared towards professionals working in these fields.

Arizona State University   B, M

Distance Learning Technology
Tempe, AZ 85287-0501
Fields offered: Engineering, history
Year founded: 1885
Accreditation: Regional
Phone: (480) 965 6738
Fax: (480) 965 1371

Email: distance@asu.edu
Web site: www.dlt.asu.edu

Offers courses through the World Wide Web, cable, public television, satellite, microwave, and independent learning. An M.S. in engineering is available via ITFS in the Phoenix area, and a Master of Engineering, in collaboration with Northern Arizona University and University of Arizona, is available on the Web and via videotape. A B.A. in history is offered through interactive television and Web with two evening on-campus courses.

Aston University   M

Language Studies Unit
Aston Triangle
Birmingham B4 7ET, United Kingdom
Fields offered: Teaching English, TESOL
Year founded: 1895
Accreditation: International (GAAP)
Phone: +44 (121) 359 3611
Email: s.m.morton@aston.ac.uk
Web site: www.les.aston.ac.uk/lsu

The M.Sc. programs in teaching English are designed for persons already teaching the English language—the school stresses that it is *not* a teacher training program. Assignments and the dissertation relate directly to the student's own professional environment; topics studied include pedagogic principles, language learning theory, and production of original materials, among others. Applicants should hold an approved bachelor's degree or equivalent and have at least three years' professional experience. Aston also offers a distance-learning MBA, but only within the United Kingdom and Germany.

Athabasca University   B, M

1 University Dr.
Athabasca, AB T9S 3A3, Canada
Fields offered: Administration, arts & sciences, general studies, commerce, nursing, computing & information systems, business administration, health studies, distance learning, integrated studies, counseling
Year founded: 1970
Accreditation: International (GAAP)
Phone: (780) 675 6100 ▪ (800) 788 9041
Fax: (780) 675 6145
Email: auinfo2@athabascau.ca
Web site: www.athabascau.ca

An open distance-education institution serving more than 20,000 students around the world. Degree programs include a Bachelor of Administration, Bachelor of Arts, Bachelor of Commerce, Bachelor of General Studies, Bachelor of Nursing, Bachelor of Professional Arts, Bachelor of Science, and Bachelor of Science in Computing & Information Systems. Graduate degrees include an MBA program (which requires three short visits to the campus), Master of Health Studies, Master of Distance Education, Master of Arts in Integrated Studies, and a Master of Counseling. All distance-education courses are offered through sophisticated home-study packages. Students set up their own study schedules and work at their own pace. All students are assigned a telephone tutor to whom

they have tollfree access from anywhere in North America. (Students residing outside of North America must pay their own long-distance charges.) Some courses are delivered completely online; others are supplemented by radio and television programs, audio- and videocassettes, seminars, laboratories, or teleconference sessions.

Atlantic University (Virginia)   M

397 Little Neck Rd.
Building 3300, Suite 100
Virginia Beach, VA 23452
Fields offered: Spiritual mentoring, transpersonal studies
Year founded: 1930
Accreditation: National (DETC)
Phone: (757) 631 8101 ▪ (800) 428 1512
Fax: (757) 631 8096
Email: info@atlanticuniv.edu
Web site: www.atlanticuniv.edu

Originally established in 1930 by the Edgar Cayce Foundation, but dormant from 1932 to 1985. The program is interdisciplinary, exposing learners to the transpersonal aspects of psychology, science, and various spiritual traditions. The M.A. can be earned through ten correspondence or online courses; concentrations are available in archetypal studies, holistic health & living, intuitive studies, spiritual mentoring, transpersonal counseling, and visual arts from a transpersonal approach. A six-course noncredit certificate in spiritual mentoring is also available.

Australian Catholic University   B

McAuley Campus
P.O. Box 247
Everton Park, Queensland 4053, Australia
Fields offered: Education
Year founded: 1991
Accreditation: International (GAAP)
Phone: +61 (7) 3855 7135
Fax: +61 (7) 3855 7249
Email: admissions@mcauley.acu.edu.au
Web site: www.acu.edu.au

Offers a Bachelor of Education covering the basic professional training needed for teachers at the primary and/or secondary level, particularly those seeking a career in Catholic education, with a focus on the philosophy of Catholic education, the nature of Catholic school, and the teaching of religion.

Baker College   B, M

1050 West Bristol Rd.
Flint, MI 48507-5508
Fields offered: Business administration
Year founded: 1888
Accreditation: Regional
Phone: (800) 469 4062
Email: adm-ol@baker.edu
Web site: www.baker.edu

Baker College On-Line is part of Michigan's largest (nine-campus) private college system. The BBA is available with an optional specialization in human resource management; the MBA is available with optional specialization in computer information systems, health care management, human resource management, industrial management, integrated health care, international business, leadership studies, or marketing. The bachelor's degree requires an associate's degree or equivalent, and takes approximately two years to complete. The master's degree can be completed in 18 months. Interaction occurs by email. Coursework can then be completed off-line. Each course takes place in a "virtual classroom," and students are provided 24-hour access to their "classes," as well as a private mailbox. Each course takes six weeks.

Belhaven College   A

1500 Peachtree St.
Jackson, MS 39202
Fields offered: A.A. for home schoolers
Year founded: 1894
Accreditation: Regional
Phone: (601) 968 5940 ▓ (800) 960 5940
Fax: (601) 968 8946
Email: admissions@belhaven.edu
Web site: www.belhaven.edu

The Presbyterian college, "dedicated to the belief that only the Christian liberal arts institution can educate men and women capable of totally purposeful action and direction," offers a general associate's degree entirely online and specifically designed for home-schooled students.

Bellevue University   B, M

1000 Galvin Rd., S
Bellevue, NE 68005
Fields offered: Business administration, business information systems, criminal justice administration, e-business, leadership, management, management information systems, management of human resources
Year founded: 1965
Accreditation: Regional
Phone: (402) 291 8100 ▓ (800) 756 7920
Fax: (402) 293 3730
Email: online-u@scholars.bellevue.edu
Web site: www.bellevue.edu

Bachelor's degrees are available in business information systems, criminal justice administration, e-business, leadership, management, management information systems, and management of human resources. An MBA and M.A. in leadership are also offered, both requiring 36 hours credit hours and about 18 months of study.

Bemidji State University   B

Center for Extended Learning, Deputy Hall 335
Bemidji, MN 56601
Fields offered: Criminal justice, history, social studies
Year founded: 1913
Accreditation: Regional
Phone: (218) 755 2030 ▓ (800) 475 2001
Fax: (218) 755 4604
Email: admissions@vax1.bemidji.msus.edu
Web site: www.bemidji.msus.edu

This program is available to U.S. citizens only. Some credit for life experience and prior learning may be applied toward the degree requirements. Credit is earned through on-campus classes, extension classes in other Minnesota cities, and independent guided home study. Learning packages (a syllabus, books, and sometimes audio- or video-cassettes) are provided. Continued contact with BSU is maintained by mail, telephone, email, exchange of cassettes, and conferences with academic advisors. As the Coordinator of External Studies put it, "Unique solutions exist for unique situations."

Berean University of the Assemblies of God

See: Global University of the Assemblies of God

Boise State University   M

1910 University Dr.
Boise, ID 83725
Fields offered: Instructional & performance technology
Year founded: 1932
Accreditation: Regional
Phone: (208) 426 1709 ▓ (800) 824 7017
Fax: (208) 385 3647
Email: bsuipt@micron.net
Web site: www.boisestate.edu/conted

Totally nonresident M.S. in instructional & performance technology (the study of human performance problems in various business and industry settings), offered via real-time computer conferencing courses. Applicants must have access to a compatible computer and modem for at least two hours a day, five days a week, and preferably a fax machine as well.

Brock University   B

500 Glenridge Ave.
St. Catherines, ON L2S 3A1, Canada
Fields offered: Adult education
Year founded: 1964
Accreditation: International (GAAP)
Fax: +1 (905) 688 5550
Email: liaison@dewey.ed.brocku.ca
Web site: adult.ed.brocku.ca

Offers a Bachelor of Education in adult studies; courses are delivered online or by videotape, and students respond via mail, phone, email, or fax.

Brunel University   B, M

Uxbridge
Middlesex UB8 3PH, United Kingdom
Fields offered: Advanced manufacturing systems, building services engineering, youth & community studies, communication systems, packaging technology
Year founded: 1966
Accreditation: International (GAAP)
Phone: +44 (1895) 274 000
Fax: +44 (1895) 203 084
Email: admissions@brunel.ac.uk
Web site: www.brunel.ac.uk

Degrees include an M.S. in advanced manufacturing systems, an M.S. in building services engineering, a B.A. or M.A. in youth & community studies, and M.S.'s in communication systems and packaging technology. Some courses may require some classroom attendance.

California College for Health Sciences   A, B, M

222 West 24th St.
National City, CA 91950
Fields offered: Health services, business
Year founded: 1979
Accreditation: National (DETC)
Phone: (619) 477 4800 ▦ (800) 221 7374
Fax: (619) 477 4360
Email: cchsinfo@cchs.edu
Web site: www.cchs.edu

Entirely through home-study courses, California College offers a B.S. in health services management, respiratory care, and business; an A.S. in respiratory therapy, early childhood education, medical transcription, electroencephalographic technology, and business; and master's degrees in health services, health care administration, and public health, as well as an MBA concentrating in health care. CCHS is a part of the large Harcourt education company, and is accredited by the Distance Education and Training Council (DETC).

California National University
for Advanced Studies   B, M

16909 Parthenia St.
North Hills, CA 91343
Fields offered: Business administration, engineering, computer science, quality assurance science, human resource management, health care management
Year founded: 1993
Accreditation: National (DETC)
Phone: (800) 782 2422
Email: cnuadms@mail.cnuas.edu
Web site: www.cnuas.edu

CNU offers bachelor's degrees in engineering (computer, electrical, environmental, mechanical), business administration (accounting, finance, international business, management, MIS, marketing, and health care management), computer science, and quality assurance science. Master's in business administration, engineering, health care management, MIS, and human resource management. All degrees can be earned wholly through distance learning, and students from around the world are welcomed. Up to 75% of credit towards a bachelor's degree can come from transfer credit, challenge exams such as CLEP, and life experience assessment.

California State University—Chico   B, M

Center for Regional and Continuing Education
Chico, CA 95929-0250
Fields offered: Computer science, creative writing, interdisciplinary study, psychology, telecommunications
Year founded: 1887
Accreditation: Regional

Phone: (916) 898 6105 ▦ (800) 780 4837
Email: rce@csuchico.edu
Web site: www.rce.csuchico.edu

Chico State offers a B.S. and an M.S. in computer science to corporate subscribers across the nation, entirely through interactive satellite TV and videotape. In addition, an online M.A. program in psychology has recently been developed. An M.F.A. in creative writing is also available through online courses and two-week summer residencies. Finally, an M.S. in interdisciplinary studies with emphasis in telecommunications is available through videocourses and short residency seminars.

California State University—
Dominguez Hills   B, M

1000 E. Victoria St.
Carson, CA 90747
Fields offered: Humanities, business administration, negotiation & conflict management, nursing, quality assurance
Year founded: 1960
Accreditation: Regional
Phone: (310) 243 3741 ▦ (877) 464 4557
Fax: (310) 516 3971
Email: eereg@csudh.edu
Web site: www.csudh.edu

Degrees available via the Internet include an MBA; a Master of Science in Quality Assurance, with a concentration on manufacturing, service, or health care; a Master of Arts in Behavioral Science focusing on negotiation & conflict management, and a Bachelor of Science in Nursing. The school also offers an M.A. in the Humanities via correspondence: a rare opportunity to earn an accredited master's degree in the humanities nonresidentially, with a specialization in philosophy, history, music, art, or religion. (We are biased. The authors' wife and mother, respectively, Marina Bear, completed her M.A. here in 1985 while living in a remote location and taking care of three young children.) Dominguez Hills is also expanding their degree offerings, expecting to have an M.S. in Nursing, a B.S. in Quality Assurance, and a B.S. in Applied Studies online by the fall of 2001.

California State University—Fresno   B, M

AIC - Distance Learning
5241 N. Maple Ave
McKee Fisk Bldg, Room 110
Fresno, CA 93740-8027
Fields offered: Business administration, criminology (corrections, law enforcement, victimology), education (administration & supervision), liberal studies, management
Year founded: 1911
Accreditation: Regional
Phone: (559) 278 2058
Fax: (559) 278 7026
Web site: www.csufresno.edu

Offers a B.S. in business administration, B.S. in criminology (emphasis corrections, law enforcement, or victimology), and B.A. in liberal studies entirely through off-campus extension courses, which are gradually being made available through online distance learning. An M.A. in education (emphasis administration & supervision) is under development.

California State University—Hayward   M

Continuing Education
25800 Carlos Bee Blvd.
Hayward, CA 94542-3012
Fields offered: Education
Year founded: 1957
Accreditation: Regional
Phone: (510) 885 3605
Fax: (510) 885 4817
Email: online@csuhayward.edu
Web site: www.online.csuhayward.edu

Offers an online M.S. in education with emphasis on online teaching and learning. Online certificate programs are also available in online teaching and learning, technical and professional communication, and cross-cultural linguistic academic development.

California State University—Los Angeles   B

5151 State University Dr.
Los Angeles, California 90032-4226
Fields offered: Fire protection administration
Year founded: 1947
Accreditation: Regional
Phone: (213) 343 4550
Fax: (213) 343 4571
Web site: www.calstatela.edu

Bachelor of Science in fire protection administration & technology through a variety of nontraditional means, including interactive televised courses broadcast to workplaces or various public sites, teleconferencing, and videocassette. Enrollment limited to the Los Angeles basin and surrounding counties.

California State University—Northridge   M

College of Extended Learning
18111 Nordhoff St
Northridge, CA 91330-8343
Fields offered: Public administration, speech pathology
Year founded: 1958
Accreditation: Regional
Phone: (818) 677 2786
Email: exl@csun.edu
Web site: www.csun.edu

CSUN offers a master's degree in speech pathology based completely on online study. Undergraduate and graduate level extension courses are also available.

Canadian School of Management   B, M

335 Bay St., #1120
Toronto, ON M5H 2R3, Canada
Fields offered: Business, management, health services, tourism
Year founded: 1976
Accreditation: National (DETC)
Phone: (416) 360 3805 ▪ (888) 508 7642
Fax: (416) 360 6863

Email: csm@c-s-m.org
Web site: www.c-s-m.org

Offers Internet courses in business, management, health services, and tourism that qualify the student to earn DETC-accredited bachelor's and master's degrees from CSM's U.S.-based partner, the University of Action Learning (see listing in this chapter). Both CSM and UAL are owned by International Management Centres (also listed in this chapter).

Canadian Virtual University   B, M

Year founded: 2000
Accreditation: International (GAAP)
Phone: +1 (780) 675 6791
Web site: www.cvu-uvc.ca

Seven Canadian universities with distance learning programs formed a consortium in 2000 to permit students to "mix and match" courses in working on a wide range of bachelor's and master's degree programs offered by consortium members. The degrees will be awarded by the individual schools, which are each described in this chapter: Athabasca, Brandon, U. of Manitoba, U. of Victoria, British Columbia Open U., Laurentian, and Royal Roads. Diplomas and certificates are also available.

Capella University   M, D

222 South 9th St., 20th Floor
Minneapolis, MN 55402-3389
Fields offered: Business administration, education, human services, information technology, psychology
Year founded: 1993
Accreditation: Regional
Phone: (612) 339 8650 ▪ (888) 227 3552
Fax: (612) 337 5396
Email: info@capella.edu
Web site: www.capellauniversity.edu

A major, well-funded, and regionally-accredited institution devoted entirely to nontraditional education. Offers Internet-based master's and doctorate degree programs in business, education, human services, information technology, and psychology. The MBA and most master's programs require no residency. All Ph.D. programs include a minimal residency component, typically involving one-to two-week intensive summer sessions. Formerly called the Graduate School of America.

Capitol College   B, M

11301 Springfield Rd.
Laurel, MD 20708
Fields offered: Software & Internet applications, information & telecommunications systems, e-commerce management
Year founded: 1932
Accreditation: Regional
Phone: (301) 369 2800 ▪ (800) 950 1992
Fax: (301) 953 3876
Email: admissions@capitol-college.edu
Web site: www.capitol-college.edu

Specializing in engineering and technology fields, Capitol's distance-learning offerings include a B.S. in software &

Internet applications, M.S. in information & telecommunication systems, and M.S. in e-commerce management. Both asynchronous and live classes are delivered entirely over the Web.

Cardean University M

500 Lake Cook Rd. Suite 150
Deerfield, IL 60015
Fields offered: Business administration
Year founded: 1999
Accreditation: National (DETC)
Phone: (847) 444 8282
Email: info@cardean.edu
Web site: www.cardean.edu

A degree-granting division of UNext.com, an ambitious and deep-pocketed Internet education corporation. Develops Web-based business courses in partnership with a who's who list of business schools—Carnegie Mellon, Columbia Business School, London School of Economics, Stanford University, and University of Chicago—and sells these courses to companies for their employees. 45 credits qualifies a student for a DETC-accredited MBA degree. They plan to offer their program to non–corporate-sponsored individuals in the future.

Carnegie Mellon University M

School of Computer Science - ISRI
5000 Forbes Ave
Pittsburgh, PA 15213-3891
Fields offered: Software engineering, software information technology
Year founded: 1967
Accreditation: Regional
Phone: (412) 268 1593
Fax: (412) 268 5413
Email: distance-info@cs.cmu.edu
Web site: www.distance.cmu.edu

Regarded as one of the most prestigious research universities in the country, Carnegie Mellon University offers a Master of Software Information Technology (M.S.I.T.) entirely through online classes with no on-campus residency whatsoever. A certificate in software engineering may also be completed online, and courses from the certificate may (to a limited extent) be transferred to the Master of Software Engineering (M.Sw.E.) program. We have heard rumors that the M.Sw.E. may itself be available through online study eventually, and the program can already be completed through a mix of online coursework and extension classes.

Catholic Distance University M

120 East Colonial Highway
Hamilton, VA 20158-9012
Fields offered: Religious studies
Year founded: 1983
Accreditation: National (DETC)
Phone: (540) 338 2700 ▪ (888) 254 4238
Fax: (540) 338 4788
Email: cdu@cdu.edu
Web site: www.cdu.edu

CDU's mission is to provide education in the Catholic faith through distance education. Offers master's degrees in religious studies. Accreditation from the Distance Education and Training Council (DETC).

Central Michigan University B, M, D

CMU-DDL
CEL-North
Mt. Pleasant, MI 48859
Fields offered: Administration, audiology, community development, industrial administration, health sciences, nutrition & dietetics
Year founded: 1892
Accreditation: Regional
Phone: (517) 774 3505 ▪ (800) 688 4268
Fax: (517) 774 3491
Email: connie.detwiler@cmich.edu
Web site: www.ddl.cmich.edu

The College of Extended Learning offers distance-learning B.S. degrees in administration, community development, health sciences, and industrial administration. The degree is awarded for a combination of previously earned college credit, credit for other prior learning, and distance education. At the graduate level, online M.S. degrees in administration and in nutrition & dietetics are available; a Doctor of Audiology (Au.D.), designed in consultation with Vanderbilt University, may also be completed by distance learning.

Central Missouri State University M

403 Humphreys
Warrensburg, MO 64093
Fields offered: Aviation safety, criminal justice, industrial safety management
Year founded: 1871
Accreditation: Regional
Phone: (660) 543 4984 ▪ (800) 729 2678
Fax: (660) 543 8333
Web site: www.cmsu.edu

Courses leading to master's degrees in aviation safety, criminal justice, and industrial safety management sent via television, videotape, videoconference, and Internet to students in Missouri.

Central Queensland University B, M, D

Bruce Highway
Rockhampton, Queensland 4702, Australia
Fields offered: See below
Year founded: 1967
Accreditation: International (GAAP)
Phone: +61 (7) 4930 9719
Fax: +61 (7) 4930 9792
Email: ddce-enquiries@cqu.edu.au
Web site: www.ddce.cqu.edu.au

Distance learning programs offer degrees at all levels through methods including written study materials, audiotapes, home laboratory kits, and computer-aided learning packages. Students also get support through teleconferencing, access to tutors, and regional study centers.

Bachelor's programs are as follows: Bachelor of Accounting; B.A. in Aboriginal and Torres Strait Islander studies, Asia & Pacific studies, Australian studies, drama & literary studies, drama & theater studies, environmental studies, film studies, geography, history, Japanese language, literary & cultural studies, literary studies, methods of social research, sociology, and welfare; Bachelor of Building Design; Bachelor of Building Surveying; Bachelor of Business (in accounting, human resources management, management, marketing, or purchasing & materials management); BBA; Bachelor of Communication; Bachelor of Construction Management; Bachelor of Education (in early childhood studies, languages other than English, primary education, or secondary education); Bachelor of Engineering Technology; Bachelor of Human Movement Science; Bachelor of Information Systems; Bachelor of Multimedia Studies; Bachelor of Quantity Surveying; B.S. in biology, chemical sciences, environmental sciences, mathematics, and physics; Bachelor of Tourism; and Bachelor of Vocational Education and Training.

Master's programs are as follows: Master of Accounting, Master of Arts Administration (significant residency required), MBA (with an optional track in health services management), Master of Education Studies, Master of Financial Management, Master of Health Administration & Information Systems, Master of Human Resources Management, Master of Information, Master of Letters (in cultural studies or history), Master of Maintenance Management, Master of Primary Health Care, Master of School Management, and an M.S. in communication.

An Ed.D. is also available (by research or coursework-and-research), as are research Ph.D. programs in business & law, communication, computing, education & creative arts, engineering & physical systems, health sciences, journalism, mathematics, and nursing.

Champlain College   B

163 South Willard St.
Burlington, VT 05402-0670
Fields offered: Accounting, business, computer information systems, computer programming, hotel-restaurant management, management, professional studies, telecommunications, Web site development & management
Year founded: 1878
Accreditation: Regional
Phone: (888) 545 3459
Email: online@champlain.edu
Web site: www.champlain.edu

Champlain offers bachelor's degrees in the fields listed above. Often serves as a degree completion program; allows students to transfer in either an A.A. or a certain number of credits, and then finish the degree online. Also offers associate's degrees and professional certificates.

Charles Sturt University   B, M, D

International Division
Locked Bag 676
Wagga Wagga, NSW 2678, Australia
Fields offered: See below

Year founded: 1989
Accreditation: International (GAAP)
Phone: +61 (2) 6933 2666
Fax: +61 (2) 6933 2799
Email: inquiry@csu.edu.au
Web site: www.csu.edu.au

In 1989, Mitchell College of Advanced Education and Riverina-Murray Institute of Higher Education merged to CSU, now the largest distance-education provider in Australia. Most programs can be completed by correspondence courses, online classes, residential workshops, or some mix of the three. Relatively few require actual on-campus residency.

Bachelor's degrees include: Bachelor of Applied Science in agriculture, ecotourism, environmental horticulture, equine studies, food science, medical & applied biotechnology, medical imaging, parks recreation & heritage, and viticulture & wine science; Bachelor of Arts in individualized fields or with a major in psychology; Bachelor of Business (with optional specialization in accounting); Bachelor of Education (in early childhood education, primary education, or vocational education); Bachelor of Health Science (in community & public health, complementary medicine, gerontology, leisure & health, mental health, nursing, or pre-hospital care); Bachelor of Information Technology; Bachelor of Medical Science; Bachelor of Nursing; Bachelor of Policing (with specialization in investigations or prosecutions); Bachelor of Science in analytical chemistry, mathematics, plant biotechnology, and remote sensing; Bachelor of Social Science in emergency management, habilitation, justice studies, leisure & health, pre-hospital care, psychology, and social welfare; Bachelor of Social Work; Bachelor of Spatial Information Systems; Bachelor of Teaching (emphasis birth to five years); Bachelor of Theology; and Bachelor of Vocational Education and Training.

Master's degrees include: Master of Accountancy, Master of Aged Services Management, Master of Applied Finance, Master of Applied Science (in agriculture, environmental management & restoration, library & information management, medical imaging, medical laboratory science, medical ultrasound, parks recreation & heritage, respiratory science, or teacher librarianship), Master of Arts (in child protection investigation, communication, compliance, criminal intelligence, cultural heritage studies, fraud investigations, investigations management, journalism, organizational communication, police negotiation, or visual & performing arts), MBA (with optional specialization in global trade management, international business, or operations management), Master of Child & Adolescent Welfare, Master of Commerce (with optional emphasis in accounting), Master of Correctional Administration, Master of Correctional Management, Master of Education (with optional emphasis in special education or teacher librarianship), Master of Emergency Management, Master of Ethics & Legal Studies, Master of Health Science (with optional emphasis in asthma education, genetic counseling, or nursing), Master of Health Services Management, Master of Human Resource Management, Master of Human Services Management, Master of Industrial Relations, Master of Information Technology, Master of

Management, Master of Marketing, Master of Mental Health, Master of Ministry (M.Min.), Master of Police Practice, Master of Psychology (M.Psy.), Master of Public Policy & Administration, Master of Social Policy & Planning, Master of Social Science (with an optional emphasis in criminology), Master of Social Work, Master of Strategic Marketing, and Master of Theology (Th.M.).

Doctorates include the DBA (coursework plus research), Doctor of Education (coursework or research), Doctor of Psychology (coursework plus research), Doctor of Public Policy (coursework plus research), and the research Ph.D. The research Ph.D. is available in agricultural economics, agriculture, Australian history, business management, communication & culture, drama, education, environmental & information science, environmental studies, financial & management accounting, fine arts, health studies, industry & resource economics, information studies, information technology, justice studies & police studies, professional & applied ethics, psychology, rural social studies, science & technology, social welfare & social policy, social work, and wine & food sciences.

Students in the Wharton online MBA program dread the arrival of the traditional 'Dodo Box,' mailed to the student finishing last in his or her class.

Charter Oak State College A, B

55 Paul J. Manafort Dr.
New Britian, CT 06053-2142
Fields offered: Anthropology, applied arts, art history, biology, business, chemistry, child study, communication, computer science studies, criminal justice, economics, engineering studies, individualized studies, fire science technology, French, geography, geology, German, history, human services (administration, applied behavioral science, health studies), individualized studies, information systems, liberal studies, literature, mathematics, information technology, music history, music theory, optical business management, organizational management, philosophy, physics, political science, psychology, religious studies, sociology, Spanish, technology studies
Year founded: 1973
Accreditation: Regional
Phone: (860) 832 3855
Fax: (860) 832 3999
Email: info@cosc.edu
Web site: www.cosc.edu
The college is operated by the Connecticut Board for State Academic Awards and offers the B.A. and B.S. in general studies with concentrations available in the fields listed above. Each student is responsible for amassing a minimum of 120 semester units, which may come from courses taken elsewhere, equivalency examinations, military study, distance learning, correspondence courses, or portfolio assessment. The degree requires that at least half the credits be in the arts and sciences, and that the student complete a faculty-approved concentration with a minimum of 36 credits in a single subject or combination of subjects. Only students residing in the U.S. may enroll. Original name: Connecticut Board for State Academic Achievement Awards. Also offers associate's degrees.

Cheltenham Tutorial College M

292 High St.
Cheltenham GL50 3HQ, United Kingdom
Fields offered: Business administration (maritime management), cooperative management, finance, marketing
Accreditation: International (GAAP)
Phone: +44 (1242) 241 279
Fax: +44 (1242) 234 256
Email: info@cheltenhamlearning.co.uk
Web site: www.cheltenhamlearning.co.uk
A distance-learning MBA (with optional emphasis in maritime management), M.Sc. in finance or marketing, and M.A. in cooperative management are offered, through printed correspondence materials and tutorial support, in cooperation with the University of Leicester (see listing in this chapter). Applicants should have practical experience in their field, and be able to support their application with strong references. In the third year of the program, students will be asked to undertake a research project examining in depth a topic of particular relevance to their interests and/or place of work.

Christopher Newport University B

1 University Place
Newport News, VA 23606
Fields offered: Government administration, philosophy & religious studies, political science
Year founded: 1960
Accreditation: Regional
Phone: (804) 594 7015 ▦ (800) 333 4268
Fax: (804) 594 7333
Email: online@cnu.edu
Web site: cnuonline.cnu.edu
Offers online bachelor's programs in the above fields.

City University B, M

335 116th Ave. SE
Bellevue, WA 98004
Fields offered: See below

Year founded: 1973
Accreditation: Regional
Phone: (425) 637 1010 ▪ (800) 426 5596
Fax: (425) 277 2437
Email: info@cityu.edu
Web site: www.cityu.edu

Distance-learning degrees are available through online study or by more traditional means. Bachelor's degrees in accounting, business administration, commerce, computer systems (with emphasis in computer programming, internetworking, networking & telecommunications, networking technologies, or student-defined selected studies), e-commerce, general studies, humanities, management, marketing, quantitative studies, and social sciences. M.A. degrees in counseling psychology, executive leadership, and management. M.S. degrees in computer systems and project management. MBA specializations include financial management, information systems, managerial leadership, marketing, and personal financial planning. A Master of Public Administration is also available; students may also choose to undertake a joint MBA/MPA. Master of Education specializations include curriculum & instruction, educational leadership & principal certification, educational technology, guidance & counseling, and reading & literacy. A Master of Teaching completion program is also available to residents of California and Washington.

Clarkson College   B, M

101 South 42nd St.
Omaha, NE 68131
Fields offered: Business administration (health related), nursing, medical imaging
Year founded: 1888
Accreditation: Regional
Phone: (402) 552 3041 ▪ (800) 647 5500
Fax: (402) 552 6057
Email: admiss@clrkcol.crhsnet.edu
Web site: www.clarksoncollege.edu

B.S. programs in nursing, medical imaging, and health-related business administration; M.S. in nursing. Distance-learning media include teleconferencing, Internet, video/audio tapes, and fax. Distance students must live at least 75 miles from Omaha to qualify for Clarkson's programs. The nursing programs require short residencies.

Cleveland Institute of Electronics

See: World College

Cogswell College

See: National Fire Academy

College for Financial Planning   M

6161 South Syracuse Way
Greenwood Village, CO 80111-4707
Fields offered: Personal financial planning
Year founded: 1972
Accreditation: Regional
Phone: (303) 220 1200 ▪ (800) 237 9990
Fax: (303) 220 4940
Email: ssc@fp.edu

Web site: www.fp.edu

The creator of the CFP license (still its primary program) also offers an M.S. in personal financial planning with emphasis in four fields: wealth management, estate planning, tax planning, and retirement planning. The 12-course program is designed for applicants with some financial services background. Accredited by the North Central Association and the DETC. Acquired in 1997 by the Apollo Group, the company that owns the University of Phoenix.

College of Estate Management   B, M

Whiteknights
Reading, Berkshire RG6 6AW, United Kingdom
Fields offered: Estate management, business administration, construction, real estate
Year founded: 1919
Accreditation: International (GAAP)
Phone: +44 (118) 986 1101
Fax: +44 (118) 975 5344
Email: info@cem.ac.uk
Web site: www.cem.ac.uk

Through an association with the University of Reading, this school offers three distance-learning degrees: a B.S. in estate management, an MBA with a concentration in construction & real estate, and an M.S. in real estate, this last tailored to overseas students. Courses are taught through a combination of written instructional materials, audio- and videocassettes, and, where feasible, face-to-face teaching sessions.

College of West Virginia   A, B

609 South Kanawha St.
Beckley, WV 25802-2830
Fields offered: Business, criminal justice, nursing, interdisciplinary studies, travel, general studies, secretarial science, environmental studies
Year founded: 1933
Accreditation: Regional
Phone: (304) 253 7351 ▪ (800) 766 6067
Fax: (304) 253 3485
Email: saell@cwv.edu
Web site: www.cwv.edu/saell

Courses leading to an associate's or bachelor's in the above fields delivered to home, workplace, etc. by print (mainly), tapes, email, etc. Well-developed program for awarding credits based on prior learning acquired through work, independent reading, noncollegiate training, community activities, religious activities, and other experiences. At least 18 credit hours must be earned through on-campus classes or directed independent study in order to earn a degree.

Colorado State University   B, M, D

Division of Educational Outreach
Spruce Hall
Fort Collins, CO 80523-1040
Fields offered: Engineering, business administration, computer science, statistics, management, industrial hygiene, agriculture, human resources

Year founded: 1870
Accreditation: Regional
Phone: (970) 491 5288 ▪ (800) 525 4950
Fax: (970) 491 7885
Email: questions@learn.colostate.edu
Web site: www.colostate.edu

Established in 1967, the Distance Degree Program (formerly called SURGE) was the first video-based graduate education program of its kind in America. Today courses are delivered through videotape, the Internet, or a combination of the two. Master's degrees offered in such fields as agriculture, business administration, engineering (agricultural, civil, electrical, environmental, industrial, and mechanical), computer science, human resources, industrial hygiene, management, and statistics. Doctorates in electrical, industrial, mechanical, and systems engineering. A second B.S. is available in computer science.

Columbia Union College   B

7600 Flower Ave.
Wilkinson Hall, Room 336A
Takoma Park, MD 20912-7796
Fields offered: Business administration, general studies, information systems, psychology, religion, respiratory care, theology
Year founded: 1904
Accreditation: Regional
Phone: (301) 891 4124 ▪ (800) 835 4212
Email: hsi@cuc.edu
Web site: www.cuc.edu

Bachelor's degrees in the above fields can be earned entirely through correspondence study. Credit available for standard equivalency examinations and/or work experience once the student has earned at least 24 semester hours in the program. At least 30 units (between 8 and 12 courses) must be earned after enrolling. Students in the respiratory care program must complete some on-campus classes, held in two-week-long summer sessions. Every student must write a major paper, related to literature, religion, or arts, or pass a comprehensive examination, to qualify for graduation. The school is owned by the Seventh Day Adventist Church but non-church members are welcome. Students may live anywhere in the world, but all work must be done in English.

Columbia University   M

540 Mudd, MC 4719
500 W. 120th St.
New York, NY 10027
Fields offered: Computer science, electrical engineering, engineering & management systems, materials science, mechanical engineering
Year founded: 1754
Accreditation: Regional
Phone: (212) 854 6447
Fax: (212) 854 2325
Email: cvn@columbia.edu
Web site: www.cvn.columbia.edu

The engineering department offers master's programs in the above fields through the "Columbia Video Network." Course lectures are delivered to off-campus students by videotape, through videoconferencing, or over the Internet; course materials, class notes, homework assignments, and syllabi are accessed on the Web.

Columbus State University   M

4225 University Ave.
Columbus, GA 31907-5645
Fields offered: Computer science
Year founded: 1958
Accreditation: Regional
Phone: (706) 568 2035
Fax: (706) 568 2123
Email: inquiry@csuonline.edu
Web site: www.csuonline.edu

In partnership with eCollege.com, offers an M.S. in applied computer science over the Internet. Not to be confused with the unaccredited Columbus University or Columbia State University.

Connecticut Board for State Academic Achievement Awards

See: Charter Oak State College

Connecticut State University   M

501 Crescent St.
New Haven, CT 06515-1355
Fields offered: Library science
Accreditation: Regional
Phone: 203 392 5781 ▪ 888 500 SCSU
Email: mls@onlinecsu.ctstateu.edu
Web site: onlinecsu.ctstateu.edu

The four Connecticut State Universities have consolidated their distance-learning programs into an organization called OnlineCSU. Their first degree offering is a Master of Library Science. Degrees planned for the future include a master's degree in accounting, and bachelor's degrees in computer science, business administration, nursing, and justice & law administration.

Crown College   A

8739 S. Hosmer
Tacoma, WA 98444
Fields offered: Criminal justice, paralegal studies
Year founded: 1969
Accreditation: Professional
Phone: (253) 531 3123 ▪ (800) 755 9525
Fax: (253) 531 3521
Email: admissions@crowncollege.com
Web site: www.crowncollege.edu

Offers A.S. degrees in criminal justice and paralegal studies online. Accredited by the Accrediting Commission of Career Schools and Colleges of Technology (ACCSCT).

Curtin University of Technology   B, M, D

GPO Box U 1987
Perth, WA 6845, Australia
Fields offered: See below
Year founded: 1967
Accreditation: International (GAAP)
Fax: +61 (8) 9266 9266

Email: customer-service@curtin.edu.au

Web site: www.curtin.edu.au

A number of degrees are offered via distance learning. At the beginning of each semester, students are sent a package of study materials for each course in which they are enrolled—a typical package may include a course plan, a study guide, and a reader. They may also, if appropriate, have audio- or videocassettes, slides or photographs, maps or charts, and computer disks. Many required courses may now instead be undertaken online.

Distance-learning bachelor's degrees are offered in social sciences, vocational education & training, commerce (in accounting/economics/finance or accounting/finance), education, and nursing. Master's degrees in accountancy, information & library studies, information management, educational administration, environmental health, health communications, health promotion, health services management, international health, occupational health & safety, public health, rehabilitation, and occupational therapy. Master's and Ph.D. in science education.

Research-based M.Phil. and Ph.D. programs in communication & culture and Internet studies. Many other bachelor's and master's degrees are offered through short residency programs.

Dallas Baptist University   B, M

3000 Mountain Creek Pkwy

Dallas, TX 75211-9299

Fields offered: Business studies (business administration or management), business administration (e-commerce or management)

Accreditation: Regional

Phone: (214) 333 6898 ▪ (800) 460 8188

Email: online@dbu.edu

Web site: www.dbu.edu/online

Offers a Bachelor of Business Studies (with emphasis in business administration or management) and an MBA (with emphasis in e-commerce or management) entirely through online study.

Darling Downs Institute of Advanced Education

See: University of Southern Queensland

David English House

See: University of Birmingham

David N. Myers College   B

Division of Adult Learning

112 Prospect Ave.

Cleveland, OH 44115

Fields offered: Criminal justice, human resource management, management, marketing

Year founded: 1848

Accreditation: Regional

Phone: (216) 523 3856

Fax: (216) 696 6430

Email: lhice@dnmyers.edu

Web site: www.dnmyers.edu

Adult students can complete a Bachelor of Science in criminal justice, human resource management, management, or marketing. An online MBA is imminent. Options

for earning credit include online coursework, residential coursework, group study at various locations, life/work experience, proficiency exams, and/or previous credit transfer. Tuition can be greatly reduced by life/work experience credit and proficiency exams. The first such program approved by the Ohio Board of Regents, this is the oldest and largest external degree program in Ohio. Formerly Dyke College.

De Montfort University   B, M, D, Law

Centre for Independent Study

The Gateway

Leicester LE1 9BH, England

Fields offered: See below

Year founded: 1897

Accreditation: International (GAAP)

Phone: +44 (116) 255 1551

Fax: +44 (116) 257 7533

Email: enquiry@dmu.ac.uk

Web site: www.dmu.ac.uk

The former Leicester Polytechnic, which became a university in 1992, offers a variety of graduate programs through distance learning, with minimal time required on the campus in England. Most programs are based on a learning contract or agreement negotiated between the student and the university. When a student is accepted into the program, she is assigned a mentor/supervisor, usually a member of the university staff, who will guide her through their program and assist in the formulation of a research or study proposal. Normally the mentor meets with the student once during each term; for foreign (non-U.K.) students, the school generally requires the student to have a local mentor as well as the university mentor. While meetings with the university mentor are generally done in person, it is possible that foreign students can meet the requirements by telephone, mail, or email. In lieu of formal examinations, the university conducts "continuous assessments" through a variety of coursework assignments, plus a major project or thesis which will account for at least 40% of the total. An oral examination is held at the end of each program. B.Sc. and Honours B.Sc. degrees are available in chemistry, waste & environmental management, and water & environmental management. B.A. and Honours B.A. programs in business are also available. Undergraduate diplomas are available in environmental protection and legal practice. M.Sc. degrees are available in clinical pharmacy (with emphasis in community, hospital, or psychiatric pharmacy), conservation science, environmental quality management, industrial data modeling, lubricant & hydraulic technology, and polymer technology. The Master of Laws (LL.M.) is available in advanced legal practice, business law, countryside & agriculture law, environmental law, and food law. M.A. programs in health & community development (with optional emphasis in youth & community work) and in learning & teaching are also available. Postgraduate diplomas are available in all of the above fields. Research M.Phil. and Ph.D. degrees in fine art practice may also be negotiated on a nonresident or semi-residential basis.

Deakin University   B, M, D
Deakin International
336 Glenferrie Rd.
Malvern, Victoria 3144, Australia
Fields offered: See below
Year founded: 1974
Accreditation: International (GAAP)
Phone: +61 (3) 9244 5095
Fax: +61 (3) 9244 5094
Web site: www.deakin.edu.au

Deakin University offers programs to students worldwide through Deakin International, the overseas student office. Most instruction takes place online or through correspondence, although the majority of courses also require proctored final examinations. Degrees offered entirely through distance learning include bachelor's in international development studies, international relations, journalism, and public relations; master's in international relations, science & technology studies, TESOL, commerce (accounting, economics, law, management information systems, or marketing), aquaculture, distance education, international trade & investment law, computing studies, international & community development, professional education & training, environmental engineering, health science (in human nutrition or nursing), and education (in curriculum & administration studies or TESOL). Deakin offers both the Bachelor of Laws (LL.B.) and Master of Laws (LL.M.). A research-based Doctor of Health Science (D.H.Sc.) is available almost completely nonresidentially, and it may be possible to fulfill remaining residency requirements through one of Deakin's many U.S. partner universities.

Drexel University   M
3141 Chestnut St.
Philadelphia, PA 19104
Fields offered: Business administration, information systems, library & information science, management of digital information
Year founded: 1891
Accreditation: Regional
Phone: (215) 895 2000 ▪ (800) 2 DREXEL
Fax: (215) 895 1414
Email: admissions@drexel.edu
Web site: www.drexel.edu

Offers online M.S. programs in library & information science (with emphasis on management of digital information) and information systems totally by distance learning. Also a "Techno-MBA" program, with a strong focus on e-commerce and the high-tech business world, offered online except for three on-campus weekends.

Dublin City University
See: National Distance Education Centre (Ireland)

Duquesne University   M, D
600 Forbes Ave.
Pittsburgh, PA 15282
Fields offered: Leadership, liberal studies, nursing, pharmacy
Year founded: 1878

Accreditation: Regional
Phone: (412) 396 6000 ▪ (800) 456 0590
Fax: (412) 396 5644
Web site: www.duq.edu

The Division of Continuing Education offers an online Master of Arts in Leadership & Liberal Studies. The School of Nursing offers an RN/BSN and Ph.D. totally online as well as a number of courses for their bachelor's and master's degrees. And the Mylan School of Pharmacy offers a distance-learning Doctor of Pharmacy program designed for working pharmacy practitioners. For information on Dusquesne's short-residency master's in music program, see the listing in the next chapter.

Dyke College
See: David N. Myers College

East Carolina University   M
East Fifth St.
Greenville, NC 27858-4353
Fields offered: Industrial technology (digital communication technology, manufacturing, planning)
Year founded: 1907
Accreditation: Regional
Phone: (252) 328 6704
Web site: www.sit.ecu.edu

A wholly nonresident M.S. in industrial technology with concentrations in digital communication technology, manufacturing, and planning. Students complete all coursework over the Internet. Students with three or more years' experience in the field may take the Practitioner's Option, which excuses them from thesis, internship, and research project, but must take two additional advanced classes and submit a work portfolio.

Eastern Illinois University   B
School of Adult and Continuing Education
600 Lincoln Ave
Charleston, IL 61920
Fields offered: Individualized major
Year founded: 1895
Accreditation: Regional
Phone: (217) 581 5618
Email: lkwoodward@eiu.edu
Web site: www.eiu.edu/~adulted

Bachelor of Arts, with a minimum of 15 units to be earned on campus or at sites approved by the director. This non-traditional program is designed to allow working adults who are 25 years of age or older the chance to complete most of their requirements off-campus, through independent study, equivalency examinations, and credit for life experience. A major is not required. Skills and knowledge acquired by nonacademic means can be evaluated for academic credit.

Eastern Oregon University   B, M
Division of Distance Education (DDE)
1 University Blvd.
La Grande, OR 97850-2889

Fields offered: Business, economics, fire services administration, liberal studies, nursing, philosophy/politics/economics, physical education & health, school administration, teacher education
Year founded: 1929
Accreditation: Regional
Phone: (541) 962 3614 ▪ (800) 452 8639
Fax: (541) 962 3627
Email: jhart@eou.edu
Web site: www2.eou.edu/dde

Eastern Oregon offers B.S. and B.A. degrees by distance learning to students nationwide in the following fields: business & economics, fire services administration, liberal studies (with a concentration in virtually anything), philosophy/politics/economics (combined program), and physical education & health. An A.S. in office administration is also available. Credit is awarded for online coursework, residential coursework, independent study, cooperative work experience, assessment of prior learning, weekend college, and examination. All of these programs may be completed 100% by distance learning. Eastern Oregon does not charge out-of-state tuition. Oregon residents are also eligible for a bachelor's in nursing, an M.S. in social work, and a Master of Teacher Education (M.T.E.) through a mix of distance learning, extension coursework, and short residency.

THE DISCOVER CHANNEL

"In this video, we will learn how centrifugal force works by spinning eggs."

Edith Cowan University   **B, M, D**
International Students Office
Claremont, WA 6010, Australia
Fields offered: See below
Year founded: 1990
Accreditation: International (GAAP)
Phone: +61 (9) 273 8681
Email: extstudi@echidna.cowan.edu.au
Web site: www.cowan.edu.au

Distance-learning methods employed may include workbooks and/or study guides, additional readings, audio-visual materials, online study, and other instructional media. In addition, students may be directed to obtain and read various necessary texts and journal articles. External bachelor's degrees in aboriginal studies, justice studies, psychology, accounting, information systems, management, marketing, advertising, education (with an optional track in special education), nursing (completion program), addiction studies, applied anthropology & sociology, applied women's studies, children & family studies, disability studies, gerontology, health promotion, human services, indigenous studies, justice studies, leisure studies, police studies, psychology, and youth work.

Master's degrees in applied linguistics, business administration (with optional emphasis in health services management, justice administration, or sport management), education (in career education, children with special needs, early childhood studies, educational computing, educational policy & administrative studies, interactive multimedia, language & literacy, mathematics education, music education, religious education, science education, society & environment education, teaching & learning, or technology & enterprise education), health science (with optional emphasis in health promotion or occupational safety & health), medicine for practicing physicians (in family medicine, palliative care, or sports medicine), nursing, accounting, public health, information science, social science (with optional emphasis in development studies or leisure studies), and sport management.

External research Ph.D.'s are available in development studies, education, interdisciplinary studies, nursing, and occupational health & safety. Formerly Western Australian College of Advanced Education.

Empire State College   **B**
Center for Distance Learning
3 Union Ave.
Saratoga Springs, NY 12866-4391
Fields offered: Business, management, accounting, fire service, emergency management, human services, health services, criminal justice, interdisciplinary studies, labor studies, public affairs
Year founded: 1971
Accreditation: Regional
Phone: (518) 587 2100 ▪ (800) 847 3000
Fax: (518) 587 2660
Email: cdl@esc.edu
Web site: www.esc.edu

A part of the State University of New York (SUNY) system, Empire State College has been a longtime leader in individualized academic programs. Through its Center for Distance Learning, students can develop an individualized bachelor's degree program that builds upon their interests, life experiences, needs, and goals in one of the general areas listed above. Coursework is done entirely through independent study guided by a faculty mentor who communicates with the student by phone, mail, fax, or email. The bachelor's degree in business can be earned entirely over the Internet. For information on Empire State's short-residency master's programs, see the next chapter.

Emporia State University   B, M
1200 Commercial
Box 4052
Emporia, KS 66801-5087
Fields offered: Integrated studies, physical education
Year founded: 1863
Accreditation: Regional
Phone: (316) 341 5385
Fax: (316) 341 5744
Email: lifelong@emporia.edu
Web site: lifelong.emporia.edu

Two degree programs are available online: a Bachelor of Integrated Studies (degree completion program) and a Master of Science in physical education.

Excelsior College   A, B, M
7 Columbia Circle
Albany, NY 12203-5159
Fields offered: Business, liberal arts, liberal studies, science, nursing, technology
Year founded: 1784
Accreditation: Regional
Phone: (518) 464 8500 ■ (888) 647 2388
Fax: (518) 464 8777
Web site: www.excelsiorcollege.edu
Please note: Excelsior College was formerly known as Regents College. At the time we went to press, the name change had just been announced, so the transition (updating the school's literature, Web site, etc.) was far from complete. If the new name doesn't seem to be working for you in whatever context you're using it, swapping "Regents" for "Excelsior" will probably solve the problem.

The largest and, along with Thomas Edison State College, the most popular nonresident degree programs in the U.S. Offers associate's and bachelor's degrees in arts, science, business (including accounting, finance, management, and marketing), nursing, and technology (including computer information systems, nuclear engineering, and electronics engineering). Master's degrees in liberal studies and nursing.

Excelsior College itself does not offer distance-learning courses (except for its master's programs); rather it awards degrees to persons who have accumulated sufficient credits by a broad variety of means: Accepts course credit from regionally accredited colleges (both distance and classroom). Offers credit for many noncollege learning experiences, including corporate training programs, military training, and professional licenses. (For example, the technology degree program offers credit for Microsoft

certifications.) Recognizes many equivalency exams (CLEP, DANTES, GRE, etc.) as well as offering its own nationally recognized exam program (see chapter 12, "Equivalency Examinations"). Recognizes portfolios as evaluated through partnerships with Ohio University, Charter Oak State College, and Empire State College. If nonschool learning experiences cannot be assessed easily at a distance, or by exam, the student may go to Albany, New York, for an oral examination.

Excelsior was formerly known as Regents College. It began as an integral part of the University of the State of New York, and the degrees were awarded by the latter. In a controversial move in 1998, Regents College purchased its independence and became a private institution. As part of the separation, it was required to change its name: thus the switch from Regents to Excelsior.

Faith Bible College   B
4501 Shed Rd.
Bossier City, LA 71111
Fields offered: Bible studies/theology, religious education
Year founded: 1976
Accreditation: National (DETC)
Phone: (318) 746 8400
Fax: (318) 747 9634
Email: info@ici.edu

While FBC offers its own unaccredited degrees, it also has a joint degree with Global University of the Assemblies of God, which is accredited by the Distance Education and Training Council. The joint degree is more expensive.

FernUniversität   B, M, D
Feithstrasse 140
D-58084 Hagen, Germany
Fields offered: Arts & social sciences, business & economics, computer science, education, engineering, law, mathematics
Year founded: 1974
Accreditation: International (GAAP)
Phone: +49 (2331) 987 2444
Fax: +49 (2331) 987 399
Email: studentensekretariat@fernuni-hagen.de
Web site: www.fernuni-hagen.de

Germany's only international distance teaching university offers about 1,700 distance courses, leading to the equivalent of bachelor's, master's and doctoral degrees, as well as postdoctoral theses. Fields of study span economics, humanities, and sciences, including computer science, education, history, modern German literature, political science, social behavioral sciences, electrical engineering, math, law, and more. Home-study materials are mainly printed lessons sent by mail, although they may also include complementary materials delivered via Internet, CD-ROM, multimedia, audio- and videotapes, etc. The university operates 64 study centers in Germany, Austria, Switzerland, and Hungary for the assistance and guidance of students. All instruction in German, although a nice color brochure is available in English. More than 3,100 of FernUniversität's over 55,000 students live outside of Germany.

Flinders University   B, M, D

GPO Box 2100
Adelaide, SA 5001, Australia
Fields offered: Special education, nursing,
midwifery, primary health care
Year founded: 1966
Accreditation: International (GAAP)
Phone: +61 (8) 201 2727 ▪ (800) 686 3562
Fax: +61 (8) 201 3177
Email: intl.office@flinders.edu.au
Web site: www.flinders.edu.au

Offers several distance-learning programs: a Bachelor
and Master of Special Education, Bachelor and Master
of Nursing, Bachelor and Master of Midwifery, Master of
Primary Health Care, as well as a Ph.D. in education.
Courses are delivered using Web-based programs and
printed correspondence texts, supplemented by study
guides, other readings, and sometimes audiocassettes
and software.

Florida Gulf Coast University   B, M

Distance Learning Program
10501 FGCU Blvd.
Fort Myers, FL 33908-4500
Fields offered: Business administration, criminal
justice, curriculum & instruction (educational
technology), health science, public administration,
TESOL
Year founded: 1997
Accreditation: Regional
Phone: (941) 590 2315
Email: tdugas@fgcu.edu
Web site: www.fgcu.edu/DL

Distance-learning programs are offered through online
classes, compressed video, television, and traditional
correspondence. Offers B.S. completion programs in
criminal justice and health sciences, an MBA, a Master of
Public Administration (MPA), and M.S. programs in
health science and curriculum & instruction (emphasis
educational technology). A certificate in TESOL for K-12
teachers is also available.

Florida Institute of Technology   M

150 W. University Blvd.
Melbourne, FL 32901
Fields offered: Business administration, public
administration, health management, human
resources, management
Year founded: 1958
Accreditation: Regional
Phone: (407) 674 8000 ▪ (800) 944 4348
Fax: (407) 984 8461
Email: segs@segs.fit.edu
Web site: www.fit.edu

A number of online graduate degree programs in business-
related fields, including an MBA, an M.S. in public administration, an M.S. in health management, an M.S. in
management (seven concentrations), and an M.S. in systems management (two concentrations). In addition to these,
graduate computer and engineering degrees are offered
to military and civilians at 15 locations in Florida, New

Jersey, Alabama, New Mexico, Virginia, Louisiana, and
Maryland. FIT once threatened to sue us for mentioning,
in earlier editions, the circumstances under which the
then-chairman of their board of trustees resigned—an
event described in detail in Florida newspapers at the time,
but we've decided to let the matter rest.

Florida State University   B, M

Tallahassee, FL 32306
Fields offered: Computer science, information
studies, software engineering, criminology,
engineering, information studies, distance learning,
social science
Year founded: 1851
Accreditation: Regional
Phone: (850) 645 0393 ▪ (877) 357 8283
Email: students@oddl.fsu.edu
Web site: www.fsu.edu

For students with an A.A. degree or higher, FSU's "2+2
Distance Learning Initiative" offers a bachelor's degree
completion program in computer science, information
studies, interdisciplinary social science, and software
engineering. Online master's degrees can be earned in
information & library studies, criminal justice studies,
mechanical engineering, and open & distance learning (a
program in collaboration with Open University of the United
Kingdom). Courses leading to a Master's in Engineering
are broadcast by video to industrial, business, and military
sites all over Florida.

Fort Hays State University   B, M

600 Park St.
Hays, KS 67601
Fields offered: General studies, liberal studies
Year founded: 1902
Accreditation: Regional
Phone: (785) 628 4291 ▪ (888) 351 3587
Fax: (785) 628 4037
Email: celliott@fhsu.edu
Web site: www.fhsu.edu

Online degree programs include a Bachelor of General
Studies and a Master of Liberal Studies. Students can
transfer up to 95 credit hours for the B.G.S. and 21 credit
hours for the M.L.S. from any accredited institution. No
ACT, SAT, or graduate exam required.

Franklin University   B, M

201 S. Grant Ave.
Columbus, OH 43215
Fields offered: Business administration, computer
science, health care management, management
information systems, public safety management,
technical management
Accreditation: Regional
Phone: (888) 341 6237
Email: alliance@franklin.edu
Web site: www.alliance.franklin.edu

Offers online B.S. completion programs in the above
fields, in cooperation with a number of community colleges. An online MBA is also available.

General Motors Institute

See: Kettering University

George Fox University   B

Admissions Office
414 North Meridian St. #6306
Newberg, OR 97132-2697
Fields offered: Management & organizational leadership
Year founded: 1891
Accreditation: Regional
Phone: (503) 554 2270 ▪ (888) 888 0178
Fax: (503) 554 3867
Email: conted@georgefoxonline.org
Web site: www.georgefoxonline.org

Offers an online, 18-month B.A. completion program in management & organizational leadership. The program is organized primarily around a cohort model whereby students progress through requirements at a more or less uniform pace.

George Washington University   B, M

GWTV – Distance Learning
801 22nd St. NW, Suite 350
Washington, DC 20052
Fields offered: Educational technology leadership, health sciences, project management
Year founded: 1821
Accreditation: Regional
Phone: (202) 994 8233
Fax: (202) 994 5048
Email: webmaster@gwtv.gwu.edu
Web site: www.gwu.edu/~distance

Offers a bachelor's program in health sciences (with specialization in clinical health sciences, clinical management & leadership, clinical research administration, or EMS management) to professionals who work in the field. The distance-learning M.A. in educational technology is available through a range of nontraditional teaching methods, including cable television, the Internet, computer conferencing, listservs, email, and videocassettes. Also offers a distance-learning M.S. in project management with just a one-week residency requirement in Washington, DC, and an M.S. in health sciences (specialization in clinical leadership) for certified Physician Assistants.

Georgia Institute of Technology   M

Center for Distance Learning
Atlanta, GA 30332
Fields offered: Electrical & computer engineering, environmental engineering, health physics, radiological engineering, industrial engineering, mechanical engineering
Year founded: 1885
Accreditation: Regional
Phone: (404) 894 8572
Fax: (404) 894 8924
Email: cdl@conted.gatech.edu
Web site: www.conted.gatech.edu/distance

This school's distance-learning instruction system allows working professionals to earn master's degrees in the above fields entirely through online (or videotaped) classes and proctored exams from anywhere in the U.S. (and, in some cases, from other countries as well). While the degree is expensive, many companies have tuition-reimbursement plans for their employees.

Glasgow Caledonian University   M

City Campus, Cowcaddens Rd.
Glasgow G4 0BA, United Kingdom
Fields offered: Bulk solids handling technology
Year founded: 1971
Accreditation: International (GAAP)
Phone: +44 (141) 331 3000
Fax: +44 (141) 331 3005
Email: international@gcal.ac.uk
Web site: www.gcal.ac.uk

A Master of Science in bulk solids handling technology is offered through a series of comprehensive distance-learning packages. Offered by the school's Department of Physical Sciences, which in 1993 merged with the Centre for Industrial Bulk Solids Handling, the course of study consists of 12 modules and an industrially based project. While no residency is required, students are welcome to attend any of a number of short courses on the Glasgow campus. Applicants should have an undergraduate degree in an engineering or technological field; experience in bulk solids or a related field will be considered as part of the application.

Global University of the Assemblies of God   B, M

1211 S. Glenstone Ave.
Springfield, MO 65804
Fields offered: Biblical studies, Christian counseling, Christian education, leadership, ministerial studies, missions & evangelism, pastoral ministries, theology
Year founded: 2000
Accreditation: National (DETC)
Phone: (800) 443 1083
Fax: (417) 862 0863
Email: info@globaluniversity.edu
Web site: www.globaluniversity.edu

Offers B.A. degrees in Biblical studies (with specialization in Christian counseling, Christian education, missions & evangelism, pastoral ministries, or theology), Bible & theology, missions, and religious education. M.A. degrees are available in Biblical studies (with optional emphasis in New Testament), Christian counseling, and ministerial studies (with specialization in education, leadership, or missions). All courses can be completed by online study or correspondence; credit can also be earned by examination and for life experience. While the above programs are conducted in English, many courses are available in Spanish, and a special degree—the B.A. in development—can be completed entirely through Spanish coursework. Established in 2000 by the merging of Berean University of the Assemblies of God and ICI University.

Golden Gate University — B, M

536 Mission St.
San Francisco, CA 94105
Fields offered: Accounting, business administration, healthcare administration, finance, marketing, taxation, telecommunications management, public administration
Year founded: 1901
Accreditation: Regional
Phone: (415) 369 5250 ▪ (888) 874 2923
Fax: (415) 227 4502
Email: cybercampus@ggu.edu
Web site: cybercampus.ggu.edu

Golden Gate University's CyberCampus delivers a number of degree programs entirely over the Internet. Master's degrees can be earned in accounting, healthcare administration, finance, marketing, taxation, telecommunications management, and public administration. An online version of Golden Gate's large and well-respected MBA program is also available. At the undergraduate level, a degree completion program is offered for a Bachelor of Public Administration. Courses are taught asynchronously through syllabus/modules and interactive conferences.

Governors State University — B

BOG Program
University Park, IL 60466
Fields offered: Individualized
Year founded: 1969
Accreditation: Regional
Phone: (708) 534 4092 ▪ (800) GSU 8 GSU
Fax: (708) 534 1645
Email: gsubog@govst.edu
Web site: www.govst.edu/bog

B.A. may be earned through weekend, evening, and summer programs, as well as by various telecourses. Students design an individualized major field with faculty assistance. 15 credit hours must be completed through Governors State. These units may be earned through independent study, telecourses, classes offered online, and on- or off-campus courses, so it is possible to earn this degree without ever setting foot on campus. Credit is awarded for nonacademic prior learning and CLEP proficiency exams.

Graduate School of America

See: Capella University

Grand Canyon University — M

3300 West Camelback Rd.
Phoenix, AZ 85017
Fields offered: Executive fire service leadership, teaching
Year founded: 1949
Accreditation: Regional
Phone: (602) 589 2746 ▪ (800) 600 5019
Email: admiss@grand-canyon.edu
Web site: www.grand-canyon.edu

Offers a videocassette-based or online M.A. in teaching, geared to K-12 teachers. An online M.S. in executive fire service leadership is also available.

Grantham College of Engineering — B

34641 Grantham College Rd.
Slidell, LA 70460
Fields offered: Computer science, engineering technology (computer or electronic)
Year founded: 1951
Accreditation: National (DETC)
Phone: (504) 649 4191 ▪ (888) 423 4242
Fax: (504) 649 4183
Email: gce@grantham.edu
Web site: www.grantham.edu

Grantham offers nonresident B.S. degrees in computer science and engineering technology (with specialization in computer engineering technology or electronic engineering technology). The first requires very minimal prior experience; the latter two are geared to students with practical and/or work experience. Students are given up to 15 months to complete each distance-learning semester (8 in all), but the average student takes something closer to 8 months each. Credit granted for prior college work, military and job training, approved exams (CLEP, etc.), and, in the engineering technology program, work experience and laboratory proficiency. All students must have access to an IBM-compatible computer. All lessons are delivered via traditional correspondence, but tests may be submitted by email. Foreign students are welcome, but must be fluent in English. Accredited by the Distance Education and Training Council (DETC).

Greenwich School of Theology — B, M, D

29 Howbeck Lane
Clarborough, Notts DN22 9LW, United Kingdom
Fields offered: Theology
Year founded: 1958
Accreditation: International (GAAP)
Phone: +44 (1777) 703 058
Fax: +44 (1777) 703 526
Email: byrone@netcomuk.com
Web site: www.odlqc.org.uk/green.htm

Offers degrees at all levels in theology, in conjunction with the accredited South African Potchefstroom University for Christian Higher Education. Also accredited by the Open and Distance Learning Quality Council in London. Originally established as the Geneva Theological College, the school affiliated with the unaccredited Greenwich University, located in Hawaii (see listing in chapter 21), and took the name "Greenwich." In 1998, Greenwich School of Theology became an affiliated college of Potchefstroom University for Christian Higher Education, an old (founded 1869) residential university in South Africa, and terminated its relationship with Greenwich in Hawaii. The Greenwich School of Theology conducts training by distance learning, and the degrees are awarded by Potchefstroom. For his help with Greenwich's development, John Bear was offered the honorary presidency of the Greenwich School of Theology, a totally honorary role with no involvement whatsoever in the operation or marketing of the school.

Griffith University   B, M

Nathan
Queensland 4111, Australia
Fields offered: Adult education, justice
administration, education, special education,
technology management
Accreditation: International (GAAP)
Phone: +61 (7) 3382 1339
Email: student_enquiry@gu.edu.au
Web site: www.gu.edu.au

Bachelor of Adult & Vocational Teaching, Bachelor of
Arts, Bachelor of Arts in justice administration, Bachelor
of Education, Master of Special Education, Master of
Technology Management, and various diploma and
certificate programs, all through distance learning.

Griggs University   B

12501 Old Columbia Pike
Silver Spring, MD 20904-6600
Fields offered: Church business management,
religion, religious education, theological studies
Year founded: 1909
Accreditation: National (DETC)
Phone: (301) 680 6570 ▣ (800) 782 4769
Fax: (301) 680 5157
Email: 74617,3325@compuserve.com
Web site: www.griggs.edu

The venerable Home Study International, which has
offered correspondence courses for decades, now has a
degree-granting university, offering a B.A. in religion or
theological studies, and a B.S. in religious education or
church business management. Accredited by the Distance
Education and Training Council (DETC).

Hampton University   B

Hampton, VA 23668
Fields offered: Business, general studies, systems
organization & management
Year founded: 1868
Accreditation: Regional
Phone: (757) 727 5000 ▣ (800) 624 3328
Fax: (757) 727 5085
Web site: www.hamptonu.edu

Bachelor's degrees in the above fields.

Harcourt Learning Direct   A

Student Service Center
Department GDGS80S
925 Oak St.
Scranton, PA 18540-9886
Fields offered: Accounting, applied computer
science, business management, civil engineering
technology, electrical engineering technology,
electronics technology, hospitality management,
industrial engineering technology, mechanical
engineering technology
Year founded: 1890
Accreditation: National (DETC)
Phone: (800) 275 4409
Email: info@harcourt-learning.com
Web site: www.harcourt-learning.com

Part of the world's largest correspondence institution,
ICS Learning Systems; offers a large number of voca-
tionally targeted courses, as well as two associate's degrees,
with a number of specializations. The degrees are an
Associate in Specialized Business, with concentrations in
accounting, applied computer science, business management, management, finance, marketing, or hospitality
management; also, an Associate in Specialized Technology,
with concentrations in civil engineering technology, electrical engineering technology, electronics technology,
industrial engineering technology, and mechanical
engineering technology. Original name: International
Correspondence Schools, established in the late 19th century to offer home study courses to disabled coal miners.

Heriot-Watt University   B, M

U.S. agent: FT Knowledge Inc.
Student Services
2 World Trade Center, Suite 1700
New York, NY 10048
Fields offered: Business administration,
management
Year founded: 1821
Accreditation: International (GAAP)
Phone: (212) 390 5030 ▣ (800) 622 9661
Fax: (212) 344 3469
Email: info@hwmba.net
Web site: www.hwmba.edu

Heriot-Watt offers the only accredited MBA program that
explicitly does not require a bachelor's degree or entrance
examinations and that can be done entirely by home
study. With more than 8,000 students in over 120 countries (including more than 4,000 in the U.S. and Canada),
it is one of the largest MBA programs in the world. The
only requirement for earning the degree is passing nine
rigorous three-hour exams, one for each of the required
nine courses (marketing, economics, accounting, finance,
strategic planning, etc.). The exams are given twice a
year on hundreds of college campuses. Students buy the
courses one at a time, as they are ready for them. The courses
consist of looseleaf textbooks (average: 500 pages) written
by prominent professors specifically for this program.
Courses are not interactive: there are no papers to write,
quizzes, or other assignments, and no thesis. Each course
averages about 160 hours of study time, so the entire
MBA can be completed in one year, but 18 to 24 months
is more common. Hundreds of major corporations recognize
and pay for the degree. An examination-based bachelor's
in management education is also offered in cooperation
with Financial Times Management. Heriot-Watt also
offers a postgraduate diploma in malting & brewing by
distance learning.

Financial Times Management is the sole distributor of
Heriot-Watt courses in North America; there are also
agents and distributors in twenty other countries. For
information on the MBA, write to Financial Times
Management in New York. For information on other programs, write to the main campus: Heriot-Watt University,
Edinburgh EH14 4AS, Scotland, or go to *www.hw.ac.uk*.

Holborn College   B, M, Law

200 Greyhound Rd.
London W14 9RY, United Kingdom
Fields offered: Law, business
Year founded: 1970
Accreditation: International (GAAP)
Phone: +44 (171) 385 3377
Email: hlt@holborncollege.ac.uk
Web site: www.holborncollege.ac.uk
Holborn College offers law degrees at the LL.B. (Honours) and postgraduate LL.M. levels, through an association with the University of Wolverhampton. The LL.B. may qualify graduates to take the Bar in England. Both programs take a minimum of three years to complete, and were originally tutorials for the University of London's exams. Holborn's catalog notes that its degrees, legitimate in their own right, "can also be used by students as an access program" to the prestigious London degrees. The LL.B. can be completed entirely by mail, with the exception of exams held yearly in London, Hong Kong, Kuala Lumpur, and elsewhere by special arrangement.

Holy Apostles College and Seminary

See: International Catholic University

Hope International University   B, M

2500 East Nutwood Ave.
Fullerton, CA 92831
Fields offered: Human development, organizational management, business administration, ministry, intercultural studies
Year founded: 1928
Accreditation: Regional
Phone: (714) 879 3901
Fax: (714) 526 0231
Email: palexander@hiu.edu
Web site: www.hiu.edu
As a degree completion program designed for working adults, Hope International offers a B.S. in human development or organizational management. Distance-learning master's degrees include an MBA in international development or nonprofit management and a Master of Arts/Ministry in intercultural studies. Courses are delivered mostly over the Internet; some video. Programs are Christian-focused.

Howard University   M

Graduate School Office of Admissions
Fourth and College, NW
Washington, DC 20059
Fields offered: Business administration, environmental engineering
Year founded: 1867
Accreditation: Regional
Phone: (202) 806 7793
Fax: (202) 462 4053
Email: hugsadmission@howard.edu
Web site: www.howard.edu
Offers an MBA and master's in environmental engineering entirely through online study.

ICI University

See: Global University of the Assemblies of God

Illinois Institute of Technology   M

3300 South Federal St.
Chicago, IL 60616
Fields offered: Chemistry, health physics
Year founded: 1890
Accreditation: Regional
Phone: (312) 567 3167
Fax: (312) 567 5913
Email: hewitt@iit.edu
Web site: www.iit-online.iit.edu
An M.S. in analytical chemistry or an M.S. in materials & chemical synthesis can be earned entirely over the Internet or by video. Both programs take about two and a half years of part-time study. The M.S. in health physics requires one week of residency for a short course; the other 10 courses are offered online.

Indiana State University   M

Terre Haute, IN 47809
Fields offered: Criminology, human resource development
Year founded: 1865
Accreditation: Regional
Phone: (812) 237 2642 ▪ (800) 444 4723
Fax: (812) 237 4292
Email: admissions@indstate.edu
Web site: www-isu.indstate.edu
An M.S. or M.A. in criminology and an M.S. in human resource development is delivered by Internet and/or televised courses broadcast at 300 sites all over Indiana. Indiana State also offers some short-residency degree programs, including a Ph.D. in technology management. See the next chapter for details.

Indiana University   A, B, M

School of Continuing Studies
Owen Hall 001

Bloomington, IN 47405
Fields offered: General studies, labor studies, adult education, language & literacy education, nursing
Year founded: 1912
Accreditation: Regional
Phone: (812) 855 8995 ▪ (800) 334 1011
Fax: (812) 855 8997
Email: scs@indiana.edu
Web site: scs.indiana.edu

Indiana University has been offering distance-learning courses since 1912. Bachelor's degrees are offered in general studies and in labor studies; master's in adult education, language & literacy education, nursing (requires a prior BSN), and therapeutic recreation. Programs employ the full spectrum of communications possibilities.

Institute for Educational Studies M

8115 McCormick Ave.
Oakland, CA 94605
Fields offered: Integrative learning
Year founded: 1996
Accreditation: Regional
Phone: (510) 638 2300
Fax: (510) 638 4242
Email: ties@endicott.edu
Web site: ties-edu.org

The M.A. in integrative learning is a three-semester program focusing on building a "compassionate community—drawing forth the inherent wisdom of each participant through the influences of spirit, mind, and body." "Colloquium-based learning" can take place entirely over the Internet; two week-long residential seminars are optional. Students must complete a research-based paper or project. Degree is awarded by the regionally accredited Endicott College in Beverly, MA.

Institute of Transpersonal Psychology M

744 San Antonio Rd.
Palo Alto, CA 94303
Fields offered: Transpersonal psychology, transpersonal studies
Year founded: 1975
Accreditation: Regional
Phone: (650) 493 4430
Fax: (650) 493 6835
Email: itpinfo@itp.edu
Web site: www.itp.edu

This school offers a Master of Transpersonal Psychology, an M.A. in transpersonal studies, and various certificate programs (with concentrations in fields such as women's spirituality, wellness counseling, and creative development). Study generally begins with a seminar held somewhere near the student's home area, and continues through mentored independent studies.

International Catholic University M

Box 495
Notre Dame, IN 46556
Fields offered: Philosophy, theology
Year founded: 1994
Accreditation: Regional

Phone: (800) 771 7346
Email: icu@skyenet.net
Web site: www.catholicity.com/school/icu

Offers distance-learning M.A. programs in philosophy and theology, in partnership with Holy Apostles College & Seminary in Connecticut. ICU designs the coursework (video, required readings, etc.), and HAC&S provides the professor who guides the student's progress and determines the grade. Regionally accredited HAC&S grants the degree.

International Management Centres Inc. B, M, D

Marriotts, Castle St.
Buckingham MK18 1BP, United Kingdom
Fields offered: Management, business administration, training & development, professional studies
Year founded: 1964
Accreditation: National (DETC)
Phone: +44 (1280) 817 222
Fax: +44 (1280) 813 297
Email: imc@imc.org.uk
Web site: www.i-m-c.org

The parent corporation for a worldwide network of business and management schools, including the Canadian School of Management and the University of Action Learning in the U.S. (see listings in this chapter). Offers degrees at all levels in management, business administration, training & development, and professional studies. Under the school's philosophy of "action learning," the employer-sponsored programs are based in the workplace where lessons can be directly applied. Apparently one of the few doctorate-granting schools accredited by the Distance Education and Training Council (DETC).

International School of Information Management

See: ISIM University

International University College

See: Jones International University

International University (Colorado)

See: Jones International University

Internet Distance Education Associates

See: Advance Learning Network

ISIM University M

501 South Cherry St.
Room 350—Admissions Office
Denver, CO 80246
Fields offered: Business administration, information management, information technology
Year founded: 1987
Accreditation: National (DETC)
Phone: (303) 333 4224 ▪ (800) 441 4746
Fax: (303) 336 1144
Email: admissions@isim.edu
Web site: www.isimu.edu

An M.S. in information management, an M.S. in information technology, and an MBA are offered via an electronic campus, where instructor-guided learning takes place using the school's own telecommunications network and computer bulletin-board service. A thesis or major independent study project is required of every student. Formerly called International School of Information Management. ISIM University is a division of Cardean University, a subsidiary of UNext.com, a large education corporation.

James Cook University   M, D
Townsville, Queensland 4811, Australia
Fields offered: Social policy, social work
Year founded: 1961
Accreditation: International (GAAP)
Phone: +61 (7) 4781 4407
Fax: +61 (7) 4781 5988
Email: internationalaffairs@jcu.edu.au
Web site: www.oia.jcu.edu.au

M.S. programs in social policy and social work are available by distance learning; coursework is delivered largely via printed correspondence materials, with some audiovisual support. It is also possible to complete the preliminary research coursework for a Ph.D. in community welfare and social work through distance learning; the subsequent dissertation may then very likely be undertaken through a nonresidential arrangement of some kind. Contact the school for details.

Jones International University   B, M
9697 East Mineral Ave.
Englewood, CO 80112
Fields offered: Business administration, business communication
Year founded: 1995
Accreditation: Regional
Phone: (303) 784 8045 ▩ (800) 811 5663
Fax: (303) 784 8547
Email: info@international.edu
Web site: www.international.edu

In 1999 Jones International University became the first completely virtual university to be accredited by one of the six regional accrediting agencies. Offers an MBA, as well as a B.A. and M.A. in business communication. All discussions, interactions, lectures, and assignments are over the Internet. Formerly known as International University, which in turn was originally International University College.

Judson College   B
302 Bibb St.
Marion, AL 36756
Fields offered: Business administration, management information systems, criminal justice, elementary education, English, history, individualized major, music, music education, psychology, religious education, secondary education
Year founded: 1838
Accreditation: Regional
Phone: (334) 683 5169 ▩ (800) 447 9472
Fax: (334) 683 5147

Email: adultstudies@future.judson.edu
Web site: www.judson.edu

Wholly nonresident bachelor's degrees in the above fields, for women over the age of 21 only, through an individualized study program based on a learning contract. Credit for prior life learning through portfolio assessment, standard equivalency exams, and proficiency tests prepared by Judson faculty.

Kansas State University   B, M
13 College Court
Manhattan, KS 66506
Fields offered: Interdisciplinary social science, agriculture, animal sciences & industry, engineering, business, industrial/organizational psychology
Year founded: 1863
Accreditation: Regional
Phone: (785) 532 5686 ▩ (800) 622 2578
Fax: (785) 532 5637
Email: info@dce.ksu.edu
Web site: www.dce.ksu.edu

Kansas State offers a degree completion program for a B.S. in interdisciplinary social science, animal sciences & industry, or general business. Students may earn credit through audio and video courses, Internet courses, and/or courses taken at other universities. Master's programs include agribusiness, engineering (electrical, civil, chemical, and software), and industrial/organizational psychology.

Kaplan College   A, B, Law
1801 Clint Moore Rd., Suite 215
Boca Raton, FL 33487
Fields offered: Criminal justice, management, information technology, nursing, law
Year founded: 1976
Accreditation: National (DETC)
Phone: (561) 994 2522 ▩ (800) 669 2555
Fax: (561) 988 2223
Email: info@kaplancollege.com
Web site: www.kaplancollege.com

Owned and operated by the very large Kaplan test preparation company which is, itself, a part of the very much larger Washington Post company. Offers bachelor's degrees in criminal justice, management (emphasis: applied management or information technology management), and nursing (for registered nurses), as well as diploma programs in paralegal studies and nursing-related legal issues. A division of Kaplan College called Concord Law School offers an online J.D. that qualifies its graduates to sit for the California Bar exam; more information about this program can be found in chapter 25, "Law Schools." The "Executive" J.D. is designed for business managers interested in learning about but not practicing law. All of Kaplan's programs are delivered through their Web site.

Keele University   M
Postgraduate Admissions & Recruiting Office
Department of Academic Affairs
Staffordshire ST5 5BG, United Kingdom
Fields offered: Advanced therapeutics, business administration (emphasis

health/population/nutrition in developing countries), educational improvement & effectiveness, education management, European industrial relations & human resource management, human resources in health, industrial relations, pharmacy
Year founded: 1949
Accreditation: International (GAAP)
Phone: +44 (1782) 584 002
Fax: +44 (1782) 632 343
Email: aaa12@admin.keele.ac.uk
Web site: www.keele.ac.uk

Master's degrees in the above fields tailored to working professionals seeking career development. While courses are generally available only to persons resident in Great Britain, exceptions can be made. A variety of postgraduate diploma and certificate programs are also available.

Keller Graduate School of Management   M

One Tower Lane
Oakbrook Terrace, IL 60181
Fields offered: Business administration, telecommunications management, accounting & financial management, information system management, project management, human resource management
Year founded: 1973
Accreditation: Regional
Phone: (630) 574 1960 ▦ (888) 535 5378
Fax: (630) 574 1969
Email: sbranick@keller.edu
Web site: www.keller.edu

Offers master's degrees in the above fields, entirely online, and in 32 regional centers around the United States. (Keller acquired the multi-campus DeVry Institute, now DeVry University, in 1987.) Students read course materials, write papers, conduct applied research, and take exams, all online.

Kentucky Commonwealth
Virtual University   A, B, M

Fields offered: Communication disorders, information technology, nursing
Year founded: 1999
Accreditation: Regional
Phone: (877) 740 4357
Email: kcvu@mail.state.ky.us
Web site: www.kcvu.org

A clearinghouse for online courses offered by public and private universities and colleges in the state of Kentucky. Available degree programs include an associate in arts, a master's in communication disorders, an A.S. in IT, and a bachelor's in nursing.

Kettering University   M

1700 West Third Ave.
Flint, MI 48504
Fields offered: Automotive systems engineering, engineering, manufacturing management, manufacturing systems engineering, mechanical design, operations management

Year founded: 1919
Accreditation: Regional
Phone: (810) 762 7494 ▦ (800) 955 4464
Fax: (810) 762 9935
Email: gradoff@kettering.edu
Web site: www.kettering.edu

Formerly known as General Motors Institute, Kettering offers three graduate degrees: an M.S. in engineering (with specialization in automotive systems engineering, manufacturing systems engineering, and mechanical design), an M.S. in manufacturing management, and an M.S. in operations management. These programs are offered through learning centers located at GM plants and other facilities around the country. Learning is video-based, and the school stresses that this is a rigorous program. Establishment of a learning center is a function of demand; if enough people in a work place are interested in the program, a learning center can be established there. If only a few people are interested, Kettering may be able to arrange for them to study at a nearby site.

Lakehead University   B, M

955 Oliver Rd.
Thunder Bay, Ontario P7B 5E1, Canada
Fields offered: Education, forestry, general studies, nursing, social work
Accreditation: International (GAAP)
Phone: +1 (807) 346 7730
Fax: +1 (807) 343 8008
Web site: www.lakeheadu.ca

Bachelor's in general studies, education, social work, and nursing; master's in education and forestry. Each course package includes a manual, audio- and/or videocassettes, and possibly supplementary reading and self-test materials. Students mail in up to six assignments per course, and take examinations on specified dates at about 30 locations in northern Ontario and other Canadian locations by special arrangement. Students are encouraged to participate in group tutorials through telephone conferences.

Lansbridge University   M

10 Knowledge Park Dr., Suite 120
Fredericton, New Brunswick E3C 2M7, Canada
Fields offered: Business administration
Year founded: 1999
Accreditation: International (GAAP)
Phone: +1 (506) 443 0780 ▦ (800) 980 9926
Fax: +1 (506) 459 2909
Email: admissions@lansbridge.com
Web site: www.lansbridge.com

Owned and operated by Learnsoft Corporation, claims to be "Canada's first Internet University." The name was changed from Unexus University following a nudge from the unconnected Unext company, which also operates distance-learning schools. Online executive MBA program is designed specifically for professionals in a technology or technology-affected industry. There is a dual degree option with the Arthur D. Little School of Management, in which one simultaneously works on the Lansbridge MBA and the M.S. in management from ADL. Intriguingly, the Web site description of this joint program does not mention the tuition, but offers information on how to borrow money to pay for it.

Laurentian University   B

Centre for Continuing Education
935 Ramsey Lake Rd.
Sudbury, Ontario P3E 2C6, Canada
Fields offered: Family life studies & human sexuality, gerontology, liberal sciences, native studies, nursing, psychology, religious studies, social work, sociology, women's studies
Accreditation: International (GAAP)
Phone: +1 (705) 673 6569
Fax: +1 (705) 675 4897
Email: cce_l@nickel.laurentian.ca
Web site: www.laurentian.ca

Canada's largest bilingual distance-education provider offers courses in English and French through a wide variety of methods, including printed course materials, teleconferencing, and the Internet. Bachelor's degrees available in the above fields.

Lee University   B

100 Eighth St., NE
Cleveland, TN 37311
Fields offered: Christian ministry
Year founded: 1918
Accreditation: Regional
Phone: (423) 614 8370 ▪ (800) 256 5916
Fax: (423) 614 8377
Email: inquiry@leeonline.org
Web site: www.leeonline.org

Lee University offers an external studies program based entirely on online study for those who cannot pursue a traditional residential program; its basic purpose is to prepare Christian workers in the area of biblical studies, theology, pastoral studies, music, missions, and evangelism.

Lehigh University   M

Office of Distance Education
205 Johnson Hall
36 University Dr.
Bethlehem, PA 18015
Fields offered: Chemistry, chemical engineering, molecular biology, quality engineering, technology management, environmental engineering, business administration
Year founded: 1865
Accreditation: Regional
Phone: (610) 758 5794
Fax: (610) 758 6269
Email: online@lesn.lehigh.edu
Web site: www.distance.lehigh.edu

M.S. in chemistry, chemical engineering, pharmaceutical chemistry, molecular biology, quality engineering, polymer science & engineering, management of technology, and environmental engineering, as well as an MBA, through a highly innovative program that is, at present, available only to corporate-sponsored groups. Classes are delivered nationwide via satellite television, and students can interact in real time by in-class phone bridge, fax, or online message center/electronic whiteboard.

Leicester Polytechnic

See: De Montfort University

Lesley University   M

29 Everett St.
Cambridge, MA 02138-2790
Fields offered: Education, independent study (individualized major), management
Year founded: 1909
Accreditation: Regional
Phone: (617) 349 8320 ▪ (800) 999 1959
Fax: (617) 349 8313
Email: info@mail.lesley.edu
Web site: www.lesley.edu

Wholly nonresident master's degrees (M.A., M.Ed., or M.S. in management) are offered through the Independent Study Degree program, which offers individualized degree programs that can be studied from anywhere in the world. Students work with a team of faculty advisors and are encouraged to concentrate on a specialized field that might not be available in a traditional program. Also offers a master's in technology in education entirely over the Internet. The program includes courses in emerging technologies, curriculum areas and issues, emphasizing technology as a catalyst for educational reform. Lesley's short-residency programs are described in the next chapter. Formerly Lesley College.

Loma Linda University   M

School of Public Health
Office of Extended Programs
Nichol Hall, #1706
Loma Linda, CA 92350
Fields offered: Public health
Year founded: 1905
Accreditation: Regional
Phone: (909) 558 4595 ▪ (800) 854 5661
Fax: (909) 558 4577
Email: sphinfo@sph.llu.edu
Web site: www.llu.edu

The Extended Program at Loma Linda University's School of Public Health offers a unique and practical way for midcareer health professionals to obtain a Master of Public Health (M.P.H.) degree in either health promotion or health administration while maintaining their present employment. The format includes a combination of independent study (pre- and post-lecture assignments) and extensive student/instructor contact. The student is not required to spend time on campus at LLU. Instead, instructors travel to various sites in the United States to meet with students in intensive three-day class sessions; one per quarter at each site. The program is geared to the needs of physicians, dentists, nurses, and other health professionals who wish to become qualified to organize health programs, engage in health promotion activities, and so on.

Loyola University (Louisiana)   M
6363 St. Charles Ave.
Box 67
New Orleans, LA 70118
Fields offered: Criminal justice, pastoral studies, nursing, religious education
Year founded: 1912
Accreditation: Regional
Phone: (504) 865 3728 ▪ (800) 777 5469
Fax: (504) 865 2066
Email: lim@loyno.edu
Web site: www.loyno.edu

Master of Religious Education or of Pastoral Studies, through off-campus programs administered through host sponsoring agencies, typically Roman Catholic dioceses. Students meet in their host site to view videotaped lectures, discuss assigned reading, and get assistance. Additional coursework is done as independent study; no visit to campus is required. Loyola also offers some off-campus programs for Louisiana residents only: a B.S. in nursing for licensed RNs, and a Bachelor of Criminal Justice for Louisiana police officers.

Lund Virtual University
Box 118
Lund 221 00, Sweden
Year founded: 1666
Accreditation: International (GAAP)
Web site: lvunt.citu.lu.se/lvudemo

The good news is that Sweden's very old and traditional Lund University has established LVU to offer hundreds of courses, in the English language, to online students worldwide. They say that "you will find everything you need [on the Web]: course literature, lectures, exercises, workgroups and examinations." The better news is that "the education at LVU is free of charge for the citizen of the world." But the disappointing news is that the Web site was only barely operational at press time, with most of the links inoperative, so our information now is very sparse. But the price is right, so it is worth checking back.

Macquarie University   B, M, D, Law
Centre for Open Education
Building X5B
Sydney, NSW 2109, Australia
Fields offered: See below
Year founded: 1964
Accreditation: International (GAAP)
Phone: +61 (2) 9850 7470
Fax: +61 (2) 9850 7480
Email: coe@mq.edu.au
Web site: www.coe.mq.edu.au

A number of degrees are offered through distance-learning methods that include specially prepared study guides, audiocassettes, assigned readings, and regular written assignments. While the programs are designed for Australian residents, applicants from abroad are admitted if they have proper qualifications (contact school for details). At the bachelor's level, programs include the B.A. in ancient history, early childhood education, English, European languages, modern history, and politics; Bachelor

of Education (in early childhood education); Bachelor of Laws (LL.B.); and the B.S. in biology, earth & planetary sciences (with emphasis in geology or geophysics), and human geography. Master's programs offered in applied linguistics (with optional emphasis in literacy or TESOL), applied statistics, communication disorders, environmental & life sciences, early childhood education, early Christian & Jewish studies, history, modern history, commercial law, early childhood education, environmental & local government law, financial services law, geoscience, geology, paleobiology, and speech & language processing. Research Ph.D. programs are available in early childhood education and in environmental & life sciences.

Madurai Kamaraj University   B, M, Law
Directorate of Distance Education
Palkalainagar
Madurai 625 021, Tamil Nadu, India
Fields offered: Advertising & public relations, business administration, commerce, computer science, economics, English literature, entrepreneurship, Gandhian thought, history, journalism & mass communication, labour management, laws, library & information science, mathematics, philosophy & religion, political science, public administration, social science, sociology, Tamil literature
Year founded: 1971
Accreditation: International (GAAP)
Phone: +91 (45) 858 471
Fax: +91 (45) 0452 859 185

Madurai Kamaraj University offers a variety of examination-based (or, in the case of the master's degrees, sometimes research-based) programs in both English and Tamil. The university has tentative plans for a U.S. agency. Three-year B.A. programs are available in economics, English literature, history, political science, social science, and Tamil literature. Also available are the B.S. in mathematics or computer science, the one-year B.Lit. (Bachelor of Letters) in Tamil, the BBA, the Bachelor of General Laws (B.G.L.), the Bachelor of Library & Information Science (B.L.I.Sc.), and the Bachelor of Commerce (B.Com.). M.A. programs are available in advertising & public relations, economics, English literature, Gandhian thought, history, journalism & mass communication, labour studies, philosophy & religion, political science, public administration, sociology, and Tamil literature. An M.S. in mathematics is also available. Professional master's degrees available by examination include the Master of Bank Management, the MBA, the Master of Commerce, the Master of Labour Management, the Master of Library & Information Science, and the Master of Tourism Management. The Master of Philosophy (M.Phil.) is a post-master's research degree available in commerce, economics, education, English, entrepreneurship, Gandhian thought, history, labour studies, mathematics, political science, public administration, and Tamil.

Maharishi International University
See: Maharishi University of Management

Maharishi University of Management   M

1000 North 4th St.
Fairfield, IA 52557
Fields offered: Business administration
Year founded: 1971
Accreditation: Regional
Phone: (515) 472 7000
Fax: (515) 472 1189
Email: admissions@mum.edu
Web site: www.mum.edu

Founded by the Maharishi Mahesh Yogi, this nontraditional business school offers an MBA entirely by distance learning. Formerly Maharishi International University.

Manchester Metropolitan University   B

All Saints Building
Manchester M15 6BH, United Kingdom
Fields offered: Fashion, geographic information systems, leadership
Year founded: 1970
Accreditation: International (GAAP)
Phone: +44 (161) 247 2000
Fax: +44 (161) 247 6390
Email: educational-services@mmu.ac.uk.
Web site: www.mmu.ac.uk

Offered via distance learning is an M.S. in geographic information systems and a bachelor's degree in the fields of fashion marketing and clothing manufacture. Applicants for the B.A. in clothing should hold the school's diplomas in Clothing and Footwear Institute, parts I & II; the program takes a year, culminating in an honors dissertation. The B.A. in practitioner leadership is offered largely through distance learning, with required one-day workshops approximately every ten weeks. This degree program is designed for people working in management in the healthcare field. Assessment is continuous, and includes project reports, journals, case studies, research reports, and other assignments.

Marist College   M

290 North Rd.
Poughkeepsie, NY 12601
Fields offered: Business administration
Year founded: 1946
Accreditation: Regional
Phone: (914) 575 3000
Fax: (914) 471 6213
Email: admissions@marist.edu
Web site: www.marist.edu

Offers a totally online MBA program. Eight-week courses are taken sequentially, not concurrently.

Marlboro College   M

Graduate Center
28 Vernon St., Suite 5
Brattleboro, VT 05301
Fields offered: Internet strategy management, Internet engineering, teaching with Internet technologies
Year founded: 1946
Accreditation: Regional
Phone: (802) 258 9200 ▪ (888) 258 5665
Fax: (802) 258 9201
Email: gradcenter@marlboro.edu
Web site: www.gradcenter.marlboro.edu

The Graduate Center of Marlboro College offers a Master of Science in both Internet strategy management and Internet engineering, as well as a Master of Arts in teaching with Internet technologies. This program takes place every other weekend and is completely online. To qualify for the ISM and MAT programs, students must have a B.A. and some familiarity with computers and the Internet. To qualify for the MSIE program, students must have a B.A., programming experience, and command of at least one programming language.

Medical College of Georgia   B

Department of Radiologic Sciences
Bldg. AE-1003
Augusta, GA 30912-0600
Fields offered: Radiologic sciences
Year founded: 1828
Accreditation: Regional
Phone: (706) 721 3691
Fax: (706) 721 8293
Email: gpassmor@mail.mcg.edu
Web site: www.mcg.edu/sah/RadSci

Offers a B.S. completion ("2+2") program in radiologic sciences which may be completed off-campus; students must have access to a suitable work environment and possess at least 60 hours of liberal arts credit to qualify for the program. Concentrations are available in diagnostic medical sonography, medical dosimetry, nuclear medicine technology, radiography, and radiation therapy technology. Credit may be awarded based on prior certifications.

Memorial University of Newfoundland   B

Division of Continuing Studies
Room E2000, G. A. Hickman Building
St. John's, NF A1B 3X8, Canada
Fields offered: Business administration, commerce, nursing, social work, technology
Accreditation: International (GAAP)
Phone: +1 (709) 737 8700
Email: cstudies@morgan.ucs.mun.ca
Web site: www.ce.mun.ca

This school offers bachelor's degrees in the above fields, as well as a number of certificate and diploma programs (business administration, public administration, Newfoundland studies, municipal administration, and criminology) through distance learning. Students study independently, either online or by completing correspondence assignments at home supported by video- and/or audiotapes, as well as teleconferencing sessions. Assessment is by assignments and examination.

Mercy College   B, M

555 Broadway
Dobbs Ferry, NY 10522
Fields offered: Business, psychology, computer science, banking, e-commerce, marketing

Year founded: 1950
Accreditation: Regional
Phone: (914) 693 7600 ▪ (800) 637 2969
Fax: (914) 674 7382
Email: admissions@merlin.mercynet.edu
Web site: www.mercynet.edu

Mercy's online campus, known as "MerLIN," offers an associate's in liberal studies, bachelor's degrees in business, psychology, and computer science, and master's degrees in direct marketing, banking, business administration, and e-commerce.

Monash University   B, M, D

Distance Education Centre
Gippsland Campus
Northways Rd.
Churchill, Victoria 3842, Australia
Fields offered: See below
Year founded: 1961
Accreditation: International (GAAP)
Phone: +61 (3) 9902 6200
Fax: +61 (3) 9902 6300
Email: course.inquiries@celts.monash.edu.au
Web site: www.monash.edu.au/de

Monash offers a wide range of bachelor's and master's degree programs wholly by distance education. Coursework is accomplished through a range of methods, including audio- and videotape, written lessons, online study, and correspondence. Foreign students are welcome, although those for whom English is not a first language need to prove fluency. Most degrees may be completed without campus visits, although some (notably science or engineering programs) may require a fixed or negotiable amount of residency.

Bachelor's offered in Australian studies, communication, community studies, gender studies, history & politics, Indonesian, journalism, Koorie studies, mass communications, psychology, psychology & humanities, sociology & social research, writing, behavioral science, business (in banking & finance or retail management), business & commerce (in accounting, business law, economics, e-commerce, human resources, international management, marketing, services management, or tourism), computing (with an optional minor in multimedia technology), educational studies, engineering (in civil engineering, electrical engineering, information engineering, interdisciplinary engineering, mechanical engineering, or mechatronics), multimedia computing, nursing (for registered nurses), applied biology, applied chemistry, applied statistics, biotechnology, environmental management, human physiology, mathematics & modeling, resource & environmental management, social welfare (with optional specialization in community studies, Koorie studies, psychology, or sociology), and social work. Dual-degree tracks are encouraged.

Master's degrees offered in applied linguistics, bioethics, business (in retail and wholesale), business systems, clinical medicine (for licensed physicians), diplomacy & trade, education (with an optional specialization in international education), engineering & maintenance management, family medicine (for licensed physicians), general practice psychiatry (for licensed physicians), health services management, information management (with specialization in decision support systems, electronic record keeping & archiving, information management, information systems development, information technology management, library & information services, or multimedia), information technology, multimedia computing, network computing, nursing (for registered nurses), occupational & environmental health, psychology (with emphasis in counseling or health), public policy & management, rural health, and transport & traffic. A variety of postgraduate certificates and diplomas are also available in fields such as child psychotherapy, tourism management, civil ceremonies, forensic medicine, and health informatics. It may also be possible to negotiate research doctorates on a case-by-case basis.

Montana State University—Billings   B

MSU-B Online Coordinator
1500 North 30th St., Apsaruke 116
Billings, MT 59101-0298
Fields offered: Communication, liberal studies
Accreditation: Regional
Phone: (406) 657 2294
Fax: (406) 657 2254
Email: klacy@msubillings.edu
Web site: www.msubonline.org

Offers a B.A. in communication and B.S. in liberal studies (also available as an accelerated degree completion program) entirely through online study.

Montana State University
College of Technology   B

P.O. Box 6010
Great Falls, MT 59406
Fields offered: General studies
Year founded: 1932
Accreditation: Regional
Phone: (406) 771 4300 ▪ (800) 446 2698
Email: information@msugf.edu
Web site: www.msugf.edu

Offers a B.A. in general studies; students may transfer in a substantial amount of prior credit, then complete remaining degree requirements through a mix of life experience evaluation, online coursework, residential coursework, and credit by examination.

Montana State University—Northern   B

College of Nursing
P.O. Box 6010
Great Falls, MT 59406
Fields offered: Nursing
Accreditation: Regional
Phone: (406) 771 4437 ▪ (800) 446 2698
Email: inquiry@msunonline.org
Web site: www.msunonline.org

Offers an online BSN completion program to registered nurses. Other online programs are under development.

Monterrey Institute for Graduate Studies   M, D

The Center of University Studies
Virtual Graduate School (MIGS)
511 N.E. Third Ave., 2nd Floor
Ft. Lauderdale, FL 33301
Fields offered: See below
Year founded: 1998
Accreditation: Confirmation Pending
Phone: (954) 572 5493 ▪ (800) 459 1738
Fax: (954) 742 3306
Web site: www.degree.com

The online, U.S.-based graduate school of Centro de Estudios Universitarios (CEU), a 30-year-old school in Monterrey, Mexico. Offers master's and doctorates entirely through online study with no required residency. Instruction is available in English and Spanish.

M.S. degrees are offered in business (with emphasis in e-commerce, financial services, healthcare administration, human resource management, international business, management, management of technology, or sales & marketing management), education (with emphasis in educational leadership, educational psychology, exceptional education, or instruction & learning), and psychology (with emphasis in addiction, behavioral science, criminal justice, health psychology, or social & family systems; the Web site stresses that this program is not designed to fulfill counseling licensure requirements). A bachelor's degree is not necessarily required for admission.

Ph.D. programs are available in business (with emphasis in finance, financial services, international business, management, marketing, or organizational behavior), education (with emphasis in educational leadership, educational psychology, exceptional education, or higher education), health sciences research, and psychology (with emphasis in behavioral healthcare, chemical dependency, criminal justice & forensic psychology, geriatric psychology, health psychology, management & evaluation, management psychology, psychopathology, social & family systems, social & personality psychology, or spiritual psychology; the Web site stresses that this is not a clinical program). Advanced standing may be granted to students who have achieved ABD status in another accredited program.

Morehead State University   M

150 University Blvd.
Morehead, KY 40351
Fields offered: Business administration
Year founded: 1922
Accreditation: Regional
Phone: (606) 783 2221 ▪ (800) 585 6781
Fax: (606) 783 5025
Email: admissions@morehead-st.edu
Web site: www.morehead-st.edu

Morehead's entire MBA program is offered online or via two-way interactive audio/video at a variety of sites in the eastern Kentucky service area. Those persons with undergraduate degrees in business disciplines may complete the MBA degree with a minimum of 36 semester hours; 50 hours for those whose degrees are in other areas.

Murdoch University   B, M

External Studies Unit
90 South St.
Murdoch, WA 6150, Australia
Fields offered: See below
Year founded: 1973
Accreditation: International (GAAP)
Phone: +61 (8) 9360 2498
Email: p_martin@cleo.murdoch.edu.au
Web site: www.murdoch.edu.au

This large university offers degree programs through correspondence and online study to students worldwide. Most programs described below may be completed with no campus residency whatsoever.

Murdoch offers bachelor's programs in Aboriginal and Islander studies, Asian studies, communication studies, education, English & comparative literature, general studies, history, philosophy, politics & international studies, theology, women's studies, applied computational physics, chemistry, computer science, education, environmental science, general studies, mathematics & statistics, mineral science (emphasis in extractive metallurgy), sustainable development, education (with emphasis in primary or secondary education), applied science, policy studies (in city policy, public policy, or science & technology policy), computer studies, development studies, ecological public health, ecologically sustainable development, economics, education studies (with optional emphasis on teaching languages other than English), engineering, software engineering, environmental impact assessment, environmental science, professional studies, social research & evaluation, sociology, and theology.

Master's programs in Asian studies, city policy, development studies, ecological public health, ecologically sustainable development, science & technology policy, environmental science, renewable energy technology, telecommunications management, education (in primary or secondary education), software engineering, and veterinary studies (in small animal medicine).

National American College   B

321 Kansas City St.
Rapid City, SD 57701
Fields offered: Applied management, business administration (accounting), computer information systems, computer technology, financial accounting, financial management, management information systems (network management, Microsoft), managerial accounting, marketing
Year founded: 1941
Accreditation: Regional
Phone: (605) 394 4827 ▪ (800) 843 8892
Fax: (605) 394 4871
Web site: www.nationalcollege.edu

Offers online bachelor's degrees in the above fields, as well as a number of associate's degrees.

National Distance Education Centre (Ireland)   B, M

Dublin City University
Glasnevin, Dublin 9, Ireland

Fields offered: Humanities, information technology, nursing, operations management
Year founded: 1982
Accreditation: International (GAAP)
Phone: +353 (1) 704 5813
Fax: +353 (1) 704 5494
Email: ndec@dcu.ie
Web site: www.dcu.ie/ndec

This program offers a humanities-centered B.A. in Arts (comprising studies in history, literature, philosophy, psychology, and sociology), as well as a B.S. in information technology, a Bachelor of Nursing Studies, an M.S. in operations management, and an M.S. in management & applications of information technology in accounting. Students register as a student at one of six Irish universities (Dublin City University, St. Patrick's College at Maynooth, University College Cork, University College Galway, Trinity College, or University of Limerick), but all study a common program administered by the National Distance Education Centre. Courses are presented in modules, allowing students to tailor the rate at which they progress through the program—it is possible to finish in three years, and 85% of students finish within six. Students who can demonstrate prior learning may be exempted from up-to-four modules; such exemptions will be considered on a case-by-case basis. Coursework is done entirely at a distance, although theoretically one is supposed to be a resident of Ireland. Students who move out of Ireland during their course of study are required to maintain an Irish address for correspondence.

National Extension College

18 Brooklands Ave.
Cambridge CB2 2HN, United Kingdom
Accreditation: International (GAAP)
Phone: +44 (1223) 450 200
Fax: +44 (1223) 313 586
Email: info@nec.ac.uk
Web site: www.nec.ac.uk

While this school does not offer any degree programs of its own, it does provide full tutoring and coursework for persons enrolled in the following University of London programs: B.A. in English, French, geography, German, Italian, philosophy, Spanish & Latin American studies, and joint modern languages (French & German, German & Italian, or Italian & French); B.S. in economics, management, and management & law; Bachelor of Laws; and Bachelor of Divinity (B.D.). Students must first register with the University of London, then they can complete their studies with the extra guidance provided by NEC. The degree is awarded by London.

National Fire Academy   B

16825 South Seton Ave.
Emmitsburg, MD 21727-8998
Fields offered: Fire administration, fire prevention technology
Year founded: 1977
Accreditation: Regional
Phone: (301) 447 1000
Fax: (301) 447 1052

Web site: www.usfa.fema.gov/nfa

The National Fire Academy's "Degrees at a Distance Program" offers a regionally accredited bachelor's degree in fire administration or fire prevention technology. Independent study courses are taken from one of the program's seven regional partners: Cogswell College (CA), University of Cincinnati, University of Memphis, Western Oregon University, University of Maryland, Western Illinois University, or Empire State College. Students are sent a course guide, required textbooks, and their assignments. They communicate with instructors by mail and telephone. Supervised exams can be taken locally.

National Institute of Nutritional Education

See: American Health Science University

National Technological University   M

700 Centre Ave.
Fort Collins, CO 80526
Fields offered: Business administration, chemical engineering, computer engineering, computer science, electrical engineering, engineering management, environmental systems management, individualized major, information systems, international business, management of technology, manufacturing systems engineering, materials science & engineering, mechanical engineering, optical science, project management, software engineering, systems engineering
Year founded: 1984
Accreditation: Regional
Phone: (970) 495 6400 ▪ (800) 582 9976
Fax: (970) 484 0668
Email: Admissions@mail.ntu.edu
Web site: www.ntu.edu

It is now possible to complete an NTU M.S. in computer engineering, computer science, software engineering, or systems engineering entirely through online study. These and other master's programs are also available through the more traditional NTU distributed learning network. Courses are transmitted by satellite digital compressed video from 45 university campuses, from Alaska to Florida, to corporate, government, and university work sites. Working professionals and technical managers take the classes, often in "real time" (as they are being taught on the campuses), with telephone links to the classrooms. NTU offers master's degrees in chemical engineering, computer engineering, computer science, electrical engineering, engineering management, environmental systems management, information systems (in conjunction with Northeastern University), management of technology, manufacturing systems engineering, materials science & engineering, mechanical engineering, optical science, project management, software engineering, and systems engineering. Students may also design an individualized M.S. program based on courses offered for any of the above programs. An MBA, focusing on international business, is also available.

In addition, about 400 short courses are broadcast on the NTU Network each year.

National Universities Degree Consortium

Accreditation: Regional
Web site: www.nudc.org

The National Universities Degree Consortium offers online and videocassette-based courses which can be applied towards degrees at any of its nine member institutions: Colorado State University, Kansas State University, Mississippi State University, Oklahoma State University, University of Alabama, University of Maryland University College, University of New Orleans, University of South Carolina, and Washington State University.

National University (California)   B, M

11255 North Torrey Pines Rd.
La Jolla, CA 92037-1011
Fields offered: Global studies, business administration, e-commerce, nursing
Year founded: 1971
Accreditation: Regional
Phone: (619) 563 7100 ▪ (800) 628 8648
Fax: (619) 642 8714
Email: getinfo@nu.edu
Web site: www.nu.edu

Online programs include bachelor's degrees in global studies, business, and nursing; master's degrees in business administration, electronic commerce, and nursing. Weekly audio and video lectures and online discussion sessions with classmates.

National-Louis University   B, M

2840 Sheridan Rd.
Evanston, IL 60201
Fields offered: Management, adult education
Year founded: 1886
Accreditation: Regional
Phone: (847) 256 5156 ▪ (800) 443 5522
Fax: (847) 256 1057
Email: nluinfo@wheeling1.nl.edu
Web site: www.nl.edu

Offers two programs entirely online: a master's in adult education and a B.S. in management. Other (MBA, M.S. in electronic commerce) degrees combine online courses with in-person meetings of cohort groups at various locations nationwide. See short-residency listing in the next chapter. Original name: National College of Education.

Naval Postgraduate School   M

1 University Circle
Monterey, CA 93943
Fields offered: Engineering (electrical, computer, mechanical, software), systems management
Year founded: 1909
Accreditation: Regional
Phone: (831) 656 2441
Fax: (831) 656 2921
Email: grad-ed@nps.navy.mil
Web site: www.nps.navy.mil

For officers in all branches of the military, as well as federal employees sponsored by their agencies, the Naval Postgraduate School offers distance-learning master's degree programs in the above fields.

New Jersey Institute of Technology   B, M

Office of Distance Learning
University Heights, NJ 07102
Fields offered: Information systems, engineering management, computer science
Year founded: 1881
Accreditation: Regional
Phone: (973) 596 3177 ▪ (800) 624 9850
Fax: (973) 596 3203
Email: dl@njit.edu
Web site: www.njit.edu

Bachelor's in information systems and computer science, master's in information systems, computer science, and engineering management, offered entirely through distance learning, using videotaped courses, online conferencing, fax, and phone. Distance students study along with on-campus students, on the same schedule, and examinations can be administered in remote locations by an approved proctor. Students must have access to a PC and modem.

New School for Social Research

See: New School University

New School University   B, M

68 Fifth Ave.
New York, NY 10011
Fields offered: Liberal studies, media studies
Year founded: 1919
Accreditation: Regional
Phone: (212) 229 5880
Fax: (212) 989 2928
Email: admissions@dialnsa.edu
Web site: www.dialnsa.edu

M.A. in media studies which combines theoretical offerings with advanced production coursework, designed for both media professionals and students considering further graduate study. Evening and independent study. Students can take classes online. Also offers a wholly nonresidential, self-paced, bachelor's–degree completion program in liberal studies. Applicants must have already completed 60 units through an accredited school. Online certificate programs are available in Web page design, media management, group practice management, and TESOL. Formerly the New School for Social Research.

New York Institute of Technology   B, M

211 Carleton Ave.
Central Islip, NY 11722
Fields offered: Business administration, interdisciplinary studies, hospitality management, behavioral sciences, energy management
Year founded: 1955
Accreditation: Regional
Phone: (631) 348 3200 ▪ (800) 345 6948
Fax: (631) 348 0912
Web site: www.nyit.edu

Through the Online Campus, NYIT offers an MBA and BBA; B.A., B.S., and B.P.S. in interdisciplinary studies; B.P.S. in hospitality management; B.S. in behavioral sciences (with four concentrations: criminal justice, community mental health, psychology, and sociology); and M.S. in energy management. Credit available for prior learning experiences, by portfolio assessment, and for equivalency exams. The off-campus programs were formerly offered through American Open University.

We have some serious concerns about NYIT's joint MBA program offered in partnership with the London Institute of Technology & Research (see listing in chapter 21), a school that has been prosecuted in English courts for making false claims regarding its accreditation and the educational background of its administrators.

North Central Bible College
See: North Central University (Minnesota)

North Central University (Minnesota)   B
Carlson Institute
910 Elliot Ave.
Minneapolis, MN 55404
Fields offered: Christian education, church ministries
Year founded: 1930
Accreditation: Regional
Phone: (612) 343 4430 ▓ (800) 446 1176
Fax: (612) 343 4435
Email: carlinst@northcentral.edu
Web site: www.northcentral.edu
Wholly nonresident B.A. or B.S. in church ministries or Christian education. Credit available for life-experience learning through portfolio assessment, and for equivalency exams. 27 of the 130 credits required must be earned from North Central; this can be accomplished through their correspondence courses. Formerly North Central Bible College. No relation to the unaccredited North Central University in Prescott, Arizona.

Northern Territory University   B, M
Darwin, NT 0909, Australia
Fields offered: Education, nursing
Year founded: 1988
Accreditation: International (GAAP)
Phone: +61 (8) 8946 6004
Fax: +61 (8) 8946 6644
Email: marketing@ntu.edu.au
Web site: www.ntu.edu.au
Degrees offered are a Bachelor of Education, Bachelor of Nursing, and Master of Educational Studies. Coursework is specially tailored to distance-learning students, who receive both print and multimedia materials for each semester-long unit. Additional support is available via audioconferencing, residential periods, and workshops.

Ohio University   B
External Student Program
301 Tupper Hall
Athens, OH 45701
Fields offered: Specialized studies
Year founded: 1804
Accreditation: Regional
Phone: (740) 593 2150 ▓ (800) 444 2420
Fax: (740) 593 0452
Email: external.student@ohio.edu
Web site:
www.cats.ohiou.edu/adultlearning/esp.htm
The Bachelor of Specialized Studies (B.S.S.) can be earned entirely though nonresident study. The External Student Program provides a counseling and advising service, and also acts as a liaison in dealing with other university offices. Credit for the degree can come from assessment of prior learning experiences, correspondence courses, independent study projects, and courses on television. In many correspondence courses, one can take the examination only. If you pass, credit for the course is given. These exams can be administered anywhere in the world and must be supervised. Forty-eight quarter hours of credit must be completed after enrolling at Ohio. Ohio's short-residency MBA is profiled in the next chapter. The university also has offered a college program for the incarcerated, at unusually low cost.

Old Dominion University   B, M
5215 Hampton Blvd.
Norfolk, VA 23529
Fields offered: See below
Year founded: 1930
Accreditation: Regional
Phone: (757) 683 3000 ▓ (800) 968 2638
Fax: (757) 683 5492
Email: admit@odu.ed
Web site: web.odu.edu
The TELETECHNET program delivers degree programs to over 50 sites—mainly community colleges, military installations and corporations—in Virginia, Indiana, Washington, North Carolina, and Arizona. Students at the remote sites can participate interactively in the classes. Bachelor's in business administration (emphasis accounting, finance, information systems, international business, management, or marketing); civil, mechanical, or electrical engineering technology; nursing; computer science; criminal justice; health sciences; human service counseling; occupational & technical studies; and interdisciplinary studies. Graduate degrees include Master of Engineering Management, M.S. in education (emphasis special education), M.S. in occupational & technical studies, M.S. in nursing (for the family nurse practitioner), and Master of Taxation.

Open Learning Institute of Hong Kong
See: Open University of Hong Kong

Open University and Open College   A, B
Open Learning Agency
4355 Mathissi Place
Burnaby, BC V5G 4S8, Canada
Fields offered: See below
Year founded: 1978

Accreditation: International (GAAP)
Phone: +1 (604) 431 3000 ▦ (800) 663 1663
Fax: +1 (604) 431 3333
Email: olainfo@ola.bc.ca
Web site: www.ola.bc.ca

The Open University and Open College are services of Canada's Open Learning Agency; the university's courses lead to associate's and bachelor's degrees, the college's to certificates and diplomas. Coursework is delivered via online instruction, computer conferencing, videocassettes, televised classes, printed materials, telephone, and video.

Bachelor's degrees offered to students worldwide include general studies, English, history, psychology, sociology, business administration (with an optional specialization in public sector management; offered in cooperation with the University of Victoria), general science, chemical science, earth science, engineering science, life science, mathematics, and physical science.

Additional bachelor's degrees available to residents of Canada include fine arts, health science (emphasis physiotherapy, psychiatric nursing, or respiratory therapy), and music (emphasis jazz or performance). Formerly the British Columbia Open University.

Open University (England)   B, M, D

Walton Hall
Milton Keynes MK7 6AA, United Kingdom
Fields offered: Arts, law, math, computing, science, social science, technology, education, health & social welfare, business school, languages
Year founded: 1969
Accreditation: International (GAAP)
Phone: +44 (1908) 274 066
Fax: +44 (1908) 653 744
Email: ces-gen@open.ac.uk
Web site: www.open.ac.uk

Established in 1969, the Open University is now one of the largest distance-education institutions in the world. Indeed, similar ventures around the world now model themselves on this highly successful educational experiment. Students study in their own homes and on their own schedules, using a combination of correspondence texts and audio- and videocassettes, software, email, and, increasingly, the Internet. Study can lead to a degree, a certificate, or a diploma. Credit is earned through a combination of achieving a specified level of continuous assessment and passing the course examination. Some courses have week-long summer schools or weekend residential schools, and some require that the applicant be a resident of the U.K. or other European country. The school is actively involved in establishing a presence in the U.S. See: United States Open University (listing in this chapter).

Open University of Hong Kong   B, M, D

30 Good Shepherd St.
Ho Man Tin, Kowloon, Hong Kong
Fields offered: Business, education, humanities, international studies, languages, social science, economics, computer science, electronics, engineering, communications technology, environmental studies, mathematics, nursing
Year founded: 1989
Accreditation: International (GAAP)
Phone: +852 2768 6000
Fax: +852 2715 0760
Email: regwww@ouhk.edu.hk
Web site: www.ouhk.edu.hk

This school was originally created to serve Hong Kong students, but it is expanding into the rest of China and eventually plans to enroll students from other parts of the world. Accredited by the Hong Kong Council for Academic Accreditation, this school offers a number of bachelor's, master's, and doctoral programs via distance learning, through a combination of transfer credits (up to 60 credits, or 80 in an honors program), comprehensive self-study packs, and supplementary audio-visual materials. In some cases tutorials are arranged, but they are not required, and may be subject to geographic limitations. Postgraduate degrees include an MBA, an M.Ed., and an Ed.D. While exams are generally administered at the Hong Kong campus, arrangements can be made to take them elsewhere. The school was modeled on the Open University (England) and uses some of that school's course materials. The majority of the instruction is in English, although an increasing number of programs are available in Chinese. Formerly the Open Learning Institute of Hong Kong.

Open University of Israel   B

U.S. office: American Friends of the Open University
180 W. 80th St.
New York, NY 10024
Fields offered: Computer science, cultural enrichment, education, humanities, international relations, Jewish studies, life sciences, management, mathematics, natural sciences, social sciences, video production
Year founded: 1974
Accreditation: International (GAAP)
Phone: (212) 712 1800
Fax: (212) 496 3296
Email: infodesk@oumail.openu.ac.il
Web site: www.openu.ac.il

Israel's first open university offers the bachelor's degree on completion of 18 home study courses. Each course consists of a home-study kit, which may include written materials (in Hebrew only), laboratory equipment, simulation games, videotapes, etc. Each course requires 16 to 18 weeks to complete, with a 15- to 18 hours-a-week time commitment. Study group formation is encouraged, and tutorial sessions are held in study centers throughout Israel.

Oral Roberts University   B

ORU Adult Learning Service Center
ATTN: SLLE Admissions
7777 S. Lewis Ave.
Tulsa, OK 74171

Fields offered: Business administration, Christian care & counseling, church ministries, elementary Christian school education, liberal studies
Accreditation: Regional
Phone: (800) 643 7976
Email: slle@oru.edu
Web site: www.oru.edu

B.S. degrees in the above fields, as well as degree-completion programs in Christian school administration, Christian school curriculum, and Christian school teaching, can be completed entirely through distance learning. There are also semi-residential and weekend college options. Credit is given for experiential learning, independent study, transfer courses, and equivalency exams. Applicants must sign a pledge stating they will abstain from tobacco, alcohol, lying, cheating, cursing, stealing, homosexual activity, and immorality. In addition, they must promise to participate in an aerobics program, attend church, and commit their lives to Jesus Christ.

Pennsylvania State University　　　A, B, M

207 Mitchell Building
University Park, PA 16802-3601
Fields offered: Business administration, letters & sciences, dietetic management, liberal studies, hotel/restaurant management, human development & family studies, adult education
Year founded: 1855
Accreditation: Regional
Phone: (814) 865 5403 ■ (800) 252 3592
Fax: (814) 865 3290
Email: psude@cde.psu.edu
Web site: www.outreach.psu.edu

Offers a bachelor's degree completion program in letters, arts, & sciences; courses, focusing on organizational leadership, are delivered by printed text and email. Also a Bachelor of Liberal Studies offered in partnership with University of Iowa, a distance-learning program known as LionHawk; the associate's is awarded from Penn State, the bachelor's from Iowa. Distance-learning associate's degrees, both by Internet and through independent study, can be earned in hotel/restaurant management; dietetic management; letters, arts, & sciences; business administration; and human development & family studies. The online M.Ed. in adult education consists of 33 credits, 12 of which can be transferred in from another institution.

Pfeiffer University　　　M

School of Graduate Studies
4701 Park Rd.
Charlotte, NC 28209
Fields offered: Business administration, health administration, organizational management
Year founded: 1885
Accreditation: Regional
Phone: (704) 521 9116
Fax: (704) 521 8617
Email: admissions@poe.pfeiffer.edu
Web site: poe.pfeiffer.edu

Offers an MBA, Master of Health Administration (MHA), and M.S. in organizational management entirely through online study. The MBA and MHA may be taken as a single joint program.

Potchefstroom University for Christian Higher Education　　　B, M

Privaatsak X6001
Potchefstroom 2520, South Africa
Fields offered: Business administration, engineering, law, legal studies, nursing, pharmacology, public management & governance, theology
Year founded: 1869
Accreditation: International (GAAP)
Phone: +27 (18) 299 1465
Fax: +27 (18) 299 1442
Email: tlscv@puknet.puk.ac.za
Web site: www.puk.ac.za

Offers the BBA and MBA, the LL.B. (Bachelor of Laws), Bachelor Curationis (Bachelor of Nursing), Bachelor of Engineering, B.A. in legal studies and theology, a B.Sc. in pharmacology, and an M.A. in public management & governance entirely by distance learning. Also offers a variety of theology-related distance-learning programs in conjunction with Greenwich School of Theology in the United Kingdom (see listing in this chapter).

Queen's University of Belfast　　　M

Belfast BT9 7BL, Northern Ireland
Fields offered: Pharmacy
Year founded: 1845
Accreditation: International (GAAP)
Phone: +44 (1232) 242 041
Fax: +44 (1232) 247 794
Email: b.mccaw@qub.ac.uk
Web site: www.qub.ac.uk/pha/dl

Master of Science in either clinical pharmacy or community pharmacy, through a program tailored specifically to the needs of working pharmacists. Applicants must have an undergraduate degree in pharmacy, and be working in the field. Coursework is done by correspondence, with tutorial support by telephone.

Queens University　　　B

99 University Ave.
Kingston, ON K7L 3N6, Canada
Fields offered: German, history, political studies, psychology
Year founded: 1841
Accreditation: International (GAAP)
Phone: +1 (613) 533 2471
Fax: +1 (613) 533 6805
Email: cds@post.queensu.ca
Web site: www.queensu.ca/pts

A Bachelor of Arts degree (15 courses in total) concentrating in German, history, political studies, or psychology can be completed entirely through correspondence. Study involves use of textbooks, tapes, course notes written by instructors, and in some courses, CD-ROM textbooks and use of the Internet. Students submit assignments for grading and write final examinations under supervision at various centers worldwide. Telephone contact with instructors is possible. Other concentrations can be fulfilled by taking a combination of correspondence courses through Queens and by transferring Queens-approved courses from other universities to complete degree requirements.

Regent University   M, Law

1000 Regent University Dr.
Virginia Beach, VA 23464-9800
Fields offered: Communication, journalism, education, organizational leadership, law, taxation
Year founded: 1977
Accreditation: Regional
Phone: (757) 226 4127 ▧ (800) 373 5504
Fax: (757) 424 7051
Email: admissions@regent.edu
Web site: www.regent.edu

Distance-learning programs, largely Web-based, include an M.A. in communication, M.A. in journalism, M.A. in computer mediated communication, an M.Ed., an M.A. in organizational leadership, and an LL.M. in international taxation. Founded as CBN University (named after university founder Pat Robertson's Christian Broadcasting Network). Regent University integrates traditional Judeo-Christian ethical principles in the teaching of its courses. See the next chapter for information on Regent's short-residency master's and doctoral programs.

Regents College

See: Excelsior College

Regis University   B, M

3333 Regis Blvd.
Denver, CO 80221
Fields offered: Business administration, computer information systems, insurance, nonprofit management, nursing
Year founded: 1877
Accreditation: Regional
Phone: (303) 458 4900
Email: regisadm@regis.edu
Web site: www.regis.edu

Regis's School for Professional Studies offers a variety of nontraditional adult programs at the graduate and undergraduate levels in a number of learning formats, including the following programs which may be completed entirely through online study: the B.S. in business management (with optional specialization in insurance), the M.S. in computer information systems (designed in consultation with Sun Microsystems and available with specialization in databases, networking, or object-oriented technologies), the MBA, and a Master of Nonprofit Management.

Rensselaer Polytechnic Institute   M

Professional and Distance Education
CII Suite 4011
110 8th St.
Troy, NY 12180-3590
Fields offered: Business administration, computer & systems engineering, computer science, electrical engineering, electric power engineering, engineering

"Attention. Attention. Your online electrical engineering exam begins … now!"

(management of technology), engineering science (manufacturing systems engineering, microelectronics manufacturing engineering), individualized major, industrial & management engineering (quality engineering, service systems), information technology, management, mechanical engineering, technical communication
Year founded: 1824
Accreditation: Regional
Phone: (518) 276 7787
Fax: (518) 276 8026
Email: rsvp@rpi.edu
Web site: www.rsvp.rpi.edu

Distance-learning master's degrees offered in the above fields. Students may also (with faculty approval) design an individualized "Professional M.S." out of available distance-learning courses. All program materials are delivered to individuals or participating corporate sites by satellite, videoconferencing, and videotape, enhanced by Internet sites and optional classroom participation. A variety of technology-related certificate programs are also available.

Rhodec International   B

35 East St.
Brighton BN1 1HL, United Kingdom
Fields offered: Interior design
Year founded: 1960
Accreditation: National (DETC)
Phone: +44 (1273) 327 476
Fax: +44 (1273) 821 668
Email: contact@rhodec.com
Web site: www.rhodec.com

Rhodec offers diplomas in interior design wholly through distance learning. Once the diploma has been earned, typically two years, students may submit the work, plus additional projects, to London Guildhall University, and earn a B.A. with honours in interior design. Rhodec is accredited by the Distance Education and Training Council (DETC).

Roger Williams University   B

1 Old Ferry Rd.
Bristol, RI 02809-2921
Fields offered: Criminal justice, business management, industrial technology, public administration
Year founded: 1956
Accreditation: Regional
Phone: (401) 254 3530
Fax: (401) 254 3480
Web site: www.rwu.edu

Through the "Open Program," students can earn a distance-learning B.S. in administration of justice, business management, industrial technology, or public administration. Credit given for prior-learning assessment, military training, CLEP and other exams, and prior college attendance. While enrolled, one may earn credit from external courses, independent studies, internships, and day, evening, summer, and special classroom courses. Some courses may also involve guided instruction via phone, fax, mail, or email, or otherwise over the Internet. Each external course generally ends with a proctored exam, taken in the student's local area under an approved proctor. Preference is given to students who are able to enter with advanced standing, based on credits earned elsewhere, CLEP exams, military, and/or job training.

Saint Patrick's College, Maynooth

See: National Distance Education Centre (Ireland)

Simon Fraser University   B

8888 University Dr.
Burnaby, BC V5A 1S6, Canada
Fields offered: General studies, criminology
Year founded: 1964
Accreditation: International (GAAP)
Phone: +1 (604) 291 3524
Fax: +1 (604) 291 4964
Email: cde@sfu.ca
Web site: www.sfu.ca/cde

Offers a Bachelor of General Studies and a B.A. in criminology wholly through distance learning, as well as a number of diplomas, certificates, and additional correspondence courses in a wide range of subjects. Students receive a "complete learning package" for each course, which includes lecture notes as well as, as appropriate, audio- and videocassettes, slides, textbooks, and supplementary reading guides. Some courses also integrate televised materials and/or Internet resources as well. The school assumes a high level of interactivity between students and faculty. Tuition is waived for Canadian citizens sixty years old and over. As distance students study along with classroom courses, there are many close deadlines, and the school discourages persons outside Canada from enrolling, as mail and phone costs will be high.

Sir Joseph Banks College

P.O. Box 52
Crafers, South Australia 5152, Australia
Fields offered: Human resources
Accreditation: International (GAAP)
Phone: +61 (8) 8212 3616
Fax: +61 (8) 8339 3919
Email: josephbanks@lynx.net.au
Web site: www.lynx.net.au/~joseph-banks

Their graduate diploma in human resources is accredited by the Australian government and qualifies its graduates to apply for master's programs in similar disciplines. Credit is given for prior learning, including that which took place in the workplace. Studies take place through a combination of multimedia, mail, fax, phone, email, and Internet. They say they have applied for accreditation for their own master's degree in human resources.

Southern Christian University   M, D

1200 Taylor Rd.
Montgomery, AL 36117
Fields offered: Biblical studies, counseling & family therapy, divinity, marriage & family therapy, ministry, organizational leadership
Year founded: 1967
Accreditation: Regional
Phone: (334) 387 3877 ▪ (800) 351 4040
Fax: (334) 387 3878
Email: admissions@southernchristian.edu
Web site: www.southernchristian.edu

Offers an M.A. in biblical studies; M.S. in Christian ministry, counseling & family therapy, or organizational leadership; Master of Divinity; and Doctor of Ministry through online study. Except for the M.S. in counseling & family therapy (which requires a supervised internship in accordance with Alabama state counseling licensure requirements) and the Doctor of Ministry (which requires two one-week sessions on campus), all programs may be completed entirely online. To the best of our knowledge, Southern Christian University is the only regionally accredited school to offer a Master of Divinity entirely by distance learning. Concentrations are available in Christian ministry and marriage/family therapy; students who choose the latter track are encouraged, but not required, to attend a one-week session on campus.

Southwest Missouri State University   M

901 South National St.
Springfield, MO 65804
Fields offered: Computer information systems, administrative studies
Year founded: 1906
Accreditation: Regional
Phone: (417) 836 6111 ▪ (888) 767 8444
Fax: (417) 836 6494
Email: smsuonline@mail.smsu.edu
Web site: smsuonline.smsu.edu

Online master's degrees in the above fields. The M.S. in administrative studies can be earned entirely over the Internet; the M.S. in computer information systems requires four 7-day sessions on campus.

Spertus College   M, D

618 S. Michigan Ave.
Chicago, IL 60605
Fields offered: Jewish studies, Jewish education
Year founded: 1924
Accreditation: Regional
Phone: (312) 322 9012 ▪ (888) 322 1769
Fax: (312) 922 6406
Email: sijs@spertus.edu
Web site: www.spertus.edu

Distance-learning programs include an M.S. in Jewish Studies (M.S.J.S.) or Jewish education (M.S.J.E.), a Doctor of Jewish Studies (D.J.S.), and a Doctor of Science in Jewish Studies (D.S.J.S.). Master's degrees are designed for students interested in additional knowledge of Jewish subjects or as a professional credential for work in Jewish education or communal service. The doctoral programs are designed for Jewish clergy, educators, and communal service workers who desire to make a "cutting edge" contribution to their respective fields. Courses are delivered in a number of ways, including distance-learning packages, intensive seminars, and independent study. Students are encouraged to spend at least six days a year at the Chicago campus for intensive seminars.

Stanford University   M

Stanford Center for Professional Development
496 Lomita Mall, Durand Building, Room 401
Stanford, CA 94305-4036
Fields offered: Electrical engineering, engineering, computer science
Year founded: 1885
Accreditation: Regional
Phone: (650) 725 3000
Fax: (650) 725 2868
Email: sitn-registration@stanford.edu
Web site: scpd.stanford.edu

In the fall of 1998, Stanford became the first major U.S. research university to offer a master's degree wholly on the Internet: an M.S. in Electrical Engineering with an emphasis on telecommunications. In order to satisfy the 45-unit requirement for the master's, students must select approximately 15 online, asynchronous courses out of 30 options made available. Stanford also offers a distance-learning M.S. in engineering or computer science to corporate and government subscribers, through closed-circuit television, teleconferencing, Internet, and other nontraditional methods. It is recommended, though not required, that students outside the live broadcast area spend one quarter in residency.

State University of New York Institute of Technology at Utica/Rome   M

P.O. Box 3050
Utica, NY 13504
Fields offered: Accounting
Accreditation: Regional
Phone: (315) 792 7500 ▪ (800) 786 9832
Fax: (315) 792 7222
Email: admissions@sunyit.edu
Web site: www.sunyit.edu/~ftjt/msa-online.htm

Online M.S. in accountancy prepares students for the CPA and CMA exams or satisfies Continuing Professional Education requirements for current CPAs and CMAs.

Strathclyde Graduate Business School   M

199 Cathedral St.
Glasgow G4 0QU, United Kingdom
Fields offered: Business administration
Year founded: 1947
Accreditation: International (GAAP)
Phone: +44 (141) 553 6000
Fax: +44 (141) 552 8851
Email: info@worldclassmba.com
Web site: www.worldclassmba.com

Master's programs in business administration, management, facilities management, business information systems management, business technology systems, leadership studies, and procurement management.

Strayer University   A, B, M

1025 15th St. NW
Washington, DC 20005
Fields offered: Accounting, business, economics, computer information systems, general studies, marketing
Year founded: 1892
Accreditation: Regional
Phone: (703) 339 1850 ▪ (800) 422 8055
Fax: (703) 339 1852
Email: jct@strayer.edu
Web site: www.strayer.edu

Strayer University offers online, business-related degrees at the associate's, bachelor's, and master's level, including an MBA. Strayer has a liberal policy regarding transfer credits from other colleges and universities, passing scores on CLEP and DANTES, and military experience.

Suffolk University   M

Beacon Hill
Boston, MA 02108
Fields offered: Business administration
Year founded: 1906
Accreditation: Regional
Phone: (617) 573 8000
Fax: (617) 573 8353
Email: admissions@admin.suffolk.edu
Web site: www.suffolk.edu

The eMBA program, which can be completed entirely online, consists of 11 to 16 courses, which include 9 electives.

Technikon of Southern Africa   B, M, D

Private Bag X6
Florida, 1710, South Africa
Fields offered: Accounting, communications, sciences, business, education, human resources, engineering, information technology, law, management, marketing, correctional services
Accreditation: International (GAAP)
Phone: +27 (11) 471 2000
Fax: +27 (11) 471 2134

Email: info@tsa.ac.za
Web site: www.tsa.ac.za

South Africa's only distance-education technikon (technical university) offers a variety of degrees at all levels in the above fields. Study takes place through self-paced materials sent to students as well as over the Internet. Students combine workplace experience with guided study, and take year-end examinations at approved examination centers. The school offers many support services to distance-learning students, including self-esteem courses, job-hunting assistance, assertiveness training, and more.

Télé-université   B

2600 boulevard Laurier
Tour de la Cite 7e etage
Case postale 10700
Sainte-Foy, QB G1V 4V9, Canada
Fields offered: Administration, communications, human resources
Accreditation: International (GAAP)
Phone: +1 (418) 657 2262 ▪ (888) 843 4333
Fax: +1 (418) 657 2094
Email: info@teluq.uquebec.ca
Web site: www.teluq.uquebec.ca

The Télé-université is one of eleven institutions that together form the University of Quebec network. It also collaborates with Athabasca University in Alberta and the Open Learning Agency of British Columbia in the exchange of course materials. The only French-speaking university in North America that specializes in distance education.

Texas A & M University—Commerce   M

P.O. Box 3011
Commerce, TX 75429
Fields offered: Business administration
Year founded: 1889
Accreditation: Regional
Phone: (903) 886 5102
Fax: (903) 886 5888
Email: mba@tamu-commerce.edu
Web site: mbaonline.tamu-commerce.edu

Students can complete the MBA degree by taking ten online courses (or 30 semester hours of coursework). Some tests may require travel to a nearby testing facility.

Texas Christian University   M

Office of Graduate Studies and Research
TCU Box 297023
Fort Worth, TX 76129
Fields offered: Liberal arts, nursing (clinical nurse specialist)
Year founded: 1873
Accreditation: Regional
Phone: (817) 257 7515
Email: p.yarbrough@tcu.edu
Web site: www.tcuglobal.edu

Offers a Master of Liberal Arts and an MSN (in clinical nursing) through online classes and, in the case of the MSN, short intensive residencies. An undergraduate program may be under development.

Texas Tech University   B, M

Outreach and Extended Studies
6901 Quaker Ave.
Lubbock, TX 79413
Fields offered: General studies, technical communication, engineering
Year founded: 1923
Accreditation: Regional
Phone: (806) 742 7200 ▪ (800) 692 6877
Fax: (806) 742 7222
Email: distlearn@ttu.edu
Web site: www.ttu.edu

Texas Tech offers these degrees entirely by distance learning: Bachelor of General Studies (*www.dce.ttu.edu*), Master of Arts in Technical Communication (*www.english.ttu.edu/tc/dl*), a general Master of Engineering, and M.S. degrees in systems & engineering management, software engineering, and petroleum engineering (*aln.coe.ttu.edu*).

Texas Wesleyan University   M

1201 Wesleyan
Fort Worth, TX 76105-1536
Fields offered: Education
Year founded: 1890
Accreditation: Regional
Phone: (817) 531 4444 ▪ (800) 580 8980
Fax: (817) 531 4425
Email: info@txwesleyan.edu
Web site: www.txwesleyan.edu

Texas Wesleyan offers an M.Ed. designed for classroom teachers, through a video-based program of instruction. Applicant must be a full-time teacher with access to email. The school puts distance-learning students in touch with others in their area for learning groups, guided by a faculty mentor. A maximum of 6 of the 36 semester hours required for the degree can be transferred from another accredited institution. Weekend programs are also available for a number of graduate and undergrad degrees.

Thomas Edison State College   A, B

101 West State St.
Trenton, NJ 08608-1176
Fields offered: Accounting, administrative office management, administration of justice, advertising management, air traffic control, anthropology, architectural design, art, aviation flight technology, aviation maintenance technology, banking, biomedical electronics, biology, chemistry, child development services, civil & construction engineering technology, civil engineering technology, clinical laboratory science, communications, community services, computer information systems, computer science, computer science technology, construction, dietetic sciences, dental assisting sciences, dental hygiene, economics, electrical technology, electronic engineering technology, emergency disaster management, engineering graphics, English, environmental sciences, environmental studies, finance, fire protection science, foreign language, forestry, general management, gerontology, health &

nutrition counseling, health professions education, health services, health services administration, health services education, health services management, history, horticulture, hospital health care administration, hotel/motel/restaurant management, human resource management, humanities, imaging science, insurance, international business, journalism, labor studies, laboratory animal science, legal services, liberal studies, logistics, manufacturing engineering technology, marine engineering technology, marketing, mathematics, mechanical engineering technology, medical imaging, mental health & rehabilitative services, music, natural sciences & mathematics, nondestructive testing technology, nuclear engineering technology, nuclear medicine technology, nursing, operations management, organizational management, perfusion technology, philosophy, photography, physics, political science, procurement, psychology, public administration, purchasing & materials management, radiation protection, radiation therapy, radiologic technology, real estate, recreation services, religion, respiratory care, respiratory care sciences (advanced), retailing management, small business management & entrepreneurship, social sciences & history, social services, social services administration, social services for special populations, sociology, surveying, theater arts, transportation & distribution management
Year founded: 1972
Accreditation: Regional
Phone: (609) 292 6565 ▪ (888) 442 8372
Fax: (609) 984 8447
Email: admissions@tesc.edu
Web site: www.tesc.edu
Bachelor's and associate's degrees in the above areas of specialization. Unlimited credit can be earned through portfolio assessment; Thomas Edison's own exams in dozens of subjects; guided study (distance-learning courses using texts and videocassettes); the "On-Line Computer Classroom" (many courses available through Edison's innovative CALL system: Computer Assisted Lifelong Learning); equivalency exams; military, business, and industry courses and training programs; telecourses (centered on, for example, PBS's The Civil War, etc.); licenses and certificates; and transfer credit from accredited colleges. Unique academic advising available to enrolled students on an 800 number. Foreign students are welcome, with certain restrictions. Edison is in the process of developing an online M.A. in professional studies. A short-residency M.S. in management is already available; see the Thomas Edison State College listing in the short-residency chapter.

Touro College
See: Touro University International

Touro University International   B, M, D
10542 Calle Lee, Suite 102
Los Alamitos, CA 90720

Fields offered: Business administration, health sciences
Accreditation: Regional
Phone: (714) 816 0366
Fax: (714) 816 0367
Email: info@tourou.edu
Web site: www.tourouniversity.edu
Their slogan—"world's leading Internet university in every aspect"—may be a bit of hyperbole, but TUI was the first regionally accredited American university to offer doctoral programs that can be earned 100% online: one in business administration, another in health sciences. There are also online bachelor's and master's degrees in these fields. TUI is a branch campus of Touro College, New York, which identifies itself as "a Jewish-sponsored independent institution of higher and professional education." Touro College does not, itself, have a doctoral program. The notion of a "college" without doctoral programs having a "university" branch campus in another state with doctoral programs may be unique in American higher education, but TUI's doctorates are definitely regarded as accredited by the Middle States Association, the regional accreditor that deals with New York schools. The master's programs can be completed in a year, the doctorates in two.

Trinity College (Ireland)
See: National Distance Education Centre (Ireland)

Troy State University Montgomery   B
P.O. Drawer 4419
Montgomery, AL 36103-4419
Fields offered: Professional studies, international relations
Year founded: 1887
Accreditation: Regional
Phone: (334) 241 9553 ▪ (800) 355 8786
Fax: (334) 241 5465
Email: edp@tsum.edu
Web site: www.tsum.edu
Bachelor of Arts or Science in professional studies can be earned through a combination of learning contracts, television courses, transfer credit from and transient credit at other regionally accredited colleges/universities, and prior learning assessment (credit by examination; evaluation of previous training in military, business and/or industry; and portfolio assessment). Majors are available in resource management (business), English, history, political science, social science, and psychology. Students must complete a minimum of 50 quarter hours under TSUM sponsorship. Also offers an M.S. in international learning, using video-based study.

Tulane University   M
6823 St. Charles Ave.
New Orleans, LA 70118
Fields offered: Public health, occupational health, safety management
Year founded: 1834
Accreditation: Regional
Phone: (504) 584 1774 ▪ (800) 862 2122

Fax: (504) 587 7352
Email: dldirect@mailhost.tcs.tulane.edu
Web site: caeph.tulane.edu
Designed for midcareer health professionals, a Master of Public Health (MPH) in occupational health and/or safety management is offered through live Internet classes held once or twice a week.

Unexus University
See: Lansbridge University

United States Open University   B, M
901 Market St., Suite 410
Wilmington, DE 19801
Fields offered: Business administration, computing, English, European studies, humanities, information technology, international studies, liberal arts, social sciences
Accreditation: Candidate for Regional
Phone: (302) 778 0300 ▪ (800) 232 7705
Fax: (302) 429 5953
Email: info@open.edu
Web site: www.open.edu
The U.S. branch of the Open University in England, one of the leading distance-education institutions in the world. At press time, USOU was a candidate for accreditation with the Middle States Association. We have chosen to include them in the GAAP chapter, since we believe that their eventual full accreditation is as certain as anything can be in this field; however, it might be appropriate to confirm their current status before enrolling. USOU has been set up in an effort to make Open University's much-emulated programs more available to students in the United States. Degrees offered include bachelor's degrees in business administration (B.S.), computing (B.S.), English (B.A.), European studies (B.A.), humanities (B.A.), information technology (B.S.), international studies (B.A.), liberal arts (B.A.), and social sciences (B.A.). An MBA is also offered, as is an M.S. in computing. See also: Open University (England)

Universidad Estatal a Distancia   B, M
Apartado 474-2050 de Montes de Oca
San Jose, Costa Rica
Fields offered: Education, health fields, social services, business & financial fields, administration
Year founded: 1977
Accreditation: International (GAAP)
Phone: +506 234 1909
Email: vacademic@arenal.uned.ac.cr
Web site: www.uned.ac.cr
Costa Rica's state university for distance learning offers correspondence study consisting of written units, audio- and videocassettes, computer-assisted instruction, telephone counseling, electronic classes, videoconferencing, and more. Degrees awarded are equivalent to the bachelor's and master's in the following fields: elementary teaching, educational administration, administration of child social services, civic education, administration of health services, rehabilitation, university studies, business administra-

tion, administration of cooperatives, agrarian administration, banking & financial administration, accountancy, and organization management. A bachelor's can be earned in about two years of study.

University College Cork
See: National Distance Education Centre (Ireland)

University College Galway
See: National Distance Education Centre (Ireland)

University of Action Learning   B, M
1650 38th St., Suite 205W
Boulder, CO 80301
Fields offered: Management, administration
Year founded: 1999
Accreditation: National (DETC)
Phone: (303) 442 6907
Fax: (303) 442 6815
Email: ual@u-a-l.org
Web site: www.u-a-l.org
The U.S. division of British-based International Management Centres. Offers bachelor's and master's courses in general management and administration specialties, e.g., health care, hospitality, quality management, etc. Accredited by the Distance Education and Training Council (DETC).

University of Baltimore   B, M, D
Charles at Mount Royal
Baltimore, MD 21201
Fields offered: Business administration
Year founded: 1925
Accreditation: Regional
Phone: (410) 837 4200 ▪ (877) 277 5982
Fax: (410) 539 3714
Email: admissions@ubmail.ubalt.edu
Web site: www.ubalt.edu
MBA program offered entirely over the Internet. Regional and AACSB accreditation.

University of Birmingham   B, M
Edgbaston
Birmingham B15 2TT, United Kingdom
Fields offered: Special education
Year founded: 1900
Accreditation: International (GAAP)
Phone: +44 (121) 414 4856
Email: d.eaton@bham.ac.uk
Web site: www.edu.bham.ac.uk/CPD
Bachelor's and master's degrees are offered in special education with a wide range of specializations, including multisensory impairment, emotional & behavioral difficulties, teaching hearing-impaired children, and more. Undergraduate study leads to a B.Phil.; the graduate program, tailored to teachers already working with learning-impaired pupils, leads to an M.Ed. Students from outside the U.K. are occasionally admitted, with, the school tells us, "careful consideration of the support available to them for their study."

The university also offers a distance M.A. in the teaching of English as a foreign (or second) language in association with David English House in Hiroshima, Japan, through a two-year wholly nonresidential module program. Applicants should have "normal teaching experience," a "good first degree or equivalent," and, if English is not their first language, a score of 550 or better on the TOEFL. A dissertation is required, and it is hoped that students will be able to base this final project on practical classroom issues.

University of Bridgeport   B, M, D

126 Park Ave.
Bridgeport, CT 06601
Fields offered: Nutrition
Year founded: 1927
Accreditation: Regional
Phone: (203) 576 4552 ▪ (800) 470 7307
Fax: (203) 576 4941
Email: ubonline@bridgeport.edu
Web site: www.bridgeport.edu

Bridgeport offers a wholly online M.S. in human nutrition through courses posted on the Internet. Applicants should have an accredited bachelor's degree and have taken certain prerequisites. At the completion of the eight-course program, students must travel to the Connecticut campus for a single two-day exam. This is the only residency requirement. Up to six semester units of credit can be transferred in, with the dean's approval. Financial aid is available.

Bridgeport also offers a number of nontraditional residential programs, including associate's, bachelor's, master's, and doctoral programs through evening and weekend programs, in fields including engineering, business administration, education, computer science, chiropractic, naturopathic medicine, and nutrition. The IDEAL program allows people who have completed two years of college to complete a bachelor's degree in five weeks of residential study.

University of British Columbia

Distance Education and Technology
1170 - 2329 West Mall
Vancouver, BC V6T 1Z4, Canada
Fields offered: Intercultural studies, technology-based distributed learning, turfgrass management, watershed management
Year founded: 1908
Accreditation: International (GAAP)
Phone: +1 (604) 822 6565
Fax: +1 (604) 822 8636
Email: det@cstudies.ubc.ca
Web site: det.cstudies.ubc.ca

Established as the Department of University Extensions at UBC in 1949, the Distance Education & Technology (DE&T) unit brings together resources from a number of UBC faculties to provide certificates in the above fields as well as for-credit distance-learning courses in agricultural sciences, arts, education, forestry, nursing, computer science, civil engineering, health sciences, applied science, and environmental studies. Courses are delivered using print-based materials, audio, video, CD-ROM, and the Internet.

University of Central Florida   B, M

P.O. Box 160000
Orlando, FL 32816
Fields offered: Vocational education, nursing, liberal studies, health services administration, engineering, forensic science
Year founded: 1963
Accreditation: Regional
Phone: (407) 823 2000
Fax: (407) 823 3419
Email: distrib@mail.ucf.edu
Web site: www.ucf.edu

B.S., M.S., or M.A. in vocational education, RN to BSN in nursing, B.A. or B.S. in liberal studies (with an optional track in information technology), and B.S. in health services administration (a degree completion program) are offered over the Internet. The B.S. in engineering technology is offered by videocassette at designated centers throughout Florida.

University of Colorado at Boulder   M

Boulder, CO 80309
Fields offered: Engineering, computer science, engineering management, telecommunications
Year founded: 1876
Accreditation: Regional
Phone: (303) 492 6331
Fax: (303) 492 5987
Email: catecs-info@colorado.edu
Web site: www.colorado.edu/CATECS

M.S. and Master of Engineering offered to working adults in the following concentrations: aerospace engineering, electrical/computer engineering, engineering management, mechanical engineering, telecommunications, and computer science. Students take one class per semester, finishing the degree in 3½ to 5 years. Distance-learning options include videocassettes and television courses.

University of Colorado at Colorado Springs   M

1420 Austin Bluffs Parkway
Colorado Springs, CO 80933
Fields offered: Business administration
Year founded: 1965
Accreditation: Regional
Phone: (719) 262 3408 ▪ (800) 990 8227
Email: busadvsr@mail.uccs.edu
Web site: web.uccs.edu/business/dmbamain.htm

Offers an MBA via distance-learning methods, in cooperation with Jones Knowledge Group. This individually tailored program uses a number of technologies, including video delivered over satellite and cable systems by the Learning Channel. The majority of the coursework, however, is accomplished over the Internet, as is student/faculty interaction. This is one of the few distance MBAs that is accredited by the AACSB (the International Association for Management Education).

University of Dallas   M

Graduate School of Management
1845 East Northgate Dr.
Irving, TX 75062
Fields offered: Business administration,
management
Year founded: 1956
Accreditation: Regional
Phone: (800) 832 5622
Fax: (972) 721 4009
Email: cfdl@gsm.udallas.edu
Web site: imba.udallas.edu

Offers an MBA and Master of Management through
online study; either program may be tailored to focus on
e-commerce, information technology, sport management,
or telecommunications.

University of Denver   M

University College
2211 South Josephine St.
Denver, CO 80208
Fields offered: Environmental policy &
management, telecommunications
Year founded: 1864
Accreditation: Regional
Phone: (303) 871 3155 ▪ (800) 347 2042
Fax: (303) 871 3303
Email: ucolinfo@du.edu
Web site: www.universitycollege.du.edu

Both master's degrees and certificates in the fields of
environmental policy & management and telecommunications. Delivery of course curriculum is both text-based
and online and may include occasional use of audio- or
videotapes. Distance-learning students have access to
the same resources as traditional ones, including financial
aid and the career center.

University of Dundee   M

Dundee DD1 4HN, United Kingdom
Fields offered: Medical fields, nursing, town &
country planning
Year founded: 1981
Accreditation: International (GAAP)
Phone: +44 (1382) 348 111
Fax: +44 (1382) 345 500
Email: srs@dundee.ac.uk
Web site:
www.dundee.ac.uk/prospectus/distlearning

Nonresident degrees include a Master of Medical Education,
M.Sc. degrees in palliative care and primary care, and an
M.A. in town & country planning, as well as courses in
a variety of health-related fields, and both a certificate and
a diploma in medical education. There is also a Bachelor
of Nursing and a Bachelor of Midwifery, both of which
require a minimum of five 1-week sessions on campus (one
per module; it can take up to three years to complete all
modules). The M.S. in orthopedic & rehabilitation technology also requires a brief campus stay, although the school's
materials do not make it clear exactly how long this stay
needs to be. Students from around the world are accepted
into this program.

University of Florida   D

Gainesville, FL 32611
Fields offered: Audiology, pharmacy
Year founded: 1853
Accreditation: Regional
Phone: (352) 392 3261
Fax: (352) 392 8791
Email: gradinfo@ufl.edu
Web site: www.fcd.ufl.edu

Doctoral programs in audiology and pharmacy for working professionals. For information on Florida's short-
residency degree programs, see the next chapter.

University of Glasgow   M, D

22 Western Court
Glasgow G12 8SQ, United Kingdom
Fields offered: Business administration, digital
preservation, medical law, oncology, pain
management, philosophy, public health, religious
education, Scottish literature, travel medicine
Accreditation: International (GAAP)
Phone: +44 (141) 330 3870
Fax: +44 (141) 330 4079
Email: guide@mis.gla.ac.uk
Web site: www.gla.ac.uk/Inter/GUIDE

Master's degrees are currently available by distance learning in medical law, religious education, Scottish literature,
and travel medicine. MBA and DBA programs are under
development, as are master's programs in digital preservation, oncology, pain management, philosophy, and
public health; all of these programs should be completely
available to students worldwide by the end of 2001. It has
also been suggested that Glasgow may be willing to
negotiate research doctorates on a case-by-case basis.

University of Houston   B, M

Distance Education
4800 Calhoun Rd.
Houston, TX 77024
Fields offered: See below
Year founded: 1927
Accreditation: Regional
Phone: (281) 395 2810 ▪ (800) 687 8488
Email: deadvisor@uh.edu
Web site: www.uh.edu/uhdistance

University of Houston's distance-education program
offers a number of degrees through online compressed video,
microwave, and/or satellite courses beamed to remote
locations, as well as through videotape, cable or public
TV broadcast, and Internet courses. Bachelor's completion
programs are available in computer drafting & design, earth
science, English, history, hotel & restaurant management,
industrial supervision, and psychology. The following
master's programs are available: Master of Education
(M.Ed.) in curriculum & instruction (emphasis reading &
language arts), Master of Electrical Engineering, Master
of Hospitality Management, Master of Industrial Engineering,
and an M.S. in computer science or occupational technology.
A reading specialist certificate for teachers is also available.

University of Huddersfield   M

Queensgate
Huddersfield HD1 3DH, United Kingdom
Fields offered: Geographic information systems
Year founded: 1841
Accreditation: International (GAAP)
Phone: +44 (1484) 472 246
Email: d.e.reeve@hud.ac.uk
Web site: www.hud.ac.uk/sas/ges/mgis.htm
Huddersfield offers both a master's degree and a post-
graduate diploma in geographic information systems
(GIS) through distance learning.

University of Idaho   M

Engineering Outreach Program
P.O. Box 441014
Moscow, ID 83844-1014
Fields offered: Biological & agricultural engineering,
civil engineering, computer engineering, computer
science, electrical engineering, engineering
management, geological engineering, human factors
psychology, mining engineering, mechanical
engineering, metallurgical engineering, teaching
mathematics
Year founded: 1889
Accreditation: Regional
Phone: (800) 824 2889
Email: outreach@uidaho.edu
Web site: www.uidaho.edu/evo
Master's degrees in the above fields are offered nonresidentially via the Engineering Outreach program. The
school stresses that this is an intensive program that
requires high levels of discipline and commitment from
students. International students are accepted; those whose
native language is other than English must present a
minimum score of 525 on the TOEFL.

University of Illinois at Springfield   B, M

P.O. Box 19243
Springfield, IL 62794
Fields offered: Liberal studies, management
information systems
Year founded: 1969
Accreditation: Regional
Phone: (217) 206 6600
Fax: (217) 206 7188
Email: admissions@uis.edu
Web site: www.uis.edu
Bachelor's degree completion program in liberal studies
and an M.S. in management information systems, both
offered over the Internet.

University of Illinois at Urbana-Champaign   M

Urbana, IL 61801
Fields offered: Engineering, computer science,
education, human resources
Year founded: 1867
Accreditation: Regional
Phone: (217) 333 1000
Fax: (217) 333 9758
Email: graduate@admissions.uiuc.edu

For an added fee, Cramwell University
will install a private telephone line from
our campus to your home.

Web site: www.uiuc.edu
Master's in computer science, education, human resources,
and a number of engineering fields (mechanical, general,
electrical, or theoretical) via the Internet. Courses are also
available in mathematics and materials science. Admission
to this program is highly competitive.

University of Iowa   B

Division of Continuing Education
116 International Center
Iowa City, IA 52242-1802
Fields offered: Liberal studies
Year founded: 1847
Accreditation: Regional
Phone: (319) 335 2575 ▪ (800) 272 6430
Fax: (319) 335 2740
Email: credit-programs@uiowa.edu
Web site: www.uiowa.edu
Offers a degree completion program by guided inde-
pendent study for a Bachelor of Liberal Studies. As part
of the "LionHawk" partnership between Iowa and Penn
State, students with an A.A. from Penn State automati-
cally qualify for admission. See also: Pennsylvania State
University

University of Leicester M

University Rd.
Leicester LE1 7RH, United Kingdom
Fields offered: Applied linguistics, archaeology, organizational development, criminal justice, European Union law, finance, forensic & legal psychology, law & employment relations, business administration, marketing, mass communications, museum studies, primary education, public order studies, risk & crisis management, security & crime risk management, sport sociology, human resources
Year founded: 1921
Accreditation: International (GAAP)
Phone: +44 (116) 252 2298
Fax: +44 (116) 252 2200
Email: higherdegrees@le.ac.uk
Web site: www.le.ac.uk

Offers well-established distance-learning master's degrees in the above fields, available worldwide. Coursework is assessed by written assignment or by examination. Dissertation required. The M.S. in training and in training & human resource management is offered by the university's Centre for Labour Market Studies, which has made a special outreach to the North American and the Asia Pacific markets, with specially prepared course materials and regular faculty visits for optional meetings with students. The Centre is accredited by the Distance Education and Training Council (DETC).

University of Limerick

See: National Distance Education Centre (Ireland)

University of London B, M, D, Law

The External Programme
Senate House, Malet St.
London WC1E 7HU , England
Fields offered: See below
Year founded: 1836
Accreditation: International (GAAP)
Phone: +44 (20) 7862 8360
Fax: +44 (20) 7862 8358
Email: enquiries@external.lon.ac.uk
Web site: www.lon.ac.uk/external

London had the world's first external degree program and, after more than a century and a half, it is still among the most popular. Degrees are completed via examinations (proctored at Sylvan Learning Centers worldwide) and sometimes by thesis. Tutoring by correspondence is available but not required.

B.A. degrees are available in English, French, geography, German, Italian, Jewish history, philosophy, and Spanish & Latin American studies. Students are permitted to undertake joint language degrees (French & Italian, Italian & German, and so forth).

B.S. degrees are available in accounting & finance, banking & finance, computing & information systems, computing & statistics, economics (with optional emphasis in geography, sociology, or politics & international relations), information systems & management, law & management, management, mathematics & computing, and

mathematics & statistics. Other bachelor's degrees include the Bachelor of Divinity and the Bachelor of Laws.

Master's degrees are available in business administration, law, distance education, geography, agricultural development, agricultural economics, applied environmental economics, community dental practice, dental public health, dental radiology, clinical dentistry (for practicing dentists), development finance, drug and alcohol policy & intervention, environment & development, environmental management, epidemiology, financial economics, financial management, food industry management & marketing, health systems management, infectious diseases, livestock health & production, managing rural change, materials science & engineering, occupational psychology, organizational behavior, public policy & management, and sustainable agriculture & rural development.

University of Luton D

Park Square
Luton, Bedfordshire LU1 3JU, United Kingdom
Fields offered: Applied social studies, architecture/surveying/construction, biological sciences, business strategy & entrepreneurship, business systems & operations, computing, design & manufacturing, environment/geography/geology, electronics, foreign languages, health studies, history, human resource management, linguistics, literary studies, marketing & international business, media arts, politics & public policy, psychology, social studies, tourism & leisure
Accreditation: International (GAAP)
Phone: +44 (1582) 743 700
Fax: +44 (1582) 743 400
Email: admissions@luton.ac.uk
Web site: www.luton.ac.uk

A "Ph.D. by published work" is offered in the above fields, based on "extensive research record and substantial publications." This is unusual; other programs require the research for the Ph.D. to be completed *after* entry into a program. LL.D. and D.Sc. degrees may be awarded to candidates who already possess a Ph.D. degree and can document an unusually strong publication record. More traditional research Ph.D.'s are also available; contact the school for details. Luton is one of the former polytechnics, just north of London.

University of Manitoba B

Winnipeg, Manitoba R3T 2N2, Canada
Fields offered: Canadian studies, economics, geography, history, nursing, philosophy, political studies, psychology, social work, sociology
Year founded: 1877
Accreditation: International (GAAP)
Phone: +1 (204) 474 8012
Fax: +1 (204) 474 7660
Email: stuvcs_ced@umanitoba.ca
Web site: www.umanitoba.ca/coned/de

The University of Manitoba offers bachelor's programs in the fields listed above. Instruction takes place in both English and French, and coursework is accomplished via special course manuals, sometimes supplemented with audiotapes.

University of Maryland   B, M

University College
3501 University Blvd. East
Adelphi, MD 20783
Fields offered: See below
Year founded: 1856
Accreditation: Regional
Phone: (301) 985 7000 ▨ (800) 888 8682
Fax: (301) 454 0399
Email: umucinfo@umuc.edu
Web site: www.umuc.edu

University College, the continuing higher education campus of the University of Maryland System, offers online bachelor's degrees in 15 academic areas (accounting, behavioral & social sciences, business & management, communication studies, computer & information science, computer studies, English, environmental management, fire science, history, humanities, information systems management, management studies, paralegal studies, and psychology). Online master's degrees include an M.S. in computer systems management, M.S. in technology management (with optional tracks in biotechnology management or technology systems management), M.S. in telecommunications management, M.S. in e-commerce, M.S. in environmental management, M.S. in Management, Master of Software Engineering, Master of International Management, Master of Distance Education, and a Master of Business Administration (MBA).

University of Massachusetts—Amherst   M

Amherst, MA 01003
Fields offered: Computer science, electrical & computer engineering, engineering management
Year founded: 1863
Accreditation: Regional
Phone: (413) 545 0063
Fax: (413) 545 1227
Email: vip@vip.ecs.umass.edu
Web site: www.umass.edu

The Video Instructional Program (VIP) is an established distance-learning program providing graduate education to working engineers across the country. Using videotaped lectures and/or satellite broadcasts, professionals can enroll in the same classes offered to on-campus students, in both degree and nondegree formats. Master of Science degrees are offered in the above fields, and noncredit/training courses are offered in a variety of engineering-related disciplines.

University of Massachusetts—Lowell   A, B

One University Ave.
Lowell, MA 01854
Fields offered: Information systems
Year founded: 1894
Accreditation: Regional
Phone: (978) 934 2467 ▨ (800) 480 3190
Fax: (978) 934 3087
Email: cybered@uml.edu

Web site: cybered.uml.edu

The CyberEd division offers an A.S. and a B.S. in information systems totally over the Internet. Students can also enroll in one of four online certificate programs—Multimedia Applications, Intranet Development, Fundamentals of Information Technology, and UNIX—which can be applied to the A.S. and B.S. degrees. Students and faculty use the World Wide Web, email, chat, and other Internet resources to review assignments, collaborate on projects, collect reference materials, and complete homework.

University of Melbourne   M, D

Victoria, 3010, Australia
Fields offered: Accounting & finance, actuarial studies, agribusiness, agricultural animal medicine & production, American studies, anatomy, ancient & medieval studies, ancient Greek, animal production, anthropology, applied linguistics, Arabic studies, archaeology, architecture, art curatorship, art history, Asian economics, Asian studies, atmospheric science, audiology, Australian studies, behavioral science, biochemistry, biology, botany, business, Catalan, cell biology, ceramics, chemical engineering, chemistry, Chinese, cinema studies, civil engineering, classical studies, commerce, communication skills, complementary languages, computer applications in the social sciences & humanities, computer-assisted language learning, computer education, computer science, construction management, creative arts, creative writing, criminology, crop production, cultural studies, dance, dental science, drama, drawing, development studies, earth sciences, econometrics, economics, economics & commerce, education, electrical & electronic engineering, engineering, English, English as a second language, English language, environmental engineering, environmental horticulture & resource management, environmental science, environmental studies, European studies, evaluation, film & television, fine arts, food science & agribusiness, forestry, French, genetic counseling, geology, genetics, geography, geomatics, German, health & physical education, Hebrew, history, history & philosophy of science, immunology, Indonesian, information systems, Islamic studies, Italian, Japanese, Jewish studies, land & food resources, landscape architecture, Latin, law, legal studies, linguistics, management, manufacturing engineering, marketing, mathematics & statistics, mathematics education, mechanical engineering, media arts, medieval studies, medical biology, meteorology, microbiology, modern Greek, molecular biology, music, nursing, optometry & vision sciences, painting, parisitology, pathology, pharmacology, philosophy, photography, physical therapy, physics, physiology, physiology & pharmacology, physiotherapy, Polish, political science, Portuguese, print making, project management, property & construction, psychology, public health, reproduction, rural health, Russian, science education, sculpture, Semitic languages,

Slavic studies, social research methods, social theory, social work, sociology, software engineering, Spanish, Swedish, Thai, theater studies, Ukrainian, urban planning, visual arts, veterinary science, women's health, women's studies, zoology
Year founded: 1989
Accreditation: International (GAAP)
Phone: +61 (3) 8344 8670
Email: j.gilbert@sgs.unimelb.edu.au
Web site: www.unimelb.edu.au/research

The University of Melboune offers research-based master's and Ph.D. programs in the above fields. Remote students must find a suitable nearby university or medical school research facility and a suitable supervisor in the relevant field(s) of study. The Ph.D. requires at least one year of supervised full-time research (or two years of supervised part-time research) at this remote facility. The list of colleges approved as remote facilities is large and growing; students who do not live near an approved site may petition to have their nearby site added to the list of approved schools. Common sense would logically dictate one's success rate; for example, a petition to study doctoral-level electrical and electronic engineering at a small four-year liberal arts college would probably not be feasible, while a petition to study for a Ph.D. in Japanese under an established scholar in the field at a major state university would probably be accepted with no serious controversy at all.

University of Memphis   M

Department of Journalism
Memphis, TN 38152-6661
Fields offered: Journalism (news editorial, broadcasting, advertising, public relations, magazine)
Year founded: 1912
Accreditation: Regional
Phone: (901) 678 2401
Fax: (901) 678 4287
Email: cphilpot@memphis.edu
Web site: umvirtual.memphis.edu

Offers an online Master of Arts in journalism, wherein distance-learning students follow the same program as those on campus. Formerly Memphis State University. See also: National Fire Academy

University of Nebraska—Lincoln   M

Dept. of Entomology
202 Plant Industry Bldg.
Lincoln, NE 68583-0816
Fields offered: Biology (entomology)
Year founded: 1869
Accreditation: Regional
Phone: (402) 472 8689
Email: lhigley1@unl.edu
Web site: ianrwww.unl.edu/ianr/entomol/educatn/distancems.htm

An M.S. in entomology available totally by distance learning. Courses delivered by video and Internet. As a terminal, non-thesis degree, this program is not useful to those who plan to pursue a Ph.D. in entomology. For University of Nebraska's short-residency and in-state degree programs, see the listing in the following chapter.

University of New England   B, M, D, Law

Armidale, New South Wales 2351, Australia
Fields offered: See below
Year founded: 1938
Accreditation: International (GAAP)
Phone: +61 (2) 6773 3333
Fax: +61 (2) 6773 3122
Email: ipo@metz.une.edu.au
Web site: www.une.edu.au

This school offers a truly vast number of bachelor's and master's degrees, as well as a number of research doctorates; some programs require a visit to Australia, but many do not. Learning takes place via printed correspondence texts, audio- and videotapes, radio and television broadcasts, and Internet. UNE is Australia's oldest distance-education provider, and has thousands of students enrolled in external programs.

Bachelor's degrees are offered in agriculture, Aboriginal studies, ancient history, archaeology, paleoanthropology, Asian societies, Chinese, classical studies, communication studies, composition, economic history, economics, English, social science, ethnomusicology, European cultures, French, geography & planning, German, Greek, history, Indonesian, international relations, Italian, Japanese, Latin, linguistics, mathematics, modern Greek, musicology, philosophy, political science, psychology, sociology, studies in religion, theater studies, women's & gender studies, Asian studies, commerce, computer science (online), engineering technology (audio or electronics), environmental science, financial administration (online), law (LL.B.), natural resources, rural science, general science, biomedical science, biosystematics, ecology, horticultural science, molecular biology, technology, and urban & regional planning (online).

Master's degrees include the fields of ancient history, archaeological heritage, Asian societies, Chinese, communication studies, defense studies, English, French, German, geography & planning, history, Indonesian, Islamic studies, Japanese, philosophy, peace studies, political science, public policy, sociology, studies in religion, women's & gender studies, Asian studies, business administration (with emphasis in agribusiness management, association management, human resource management, international business, local government, marketing, professional accounting, or public sector management), commerce (in accounting, agribusiness, finance & banking, or small business & entrepreneurship), computer studies, economic studies (in agricultural & resource economics, economic analysis, economic development, economic history, economics, or efficiency & productivity analysis), law (LL.M.), American studies, biology, classics, development studies, education, ethnomusicology, European cultures, Greek, international relations, Italian, Latin, linguistics, mathematics, musicology, statistics, theater studies, computer science, mathematics, molecular & cellular biology, and zoology.

External research Ph.D.'s are available with a vast array of specializations, and administered by faculties in the following subject areas: arts, biological sciences, business, classics, communication, computer science, cultures, economics, education, engineering, English, health, history, human & environmental studies, languages, law, linguistics, mathematics, music, physical sciences, professional studies, religion, and theater.

University of Northern Colorado   B, M

Greeley, CO 80639
Fields offered: Special education, school psychology, communication disorders, nursing
Year founded: 1889
Accreditation: Regional
Phone: (970) 351 1936 ▪ (800) 232 1749
Fax: (970) 351 2519
Web site: www.unco.edu/center/oes

M.A. in special education, Ed.S. in school psychology, M.A. in communication disorders, and an RN to BSN nursing program. Distance methods are based primarily on online courses and independent study.

University of Northern Iowa   B, M

1227 West 27th St.
Cedar Falls, IA 50614
Fields offered: Education-related fields (see below), English, industrial technology, liberal studies, library science, public relations
Year founded: 1847
Accreditation: Regional
Phone: (319) 273 2121 ▪ (800) 772 1746
Email: contined@uni.edu
Web site: www.uni.edu

Bachelor's completion programs in liberal studies, elementary education, and industrial technology. Credit is earned primarily through guided correspondence study courses, but other options include on-campus evening and week-end courses, televised courses, off-campus course sites throughout Iowa, courses from other regionally accredited four-year colleges (both on-campus and correspondence), and online courses. To qualify for admission, a student must live in the United States and have completed 62 transferable units or have an associate's degree.

Distance-learning M.A. programs are available in communication education, education (with emphasis on educational leadership, elementary reading & language arts, middle school education, or special education), educational technology, English, industrial technology, library science, middle school mathematics, and public relations. An M.Mus. in music education is also available. Most programs require no on-campus residency.

University of Northumbria at Newcastle   M

Flexible Management Learning Centre
Newcastle Business School
Northumberland Building
Newcastle Upon Tyne NE1 8ST, United Kingdom
Fields offered: Business administration
Year founded: 1969
Accreditation: International (GAAP)
Phone: +44 (191) 227 4942
Fax: +44 (191) 227 4684

Email: d.thompson@unn.ac.uk
Web site: fmlc.unn.ac.uk

Internet-based MBA program is available internationally. Challenge papers are posted on the Web for discussion, and students are assigned to "buddy" groups.

University of Otago   B, M

P.O. Box 56
Dunedin, New Zealand
Fields offered: Theology, ministry, social welfare, consumer & applied sciences
Year founded: 1869
Accreditation: International (GAAP)
Phone: +64 (3) 479 8247
Fax: +64 (3) 479 7377
Email: external-relations@otago.ac.nz
Web site: www.otago.ac.nz

In addition to a vast array of postgraduate diploma and certificate programs, New Zealand's oldest university offers a Bachelor of Theology (Th.B.), Master of Ministry (M.Min.), Master of Consumer & Applied Sciences in Community and Family Studies, and Master of Social Welfare. Many of these are based on audioconference class sessions supplemented by written course materials supported by references, assignments, tapes, self-assessment exercises and, of course, regular contact with tutors by letter, phone, or electronic means. Postgraduate certificates are equivalent to one semester (six months) full-time work, postgraduate diplomas are equivalent to 12 months' full-time work, and master's degrees are equivalent to two years of full-time work.

University of Phoenix   B, M, D

4615 East Elwood St.
Phoenix, AZ 85072
Fields offered: Business (see fields below), management, information technology, education, nursing
Year founded: 1976
Accreditation: Regional
Phone: (480) 966 9577 ▪ (800) 742 4742
Fax: (480) 829 9030
Web site: www.phoenix.edu

In 1989, the Arizona-based University of Phoenix, the largest private university in the U.S., began offering degrees entirely via computer. Online students get their assignments, have group discussions, and ask questions of their professors all over the Internet. Each class meeting is spread out over an entire week, allowing students to complete their work at their convenience. Bachelor's in business/accounting, business/administration, business/information systems, business/management, business/marketing, e-business, information technology, and nursing. Master's in education, organizational management, computer information systems, and nursing. The MBA, with optional concentrations in accounting, global management, technology management, or e-business, can be taken by text-based correspondence rather than online. Also available is a short-residency Doctor of Management in Organizational Leadership.

University of Plymouth

The International Office
Drake Circus
Plymouth PL4 8AA, United Kingdom
Fields offered: Perfumery
Accreditation: International (GAAP)
Phone: +44 (1752) 233 345
Email: intoff@plymouth.ac.uk
Web site: www.plymouth.ac.uk

Offers a diploma in perfumery to students worldwide via correspondence.

University of Pretoria   B, M, D, Law

Pretoria 0002, South Africa
Fields offered: See below
Year founded: 1930
Accreditation: International (GAAP)
Phone: +27 (12) 420 3884
Fax: +27 (12) 362 5168
Email: telehelp@postino.up.ac.za
Web site: www.up.ac.za/telematic

Offers degrees through online Web-based coursework, interactive television, traditional paper correspondence, workshops, block residencies, or any mix of the above methods.

The B.A. is generally offered through paper correspondence or online coursework with no required residency, and is offered in the following fields: accounting, augmentative & alternative communication, biblical studies, education, general literature science, general studies, information science & library science, language (Afrikaans, English, Ndebele, Pedi, Tswana, or Zulu), Old Testament, recreation & sport management, and social sciences.

The Bachelor of Engineering (B.Ing.) generally requires extensive block residencies, although the exact location of these residencies may or may not be negotiable. It is available in the following fields: applied sciences, bioengineering, biosystems, computer engineering, electrical engineering, electronic engineering, electronics, electrotechnics, microelectronics, and process industry.

Other degrees offered at the undergraduate level include the Bachelor of Agriculture (B.Inst.Agrar.), Bachelor of Commerce (in aviation management, communication management, or marketing management), Bachelor of Education (B.Ed.), Bachelor of Home Economics, Bachelor of Laws (LL.B.), and Bachelor of Nursing (B.Cur.). A variety of undergraduate diploma and certificate programs are also available.

Master's programs are offered in augmentative & alternative communication, biblical studies, environmental psychology, linguistics (emphasis on Pedi or Zulu), research psychology, financial management, taxation, diplomatic studies, divinity, education (optional emphasis in computer-assisted education, education management, or potential development in education and training), engineering (bio-, computer, electrical, electronic, or microelectronic), music education, political policy studies, public affairs (emphasis on international management), leadership development, public finance management, urban & regional management, public health, applied sciences, biosystems, electrotechnics, engineering man-

agement, orthodontics, project management, real estate, and security studies.

Ph.D. programs are available in augmentative & alternative communication, biblical studies, electrical engineering, electronic engineering, Old Testament, and public affairs. A short residency D.Phil. in psychotherapy is also available.

University of Reading

See: College of Estate Management

University of Saint Francis (Illinois)   B, M

500 Wilcox St.
Joliet, IL 60435
Fields offered: Business administration, health services
Year founded: 1920
Accreditation: Regional
Phone: (815) 740 3360 ▪ (800) 735 7500
Fax: (815) 740 4285
Email: admissions@stfrancis.edu
Web site: www.stfrancis.edu

B.S. in health arts is a degree completion program for health care professionals such as registered nurses, radiologic technologists, dental hygienists, etc. Online master's degrees include an MBA (with a concentration in management or health services) and an M.S. in health services administration.

University of Saskatchewan   B

Extension Credit Studies
326-117 Science Place
Saskatoon, SK S7N 5C8, Canada
Fields offered: Adult education, agriculture, anthropology, archaeology, biology, computer science, ecological education, English, French, geography, geology, history, horticulture, mathematics, microbiology, music, Native studies, nursing, philosophy, psychology, religious studies, sociology, TESOL
Year founded: 1907
Accreditation: International (GAAP)
Phone: +1 (306) 966 5563
Fax: +1 (306) 966 5590
Email: extcred@usask.ca
Web site: www.extension.usask.ca

A wide variety of undergraduate certificate programs are offered via independent study, and bachelor's programs may be completed by a mix of independent study, transfer credit, credit by examination, and life experience. There is also a special B.S. in nursing for holders of nursing diplomas currently registered and working in Canada.

University of South Africa   B, M, D

P.O. Box 392
Unisa 0003, South Africa
Fields offered: See below
Year founded: 1873
Accreditation: International (GAAP)
Phone: +27 (12) 429 3111
Fax: +27 (12) 429 3221
Email: study-info@alpha.unisa.ac.za

Web site: www.unisa.ac.za

UNISA offers a huge number of courses, degrees, and certificates at all levels, and nearly all of them are available entirely by distance learning (largely via guided research and correspondence, although UNISA has recently begun to offer online courses as well). Examinations may be taken at South African embassies and consulates worldwide. At one time, UNISA offered the least expensive distance-learning programs in the world; this was due to the fact that, until recently, UNISA subsidized students worldwide. This practice is being phased out at press time, although UNISA's unsubsidized rates are still fairly low.

The honours (four-year) bachelor's is available in accounting, accounting science, African languages (with optional emphasis in northern Sotho, Shona, southern Sotho, Swati, Tsonga, Tswana, Venda, Xhosa, or Zulu), African politics, Afrikaans, ancient history, anthropology, applied mathematics, Arabic, art history, astronomy, auditing, Biblical studies, business management, chemistry, church history, classics, commerce, communication, computer science, criminology, development administration, economics, education, educational management, English, French, gender studies, geography, German, gifted child education, Greek, guidance & counseling, history, industrial psychology, information science, information systems, international politics, Islamic studies, Italian, Judaica, Latin, law, linguistics, mathematics, missiology, modern Hebrew, musicology, New Testament, Old Testament, operations research, penology, philosophy, physics, police science, politics, Portuguese, practical theology, preprimary education, primary education, psychology, public administration, quantitative management, religious studies, Romance languages, Russian, secondary education, Semitic languages, social science (with specialization in criminology, development administration, psychology, social work, or sociology), Spanish, statistics, systematic theology, theological ethics, theory of literature, and transport economics.

Master's degrees are available in most of the fields listed above, as well as ancient languages & cultures, archaeology, banking law, business leadership, Christian spirituality, clinical psychology, commercial law, comparative education, corporate law, counseling psychology, criminal law & criminal procedure, didactics, educational management, environmental education, history of education, insurance law, intellectual property law, international communication, international economic law, labor law, mathematics education, mental health, natural science education, nursing science (with specialization in clinical nursing science, community health, health sciences education, health services management, or nursing ethos and professional practice), pastoral therapy, philosophy of education, philosophy of law, psychology of education, socio-education, sociolinguistics, urban ministry, and visual arts.

Doctorates are available in nearly all of the fields listed above.

U.S. students interested in UNISA should contact UNISA's U.S. agent: American International Higher Education Corporation (AIHEC), 5808 Misty Hill Cove, Austin, Texas 78759; phone: (512) 343 2031; fax: (512) 343 8644; email: *jcraparo@aihec.com*; Web site: *www.aihec.com*.

University of South Alabama   B, M

Office of Admissions
182 Administrative Bldg.
Mobile, AL 36688-0002
Fields offered: Advanced gerontological nursing, business administration, education, educational administration, educational media, instructional design & development, nursing, nursing education, special education (collaborative teaching or gifted education)
Accreditation: Regional
Phone: (334) 460 6141 ▪ (800) 872 5247
Fax: (334) 460 7876
Email: admiss@usamail.usouthal.edu
Web site: usaonline.southalabama.edu

Offers the following programs through online study: a BSN completion program for registered nurses; an MBA; a Master of Education in educational administration, educational media, or special education (with emphasis on collaborative teaching or gifted education); an M.S. in instructional design & development; and an M.S. in nursing (with emphasis on advanced gerontological nursing or nursing education). A variety of Class A teaching certificates are also available through online study. Some programs may require brief residency sessions.

University of South Australia   B, M, D

GPO Box 2471
Adelaide, SA 5001, Australia
Fields offered: Accountancy, business administration, business & management, business banking & finance, communication & media management, computer & information science, counseling, early childhood education, education, information technology, manufacturing management, nursing, pharmacy, project management
Year founded: 1991
Accreditation: International (GAAP)
Phone: +61 (8) 8302 0114
Fax: +61 (8) 8302 0233
Email: international.office@unisa.edu.au
Web site: www.unisa.edu.au

This school offers a wide range of programs through distance-learning methods. The following degrees are available to overseas students: the Bachelor of Accountancy, Bachelor of Business Administration (BBA), Bachelor of Business Banking & Finance, B.A. in communication and media management, Bachelor of Computer & Information Science, Bachelor of Education in early childhood education, Bachelor of Nursing, Bachelor of Pharmacy, Master of Business Administration (MBA), Master of Manufacturing Management, Master of Project Management, Master of Social Science in counseling, Doctor of Business Administration (DBA), and Doctor of Education. Nonresidential research Ph.D. programs are available in business and management and in education (with optional specializations in a variety of fields, including art education, curriculum leadership, distance education, early childhood education, religious education, and women in education).

University of Southern California   M

University Park
Los Angeles, CA 90089-0012
Fields offered: Gerontology
Year founded: 1880
Accreditation: Regional
Phone: (213) 740 1364 ▪ (800) 331 0558
Fax: (213) 740 7254
Web site: www.usc.edu

Online M.A. in gerontology designed for working professionals involved in the care of the elderly.

University of Southern Colorado   B

2200 Bonforte Blvd.
Pueblo, CO 81001-4901
Fields offered: Social science (sociology, psychology, history, political science, anthropology, economics)
Year founded: 1933
Accreditation: Regional
Phone: (719) 549 2316 ▪ (877) 872 9653
Email: coned@uscolo.edu
Web site: www.uscolo.edu/coned

Bachelor of Science in social science through a combination of correspondence courses, transfer credits, and exams. While this is primarily a degree-completion program, the school will help students to choose courses at local institutions (or correspondence courses from other schools) to meet their requirements. Degree-completion students must complete at least 32 credits with USC; a maximum of 96 credits can be transferred in, and 64 of those can be from junior colleges.

University of Southern Queensland   B, M, D

International Office
Toowoomba Qld, Queensland 4350, Australia
Fields offered: See below
Year founded: 1967
Accreditation: International (GAAP)
Phone: +61 (74) 631 2362
Fax: +61 (74) 636 2211
Email: international@usq.edu.au
Web site: www.usqonline.com.au

The University of Southern Queensland evolved from the Darling Downs Institute of Advanced Education. They offer degrees at all levels in an immense array of fields, and new programs are regularly added. Programs are offered through two distance learning mediums: correspondence and online.

Degrees offered at the undergraduate level include the B.A. (major in anthropology, Asian studies, communication & media studies, English literature, Indonesian language, international relations, journalism, or public relations), B.S. (major in applied mathematics, computing, mathematics, psychological studies, psychology, or statistics), the Bachelor of General Studies, the Bachelor of Business (major in administrative management, applied economics & resource management, computer software development, human resource management practices, information technology management, logistics & operations management, marketing, or strategic human resource management), the Bachelor of Business Administration (BBA), the Bachelor of Commerce (with optional specialization in accounting, banking, or finance), the Bachelor of Engineering (with major in agricultural engineering, civil engineering, computer systems engineering, electrical & electronic engineering, environmental engineering, instrumentation & control, mechanical engineering, mechatronic engineering, mining, or software engineering), the Bachelor of Technology (in geographic information systems or surveying), the Bachelor of Engineering Technology (in building & construction management, civil engineering technology, electrical & electronic engineering technology, environmental engineering technology, or mechanical engineering technology), the Bachelor of Information Technology (in applied computer science, computer software development, industrial computing, information technology management, networking, or software engineering), the Bachelor of Education (with an optional specialization in further education and training), the Bachelor of Education Studies, the Bachelor of Further Education & Training, the Bachelor of Applied Finance, the Bachelor of Surveying, and the Bachelor of Nursing. Double majors are permitted in most reasonable cases. Credit for prior learning is also available.

Degrees at the master's level include the Master of Business Administration (MBA), Master of e-business, Master of Business (in environmental management, human resource management, information systems, international business, leadership, marketing, occupational health & safety, or project management), Master of Commerce (in accounting, business law, or finance), Master of Business Information Technology, Master of Management, Master of Information Technology, Master of Engineering (in agricultural engineering, computer systems engineering, electrical & electronic engineering, environmental engineering, instrumentation & control, or mechatronics), Master of Engineering Technology (in agricultural technology, computer systems engineering technology, electrical & electronic engineering technology, environmental engineering technology, instrumentation & control technology, or mechatronic engineering technology), Master of Education (in advanced studies in teaching, children's literature, cross-disciplinary studies, curriculum, education technology, educational management, further education & training, guidance & counseling, online education, open & distance learning, special education, or teaching second languages), Master of Educational Technology, Master of Open & Distance Learning, Master of Online Education, Master of Arts Management, Master of Professional Communication (in applied communication, multimedia studies, or public relations), Master of Applied Linguistics, Master of Editing & Publishing, Master of Applied Finance, Master of Commercial Law, Master of Professional Accounting, Master of Professional Computing, Master of Geomatics, Master of Health Communication Systems, Master of Nursing, Master of Midwifery, Master of Health in rural & remote health, and Master of Occupational Health & Safety Nursing.

At the doctoral level, students may choose the Doctor of Business Administration (DBA) or the Doctor of Education in professional leadership. It may be possible to negotiate a research M.Phil. or Ph.D. on a case-by-case basis.

University of Strathclyde   M

International Office
Level 4, Graham Hills Bldg.
50 George St.
Glasgow G1 1QE, United Kingdom
Fields offered: Law (information technology law)
Year founded: 1796
Accreditation: International (GAAP)
Phone: +44 (141) 548 3291
Fax: +44 (141) 553 1546
Email: international@mis.strath.ac.uk
Web site: itlaw.law.strath.ac.uk

The Master of Law (LL.M) with a specialty in information technology is offered over the Internet. Distance-learning options are also available for the MBA and M.S. in international marketing, but only for students within traveling distance of a learning center. For locations of these centers, contact the school directly.

University of Sunderland   B, M

Langham Tower, Ryhope Rd.
Sunderland SR2 7EE, United Kingdom
Fields offered: Engineering, business, business information technology, computer information systems, education, podiatric medicine
Accreditation: International (GAAP)
Phone: +44 (191) 515 2000
Fax: +44 (191) 515 2147
Email: international@sunderland.ac.uk
Web site: www.sunderland.ac.uk

Sunderland offers a number of specialized distance-learning degrees, as well as a research doctorate option. The B.A. in business studies and business information technology can be earned through completion of 18 modules, using print study materials, with support by fax, email, and Internet. Assessment is by examination, usually in the U.K., although arrangements can be made for students who do not wish to travel there. A B.Eng. is available through independent study; some attendance at approved learning centers is required, but the school is flexible. A B.S. in podiatric medicine requires attendance at residential weeks, but these can be arranged to suit learners, if there are sufficient numbers with similar needs. A B.A. in education usually requires some residency, but tutorial sessions may be able to be accomplished through videoconferencing. At the graduate level, there is an MBA offered via distance learning through centers in Saudi Arabia, Greece, and Malaysia. The M.S. in computer-based information systems is available by distance learning, with study centers in the U.K., Hong Kong, Bahrain, Saudi Arabia, Greece, Israel, and Malaysia.

University of Surrey   M

Guildford
Surrey GU2 7XH, United Kingdom
Fields offered: Bridge engineering, business administration, business management, general practitioner training, medical education, structural engineering
Year founded: 1891
Accreditation: International (GAAP)
Phone: +44 (1483) 300 800
Fax: +44 (1483) 300 803
Email: information@surrey.ac.uk
Web site: www.surrey.ac.uk/Postgrad

Most of the degree programs consist of modules based on printed materials, audiocassette, computer programs, Internet, and workshops. It is possible to complete these programs entirely through distance learning—some modules do not have the workshop requirements, and in those that do, it may be possible to fulfill them by meeting with approved staff in your area. These degrees include an MBA, an M.A. in medical education, and M.S. programs in bridge engineering, general practitioner training, and structural engineering. Surrey is also making a promising foray into online distance education; two degree programs, the MBA and M.S. in business management, may be completed entirely online with no workshops. Surrey does accept students from other countries. Nonnative speakers are required to produce confirmation of English ability.

University of Tasmania   M, D

Board of Graduate Studies by Research
Churchill Ave., Sandy Bay
G.P.O. Box 252-45
Hobart, Tasmania 7001, Australia
Fields offered: Accounting & finance, agricultural science, aquaculture, architecture, computing, economics, education, engineering, environmental studies, fine arts, humanities & social science, information systems, law, management, medical science, music, pharmacy, psychology, science, surveying
Accreditation: International (GAAP)
Phone: +61 (3) 6226 2762
Fax: +61 (3) 6226 7497
Email: international.office@utas.edu.au
Web site: www.international.utas.edu.au

Research-based master's and Ph.D. programs are available in all of the fields listed above. Students may complete the programs through independent study combined with a number of residencies in Tasmania, or (of more interest to our readers) on the basis of prior written work (published or unpublished).

University of Technology, Sydney   D

P.O. Box 123
Broadway, NSW 2007, Australia
Fields offered: Accounting, adult & vocational education, applied physics, architecture, bioethics, building studies, cell & molecular biology, chemistry, civil engineering, computer science, computer systems engineering, constitutional law, corporate governance, cultural studies, design, economics, electrical engineering, environmental sciences, finance, forensic sciences, health services management, information studies, information

Uh-oh. Lesson 4 in Pablito's home-study
meteorology course seems to be going awry.

systems, international commerce law, international
law, international studies, language & literacy,
leisure sport & tourism, management,
manufacturing, marketing, materials science,
mechanical engineering, media arts, medical
biomedical & health sciences, midwifery, nursing,
operations research, pure & applied mathematics,
social sciences, statistics, sustainable futures, teacher
education, telecommunications engineering
Accreditation: International (GAAP)
Phone: +61 (2) 9514 2000
Email: info.office@uts.edu.au
Web site: www.gradschool.uts.edu.au/courses/
phdpub_info.html
The Ph.D. by Publication program awards doctoral
degrees to established researchers on the basis of their record
of academic publication and their original scholarly
contribution to knowledge. An applicant must submit his
or her published works and an extended paper integrating
the work.

University of Texas System   M

Office of Information Technology and Distance
Education
201 West Seventh St.
Austin, TX 78701
Fields offered: Educational technology, business
administration, kinesiology, computer science,
electrical engineering, reading
Year founded: 1973
Accreditation: Regional
Phone: (512) 499 4207 ▪ (888) 786 9832
Email: telecampus@utsystem.edu
Web site: www.telecampus.utsystem.edu
The UT TeleCampus pools the distance-learning offerings
of the 15-campus University of Texas system. Online
degree programs include an MBA in general management,
M.Ed. in educational technology, Master's in Kinesiology,
M.S. in computer science, M.S. in electrical engineering,
and M.Ed. in ESL reading.

University of the State of New York
See: Excelsior College

University of Victoria   B

P.O. Box 1700 STN CSC
Victoria, BC V8W 2Y2, Canada
Fields offered: Child & youth care, social work,
nursing
Accreditation: International (GAAP)
Phone: +1 (250) 721 7211
Fax: +1 (250) 721 6603
Email: srsad13@uvvm.uvic.ca
Web site: www.uvic.ca
Students at a distance receive instruction through print
packages, audiotapes, computer-assisted learning, and video-
tapes. Instructors lead group discussions, using audio
or computer conferencing, and tutors answer queries
and discuss assignments by phone and/or email. Degrees
offered are a B.A. in child & youth care, a Bachelor of Social
Work, and a B.S. in nursing.

University of Virginia   M

Televised Graduate Engineering
Thornton Hall
Charlottesville, VA 22903
Fields offered: Engineering
Year founded: 1819
Accreditation: Regional
Phone: (804) 982 2313
Fax: (804) 924 4086
Email: rfk2u@virginia.edu
Web site: watt.seas.virginia.edu/~rfk2u
Master of Engineering in a number of fields, including
chemical, civil, electrical, materials science, mechanical &
aerospace, and systems engineering, available by satellite.
Classes are televised live to numerous locations throughout
the U.S. in the evening hours, four days a week.

University of Wales—Lampeter   M, D

Ceredigion, Wales SA48 7ED, United Kingdom
Fields offered: See below
Year founded: 1822
Accreditation: International (GAAP)
Phone: +44 (1570) 424 748
Fax: +44 (1570) 422 840
Email: pg-office@lampeter.ac.uk
Web site: www.lamp.ac.uk
Offers taught master's degrees and research doctorates
entirely nonresidentially, although students are asked to

visit Wales at least once a year if at all possible. The Th.M. in church history is available through distance learning. Taught M.A. degrees are available in British Empire & Commonwealth studies, Celtic Christianity, death & immortality, ethics of life & death, religion politics & international relations, religious experience, and visual representations in history; distance-learning M.A. degrees in death studies, feminist theology, and study of religion may also be arranged on a case-by-case basis. Research M.Phil. and Ph.D. programs are available in anthropology, archaeology, classics, English, geography, history, Islamic studies, philosophy, religious studies, and theology. Formerly St. David's College.

University of Waterloo   B, M
Waterloo, ON N2L 3G1, Canada
Fields offered: See below
Year founded: 1957
Accreditation: International (GAAP)
Phone: +1 (519) 888 4050
Fax: +1 (519) 746 6393
Email: distance@admmail.uwaterloo.ca
Web site: dce.uwaterloo.ca

Distance-learning bachelor's degrees with the following major options: Canadian studies, classical studies, economics, English, environmental studies, French, geography, history, medieval studies, philosophy, psychology, religious studies, social development studies, or sociology. Master's degree available in management of technology. Credit is considered for prior academic experience, but none for experiential learning. The programs are available to people residing in Canada and the United States, but U.S. citizens pay three to four times as much tuition. All courses are offered on a rigid time schedule, in which papers and exams must be done by very specific times. As a result, there have been postal delivery problems with some U.S. students.

University of Wisconsin—Madison   M
College of Engineering
432 North Lake St.
Madison, WI 53706
Fields offered: Engineering (technical Japanese)
Year founded: 1849
Accreditation: Regional
Phone: (608) 262 2061 ▪ (800) 462 0876
Fax: (608) 263 3160
Email: custserv@epd.engr.wisc.edu
Web site: www.engr.wisc.edu

A one year program, the Master of Engineering in Technical Japanese teaches skills and knowledge to interact effectively with Japanese counterparts in the technical or business arena. Also available from the engineering school is a Professional Development Degree, a post-bachelor's degree geared to helping engineers reach personal professional objectives.

University of Wisconsin—Milwaukee   M
P.O. Box 413
Milwaukee, WI 53211
Fields offered: Library science

Year founded: 1885
Accreditation: Regional
Phone: (414) 229 4707 ▪ (888) 349 3432
Fax: (414) 229 4848
Email: info@slis.uwm.edu
Web site: www.slis.uwm.edu

Master of Library & Information Science offered over the Internet and by compressed video.

University of Wisconsin—Platteville   B, M
1 University Plaza
Platteville, WI 53818
Fields offered: Business administration, criminal justice, engineering, project management
Year founded: 1866
Accreditation: Regional
Phone: (608) 342 1491 ▪ (800) 362 5460
Fax: (608) 342 1232
Email: disted@uwplatt.edu
Web site: www.uwplatt.edu

Master's programs—M.S. in criminal justice, Master of Engineering, and M.S. in project management—are offered exclusively over the Internet. For the B.S. in business administration, students have the option of earning the degree online or taking print-based courses.

University of Wisconsin—Stout   M
448 Home Economics Building
Menomonie, WI 54751
Fields offered: Hospitality & tourism
Year founded: 1891
Accreditation: Regional
Phone: (715) 232 1480
Email: daviesb@uwstout.edu
Web site: www.uwstout.edu/programs/msht/ghm

The online M.S. in hospitality & tourism concentrates in global hospitality management. Students must meet together at least twice, at the beginning and end of the program, at a site determined by the geographic location of the students.

University of Wisconsin—Superior   B
Extended Degree Program
Erlanson 105
P.O. Box 2000
Superior, WI 54880
Fields offered: Individualized
Year founded: 1893
Accreditation: Regional
Phone: (715) 394 8487
Fax: (715) 394 8139
Email: extdegree@uwsuperior.edu
Web site: edp.uwsuper.edu

Bachelor of Science can be completed entirely through off-campus, independent, faculty-guided study. However, on-campus conferences with faculty are required. The student designs an individualized major based on personal or career goals. Self-paced courses developed by the university faculty in a wide variety of fields are the primary mode of learning, in addition to learning contracts. The student has the option of requesting credit for prior learning through the development of a portfolio.

University of Wisconsin—Whitewater M
On-Line MBA
4033 Carlson Hall
College of Business and Economics
Whitewater, WI 53190
Fields offered: Business administration
Year founded: 1868
Accreditation: Regional
Phone: (414) 472 1945
Fax: (414) 472 4863
Email: zahnd@uwwvax.uww.edu
Web site: www.uww.edu/business/onlinemba
A wholly online MBA with emphases in finance, management, and marketing. (A number of other emphases, from healthcare to international business, are offered through a combination of on-campus and on-line courses.) Faculty contact is by phone, fax, and email, and the university makes a point of its faculty being interested in a high level of student contact.

University of Wolverhampton
See: Holborn College

Upper Iowa University B, M
P.O. Box 1861
Fayette, IA 52142
Fields offered: Accounting, business, human services, human resources management, management, marketing, social sciences, public administration
Year founded: 1857
Accreditation: Regional
Phone: (319) 425 5252 ▪ (888) 877 3742
Fax: (319) 425 5353
Email: extdegree@uiu.edu
Web site: www.uiu.edu
Upper Iowa's External Degree Program offers the opportunity to earn a B.S. majoring in one of the above fields, entirely through self-paced directed independent study, with learning packets containing assignments and other course materials. Frequent interaction with the faculty by phone, fax, email, or regular post is encouraged. Previous college work, job and military training, and other educational experience is evaluated for credit. Offered online is an M.A. in business leadership.

Utah State University M
School of Graduate Studies
Graduate Office, Old Main 164
Logan, UT 84322
Fields offered: Technical writing
Year founded: 1888
Accreditation: Regional
Phone: (435) 797 1189
Fax: (435) 797 1192
Email: gradsch@cc.usu.edu
Web site:
english.usu.edu/dept/instruction/online/TechWriting
Totally online master's degree in technical writing. Designed for working technical/professional communi-

cators who want to enhance their credentials and build a theoretical understanding of their profession.

Valdosta State University M
Valdosta, GA 31698
Fields offered: Public administration
Year founded: 1906
Accreditation: Regional
Phone: (912) 245 3842
Fax: (912) 333 5397
Email: smcclain@valdosta.edu
Web site: valdosta.ecollege.com
Offers an online Master of Public Administration (MPA) through eCollege.com.

Victoria University M
P.O. Box 600
Wellington 6001, New Zealand
Fields offered: Communications studies
Year founded: 1899
Accreditation: International (GAAP)
Phone: +64 (4) 495 5266
Fax: +64 (4) 495 5235
Email: lalita.rajasingham@vuw.ac.nz
Web site:
www.vuw.ac.nz/comms/courses/mcomms.htm
This New Zealand university offers a master's degree in communication entirely over the Internet, using audio, video, and interactive graphics.

Virginia Polytechnic Institute and State University M
Blacksburg, VA 24061
Fields offered: Engineering, political science, business administration
Year founded: 1872
Accreditation: Regional
Phone: (540) 231 6000
Fax: (540) 231 9263
Email: gradsect@vt.edu
Web site: www.vt.edu
M.S. or M.E. in various engineering fields (electrical, mechanical, system, civil, industrial, ocean, and aerospace) though satellite courses available nationwide. M.A. in political science is delivered entirely over the Internet. The Satellite MBA program is broadcast to sites all over Virginia.

Walden University M
155 Fifth Ave. South
Minneapolis, MN 55401
Fields offered: Educational technology, psychology
Year founded: 1970
Accreditation: Regional
Phone: (612) 338 7224 ▪ (800) 925 3368
Fax: (612) 338 5092
Email: info@waldenu.edu
Web site: www.waldenu.edu
Master's programs in the above fields can be completed entirely over the Internet. Each student is guided by a faculty mentor. For information on Walden's short-residency doctoral programs, see the next chapter.

Washington State University   B, M, D

Extended Degree Programs
Van Doren Hall 204
P.O. Box 645220
Pullman, WA 99164-5220
Fields offered: Agriculture, business administration,
criminal justice, education, engineering
management, human development, manufacturing
engineering, pharmacy, social sciences
Year founded: 1890
Accreditation: Regional
Phone: (509) 335 3557 ▓ (800) 222 4978
Fax: (509) 335 4850
Email: edp@wsu.edu
Web site: www.eus.wsu.edu/edp

Washington State University offers distance-learning
bachelor's programs in agriculture, business administration, criminal justice, human development, and social
sciences, designed primarily for students who have
completed the equivalent of the first two years of college.
An M.S. in agriculture is also available. These degrees can
be earned entirely nonresidentially through a variety of
distance-learning methods, including correspondence
and television courses, guided independent study, audio-
and videocassettes, and telephone instruction. Washington
State also offers a B.A. in education (with teaching certificate),
a B.S. in manufacturing engineering, a Master of Engineering
Management, and a Doctor of Pharmacy to residents of
Washington through a combination of distance learning
and on-site study.

Webster University (Missouri)   M

470 E. Lockwood Ave.
St. Louis, MO 63119
Fields offered: Business administration
Year founded: 1915
Accreditation: Regional
Phone: (314) 968 7100 ▓ (800) 981 9801
Fax: (314) 968 7116
Email: gadmit@webster.edu
Web site: www.webster.edu

Offers an online MBA. Also offers master's degrees by
extension in several fields to sites nationwide.

Western Australian College of Advanced Education

See: Edith Cowan University

Western Illinois University   B

Non-Traditional Programs
5 Horrabin Hall
1 University Circle
Macomb, IL 61455
Fields offered: Individualized
Year founded: 1899
Accreditation: Regional
Phone: (309) 298 1929
Fax: (309) 298 2226
Email: np-bot@wiu.edu
Web site: www.wiu.edu/users/mintp

The Board of Trustees B.A. can be earned entirely by
correspondence study. 15 of 120 semester hours must be
earned through Western Illinois University, and 40 must
be upper division. The 15 units that must be earned
through enrollment at Western Illinois University can be
done by correspondence, on campus in Macomb, or
through extension courses at locations around the state.
Students who did not graduate from an Illinois high
school must pass an exam on the U.S. and Illinois state
constitutions, or take an equivalent course in political
science. All students must pass a university writing exam.
Western Illinois provides a helpful guide to the preparation of a prior learning portfolio. Credit for learning
experiences and many equivalency exams. The total cost
of the program depends on the number and type of
courses taken. Students from other countries are admitted,
but they must have a U.S. address to which materials can
be sent. See also: National Fire Academy

Western Oregon University

See: National Fire Academy

Wolverhampton Polytechnic

See: Holborn College

Worcester Polytechnic Institute   M

Advanced Distance Learning Network
100 Institute Rd.
Worcester, MA 01609-2280
Fields offered: Business administration, civil &
environmental engineering, fire protection
engineering, management of technology
Year founded: 1865
Accreditation: Regional
Phone: (508) 831 5220
Fax: (508) 831 5881
Email: adln@wpi.edu
Web site: www.wpi.edu/Academics/ADLN

Videotape- and Internet-based courses and programs.
The MBA focuses on the management of technology and
features a highly integrative curriculum that emphasizes
leadership, ethics, communication, and a global perspective. The M.S. in fire protection engineering is designed to
teach students current standards of practice and expose them
to state-of-the-art research. The M.S. in civil & environmental
engineering focuses on today's environmental issues and
their relationship to engineering business and law.

World College   B

Cleveland Institute of Electronics
1776 East 17th St.
Cleveland, OH 44114-3679
Fields offered: Electronic engineering technology
Accreditation: National (DETC)
Phone: (800) 243 6446
Fax: (216) 781 0331
Email: administration@cie-wc.edu
Web site: www.cie-wc.edu

World offers a Bachelor of Electronic Engineering Technology
through independent study. All lab equipment, parts,
and software are provided (student must have access to
a computer), and the program's 300-plus experiments
can be completed in the home.

Independent Study

Robert Nunnally

Learning, like gifts, deserves a bit of fancy wrap
a ribbon of degrees, a bow of accreditation,
the sense that when you rip through all the fancy paper,
there's something different and solid inside,
perhaps a fruitcake or exotic nuts.

In his workaday world there was no room for school,
no student unions in the dark satanic mills,
whose forges burn, heedless of the liberal arts,
melding souls into more useful things,
like plyboard or plasticine.

His dreams were not bounded by paychecks or promotions,
he saw himself giving speeches in small museums,
brick meeting halls once owned by utopian communities,
but now filled with many people—mostly sane—
politely applauding his talks on local history, and where people lived
when they died.

So he headed to the bookstore with the computer terminals and clerks
whose faces are stamped, as if by a punch-press, with the expression that says
a major corporation may own this shop, but I still wear berets and drink cappuccino,
as they add to the bottom line of corporations whose annual reports
speak in units sold rather than volumes read.

He found a pantheon of gods of correspondence study,
all the "doctor bear's" and "degree by mail" and "campus-free degree"
books one could imagine, promising secrets, perhaps mystic,
for entering into secret pacts with remote universities,
accredited ways to prove that one learned what one knows.

For in our curious world one is not entitled to profess to others
unless the letters on one's plaque say the right things;
"P's," "H's" and "D's" rather than "B's" or "A's;"
just as a surgeon wields no scalpel based on skill alone,
but based instead upon "M.D."

Now he labors, in his attic, his mouse upon his rolltop desk,
a scholar and postage-stamp purchaser,
sending mentors he's never met
manuscripts about obscure things,
so that someday these strangers will tell him he has knowledge.

CHAPTER 19

Accredited Schools with
Short Residency Programs

I forget what I was taught. I only remember what I learned.

Patrick White

All schools in this chapter meet the standards of GAAP, Generally Accepted Accreditation Principles (explained in detail on page 95) and are therefore likely to be accepted as accredited in the worlds of business, government, and academia.

The degree programs listed in this chapter can be completed mostly through distance-learning methods; however, they do require some sort of campus attendance at some point in the program.

The basic format of each listing is as follows:

Name of School	Associate's, **B**achelor's, **M**aster's, **D**octorate, **Law**

Postal Address (United States if country not specified)
Fields of study **offered**
Year founded
Accreditation (Regional, National, Professional, or International; see chapter 8 for an explanation of these terms)
Phone ▨ Tollfree phone (If a U.S. number, country code (+1) not included)
Fax
Email address
Web site URL
Description of programs

Information in this book, especially the listings, changes fast. Updates and corrections are posted on our Web site at *www.degree.net/updates/bearsguide14*.

And remember, our readers play a huge role in helping us keep this book up to date. Please, whether it's a defunct area code or a hot new distance-learning program, bring it to our attention at *johnandmariah@degree.net* or *Bears' Guide*, P.O. Box 7123, Berkeley, CA 94707.

Acadia University   **B**

Wolfville, NS BOP 1X0, Canada
Fields offered: Biology, business, chemistry, computer science, economics, education, English, geology, history, Latin, math, nutrition, physics, political science, psychology, sociology
Year founded: 1838
Accreditation: International (GAAP)
Phone: +1 (902) 585 1434
Email: ask.acadia@acadiau.ca
Web site: www.acadiau.ca

Although many courses are offered by distance learning, and a limited number of courses may be transferred from elsewhere, the school wants prospective students to be aware that it is not possible to complete all degree requirements nonresidentially.

American College   **M**

270 South Bryn Mawr Ave.
Bryn Mawr, PA 19010
Fields offered: Financial services
Year founded: 1927
Accreditation: Regional
Phone: (610) 526 1490 ▨ (888) AMERCOLL
Fax: (610) 526 1465
Email: studentservices@amercoll.edu
Web site: www.amercoll.edu

Offers a Master of Science in Financial Services through a combination of mailed correspondence courses and two 1-week residency programs. Also offered are the Certified Financial Planner (CFP), Chartered Life Underwriter (CLU), Chartered Financial Consultant (ChFC), Registered Health Underwriter (RHU), and Registered Employee Benefits Counselor (REBC) designation programs.

Andrews University   A, B
Nethery Hall
Berrien Springs, MI 49104-0070
Fields offered: General studies, religion
Year founded: 1874
Accreditation: Regional
Phone: (800) 782 4769
Email: enroll@andrews.edu
Web site: www.andrews.edu

Offers A.A. and B.A. degrees in general studies, and a B.A. in religion, in cooperation with DETC-accredited Home Study International.

Antioch University   M, D
800 Livermore St.
Yellow Springs, OH 45387
Fields offered: See below
Year founded: 1852
Accreditation: Regional
Phone: (937) 767 6321
Fax: (937) 767 6461
Web site: www.antioch.edu

Antioch University offers nontraditional educational programs through campuses in Yellow Springs (OH), Los Angeles, Santa Barbara, Seattle, and Keene (NH).

Students can design their own programs leading to a Master of Arts degree; requires two 5-day seminars on Antioch's Yellow Springs campus. Each student develops an individualized curriculum under the direction of two degree committee members who are recruited by the student and approved by Antioch University, then completes the coursework in his or her own community. Coursework may include independent study, research, practicums, workshops, conferences, tutorials, and traditional courses at other institutions. Thesis is required. Popular fields include conflict resolution, peace studies, counseling, applied psychology, creative writing, environmental studies, women's studies, and education.

The Los Angeles campus offers a short-residency M.F.A. writers program. This two-and-a-half-year program includes five 10-day residencies in Los Angeles, and ongoing communication with faculty mentors over the Internet.

Antioch also offers a low-residency (four times per year) Ph.D. in leadership & professional studies, available through all its campuses.

Argosy University
See: University of Sarasota

Atlantic Union College   B, M
South Lancaster, MA 01561
Fields offered: See below
Year founded: 1882
Accreditation: Regional
Phone: (978) 368 2300 ▪ (800) 282 2030
Fax: (978) 368 2514
Email: adp@atlanticuc.edu
Web site: www.atlanticuc.edu

Students take one "unit" each semester. A "unit" is a six-month study project, requiring 9–11 days on campus,

and the balance of the time in independent study. A minimum of at least two units must be taken within the Adult Degree Program. Bachelor's degrees are offered in art, behavioral science, communications, computer science, education (with emphasis on early childhood and elementary education), English, history, interior design, modern languages, personal ministries, physical education, psychology, religion, theology, and women's studies. Experiential learning credit through portfolio appraisal. A Master of Education degree is also offered with concentrations in curriculum & instruction, as well as administration.

Auburn University   M
Graduate Outreach Program
106 Hargis Hall
Auburn, AL 36849-5122
Fields offered: Accounting, business administration, engineering
Year founded: 1856
Accreditation: Regional
Phone: (334) 844 4700
Fax: (334) 844 4348
Email: gradadm@mail.auburn.edu
Web site: www.auburn.edu

Auburn offers an almost totally nonresident Master of Accounting, MBA, and Master of Engineering in a range of fields, including aerospace, chemical, civil/environmental, computer science, industrial, materials, and mechanical engineering. Graduate courses are taped in on-campus classrooms and mailed to distance students, who must keep the same pace as resident students. The MBA requires three days on campus for a team case analysis; the engineering degrees require one day for oral exams. The program is limited to U.S. residents; the only overseas students are U.S. military personnel with APO/FPO addresses.

Australian Graduate School of Business   M
University of New South Wales
Sydney 2052, NSW, Australia
Fields offered: Business administration, general management with an emphasis on strategy
Year founded: 1977
Accreditation: International (GAAP)
Phone: +61 (2) 9931 9412
Fax: +61 (2) 9931 9205
Email: emba@agsm.unsw.edu.au
Web site: www.agsm.unsw.edu.au

MBA available through a combination of distance-learning courses taken at sites around Australia, and four 6-day residencies in Sydney during the final year. The program is only available to managers working in the six-city network. Class attendance is mandatory.

Bennington College   M
Bennington, VT 05201-9993
Fields offered: Fine arts
Year founded: 1925
Accreditation: Regional
Phone: (802) 442 5401 ▪ (800) 833 6845
Fax: (802) 442 6164
Email: admissions@bennington.edu

Web site: www.bennington.edu

The Master of Fine Arts is offered in a short-residency model, requiring five 10-day visits to the campus each January and June over a two-year period.

Brigham Young University   B

315 Harman Continuing Education Bldg.
P.O. Box 21515
Provo, UT 84602-1515
Fields offered: Independent studies
Year founded: 1875
Accreditation: Regional
Phone: (801) 378 4351 ■ (888) 298 3137
Email: bgs@byu.edu
Web site: ce.byu.edu/bgs

The Bachelor of General Studies (B.G.S.) program involves independent study and a short period of on-campus study. The degree requires attendance at a maximum of five 2-week on-campus seminars—one for each of five areas of study—plus a one-week "closure seminar" prior to graduation. Prior college credits can be transferred into the program, where they will be applied towards B.G.S. course requirements, as applicable.

Burlington College   B

95 North Ave.
Burlington, VT 05401
Fields offered: Cinema studies, fine arts, individualized major, psychology, transpersonal psychology, writing, literature
Year founded: 1972
Accreditation: Regional
Phone: (802) 862 9616 ■ (800) 862 9616
Fax: (802) 660 4331
Email: admissions@burlcol.edu
Web site: www.burlcol.edu/distance.htm

Bachelor of Arts offered in the fields listed above through the primarily nonresident "Independent Degree Program" (IDP). IDP students must have completed 45 college credits and have "strong writing skills and a track record in independent study," and must be able to spend four days on the Vermont campus at the beginning of each semester. IDP students must complete a minimum of 30 credits through the program, regardless of prior experience. Although programs are highly individualized, the school specifically encourages applicants whose interests fall in the fields of fine arts, humanities, psychology, transpersonal psychology, or "almost any liberal arts area(s) of study." Formerly Vermont Institute of Community Involvement.

Caldwell College   B

9 Ryerson Ave.
Caldwell, NJ 07006-6195
Fields offered: Accounting, art, business administration, computer information systems, communication arts, criminal justice, English, history, international business, management, marketing, political science, psychology, religious studies, social studies, sociology
Year founded: 1979

Accreditation: Regional
Phone: (973) 618 3385 ■ (888) 864 9518
Fax: (973) 618 3660
Email: agleason@caldwell.edu
Web site: www.caldwell.edu/adult-ed

Bachelor's degrees in the above fields. This is primarily an off-campus, independent study program that utilizes tutorial relationships with professors. Applicants must be 23 years of age or older. Students spend one weekend per semester on campus (and, for the art and computer information systems majors, must take a few intensive residential courses). Credit is given for life experience assessment and by examination.

California Institute of Integral Studies   B, M, D

1453 Mission St.
San Francisco, CA 94103
Fields offered: East-west psychology, philosophy, religion, anthropology, counseling
Year founded: 1968
Accreditation: Regional
Phone: (415) 575 6100
Fax: (415) 575 1264
Email: info@ciis.edu
Web site: www.ciis.edu

Master's degrees are offered in counseling psychology (with concentrations in drama therapy, expressive arts therapy, integral counseling psychology, and somatic psychology), East-West psychology, cultural anthropology & social transformation, and philosophy & religion (with concentrations in Asian & comparative studies, philosophy, cosmology & consciousness, and women's spirituality). The Ph.D. is available in East-West psychology, philosophy & religion, social & cultural anthropology, and transformative learning. Psy.D. is available in clinical psychology. Also offered is a B.A. completion program geared to working adults who need up to 45 credits to finish their degree (credit available for life-experience learning). Most programs involve a combination of intellectual study, online interaction, personal experience of psycho-spiritual growth processes, and practical fieldwork in counseling, community service, teaching, or creative independent study. Formerly California Institute of Asian Studies.

Capital University   B

Columbus Center
2199 E. Main St.
Columbus, OH 43209-2394
Fields offered: Accounting, computer science, criminology, economics, English, general studies, individualized major, international studies, management, nursing, organizational communications, philosophy, political science, psychology, public relations, religion, social work, sociology
Year founded: 1850
Accreditation: Regional
Phone: (614) 236 6996
Fax: (614) 236 6171
Email: rashbroo@capital.edu
Web site: www.capital.edu

A University Without Walls program begun in 1976 by the Union for Experimenting Colleges and Universities and taken over in 1979 by the venerable Capital University. Beginning students must complete the equivalent of 124 semester credit hours, largely through guided independent study. Bachelor's are available in every field listed above. All students must complete a senior project, showing bachelor's-level abilities and serving as a learning experience. The university maintains Adult Degree Program offices in Cleveland and Dayton as well. Offers credit for experiential learning through portfolio assessment.

Case Western Reserve University   M, D
Frances Payne Bolton School of Nursing
2121 Abington Rd.
Cleveland, OH 44106
Fields offered: Nursing
Year founded: 1826
Accreditation: Regional
Phone: (216) 368 4700
Email: admissions@fpb.cwru.edu
Web site: fpb.cwru.edu

According to a correspondent, the venerable Case Western has joined the ranks of the nontraditionalists, but hasn't advertised the programs, as they fill up on word of mouth alone. They offer an intensive M.S. in nursing for RNs who have a B.S. in nursing and hold certification as a nurse practitioner. Candidates who meet these criteria can be awarded as much as 22 semester hours of graduate credit. To complete the degree, Case offers four weeks of intensive classes on campus (presented between traditional semesters), and a final class completed independently. Nurse practitioners from across America—including Hawaii—are enrolled in the program. Students fly into Cleveland for a week of intensive classes at a time, staying in dorm rooms for $10 per night. A Nursing Doctorate (N.D.) is also available in this intensive format. The programs are a bit pricey but lead to degrees from one of America's most prestigious nursing schools.

CBN University
See: Regent University

College of Saint Scholastica   B, M
1200 Kenwood Ave.
Duluth, MN 55811
Fields offered: Education
Year founded: 1912
Accreditation: Regional
Phone: (218) 723 6000 ■ (800) 447 5444
Fax: (218) 723 5991
Email: admissions@css.edu
Web site: www.css.edu

Except for a two-day on-campus class at the beginning and end of the program, a Master of Education can be earned by distance learning. All of the required instructional materials for each course are mailed to the student at the beginning of each term. Students and faculty communicate by mail, email, telephone, and fax.

Columbia University   M, D
Teachers College
525 W. 120th St.
New York, NY 10027
Fields offered: Education
Year founded: 1887
Accreditation: Regional
Phone: (212) 678 3000
Fax: (212) 678 4048
Web site: www.tc.columbia.edu

The Doctor of Education is offered through an innovative program called AEGIS: Adult Education Guided Independent Study. The program requires two years to complete, largely through guided independent study, with advisement by correspondence, telephone, or optional campus visits. Participants must attend a seminar on campus one Saturday each month, plus a three-week intensive summer session for both summers of enrollment. The program is designed for experienced, self-directed professionals with at least five years of experience in program development or administration of adult education or training. Admission is highly competitive; about 20 students are admitted every other year. The M.A. in technology & education is offered through independent study, with two or three summer sessions. Concentrations include multimedia development in education, telecommunications & global issues, and teaching & learning with technology.

Concordia University (Minnesota)   B, M
275 Syndicate St. North
St. Paul, MN 55104
Fields offered: School-age child care, child & youth development, human services, criminal justice, parish education
Year founded: 1893
Accreditation: Regional
Phone: (651) 641 8897 ■ (800) 211 3370
Fax: (651) 603 6144
Email: schoolage@luther.csp.edu
Web site: www.csp.edu/hspd

Bachelor's and master's degrees in school-age care (a field involving the care of children before and after school), child & youth development, human services, criminal justice, family studies, and parish education. Except for a five-day orientation residency, coursework takes place through email, online discussion groups, bulletin boards, phone conferences, and audio- and videotapes.

Dalhousie University   M
6100 University Ave.
Halifax, NS B3H 3J5, Canada
Fields offered: Business administration (financial services)
Accreditation: International (GAAP)
Phone: +1 (902) 494 2526
Fax: +1 (902) 494 6875
Email: henson-info@dal.ca
Web site: mbafs.mgmt.dal.ca

Offers an MBA with emphasis in financial services, in association with the Institute of Canadian Bankers. Most

"So far, this distance-learning course in tennis is all right, but I can hardly wait until lesson 2 when they send us the balls."

of the program can be completed by distance learning, although significant on-campus and seminar residencies are required.

Drew University   D

36 Madison Ave.
Madison, NJ 07940
Fields offered: Ministry
Year founded: 1866
Accreditation: Regional
Phone: (973) 408 3000
Fax: (973) 408 3939
Email: theoadm@drew.edu
Web site: www.drew.edu

The Global/Online Doctor of Ministry (D.Min.) program is open to ministerial leaders anywhere in the world who meet qualifications for admission. Students can specialize in leadership development, campus ministry & college chaplaincy, or military chaplaincy. Requires attendance at one 4-week summer intensive on the Drew campus.

Duke University   M

The Fuqua School of Business
Box 90120
Durham, NC 27708-0120
Fields offered: Business administration (global)
Year founded: 1838
Accreditation: Regional
Phone: (919) 660 7700
Fax: (919) 684 2818
Email: fuqua-execed@mail.duke.edu
Web site: www.fuqua.duke.edu

Duke's Global Executive MBA (GEMBA) program is a 19-month program designed for experienced managers who want to learn more about global management. It combines five 2-week residential sessions at sites in Europe, Asia, and North and South America with continuing distance education using a wide range of interactive communication tools. The majority of learning is done over the Internet using Lotus Notes or equivalent technology. In addition to using bulletin boards and email for case discussion, students use multimedia lesson plans and Web pages, among other methods, to communicate, research, and learn.

Duquesne University   M

600 Forbes Ave.
Pittsburgh, PA 15282
Fields offered: Music Education
Year founded: 1878
Accreditation: Regional
Phone: (412) 396 6000 ▪ (800) 456 0590
Fax: (412) 396 5644
Web site: www.duq.edu

For Duquesne's Master of Music in Music Education degree, 16 of the 30 credits are offered online. The remaining 14 are taken on campus as summer workshops. For information on Duquesne's totally online degree programs, see the listing in the previous chapter.

Eastern New Mexico University   B, M

Station #9
Portales, NM 88130
Fields offered: See below
Year founded: 1934
Accreditation: Regional
Phone: (505) 562 2165 ▪ (800) 537 5376
Fax: (505) 562 2168
Email: a.schreoder@enmu.edu
Web site: www.enmu.edu

BBA, MBA, BSN, B.S. in university studies, B.Ed., M.Ed., M.A. in English, and M.S. in communication disorders offered via distance learning and extension courses to students in southeastern New Mexico only.

Elizabethtown College   B

1 Alpha Dr.
Elizabethtown, PA 17022-2298
Fields offered: Professional studies (with concentrations; see below)
Year founded: 1899
Accreditation: Regional
Phone: (717) 361 1411 ▪ (800) 877 2694
Email: admissions@acad.etown.edu
Web site: www.etown.edu

Bachelor of Professional Studies offered through the EXCEL program. Majors offered include business administration, communications, criminal justice, early childhood education, human services, and public administration. Applicants must have a minimum of seven years' work experience related to the major field of study, have completed at least 50 semester hours of college study, grade C or better, at regionally accredited institutions, and reside within 400 miles of the college. Credit awarded for

CLEP/DANTES exams, certain structured noncredit learning, and (up to 32 semester hours) experiential learning in the major field of study.

Empire State College   M

One Union Ave.
Saratoga Springs, NY 12866-4391
Fields offered: Business administration, business & policy studies, labor & policy studies, social policy, liberal studies
Year founded: 1971
Accreditation: Regional
Phone: (518) 587 2100 ■ (800) 847 3000
Fax: (518) 587 2660
Email: cdl@esc.edu
Web site: www.esc.edu

A part of the State University of New York (SUNY) system, Empire State offers an MBA that allows distance learners to test out of almost half of the required credits through assessment of prior knowledge, workplace training, and managerial experience. Remaining credits are earned through Internet courses, independent study, and two weekend residencies in New York state per year. Empire State also offers Master of Arts programs in business & policy studies, labor & policy studies, social policy, and liberal studies. Primarily earned through independent study, with three weekend residencies per year at one of 45 locations across New York state. For information on Empire State's distance-learning bachelor's degree programs, see the preceding chapter.

Empresarial University   B, M, D

Apartado 1810-1250 Escazu
San Jose, Costa Rica
Fields offered: See below
Year founded: 1992
Accreditation: International (GAAP)
Phone: (770) 554 0630
Fax: (770) 978 3369
Email: info@unem.edu
Web site: www.unem.edu

Started as the International Post-Graduate School, a doctorate-granting division of Costa Rica's University of San Jose. After becoming independent of USJ, was known briefly as International University of Costa Rica before it switched to its current name. Offers nonresidential instruction in English or Spanish (according to the student's language preference) with a two-week on-campus residency requirement.

Bachelor's are as follows: B.A.'s in anthropology, communications, economics, English, English literature, French, German, history, Latin American studies, philosophy, political science, psychology, religious studies, sociology, Spanish, and Spanish literature; BBAs in accounting, finance, human resources, international business, management, and marketing; and B.Ed.'s in early childhood education, elementary education, guidance & counseling, secondary education, and special education.

Master's and doctorates are available in administrative science, behavioral science, education, biological science (Ph.D. only), humanities, psychology (Ph.D. only),

and social science. The master's program must be completed in less than three years, the doctorate in less than five. Two study options are offered: a curriculum-based program for students who have the need to take traditional coursework in addition to the thesis/dissertation, and a research-based program for qualified students who already possess the necessary theoretical knowledge and experience in their area of expertise.

Fielding Institute   M, D

2122 Santa Barbara St.
Santa Barbara, CA 93105
Fields offered: Clinical psychology, human & organizational development, educational leadership & change, organizational management
Year founded: 1974
Accreditation: Regional
Phone: (805) 687 1099 ■ (800) 340 1099
Email: admissions@fielding.edu
Web site: www.fielding.edu

Students must attend a five-day admissions workshop in Santa Barbara (held March, June, and September) before enrolling. This is the only required residency. Regional research sessions and academic seminars are offered at various locations throughout the year. Offers an Ed.D. in educational leadership & change, a Ph.D. in human & organizational systems or human development, a master's in organizational development, and a Ph.D. in clinical psychology. The degrees are neither fast nor easy, but are designed to enable mid-career professionals to attain advanced degrees. It typically takes three to six years to complete the requirements for a doctoral degree. The psychology program has a residency requirement that can be completed through attendance at local student meetings. All students and faculty must have access to an electronic network which offers email, bulletin board service, and academic seminars. A correspondent tells us that this is the only primarily distance program in clinical psychology recognized by the APA under its new "provisional accreditation" guidelines. Short residency certificates are also available in neuropsychology and psychopharmacology, and a clinical psychology retooling program is available for students who hold a non-APA-approved Ph.D. and would like to fulfill remaining requirements.

Framingham State College   B

100 State St., P.O. Box 9101
Framingham, MA 01701
Fields offered: Liberal studies
Year founded: 1839
Accreditation: Regional
Phone: (508) 620 1220
Fax: (508) 626 4592
Web site: www.framingham.edu

Bachelor of Arts in liberal studies in which units may be earned through equivalency exams, independent study, correspondence study, prior learning experiences, and "noncredit educational experiences." The remaining units must be earned by taking courses on campus, through a series of weekend or summer seminars, or by making other arrangements satisfactory to the advisory committee.

Franciscan University of Steubenville   M

1235 University Blvd.
Steubenville, OH 43952
Fields offered: Theology
Year founded: 1946
Accreditation: Regional
Phone: (740) 283 3771 ▪ (800) 466 8336
Fax: (740) 283 6472
Email: admissions@franuniv.edu
Web site: www.franuniv.edu

Thirty of the 36 credits required for the M.A. in theology & Christian ministry can be earned at a distance, mostly by audiotapes and support materials; the rest during two 3-week summer residencies.

Goddard College   B, M

123 Pitkin Rd.
Plainfield, VT 05667
Fields offered: Fine arts (writing), individualized major
Year founded: 1938
Accreditation: Regional
Phone: (802) 454 8311
Email: admissions@goddard.edu
Web site: www.goddard.edu

Goddard has been a pioneer in nontraditional, progressive education for more than 60 years. They offer nontraditional bachelor's and master's, with predesigned tracks for study in business & organizational leadership, education, psychology & counseling, natural & physical sciences, feminist studies, visual & performing arts, literature & writing, and social & cultural studies (history, philosophy, religious studies). An M.F.A. in writing is also available. The first eight days of each semester are spent in residency, where the work of the coming semester is planned. Students may choose to do the majority of their coursework off-campus while maintaining contact by mail every three weeks. Both bachelor's and master's programs require a minimum enrollment: two semesters for the bachelor's, three for the master's. Credit is available for prior learning, but life-experience credit is given only at the bachelor's level.

Goucher College   M

1021 Dulaney Valley Rd.
Baltimore, MD 21204
Fields offered: Fine arts (creative nonfiction), historic preservation
Year founded: 1885
Accreditation: Regional
Phone: (410) 337 6000
Email: center@goucher.edu

The Master's degree in creative nonfiction (M.F.A.) or historic preservation is available to U.S. students and Canadians only. Courses are delivered to the student's home, and three 2-week summer sessions are required over the course of study.

Graceland College   B, M

1 University Place
Lamoni, IA 50140
Fields offered: Nursing, liberal studies, addiction studies
Year founded: 1895
Accreditation: Regional
Phone: (515) 784 5196 ▪ (800) 537 6276
Fax: (515) 784 5480
Email: bsn@gc-outreach.com
Web site: www.gracelandoutreach.net

B.S. and M.S. in nursing designed for working nurses, and B.A. in liberal studies. Courses include projects, home study texts, learning guides (developed by Graceland faculty), videotapes, tests, and a final proctored exam. Students are provided a tollfree number for contact with instructors. Up to 64 credit hours can come from evaluation of prior education and experience. BSN and MSN programs have clinical components; students can come to campus to fulfill these or find a college-approved preceptor to monitor their progress in their own community. There are mandatory two-week residency sessions twice a year.

Harvard University   B, M

Division of Continuing Education
51 Brattle St.
Cambridge, MA 02138
Fields offered: Anthropology, archaeology, biology, languages, humanities, drama, government, history, psychology, religion, studio arts, women's studies, information technology
Year founded: 1636
Accreditation: Regional
Phone: (617) 495 4024
Fax: (617) 495 0500
Email: ext@hudce.harvard.edu
Web site: extension.dce.harvard.edu

Harvard's Extension School offers more than 600 courses in 50 fields of study on an open-enrollment basis. It offers the undergraduate degrees of Associate in Arts and Bachelor of Liberal Arts and the graduate degree of Master of Liberal Arts in 21 fields of concentration (including the popular program in information technology). For international students planning to pursue graduate studies at English-speaking institutions, there's a Diploma in English for Graduate and Professional Studies. Although you can't get a Harvard Extension degree without spending some time in Cambridge, a growing number of individual courses are offered over the Internet, especially in the computer sciences.

Henley Management College   M, D

Greenlands
Henley-on-Thames
Oxfordshire RG9 3AU, United Kingdom
Fields offered: Business administration, project management
Year founded: 1945
Accreditation: International (GAAP)
Phone: +44 (1491) 571 454
Fax: +44 (1491) 571 635
Email: enquiries@henleymc.ac.uk
Web site: www.henleymc.ac.uk

Henley bills itself as the oldest independent management college in Europe. It has about 7,000 distance-learning MBA students in some 80 countries. Applicants must be 27 or older, have a bachelor's degree from a recognized university, and have three years of relevant business/managerial experience. The average student age is 34, and the school stresses that this is not a program for the young and/or inexperienced. Henley itself has facilities in 23 countries to provide local support, tutoring, workshops, etc. Elsewhere (including the U.S.) students can join what the school calls its "International Stream," which allows them to consolidate workshop attendance into one-week blocks. All students access electronic support via Lotus Notes. A final dissertation of 15,000 words is required for the MBA. They also offer a DBA in full-time, part-time, modular, distance-learning, company, and consortium modes. While much of the work can be completed by independent study, it is not a wholly distance degree; an annual residential study week is required at one of the school's centers (in the U.K., France, or Singapore). An M.S. in project management is also available.

Human Relations Institute
See: Pacifica Graduate Institute

Humanistic Psychology Institute
See: Saybrook Graduate School

Indiana State University   M, D
Terre Haute, IN 47809
Fields offered: Health & safety, student affairs administration, nursing, technology management
Year founded: 1865
Accreditation: Regional
Phone: (812) 237 2642 ■ (800) 444 4723
Fax: (812) 237 4292
Email: admissions@indstate.edu
Web site: www-isu.indstate.edu

Making extensive use of Internet delivery, a Ph.D. in technology management is offered through a consortium of universities led by Indiana State and including University of Wisconsin, Bowling Green State, Texas Southern, and Central Missouri State. Minimal residency requirements. Other short-residency graduate degrees include an M.S. in health & safety, an M.A. or M.S. in student affairs administration, and an M.S. in nursing. For information on Indiana State's nonresidential degree programs, see the listing in the previous chapter.

Institute for Financial Management
See: University of Wales—Bangor

Institute of Canadian Bankers
See: Dalhousie University

Institute of Physical Therapy
See: University of Saint Augustine for Health Sciences

International Post-Graduate School
See: Empresarial University

International University of Costa Rica
or Universidad Internacional de Costa Rica. See: Empresarial University

Iowa State University   B, M
Off-Campus and Adult Student Services
B6 Memorial Union
Ames, IA 50011-2010
Fields offered: Agriculture, business administration, liberal studies
Year founded: 1858
Accreditation: Regional
Phone: (515) 294 2364
Fax: (515) 294 6331
Email: ocass@iastate.edu
Web site: www.ocass.iastate.edu

The university offers an external degree called the Bachelor of Liberal Studies, primarily for residents of Iowa who are able to attend one of the off-campus centers around the state or occasional courses on the Ames campus. In addition, evening and weekend courses are offered toward degrees in agriculture, business, design, education, engineering, family & consumer sciences, and liberal arts & sciences. Upper-division B.S. in agriculture (for students who have completed their first two years of study elsewhere) and Master of Agriculture (M.Ag.) are offered largely through locally available satellite and cable television programs, as well as videotaped programs. A Saturday MBA program is also available. Many courses require one Saturday on campus per credit, plus one week during the summer.

Lesley University   B, M
29 Everett St.
Cambridge, MA 02138
Fields offered: See below
Year founded: 1909
Accreditation: Regional
Phone: (617) 349 8300 ■ (800) 999 1959
Email: info@lesley.edu
Web site: www.lesley.edu

Lesley offers a range of nontraditional programs, including weekend bachelor's degree programs, and an Intensive Residency Option, in which B.A. and B.S. students attend twice-yearly nine-day residencies in Massachusetts, then complete coursework on their own in between. For information on Lesley's wholly nonresidential graduate degrees, see the previous chapter.

Also, there is a B.S. in environmental studies and an M.S. in environmental education, offered in cooperation with the National Audubon Society's Expedition Institute. These programs involve a combination of on-campus coursework and off-campus expeditions: camping, hiking, canoeing, skiing, backpacking, and cycling all over America. Students gain practical knowledge of astronomy, anthropology, ecology, etc.

Liberty University   B, M, D
1971 University Blvd.
Lynchburg, VA 24502-2269

The arrival of Mlle. La Roux to deliver the commencement address by streaming video was an annual
highlight at the La Roux Online Institute of Haute Coutour & Drafting.

Fields offered: Religion, business, psychology,
education
Year founded: 1971
Accreditation: Regional
Phone: (804) 582 2000 ▦ (800) 424 9595
Fax: (804) 582 2304
Email: admissions@liberty.edu
Web site: www.liberty.edu
Liberty's "External Degree Program" offers accredited
bachelor's, master's, and doctoral degrees through a
combination of home study and approximately one week
of residency per year (two weeks for education degrees).
Bachelor's degrees can be earned in business, psychology,
and religion; master's in counseling, religion, business
administration, and education; an Ed.D. in educational
leadership. While residential students at Liberty must
have accepted Jesus Christ as their personal savior, external
students are not required to have done so. The founder
of Liberty is the Rev. Jerry Falwell.

Liverpool John Moores University   B
2 Rodney St.
Liverpool L3 5UX, United Kingdom
Fields offered: Health care (quality assurance in
nursing)
Year founded: 1970
Accreditation: International (GAAP)
Phone: +44 (151) 231 3522
Web site: www.livjm.ac.uk
The former Liverpool Polytechnic offers a B.A. in health
care (specifically, quality assurance in nursing) through
a combination of distance and residential learning. They

also offer entirely nonresident diplomas in health care and
community health care.

Liverpool Polytechnic
See: Liverpool John Moores University

Maine College of Art   M
97 Spring St.
Portland, ME 04101
Fields offered: Art
Year founded: 1882
Accreditation: Regional
Phone: (207) 775 3052 ▦ (800) 639 4808
Fax: (207) 775 5069
Email: comm@meca.edu
Web site: www.meca.edu
A 24-month Master of Fine Arts, combining intensive
residencies (two months in the summer and ten days in
the winter) with tutored independent study. The intent
was to create a program that "meets or exceeds the rigors
and vitality of the traditional model as the 'terminal'
professional degree for studio art and design, [and] that
accommodates well-qualified and motivated individuals
for whom a program of two 9-month residency periods
of study is not feasible."

Malone College   B
515 25th St. NW
Canton, OH 44709
Fields offered: Management
Year founded: 1957

Accreditation: Regional
Phone: (330) 471 8242 ▪ (800) 867 6267
Email: inquiry@malone-online.org
Web site: www.malone-online.org

Offers a B.A. completion program in management. Although this has not been established as an online program per se, an indefinite amount of online coursework may be applied towards the degree to fulfill necessary graduation requirements.

Manchester Business School
See: University of Wales—Bangor

Mary Baldwin College   B
Staunton, VA 24401
Fields offered: Applied mathematics, art, art & communications, arts management, Asian studies, biochemistry, biology, business administration, business administration & economics, chemistry, communication, computer science & business administration, economics, English, French, German, health care administration, history, international relations, marketing communications, mathematics, music, philosophy, philosophy & religion, physics, political science, psychology, sociology, Spanish, theater
Year founded: 1842
Accreditation: Regional
Phone: (540) 887 7003 ▪ (800) 822 2460
Email: adp@mbc.edu
Web site: www.mbc.edu/adp

Bachelor of Arts program for residents of Virginia, in which work can be done independently, with very few visits required. Students need to come to the campus for a day of orientation, and to regional centers twice a year for conferences with advisors. Advanced standing may be given for work done at other schools, CLEP examinations, and the assessment of prior learning by portfolio. The degree program has regional offices in Richmond, Charlottesville, Weyers Cave, and Roanoke, Virginia, in addition to the main office in Staunton.

Maryvale Institute   B, M, D
Maryvale House, Old Oscott Hill
Kingstanding
Birmingham B44 9AG, United Kingdom
Fields offered: Catholic studies, theology, religious education
Accreditation: International (GAAP)
Phone: +44 (121) 360 8118
Web site: www.maryvale.ac.uk

Offers degrees in a range of fields involving Catholic theology and religious education, including B.Phil., M.Phil., and D.Phil. research degrees. Programs are largely distance learning, but most require short residential sessions. The degrees awarded by Maryvale are validated by the Pontifical University in Ireland, which was specifically commended by Pope John Paul II when he visited the campus, which should be a sufficient level of acceptance to satisfy Catholic theologians.

Marywood University   B
2300 Adams Ave.
Scranton, PA 18509-1598
Fields offered: Business administration, accounting
Year founded: 1915
Accreditation: Regional
Phone: (570) 348 6235 ▪ (800) 836 6940
Fax: (570) 961 4751
Email: ocdp@ac.marywood.edu
Web site: www.marywood.edu

The Bachelor of Science degree in accounting or business administration (with concentrations in management, financial planning, or marketing) is earned through a combination of directed correspondence study (114 credits) and four weeks of residency (12 credits) held on the campus in one-week, two-week, and weekend sessions. Transfer credit is available through the evaluation of prior learning; a minimum of 60 of the required 126 credits must be earned after enrolling at Marywood.

Massachusetts Institute of Technology   M
77 Massachusetts Building 9
Cambridge, MA 02139-4307
Fields offered: Engineering, management
Year founded: 1861
Accreditation: Regional
Phone: (617) 253 7408
Email: caes-info@mit.edu
Web site: www-caes.mit.edu

Students must have company sponsorship and be on campus for the first January of the program, and for one semester during the course of the program.

McGill University   M
1020 Pine Ave. West, Room 16
Montreal, Quebec H3A 1A2, Canada
Fields offered: Occupational health sciences
Year founded: 1821
Accreditation: International (GAAP)
Phone: +1 (514) 398 6989
Fax: +1 (514) 398 7153
Email: distocch@epid.lan.mcgill.ca
Web site: www.mcgill.ca/occh/distance

Master of Applied Science in Occupational Health Sciences in a program specifically for persons holding a degree in medicine or nursing. Study takes place via printed materials and videotapes, but students are required to attend six 3-day practicums towards the beginning of study.

Michigan Technological University   B, D
1400 Townsend Dr.
Houghton, MI 49931
Fields offered: Mechanical engineering, surveying
Year founded: 1885
Accreditation: Regional
Phone: (906) 487 1885 ▪ (888) 688 1885
Email: mtu4u@mtu.edu
Web site: www.mtu.edu

The ABET-accredited B.S. in surveying can be completed almost fully by distance learning. There is also a doctoral program in mechanical engineering. Students must be sponsored by a corporation or business and spend approximately six weeks on campus for examinations and dissertation defense.

Mississippi State University   M
Mississippi State, MS 39762
Fields offered: Broadcast meteorology, business administration (project management), chemical engineering, civil engineering, computer science, electrical & computer engineering, industrial engineering, mechanical engineering, operational meteorology
Year founded: 1878
Accreditation: Regional
Phone: (662) 325 7400
Email: grad@grad.msstate.edu
Web site: www.msstate.edu
Offers master's degrees in the above fields, with courses delivered via Internet, video- and/or audio-streaming, video-conferencing, and videotape. Except for the online MBA in project management, all master's programs require one campus visit for an oral exam. An online graduate certificate in materials engineering is also available.

Mississippi University for Women   B
2170 S. Eason Blvd.
Tupelo, MS 38804
Fields offered: Nursing
Year founded: 1884
Accreditation: Regional
Phone: (662) 844 0284
Fax: (662) 844 1927
Email: kmcshane@muw.edu
Web site: www.muw.edu
Nursing program for RNs with associate or diploma degrees who want to upgrade to a bachelor's. Courses delivered via modules, computer-assisted programs, email, and Internet. Students must visit the Tupelo campus every few weeks.

Montana State University—Bozeman   B, M
Bozeman, MT 59717-2000
Fields offered: Curriculum & instruction (technology education), elementary school administration, mathematics, nursing, science education, secondary school administration
Year founded: 1893
Accreditation: Regional
Phone: (406) 994 4145
Email: gradstudy@montana.edu
Web site: www.montana.edu
Offers a BSN completion program for registered nurses, Master of Nursing, Master of Education (in curriculum & instruction with emphasis on technology education, in elementary school administration, or in secondary school administration), and M.S. programs in mathematics and science education. Online and videocourse-based study with short summer residencies.

Murray State University   B, M
P.O. Box 9

Murray, KY 42071
Fields offered: Independent studies, nursing
Year founded: 1922
Accreditation: Regional
Phone: (270) 762 5322 ▪ (800) 669 7654
Email: marla.poyner@murraystate.edu
Web site: www.mursuky.edu
Bachelor of Independent Studies through correspondence study, television, and contract-learning courses. Some weekend and evening classes are available. 32 of the 128 required semester hours must be taken with Murray State. Departmental challenge exams are available in some fields. All students must attend a day-long seminar, held on Saturdays in April, August, and December. Admission to the program is based on satisfactory completion of the seminar. All students must earn credit in basic skills, humanities, science, social sciences, and electives, and complete a study project. Overseas applicants are not accepted, and the B.I.S. director tells us that this program seems to work best for students who live within commuting range of Murray State. Also, an M.S. for RNs who already have a B.S. in nursing, offered by remote television at three sites within a 100-mile radius of the campus.

Napier University   M
The International Office
Craighouse Campus
Edinburgh EH10 5LG, United Kingdom
Fields offered: Business administration, information systems
Year founded: 1964
Accreditation: International (GAAP)
Phone: +44 (131) 455 6331
Fax: +44 (131) 455 6334
Web site: www.napier.ac.uk
Edinburgh's third-oldest university offers an "open learning" MBA, mainly geared to managers operating in Europe, which allows students to gain an MBA "after approximately two years' hard work." Participants work full-time and study using specially prepared study materials, backed up with local study groups, and eight study weekends at the Edinburgh campus. Selection procedure is rigorous, designed to select only those applicants with sufficient business experience. There is also an M.S. in information systems, available largely through distance learning, with several one-day "surgery sessions." Learning takes place through printed correspondence texts, telephone and email tutoring, and various Internet functions.

Naropa University   M
2130 Arapahoe Ave.
Boulder, CO 80302
Fields offered: Transpersonal studies
Accreditation: Regional
Phone: (303) 444 0202
Fax: (303) 444 0410
Email: admissions@naropa.edu
Web site: www.naropa.edu
Beginning in the fall of 2001, Naropa University will offer an M.A. in transpersonal studies through a short-residency,

online format. Rumors of a short-residency M.F.A. in writing or poetics have not been confirmed. Also offers a number of interesting nontraditional residential programs. Education at Naropa combines the disciplines of the classroom with those of personal awareness through contemplative practices such as sitting meditation, akido, t'ai chi, and others.

National-Louis University M, D

2840 Sheridan Rd.
Evanston, IL 60201
Fields offered: Adult education, e-commerce
Year founded: 1886
Accreditation: Regional
Phone: (847) 256 5156 ▪ (800) 443 5522
Fax: (847) 256 1057
Email: nluinfo@wheeling1.nl.edu
Web site: www.nl.edu

An Ed.D. in adult education can be earned through three years of guided independent study with monthly on-campus weekends and a three-week summer session. The M.S. in electronic commerce is delivered by online courses, with four short residencies spread through the program. Nonresidential programs detailed in the previous chapter. Original name: National College of Education.

New Mexico State University B, M

Box 30001, Department 3WEC
Las Cruces, NM 88003-8001
Fields offered: Business, education, engineering
Year founded: 1888
Accreditation: Regional
Phone: (505) 646 5837 ▪ (800) 821 1574
Fax: (505) 646 2044
Email: distance@nmsu.edu
Web site: www.nmsu.edu

BBA for students in the local area, an M.S. in education for in-state students, and a nonresidential M.S. in engineering.

Northeastern Illinois University B, M

5500 N. St. Louis Ave.
Chicago, IL 60625-4699
Fields offered: Liberal arts, education, business
Year founded: 1961
Accreditation: Regional
Phone: (773) 794 6684
Email: admrec@neiu.edu
Web site: www.neiu.edu

Bachelor of Arts with a minimum residency requirement of 15 semester hours, which can be completed in four months on campus. Also has two MBA programs, one for business majors, the second for graduate students with bachelor's degrees in other fields. Credit may be awarded for life experience and all prior learning experiences. New credit may be earned through regular courses at any of the five schools in the program, or by correspondence study and independent study.

Northwood University B

University College
4000 Whiting Dr.

Midland, MI 48640
Fields offered: Management
Year founded: 1959
Accreditation: Regional
Phone: (517) 837 4411 ▪ (800) 445 5873
Fax: (517) 837 4600
Email: uc@northwood.edu
Web site: www.northwood.edu

Offers a bachelor's in management through tailored independent study. Optional concentrations in automotive marketing, computer science, and marketing are available. The program is targeted at students 25 and older. Previous learning experience may be transferred toward the degree. Students near an outreach center (14 nationwide) may attend class there, and a residency of two 3-day seminars is required.

Norwich University B, M

Vermont College
College St.
Montpelier, VT 05602
Fields offered: Art therapy, education (individualized specialization), individualized major, visual arts, writing, writing for children
Year founded: 1834
Accreditation: Regional
Phone: (802) 828 8500 ▪ (800) 336 6794
Fax: (802) 828 8855
Email: vcadmis@norwich.edu
Web site: www.norwich.edu/vermontcollege

Vermont College of Norwich University offers several of the longest-running external degree programs for adult learners in North America. The programs are structured to allow students great latitude in designing their studies in conjunction with faculty mentors. The Adult Degree Program (B.A.), begun in 1963, features short residencies in Vermont (9 days every six months or one weekend a month) alternating with study at home. Faculty members guide and support student work in the liberal arts, including psychology, counseling, literature, writing, management, and education.

The Graduate Program, started in 1969, offers self-designed studies in the humanities, arts, education, and social sciences (including psychology and counseling). Regional meetings with program faculty are held quarterly or monthly; students who prefer not to attend regional meetings may choose an online option (although a five-day seminar is still required at the beginning of the program). Students work with two advisors: a core faculty member who is responsible for a geographical region of the country and a field advisor who is a local expert in the student's field of study.

The M.A. in art therapy is a 15-month program which includes summer residencies in Vermont. An M.F.A. in writing or visual arts is offered through off-campus programs with nine-day residencies twice a year. The M.F.A. in music performance requires short, intensive summer- and winter-residency sessions alternating with six-month nonresident study projects.

Finally, there's a program designed for "traditional age students" that combines brief on-campus stays with off-campus travel, internships, and relevant jobs. Each student is given a notebook computer, and she stays in touch with a faculty mentor and with other students via the Internet.

Nova Southeastern University   B, M, D
3301 College Ave.
Fort Lauderdale, FL 33314
Fields offered: See below
Year founded: 1964
Accreditation: Regional
Phone: (954) 262 8500 ▪ (800) 541 6682
Email: cwis@nova.edu
Web site: www.nova.edu

Offers B.S. completion programs in education (with emphasis on early childhood education, elementary education, exceptional education, middle school science, or secondary education) and professional studies, consisting of online study supplemented with intensive seminars.

At the master's level, most programs require some residency in the form of cluster groups (extension courses). Programs are as follows: Master of Accounting, MBA (with emphasis in finance, management information systems, or marketing), Master of Medical Science, and M.S.'s in child & youth studies, computer information systems, computer science, computing technology in education, curriculum instruction & technology, dispute resolution, educational media, education with emphasis on teaching in learning, instructional technology & distance education, management & administration of educational programs, management information systems, and social studies education.

Nova Southeastern University also offers some of the more nontraditional doctoral programs ever to achieve regional accreditation. The typical student attends one group meeting a month (generally two or three days), plus two 1-week residential sessions, and from three to six practicums which emphasize direct application of research to the workplace. Total time: about three-and-a-half years. A major part of instruction in this program is through teleconferencing and Web-based study. Residential work has been offered in 23 states. Nova will consider offering the program in the continental United States wherever a cluster of 20–25 students can be formed. Ed.D. programs are available in computing technology in education and educational leadership. Ph.D. programs are available in child & youth studies, computer information systems, computer sciences, computing technology in education, dispute resolution, information science, information systems, instructional technology & distance education, occupational therapy, and physical therapy. The degrees of Doctor of Occupational Therapy and Doctor of Physical Therapy are also available.

Formerly Nova University, they merged with Southeastern Medical School, hence the name change.

Nova University
See: Nova Southeastern University

Ohio University   M
College of Business
Copeland Hall

Athens, OH 45701
Fields offered: Business administration
Year founded: 1804
Accreditation: Regional
Phone: (740) 593 2072 ▪ (800) 622 3124
Fax: (740) 593 0319
Email: milter@ohiou.edu
Web site: mbawb.cob.ohiou.edu

Ohio University's MBA Without Boundaries is designed primarily for working managers. Several on-campus seminars are required, but nearly all study takes place online. A number of completely off-campus bachelor's completion programs are also available; for more information, see the Ohio University listing in the previous chapter.

Oklahoma City University   B
2501 N. Blackwelder
Oklahoma City, OK 73106-1493
Fields offered: Individualized major
Year founded: 1901
Accreditation: Regional
Phone: (405) 521 5265
Email: plus@okcu.edu
Web site: www.okcu.edu/plus

A Bachelor of Arts or Science degree can be earned by utilizing a combination of alternative methods: independent study, seminars, assessment of prior learning, and traditional courses. Each student must visit the campus to attend an orientation workshop, and additional campus visits may be necessary. The university has asked us to point out that the program may be suitable for some distance students; however, it may not meet the needs of others. An evaluation of each student's educational situation is necessary.

Open Theological College
See: Spurgeon's College

Open University of the Netherlands   B, M, D
P.O. Box 2960
6401 DL Heerlen, Netherlands
Fields offered: Business & public administration, cultural studies, economics, environmental science, Dutch law, psychology, information science
Year founded: 1984
Accreditation: International (GAAP)
Phone: +31 (45) 576 2222
Fax: +31 (45) 576 2766
Email: lilian.janssen-grootenboer@ou.nl
Web site: www.ouh.nl

The Netherlands' first nontraditional university offers a wide range of self-study courses in the fields listed above. In this program, modeled on Britain's Open University, credit is earned solely by passing examinations, and tutoring is available in study centers around Holland, or by telephone anywhere in the world. For foreign students, however, the school stresses two difficulties: 1) all examinations are administered in the Netherlands and 2) most of the courses are taught in Dutch. However, there is an MBA being offered in English, with an emphasis on European business and European law. (There's also a certificate in European law.) For information on this program, check out *www.euromba.org*.

Ottawa University B, M

1001 South Cedar St.
Ottawa, KS 66067-3399
Fields offered: Human resources, health services, police science
Year founded: 1865
Accreditation: Regional
Phone: (785) 242 5200 ▪ (800) 755 5200
Fax: (785) 242 7429
Email: ottawainfo@aol.com
Web site: www.ottawa.edu

Distance-learning degree programs—a B.A. in health services and an M.A. in human resources—require three weekends per year in Kansas City. Also offers, in partnership with Rio Salado Community College, a distance B.A. in police science.

Oxford Brookes University M

Gipsy Lane Campus, Headington
Oxford OX3 0BP, United Kingdom
Fields offered: Business administration, education
Year founded: 1970
Accreditation: International (GAAP)
Phone: +44 (1865) 485 962
Fax: +44 (1865) 485 830
Email: mba-bus@brookes.ac.uk
Web site: www.brookes.ac.uk

A distance MBA conducted over two years of open-learning study. Uses a variety of distance-learning methods, including printed text, audio- and videotapes, computer conferencing, and study groups. Three short residential sessions required.

Pace University M

1 Pace Plaza
New York, NY 10038
Fields offered: Business administration
Year founded: 1906
Accreditation: Regional
Phone: (212) 346 1200 ▪ (800) 874 7223
Fax: (212) 346 1933
Email: online@pace.edu
Web site: www.pace.edu

Executive MBA program combines online learning with nine short residencies, totaling 28 days over two years.

Pacifica Graduate Institute M, D

249 Lambert Rd.
Carpinteria, CA 93013
Fields offered: Psychology, mythology
Year founded: 1974
Accreditation: Regional
Phone: (805) 969 3626
Fax: (805) 565 1932
Email: admissions@pacifica.edu
Web site: www.pacifica.edu

Pacifica's stated mission is "to foster research in the fields of psychology and mythological studies, framed in the traditions of depth psychology." M.A. and Ph.D. students attend on-campus courses once a month, in the form of a three-day learning retreat. In most of the degree programs, there is also a one-week summer session. In between the on-campus sessions, students continue their coursework through directed readings, research, and practicums in their local areas. Formerly the Human Relations Institute.

Park College B

8700 River Park Dr.
Parkville, MO 64152
Fields offered: Management, criminal justice, computer information systems
Year founded: 1875
Accreditation: Regional
Phone: (816) 741 2000 ▪ (800) 745 7275
Fax: (816) 746 6423
Email: admissions@mail.park.edu
Web site: www.park.edu

Online B.S. degree completion programs in the above fields. Students who come to these programs with an associate's degree or equivalent can complete the B.S. degree nonresidentially except for two in-class courses (six hours) on Park's campus or at one of Park's extended learning sites on or near military bases all over the country.

Pennsylvania State University M

207 Mitchell Building
University Park, PA 16802-3601
Fields offered: Acoustics, elementary education
Year founded: 1855
Accreditation: Regional
Phone: (814) 865 5403 ▪ (800) 252 3592
Fax: (814) 865 3290
Email: psude@cde.psu.edu
Web site: www.psu.edu

Master of Science in acoustics through a special program for employees of the U.S. Navy and its contractors nationwide. Learning takes place through compressed-video television courses; one 2-week summer session required. M.Ed. in elementary education also available. For information on Penn State's wholly distance-learning programs, see its listing in the previous chapter.

Pepperdine University M, D

24255 Pacific Coast Hwy.
Malibu, CA 90263
Fields offered: Educational technology
Year founded: 1937
Accreditation: Regional
Phone: (310) 456 4000
Fax: (310) 456 4357
Email: admission-seaver@pepperdine.edu
Web site: www.pepperdine.edu

Online M.A. and Ed.D. in educational technology. Residency requirements for the master's include a five-day seminar at the beginning and end of the program and participation in a national conference; for the doctorate, four weeks and six weekends each year.

Prescott College   B, M

220 Grove Ave.
Prescott, AZ 86301
Fields offered: See below
Year founded: 1966
Accreditation: Regional
Phone: (520) 778 2090 ▓ (800) 628 6364
Email: admissions@prescott.edu
Web site: www.prescott.edu

Prescott's Adult Degree Program for B.A. completion (in counseling, human services, liberal arts, management, or teacher education) offers a student-centered, independent-study format, using instructors from a student's home community. Students normally take two courses every three months, meeting weekly with local instructors wherever they live. (Prescott helps locate them.) Students must come to the college for a weekend orientation at the beginning of their program, and for an additional liberal arts seminar, also held on a weekend. Degree programs can be individually designed to meet students' goals. Entering students normally have a minimum of 30 semester hours of prior college work. One year enrollment with Prescott is required to earn the degree. Credit for prior college-level learning can be awarded through the writing of a life-experience portfolio. Prescott also offers flexible, short-residency M.A. programs in adventure education, counseling & psychology, education, environmental studies, and humanities.

Purdue University   A, M, D

West Lafayette, IN 47907
Fields offered: Education, engineering, technology, management, pharmacy, agriculture, veterinary medicine, science, liberal arts, business administration
Year founded: 1869
Accreditation: Regional
Phone: (765) 494 1776
Fax: (765) 494 0544
Web site: www.cll.purdue.edu/dls

All of the programs require some residency, some more than others. Offers an A.S. in veterinary technology, MBA in food & agribusiness, and M.S. programs in accountancy, engineering, international management, management, and technology; at the doctoral level, a cohort-model Ed.D. in educational administration and a low-residency Doctor of Pharmacy.

Regent University   M, D

1000 Regent University Dr.
Virginia Beach, VA 23464-9800
Fields offered: Business administration, management, communications, theology, education, public policy, political management, public administration, organizational leadership
Year founded: 1977
Accreditation: Regional
Phone: (757) 226 4127 ▓ (800) 373 5504
Fax: (757) 424 7051
Email: admissions@regent.edu
Web site: www.regent.edu

Following a three-day on-campus orientation, the MBA and M.A. in management can be earned through a combination of Internet courses, guided independent study, audio- and videocassettes, and instruction by telephone and mail. M.A. programs in practical theology and biblical studies start with a nine-day residency. M.Ed. programs in educational leadership and Christian schools require summer residencies. The School of Government has master's programs in public policy, political management, and public administration; two weeks of residency per year. Distance-learning doctoral programs in communications as well as organizational leadership require two- to four-week summer sessions. Founded as CBN University (named after university founder Pat Robertson's Christian Broadcasting Network). Regent University integrates traditional Judeo-Christian ethical principles in the teaching of its courses. See the previous chapter for information on Regent's wholly distance-learning programs.

Robert Gordon University   B, M

Schoolhill
Aberdeen AB10 1FR, United Kingdom
Fields offered: See below
Year founded: 1750
Accreditation: International (GAAP)
Phone: +44 (1224) 262 000
Email: i.centre@rgu.ac.uk
Web site: www.rgu.ac.uk

While degree programs are largely completed via distance learning, most require a one- or two-week on-campus residency for a taught course held at the university. The degrees available are a B.A. in community health nursing (concentration in community psychiatric nursing, district nursing, health visiting, general practice nursing, occupational health nursing, or school nursing), a B.A. in midwifery studies, a B.A. in nursing specialist practice (concentration in blood transfusion, cancer nursing, critical care nursing, gerontological nursing, or hematological nursing), a B.A. in nursing studies, a B.A. in occupational health & safety management, and M.S.'s in clinical pharmacy and nursing.

Rochester Institute of Technology   B, M

91 Lomb Memorial Dr.
Rochester, NY 14623-5603
Fields offered: See below
Year founded: 1829
Accreditation: Regional
Phone: (716) 475 5089 ▓ (800) 225 5748
Fax: (716) 475 5077
Email: online@rit.edu
Web site: distancelearning.rit.edu

Offers a variety of degrees and certificate programs primarily through online study, although short residencies (usually laboratory seminars) are required. The B.S. is offered in applied arts & sciences, electrical & mechanical engineering technology, and environmental management & technology. The M.S. is offered in applied statistics, cross-disciplinary professional studies (with individualized focus area), environmental health & safety management, health systems administration, information technology, and software development management.

Royal Roads University   M

2005 Sooke Rd.
Victoria, BC V9B 5Y2, Canada
Fields offered: Business administration, leadership & training, distributed learning, conflict analysis & management, environment & management
Year founded: 1995
Accreditation: International (GAAP)
Phone: +1 (250) 391 2600 ▧ (800) 788 8028
Email: registrar-inquiries@royalroads.ca
Web site: www.royalroads.ca

A public university "for mid-career learners working in the global economy," created in 1995 by the British Columbia Legislature. Distance-learning master's degree programs in the above fields are Internet-based, but all involve multi-week residential sessions.

Rudolf Steiner College   B, M

9200 Fair Oaks Blvd.
Fair Oaks, CA 95628
Fields offered: Education, human development, arts
Year founded: 1976
Accreditation: Regional
Phone: (916) 961 8727
Fax: (916) 961 8731
Email: rsc@steinercollege.edu
Web site: www.steinercollege.edu

Rudolf Steiner College offers regionally accredited degree programs in association with regionally accredited universities, involving dual enrollment: with St. Mary's University of Minnesota for an M.A. in human development, and with the Union Institute for a bachelor's. In addition, they have their own state-approved (but not regionally accredited) B.A. in anthroposophical studies and in Waldorf education, and an M.A. in Waldorf education. They also offer a wide range of nondegree courses in topics ranging from Goethean studies to biodynamic gardening, and a three-year part-time course in Waldorf teacher education, offered in Fair Oaks and San Francisco.

Saint Francis Xavier University   B, M

P.O. Box 5000
Antigonish, NS B2G 2W5, Canada
Fields offered: Nursing, education
Year founded: 1853
Accreditation: International (GAAP)
Phone: +1 (902) 863 3300
Fax: +1 (902) 867 5154
Email: admit@stfx.ca
Web site: www.stfx.ca

A bachelor's degree program for working nurses who have one year of clinical experience and a high school diploma. Courses are built around correspondence materials (home-study readings and assignments, supplemented by audio- and videocassettes and telephone tutoring), but there is one annual visit to the campus required for orientation and counseling. Master's degree in education is offered through a short residency and guided independent study.

Saint Joseph's College   B, M

278 White's Bridge Rd.
Standish, ME 04084-5263
Fields offered: See below
Year founded: 1912
Accreditation: Regional
Phone: (800) 752 4723
Email: admiss@sjcme.edu
Web site: www.sjcme.edu/cps

Offers bachelor's completion programs in business, criminal justice, education, health care, liberal studies, and nursing. At the graduate level, St. Joseph's offers a Master of Health Services Administration, an M.A. in pastoral studies, an M.S. in nursing, an M.S. in education (with emphasis on lifelong teaching & learning). Most programs require one 2-week summer residency (except for the B.S. in nursing program which requires weekly clinicals in southern Maine). Video- and audiotapes, computer software, and email delivery of course materials.

Saint Mary-of-the-Woods College   B, M

Saint Mary-of-the-Woods, IN 47876
Fields offered: See below
Year founded: 1840
Accreditation: Regional
Phone: (812) 535 5106 ▧ (800) 926 7692
Email: adm-smwc@smwc.edu
Web site: www.smwc.edu

Majors offered at the bachelor's level (for women only) include accounting, business administration, computer information systems, early childhood, elementary education, English, gerontology, human resource management, human services, humanities, journalism, K-12 education, K-3 education, marketing, mathematics, paralegal studies, philosophy, psychology, science, secondary education (English or social studies), special education (learning disabilities or mild mental handicaps), and theology. Master's degree (coeducational) available in pastoral theology. Life-experience credit awarded to those with college-level knowledge acquired other than in a classroom environment. Students are guided by faculty via mail and phone in off-campus independent study, punctuated with brief on-campus residencies (an average of one day per semester).

Salve Regina University   B, M

100 Ochre Point Ave.
Newport, RI 02840-4192
Fields offered: International relations, management, business, human development, liberal studies, nursing
Year founded: 1934
Accreditation: Regional
Phone: (401) 847 6650 ▧ (800) 637 0002
Fax: (401) 341 2938
Email: sruadmis@salve.edu
Web site: www.salve.edu

A B.A. in liberal studies and a B.S. in both business and nursing, available to adult students who have already completed at least 45 credit hours elsewhere. At least 60 of the 120 credits required for the degree must then be completed through Salve Regina within six years, with a G.P.A. of 2.0 or higher. Master's degrees are offered in management, business administration, international relations, and human development. These programs require 36 units to complete. The school says that "the usual number of transfer credits is 6," but that exceptions are made for graduates of U.S. military colleges, who may transfer in a maximum of 18 earned credits, as well as for CPCUs, who can transfer up to 12 units towards the management degree. In all programs, instruction is by correspondence courses and guided independent study, supported by regular mail, email, and telephone contact with faculty. All programs require a brief residency, usually for five days in the summer.

San Jose State University   M

One Washington Square
San Jose, CA 95192
Fields offered: Library & information sciences, nursing, occupational therapy, transportation management
Year founded: 1857
Accreditation: Regional
Phone: (408) 924 1000
Fax: (408) 924 1018
Email: info@soar.sjsu.edu
Web site: www.sjsu.edu

Master's degrees in the above fields. Distance-learning methods vary. Short residencies involved.

Saybrook Graduate School   M, D

450 Pacific, 3rd Floor
San Francisco, CA 94133
Fields offered: Human science, organizational systems inquiry, psychology
Year founded: 1970
Accreditation: Regional
Phone: (415) 433 9200 ▪ (800) 825 4480
Fax: (415) 433 9271
Email: saybrook@saybrook.edu
Web site: www.saybrook.edu

Offers M.A. and Ph.D. programs in the above fields; courses are offered in a distance-learning format. A course guide is provided, specifying the required readings and including written lecture materials prepared by the faculty. Students may design their own courses as well. Student work focuses within nine areas of concentration: clinical inquiry, systems inquiry, health studies, peace & conflict resolution, creativity & art, organizational inquiry, social philosophy & political psychology, humanistic & transpersonal psychology, and consciousness studies. All students must attend a five-day planning seminar in San Francisco, and two 1-week national meetings each year. Degrees can take from two to six years to complete. Many well-known psychologists have been associated with Saybrook (Rollo May, Stanley Krippner, Richard Farson, Nevitt Sanford, Clark Moustakas, etc.). Saybrook, until 1982, was called the Humanistic Psychology Institute; later, it was known as Saybrook Institute.

Seton Hall University   M

400 South Orange Ave.
South Orange, NJ 07079-2697
Fields offered: Counseling, education, educational administration, Catholic school leadership, healthcare administration, higher education, human resources, law enforcement, strategic communication
Year founded: 1874
Accreditation: Regional
Phone: (973) 642 8500 ▪ (888) 738 6699
Fax: (973) 761 9234
Email: setonworldwide@shu.edu
Web site: www.setonworldwide.net

Offers online master's degrees in the above fields. At matriculation, students join a cohort and proceed as a group through the program. Extensive use of online seminar techniques using asynchronous computer conferencing. Short residencies, usually three long weekends spread over the program, help students bond with peers and faculty facilitators.

Sheffield Hallam University   B, M

City Campus, Howard St.
Sheffield S1 1WB, United Kingdom
Fields offered: Applied statistics, applied statistics with statistical education, business administration (enterprise & entrepreneurship, European management, financial management, financial services management, human resources management, information technology management, international management, management consultancy, marketing management), countryside recreation management, enterprise network management, food management, hospitality & tourism management, hospitality management, imperialism & culture, information technology & management, international hospitality management, international tourism management, management, networked information engineering, operations research, outdoor management development, technical authorship, total quality management & business excellence, tourism management
Year founded: 1969
Accreditation: International (GAAP)
Phone: +44 (1142) 252 127
Email: dl.support@shu.ac.uk
Web site: www.shu.ac.uk

This school offers master's degrees in the above fields, with several short residency periods for an annual study school and for exams every six months. Coursework is done by correspondence, supported by tutorial assistance and audiotapes. An Honours B.S. in hospitality management is also available.

Skidmore College   B, M

University Without Walls
815 North Broadway
Saratoga Springs, NY 12866
Fields offered: Individualized major, liberal studies

Year founded: 1911
Accreditation: Regional
Phone: (518) 580 5450
Fax: (518) 580 5449
Email: uww@skidmore.edu
Web site: www.skidmore.edu

Skidmore is one of the pioneers of the nontraditional movement, having offered a University Without Walls program since 1970. It is possible to earn a Bachelor of Arts or Bachelor of Science with a total of three days on campus: one for an admissions interview, a second for advising and planning, and the third to present a degree plan to a faculty committee. Skidmore makes it clear that they hold their graduates to "standards of knowledge, competence, and intellectual attainment which are no less comprehensive and rigorous than those established by traditional . . . programs." In addition to fulfilling all other requirements in the degree plan, each student completes a final project demonstrating competence in one's field. Students can major in any of the dozens of fields offered by Skidmore or, with the assistance of faculty advisors, devise a self-determined major. In 1992 Skidmore launched a master's program in interdisciplinary studies, modeled on its undergraduate program.

South Bank University M, D

103 Borough Rd.
London SE1 0AA, United Kingdom
Fields offered: Environment & development, business, chemical engineering, comparative social policies, computing, construction economics & international studies, construction management, construction technology, education, engineering, families, food & nutrition, gender & women's studies, geotechnics, health & illness, health & social care, media, politics, postcolonial literatures, race relations, sexualities, social policy & sociology, social psychology, socio-legal studies, sports & exercise science, Third World studies, transport & highways, water & environmental engineering, welfare & development studies
Accreditation: International (GAAP)
Phone: +44 (20) 7815 6137
Fax: +44 (20) 7815 6199
Email: internat@sbu.ac.uk
Web site: www.southbank-university.ac.uk

Offers a M.S. in environment & development largely by correspondence, with occasional Saturday sessions on campus. Students receive all required course materials (including textbooks) as a bulk packet. Also offers research-based M.Phil. and Ph.D. degrees in the above fields to candidates who have properly demonstrated their research of a topic to the satisfaction of a board of examiners. Supervised research at remote locations can be formally approved by the school, and it will consider non-U.K. students, provided they can demonstrate access to appropriate research facilities. Students are expected to spend some six weeks a year on the school's London campus, although some exceptions may be possible. While oral exams are generally held in the U.K., approval may be given in special cases for the examination to take

"In lieu of a textbook for your home-study course in classical Japanese art, we are sending you instead Mr. Fred Fukugawa."

place abroad. There is also an option under which a candidate may be awarded a Ph.D. on the basis of previously published work; such candidates are also expected to "have a significant connection with the University."

Southern Baptist Theological Seminary D

2825 Lexington Rd.
Louisville, KY 40280
Fields offered: Education
Accreditation: Regional
Phone: (502) 897 4011 ▪ (800) 626 5525
Fax: (502) 897 4880
Web site: www.sbts.edu

Ed.D. in leadership with little residency. Extensive use of Internet and email.

Southern Cross University B, M, D

P.O. Box 157
Lismore, NSW 2480, Australia
Fields offered: See below
Year founded: 1989
Accreditation: International (GAAP)
Phone: +61 (2) 6620 3000
Fax: +61 (2) 6620 1300
Email: sservice@scu.edu.au
Web site: www.scu.edu.au

Degrees at all levels are offered in a broad range of fields. Instruction is by the same faculty that teach on-campus courses, and is via various media, including printed lecture notes, interactive TV and radio, and video- and audio-cassettes. Some subjects require students to attend a certain number of short residential sessions on campus; voluntary weekend sessions are also available, the majority of them in Sydney. Enrollment in some programs is restricted to full-time residents of Australia, or Australians with resident status who are temporarily overseas. Degrees offered by correspondence include Bachelor of Business in tourism, Bachelor of Education, Bachelor of Health Science in nursing, Bachelor of Social Science, Master of Accounting Studies, M.A. and M.S. in many fields, MBA, Master of Business, Master of Education with an optional specialization in training & development, Master of Health Science, Master of International Tourism Management, Master of Laws, Master of Organizational Development & Training, and Doctor of Business Administration. Southern Cross University is developing its online program division; bachelor's degrees in emergency management, paralegal studies, and school & workforce development may be completed entirely through Web-based study.

Southern Methodist University   M

6425 Boaz Lane
Dallas, TX 75205
Fields offered: Business administration, computer science, electrical engineering, engineering management, environmental systems management, hazardous & waste materials management, materials science & engineering, manufacturing systems management, mechanical engineering, software engineering, systems engineering, telecommunications
Year founded: 1911
Accreditation: Regional
Phone: (214) 768 2000
Fax: (214) 768 1001
Email: tdowning@mail.smu.edu
Web site: www.smu.edu/distance
Offers master's programs in the above fields primarily through online study and videocourses, with minimal on-campus residency required.

Southern Oregon State College

See: Southern Oregon University

Southern Oregon University   B, M

1250 Siskiyou Blvd.
Ashland, OR 97520
Fields offered: Business & management, criminology, education, human services, nursing
Year founded: 1926
Accreditation: Regional
Phone: (541) 552 6332 ▪ (800) 552 5388
Fax: (541) 552 6047
Email: admissions@sou.edu
Web site: www.sou.edu
Off-campus bachelor's degree completion programs in business & management, human services, nursing, and criminology, and an M.Ed. for working teachers, mainly through courses viewed at distant sites, videocassette, computer conferencing, and telephone instruction. Most

programs are offered evenings and weekends, or by "multiple technologies." Summer sessions and occasional campus visits are required in many programs. This program serves only the southern Oregon region. Formerly Southern Oregon State College.

Southwestern Adventist College

See: Southwestern Adventist University

Southwestern Adventist University   B

Keene, TX 76059
Fields offered: Business administration, individualized major
Year founded: 1893
Accreditation: Regional
Phone: (817) 556 4705 ▪ (800) 433 2240
Fax: (817) 556 4742
Email: admissions@swau.edu
Web site: www.swau.edu
B.A., B.S., and Bachelor of Business Administration through the Adult Degree Program (ADP). Virtually all work can be completed at a distance, following a six-day admission seminar, held each March, June, and October. Credit is earned by transfer of credit, proficiency exams, credit for prior learning (portfolio), and independent study by mail, computer, and telephone. ADP students pay 80% of the tuition of on-campus students. Majors include business, communication, education, English, office administration, computer science, religion, social science, and history. Formerly Southwestern Adventist College.

Southwestern Assemblies of God University   B

1200 Sycamore
Waxahachie, TX 75165
Fields offered: Individualized major
Year founded: 1927
Accreditation: Regional
Phone: (972) 937 4010 ▪ (888) 937 7248
Fax: (972) 923 0488
Email: info@sagu.edu
Web site: www.sagu.edu/sde
Bachelor's degree through a largely nonresidential program open to anyone who makes a statement of Christian faith. Instruction is through audio- and videocassette, teleconferencing, and computer conferencing; students must spend two days on campus at the beginning of each semester, for registration.

Spurgeon's College   M

189 South Norwood Hill
London SE25 6DJ, United Kingdom
Fields offered: Theology, ministry
Year founded: 1856
Accreditation: International (GAAP)
Phone: +44 (181) 653 0850
Fax: +44 (181) 771 0959
Email: enquiries@spurgeons.ac.uk
Web site: www.spurgeons.ac.uk
In partnership with the Open Theological College and University of Wales, offers master's degrees in theology

by open learning. Degrees are awarded by the University of Wales.

Stephens College   B, M

Columbia, MO 65215
Fields offered: Business administration, education, English, health information administration, individualized major, law/philosophy/rhetoric, psychology
Year founded: 1833
Accreditation: Regional
Phone: (573) 876 7125 ▪ (800) 388 7579
Fax: (573) 876 7248
Email: sce@wc.stephens.edu
Web site: www.stephens.edu

Bachelor's in any of the above fields, or in a student-initiated major. Degree requirements can be met through independent study and online courses. Students may also earn credits through short-term, intensive courses, CLEP exams, prior learning portfolios, approved courses taken locally, etc. Students attend an introductory liberal studies seminar at Stephens College prior to admission. The course is offered in seven-day or double-weekend formats several times throughout the year. A minimum of 36 semester hours must be completed with Stephens College faculty. Open to applicants 23 years of age and older.

Syracuse University   B, M

Independent Study Degree Programs
700 University Ave.
Syracuse, NY 13244-2530
Fields offered: See below
Year founded: 1870
Accreditation: Regional
Phone: (315) 443 3480 ▪ (800) 442 0501
Fax: (315) 443 4174
Email: suisdp@uc.syr.edu
Web site: www.yesu.syr.edu

Syracuse independent study degree programs combine correspondence and online study with yearly residencies ranging from one to four weeks. Offers an A.A. and B.A. in liberal arts, MBA, Master of Library Science, Master of Social Science, M.A. in advertising design or illustration, and M.S.'s in communications management, engineering management, information resources management, nursing, and telecommunications & network management.

Taylor University   A

1025 West Rudisill Blvd.
Fort Wayne, IN 46807-2197
Fields offered: Biblical studies, Christian work, justice administration, justice & ministry, liberal arts
Year founded: 1846
Accreditation: Regional
Phone: (219) 744 8750 ▪ (800) 845 3149
Email: wwcampus@tayloru.edu
Web site: www.tayloru.edu

Offers online associate's degrees in biblical studies, justice administration, and liberal arts. Two certificates may also be earned through online study: a Christian Workers Certificate and a Justice & Ministry Certificate. The latter requires two 1-week summer residencies on the Fort Wayne Campus through Taylor's American Chaplaincy Training School.

Technical University of British Columbia   M, D

1063 Surrey Place Mall
Surrey, BC V3T 2W1, Canada
Fields offered: Software technology, information technology, management & technology, interactive arts, applied science
Year founded: 1998
Accreditation: International (GAAP)
Phone: +1 (604) 586 6000
Fax: +1 (604) 586 6003
Email: techbc@techbc.ca
Web site: www.techbc.ca

TechBC offers residential bachelor's programs and highly flexible master's and doctoral degree programs in applied science, management & technology, software technology, and related fields. The graduate degree programs, starting in fall 2001, seem comparable to British and Australian research degrees, in that they are individually designed, are based largely or entirely on a research project, and can be, as TechBC describes them, "location friendly" and "schedule friendly."

Teikyo Loretto Heights College   B

3001 S. Federal Blvd.
Denver, CO 80236
Fields offered: Liberal studies
Year founded: 1918
Accreditation: National (ACICS)
Phone: (303) 936 8441
Web site: www.tlhu.edu

Loretto offers a University Without Walls program that allows enrollees to earn the Bachelor of Arts with little or no time spent on campus. The SAAD (Students at a Distance) program is available to students of all ages in the Rocky Mountain area. The degree requires 128 semester units, of which at least the final 30 hours must be earned consecutively after enrolling. But these can be earned through a variety of nontraditional means: independent reading and research, seminars in the field, independent field practicums, assessment of prior learning experiences, CLEP and challenge exams, etc. Students are expected to meet periodically with faculty advisors, but those advisors are sometimes able to travel to a student's home location.

Texas A & M University—Commerce   D

P.O. Box 3011
Commerce, TX 75429
Fields offered: Educational psychology
Year founded: 1889
Accreditation: Regional
Phone: (903) 886 5102
Fax: (903) 886 5888
Email: dean_ginther@tamu-commerce.edu
Web site:
www.tamu-commerce.edu/coe/psy/Psyphd.htm

Ph.D. and master's degree programs in educational psychology with a curriculum focus on learning technologies, human cognition, and research and evaluation. A short on-campus residency (two summer sessions of five weeks) is required; classes available both on campus and over the Internet.

Thomas Edison State College   M
101 West State St.
Trenton, NJ 08608-1176
Fields offered: Management
Year founded: 1972
Accreditation: Regional
Phone: (609) 292 6565 ▪ (888) 442 8372
Fax: (609) 984 8447
Email: admissions@tesc.edu
Web site: www.tesc.edu

Offers an M.S. in management through a program of study that requires two brief residential periods. An online M.A. in professional studies is also under development. For information on Edison's wholly nonresident bachelor's and associate's degrees (available in 118 fields), see listing in the previous chapter.

Trinity University   M
715 Stadium Dr.
San Antonio, TX 78212
Fields offered: Health care administration
Year founded: 1869
Accreditation: Regional
Phone: (210) 999 7207
Fax: (210) 999 8164
Email: admissions@trinity.edu
Web site: www.trinity.edu

Master's in health care administration available almost entirely through home study. Each course begins with an intensive three-day on-campus program, followed by independent home study. Support is offered in the form of regular teleconferencing sessions with the instructor.

Tulane University   D
6823 St. Charles Ave.
New Orleans, LA 70118
Fields offered: Health systems management
Year founded: 1834
Accreditation: Regional
Phone: (504) 588 5387
Fax: (504) 584 3783
Email: edoc@hsm.tulane.edu
Web site: hsm.tulane.edu

Offers a Doctor of Science (Sc.D.) in Health Systems Management designed for practicing health care executives. Requires a dissertation and five weekend sessions per semester.

Union Graduate School
See: Union Institute

Union Institute   B, D
440 East McMillan St.
Cincinnati, OH 45206-1925

Fields offered: Individualized major, professional psychology
Year founded: 1964
Accreditation: Regional
Phone: (513) 861 6400 ▪ (800) 486 3116
Fax: (513) 861 0779
Email: admission@tui.edu
Web site: www.tui.edu

Union began in 1964 as the Union for Experimenting Colleges and Universities, a consortium that included some large state universities. When the consortium was dissolved, Union, renamed Union Graduate School, remained, and began to grant doctorates. (When bachelor's degrees were introduced, the name changed again, to the Union Institute.) At the undergraduate level, students can either study at one of the school's five academic centers (in Cincinnati, Miami, Los Angeles, Sacramento, and San Diego), or work through the Center for Distance Learning, combining brief residencies with a variety of other learning methods, including the Internet. Students design their own program in the fields of arts and sciences, business, criminal justice studies, or psychology; credit is available for prior academic and experiential learning. 30 of the 128 units needed for the degree must be earned while enrolled at Union.

The Graduate College offers independent study and research programs leading to a doctorate in interdisciplinary studies or professional psychology. No transfer or life-experience credit is accepted, and applicants must have a master's degree. A total of 35 days of required residency can be accomplished through participation in university-sponsored activities held around the country. The program also requires an internship, and culminates in a dissertation-level work, the "project demonstrating excellence," which can be traditional or nontraditional. Length of time to complete the doctorate varies, but a minimum of two years' enrollment is required; three to four years is typical. Note: Yet another name change is in the cards for 2001, but details were not available at press time.

United States Sports Academy   M
1 Academy Dr.
Daphne, AL 36526-7055
Fields offered: Sport science (recreation management)
Year founded: 1972
Accreditation: Regional
Phone: (334) 626 3303
Fax: (334) 621 2527
Email: academy@ussa.edu
Web site: www.sport.ussa.edu

Offers the Master of Sport Science (M.S.S.) in recreation management. This program involves two summers on the Academy's Daphne, Alabama, campus and a "mentorship" in the student's home community. It is also offered via distance learning: students can begin at any time during the year and must travel to the campus only at the program's end for exams. Courses are delivered through a variety of media including printed media, mentorship, internships, video- and audio-tape, computer-mediated instruction, interactive computer media, bulletin boards, databases, fax, phone, and various forms of directed study. For those students more comfortable in a group study environment, the Academy offers cluster study in various parts of the United States.

Universidad de Monterrey   M
Avenida Ignacio Morones Prieto 4500 Pte.
San Pedro, Garza Garcia
Nuevo Leon 66238, Mexico
Fields offered: Adult education
Year founded: 1969
Accreditation: International (GAAP)
Phone: +52 (8) 338 50 50
Web site: www.udem.edu.mx
A master's in adult education for persons who have at least two years of experience in the field. Instruction takes place via directed reading, audio- and videocassettes, telephone tutoring, teleconferencing, practical fieldwork, and some on-campus tutoring.

Universidad de San Jose
See: Empresarial University

Universidad Nacional
de Educacion a Distancia   M, D
Calle Conde de Penalver 38, Third Floor
Madrid 28006, Spain
Fields offered: See below
Year founded: 1972
Accreditation: International (GAAP)
Phone: +34 (1) 398 6545
Fax: +34 (1) 398 8086
Web site: www.uned.es
Spain's national open university offers degrees in a wide range of academic subjects. Instruction is in Spanish. Students study primarily through audio and video correspondence, although face-to-face and classroom sessions are also an essential component of many programs. Students enrolled in UNED need never actually travel to Spain; nine full Study Centres have been established in other countries (including Mexico), and approved examination centers, including New York, may be used to fulfill many residency requirements. Degrees offered include the Master of Behavior Therapy, the Master of Environmental Education, the Master of Human Sexuality, and doctorates offered through faculties in the following fields: economics and business administration (with five specializations), education (with eight specializations), geography and history (with nine specializations), industrial engineering (with five specializations), law (with seven specializations), philosophy (with four specializations), political and social science (with four specializations), and science (with eight specializations). Many intensive five- to seven-month graduate certificate courses are also available.

University of Alabama   B
Tuscaloosa, AL 35487-0001
Fields offered: Interdisciplinary studies
Year founded: 1831
Accreditation: Regional

Phone: (205) 348 3019
Email: info@exd.ccs.ua.edu
Web site: bama.ua.edu/~exd
The Bachelor of Arts or Bachelor of Science may be earned entirely through nonresident independent study, with the exception of a three-day degree-planning seminar on the campus at the start of the program. At least 32 semester hours of work must be completed after admission. This can be by out-of-class contract learning, correspondence courses, television courses, weekend college, prior-learning evaluation, or on-campus courses at the university. Interdisciplinary degrees offered in human services, humanities, social sciences, natural sciences, applied sciences, administrative sciences, and communication. A 12-semester-hour senior project is required of all students. Academic advising and planning can be done by telephone.

University of Arizona   M
Tucson, AZ 85721
Fields offered: Information resources & library science
Year founded: 1885
Accreditation: Regional
Phone: (520) 621 8632 ▪ (800) 478 9508
Fax: (520) 621 3269
Email: distance@u.arizona.edu
Web site: www.eu.arizona.edu/dist
A master's in library science is available through courses offered over the Internet, supplemented by cablecast lectures (students must have graphical Web access and provide an email address upon registration). A minimum of 12 units of coursework on campus at Tucson is required, but these may be done during the summer sessions.

University of Bath   M
Bath BA2 7AY, United Kingdom
Fields offered: Construction management, integrated environmental management, electrical power systems, sports medicine, rheumatology
Year founded: 1894
Accreditation: International (GAAP)
Phone: +44 (1225) 826 878
Fax: +44 (1225) 826 849
Email: dcde@bath.ac.uk
Web site: www.bath.ac.uk/Departments/DCDE
The University of Bath's Department of Continuing and Distance Education offers three M.S. programs: construction management, integrated environmental management, and electrical power systems. Degree programs are offered in six to eight modules, depending on the programs which are generally completed over a period of three to five years, by distance-learning methods including correspondence, workbooks, audio- and videotapes, and regular contact with tutors. Distance students worldwide are offered a support network including a newsletter, a Website, counseling, and the like. The average program requires about 20 days residency—one 10-day session spent on the British campus in each of the first two years. Also offers two health-related postgraduate diploma courses for doctors: one in sports medicine, and one in

primary care rheumatology. Both can be accomplished largely through distance learning, with some clinical weekends.

University of Bradford   M, D

Student Registry, Postgraduate
Richmond Rd.
Bradford BD7 1DP, United Kingdom
Fields offered: Applied social sciences, archaeological sciences, biomedical sciences, cancer research, chemical engineering, chemistry, civil & environmental engineering, computing, cybernetics, development & project planning, education, electronic & electrical engineering, electronic imaging & media communications, environmental science, European studies, gender & women's studies, health studies, industrial technology, interdisciplinary human studies, management, mathematics, mechanical & medical engineering, modern languages, optometry, peace studies, pharmacy, polymer engineering, social & economic studies
Year founded: 1957
Accreditation: International (GAAP)
Phone: +44 (1274) 233 042
Fax: +44 (1274) 235 810
Email: pg-admissions@bradford.ac.uk
Web site: www.brad.ac.uk
Research-based M.Phil. and Ph.D. programs in all of the above fields by distance learning, with about two weeks of residency per year. Students must register initially for the M.Phil. before they are given the option of advancing to Ph.D. candidacy.

University of Calgary   B, M

2500 University Dr. NW
Calgary, Alberta T2N 1N4, Canada
Fields offered: Continuing education (workplace learning, leadership & development), education (adult/community/higher education, curriculum teaching & learning, educational leadership, educational technology)
Year founded: 1980
Accreditation: International (GAAP)
Phone: +1 (403) 220 6920
Fax: +1 (403) 210 0043
Email: uofcinfo@ucalgary.ca
Web site: www.ucalgary.ca
M.Ed. (in adult/community/higher education, curriculum teaching & learning, educational leadership, or educational technology) and Master of Continuing Education (emphasis leadership & development or workplace learning) are available largely through distance learning. The first requires one 6-week summer session on campus, the latter a 3-week orientation at the program's beginning. Courses are delivered via a range of media, including tele- and videoconferencing, computer networks, videocassette, telephone, fax, and email.

University of California—Irvine   M

Graduate School of Management
Irvine, CA 92697-3125

Fields offered: Business administration (health care)
Year founded: 1965
Accreditation: Regional
Phone: (949) 824 4622
Email: oars@uci.edu
Web site: www.gsm.uci.edu
This part-time MBA with a focus on health care (it's called the Health Care Executive MBA) takes two years to complete. Much of the work is done over the Internet; students meet once a month for three and a half days; the school points out that their campus is only minutes from a major airport, making this a reasonable distance-learning program for someone at an executive level.

University of Colorado at Denver   M

P.O. Box 480006
Denver, CO 80248-0006
Fields offered: Business administration (health administration)
Year founded: 1912
Accreditation: Regional
Phone: (303) 623 1888 ▪ (800) 228 5778
Fax: (303) 623 6228
Email: peter_taffe@ceo.cudenver.edu
Web site: www-bus.colorado.edu/execed
MBA in health administration for working health care professionals, through a combination of computer conferencing and on-campus instruction. Students must attend five intensive on-campus sessions in Denver during the two-year program. Instruction takes place largely online. Students in the executive program come from a variety of backgrounds, and include physicians, nurses, pharmacists, group-practice administrators, managed-care administrators, and hospital and long-term care administrators.

University of Delaware   B

Newark, DE 19716
Fields offered: See below
Year founded: 1833
Accreditation: Regional
Phone: (302) 831 6442
Email: maryvp@udel.edu
Web site: www.udel.edu/ce
Offers a BSN for working registered nurses primarily through online study. (This course involves three weekends on the Delaware campus.) Also offers a B.S. in hotel, restaurant, & institutional management, a Master of Mechanical Engineering, an MSN, and a certificate in e-commerce through a mix of online study and short residency sessions.

University of Durham   M, D

Business School, Mill Hill Lane
Durham City DH1 3LB, United Kingdom
Fields offered: Business administration
Year founded: 1832
Accreditation: International (GAAP)
Phone: +44 (1913) 742 216
Fax: +44 (1913) 743 389
Email: mbadl.enq@durham.ac.uk

Web site: www.dur.ac.uk/dubs/mbadl

In mid-1988 Durham introduced a distance-learning MBA (they have offered a traditional MBA since 1967). The program is administered by the University Business School to students in more than 40 countries. The three-to-four-year course of study combines specially written distance-learning materials, annotated texts, audiotapes, and one week per year of intensive residential seminars (first year excluded).

University of Florida   B, M

Gainesville, FL 32611
Fields offered: Business administration, electrical engineering, fire & emergency services, agriculture, health administration
Year founded: 1853
Accreditation: Regional
Phone: (352) 392 3261
Fax: (352) 392 8791
Email: gradinfo@ufl.edu
Web site: www.fcd.ufl.edu

Distance-learning M.S. and B.S. in electrical engineering, B.S. and M.S. in fire & emergency services, Master of Agriculture, master's in health administration, and an Internet MBA program (which has a one-year track for students who already have a business degree). Courses delivered by Internet and video. Short residencies vary by program. For information on Florida's wholly distance-learning degrees, see the preceding chapter.

University of Guelph   M

Room 221, MacLachlan Building
Guelph, Ontario N1G 2W1, Canada
Fields offered: Business administration (agribusiness)
Year founded: 1964
Accreditation: International (GAAP)
Phone: (888) 622 2474
Fax: +1 (519) 767 1510
Email: mbaagri@uoguelph.ca
Web site: www.mbaagri.uoguelph.ca

The University of Guelph offers a computer-based MBA in agriculture in conjunction with Athabasca University. Students interact and discuss assignments using Lotus Notes. The program is divided into three distinct phases. After the first phase is completed, the student is awarded the Advanced Graduate Diploma in Management. Phase two consists of agribusiness courses. Phase three is a dissertation. The program takes two to three years to complete.

University of Illinois at Chicago   M

Chicago, IL 60612
Fields offered: Engineering, health education
Year founded: 1891
Accreditation: Regional
Phone: (312) 996 7000
Email: uicadmit@uic.edu
Web site: www.uic.edu

Master of Engineering offered primarily by the Internet, but also using videocassette courses and/or audio-video teleconferencing. The online Master of Health Professions Education prepares health professionals (doctors, nurses, pharmacists, etc.) for roles in education. Annual five-day conference held on campus.

University of Illinois at Urbana-Champaign   M

Graduate School of Library and Information Science
501 E. Daniel St.
Champaign, IL 61820
Fields offered: Library & information science
Year founded: 1867
Accreditation: Regional
Phone: (217) 333 7197 ▪ (800) 982 0914
Fax: (217) 244 3302
Email: leep@alexia.lis.uiuc.edu
Web site: www.lis.uiuc.edu

An M.S. in library & information sciences tailored to working students. Study begins with a two-week residency, after which students study by distance-learning methods. There is at least one more residential requirement, a three-day weekend. Part-time students are expected to take two to five years to complete this degree. Study takes the form of correspondence, heavy Internet use, a practicum in a local information center, independent study, and courses transferred in.

University of Kent at Canterbury   M, D, Law

The Registry
Canterbury, Kent CT2 7NZ, United Kingdom
Fields offered: Accounting, actuarial science, American studies, applied language studies in computing, applied linguistics, applied mathematics, biochemistry, biodiversity management, biotechnology, cartoons & caricature, chemistry, classical archaeology, classical studies, communication & image studies, comparative literary studies, computer science, drama, economics, electronic engineering, English, environmental anthropology, environmental law & conservation, environmental social science, European studies, feminist legal studies, film studies, forensic psychology, German, health psychology, history, history & cultural studies of science, history & theory of art, industrial relations, international conflict analysis, international relations, Italian, law, law & philosophy, learning disability, management, management science, medicine & health sciences, medieval & Tudor studies, mental health, microbiology, operations research, personal social services, philosophy, physics, politics & government, postcolonial studies, psychology, psychotherapy, pure mathematics, social anthropology, social policy, social psychology, social work, sociolegal studies, sociology, Spanish, statistics, theology & religious studies, urban studies, women's studies
Year founded: 1965
Accreditation: International (GAAP)
Phone: +44 (1227) 824 040
Fax: +44 (1227) 452 196
Email: graduate-office@ukc.ac.uk
Web site: www.ukc.ac.uk

Offers research-based M.Phil., Ph.D., and (in the case of feminist legal studies, law, or sociolegal studies) LL.M. programs in the above fields. Students must choose a nearby institution to act as a satellite research site and generally make yearly residencies at the Kent campus itself, usually of about six weeks duration.

University of Manchester   M

Oxford Rd.
Manchester M13 9PL, United Kingdom
Fields offered: Pharmaceutical engineering
Year founded: 1851
Accreditation: International (GAAP)
Phone: +44 (161) 275 2484
Fax: +44 (161) 275 2423
Email: piat@fs1.pa.man.ac.uk
Web site: www.man.ac.uk

Manchester offers an M.S. in pharmaceutical engineering to students worldwide through the PEAT Programme. Students complete 12 modules by correspondence and a culminating master's dissertation. Two weeks or so of on-campus residency is required.

University of Montana   M, D

Missoula, MT 59812
Fields offered: Education, pharmacy, business administration
Year founded: 1893
Accreditation: Regional
Phone: (406) 243 0211 ▪ (800) 462 8636
Fax: (406) 243 2797
Email: ckelly@selway.umt.edu
Web site: www.umt.edu/ccesp

Two-year Ed.D. in educational leadership prepares working educators and administrators for executive roles in universities and K-12 schools. Students must come to Missoula six weekends each semester and for three weeks in the summer. Doctor of Pharmacy delivered via the Internet requires two on-campus weekends each year. For in-state students, an MBA and M.Ed. in curriculum studies is delivered by televised courses to sites all over Montana.

University of Nebraska—Lincoln   M, D

334 Nebraska Center
Lincoln, NE 68583-9805
Fields offered: Engineering, business administration, education, journalism, human resources, family sciences
Year founded: 1869
Accreditation: Regional
Phone: (402) 472 6550
Fax: (402) 472 1901
Email: jgunn2@unl.edu
Web site: dcs.unl.edu

Ed.D. or Ph.D. in administration, curriculum, & instruction, specializing in educational leadership in higher education, delivered by the Internet and interactive television or by Lotus Notes. Twenty weeks of summer residency required over the course of the program. Degrees available in-state by teleconferencing include an MBA, M.S. in human resources & family sciences, M.S. in industrial & management systems engineering, M.S. in manufacturing systems engineering, and an M.A. in journalism & mass communications.

University of North Dakota   B, M

P.O. Box 9021
Grand Forks, ND 58202
Fields offered: Space studies, engineering, business, public administration, social work, education
Year founded: 1883
Accreditation: Regional
Phone: (701) 777 4884 ▪ (877) 450 1842
Fax: (701) 777 3650
Email: ext_degree@mail.und.nodak.edu
Web site: www.conted.und.edu

M.S. in space studies (partially sponsored by NASA) offered over the Internet with a one-week on-campus requirement at the end of the program. B.S. in engineering (mechanical, chemical, or electrical) delivered by videotape to corporate-sponsored students at company sites. Master's in business, public administration, educational leadership, special education, elementary education, and social work are available to students at sites across North Dakota.

University of Oklahoma   B, M

College of Liberal Studies
1700 Asp Ave., Suite 226
Norman, OH 73072-6400
Fields offered: Liberal studies
Year founded: 1890
Accreditation: Regional
Phone: (405) 325 1061 ▪ (800) 522 4389
Fax: (405) 325 7132
Email: cls@ou.edu
Web site: www.ou.edu/cls

Bachelor and Master of Liberal Studies through directed independent study with two or three weeks each year on campus. There are no majors; students work in three general areas: humanities, natural sciences, and social sciences. The M.L.S. is largely for people with specialized bachelor's degrees who wish a broader education. Some of the on-campus residencies may be waived based on prior study or passing of an equivalency exam.

University of Pittsburgh   B, M

4200 Fifth Ave.
Pittsburgh, PA 15260
Fields offered: Psychology, economics, history, humanities, social sciences, business administration
Year founded: 1787
Accreditation: Regional
Phone: (412) 624 7210
Fax: (412) 624 7213
Email: ciddeweb+@pitt.edu
Web site: www.pitt.edu/~ciddeweb

The University External Studies Program offers bachelor's degrees in economics, history, psychology, humanities, and social science through independent study and Saturday workshops. The Katz School of Business offers a FLEX-

MBA program designed for working business executives; two weeks of residency required per term, adding up to 13 weeks over the two-year program.

University of Saint Augustine
for Health Sciences   M, D
1 University Blvd.
St. Augustine, FL 32086-5783
Fields offered: Health science, physical therapy
Year founded: 1979
Accreditation: National (DETC)
Phone: (904) 826 0084 ■ (800) 241 1027
Fax: (904) 826 0085
Email: advanced@usa.edu
Web site: www.usa.edu
Master of Health Science, Doctor of Health Science, and Doctor of Physical Therapy are offered through a combination of week-long residential seminars and home study. Formerly known as the Institute of Physical Therapy.

University of Saint Thomas   M
2115 Summit Ave.
Saint Paul, MN 55105
Fields offered: Business administration (health care management)
Year founded: 1885
Accreditation: Regional
Phone: (651) 962 4135 ■ (800) 328 6819
Email: shagel@stthomas.edu
Web site: www.stthomas.edu
Saint Thomas's MBA program in medical group management covers all of the basic concepts common to business administration, and then applies them to the health care profession and medical group environment. Internet-based courses are combined with two 1-week sessions on campus each year. The program takes between two and three years.

University of San Jose
or Universidad de San Jose. See: Empresarial University

University of Sarasota   M, D
5250 17th St.
Sarasota, FL 34235
Fields offered: See below
Year founded: 1969
Accreditation: Regional
Phone: (941) 379 0404 ■ (800) 331 5995
Fax: (941) 379 9464
Email: uofs@embanet.com
Web site: www.sarasota.edu
Note: We heard reports that University of Sarasota may change its name to Argosy University (the school is owned by the Argosy Education Group), but the matter was still not settled when we went to press.

B.S. programs in business administration and organizational management; M.A. programs in counseling psychology, education, guidance counseling, and mental health counseling; MBA in finance, health care administration, human resources, international business, international trade, and marketing; Ed.S. in curriculum & instruction,

educational leadership, and school counseling; DBA in accounting, information systems, international business, management, and marketing; and Ed.D. in counseling psychology, curriculum & instruction, educational leadership, organizational leadership, and pastoral community counseling.

For all of these programs, a minimum of eight weeks' residence is required at one of Sarasota's three campuses (Sarasota and Tampa in Florida, or Orange, California); this requirement is split up over traditional winter, summer, and spring break periods. The university's programs consist of seminars, supervised individual research, and writing, combined with the residential sessions. Master's candidates either write a thesis or complete a directed independent study project. Doctoral students must write a dissertation. Many of the students are teachers and school administrators.

Originally known as Laurence University, the predecessor of the Laurence University that opened in California and is now the University of Santa Barbara.

University of Sheffield   M, D
Western Bank
Sheffield S10 2TN, United Kingdom
Fields offered: Psychoanalytic studies, research docs
Year founded: 1828
Accreditation: International (GAAP)
Phone: +44 (114) 222 2000
Fax: +44 (114) 273 9826
Email: cics@sheffield.ac.uk
Web site: www.shef.ac.uk
Sheffield permits candidates for M.Phil. and Ph.D. research degrees to pursue a majority of their studies away from the university; specifics must be worked out with the student's faculty advisor. In addition, the Centre for Psychotherapeutic Studies offers a distance-learning M.A. in Psychoanalytic Studies. The degree is a two-year part-time program with a compulsory one-week residential course per year. See *www.shef.ac.uk/~psysc*.

University of South Carolina   M
Columbia, SC 29208
Fields offered: Engineering (chemical, civil & environmental, computer, electrical, mechanical)
Year founded: 1801
Accreditation: Regional
Phone: (803) 777 4192
Web site: www.engr.sc.edu/apogee
Offers a Master of Engineering and an M.S. in engineering in the above concentrations through a videocourse-based program; students may choose to attend a broadcast extension site near them or to view the tapes at home.

University of South Florida   B
4202 East Fowler Ave.
Tampa, FL 33620
Fields offered: Independent studies
Year founded: 1956
Accreditation: Regional
Phone: (813) 974 4058

Fax: (813) 974 5101
Email: issdept@nosferatu.cas.usf.edu
Web site: www.cas.usf.edu/bis

The Bachelor of Independent Studies program requires from four to six weeks on campus, spread out over three summers. All students must have knowledge across broad areas of study: social sciences, natural sciences, and humanities. Each area has an extensive program of guided independent study and a two-week on-campus seminar for research, writing, peer interaction, and, when relevant, laboratory experience. The average student takes about five years to complete the degree.

University of Stirling   M

Stirling FK9 4LA, United Kingdom
Fields offered: Business administration (retailing), entrepreneurial studies
Year founded: 1967
Accreditation: International (GAAP)
Phone: +44 (1786) 473 171
Web site: www.stir.ac.uk

Stirling offers several largely distance-learning master's degrees, geared to working professionals. The M.S. in entrepreneurial studies is designed for students in the U.K. and abroad; applicants who lack an undergraduate degree but have significant experience in small business may be admitted if they can prove ability to take on postgraduate-level study. The MBA in retailing is for persons with high levels of experience; the typical student has at least 10 years of work experience in the distributive trades. Face-to-face tutorials are expected in some programs.

University of Teesside   M, D

Middlesbrough, Cleveland TS1 3BA, United Kingdom
Fields offered: Accountancy, art & design, business, computing & media, criminology & law, education, engineering, English & cultural studies, health & nursing, history, leisure tourism & heritage, marketing & public relations, media, psychology, science, social sciences, social work, sport
Year founded: 1929
Accreditation: International (GAAP)
Phone: +44 (1642) 384 408
Web site: www.tees.ac.uk

Offers the M.Phil. and Ph.D. through a research model, which means that it is possible for students to register with the university but work largely outside the U.K. if the facilities available are satisfactory and if the arrangements for supervision will provide frequent and substantial contact between the student and the U.K.-based supervisor. Required number of visits with supervisor vary by program. A minimum of six weeks per year in the U.K. is required. A Ph.D. by published work is also available.

University of Tennessee—Knoxville   M

Knoxville, TN 37996
Fields offered: Information sciences, business administration (for physicians)
Year founded: 1794
Accreditation: Regional
Phone: (865) 974 1000

Fax: (865) 974 3536
Email: disteducation@utk.edu
Web site: www.outreach.utk.edu

Except for a week of orientation and an end-of-program exam or thesis defense, the M.S. in information sciences can be earned off-campus over the Internet. The Physician Executive MBA, designed for doctors seeking management and business operation skills, requires four 1-week residencies during the 12-month program; all other courses available over the Internet.

University of Texas at Dallas   M

P.O. Box 830688
Richardson, TX 75083-0688
Fields offered: Business administration (global leadership), international management
Year founded: 1969
Accreditation: Regional
Phone: (972) 883 6467
Email: glemba@utdallas.edu
Web site:
www.utdallas.edu/dept/mgmt/mims/mims.html

The University's MIMS program awards both an M.A. in international management and an MBA with a strong emphasis on international business. The MIMS program uses the Internet to deliver the curriculum through a variety of audio and video technologies. A substantial portion of the MIMS curriculum is delivered during four 2-day retreats in a traditional lecture/seminar format and one 10-day foreign study tour in the latter half of July.

University of Wales—Aberystwyth   B, M, D

Old College, King St.
Aberystwyth, Ceredigion
Wales SY23 2AX, United Kingdom
Fields offered: See below
Year founded: 1872
Accreditation: International (GAAP)
Phone: +44 (1970) 622 090
Fax: +44 (1970) 622 921
Email: rlw@aber.ac.uk
Web site: www.aber.ac.uk

The Aberystwyth campus of the University of Wales system offers a number of programs though distance learning and brief residency: a B.S. in economics, with a specialization in library & information studies; M.S. in economics with a specialization in the management of library & information systems, health information management, or records management; LL.M. in environmental law & management; and M.S.'s in environmental impact assessment, environmental auditing, environmental management, and protected landscape management. In addition, there are M.Phil. and Ph.D. degrees that can be studied on a part-time basis, with students traveling to Wales for a couple of weeks a year, or handled full-time through a place of employment. This option is available in the following departments: accounting & finance, art, biological sciences, computer science, economics, education, English, European languages, geography & earth studies, history & Welsh history, information & library sciences, international politics, law, mathematics, physics, rural agriculture, theater, film, & television studies, and Welsh (Celtic) studies.

University of Wales—Bangor M

Institute for Financial Management
Bangor, Gwynedd LL57 2DG, United Kingdom
Fields offered: Business administration
Accreditation: International (GAAP)
Phone: +44 (1248) 371 408
Fax: +44 (1248) 370 769
Email: abs046@bangor.ac.uk
Web site: www.ifm.bangor.ac.uk

In partnership with Manchester Business School, offers a distance-learning MBA program (with a concentration in financial management and financial services) designed specifically for financial managers and "finance sector professionals." Managers from some 50 countries worldwide are currently enrolled. The module-based program culminates in a final work-related project. Two yearly 6-day residential sessions provide peer-group support and networking, as well as face-to-face faculty contact. Individual students are permitted to vary their program schedules to meet the demands of their specific professional and personal needs.

University of Warwick M

Coventry CV4 7AL, United Kingdom
Fields offered: Business administration
Year founded: 1965
Accreditation: International (GAAP)
Phone: +44 (2476) 524 306
Fax: +44 (2476) 523 719
Email: inquiries@wbs.warwick.ac.uk
Web site: www.warwick.ac.uk

Warwick offers the MBA through a largely distance-learning format, although three "induction days" are required at the beginning of each of the program's three parts, plus one compulsory eight-day residential seminar. These residencies may be taken on campus in England or in Hong Kong, Singapore, or Malaysia. The school offers telephone and email tutorial support, and comprehensive correspondence study materials.

University of Westminster M

309 Regent St.
London W1R 8AL, United Kingdom
Fields offered: Business administration (design management), international business & management
Year founded: 1838
Accreditation: International (GAAP)
Phone: +44 (171) 911 5000
Fax: +44 (171) 911 5175
Email: international-office@wmin.ac.uk
Web site: www.wmin.ac.uk

Westminster offers an MBA with a concentration in design management and a Master of Arts in international business & management, both by distance learning. The MBA is module-based, with a four-day workshop at the end of each course of study; the M.A. has no required residency, although an optional residential week in July is offered.

University of Wisconsin—Green Bay B

2420 Nicolet Dr.
Green Bay, WI 54311-7001

Angela recycled her Open University paleontology project for her son's second birthday.

Fields offered: Interdisciplinary studies
Year founded: 1978
Accreditation: Regional
Phone: (920) 465 2423 ▪ (800) 621 2313
Fax: (920) 465 2643
Email: gbextdeg@uwgb.edu
Web site: www.uwgb.edu

Nontraditional program is available only to Wisconsin residents. B.A. in interdisciplinary studies requires at least two seminars held on-campus on Saturdays. Program includes independent study, research projects, internships, online courses, radio and television broadcasts, and other learning methods.

University of Wisconsin—Madison M, D

500 Lincoln Dr.
Madison, WI 53706
Fields offered: Engineering (computer, electrical, mechanical, professional practice), administrative medicine, pharmacy
Year founded: 1849
Accreditation: Regional
Phone: (608) 262 1234
Fax: (608) 262 0123
Email: gradadmiss@bascom.wisc.edu
Web site: www.wisc.edu

Short-residency master's degrees offered by the engineering school. The M.S. in computer & electrical engineering (power electronics) and the M.S. in mechanical engineering (controls) both require a three-week summer lab. The Master of Engineering in Professional Practice, likened to an engineer's version of an MBA, is designed for early- to mid-career engineers who seek to improve their professional skills. Requires a one-week on-campus summer session. These programs delivered through a variety of means, including teleconferencing and online discussions. See *www.engr.wisc.edu*.

Master's Degree in Administrative Medicine is designed for mid-career clinicians with leadership potential in medical management. Students begin and end each semester on the Madison campus, for a total of eight weeks of residency throughout the 22-month program. See *www.medsch.wisc.edu/adminmed*.

Doctor of Pharmacy is designed for licensed Wisconsin pharmacists. Coursework is delivered primarily by distance learning, with occasional on-campus or regional workshops. See *www.pharmacy.wisc.edu/ntpd*.

University of Wyoming   B, M
Laramie, WY 82071
Fields offered: Adult learning & technology, business administration, nursing, nursing education, professional child development
Year founded: 1886
Accreditation: Regional
Phone: (307) 766 1121 ▦ (800) 448 7801
Fax: (307) 766 3445
Web site: ecampus.uwyo.edu
Offers a BBA, a bachelor's in professional child development, and a B.S. completion program in nursing for registered nurses, through online study with minimal residency. Also offers master's degrees in adult learning & technology and nursing education.

Utah State University   M
Logan, UT 84322-0001
Fields offered: Special education, rehabilitation counseling
Year founded: 1888
Accreditation: Regional
Phone: (435) 797 0449
Email: info@rce.usu.edu
Web site: www.rce.usu.edu
A master's degree in vocational rehabilitation, geared to training rehabilitation counselors, is offered almost entirely through distance learning. Originally developed to serve rural Utah residents, this program now has students across the U.S. and Canada, and some overseas as well. Coursework is delivered using prepackaged, multimedia materials, two-way audio classes, and the Internet. Three 1-week summer workshops are required on campus over the course of the degree, and students must complete a supervised internship.

Vermont Institute of Community Involvement
See: Burlington College

Virginia Polytechnic Institute and
State University   M
Blacksburg, VA 24061
Fields offered: Health & physical education
Year founded: 1872
Accreditation: Regional
Phone: (540) 231 6000
Fax: (540) 231 9263
Email: rstratto@vt.edu
Web site: www.vt.edu
Except for two 2-week summer residencies, the M.A. in health & physical education is delivered over the Internet.

Walden University   D
155 Fifth Ave. South

Minneapolis, MN 55401
Fields offered: Education, health services, human services, psychology, applied management & decision sciences
Year founded: 1970
Accreditation: Regional
Phone: (612) 338 7224 ▦ (800) 925 3368
Fax: (612) 338 5092
Email: info@waldenu.edu
Web site: www.waldenu.edu
Doctoral programs in the above fields can be completed through a combination of independent study, intensive weekend sessions held regionally, personal interaction with the faculty, and a two- to three-week summer residency at Indiana University. Each student is guided by a faculty advisor, with a reader and external consultant/examiner added at the dissertation stage. For information on Walden's wholly nonresidential master's programs, see the previous chapter.

Weber State University   B
1001 University Circle
Ogden, UT 84408-1001
Fields offered: Allied health sciences
Year founded: 1889
Accreditation: Regional
Phone: (801) 626 6743
Email: admissions@weber.edu
Web site: www.weber.edu/chp
B.S. in allied health sciences, with concentrations in health administrative services, advanced radiological sciences, respiratory therapy, and advanced dental hygiene. Up to 46 credit hours for CLEP exams, and up to 15 for two full years of military service. At least 45 credit hours must be taken through WSU, through intensive workshops and independent study. Correspondence courses include textbooks, study guides, modules, video- and audiotapes, and other learning aides prepared by the instructor. Student is assigned an instructor for each course, and keeps contact by phone and mail. Student has up to six months to complete each course. Workshops are four 3- to 4-day sessions per year at various sites, including Billings, MT, and Seattle, WA, or two 6-day "super sessions" at WSU. Exact number required depends on student's field of study.

Western Baptist College   B
5000 Deer Park Dr. SE
Salem, OR 97301
Fields offered: Family studies, management & communication
Year founded: 1935
Accreditation: Regional
Phone: (503) 375 7590 ▦ (800) 764 1383
Fax: (503) 375 7583
Email: asd@wbc.edu
Web site: www.wbc.edu
Offers online bachelor's degree completion programs in family studies and management & communication. Three days of residency required at matriculation. To enroll, students need at least 60 semester hours of previous college credit and must submit to the College Statement of Faith.

So Where Did Your Regents Degree Take You?
Mine Took Me to Alcatraz!

by Martin Spillane

Having received my Regents College [now Excelsior College] B.S. in liberal studies, I embarked on the study of continuing education and one day I found myself on a wet and windy voyage to the bleak island prison of Alcatraz, which in its time has housed some of America's most violent criminals. It is not a place normally associated with education or vocational training, yet it was there that I met a self-taught scholar and medical man called Jim Quillen, otherwise known as Federal Prisoner AZ 586. He was a bulky, broad-shouldered man with gray hair, a craggy face, and the aura of a heavyweight boxer. He was sitting on the edge of a seemingly inadequate steel chair in a small, cold, harshly lit room, where the wind howled and the rain whipped between the steel bars of the square hole that served as a window. He had a pen in his hand and spectacles perched crookedly on his misshapen nose, and he was peering at the books on the table before him.

Jim Quillen had originally been sentenced to 15 years in a California state prison for robbery, but had escaped and committed other robberies whilst on the run. When cornered by the police he and another escapee had kidnapped two hostages at gunpoint and escaped in a stolen car. For this he had been sentenced to 45 years in a federal prison, with the original 15 years to be served later in the California state penitentiary. He was sent to Alcatraz, where he became embroiled in a major riot and lost all remission. Facing a lifetime in jail, he had declined all contact with his family and had become an institutionalized recluse, hidden in the steel and concrete jungle of the American penal system.

As a child he had endured an unhappy home life, an alcoholic mother, an openly hostile stepmother, separation from his sister, and life in a series of foster homes. His schooling had been limited by truancy, and as a result of petty crime he had been sent to reform school. At 20 he had joined the Marine Corps and completed his six-month basic training, only to be discharged when his criminal record came to light. His father, a former soldier, had then disowned him. However, eight years into his 60-year sentence, he had been fortunate in meeting a Roman Catholic chaplain who helped him to find a new faith and to realize that there was another way of life. Thus fortified, he was able to risk the derision of his fellow inmates and he became the prison altar-boy. The chaplain also arranged visits by his family, from whom he was to learn of the death of his mother. The effect of this news was profound, causing him to take stock of his personal attributes and situation, and he began to feel a need for knowledge.

Opportunities for education in legitimate skills were limited in Alcatraz and so he enrolled in the University of California correspondence courses to gain a high school diploma, studying at night by the light from the cell-block corridor. The authorities, recognizing his efforts, permitted him to take extra courses and rewarded his success with the gradual restoration of remission and privileges, and he achieved his high school diploma and then much more. When illness took him into the prison hospital, he gained a new interest and, having recovered, he volunteered to work there as an orderly. Through hard work and medical study, he acquired new skills and a measure of self-respect.

When I met Jim Quillen, that wet and windy day on Alcatraz, my greeting was short and to the point, "I'll bet that 50 years ago, you never thought you would be sitting here today, doing this!" In reply, he smiled broadly, shook my hand warmly, and savored the joke. For Jim Quillen, Convict AZ 586, was back in Alcatraz as a volunteer, autographing copies of his memoirs, published some years earlier by the Golden Gate National Park Association, who now operate the former jail as a national monument. His release on parole in 1960 had facilitated further study and he had gone on to gain membership by examination of the American Society of Radiological Technologists. This had given him a profession and in 11 years he rose to be Chief Technologist and Radiological Supervisor at a California hospital, a job he had held for 15 years. He married, had children and, when he retired, both the president of the United States and the governor of California had acknowledged his rehabilitation by awarding him federal and state pardons for crimes which had originally warranted 60 years in jail.

Should I ever doubt the value of continuing education, I will only have to think back to that grim island prison, and to my meeting with the man for whom such education had provided the means of escape, to a lawful and productive life.

CHAPTER 20

Accredited Schools with Nontraditional Residential Programs

I find the three major administrative problems on a campus are sex for the students, athletics for the alumni, and parking for the faculty.

Clark Kerr (when President of the University of California)

All schools in this chapter meet the standards of GAAP, Generally Accepted Accreditation Principles (explained in detail on page 95) and are therefore likely to be accepted as accredited in the worlds of business, government, and academia.

In the last edition, this was one of the largest chapters, but we came to learn that our readers have at best a modest interest in evening, weekend, and intensive summer courses. So we have reduced the size dramatically, providing only the school name, degree levels available, city, state, country, Web site address, and, for perhaps 10% of the schools, a very brief note about an unusual or special program. For the other 90%, it is safe to assume they offer nothing more unusual than evening, weekend, and/or summer degree programs—things that used to be hot stuff, but are now very commonplace.

The listings are organized geographically, first by U.S. state and then by country. The basic format of each listing is as follows:

> **Name of School**   Associate's, Bachelor's,
>   Master's, Doctorate, **Law**
>   City, State, Country (if not U.S.)
>   Web site address
>   Description (if applicable)

Schools in the U.S.

Alabama

Alabama State University   B
Montgomery, AL
www.alasu.edu

Birmingham Southern College   B, M
Birmingham, AL
www.bsc.edu

Jacksonville State University   B
Jacksonville, AL
www.jsu.edu

University of Alabama at Birmingham   M
Birmingham, AL
www.uab.edu
Offers an intensive "Executive Program" that leads to an M.S. in health administration.

Alaska

Alaska Pacific University   B, M
Anchorage, AK
www.alaskapacific.edu

University of Alaska   B, M
Fairbanks, AK
www.dist-ed.uaf.edu

Arizona

Northern Arizona University   B, M
Yuma, AZ
www.nau.edu

Western International University   B, M
Phoenix, AZ
www.wintu.edu

Arkansas

Southern Arkansas University   B
Magnolia, AR
www.saumag.edu

University of Arkansas   M
Fayetteville, AR
www.uark.edu

University of Arkansas at Little Rock   M
Little Rock, AR
www.ualr.edu

California

Armstrong University   B, M
Oakland, CA
www.armstrong-u.edu

**California School of
Professional Psychology**   M, D
San Francisco, CA
www.cspp.edu

**California State University—
Sacramento**   B, M
Sacramento, CA
www.csus.edu

Chapman University   B, M
Orange, CA
www.chapman.edu
Has campus locations throughout California, Arizona, and Washington.

Fresno Pacific University   B
Fresno, CA
www.fresno.edu

Holy Names College   B
Oakland, CA
www.hnc.edu

John F. Kennedy University   B, M
Orinda, CA
www.jfku.edu
Many innovative bachelor's and master's programs in psychology, counseling, and holistic health fields. The university sees a major role for itself in helping adults to accomplish midcareer changes.

Loyola Marymount University   M
Los Angeles, CA
www.lmu.edu

**Monterey Institute of
International Studies**   M
Monterey, CA
www.miis.edu

Mount Saint Mary's College   B
Los Angeles, CA
www.msmc.la.edu

National Hispanic University   B
San Jose, CA
www.nhu.edu
This school offers a multilingual, multicultural approach to higher education. While its programs are relatively traditional, we list it for its innovative approach to the entire question of student diversity, different cultures, and different learning styles. The school currently offers a B.A. in business administration, a B.A. in liberal studies with a concentration in child development studies or cross cultural studies, and a B.S. in computer science.

New College of California   B, M, D, Law
San Francisco, CA
www.newcollege.edu
In 1989, New College took over the nontraditional programs of Antioch University West.

Northwestern Polytechnic University   B
Fremont, CA
www.npu.edu

Pacific Oaks College   B, M
Pasadena, CA
www.pacificoaks.edu
Programs in child development, human services, counseling, and education offered in Pasadena and in Oakland, CA.

Saint Mary's College   B, M
Moraga, CA
www.stmarys-ca.edu

San Francisco State University
San Francisco, CA
www.sfsu.edu

Sonoma State University　　　　B, M
Rohnert Park, CA
www.sonoma.edu
Programs in psychology.

University of California—Berkeley　　M
Berkeley, CA
www.berkeley.edu
MBA available entirely through evening classes at Haas
School of Business.

University of California—Davis　　B, M
Davis, CA
www.ucdavis.edu

University of California—Los Angeles　　M
Los Angeles, CA
www.ucla.edu

**University of California—
Santa Barbara**　　　　B, M
Santa Barbara, CA
www.ucsb.edu

University of Creation Spirituality　　M
Oakland, CA
www.creationspirituality.com
Though unaccredited itself, this school has partnered
with Naropa University (see listing in chapter 19) to offer
an accredited Master of Liberal Arts in Creation Spirituality.

University of La Verne　　　　B, M
La Verne, CA
www.ulaverne.edu
Various regional centers, as well as campuses in Alaska
and Greece.

University of Redlands　　　　B, M
Redlands, CA
www.uor.edu

University of San Francisco　　B, M
San Francisco, CA
www.usfca.edu

**Vanguard University of
Southern California**　　　　B
Costa Mesa, CA
www.sccu.edu
Formerly Southern California College as well as Southern
California Christian University.

Woodbury University　　　　B, M
Burbank, CA
www.woodbury.edu
Also offers programs for working adults on its campuses
in Pasadena and Santa Clarita.

Colorado

Adams State College　　　　M
Alamosa, CO
www.adams.edu

Colorado Christian University　　B, M
Lakewood, CO
www.ccu.edu
Centers in various cities around Colorado. Formerly
Rockmount College. No connection whatever with a
defunct diploma mill called Colorado Christian University.

Metropolitan State College of Denver　　B
Denver, CO
www.mscd.edu

Connecticut

Albertus Magnus College　　　　B
New Haven, CT
www.albertus.edu

**Eastern Connecticut State
University**　　　　B, M
Willimantic, CT
www.ecsu.ctstateu.edu

Fairfield University　　　　B
Fairfield, CT
www.fairfield.edu

Sacred Heart University　　　　B, M
Fairfield, CT
www.sacredheart.edu

University of Connecticut　　　　B
Storrs, CT
www.uconn.edu

University of New Haven　　　　B
West Haven, CT
www.newhaven.edu

Delaware

Wilmington College　　　　B, M, D
New Castle, DE
www.wilmcoll.edu

District of Columbia

American University　　　　B, M, D
Washington, DC
www.american.edu

Southeastern University   M
Washington, DC
www.seu.edu

Florida

Barry University   B, M, D
Miami Shores, FL
www.barry.edu
Classes held in various locations throughout south and central Florida.

Bethune-Cookman College   B
Daytona Beach, FL
www.bethune.cookman.edu

Eckerd College   B
St. Petersburg, FL
www.eckerd.edu

Florida Atlantic University   M
Boca Raton, FL
www.fau.edu

International College   B
Fort Myers, FL
www.internationalcollege.edu

Jacksonville University   B, M
Jacksonville, FL
www.ju.edu

Palm Beach Atlantic College   B
West Palm Beach, FL
www.pbac.edu

Rollins College   B, M
Winter Park, FL
www.rollins.edu

Saint Leo College   B, M
St. Leo, FL
www.saintleo.edu

Schiller International University   B, M
Dunedin, FL
www.schiller.edu
Programs at ten campuses in six countries: U.S., U.K., France, Germany, Switzerland, and Spain. English is the language of instruction on all campuses.

University of Miami   B, M, D
Coral Gables, FL
www.miami.edu
Offers an intriguing honors program in medicine, biomedical engineering, law, and marine & atmospheric science. Well-qualified applicants (high school seniors) are admitted simultaneously to the bachelor's and doctoral programs.

University of Tampa   B
Tampa, FL
www.utampa.edu

University of West Florida   B, M
Pensacola, FL
www.uwf.edu

Georgia

American InterContinental University   B, M
Atlanta, GA
www.aiuniv.edu
Various programs offered at locations in Atlanta (Dunwoody and Buckhead), Washington, DC, Fort Lauderdale, Los Angeles, London, and Dubai.

Armstrong Atlantic State University   B, M
Savannah, GA
www.armstrong.edu

Brenau University   B, M
Gainesville, GA
www.brenau.edu
Courses offered at six campuses throughout the state of Georgia.

Covenant College   B
Lookout Mountain, GA
www.covenant.edu

Georgia Southern University   B
Statesboro, GA
www.gasou.edu

Georgia Southwestern University   B
Americus, GA
www.gsw.edu

University of Georgia   B, M, D
Athens, GA
www.uga.edu

Guam

University of Guam   B, M
Mangilao, Guam
www.uog.edu

Hawaii

Chaminade University   B
Honolulu, HI
www.chaminade.edu

Hawaii Pacific University   B, M
Honolulu, HI
www.hpu.edu

University of Hawaii—Manoa   B, M, D
Honolulu, HI
www.hawaii.edu

University of Hawaii—West Oahu   B
Pearl City, HI
www.uhwo.hawaii.edu

Idaho

Lewis-Clark State College   B
Lewiston, ID
www.lcsc.edu

Illinois

**American Schools of
Professional Psychology**   M, D
Chicago, IL
www.aspp.edu
Has locations in Phoenix, San Francisco, Tampa, Atlanta,
Honolulu, Chicago, Rolling Meadows (IL), Minneapolis,
Arlington, and Seattle.

Aurora University   B, M
Aurora, IL
www.aurora.edu

Barat College   B
Lake Forest, IL
www.barat.edu/academics

Bradley University   B, M
Peoria, IL
www.bradley.edu

Chicago State University   B
Chicago, IL
www.csu.edu
"University Without Walls" program involves no traditional
classroom attendance. Students must demonstrate that they
are actively engaged in their selected field of study and
must commit 20 hours per week to the program.

DePaul University   B
Chicago, IL
www.depaul.edu

East-West University   B
Chicago, IL
www.eastwest.edu

Elmhurst College   B
Elmhurst, IL
www.elmhurst.edu

Illinois Benedictine University   B, M
Lisle, IL
www.ben.edu
Formerly known as Saint Procopius College.

Loyola University of Chicago   B
Chicago, IL
www.luc.edu

North Central College   B, M
Naperville, IL
www.noctrl.edu

Northwestern University   B, M
Chicago, IL
www.nwu.edu

Quad Cities Graduate Center   M, D
Rock Island, IL
www.gradcenter.org
The center is sponsored by Augustana College, Bradley
University, Illinois State University, Iowa State University,
Marycrest International University, Northern Illinois
University, St. Ambrose University, Saint Xavier University,
University of Illinois, University of Iowa, University of
Northern Iowa, and Western Illinois University. The
degree is issued by one of these ten, depending on the
program selected.

Rockford College   B, M
Rockford, IL
www.rockford.edu

Roosevelt University   B
Chicago, IL
www.roosevelt.edu

Shimer College   B
Waukegan, IL
www.shimer.edu

**Southern Illinois University
at Carbondale**   M
Carbondale, IL
www.siu.edu/cwis

University of Chicago   M
Chicago, IL
www.uchicago.edu

Indiana

Ball State University   M
Muncie, IN
www.bsu.edu

Indiana Institute of Technology   B
Fort Wayne, IN
www.indtech.edu

Indiana University Northwest   B
Gary, IN
www.iun.edu

Indiana Wesleyan University   B, M
Marion, IN
www.indwes.edu
Formerly known as Marion College.

Manchester College   M
North Manchester, IN
www.manchester.edu

Martin University   B, M
Indianapolis, IN
www.martin.edu

University of Evansville   B
Evansville, IN
www.evansville.edu

University of Indianapolis   B, M
Indianapolis, IN
www.uindy.edu
Formerly known as Indiana Central College.

University of Notre Dame   M
Notre Dame, IN
www.nd.edu/~execprog
MBA broadcast by two-way video to remote classrooms
in Indianapolis, IN, Toledo, OH, and Chicago, IL.

University of Saint Francis   M
Fort Wayne, IN
www.sfc.edu

Valparaiso University   B, M
Valparaiso, IN
www.valpo.edu

Iowa

Briar Cliff College   B
Sioux City, IA
www.briar-cliff.edu

Drake University   B, M, Law
Des Moines, IA
www.drake.edu

Iowa Wesleyan College   B
Mt. Pleasant, IA
www.iwc.edu

Marycrest International University   B
Davenport, IA
www.mcrest.edu

Saint Ambrose University   B
Davenport, IA
www.sau.edu

Simpson College   B
Indianola, IA
www.simpson.edu

University of Dubuque   M
Dubuque, IA
www.dbq.edu

Kansas

Baker University   B, M
Baldwin City, KS
www.bakerspgs.edu

Friends University   A, B, M
Wichita, KS
www.friends.edu
Evening and weekend classes at campuses in Wichita,
Topeka, Mission, and Independence (MO).

Kansas Wesleyan University   B
Salina, KS
www.kwu.edu

Pittsburg State University   B, M
Pittsburg, KS
www.pittstate.edu
Sites around Kansas.

Saint Mary College   B, M
Leavenworth, KS
www.smcks.edu
Besides the main campus, classes held in Johnson County
and Wyandotte County.

Southwestern College   B, M
Winfield, KS
www.sckans.edu

University of Kansas   M
  Lawrence, KS
  www.ukans.edu
Some classes are held in Topeka.

Kentucky

Bellarmine College   B, M
  Louisville, KY
  www.bellarmine.edu

Campbellsville University   B
  Campbellsville, KY
  www.campbellsvil.edu

Midway College   B
  Midway, KY
  www.midway.edu

Spalding University   B
  Louisville, KY
  www.spalding.edu

University of Kentucky   B, M
  Lexington, KY
  www.uky.edu/UniversityExtension

University of Louisville   B, M, D
  Louisville, KY
  www.louisville.edu
Offers MBA programs in Athens, Hong Kong, and Singapore.

Louisiana

Centenary College   B
  Shreveport, LA
  www.centenary.edu

Louisiana State University   B, M, D
  Baton Rouge, LA
  www.lsu.edu
Locations in various cities.

Our Lady of the Lake College   B
  Baton Rouge, LA
  www.ololcollege.edu

Maine

Audubon Expedition Institute   B, M
  Belfast, ME
  www.audubon.org/educate
Bachelor or Master of Science in environmental studies and environmental education, involving community-based experiential education. Students travel, camp, and in other ways study one bioregion of the U.S. or Canada each semester.

Maine Maritime Academy   M
  Castine, ME
  www.mainemaritime.edu

University of Maine   B, M
  Orono, ME
  www.umaine.edu
Classes in Orono, as well as various off-campus extension centers.

Maryland

Bowie State University   M
  Bowie, MD
  www.bowiestate.edu
The school has a number of delivery sites around the state.

College of Notre Dame of Maryland   B, M
  Baltimore, MD
  www.ndm.edu

Hood College   B, M
  Frederick, MD
  www.hood.edu

Johns Hopkins University   B, M, D
  Baltimore, MD
  www.spsbe.jhu.edu
Campuses in Baltimore, Rockville, and Washington, DC.

Mount Saint Mary's College   B
  Emmitsburg, MD
  www.msmary.edu

Western Maryland College   M
  Westminster, MD
  www.wmdc.edu
Among other degrees, the school offers an M.S. in deaf education.

Massachusetts

American International College   B
  Springfield, MA
  www.aic.edu

Anna Maria College   M
  Paxton, MA
  www.annamaria.edu
Courses are offered on the Paxton campus and at off-campus sites in Milton, Plymouth, Springfield, West Boylston, and Worcester.

Bentley College   B
  Waltham, MA
  www.bentley.edu

Boston Architectural Center　　　　B, M
　　Boston, MA
　　www.the-bac.edu

Boston College　　　　B
　　Chestnut Hill, MA
　　www.bc.edu

Boston University　　　　B ,M
　　Boston, MA
　　web.bu.edu

Cambridge College　　　　M
　　Cambridge, MA
　　www.cambridge.edu

Clark University　　　　B, M
　　Worcester, MA
　　www.clarku.edu

Emmanuel College　　　　B, M
　　Boston, MA
　　www.emmanuel.edu
The school has eight satellite campuses.

Hampshire College　　　　B
　　Amherst, MA
　　www.hampshire.edu

Massachusetts College of Liberal Arts　　　　B
　　North Adams, MA
　　www.nasc.mass.edu
Formely North Adams State College.

Northeastern University　　　　B, M, D, Law
　　Boston, MA
　　www.neu.edu

Simmons College　　　　B
　　Boston, MA
　　www.simmons.edu

Springfield College　　　　B, M
　　Springfield, MA
　　www.spfldcol.edu

Tufts University　　　　B, M
　　Medford, MA
　　www.tufts.edu

**University of Massachusetts—
Boston**　　　　B, M
　　Boston, MA
　　www.umb.edu

**University of Massachusetts—
Dartmouth**　　　　B
　　North Dartmouth, MA
　　www.umassd.edu
Formerly known as Southeastern Massachusetts University.

Wellesley College　　　　B
　　Wellesley, MA
　　www.wellesley.edu

Western New England College　　　　B, M
　　Springfield, MA
　　www.wnec.edu

Westfield State College　　　　B, M
　　Westfield, MA
　　www.wsc.mass.edu

Michigan

Aquinas College　　　　B, M
　　Grand Rapids, MI
　　www.aquinas.edu

Eastern Michigan University　　　　M
　　Ypsilanti, MI
　　www.emich.edu

Ferris State University　　　　B
　　Big Rapids, MI
　　www.ferris.edu

Grand Valley State University　　　　B. M
　　Grand Valley, MI
　　www.gvsu.edu
Programs available throughout Michigan.

Lake Superior State Univeristy　　　　B,M
　　Sault Sainte Marie, MI
　　www.lssu.edu

Madonna University　　　　B, M
　　Livonia, MI
　　www.munet.edu

Marygrove College　　　　B, M
　　Detroit, MI
　　www.marygrove.edu

Michigan State University　　　　M
　　East Lansing, MI
　　www.msu.edu
Also has locations in Traverse City, Birmingham, Grand Rapids, and other cities. Offers an M.A. in education at centers in Thailand and France.

Siena Heights College   B

Adrian, MI

www.sienahts.edu

Degree-completion programs on the Adrian campus as well as Battle Creek, Benton Harbor, Jackson, Kalamazoo, Lansing, Monroe, and Detroit.

Spring Arbor College   B, M

Spring Arbor, MI

www.arbor.edu

University of Detroit Mercy   B, M

Detroit, MI

www.udmercy.edu

University of Michigan   M

Ann Arbor, MI

www.umich.edu

Wayne State University   B, M

Detroit, MI

www.wayne.edu

Western Michigan University   B, M, D

Kalamazoo, MI

www.wmich.edu

William Woods University   B, M

Fulton, MI

www.williamwoods.edu

Various sites throughout Missouri.

Minnesota

Augsburg College   B, M

Minneapolis, MN

www.augsburg.edu

College of Saint Catherine   B

St. Paul, MN

www.stkate.edu

Hamline University   M,D

Saint Paul, MN

web.hamline.edu

Mankato State University   B, M

Mankato, MN

www.mankato.msus.edu

Moorhead State University   B

Moorhead, MN

www.mnstate.edu/home

Northwestern College   B

St. Paul, MN

www.nwc.edu

Southwest State University   B

Marshall, MN

www.southwest.msus.edu

University of Minnesota   B

Minneapolis, MN

www.umn.edu

Winona State University   B, M

Winona, MN

www.winona.msus.edu

Mississippi

Millsaps College   B

Jackson, MS

www.millsaps.edu

University of Southern Mississippi   B, M

Hattiesburg, MS

www.usm.edu

Missouri

Avila College   B

Kansas City, MO

www.avila.edu

Columbia College   B

Columbia, MO

www.ccis.edu

The school's Extended Studies Division has locations around the country.

Drury Evening College   B

Springfield, MO

www.drury.edu

Fontbonne College   B, M

St. Louis, MO

www.fontbonne.edu

Lincoln University   M

Jefferson City, MO

www.lincolnu.edu

Lindenwood University   B, M

St. Charles, MO

www.lindenwood.edu

Maryville University of Saint Louis   B

St. Louis, MO

www.maryvillestl.edu

Research College of Nursing   **B**
Kansas City, MO
www.rockhurst.edu

Rockhurst University   **B, M**
Kansas City, MO
www.rockhurst.edu

University of Missouri at Saint Louis   **B**
St. Louis, MO
www.umsl.edu

Washington University   **B, M**
St. Louis, MO
www.wustl.edu

Montana

Rocky Mountain College   **B**
Billings, MT
www.rocky.edu

Nebraska

Chadron State College   **M**
Chadron, NE
www.csc.edu
Master's programs broadcast to various sites in western and central Nebraska.

College of Saint Mary   **B**
Omaha, NE
www.csm.edu

Creighton University   **B, M**
Omaha, NE
www.creighton.edu

Nebraska Wesleyan University   **B**
Lincoln, NE
www.nebrwesleyan.edu

University of Nebraska—Omaha   **B, M**
Omaha, NE
www.unomaha.edu

New Hampshire

Dartmouth College   **M**
Hanover, NH
www.dartmouth.edu

Franklin Pierce College   **B**
Rindge, NH
www.fpc.edu
Courses are offered at campus sites in Concord, Keene, Lebanon, Nashua, Portsmouth, and Salem.

New Hampshire College   **B, M**
Manchester, NH
www.nhc.edu
The programs in human services and social work are also offered in London, through Lansdowne College.

Plymouth State College   **M**
Plymouth, NH
www.plymouth.edu

University of New Hampshire   **B, M**
Durham, NH
www.unh.edu

New Jersey

Centenary College   **B**
Hackettstown, NJ
www.centenarycollege.edu

Fairleigh Dickinson University   **B, M, D**
Madison, NJ
www.fdu.edu
Centers located in Madison, Rutherford, and Teaneck.

Georgian Court College   **B**
Lakewood, NJ
www.georgian.edu

Kean College   **B**
Union, NJ
www.kean.edu

New Jersey City University   **M**
Jersey City, NJ
www.njcu.edu
Many of the courses for the M.A. in educational technology can be taken online; other courses take place at public schools in New Jersey.

Ramapo College of New Jersey   **B**
Mahwah, NJ
www.ramapo.edu

Rider College   **B**
Lawrenceville, NJ
www.rider.edu

Rowan College of New Jersey   **B**
Glassboro, NJ
www.rowan.edu

Rutgers University   B
    Camden, NJ
    www.rutgers.edu

Saint Peter's College   B, M
    Jersey City, NJ
    www.spc.edu
Degree programs also available at a branch campus in
Englewood Cliffs.

New Mexico

College of Santa Fe   B, M
    Santa Fe, NM
    www.csf.edu

Saint John's College   M
    Santa Fe, NM
    www.sjcsf.edu
Master's in liberal arts is offered on both the New Mexico
and Maryland campuses. The program is based on a
study of great books in Western civilization.

New York

Adelphi University   B, M, D
    Garden City, NY
    www.adelphi.edu

Alfred University   M
    Alfred, NY
    www.alfred.edu

Audrey Cohen College   B, M
    New York, NY
    www.audrey-cohen.edu
Three full semesters per year give students the option of
completing the four-year undergraduate preparation in
under three years, and the graduate degree in one year.

Bard College   B
    Annandale-on-Hudson, NY
    www.bard.edu

Baruch College   B, M
    New York, NY
    www.baruch.cuny.edu

Boricua College   B
    New York, NY
    www.greatcollegetown.com/boric.html
Bilingual (Spanish/English) college.

Canisius College   B, M
    Buffalo, NY
    gort.canisius.edu

City University of New York   B, M
    New York, NY
    www.cuny.edu

College of Mount Saint Vincent   B
    Riverdale, NY
    www.cmsv.edu

College of New Rochelle   B
    New Rochelle, NY
    www.cnr.edu
Six campus sites in the greater New York area—one in
New Rochelle and one in each of the five boroughs.

College of Saint Rose   B
    Albany, NY
    www.strose.edu

College of Staten Island   B
    Staten Island, NY
    www.csi.cuny.edu

Dominican College   B
    Orangeburg, NY
    www.dc.edu

Elmira College   B
    Elmira, NY
    www.elmira.edu

Fordham University   B
    Bronx, NY
    www.fordham.edu

**Friends World Program of
Long Island University**   B
    Southampton, NY
    www.liunet.edu
Eight centers and campuses around the world provide
students with the opportunity to live, study, and work in
other cultures while earning an accredited bachelor's.
Humanity's most pressing concerns serve as the basis of
the curriculum.

Hofstra University   B
    Hempstead, NY
    www.hofstra.edu

Hunter College   B, M
    New York, NY
    www.hunter.cuny.edu

Iona College   B
    New Rochelle, NY
    www.iona.edu

Long Island University   B, M
Brookville, NY
www.liu.edu
Office of Adult Services provides free educational and career counseling.

Marymount College   B
Tarrytown, NY
www.marymt.edu

Mount Saint Mary College   B
Newburgh, NY
www.msmc.edu

New York University   B, M
New York, NY
www.nyu.edu
Created in 1972, NYU's Gallatin Division offers mature, self-directed students the opportunity to plan an individualized program of study in more than 150 majors.

Niagara University   B, M
Lewiston, NY
www.niagara.edu

Nyack College   B
Nyack, NY
www.nyackcollege.edu

Polytechnic University   M
Brooklyn, NY
www.poly.edu
Several New York locations.

Pratt Institute   B
Brooklyn, NY
www.pratt.edu

Queens College   B
Flushing, NY
www.qc.edu

Sage Evening College   B, M
Albany, NY
www.sage.edu

Saint Francis College   B
Brooklyn Heights, NY
www.stfranciscollege.edu

Sarah Lawrence College   B
Bronxville, NY
www.slc.edu

State University of New York at Brockport   B
Brockport, NY
www.brockport.edu

State University of New York at Buffalo   B, M
Buffalo, NY
wings.buffalo.edu

State University of New York at Old Westbury   B
Old Westbury, NY
www.oldwestbury.edu

State University of New York at Plattsburgh   M
Plattsburgh, NY
www.plattsburgh.edu

North Carolina

Campbell University   B, M
Buies Creek, NC
www.campbell.edu

Elon College   B, M
Elon College, NC
www.elon.edu

Fayetteville State University   B, M
Fayetteville, NC
www.uncfsu.edu

Gardner-Webb University   B
Boiling Springs, NC
www.gardner-webb.edu

Guilford College   B
Greensboro, NC
www.guilford.edu

Mars Hill College   B
Mars Hill, NC
www.mhc.edu
Five centers in western North Carolina.

North Carolina State University   B, M, D
Raleigh, NC
www.ncsu.edu

North Carolina Wesleyan College   B
Rocky Mount, NC
www.ncwc.edu

Shaw University   B
Raleigh, NC
www.shawuniversity.edu
Nontraditional programs offered in nine cities across North Carolina.

HOME COOKING COURSE

"I can reduce the duck to ½" thick. I know I can."

North Dakota

North Dakota State University B, M
Fargo, ND
www.ndsu.nodak.edu

University of Mary B
Bismark, ND
www.umary.edu

Valley City State University B
Valley City, ND
www.vcsu.nodak.edu

Ohio

Baldwin-Wallace College B, M
Berea, OH
www.baldwinw.edu

Bowling Green State University B, M
Bowling Green, OH
www.bgsu.edu

**Cincinnati Bible College
and Seminary** B, M
Cincinnati, OH
www.cincybible.edu

Cleveland State University B, M
Cleveland, OH
www.csuohio.edu

College of Mount Saint Joseph B
Cincinnati, OH
www.msj.edu

Defiance College B
Defiance, OH
www.defiance.edu

Heidelberg College B
Tiffin, OH
www.heidelberg.edu

Hiram College B
Hiram, OH
www.hiram.edu

Lake Erie College B
Painesville, OH
www.lec.edu

Lourdes College B
Sylvania, OH
www.lourdes.edu

Marietta College B, M
Marietta, OH
www.marietta.edu

Mount Union College B
Alliance, OH
www.muc.edu

Ohio State University B, M
Columbus, OH
www.ohio-state.edu

University of Akron M
Akron, OH
www.uakron.edu

University of Cincinnati B
Cincinnati, OH
www.uc.edu

University of Findlay B, M
Findlay, OH
www.findlay.edu

University of Toledo B, M
Toledo, OH
www.utoledo.edu

Urbana University   B
Urbana, OH
www.urbana.edu

Wittenberg University   B
Springfield, OH
www.wittenberg.edu

Xavier University   B, M
Cincinnati, OH
www.xu.edu

Oklahoma

Bartlesville Wesleyan College   B
Bartlesville, OK
www.bwc.edu

Cameron University   M
Lawton, OK
www.cameron.edu

Oklahoma State University   M
Stillwater, OK
www.okstate.edu/outreach
Offers M.S. programs in engineering, technology management, business, and environmental sciences by two-way video to participating Oklahoma corporate sites.

University of Tulsa   B, M, D
Tulsa, OK
www.utulsa.edu

Oregon

Marylhurst University   B, M
Marylhurst, OR
www.marylhurst.edu

Northwest Christian College   B
Eugene, OR
www.nwcc.edu

Oregon State University   B, M
Corvallis, OR
www.orst.edu

Portland State University   B, M
Portland, OR
extended.pdx.edu
Degree programs offered through evening and weekend classes to sites all over Oregon.

Pennsylvania

Albright College   B
Reading, PA
www.alb.edu

Alvernia College   B
Reading, PA
www.alvernia.edu

Bloomsburg University
Bloomsburg, PA
www.bloomu.edu

Cedar Crest College   B
Allentown, PA
www.cedarcrest.edu

College Misericordia   B, M
Dallas, PA
www.miseri.edu

Delaware Valley College   B
Doylestown, PA
www.devalcol.edu

Edinboro University of Pennsylvania   B
Edinboro, PA
www.edinboro.edu

Gannon University   B, M
Erie, PA
www.gannon.edu

Indiana University of Pennsylvania   D
Indiana, PA
www.iup.edu

Lebanon Valley College   B
Annville, PA
www.lvc.edu

Lincoln University   M
Philadelphia, PA
www.lincoln.edu

Millersville University of Pennsylvania   B
Millersville, PA
www.millersv.edu

Neumann College   B
Aston, PA
www.neumann.edu

Pennsylvania State University—Erie   M
Erie, PA
www.pserie.psu.edu

Robert Morris College   B
Pittsburgh, PA
www.robert-morris.edu

Saint Francis College   M
Loretto, PA
www.sfcpa.edu
Class sites in Loretto, Pittsburgh, and Harrisburg.

Saint Joseph's University College   B, M
Philadelphia, PA
www.sju.edu

Thomas Jefferson University   B, M
Philadelphia, PA
www.tju.edu

University of Pennsylvania   B, M
Philadelphia, PA
www.upenn.edu

University of Scranton   B
Scranton, PA
www.scranton.edu

Villanova University   B, M
Villanova, PA
www.villanova.edu

Widener University   B
Chester, PA
www.widener.edu
A second campus is located in Wilmington, DE.

Puerto Rico

Inter-American University   B
Hato Rey, Puerto Rico
coqui.metro.inter.edu

Rhode Island

Bryant College   B, M
Smithfield, RI
www.bryant.edu

Providence College   B, M
Providence, RI
www.providence.edu

Rhode Island College   B
Providence, RI
www.ric.edu

University of Rhode Island   B, M
Providence, RI
www.uri.edu/prov

South Carolina

Coker College   B
Hartsville, SC
www.coker.edu

Converse College   B
Spartanburg, SC
www.converse.edu
Designed to encourage adult women (24 years old and up) to return to school.

Francis Marion University   B
Florence, SC
www.fmarion.edu

Medical University of South Carolina   B
Charleston, SC
www.musc.edu

Southern Wesleyan University   B, M
Central, SC
www.swu.edu

South Dakota

Augustana College   B, M
Sioux Falls, SD
www.augie.edu

South Dakota State University   B
Brookings, SD
web.sdstate.edu

University of Sioux Falls   B, M
Sioux Falls, SD
www.thecoo.edu

Tennessee

American Academy of Nutrition   A
Knoxville, TN
www.nutritioneducation.com
Also has campus in Corona del Mar, CA.

Bethel College   B
McKenzie, TN
www.bethel-college.edu

Carson-Newman College   B, M
Jefferson City, TN
www.cn.edu

East Tennessee State University   B, M, D
Johnson City, TN
www.etsu.edu

Tennessee Wesleyan College   B
  Athens, TN
  www.twcnet.edu
Classes in Athens, Chattanooga, and Knoxville.

Tusculum College   B, M
  Greeneville, TN
  www.tusculum.edu

**University of Tennessee
at Chattanooga**   B, M
  Chattanooga, TN
  www.utc.edu

**University of Tennessee
Space Institute**   M
  Tullahoma , TN
  www.utsi.edu

Vanderbilt University   M
  Nashville, TN
  www.vanderbilt.edu

Texas

Amber University   B, M
  Garland, TX
  www.amberu.edu

Howard Payne University   B
  Brownwood, TX
  www.hputx.edu

Lamar University   B, M, D
  Beaumont, TX
  www.lamar.edu

Our Lady of the Lake University   B, M
  San Antonio, TX
  www.ollusa.edu
Offers programs through its centers in San Antonio,
Houston, and Dallas.

Rice University   M
  Houston, TX
  www.rice.edu

Saint Edwards University   B, M
  Austin, TX
  www.stedwards.edu

Sam Houston State University   B, M, D
  Huntsville, TX
  www.shsu.edu

Southwest Texas State University   B
  San Marcos, TX
  www.swt.edu

**Texas A & M University—
Corpus Christi**   B, M
  Corpus Christi, TX
  www.tamucc.edu
Nursing programs delivered to various sites in Texas.

Texas A & M University—Kingsville   M
  Kingsville, TX
  www.tamuk.edu

University of Texas at Arlington   B, M, D
  Arlington, TX
  www.uta.edu

Wayland Baptist University   B, M
  Plainview, TX
  www.wbu.edu
Learning centers are located in Texas (Amarillo, Lubbock,
Wichita Falls, San Antonio, and Plainview), Alaska
(Anchorage and Fairbanks), New Mexico (Albuquerque
and Clovis), Arizona (Phoenix and Sierra Vista), and
Hawaii.

Utah

University of Utah   M
  Salt Lake City, UT
  www.utah.edu

Vermont

Castleton State College   B, M
  Castleton, VT
  www.csc.vsc.edu

Johnson State College   B
  Johnson, VT
  www.jsc.vsc.edu

Middlebury College   D
  Middlebury, VT
  www.middlebury.edu
A DML, Doctor of Modern Languages, designed for
teacher-scholars, is unique to Middlebury. Study is done
in two foreign languages and can be completed in a series
of summer sessions on the Vermont campus.

School for International Training   B, M
  Brattleboro, VT
  www.worldlearning.org
Programs combine intensive on-campus study with an overseas internship.

Southern Vermont College   B
  Bennington, VT
  www.svc.edu

Trinity College   B, M
Burlington, VT
www.trinityvt.edu

Virginia

Averett College   B, M
Danville, VA
www.averett.edu

George Mason University   B, M
Fairfax, VA
www.gmu.edu

James Madison University   B
Harrisonburg, VA
www.jmu.edu

Mary Washington College   M
Fredericksburg, VA
www.mwc.edu

Radford University   B
Radford, VA
www.runet.edu

University of Richmond   B
Richmond, VA
www.urich.edu

Virginia Commonwealth University   B, M
Richmond, VA
www.vcu.edu

Virginia State University   B
Petersburg, VA
www.vsu.edu

Washington

Bastyr University   B
Kenmore, WA
www.bastyr.edu

Central Washington University   B, M
Ellensburg, WA
www.cwu.edu

Eastern Washington University   B
Cheney, WA
www.ewu.edu

Evergreen State College   B, M
Olympia, WA
www.evergreen.edu

Fairhaven College   B
Bellingham, WA
www.ac.wwu.edu/~fhc

Heritage College   B, M
Toppenish, WA
www.heritage.edu
Formerly known as Fort Wright College.

Seattle University   B, M, D
Seattle, WA
www.seattleu.edu

University of Washington   B, M
Seattle, WA
www.washington.edu

Whitworth College   B, M
Spokane, WA
www.whitworth.edu

West Virginia

**Marshall University
Graduate College**   M, D
South Charleston, WV
www.marshall.edu/mugc
Formerly known as West Virginia Graduate College.

West Virginia University   B, M
Morgantown, WV
www.wvu.edu

Wisconsin

Alverno College   B
Milwaukee, WI
www.alverno.edu

Cardinal Stritch University   B, M
Milwaukee, WI
www.stritch.edu

Carroll College   B, M
Waukesha, WI
www.cc.edu

Columbia College of Nursing   B
Milwaukee, WI
www.ccon.edu

Concordia University   B, M
Mequon, WI
www.cuw.edu
Centers are in Mequon, Green Bay, Madison, and Kenosha, Wisconsin; Fort Wayne and Indianapolis, Indiana; St. Louis, Missouri; and New Orleans, Louisiana.

Marian College of Fond du Lac B, M
Fond du Lac, WI
www.mariancoll.edu

Marquette University B
Milwaukee, WI
www.mu.edu

Milwaukee School of Engineering B, M
Milwaukee, WI
www.msoe.edu

Silver Lake College B, M
Manitowoc, WI
www.sl.edu

University of Wisconsin—Oshkosh B
Oshkosh, WI
www.uwosh.edu

Outside the U.S.

Australia

Swinburne University of Technology B
Hawthorn, Victoria
www.swin.edu.au

Belgium

Maastricht School of Management M, D
Maastricht
www.msm.nl

Canada

Brandon University B, M
Brandon, Manitoba
www.brandonu.ca

University of Quebec B
Sainte-Foy, Quebec
www.uquebec.ca
Instruction in French.

York University B
Toronto, Ontario
www.yorku.ca

Costa Rica

Universidad Internacional de las Americas M
San Jose
www.uia.ac.cr
This legitimate Costa Rican university offers a wide range of residential courses and an MBA. But they are, as their Web site declares, "accreditada por la WAUC," which is the no reconocido and no maravilloso World Association of Universities and Colleges.

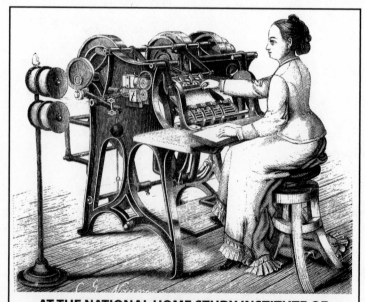

AT THE NATIONAL HOME STUDY INSTITUTE OF WEAVING, BOOKBINDING, AND WIRELESS TELEGRAPHY, YOU WILL BUILD YOUR OWN COMBO WEAVO-BINDOMATIC WITH TREADLE-POWERED E-MAIL CAPABILITY

France

American University of Paris   B
Paris
www.aup.fr

Bachelor's degrees in various fields are offered through year-round study in Paris. Instruction is in English.

Italy

European University Institute   D
San Domenico di Fiesole
www.iue.it

Students plan independent-study projects under the guidance of faculty tutors and research supervisors, and the degree of Ph.D. is awarded on completion and publication of a dissertation. Fields of study include economics, history & civilization, law, and political & social sciences.

Philippines

De La Salle University   B
Manila
www.dlsu.edu.ph

United Kingdom

Huron University   B, M
London
www.huron.edu

South Dakota-based Huron University's London program offers degrees in a variety of fields.

Kingston University   M
Surrey
www.kingston.ac.uk

Richmond College   B, M
Richmond
www.richmond.ac.uk

An accredited American college operating in London.

University of Brighton   B, M
Brighton
www.bton.ac.uk

CHAPTER 21

Other Schools with Nonresidential Programs

One could get a first-class education from a shelf of books five feet long.

Charles Eliot, when President of Harvard

The schools in this chapter do not meet the standards of GAAP, Generally Accepted Accreditation Principles (explained in detail on page 95). They are not necessarily bad, illegal, or fake, but they are unlikely to be accepted as accredited, despite the claims that many of them may make.

The degree programs listed in this chapter do not require any campus attendence; they can be completed entirely through distance-learning methods.

The basic format for each listing is as follows:

Name of School	Associate's, Bachelor's, Master's, Doctorate, **Law**

Postal Address (United States if country not specified)
Fields of study **offered**
Year founded
Phone ▪ Tollfree phone (If a U.S. number, country code (+1) not included)
Fax
Email address
Web site URL
Description of programs

Information in this book, especially the listings, changes fast. Updates and corrections are posted on our Web site at *www.degree.net/updates/bearsguide14*.

And remember, our readers play a huge role in helping us keep this book up to date. Please, whether it's a defunct area code or a hot new distance-learning program, bring it to our attention at *johnandmariah@degree.net* or *Bears' Guide*, P.O. Box 7123, Berkeley, CA 94707.

Academy of International Management   B, M, D
P.O. Box 1161
Pierre, SD 57501
Fields offered: Business administration, management

Year founded: 1999
Email: info@aaim.edu
Web site: www.aaim.edu
Offers degrees at all levels in business and management fields. Students can also design their own individualized degree programs. Run from England by Alan Jones, who also operates Fairfax University (see listing in this chapter). No listed phone number.

Academy of Natural Therapies   B, M, D
731 Makaleka Ave. C
Honolulu, HI 96816
Fields offered: Nutrition, natural therapies, naturopathy
Email: drbyrnes@powerhealth.net
Web site: www.powerhealth.net
Operated by Dr. Stephen Byrnes, who earned his Doctor of Naturopathy from the Clayton College of Natural Health (see listing in this chapter). Degree programs in the above fields are offered by distance learning with proctored finals taken in the student's area. Claims accreditation from the American Association of Drugless Practitioners, an unrecognized agency. When we asked for their mailing address, we were told that the "Academy of Natural Therapies is a 'school without walls' and has no physical address—it exists solely on the Internet." Their Web site is registered to the Hawaiian address listed above.

Acton Liberty University   B, M, D
6709 La Tijera Blvd., PMB 167
Los Angeles, CA 90045
Fields offered: Any field
Year founded: 1999
Phone: (310) 753 0733
Email: info@actonliberty.org
Web site: www.actonliberty.org
On their Web site, in the section called "Degree granting authority," they state that they are not accredited, but do

not indicate their degree-granting authority. They are not approved or licensed by the state of California. Degrees in any field, at any level, are awarded entirely based on life experience. The campus address is a mailbox rental service called Mail Connexion. We have not been able to determine if there is a connection with the equally non-wonderful Acton University.

Acton University   B, M, D, Law
350 Ward Ave., #106
Honolulu, HI 96814
Fields offered: Many fields
Year founded: 1997
Phone: (808) 263 8500 ▪ (800) 356 6768
Fax: (800) 999 9704

Some of the Acton literature is mailed from Beaumont, Texas, and the "campus" in Hawaii is a secretarial service called Kamaaina Consultants & Real Estate Fax. They offer degrees at all levels with, apparently, little or no course-work. Instead, it appears that the degree is awarded based entirely on an extended portfolio analysis and a final project or, at the doctoral level, dissertation. Originally called Edison University. Following legal action by Thomas Edison State College in New Jersey, the name was changed to Addison, and then Acton. The person who signs some of the letters to students, Natalie Handy, is the wife of Thomas Kirk, the founder of LaSalle University, who was imprisoned in Beaumont, Texas, in 1997 for his LaSalle activities. The Acton literature we have seen is almost identical to earlier LaSalle literature, but for the name change. At one time, they were accredited by the unrecognized and nonwonderful World Association of Universities and Colleges. (We wonder where the accreditation visit took place.) We have been unable to determine if there is a connection between Acton University and the equally nonwonderful Acton Liberty University.

Adam Smith University   A, B, M, D
1719 West Main St., Suite 208
Rapid City, SD 57702
Fields offered: Many fields
Year founded: 1991
Phone: (605) 394 5782 ▪ (800) 732 3796
Fax: (203) 761 9949
Email: info@adamsmith.edu
Web site: www.adamsmith.edu

Degrees based on assessment of work done at accredited schools elsewhere, and on life experience and independent study. There is no limit to the amount of credit that can be transferred from other institutions. Several readers have told us Adam Smith had offered them degrees based entirely on work previously done. The literature indicates President Donald Grunewald has his doctorate from Harvard, is former president of Mercy College, and lives in Connecticut. The university formerly operated from a mail receiving service in Louisiana, but moved to Hawaii in 1994 when it did not meet Louisiana's new standards. Grunewald pointed out what he called "one minor error" in the last edition of *Bears' Guide*, and sent us a copy of a lease showing that the Hawaii "campus" was not at a mailbox service, but was, instead, a small room (153 square

feet) rented from an executive service bureau. In 2000, after Hawaii passed a law requiring its schools to have at least one full-time employee and 25 full-time students residing in Hawaii, Grunewald moved Adam Smith's "main office and library" once again, this time to a convenience address in South Dakota. Accreditation is from the unrecognized International Accrediting Commission for Postsecondary Institutions and the equally unrecognized Global Accreditation Commission.

Adizes Graduate School   M, D
2815 East Valley Rd.
Santa Barbara, CA 93108
Fields offered: Organizational transformation
Year founded: 1973
Phone: (805) 565 2901 ▪ (800) 869 2226
Email: ags@adizes.com
Web site: www.adizes.com

Adizes's state-approved programs are geared towards consultants and other management professionals. Students collaborate in small Internet-based classrooms. During the program, students are expected to apply what they've learned in their professional life, using experience with their companies or clients as a structured internship. Two years of study leads to a master's in organizational transformation; the doctorate requires an additional two years, plus a dissertation.

Albert Schweitzer University
14, Rue de Rhone
Geneva CH1204, Switzerland
Year founded: 1999
Phone: +41 (22) 819 9472
Fax: +41 (22) 819 9473
Email: administration@albertsc.com
Web site: www.albertsc.com

Also known as Albert Schweitzer International University, they do not award degrees, but organize summer courses, and offer supplementary courses for other universities' doctoral degrees, perhaps including European Union University, also founded by Alberto Roldán Moré, a Spanish physician.

American Academy of Management
425 W. Burgundy St., Suite 1714
Highlands Ranch, CO 80126
Fields offered: Business & management studies
Phone: (720) 344 1072
Fax: (303) 265 9300
Email: firstlearn@zyworld.com
Web site: www.zyworld.com/firstlearn

"The traditional MBA has been replaced and superseded," they announce on their Web page. What has taken its place, we gather, are their two non-degree programs: the Chief Executive Officer (CEO) and Management & Business Administrator (which they abbreviate MBA) board certifications. They further state that their programs "improve on the Harvard MBA by offering them online via distance learning technologies and using the Oxford and Cambridge graduate school methodology of one-on-one consultation with and guidance from your assigned mentor." Course materials consist of the Harvard Business Review Paperback Series (which they have you purchase from Harvard Business School's Web site). Coursework consists of reading the text and, for each chapter of the books, answering questions such as "What is the author's main purpose in writing?" We leave it to the reader to decide whether or not this is an improvement of Harvard's MBA program. Formerly called Chatfield University. We note that much of this school's literature is identical to that of the short-lived Amherst University, a Les Snell operation (see Monticello University in the "Degree Mills" chapter).

American Association for Parapsychology

Box 225
Canoga Park, CA 91305
Fields offered: Hypnosis, spiritual healing, telepathy, clairvoyance
Phone: (818) 883 0887
Fax: (818) 884 1850

The small and difficult-to-read brochure from this "school" offers courses in the above fields, as well as aura reading, dermo-optic perception, and other fields, and promises that "you can start your new career for only $100." The literature refers to a "doctoral career," but apparently only certificates of completion and diplomas are awarded. A request for more information resulted in our being sent a copy of their listing from the Encyclopedia of Associations: interesting but not too helpful in assessing the academic programs.

American Coastline Christian University

See: American Coastline University

American Coastline University   B, M, D

5000 W. Esplanade, #197
Metairie, LA 70006
Fields offered: Many fields
Year founded: 1976
Phone: (504) 242 8083
Email: acuadmiss@aol.com
Web site: www.amercoastuniv.edu

Established as a religious school by Raymond Chasse, who was involved in various capacities with Pacific Western University, Summit University of Louisiana, Clayton University, University of Melchizedek, American M & N University, American Coastline Christian University, and Al-Manaf International Islamic University. The "International Communication Center" is a mailbox rental store; the actual office is in the same small building as Summit University. We apologize for writing elsewhere that Dr. Chasse played the saxophone in the Salvation Army Band. He informed us that it is, in fact, the trombone. Just before his death in March, 2000, Dr. Chasse informed us that American Coastline only grants purely religious degrees and so is exempt from the new Louisiana licensing laws that took effect in early 2000. There is a Hawaii "campus" at 733 Bishop St., #170, Honolulu 96813, a mailbox rental service. In August 2000, the telephone was in service, but not answered. The Web site was last revised in 1997.

American College of Metaphysical Theology   B, M, D

8014 Olson Memorial Highway, #210
Golden Valley, MN 55427
Fields offered: Metaphysics, divinity, biblical studies, theocentric business & ethics, comparative religion, pastoral administration, religious counseling, religious education
Phone: (612) 504 1391 ▪ (800) 689 5102
Fax: (612) 525 1566
Email: jaywise@americancollege.com
Web site: www.americancollege.com

This proudly unaccredited school offers extremely low-priced degrees (i.e., under $100 for a bachelor's degree) in a range of theological fields, including metaphysics, divinity, religious counseling, religious education, and theocentric business, with no classes required. The catalog

"My home study course in blacksmithing would be a total success, but for the fearful postage costs in mailing anvils."

lists the benefits of a Ph.D. degree, including "heightened credibility in any practice of spiritual healing . . . Psychologically, the title 'Doctor' and the word 'healing' have a natural affinity in one's mind." Ministerial credentials at no extra charge.

American College of Oxford
See: Warnborough University

American Global University   B, M, D
1603 Capitol Ave., #401
Cheyenne, WY 82001
Fields offered: Many fields
Year founded: 1996
Phone: (307) 635 0044 ▪ (800) 645 0382
Fax: (307) 635 8906
Email: achieve@americanglobalu.edu
Web site: www.americanglobalu.edu

The "campus" was a Mail Boxes Etc. store in West Des Moines, Iowa, until the fall of 1999. Moved to an office building in Cheyenne, Wyoming, after getting some bad press and drawing attention from Iowa state authorities. The name is also registered in the state of Hawaii using the address 1150 N. Mountain Ave., #101D, Upland, CA 91786. University president S.A. Samadani, Ph.D., operates the school apparently from Upland, CA. Degrees at all levels in Iranian studies, Persian literature, business, psychology, alternative medicine research, and computer fields through independent directed study. They are a member of the unrecognized and nonwonderful World Association of Universities and Colleges.

American Gulf Coast University   M
758 Kapahulu Ave., # 277
Honolulu, HI 96816
Fields offered: Business administration
Year founded: 1997
Email: a28851401@aol.com

The "campus" is a Mail Boxes Etc. store in Hawaii.

American Institute of Holistic Theology   B, M, D
5600 Market St., #10
Youngstown, OH 44512-2619
Fields offered: Divinity, metaphysics, naturology, parapsychic science, healtheology
Phone: (800) 650 4325
Email: info@aiht.edu
Web site: www.aiht.edu

They describe themselves as a "strictly non-sectarian institution of higher learning, providing non-secular education based on universal laws for those who have 'seen the light.'" They offer a Doctor of Divinity program, as well as bachelor's, master's, and Ph.D.'s in metaphysics, naturology, healtheology, and parapsychic science by home study. Five of the six listed faculty members have their advanced degrees from AIHT. The sixth is from Clayton College of Natural Health, which AIHT lists as their "sister school." This makes 100% of listed faculty with unaccredited advanced degrees. AIHT formerly claimed

accreditation from the unrecognized American Naturopathic Medical Certification and Accreditation Board (their address is a mailbox rental service), now from the unrecognized American Association of Drugless Practitioners. The Web site is registered to an address in Alabama: 2101 Magnolia, #2000, Birmingham 35205.

American Institute of Natural Sciences
226 20th St. East
Saskatoon, SK S7K 0A6, Canada
Fields offered: New age fields
Year founded: 1946
Phone: +1 (306) 384 0101 ▪ (888) 516 1212
Fax: +1 (306) 384 1103
Email: ccampus@home.com
Web site: www.mallnetglobal.com/ains

While not claiming to offer degrees, this organization does award a "Master in Mantic Arts" (M.M.A.N F.) to anyone successfully completing two courses in such fields as crystal healing, palmistry, tea cup reading, and the like.

American International Open University
See: Clayton University

American International University (Alabama)   B, M, D
415 Washington Ave.
Montgomery, AL 36104
Fields offered: Business fields
Phone: (800) 680 7474
Fax: (404) 845 0098

The campus is the address of the J & L Answering Service. This school offers business degrees at all levels, as well as what it calls professional business designation certification programs, with a large life-experience-learning component. Apparently no relationship to the defunct California degree mill or currently operating Hawaii school of the same name.

American International University (Hawaii)   B, M, D
1188 Bishop St., #3101
Honolulu, HI 96813
Fields offered: Metaphysics, parapsychology, pastoral hypnotherapy, transpersonal psychology, pastoral counseling, holistic health sciences
Phone: (808) 524 5411

The campus is a secretarial service called Tele Memo Pacific, Inc. Offers degrees at all levels in the above fields. The typed, photocopied brochure offers handy advice, such as a list of things your doctoral degree can do for you, including "Psychologically, the title 'Doctor' gives greater stature to pastoral counselors," and "Increased salary or chance for promotions," among others. Formerly located in California. There is no connection with a diploma mill of this name which operated from California in the 1970s and early 1980s or, apparently, with the unaccredited school currently operating under the same name from Alabama. We don't know if there is a connection with an identically named school on another island in Hawaii: P.O. Box 4488, Hilo 96720.

American International University (Suriname)   B, M, D

Hinterm Graben 4-10
Haiger 35708, Germany
Fields offered: Business administration
Phone: +49 (2773) 94270
Fax: +49 (2773) 94272
Email: tmt-ag@t-online.de
Web site: www.mba-study.de

A project of Denis K. Muhilly, formerly involved with the APICS accrediting agency, Eire International University, and La Jolla University, among others. Claims state recognition from the South American country of Suriname. Also has study centers (according to its Web site operated from Germany) in South Carolina, Germany, Russia, the Czech Republic, Bulgaria, "Afrika," and "other European States." Offers an MBA by distance learning, as well as diplomas based on life and work experience. The literature claims the degree is "equal to an American granted Regionally Accredited Degree." Since it meets not even one of the six standards of GAAP, Generally Accepted Accreditation Procedures, their statement is simply untrue. Formerly American University of Suriname.

American M & N University   B, M, D

Administrative Office
112 North Chandler Ave., #103
Monterey Park, CA 91754
Fields offered: Business, social work, psychology
Phone: (626) 458 4200 ▪ (800) 680 2668
Fax: (626) 570 1554
Email: uniserv@aol.com

Their English-language catalog has the finest slogan of its kind we've run across: "An alternative to education." Offers degrees at all levels through a combination of transfer credit, credit for life-experience learning, challenge exams, and directed independent study. The school says they have a presence in Shanghai, China, where it offers residential programs in business, travel, and management-related fields, as well as in New Orleans and Pearl City, Hawaii (both apparently mailbox rental services). "M" and "N" are the initials of the founders; the administrative office in Monterey Park, CA, shares the same phone number and address with M & N Traffic School. According to a 1998 article in the *Far Eastern Economic Review*, honorary doctorates awarded by American M & N helped grease major deals between Chinese and American businessmen and politicians. The man who brokered these deals, and arranged for the awarding of the degrees, was Ted Sioeng, now infamous as the key figure in the Asian fundraising scandal that racked the U.S. Democratic Party in the late '90s. Also known as Concord University.

American Pacific University (Hawaii)   B, D

615 Piikoi St., Suite 501
Honolulu, HI 96814

Fields offered: Hypnotherapy, esoteric studies
Phone: (808) 596 7765 ▪ (800) 800 6463
Fax: (808) 596 7764
Email: info@ampac.edu
Web site: www.ampac.edu

When California threatened to drop its state approval of the American Institute of Hypnotherapy if it continued to offer its doctoral programs, the owner opened up a "sister school" in Hawaii—American Pacific University—to offer these degrees. Offers bachelor's and doctoral degrees in clinical hypnotherapy and doctorates in "esoteric studies." Claims accreditation from the unrecognized International Association of Schools, Colleges, and Universities.

American Pushington University   B, M, D

3179 West Temple Ave.
Pomona, CA 91768
Fields offered: Business, Oriental medicine, arts, religion

This state-approved university seems primarily to advertise in and get students from Asia, offering degrees at all levels in business, arts, religion, and Chinese medicine. They were the subject of considerable controversy in Taiwan, as reported in the Taipei Times (*www.taipeitimes.com*) for August 31, 1999. A legislator, Dianne Lee, told the newspaper that "The practice of fraud is evident. What the students got are some meaningless sheets of paper." This is apparently because the Taiwan government only recognizes degrees offered by accredited universities. Allegations were made that the university awarded degrees. Pushington's president William Tseng vigorously denied all charges. Apparently also known as California Pushington University and International Pushington University.

American State University   B, M, D

One University Center
2165 Tenth Ave.
Honolulu, HI 96816
Fields offered: Many fields
Year founded: 1995
Phone: (808) 528 8550 ▪ (888) 528 8550
Fax: (888) 922 0927
Email: admn@amstu.edu
Web site: www.amstu.edu

The campus is a secretarial service. In late 1997, the school was sued by the state of Hawaii, claiming many violations of Hawaii law, and students were given the opportunity to claim a full refund through the state. This school offers degrees at all levels, with extremely minimal work required. In a test case, the degree was to be based on six extremely short papers (ranging from 100 words—about a paragraph—to 600) and a 2,000-word final paper on any subject. If the student is unable to write the several pages required for the dissertation, an alternate project may be proposed. The owner also operated the Higher Education Research Institute, an ostensibly impartial referral service, which referred all clients to American State. Shortly after Hawaii's law suit, there arose another "referral service" (from a Kentucky address) and "university" (from a

Wyoming address) with almost identical literature. We believe this "ARRP"/"Hamilton University" combo is the same outfit with new names.

American University in London   B, M, D

97-101 Seven Sisters Rd.
London N7 7QP, United Kingdom
Fields offered: Liberal arts, business, engineering, sciences
Year founded: 1984
Phone: +44 (171) 263 2986
Fax: +44 (171) 281 2815
Email: aul@ukbusiness.com

The university operates under the laws of the state of Iowa (which registers but does not investigate schools). Originally established as the London College of Science and Technology in 1984. Name changed to American University of London in 1986 and to American University in London in 1994. Their literature claims that AUL undergraduate credits are accepted for transfer at many accredited U.S. schools. We asked for a list of some of these, but did not receive it. Resident BBA, B.S., MBA, M.S., and Ph.D. courses are offered in London and through affiliates in Abu Dhabi, Canada, Mexico, Syria, Saudi Arabia, Lebanon, Pakistan, Bangladesh, and the U.K. Nonresident degree programs at all levels with credit for prior learning. When John visited the London campus in 1997, he found five or six large rooms in a church hall; soon after, they moved to new quarters nearby, above a bookmakers parlor. They are a member of the unrecognized and nonwonderful World Association of Universities and Colleges. No connection with the accredited school known as Richmond, the American University in London.

American University of Hawaii   B, M, D

33 North Market St.
Wailuku, HI 96793
Fields offered: Many fields
Year founded: 1994
Phone: (808) 534 0816
Fax: (808) 534 0917
Email: info@auh.edu
Web site: www.auh.edu

Accreditation is claimed from the Accreditation Association of Ametrican [sic] College [sic] and Universities (an unrecognized agency we are not familiar with). The address provided for their Web site server is a secretarial service in Honolulu. AUH claims that "multimedia" universities cannot be accredited by any recognized agency. Not so. Degrees at all levels in a broad range of fields. Generous credit for life-experience learning. They list a residential campus in the Republic of Georgia, and study centers and/or affiliate colleges with local official recognition in many nations, including Belize, Canada, Denmark, India, and Indonesia. One eyebrow-raising partnership is with Yerevan State Medical University. Through "an Agreement of Articulation" with this Armenian medical school, AUH claims to offer a Doctorate of Medicine. We note that an AUH medical degree would not qualify anyone to practice medicine in the U.S.

American University of Suriname

See: American International University (Suriname)

American World University   B, M, D

312 E. College St., #205
Iowa City, IA 52240
Fields offered: Many fields
Phone: (319) 356 6620
Fax: (319) 354 6335
Email: info@awu.edu
Web site: www.awu.edu

Dr. Maxine Asher responded to a detailed letter of inquiry about American World's program and students, saying she considered some of the questions (regarding the school's actual location and the faculty's credentials, among other claims made in the school's literature) to be an invasion of "the right-to-privacy law," and demanded not to be listed in this guide. Subsequently, according to the *New Orleans Times-Picayune*, American World failed to meet licensing standards set by the Louisiana Board of Regents, and was ordered to cease operating in the state. (Their address had been a mail service in Gretna, Louisiana.) They are accredited by the World Association of Universities and Colleges, an unrecognized and very nonwonderful agency started by Dr. Asher herself. The university address is a secretarial service called Answer Plus, Inc., in Iowa City. Dr. Asher told us the university has "substantial offices" in Iowa City, but declined to reveal their location. The Hawaii "campus" at 1142 Auahi Street, Honolulu 96814, is a service bureau called Pacific Support Center. Dr. Asher expressed annoyance that we reported that she is the author of *Ancient Energy, Key to the Universe, The Waves of Atlantis*. She has been called "the most celebrated and publicly reported Atlantean discoverer" (*Ancient Wisdom Digest*, v2, #1428) and is affiliated with the Ancient Mediterranean Research Association, which sells videotapes of underwater footage of Atlantis.

Ashington University   B, M, D

Stennard Island, Chanty Bridge, Wakefield
West Yorkshire WF1 5DL, United Kingdom
Fields offered: Many fields
Phone: +44 (1924) 217168
Email: administration@ashingtonuniversity.co.uk
Web site: www.ashingtonuniversity.co.uk

Offers unaccredited degrees based on assessment of life experience. Bachelor's ($355), master's ($575), doctorates ($700). We note that the secure order form on their Web site is hosted by an Internet server owned by the operators of Trinity College & University (U.S.) (see listing in this chapter).

Athena University   M

Virtual Online University Services, Inc.
301 E. Main St. 2F
Union, MO 63084

Fields offered: Business, English, history, computer science, computer aesthetics
Year founded: 1995
Phone: (314) 583 2282
Fax: (314) 583 2282
Email: cipher@vousi.com
Web site: www.athena.edu

This wholly online school offers unaccredited bachelor's degrees through its Athena University, and an online MBA in information strategies for new organizations, for which the degree is granted by the GAAP-accredited Ecole Superieure de Commerce—Pau in France. The Web site states that they "will seek accreditation for its other programs when regional accrediting agencies become more familiar with online education such that they can intelligently evaluate both content and delivery beyond the 'correspondence course' context."

Atlantic International University   B, M, D
13205 NE 16th Ave.
North Miami, FL 33161
Fields offered: Many fields
Phone: (305) 981 7943 ▪ (800) 993 0066
Fax: (305) 981 7943
Email: admissions@aiu.edu
Web site: www.aiu.edu

Degrees in many fields, including business administration, offered through independent study. They claim their accreditation from the nonwonderful and unrecognized Accrediting Commission International of Beebe, Arkansas, and their degree-granting authority through a convenience address in Hawaii.

Barrington College
See: Barrington University

Barrington International University
See: Barrington University

Barrington University   B, M
808 Executive Park Dr.
Mobile, AL 36606
Fields offered: Business, health sciences
Year founded: 1993
Phone: (334) 471 9977 ▪ (800) 533 3378
Fax: (888) 491 8648
Email: barrington@barrington.edu
Web site: www.barrington.edu

Barrington originally operated from an address in Vermont, although Vermont's state department of education said the school was not operating legally at that time, and the school's own literature stated "keep in mind that Barrington was chartered in 1993 in the state of Vermont but does not it's [sic] degree granting status from the state." They subsequently used addresses in New York, Florida, Iowa (where the campus was a business service agency called Rocklyn Executive Plaza), and Alabama (a mail service agency called Answering and Secretarial Service). Accreditation had been claimed from the World Association of Universities and Colleges, an unrecognized and nonwonderful agency, now from the International

Association of Universities and Schools, another unrecognized agency, with a P.O. box address in Switzerland. Originally Barrington College, then Barrington International University. They state that they are the world's largest Internet distance-learning university.

Bernadean University   B, M, D, Law
4842 Whitsett
North Hollywood, CA 91607
Fields offered: Many fields
Phone: (818) 718 2447 ▪ (800) 542 3792
Email: bernadeanuniversity@mail.com
Web site:
members.tripod.com/~bernadeanuniversity

A division of the Church of Universology, they have offered correspondence degrees in everything from theology to astronutrition to law. Bernadean used to be in Nevada but lost permission to operate in that state. Founder and president, the late Joseph Kadans, Ps.D., N.D., Th.D., Ph.D., J.D., was licensed to practice law, and at one time, Bernadean was recognized by the Committee of Bar Examiners in California. The school once offered a certificate good for absolution of all sins to its graduates. Claims accreditation from the World Council of Global Education, an unrecognized accreditor that focuses on the natural health care field. As of 2000, even though Bernadean is neither GAAP accredited nor state approved, it definitely is still in business.

Bienville University   B, M
778 Chevelle Dr.
Baton Rouge, LA 70806
Fields offered: Business administration, education, health administration, sports management, public administration, criminal justice administration, divinity, philosophy
Year founded: 1998
Phone: (225) 201 0111 ▪ (800) 473 1530
Fax: (225) 201 0222
Email: info@bienville.edu
Web site: www.bienville.edu

Bienville was cofounded by a former administrator of LaSalle University, LA. In 1999 he left Bienville when he grew concerned about how the school was evolving. Accreditation is claimed from the dreadful Accrediting Commission International of Beebe, Arkansas, with no mention of the fact that this is an unrecognized accreditor. As of 2000, Louisiana law requires unaccredited schools to be on an approved accreditation path. The school information states that admission is competitive. Not a single name of administration, faculty, or staff is mentioned in the literature. While Bienville offered doctorates at one time, they are no longer mentioned on the Web site.

Bircham International University   B, M, D
25 Beaumond St.
Oxford OX1 2NP, United Kingdom
Fields offered: Business, arts, health, psychology, technology
Year founded: 1992
Phone: (305) 668 4494

Email: info@bircham.edu
Web site: www.bircham.edu

Degrees by correspondence at all levels in business, arts, health, psychology, and technology. Web site lists "delegation" addresses in the Bahamas, Spain, England, Florida (a Mail Boxes Etc. store in Miami), New Zealand, and Taiwan. It is not clear which, if any, is the main campus. The Internet site is registered to an address in Madrid, Spain. Until 2000, this school was called Oxford International University; the name change was motivated, at least partly, by entanglements with its more venerable namesake.

Birkdale University   B, M, D

1617 Florida Ave.
West Palm Beach, FL 33401
Fields offered: Many fields
Web site: www.birkdale.org

In 1999, they appeared on the Internet as a self-styled "state of the art, nontraditional educational assessment system," offering degrees at all levels in almost any subject. No physical location is given, but the Web site is registered to a Lionel Richthofen in West Palm Beach, Florida. On the "Tuition" page of the Web site, in what appears to be a mistake, the school is referred to as Darton University. Darton was registered at a mailbox service in South Dakota. The Web site is also almost identical to that of Bridgeton University.

Boyer Graduate School of Education   D

201 East Sandpointe Ave.
Santa Ana, CA 92707
Fields offered: Education
Year founded: 1995
Phone: (888) 656 8865
Email: admissions@boyer.edu
Web site: www.boyer.edu

Offers a Doctor of Education (Ed.D.) through directed independent study. Emphasizes course work in educational leadership and management. Formerly part of William Howard Taft University. Their claim that "the institution believes it can reasonably expect to receive Candidate for Accreditation status in 2001 and initial Accreditation in 2002 or 2003" is ambitious, to say the least.

Branden University   D

35 Shady Dr. West
Mt. Lebanon, PA 15228
Fields offered: Computer and information science
Year founded: 1998
Email: office@branden.edu
Web site: www.branden.edu

This institution sends mixed messages. They were founded by the same man, Dr. Shi-Kuo Chang, who earlier founded the now-accredited Knowledge Systems Institute in Illinois. The academic model seems sound, for their online Ph.D., and many faculty with good credentials are listed. But there is no listed telephone for them in Mt. Lebanon, ostensibly the site of their "East coast regional office," nor any mention of where the "Midwest regional office" might be located. The Web site states clearly that they are not accredited, but suggests that "once accredited, a previously graduated student's degree will be recognized as an accredited degree retroactively." That would not be permitted by any recognized accreditor. Their Internet site is registered to an address in Lewes, Delaware, which seems, from a reverse yellow pages search, to be a real estate appraiser.

Breining Institute   B, M, D

8880 Greenback Lane
Orangevale, CA 95662-4019
Fields offered: Addictive disorders
Year founded: 1986
Phone: (916) 987 0662
Fax: (916) 987 8823
Email: college@breining.edu
Web site: www.breining.edu

This California state-approved school offers degrees at all levels in addictive studies. Founder Bernard G. Breining earned his bachelor's from Columbia Pacific University and his master's and doctorate from Breining Institute itself.

Bridgeton University

See: Birkdale University

British-American University   B, M, D

2026 Summer Wind
Santa Ana, CA 92704
Fields offered: Law, business
Year founded: 1997
Phone: (714) 850 1027 ▪ (800) 529 9383
Fax: (714) 850 4621
Email: info@lawprogram.com
Web site: www.british-american.edu

Offers bachelor's degrees in law and business, an MBA, and a J.D. that qualifies its graduates to sit for the California Bar exam; according to the school, students can integrate these programs and earn all four degrees in just 4 ½ to 5 years of study.

Broadmore University College of Pharmacy   D

91 North Front St.
Belize City, Belize
Fields offered: Pharmacy
Email: edu-opp@juno.com
Web site: home.infospace.com/eduopp2

Established by some pharmacists, apparently run from Canada, but using an address in the country of Belize. Program designed for holders of a B.S. in pharmacy who wish to earn a Doctor of Pharmacy by home study. After paying the nonrefundable tuition and completing the program, the student must submit a signed and notarized "Statement of Completion" before the degree is awarded. The Web site directs students to send tuition checks to Canada: "We will forward to Belize for you. Mail to and from Belize is extremely slow and unpredictable."

Cal Southern University   B, M, D

6815 Chimney Rock, #102
Bellaire, TX 77401

Web site: www.psedi.com

Well, here we are revealing a secret. Something called the Post Secondary Educational Institute arose in Texas in 2000, "founded by Christians" (they state prominently) and offering to "evaluate" one's credentials, and then award the degree of a school whose name they choose not to reveal until after the application is received, "in order to keep the integrity of the program in tact [sic]." Correspondents have blurted out the truth, telling us that the school in question is Cal Southern University, ostensibly in St. John's, Antigua, in the British West Indies, and accredited by the unrecognized International Accreditation Association of Nontraditional Colleges, also allegedly in the Caribbean, but with its Web site registered in the anonymity of the tiny South Pacific island of Niue. Here's another secret: Cal Southern doesn't reveal the cost of its degrees until after one has applied and been accepted. But The Shadow knows. They range from $350 for a bachelor's, up to $1,500 for the supersized deal of bachelor's, master's, and doctorate at the same time.

California Coast University B, M, D

> 700 N. Main St.
> Santa Ana, CA 92701
> **Fields offered:** Engineering, education, behavioral science, business, health care administration
> **Year founded:** 1974
> **Phone:** (714) 547 9625 ▪ (800) 854 8768
> **Email:** info@calcoastuniv.edu
> **Web site:** www.calcoastuniv.edu/ccu

California Coast was one of California's first nonresident universities. Degrees are offered at all levels in education, behavioral science, and business, with credit given for prior academic learning and certain equivalency exams. Although there are no engineering programs offered at the bachelor's level, new programs include an M.S. and a Ph.D. in engineering management and an M.S. in health care administration. All department heads and adjunct faculty hold degrees from traditional schools. The university operates from its own building in a Los Angeles suburb, and maintains a lending library to ensure availability of textbooks for all students, worldwide. Combined programs allow one to earn the bachelor's and master's or master's and doctorate simultaneously, although no degree can be earned in under nine months. Accreditation was at one time claimed from the National Association of Private Nontraditional Schools and Colleges, an unrecognized but legitimate agency, but the school resigned from that organization in 1996 when the agency was again rejected by the Department of Education. California Coast is approved by the state of California. Original name: California Western University.

California Pacific University B, M, D

> 9683 Terra Grande St., Room 100
> San Diego, CA 92126
> **Fields offered:** Business, management, human behavior
> **Year founded:** 1976
> **Phone:** (619) 695 3292 ▪ (800) 458 9667
> **Fax:** (619) 695 3712

Email: info@cpu.edu
Web site: www.cpu.edu

Bachelor's, master's, and doctorates in business administration, an MBA with a focus in healthcare management, and an M.A. in management & healthcare administration, entirely by correspondence study using the school's "highly structured programs." Limited experiential credit is given at undergraduate level only. Students are supplied with study guides written by university faculty, to accompany recognized textbooks in the field. The school is "committed to the training and education of business managers and leaders in the technical, quantitative, and theoretical areas of business management, without neglecting the all important human side of business enterprise." Approved by the state of California.

California Pushington University

See: American Pushington University

California Union University M

> 905 Euclid St.
> Fullerton, CA 92632
> **Fields offered:** Theology
> **Phone:** (714) 446 9133
> **Fax:** (714) 446 9106
> **Email:** info@calunion.edu
> **Web site:** www.calunion.edu

A theological seminary offering distance-learning degrees to Korean-speaking students.

California Western University

See: California Coast University

Canyon College A, B, M

> 521 West Maple St.
> Caldwell, ID 83605
> **Fields offered:** Business administration, psychology, social work, healthcare administration, counseling, theology, divinity
> **Phone:** (208) 455 0010
> **Fax:** (208) 455 0040
> **Email:** registrar@canyoncollege.edu
> **Web site:** www.canyoncollege.edu

The campus appears to be in the home of administrator John Denmark, wherein one presumably finds the School of Business, School of Psychology, School of Social Work, etc. They are not permitted to accept students living in their own state of Idaho. They offer the resumes of several dozen faculty (presumably adjunct faculty, unless Mr. Denmark's home is unusually large), many with doctorates from traditional schools, along with some from Columbia Pacific, LaSalle, Barrington, etc.

Capitol University B, M, D

> P.O. Box 3816
> Road Town, Tortola 1000, British Virgin Islands
> **Fields offered:** Any field you want
> **Phone:** +44 (207) 681 10 98
> **Email:** admissions@capitoluniversity.com
> **Web site:** www.capitoluniversity.com

'Hold still. I learned what to do in
my mail order entomology course.
I'll take care of that cockroach.'

Besides the Internet address listed above, we note that the following quite interesting URLs will also take you to Capitol University's Web site: *www.degreemill.com* (hmmm) and *surf.to/degrees* (once used by Earlscroft University; see listing in this chapter). Capitol awards degrees at all levels based on assessment of life experience. Takes "10 to 14 days in total for processing and delivery" of diploma. $399 for a bachelor's, $499 for a master's, $699 for a doctorate. Claims that its degree-granting authority comes from the "governmental British Registrar" in the British West Indies. Further states that "The United Kingdom, to which the British Virgin Islands (our jurisdiction) belong, is hardly poisoned by the existence of illegal diploma factories that are common practice in the United States and certain Asian countries. When presenting your Capitol University Degree to others, you should make very clear that you have acquired your Degree in a British distance graduation program." Claims accreditation from the Distance Graduation Accrediting Association (DGAA), an unrecognized agency that has also been claimed by Concordia College & University.

Castlebridge University
Information Services
2301 Kuhio Ave., #223-113
Honolulu, HI 96815
Fields offered: Many fields
Phone: (888) 213 1883
Degrees at all levels available in a number of fields, basically centered around the humanitites, from psychology to education to Celtic studies. See their Web site for full details, as well as a list of non-degree diplomas also available. The campus is a mailbox rental service. In mid-2000, the former Web site, at *www.castlebridgeu.org*, was not operative, but the telephone number produced an answering service message.

Center Graduate College   M
1510A Dell Ave.
Campbell, CA 95008
Fields offered: Mathematics education
Year founded: 1980
Phone: (408) 376 2400 ▦ (800) 395 6088
Email: enrollment@center.edu
Web site: www.center.edu
This state-approved school offers, by correspondence, an M.A. in education specializing in elementary mathematics.

Central Pacific University
1188 Bishop St.
Honolulu, HI 96813
Phone: (808) 524 8955
Fax: (808) 524 6924
Email: registrar@central-pacific.edu
Web site: www.central-pacific.edu
During a period when faculty and staff were identified on the Web site, we noted that among the dozen or so listed faculty, there were eight unaccredited and generally non-wonderful degrees. Registrar Nadan Drews apparently once worked for the unaccredited Honolulu University. The same person was head of the aviation and the music departments. The Web site shows photographs of a classroom facility at 1506 Piikoi Street in Honolulu, unusual for a school that seems to be 100% distance learning. Among the hundreds of home study courses listed is Music 801, Doctoral Applied Performance: A full recital/concert in the student's major area, the scope of which should be of the highest professional quality.

Central State University   B, M, D
3666 University Ave., Suite 401
Riverside, CA 92501
Fields offered: Business
Phone: (909) 276 2233 ▦ (888) 600 8833
Fax: (909) 276 1487
Email: csu@university.edu
Web site: www.university.edu
Business administration degrees at all levels, entirely by distance learning. There is "continual guidance provided by the instructor through frequent evaluation of student's mail-in answers. Each course consists of a textbook accompanied by a study guide written by the faculty." Mail-in tests are taken as well. In some cases, a term or research paper may be required. Formerly called Central University of Southern California.

Century University   B, M, D
6400 Uptown Blvd. NE #398-W
Albuquerque, NM 87110
Fields offered: Business, management, engineering, psychology, education, computer science, food marketing
Year founded: 1978
Phone: (505) 889 2711 ▦ (800) 240 6757
Fax: (505) 889 2750
Email: centuryu@nm.net
Web site: www.centuryuniversity.edu

Our major concern is that for something like 20 years, Century has claimed accreditation from the unrecognized and nonwonderful Accrediting Commission International (described in chapter 8) and does not make clear, in the literature we have seen, that the accreditation is unrecognized. Programs are by "guided independent study," which involves one-on-one faculty counseling, and credit for work experience, but no classes. Students must devote at least nine months (one academic year) to the program. More than half of the adjunct faculty hold Century University doctorates, although none of the school's five core faculty does. In 1990, Century moved its office from Los Angeles to Albuquerque, but its owner continues to work from California.

Chadwick University   B, M
2112 11th Ave. South, #504
Birmingham, AL 35205-2847
Fields offered: Many fields
Year founded: 1989
Phone: (205) 252 4483 ▪ (800) 767 2423
Fax: (205) 252 4480
Email: inform@chadwick.edu
Web site: www.chadwick.edu

Chadwick claims accreditation from the World Association of Universities and Colleges, a nonwonderful and unrecognized agency. The literature we have seen does not make clear that the accreditor is unrecognized. Nonresident self-paced degrees in many fields, including business administration, accounting, health care administration, criminal justice, environmental science, and psychology. One of four schools established and operated by Dr. Lloyd Clayton, Jr., including American Institute of Computer Science and Clayton College of Natural Healing. In the 1980s, the Alabama attorney general determined that Chadwick could operate without a state license as long as they did not accept students living in Alabama. In 1996, the state's new attorney general decided that Chadwick must have a state license in order to operate, and they quickly secured one.

City Business College
See: International University (Missouri)

City University Los Angeles   B, M, D, Law
P.O. Box 4277
Inglewood, CA 90309-4277
Fields offered: Business, education, computer science, counseling, criminal justice, engineering, journalism, humanities, political science, psychology, public administration, religious studies, nursing, environmental sciences, life science, physical therapy, law
Year founded: 1974
Phone: (310) 671 0783 ▪ (800) 262 8388
Fax: (310) 671 0572
Email: info@cula.edu
Web site: www.cula.edu

This school lost its California approval in 1995. Has since moved its corporate registration to Alabama, but appears

to still be operating from California. Claims recognition from the "Ancient and Sovereign Empire Washitaw de Dugdahmoundyah, earliest inhabitants of what is, today, Corporate United States of America (itself an 'unrecognized' corporation)." CULA is owned and operated by Evaluations and Management International, Inc., an organization that has sent out a three-page sales letter stating that for a fee, they would arrange for the degree of one's choice to be issued, but they required a 50% down payment before they would reveal the name of the school. CULA calls itself a "member in good standing" of the Association of Accredited Private Schools, an unrecognized accreditor. CULA has listed campuses in many other countries. A few we checked out were the homes or offices of alumni. They have also claimed that Muhammad Ali, Coretta Scott King, and Ethel Kennedy hold their diplomas. California residents not accepted unless they sign a waiver stating that they know CULA is not a California-approved school.

Clayton College of Natural Health   B, M, D
2140 11th Ave. South, #305
Birmingham, AL 35205
Fields offered: Holistic nutrition, alternative health
Year founded: 1980
Phone: (205) 323 8242 ▪ (800) 659 8274
Fax: (205) 323 8232
Email: inform@ccnh.edu
Web site: www.ccnh.edu

Degrees at all levels in natural health or holistic nutrition, including a Ph.D. in natural health, holistic nutrition, or holistic health sciences, and a Doctor of Naturopathy. Students entering at the graduate level must hold an undergraduate degree. Accreditation is claimed from the World Association of Universities and Colleges, a nonwonderful unrecognized agency, as well as the unrecognized American Association of Drugless Practitioners and the American Naturopathic Medical Certification and Accreditation Board, an unrecognized agency operating from a mailbox rental service. We note that in the growing number of states that regulate the practice of naturopathy (14 when we went to press), not one grants licensure to people with distance-learning credentials. Formerly Clayton School of Natural Healing and, later, American Holistic College of Nutrition.

Clayton School of Natural Healing
See: Clayton College of Natural Health

College of Security, Technology,
and Management   B, M, D
128000 South 71 Hwy.
Grandview, MO 64030
Fields offered: Law enforcement, criminal justice
Year founded: 1973
Phone: (816) 765 5551 ▪ (888) 567 6621
Fax: (816) 765 1777
Email: cstm@qni.com

Degrees at all levels are offered by distance learning in the field of executive security, law enforcement, and criminal justice. They report that their students have provided security for President Clinton, the British royal family, rock stars, and others. The school was started in association with International University of Missouri. While we had been informed it was now independent, the telephone is answered "International University."

Columbia Pacific University — B, M, D
127 E. Main
Missoula, MT 59802
Fields offered: Many fields
Year founded: 1978
Phone: (406) 728 3320 ▪ (800) 552 5522
Fax: (406) 728 3323
Email: inquiries@cpuniv.edu
Web site: www.cpuniv.edu

For many years, Columbia Pacific operated from its own building in San Rafael, and was approved by the state to offer degrees through their schools of arts & sciences, administration & management, and health & human services. In 1995, CPU's reapproval was denied. They appealed the decision and continued to operate. When the appeal was denied, the state ordered them closed, but they continued to operate. In late 1997, the state sued to shut the school down. In 1998, CPU announced they were accredited by the Paiute-Shoshone Indian Tribe of Fallon, Nevada, but that was withdrawn in 1999. CPU appealed the order to close, but this was denied in 2000. The day before this edition went to press in December, 2000, we learned that CPU is "resettling" (as they call it) in the state of Montana. A California office (885 Olive Ave., Suite C, Novato 94949) will be maintained for alumni affairs only. CPU intends to pursue legal remedies in California. Richard Crews has retired after more than 20 years as CPU president, with co-founder Les Carr assuming that position.

Columbia Southern University — B, M, D
24847 Commercial Ave.
P.O. Box 3110
Orange Beach, AL 36561
Fields offered: Occupational safety & health, human resources, health administration, environmental engineering, business administration, criminal justice, computer science
Year founded: 1993
Phone: (334) 981 3771 ▪ (800) 977 8449
Fax: (334) 981 3815
Email: csu@colsouth.edu
Web site: www.colsouth.edu

While the degree programs look impressively comprehensive, we are concerned by some of the unrecognized and non-wonderful accrediting agencies that Columbia Southern has affiliated itself with, including Accrediting Commission International and APICS. Columbia Southern applied to the recognized Distance Education and Training Council, but that application is "on hold" at the request of the school. However, the doctoral programs they had dropped, in order to make application to DETC, have been restored. Formerly the University of Environmental Sciences, and at one time operating from Silverhill, Alabama, and Pensacola,

Florida, but now from their own building in Orange Beach. Two schools of this name are also registered in Hawaii.

Columbus University — B, M, D, Law
P.O. Box 19167
New Orleans, LA 70179-0167
Year founded: 1997
Phone: (504) 486 2101
Fax: (504) 483 3265
Email: studentservices@columbusu.com
Web site: www.columbusu.com

Offers degrees at all levels with, apparently, little study. Doctorate and law program descriptions were removed from the Web site, but applications to such programs were still available. Accreditation is from the unrecognized and nonwonderful World Association of Universities and Colleges. When John went to the address at which the Web site is registered (3623 Canal Street, 2nd Floor, New Orleans, LA 70119), he found a martial arts dojo, which denied any knowledge of the university. However, corporate registration in the state shows the owner is the Kwan Tai Foundation, at the same address. Lexington University is also registered at that address. Columbus got its start by running a help wanted ad in the *Chronicle of Higher Education*, under the name Colgate University. When the real Colgate in New York squawked, the founder changed to Columbus, saying he had never heard of the New York Colgate, only the toothpaste. Columbus' motto, "Scientia, Veritas, Confectio," is translated in our Whitaker's Latin dictionary as "Science, Truth," and either "Preparation" or "Diminishing, Destroying." Two administrators of Columbus have started Lacrosse University in Louisiana.

Commonwealth Open University — B, M, D
Palm Chambers, P.O. Box 119
Road Town, Tortola, British Virgin Islands
Fields offered: Many fields
Fax: (917) 477 1321
Email: commopu@box100.com
Web site: www.commonwealth.org

Degrees at all levels through self-paced courses of study. They tell us their degree-granting authority comes from registration in the British Virgin Islands. They operate from an "International Information Center" at a P.O. box in Spain (Apartado 124, 33420 Lugones). Courses in English and Spanish. Free honorary degrees are available, based on resumes submitted. Two correspondents have sent us details of receiving such degrees based on "less than truthful" information provided.

Concord University
See: American M & N University

Concordia College & University — B, M, D
3818 South Western Ave., #886
Sioux Falls, SD 57105-6511
Fields offered: "almost any subject"
Phone: (605) 333 9381 ▪ (800) 933 1072
Fax: (605) 332 3715
Email: concordia@sjtu.edu
Web site: www.concordia-college.net

Degrees at all levels in "almost any subject" by assessment of life experience. Claims accreditation from the Distance Graduation Accrediting Association (DGAA), an unrecognized agency also claimed by Capitol University.

Cook's Institute of Electronics Engineering   B, M

4251 Cypress Dr.
Jackson, MS 39212
Fields offered: Electronics engineering, computer science, business administration
Year founded: 1945
Phone: (601) 371 1351
Fax: (601) 371 2619
Email: admissions@cooks.edu
Web site: www.cooks.edu

Offers, entirely through correspondence, a B.S. and M.S. in electronics engineering, an M.S. in computer science, and a BBA and MBA. Accreditation is from the unrecognized but legitimate National Association of Private, Nontraditional Schools and Colleges. Once, when we wrote for literature but didn't follow up, we were offered the opportunity to participate in a computer dating service under the same management.

Cornwall Independent University

15 Seton Gardens, Treswithian
Camborne, Cornwall TR14 7JS, United Kingdom
Year founded: 1992

Offers a "non-professional honorary degree classical style," in any subject, although there is apparently a particular focus on nonacademic, new age-type fields of interest.

Cyberversity

Wiesenstrasse 148
Dusseldorf 40549, Germany
Fields offered: Business, sociology, law
Phone: +49 (211) 95 45 81 0
Fax: +49 (2131) 29 57 01 1
Email: cyberversity@aer-academy.de
Web site: www.aer-academy.de/cyberversity

They seem to be a part of the Academy of European Law (Akademie für Europäisches Recht), cooperating with other institutions worldwide. A correspondent tells us they are in the process of converting entirely to a distance learning model, and seeking a convenience address in South Dakota.

Darton University

See: Birkdale University

Dominion University

See: University of Melchizedek

e Online University   B, M

P.O. Box 131765
Carlsbad, CA 92013
Fields offered: Business administration
Phone: (760) 930 0268
Fax: (760) 930 0278

Email: eou@cts.com
Web site: www.itd2000.com

BBA and MBA by directed independent study. Claims candidate status for accreditation by the International Association of Schools, Colleges, and Universities: an unrecognized and quite nonwonderful accreditor. The Web site is registered to the Institute of Training and Development, 1363 Sparrow Road, in Carlsbad. The telephone was answered, "Hello."

Earlscroft University   B, M, D

393-395 Lordship Lane
London SE22 8JN, United Kingdom
Fields offered: Any field you want, "except medicine"
Email: earlscroft@usa.net
Web site: degrees.freeyellow.com/earlscroft.htm

Send in your C.V. or resume, and Earlscroft will award you a bachelor's ($150), master's ($225), or doctorate ($320) based on your life experience. They promise a turnaround time of 14 days. Claims accreditation from The United Congress of Colleges (UCC) and The Life Experience Accreditation Association (LEAF), both unrecognized agencies for which we've never found URLs. Much of Earlscroft's literature is identical to that of Trinity College & University (U.K.), a highly suspect institution that backdates its diplomas (see listing in this chapter). Earlscroft used to be found at the Tonga-registered Internet address, *surf.to/degrees*; that URL now surfs you to Capitol University (also listed in this chapter).

EarthNet Institute   B, M

Drawer 1601
Mountain Grove, MO 65711
Fields offered: Political science, agriculture, environmental science, health & welfare, global economics, education
Email: wolford@eni.edu
Web site: www.eni.edu

Nonresident degree programs dedicated to the amelioration of major world problems (starvation, homelessness, poverty, disease, environmental devastation, etc.) through global scale education, research, and cooperation. Students pursue a three-stage apprenticeship-style program: foundational studies and core competencies; field studies on site in cooperation with organizations affiliated with EarthNet Institute; and a major project that demonstrates excellence and contributes in a genuine manner to the amelioration of major world problems. About half the listed faculty themselves have unaccredited doctorates.

Eastern American University   B, M, D

2535 Wyoming NE, Suite B
Albuquerque, NM 87112
Fields offered: Many fields
Year founded: 1993
Phone: (505) 294 2772 ▪ (800) 801 5980
Fax: (505) 294 2772
Email: judithawelker@uswest.net
Web site: www.eau.edu

Eastern American offers degrees at all levels in arts & sciences, business administration, education, human resources, and management, as well as a self-designed program in which students can create their own program. Each student works with a faculty mentor. by mail or Internet. Credit is available for life-experience learning, through exams or portfolio review. Eastern American's founder, Dr. William Welker, made some of the most hostile telephone calls John ever received, but he (Dr. Welker, not John) died soon after. Formerly Eastern University.

Eastern Nebraska Christian College
See: Saint John's University of Practical Theology

Eastern University
See: Eastern American University

Emerson College of Herbology   M
582 Cummer Ave.
Willowdale, ON M2K 2M4, Canada
Fields offered: Herbology
Master of Herbology title is awarded on successful completion of 33 correspondence lessons (a total of 550 pages), covering botanic medicine, phytotherapy, pharmabotanics and herbalism. Lessons are mailed in three at a time, graded, and returned with the next set of lessons.

Emperor's New University   B, M
P.O. Box 7070
Berkeley, CA 94707
Fields offered: Psychology of perception, clothing design, royal studies
Year founded: 1938
Fax: (510) 217 3713
Email: enu@ursa.net
ENU offers its degrees entirely by distance learning to those who can truly see the merit of its programs.

European Union University   B, M, D
C/Londres 17, bajo
Madrid 28.028, Spain
Fields offered: Many fields
Year founded: 1999
Phone: +34 (91) 725 5208
Fax: +34 (91) 725 7996
Email: euniversity@wol.es
Web site: www.eurouniversity.es.org
Founder Alfonso Roldán Moré (a Spanish medical doctor) explained to us that his Madrid-based university incorporated in Iowa (where their "Branch Office" is a secretarial service) because of the time required for Spanish approval. The New York office is also a secretarial service. Online study leading to degrees at all levels in many fields of study. Accreditation is claimed from two unrecognized agencies: the International Commission on Distance Learning (founded in Zurich by Dr. Roldán Moré) and the International Association of Educators for World Peace (no listed telephone in Huntsville, Alabama). Dr. Roldán Moré also has a Ph.D. from American World University, run from a secretarial service in Iowa. At least he had the good sense

to resign from the unrecognized and nonwonderful World Association of Universities and Colleges.

Eurotechnical Research University   B, M, D
P.O. Box 516
Hilo, HI 96721
Fields offered: Science, engineering, karate
Year founded: 1983
Established in California in 1983; moved to Hawaii in 1989, where it operated from the bedroom of university president James Holbrook's rented home. In California, we respected the quality and integrity of Eurotech's activities, primarily the awarding of doctorates based on research performed in nonacademic settings, usually an industrial or government laboratory. In 1990, however, Eurotechnical became affiliated with the Rockwell College of Applied Arts and Science, an Ohio karate school with no listed phone, run by Harold Mayle, a man whose only degrees were purchased from the Universal Life Church. Eurotechnical awarded Mayle a Ph.D. *and* a D.Sc. based on his karate skills, and has awarded other doctorates to Rockwell personnel for their karate experience. John had counted Professor Holbrook as a friend, but Holbrook refused to communicate with John after John expressed amazement at the above-mentioned developments. A diploma mill called Leiland College of Arts and Science, selling degrees for under $100, has operated from a Hawaiian post office box. Holbrook told a Hawaiian reporter he knew nothing about Leiland, but the reporter learned that Holbrook had in fact rented the box. Holbrook would not comment on this matter. Holbrook, the sole proprietor and staff member at the time, died in 1994, but the "university," clearly in other hands, has continued to operate and to advertise in martial arts magazines.

Evangel Christian University of America
909 N. 18th St., #123
Monroe, LA 71201
Fields offered: Religious fields
Phone: (318) 343 9006 ▓ (800) 346 4014
Fax: (318) 345 0350
Email: info@ecua.edu
Web site: www.ecua.edu
Degrees from bachelor's through the Ph.D. are offered in various religious fields, either by taking home study courses, or by writing two 50,000-word (or ten 10,000-word) papers. Accreditation is claimed from the unrecognized Transworld Accrediting Commission of Siloam Springs, Arkansas. The various degrees in church music are offered only in Guam.

Fairfax University   B, M, D
2900 West Fork Dr., Suite 200
Baton Rouge, LA 70827
Fields offered: Religious fields
Year founded: 1986
Phone: (225) 295 5655
Fax: (225) 298 1303
Email: info@fairfaxu.edu
Web site: www.fairfaxu.edu

"That's the beauty of home-study tennis lessons: you don't have to worry about uniforms."

Until late 2000, Fairfax offered degrees by distance learning in a wide range of fields, with students supervised by members of a large and well-credentialed adjunct faculty. Then new Louisiana regulations took force, requiring that all unaccredited schools be on an approved accreditation track. Fairfax was denied entry onto a possible accreditation track by the Distance Education and Training Council. Since only purely religious programs are exempt from the new rules, Fairfax dropped all of its nonreligious degree programs. John and his wife Marina were two of the four founders of Fairfax; they resigned two months after the first enrollment, in 1986. They thought they had parted company with school president Alan Jones amicably. But soon after, Dr. Jones attempted (unsuccessfully) to persuade California authorities to prevent John from selling this book, because he didn't like some of the things said in it. Later Jones sued John and Marina in an unsuccessful attempt to involve them in a lawsuit between Fairfax and Columbia Pacific (for whom Dr. Jones used to work). Dr. Jones has also established the Academy of International Management, based at a secretarial service in South Dakota.

Farelston College
See: Farelston & Nova Colleges

Farelston & Nova Colleges   B, M, D
P.O. Box 67004
Northland Village
Calgary, AB T2L 2L2, Canada
Fields offered: Any field
Year founded: 1977
Nova College has used various addresses in western Canada over the years, as well as in the U.S. and on the Isle of Man. Now, they say they have formed an association with Farelston College (we can find no record of such a school) to grant degrees based almost entirely on "awarding credit for demonstrated competence and knowledge no matter how or when acquired." Nova's fees may be greatly reduced for those in special circumstances (unemployed, incarcerated, etc.). Not to be confused with the accredited Nova Southeastern University (which actually has a component called Nova College).

Feather River University   B, M, D
P.O. Box 1900
Paradise, CA 95967-1900
Fields offered: Business, medical sciences, martial arts, aviation, general studies
Year founded: 1984
Web site: www.fruonline.com
Online degrees can be completed in three months. The literature announces an intention of opening a medical school by the year 2003. The Web site is registered to Roog.com, 6129 Powhite Farm Dr., Mechanicsville, VA 23111. No connection with the accredited Feather River College.

Fortune University   B, M, D
Room 488, No. 2 News Building
Shennan Center Rd.
Shenzhen 518027 Guangdong, China
Fields offered: Many fields
Phone: +86 (0755) 209.0045
Fax: +86 (0755) 209.6717
Email: saraxie@fortuneuniversity.org
Web site: www.fortuneuniversity.org
There is charming Chinese music on the Web site of this online institution, accredited by the unrecognized and nonwonderful World Association of Universities and Colleges. In the picture of diplomas and other documents, there is visible the diploma of American World University, operated by Dr. Maxine Asher, who also runs the World Association. There is mention of a dissertation "with Southwest University," but no explanation. One thing that is clear is the picture, on every page of the Web site, of bags of money against a background of good old American dollar bills.

Foundation for Economic Education   M
30 South Broadway
Irvington-on-Hudson, NY 10533
Fields offered: Economic theory, business
Phone: (914) 591 7230 ▪ (800) 452 3518
Fax: (914) 591 8910
Email: freeman@westnet.com
Web site: www.fee.org
The Foundation does not issue its own degrees, but students who complete the coursework for the M.A. in economic theory or history or for the MBA receive their degree from American Commonwealth University. According to the Foundation's literature, Professor Sennholz has served as an academic advisor and "learning resource specialist" for the unaccredited American Commonwealth University for over ten years, and this is his way of working more closely with students in his field of interest. Details of each degree program "depend primarily upon the previous preparation of the candidate," and instruction may be conducted in face-to-face classes, seminars, workshops, individual meetings, or teleconferences. At one time a Ph.D. was offered, but the school tells us that it never really got off the ground.

Frederick Taylor International University
See: Frederick Taylor University

Frederick Taylor University   B, M, D

346 Rheem Blvd., #203
Moraga, CA 94556
Fields offered: Management, business
administration
Phone: (510) 376 0900 ▓ (800) 988 4622
Fax: (510) 376 0908
Email: admissions@ftu.edu
Web site: www.ftu.edu

Degrees offered are a B.S. in management, a BBA, and an
MBA. Credit is awarded for experiential learning (up to
30 semester units at the undergraduate level, and 6 credits
for graduate degrees) as well as for challenge exams.
Financial aid and scholarships are available, and the programs are approved by the state of California. At the
same address, but as a separate institution, is Frederick
Taylor International University, a Hawaiian-registered
university. While FTU offers bachelor's and master's,
FTIU also has doctorates in business: a DBA (no dissertation required) and a Ph.D. FTIU has an affiliation with
the Academy of Professional Studies in London, in which
APS offers residential classes in London, and FTIU awards
the degree. To their credit, FTU was one of the first schools
to resign its accreditation from the nonwonderful World
Association of Universities and Colleges.

Generale University   B, M, D

1027 David St.
Vancouver, BC V6E 4L2, Canada
Phone: +1 (604) 255 6940
Fax: +1 (604) 682 8578
Web site: www.generale-canada.com

The campus address is a mailbox rental store called
Mailbox Plus. The Web site, formerly in Malaysia, identifies
four colleges, named for Thomas Edison, Alfred Sloan, Albert
Einstein, and Mohandass [sic] Gandhi. They claim to be
accredited by the Canadian National Accreditation [sic]
Commission (an organization we cannot locate), and
registered with the Ministry of Advanced Education of
British Columbia.

Glenford University   B, M, D

9541-D Brookline Ave.
Baton Rouge, LA 70809
Fields offered: Business, education, political
science, theology, social welfare, tourism
Year founded: 2000
Phone: (225) 924 4071 ▓ (800) 559 9882
Fax: (225) 924 4075
Email: glenforduv@aol.com
Web site: www.glenford.edu

Distance degrees are offered in the above fields. When we
checked the tollfree number just before publication, it
had been disconnected, as had the number for the New
York office. The phone for the Los Angeles office was
answered "Hello." The Web site is registered to Steve
Goh at a New York phone number also not in service. The
text on the Web site sounds as if it may have been translated from the Korean, perhaps by founder Ung Soo Kim:
"We are going to inform latest Glenford news." "All these
detailed information can be reviewed." Glenford can

reject an applicant based on "available of aptitude." And
so on.

Golden State University

See: Honolulu University of Arts, Sciences, and Humanities.
No connection to the diploma mill by the same name.

Greenleaf University   M, D

Communciation Processing Center
P.O. Box 7426
Alexandria, VA 22307
Fields offered: Leadership, administration, future
studies
Year founded: 1989
Phone: (314) 567 4477
Fax: (314) 567 4478
Email: admin@greenleaf.edu
Web site: www.greenleaf.edu

Offers an M.S. and Ph.D. in "leadership and administration," as well as an M.S. in future studies. The university
espouses the philosophy of "servant leadership" and
"servant institutions," as pioneered by Robert Greenleaf,
whom some consider the father of the modern empow-
erment movement. There is a non-mandatory annual
seven-day residency session. Formerly the Institute for
Professional Studies, and formerly at an address in St. Louis,
Missouri. Has claimed accreditation from the nonwonderful
and unrecognized World Association of Universities and
Colleges.

Greenwich University   B, M, D, Law

Taylors Rd.
Norfolk Island 2899, Australia
Fields offered: Many fields
Year founded: 1972
Phone: +61 (6723) 22834 ▓ (800) 367 4456
Fax: +61 (6723) 23547
Email: grnichu@aloha.net
Web site: www.greenwich.edu

Students are matched with a faculty mentor who guides
the student's independent study, consulting on all aspects
of the program, including designing the program, finding
resources, networking, arranging effective field placements,
and so on. A major paper, thesis, or dissertation is required.
Bachelor's programs are open to students with substantial
college or noncollege training and career experience in the
proposed field of study. Law programs are non-Bar qualifying. Affiliations with colleges in Indonesia, Hong Kong,
and New Zealand. Greenwich evolved from the International
Institute for Advanced Studies (established in St. Louis
in 1972, and which still exists as a part of Greenwich). John
was the first president of Greenwich, serving full-time in
the Hawaii building for 18 months (from early 1990
through mid 1991). In 1998, Greenwich moved its headquarters to Norfolk Island, which is constitutionally a British
crown colony, supervised but not owned by Australia. At
the time, Greenwich claimed accreditation, but in the
Australian sense, in which universities accredit themselves.
Greenwich became a matter of considerable controversy
in Australian higher education circles, with numerous
newspaper articles (pro and con) and parliamentary

debates. The Australian Qualifications Framework conducted a two-year investigation of Greenwich. Just before this book went to press, December 12, 2000, an AQF review committee recommended that Greenwich be denied recognition, because "the standard of its courses, quality assurance mechanisms, and academic leadership fail to meet the standards expected of Australian universities." Norfolk Island's education minister felt the report was unfair, and said Greenwich could continue to operate on Norfolk. The matter will probably remain controversial for years. (Note: The Greenwich School of Theology was once an affiliate of Greenwich University, but has changed its affiliation to a traditional South African university, Pochefstroom.)

Hamersfield College and
International University   B, M, D
2600 Turner Rd. SW, Unit 114
Marietta, GA 30064
Fields offered: "most subjects, EXCEPT medicine, law and engineering"
Web site: www.hamersfield.org

Although we waded through 18 pages of their Web-posted marketing literature, we still can't tell you much about this school. They offer degrees at all levels in just about any subject by assessment of life/work experience. No address or phone number provided, but of course they are all set up to take your credit card number. The Web site is registered to the address of a trailer park in Georgia.

Harmony College of Applied Science
See: Harmony of Life Fellowship, Inc.

Harmony of Life Fellowship, Inc.   B, M, D
1434 Fremont Ave.
Los Altos, CA 94022
Fields offered: Spiritual science, spiritual healing (which includes spiritual healing, magnetic healing, mind healing, and divine healing), philosophy, psychology, natural healing
Year founded: 1976
Phone: (650) 967 1232
Fax: (650) 961 0777

Students work through self-paced programs on a one-to-one basis with professors, keeping in touch by mail and phone. Credit available for professional and life experience, for nontraditional studies, and through a testing program. Thesis of 2,500 words required for all degrees. Formerly called Harmony College of Applied Science.

Hawthorne University (Utah)   B, M, D
2965 East 3435 South
Salt Lake City, UT 84109
Fields offered: Many fields
Year founded: 1984
Phone: (801) 485 1801
Fax: (801) 485 1563
Web site: www.hawthorne.edu

Founder and Chancellor, the late Alfred Munzert once threatened with vigor (he was yelling into the telephone) to sue us into oblivion if we said anything whatsoever about his school. We must, however, point out that the regional accreditation they have claimed relates to a high school they have operated; that the university's accreditation comes from the unrecognized and nonwonderful Accrediting Commission International, and that Chancellor Munzert's own doctorate comes, the catalog says, from the Brantwood Forest School in England. There is no such place, but there is a totally fraudulent diploma mill in England called the Brantridge Forest School. Hawthorne occupies a few rooms in a private elementary school (the Reid School) in Salt Lake City. Dr. Murphy Nmesi, Dean of Education, told a visitor that Hawthorne has campuses in Japan and South Africa, and would be opening two U.S. campuses (California and West Virginia) soon, but if that has happened, we cannot find them. The university was at one time very active in Japan, through the marketing efforts of Dr. Al-Jami.

Heed University   B, M, D, Law
3201 S. 16th St.
Milwaukee, WI 53215
Fields offered: Psychology, philosophy, education, business administration, law, religion
Year founded: 1970
Phone: (414) 297 9555 ▪ (800) 262 0175
Web site: www.heed.edu

B.A., B.S., M.A., M.S., MBA, Ph.D., Ed.D., Doctor of Arts, and Doctor of Psychology all entirely through correspondence. Heed started in Florida, then moved to the U.S. Virgin Islands, and now operates from Wisconsin. Heed also maintains Thomas Jefferson College of Law, which awards non-Bar-qualifying law degrees (J.D., LL.M., and S.J.D.) through correspondence study. Religious degree programs are offered through Heed University School of Theology, Florida.

Honolulu University of the Arts,
Sciences, and Humanities   B, M, D
1314 South King St. #750
Honolulu, HI 96814
Fields offered: Many fields
Year founded: 1987
Phone: (808) 955 7333 ▪ (888) 665 1008
Fax: (808) 946 3534
Email: honouniv@lava.net
Web site: www.honolulu-university.edu

Degrees at all levels can be earned through correspondence courses in dozens of fields of study. Formerly Golden State University, which operated from four cities in California. They suggest that most degrees can be completed in one year or less. They state they have "qualified to operate as a degree-granting institution" in Hawaii. (The state of Hawaii is adamant that unaccredited schools in the state do not suggest in any way that they are approved by the state.) The school further states that they are a "member, in full standing, of the Akademie Fuer Internationale Kultur- und Wissenschaftsfoerderung which accredits many of the foremost Universities and Colleges in Europe and the Near East." We cannot work up any enthusiasm for this organization, whose former U.S. representative, Denis Mulhilly (based in Hawaii) has written us messages we found highly insulting. Formerly shared a Honolulu address with a school called South Pacific University.

Horizons University   M, D
242 Boulevard Voltaire
75011 Paris, France
Fields offered: Business, education, science
Year founded: 1991
Email: roberta@club-internet.fr
Web site: www.h-university.com

When a reader visited the campus address in Paris, he found two businesses in the building: a driving school and a hairdresser. We do not know which one encompasses the university, which does not seem to have a listed telephone in Paris. On one page of their Web site, they claim that there is no such thing as accreditation in Europe and therefore they are not accredited. On another page, they claim that they are fully accredited by the APIX Institute, an organization we have never heard of, and cannot locate.

ICS Institute of Computer Studies
See: International University of Fundamental Studies

Ignatius University   B, M, D
3200 Cold Spring Rd.
Indianapolis, IN 46222
Fields offered: Philosophy, psychology, theology
Year founded: 1998
Phone: (718) 698 0700 ▩ (888) 862 7611
Email: ignatiusu@aol.com
Web site: members.aol.com/ignatiusu

Ignatius University is operated by the priests of the Syrian Orthodox Church. They offer distance-learning degrees at all levels in the above fields. The bachelor's program is designed so that undergraduate students do coursework which, they say, meets the requirements for a degree from the regionally accredited Excelsior College. Ignatius also offers its own master's and doctoral degrees. Formerly known as University of Antioch (which is not to be confused with Antioch University).

IMPAC University   M
800 West Marion Ave.
Punta Gorda, FL 33950
Fields offered: Business, management
Year founded: 1998
Phone: (941) 629 7512 ▩ (888) 831 9207
Email: info@impacu.edu
Web site: www.impacu.edu

This Florida-licensed institution is an outgrowth of IMPAC Corporation, a large worldwide management-engineering firm. IMPAC Corp. established IMPAC University to promulgate its approach to management, training people to become leaders in what they call "the struggle for self-actualization." The master's degrees in business, behavioral

sciences, and MIS are offered both residentially (a three-day weekend, monthly) or through online courses.

Institute of Professional
Financial Managers   M, D
25 Old Gloucester St.
Queen Square
London WC1N 3AF, United Kingdom
Fields offered: Business administration
Year founded: 1992
Phone: +44 (171) 580 9407
Fax: +44 (171) 323 1766
Email: admin@ipfm.org
Web site: www.ipfm.org

When John visited the campus in late 1997, he found it to be a one-man office (plus a small ante room) at the end of a long hall in what appeared to be a rather run-down youth hostel. A self-paced MBA and doctoral program. An association is claimed with the Irish Business School in Dublin (we could find no evidence of such a school in Ireland). Jeff Wooller College operates from the same address. According to the school, "this low-cost MBA is popular because it gives [instruction] on a one-for-one basis and payment can be made in easy installments."

Intercontinental University, Ltd.   B, M, D
546 Broad Ave.
Englewood, NJ 07631
Fields offered: Chiropractic, alternative medicine
Email: sport-dc@ix.netcom.com
Web site: www.icu.edu

It would appear from its rather sparse Web site that this school offers "post-doctoral" degrees in chiropractic and alternative medicine to people who already have a Doctor of Chiropractic. Claims that "the very existence of our University means that it is approved in the country of its charter." Ostensibly that would be Russia—they say they are headquartered in Moscow—yet no address is provided other than one in New Jersey.

Intercultural Open University   B, M, D
Yn'e Bosk House
De Hoarnen 5
9218 XC Opeinde, Netherlands
Fields offered: Many fields
Phone: +31 (512) 37 22 97
Fax: +31 (512) 37 27 03
Email: iou@iouedu.com
Web site: www.iouedu.com

They claim to have been "internationally accredited" since 1989. None of the listed accreditors is recognized. One is at the same address as the university. Another is an unrecognized agency once located in Hawaii which has written us very insulting letters. The U.S. campus is said to be in Auburn, Washington, but there is no listed telephone number there. The U.S. "homepage" turns out to be for Smith Chapel Bible College of Tallahassee, Florida, whose founder has two IOU doctorates, and all his staff members have either Smith Chapel degrees or IOU degrees. The U.S. vice president has run several unaccredited Louisiana universities. Degrees are offered in a wide range of fields, and offices or affiliated schools are listed for many countries. Also known as International Open Distance University.

International Business Foundation   M

318 North Carson St., # 214
Carson City, NV 89701
Fields offered: Business administration
Year founded: 1989
Phone: +27 (12) 548 2044
Fax: +27 (12) 548 4738
Email: info@ibfbusinessschools.com
Web site: www.ibfbusinessschools.com

Offers a "Condensed MBA program" over the Internet. From information gathered at the school's Web site, it appears that the CEO, Hannes Liebenberg, operates from South Africa and is attempting to open franchises of his school all over the world. The address of the American office is in Nevada. The Internet site is registered at P.O. Box 333, Montana Park, Pretoria 0159, South Africa.

International College of Higher Education   M

28 Saint James St.
South Petherton
Somerset TA13 5BW, United Kingdom
Fields offered: Business management
Phone: +44 (1460) 242 756
Fax: +44 (1460) 242 757
Email: email.intcol@ukonline.co.uk

Apparently operated by the same folks who run Somerset University (see listing in chapter 31), this school offers an MBA in a program "designed to meet the training needs of senior managers." The program consists of a series of modules, prepared by senior tutors and external advisors. Since they cannot operate as a degree-granting institution in the United Kingdom, we are uncertain where their authority to award degrees comes from. Somerset University has used a mailing service address in New Orleans, Louisiana.

International College of Spiritual & Psychic Sciences   B, M, D

P.O. Box 1387, Station H
Montreal, Quebec H3G 2N3, Canada
Fields offered: Therapeutic counseling
Phone: +1 (514) 937 8359
Fax: +1 (514) 937 5380
Email: info@iiihs.com
Web site: www.iiihs.com

As part of the International Institute of Integral Human Sciences, offers an independent study program in therapeutic counseling, with an emphasis in East-West spirituality, that qualifies its students to earn a degree from the Open International University for Complementary Medicine in Sri Lanka. We have some serious concerns about this Sri Lankan school; see our listing in chapter 31.

International Institute for Advanced Studies

See: Greenwich University

International Institute of Theology

See: Westbrook University

International Open Distance University

See: Intercultural Open University

International Pushington University

See: American Pushington University

International Theological University   B, M, D

P.O. Box 70018
Pasadena, CA 91117-7018
Fields offered: Philosophy, religious studies, divinity
Year founded: 1999
Phone: (626) 795 8133
Fax: (626) 568 1116
Email: admissions@accrediting.com
Web site: www.accrediting.com/itu.htm

The literature says that "Many Ideas come from the Great Spirit." One of them appears to be this online university, founded by Dr. Chief Swift Eagle of the Cherokee Western Federation Church and Tribe, operating from a P.O. box in California but with no state approval. Accredited by the International University Accrediting Association, as well as the Virtual University Accrediting Association, both agencies also founded by the self-identified Reverend Professor Doctor Chief Swift Eagle. They also claim to offer "international medical degrees" through an affiliation with the International University of Fundamental Studies of St. Petersburg, Russia.

International University (Hawaii)

7 Waterfront Plaza, #400
500 Ala Moana Blvd.
Honolulu, HI 96813

Same president as the International University in Missouri. The campus is a mail receiving and forwarding service.

International University (Missouri)   B, M, D

1301 S. Noland Rd.
Independence, MO 64055
Fields offered: Many fields
Year founded: 1973
Phone: (816) 461 3633
Web site: www.tiume.org

Degrees at all levels offered through correspondence study, with the motto, "Helping you to Rise in Career" [*sic*]. The only Web site we could find, based in the Middle East, claims (as of mid-2000) that their accreditation comes the International Accrediting Commission, the disgraced organization that was closed by the Missouri attorney general many years ago, following a sting operation. (In reality, we believe their accreditation is from ACI, the nonwonderful successor to IAC.) There has in the past been some affiliation with the Sussex College of Technology, which has been identified as a degree mill by major British newspapers and educational authorities. Apparently also some affiliation with the American University in London and with the London Institute of Technology and Research.

Campuses are listed in many countries, but the few we have visited have been the personal offices of alumni. (The Web site claims there are more than 200,000 students and alumni.)

International University of Advanced Studies

9441 East 31st. St., Suite 160
Tulsa, OK 74145
Phone: (918) 712 9980
Fax: (918) 438 2611
Email: info@new-utopia.com
Web site: www.new-utopia.com

Part of the "Principality of New Utopia," a newly conceived city-state supposedly slated for construction on a seamount in the Caribbean west of the Cayman Islands, dedicated to the principles of a free market and the philosophies of Ayn Rand and Robert Heinlein. Cofounded by Dr. Richard Crews, president of Columbia Pacific University. According to their Web site, the school was founded to impart "knowledge that will be needed in the next century for survival on Earth, the colonization of the oceans, and the exploration and colonization of space." Hailing from Tulsa, OK, New Utopia's founding father, Prince Lazarus Long, has been ordered to halt Internet sales of New Utopia bonds while under SEC investigation for investor fraud. A medical school was to have been part of the campus.

International University of Fundamental Studies

B, M, D

P.O. Box 59
St. Petersburg 191040, Russia
Fields offered: Many fields
Year founded: 1991
Phone: +7 (812) 552 8021
Fax: +7 (812) 274 4455
Email: info@iufs.edu
Web site: www.iufs.edu

They say they began in 1991, under the name ICS Institute of Computer Studies, claiming to be Russia's first private university. While they claim to offer courses to prepare for the exams of the University of London and University of Dundee, their main affiliation appears to be with the extremely dubious International Theological University, run by the Reverend Professor Doctor Chief Swift Eagle, from California, with whom they seem to offer online degrees in international medicine, forestry, aerospace, and many other fields.

International University of Professional Studies

B, M, D

P.O. Box 236
Makawao, Maui, HI 96768
Fields offered: Psychology, health, education, expressive arts therapy, transformational psychology, health & wellness services, consciousness studies, transformational education, human resources development
Year founded: 1988
Phone: (808) 573 1999 ▪ (800) 806 0317

"Even if my alma mater is under water at high tide, I am determined to attend the reunion."

Fax: (800) 806 0317
Email: iups@healthy.net
Web site: www.healthy.net/univ

Degrees at all levels in the above-mentioned fields, based on independent study and a project demonstrating excellence. Original name: Pacific University of Hawaii. Founder Irv Katz was a department chairperson at the University of Nevada and director of a graduate psychology program at Antioch University. While the Web site refers to the university being "located on the beautiful island of Maui," no address is provided other than the post office box.

IOND University

B, M, D

Central Pacific Plaza
220 South King St., Suite 1680
Honolulu, HI 96813
Fields offered: Many fields
Phone: +81 (3) 3389 7045
Fax: +81 (3) 5380 1740
Email: info@iond-univ.org
Web site: www.iond-univ.org

Based in Japan with an American campus at a mailbox rental service in Hawaii. Offers degrees at all levels. Courses are taught in both Japanese and English, although we hope the institution is more literate in the former than it seems to be in the latter. One randomly picked phrase from its catalog: "The International University that grows the grobal sense and gives the way for the restoration of the educational background" [sic]. When we drew their attention to some of these language issues, we were promised that they would use "correct english from now on." Accredited by the unrecognized and very non-wonderful World Association of Universities and Colleges (WAUC). Director General Takahashi wrote to us, "If you are willing to defame IOND University, it is no good. You may not evaluate the university's education by the standard of university's building, money, and property. Please expect our university's future." And so we do.

Irish Business School

See: Institute of Professional Financial Managers

Irish International University   B, M, D

Fields offered: Many fields
Email: iiu@postmark.net
Web site: www.iiuedu.ie

One wonders why Vice Chancellor Jeff Wooller, "a renowned educationalist," spends so much time describing Ireland—"small-beaked and wing-clipped"—in the school's prospectus. All programs are supposedly 100% distance learning, so the students don't have to go there. And the school, though "registered in Dublin," gives no Irish address in any of its literature. More than likely, it is being run from the same small London office (John visited it in 1997) that is home to the rest of Jeff Wooller's schools: Institute of Professional Financial Managers, Irish Business School, and Jeff Wooller College.

Jeff Wooller College

See: Institute of Professional Financial Managers

Kennedy-Western University   B, M, D

200 West 17th St.
Cheyenne, WY 82001-4412
Fields offered: Many fields
Year founded: 1984
Phone: (307) 635 6709 ▪ (800) 969 6906
Fax: (307) 635 7363
Email: admissions@kw.edu
Web site: www.kw.edu

People living in California cannot enroll. Students work with an academic support team consisting of a resident and adjunct faculty. Students must have five to seven years of experience in their field. Course of study involves exams and self-paced independent study, and a thesis or dissertation. Kennedy-Western moved its mail-receiving office from California to Idaho in 1990. The main office, where the president, the director of admissions, and others work, is in Thousand Oaks, California. There is an address in Boise and Wyoming (from which the degree-granting authority derives), as well as five international addresses. There was at one time a Honolulu office at 311 Ohua, #403C (c/o Ken Reiss), Honolulu, HI 96815. The Hawaii corporation was involuntarily dissolved on November 16, 1998. Online services (library, tutorial assistance) are available. More than 90% of the inquiries we get about Kennedy-Western (and there are a lot of them) come from Asia, Russia, or Spain.

Kensington International University

See: Kensington University

Kensington Pacific University

See: Kensington University

Kensington University   B, M, D

25 Kanehoe Bay Dr., 106-239
Kailua, HI 96734
Fields offered: Administration of justice, business administration, education, computer science, engineering (civil, electrical, mechanical), environmental studies, professional studies (psychology, sociology, political science)
Year founded: 1990
Phone: (808) 245 5589 ▪ (800) 423 2495
Fax: (818) 240 1707
Email: kensington@earthlink.net
Web site: www.kensington.edu

Kensington University had been a California-approved school, but their reapproval was denied in 1995. Now registered in Hawaii and Montana, although apparently still run from southern California (520 East Broadway, Suite 400, Glendale 91205). Offers degrees at all levels by independent study. Also uses the names Kensington International University and Kensington Pacific University.

Knightsbridge University   B, M, D

Grove House, Walls Hill Rd.
Torquay, Devon TQ1 3LZ, United Kingdom
Fields offered: Almost any field
Phone: +44 (803) 315 222
Fax: +44 (803) 325 774
Email: admin@knightsbridge-uni.com
Web site: www.knightsbridge-uni.com

It is hard not to like Knightsbridge, since President Henrik Fyrst Kristensen writes such charming letters, and the Web site is also well-written. The school has its only office in the United Kingdom but is not licensed there. It was once incorporated in Liberia, and is now incorporated in Antigua & Barbuda, a status which grants them the legal right to operate, but no sort of academic accreditation. President Kristensen has expressed annoyance with us for having mentioned, in previous editions, that the school was started by the owner of the University de la Romande, which we regard as a diploma mill. We agree that the new ownership would make such reference less relevant, but for the fact that the Web site continues to reference these very people: "Knightsbridge University was founded in 1986 by a group of forward thinking Academics and Administrators." To their credit, Knightsbridge voluntarily revoked its accreditation from the unrecognized and non-wonderful World Association of Universities and Colleges. Knightsbridge claims more than 300 adjunct faculty, but none is named in their literature, because "a fair amount of change is taking place on a regular basis, making it a somewhat difficult and often pointless exercise to include a list of faculty with the University's general literature."

Lacrosse University   B, M, D

P.O. Box 385
Madisonville, LA 70447-0385
Fields offered: Many fields
Year founded: 1999
Phone: (504) 845 7462
Fax: (504) 845 2690
Email: ss@lacrosseuniversity.com

Web site: www.lacrosseuniversity.com
Started in 1999 by the operators of Columbus University, also in Louisiana (see listing in this chapter). Lacrosse's Web site is registered to Dr. Harry Boyer, the founder of Columbus. The president of Lacrosse is Colleen Twomey Boyer, an administrator at Columbus. Offers degrees at all levels. "The primary source of credit for many candidates is work, occupation or professional activities (past and present)." Accredited by the unrecognized and nonwonderful World Association of Universities and Colleges (WAUC).

Lael College and Graduate School   B, M, D
3721 St. Bridget Lane
St. Ann, MO 63074
Fields offered: Behavioral studies, social services, ministry
Year founded: 1979
Phone: (314) 426 7000 ▪ (800) 321 5235
Web site:
www.netministries.org/see/charmin.exe/CM00647
Also called Lael University, this evangelical Christian school offers nonresident (residential study is also available) degrees at all levels in the above fields. The catalog states "LAEL teaches that psychology knows all the problems, Jesus Christ knows all the answers." Also: "Most courses can be completed in a few days. Send the answers in, we will mark your papers and mail your grade back to you." The examinations are unproctored. At one time, an accreditation candidate with the recognized TRACS agency, but no longer.

LaSalle University (1997 onward)
See: Orion College

Lembaga Manajemen International
Indonesia (LMII)   B, M, D
Wisma Benhil, 3rd Floor, #303
Jalan Sudirman Kav. 36
Jakarta 10210, Indonesia
Fields offered: Business administration, software engineering, management of technology
Phone: +62 (21) 570 2655
Fax: +62 (21) 570 4278
Email: lmii@indo.net.id
Web site: www.indo.net.id/lmii
This Indonesian school operates as some kind of franchise for Kennedy-Western degree programs; diplomas are issued by Kennedy-Western rather than LMII. The marketing literature states that Kennedy-Western "has one of the finest academic reputations in the United States." See the listing for Kennedy-Western University, also in this chapter.

Lexington University
Kwan Tai Foundation
3623 Canal St.
New Orleans, LA 70119
Year founded: 2000
Phone: (504) 488 8161
Fax: (504) 482 5258

In 1999, a colleague responded to a faculty-wanted notice from Columbus University (see listing in this chapter), the nonwonderful Louisiana institution whose only "public" address is a post office box, but which is registered to the Kwan Tai Foundation. In 2000, the colleague received a letter from the Kwan Tai Foundation, inviting him to apply to be on the faculty of Lexington University, which they say will be "an accredited distance learning based university with the unique purpose of offering opportunities for individuals to earn college credit while enrolled in job-training programs." Columbus University's accreditation is from the unrecognized and nonwonderful World Association of Universities and Colleges. It remains to be seen what accreditation path Lexington will follow.

Life Christian University   B, M, D
401 E. Chapman Rd.
Lutz, FL 33549
Year founded: 1995
Phone: (813) 909 9720
Fax: (813) 909 9730
Web site: www.lcus.edu
According to the literature, "established by the Lord in 1995," possibly with the assistance of the Life of Faith Ministries. They say they have campuses in 35 locations nationwide, and they are accredited by the unrecognized and less-than-wonderful Accrediting Commission International of Beebe, Arkansas.

London Institute of Technology
& Research   B, M, D
213 Borough High St.
London SE1 1JA , United Kingdom
Fields offered: Business administration, computer science, information technology
Year founded: 1987
Phone: +44 (20) 7787 4545
Fax: +44 (20) 7403 6276
Email: litrkazi@aol.com
Web site: www.litr.ac.uk
Our research into this institution has led to a number of troubling findings:

1) Although located in London, LITR claims its degree-granting authority comes from the U.S., that they are the British campus for a Stamford (that's right, Stamford with an "m") University, located in the state of New York (see listing in chapter 31). Stamford, they claim, is accredited by the New York State Education Department, the National Council for Private School Accreditation, and the International Association for Continuing Education and Training. Not one of these agencies had ever heard of Stamford University or LITR; in fact, the latter two don't even accredit higher education programs.

2) We traced Stamford University to an address in Jackson Heights, NY, home of Stamford Group USA Inc. The person who answered our calls there alternately claimed no knowledge of any university, or told us that the guy who runs the university is out of the office. We were told that Stamford Group is a "placement service" for international students.

3) In 2000, a number of LITR staff were found guilty of offenses under England's Trade Descriptions Act, specifically for falsely claiming in the school's prospectus that they held degrees from the University of London.

4) LITR was also found guilty of offenses under the Education Reform Act, for not making it clear that their degrees are not authorized by the British government.

5) Perhaps most puzzling of all, LITR offers a joint MBA degree with New York Institute of Technology, which is a regionally accredited and fully respectable American university. When we brought some of these findings to NYIT's attention, they didn't seem to have much of a response.

By the way, LITR offers business and computing degree at all levels.

London School of Business   M, D
1 Northumberland Ave.
London WCN 5BW, United Kingdom
Fields offered: Business
Phone: +44 (171) 872 5535
Fax: +44 (171) 753 2948
Email: londonmail@lsbamerica.org
Web site: www.lsbamerica.org/lsb.asp
The campus is a convenience address in London. The minimalist Web site says that their charter was granted by Queen Elizabeth in 1957. They are most emphatically not a Royal Chartered institution, and of course there is no connection with the long-established London Business School. The prospectus was "being revised" and was unavailable. No names of administrators or staff were available, although the Web site is registered to Harry Domicone in Arizona. There was a claimed affiliation with the "London School of Business in America," ostensibly in Arizona, where the campus is a mailbox rental service called Mail Box Shops in Scottsdale. Not surprisingly they are members of the unrecognized and nonwonderful World Association of Universities and Colleges.

London School of Business in America
See: London School of Business

Louisiana Capital College   B, M, D
P.O. Box 927572
San Diego, CA 92192
Fields offered: Many fields
Year founded: 1991
Web site: www.lcucollege.com
Claims that it is a "nontraditional degree granting institution of higher education in the State of Louisiana." The only address it provides is a post office box in San Diego, California. Claims that it is accredited by the Louisiana Capital Education Foundation. This organization cannot be located and appears to be an agency of the school's own creation. Claims that portfolio assessment is done by the International Education Research Foundation. The IERF is a foreign credential evaluator (see chapter 16) who told us they have never heard of Louisiana Capital College and that they don't do any experiential evaluations or evaluations of nontraditional education.

Louisiana Capital University
See: Louisiana Capital College

Madison University
P.O. Box 6627
Gulfport, MS 39506
Fields offered: Business, science, social science, law
Year founded: 2000
Phone: (228) 868 1010 ▓ (888) 661 8744
Fax: (228) 868 6624
Email: service@madisonu.com
Web site: www.madisonu.com
Degrees at all levels are offered by this new university that claims its accreditation from the dreadful and unrecognized World Association of Universities and Colleges. The street address is 424 Pass Road in Gulfport.

Magellan University
4320 N. Campbell, #230
Tucson, AZ 85718
Fields offered: Business, computer science
Year founded: 1996
Phone: (520) 299 3811 ▓ (800) 499 9338
Fax: (520) 299 3912
Email: response@magellan.edu
Web site: www.magellan.edu
After 25 years as an administrator at the University of Arizona, Dr. William Noyes founded this online university. While only certificate courses are offered online now (professional and computer areas), there are plans for bachelor's and master's degrees in business, management, history & culture, quality control, and related areas.

Maimonides University   B, M, D
16666 NE 19th Ave., #102
North Miami Beach, FL 33162
Fields offered: Psychology, theology, counseling
Year founded: 1989
Phone: (305) 949 1103
Fax: (954) 725 8414
Email: info@maimonidesuniversity.com
Web site: maimonidesuniversity.com
Established by Stefano DiMauro, whose medical degree was earned in Italy, followed by a Ph.D. from Pacific Western. Appropriately licensed by the state of Florida, but not accredited. Residential or distance degrees at all levels. The doctorate can be largely based on a "DPKE," a demonstration of professional knowledge and expertise instead of a thesis or dissertation. The literature says "The DPKE could be a series of articles, a book, a piece of music, a painting or any other valuable work; the original to remain the property of the University." Dr. DiMauro is listed as President, Chancellor, and Professor of theology, biblical studies, and religious studies. Other faculty are listed, but without the source of their degrees. Applicants are invited to apply for a bachelor's, master's, and doctorate simultaneously, and are offered a 20% discount for so doing.

Marlborough University   B, M, D
Suite 14, 8th Floor, Panjaphat Building

Surawong Rd.
Bangkok 10500, Thailand
Fields offered: Many fields
Web site: www.marled.com

Run from Thailand, "registered" in Hawaii, with an "Academic Studies Co-ordination Centre" in Gibraltar. They appear to be an assessment institution, awarding degrees upon evaluation of life experience, with "honours" degrees costing $200 extra. The prospectus says that their program "allows you to convert your work and life experience into a degree—without additional study." One merely fills out a brief application, and the school informs you what degree they consider you qualified for. For some reason, they sell this book, *Bears' Guide*, on their Web site—for about three times the cost of buying it from a bookstore or online service. Formerly used an address in Guernsey and in Sark, in the English Channel.

Masters Institute   A
50 Airport Parkway
San Jose, CA 95110
Fields offered: Systems administration
Year founded: 1974
Phone: (877) 939 0788
Fax: (916) 937 0786
Email: suggestions@mastersinstitute.edu
Web site: www.mastersinstitute.edu

A Silicon Valley school offering, among its many certificate programs for IT professionals, an Associate of Applied Science in Systems Administration. All courses delivered over the Internet. Approved by the state of California, and fairly aggressive in their marketing, once someone has made an initial inquiry.

MBA University
See: Rushmore University

Medical College of Alternative Medicines
See: Open University of Alternative Medicines

Mellen University   B, M, D
101 First St. SW
Mt. Vernon, IA 52314
Year founded: 1993
Phone: (800) 635 5368
Web site: www.mellenuniversity.edu

The university is an outgrowth of the Edwin Mellen Press. In a long cover story, the respected academic magazine *Lingua Franca* called it "a quasi-vanity press cunningly disguised as an academic publishing house . . . the brainchild of Herbert Richardson, a former University of Toronto professor of religion and one-time Moonie apologist with a Ph.D. in the sociology of religion from Harvard . . ." Richardson sued the magazine (and lost) over this article, published in the September 1993 issue (available for $6 from *Lingua Franca*, 135 Madison Avenue, New York, NY 10016; (212) 684 9884; *www.linguafranca.com*). Advertising in the *Toronto Globe and Mail*, Mellen University has offered "a fully accredited British M.Phil or Ph.D. by writing a thesis for external examination." Mellen claims to be accredited because they are chartered on the commonwealth island of Turks and Caicos, and follow the British system of "quality control (accreditation)." The catalog says "Mellen University has earned a license from the government of the Turks and Caicos Islands and, virtually, the British government." The "virtually" is presumably because Turks is a commonwealth country. *Lingua Franca* wrote that Mellen's first graduating class consisted of 11 ministers from North Carolina who "were interviewed for half an hour each by Frederic Will (whose field is comparative literature), after which Will deemed all 11 candidates qualified for Ph.D.'s." A long front-page article in the *Toronto Globe and Mail* suggested that the University of Toronto, where Professor Richardson then had tenure, was considering dismissing him, and that Richardson planned to contest this, should it happen. (They did, and he apparently didn't.) Mellen advertises a bachelor's degree based on life experience. A friend—who has two earned doctorates—left a message on their answering machine asking for a catalog. He instead received a letter saying, "Based on our conversation, achieving the degree you so richly deserve is well within your grasp. It is amazing how many are like yourself, with all the knowledge and experience, and without the recognition and credentials." Dr. Richardson announced his intent to open the University of Western Kansas in Dodge City, but the *Washington Post*, in an unflattering story on Mellen, said this plan has fallen through. In 1997, Mellen's director of admissions, John Tulip, after publicly claiming there were affiliations with accredited schools in Romania, which we challenged, wrote us proposing to "put the feud aside" and let me "convince you of the legitimacy of the Mellen program." After five reminders to Mr. Tulip, he replied simply to say that he was no longer affiliated with the school. Mellen subsequently began using an address in Iowa. This report from a colleague who visited the campus in early 2000: "It is a one-time storefront downtown, now partitioned into offices. The woman at the desk said she rents out the offices and that she's rented to Mellen University for a few years—that 'they come in occasionally to work on the computers but usually aren't there.'" When we go to Mellen's Web site, we get the message "You are not authorized to view this page."

Mesmer Institute
See: University of God's Logos System

Miami Christian University   B
9775 S.W. 87th Ave.
Miami, FL 33176-2900
Fields offered: Theological field
Phone: (305) 595 5315
Fax: (305) 596 4564
Email: greene@mcu.edu
Web site: www.mcu.edu

MCU, operated by the Jesus Fellowship of Miami, offers courses and degrees in theological fields over the Internet, through a program of mentored study. The school is authorized to operate in the state of Florida, and committed to the use of cutting-edge technology feeling, as they do, that "the Lord has created these tools to be used for the advancement of His kingdom, and MCU is in the vanguard of this move of God."

Midwestern University
See: Saint John's University of Practical Theology

National College of Complimentary
Medicine and Sciences   B, M, D
1025 Connecticut Ave. NW, #1012
Washington, DC 20036
Fields offered: Medical and scientific fields
Year founded: 1990
Phone: (202) 857 9727
Fax: (202) 635 7554
Email: nccmedsci@aol.com
Web site: members.aol.com/nccmedsci

The campus in Washington is a mailbox rental and office service company called The Office Club. This school offers unaccredited degrees at all levels in seven "interdisciplinary mission fields of study": nursing, medical/ scientific letters, ND vitalogic occupations, intrinsic naturopathy, medical & scientific stewardship, social & community health, and mission services. Regarding their name, they say that "the letter 'i' in compl-i-mentary signifies honor and benevolence." Regarding accreditation, they say they are unaccredited due to their uniqueness. OK.

New Yorker University
See: Yorker International University

newGraduate School of Architecture   M
2900 West Jackson St., Suite 202
Muncie, IN 47304
Fields offered: Architecture
Phone: (765) 286 5613
Email: newgraduate@newgraduate.org
Web site: www.newgraduate.org

Offers a Master of Architecture degree program designed for already-practicing professionals. Courses, all delivered over the Internet, focus on aspects of the profession often ignored by traditional schools, including environmental design and the business of architecture.

Newport Asia Pacific University   M
5000 Birch St., Suite 4000
Newport Beach, CA 92660
Fields offered: International business, TESOL, intercultural relations
Year founded: 1996
Phone: (949) 260 2004
Fax: (949) 260 2099
Email: edcenter@japan.cp.jp
Web site: www.asiapacificu.edu

This California-approved school offers master's degrees in the three above-named fields, entirely by online study, although non-U.S. students must attend a four-day residential session in Japan each year. The top administrators had all been associated with Kensington University. Alternative address: 444 Lunalilo Home Rd., #705,

Honolulu, HI 96825. Name changed in 2000 from Asia Pacific Open University. Students outside the U.S. deal directly with NAPU's agent, the Distance Learning Centre in Japan: *www.distance-learning.org*.

Newport International University
See: Newport University

Newport University   B, M, D, Law
20101 S.W. Birch St., Suite 120
Newport Beach, CA 92660
Fields offered: Business, education, psychology, human behavior, law, engineering, religion
Year founded: 1976
Phone: (949) 757 1155 ▪ (800) 345 3272
Fax: (949) 757 1156
Email: info@newport.edu
Web site: www.newport.edu

Students earn credit towards their degrees through directed independent study, practicums, seminars, and workshops. Web site lists administrators in countries all over the world; for the U.S. there is a South Dakota address listed in addition to the one in California. Claims accreditation from the unrecognized International Association of Schools, Colleges, and Universities, whose email domain name happens to be owned by Newport University at an address shared by Newport's office in Belgium. Originally known as Newport International University. In 1997 some assets of Newport were sold and renamed as Westport University, operating from Utah (apparently now in association with the unaccredited Hawthorne University).

North American University (Arizona)   B, M, D
13402 N. Scottsdale Rd., B-150
Scottsdale, AZ 85254-4056
Fields offered: Religious and health-related fields
Year founded: 1992
Phone: (480) 948 5100 ▪ (800) 398 8484
Fax: (480) 948 8150

NAU offers degrees at all levels in health and religious fields, including pastoral psychology, pastoral wellness, psychotherapy, Christian spirituality, and comparative religion, entirely through distance learning. Credit for life experience and equivalency exams. Its College of Wellness Science has absorbed some of the programs offered by the now defunct American College of Nutripathy. Apparently no connection with a diploma mill of the same name which operated from Arizona and Florida in the 1980s, or another diploma mill of this name which operated from Utah and Hawaii in the 1990s. The address happens to be the same as that for the branch office of Ottawa University, a properly accredited Kansas school; we are not aware of any connection between the two.

Northcentral University (Arizona)   B, M, D
505 West Whipple St.
Prescott, AZ 86301
Fields offered: Business management, psychology.
Year founded: 1996
Phone: (520) 541 7777 ▪ (800) 903 9381

Fax: (520) 541 7817
Email: enroll@ncu.edu
Web site: www.ncu.edu

Northcentral University offers bachelor's, master's, and doctorate degrees in various fields, based on self-paced learning, with faculty supervision ("guides, not teachers," they say), with a dissertation required for the Ph.D. Under the same ownership as the Southern California University for Professional Studies (a California-approved school), NCU is provisionally licensed under an Arizona law that permits schools to operate as long as they are making "reasonable and timely" progress toward recognized accreditation. The university applied to their regional accreditor, the North Central Association (no relation) in 1999; a site visit was held in early 2000, and, according to a Public Disclosure Notice written by the accreditor, and posted on the university's Web site, the application was withdrawn four months later. The university reports that the accreditation visit was generally positive, but there were some issues with the doctoral programs. The university has reduced the number of doctoral fields from four to two, and plans to apply again. When, in early 2000, John drove past the large and attractive red brick building depicted on the back of the catalog, he was surprised to note that the university occupied only a small space in that building. They have subsequently moved to their own building in Prescott. There is no connection with the regionally accredited North Central University in Minnesota.

Northland Open University   B, M

204 Lambert St., Financial Plaza, #200
Whitehorse, Yukon Y1A 3T2, Canada
Fields offered: Arts, commerce, business administration
Year founded: 1976
Phone: (800) 263 1619

Northland was established in 1976 by George Korey, founder of the Canadian School of Management, for the purpose (according to their literature) of providing mid-career professionals with access to degree-path higher learning. The address was in Yellowknife, Northwest Territories, although when John met with NWT education officials in 1986, none of them had ever heard of the university. The school has claimed to be "a standard-setting and examining body," which conducts no courses, but offers exams and evaluates prior learning. Northland has had a longtime affiliation with the Canadian School of Management and indeed appeared to operate from the same address in Toronto for a time. At one time, doctorates were offered.

Northwestern International University   B, M, D

Lautruphoj 1 – 3
Ballerup 2750, Denmark
Fields offered: Many fields
Phone: +45 (44) 20 98 30
Fax: +45 (44) 20 99 10
Email: information@universitydegree.com
Web site: www.universitydegree.com

According to its Web site, Northwestern International University is a corporation registered in Cyprus with its administrative office in Denmark. Students are awarded credit through a combination of life experience and a short course of the student's own design: "Our students are allowed to pick the textbook or textbooks that they feel are the most appropriate for their needs." All degrees cost under $400. Almost all the listed faculty members are professors in Russian universities. Accredited by the Euro-American Accreditation Agency, which is, in their own words, "a division of Northwestern International University."

Nova College

See: Farelston & Nova Colleges

Occidental University of Saint Louis

See: Greenwich University

Omega University   B, M, D

87 Sunapee St.
Newport, NH 03773
Fields offered: Hypnotherapy, holistic studies, parapsychology, divinity
Email: info@omegauniversity.com
Web site: www.omegauniversity.com

Offers degrees at all levels in hypnotherapy, holistic studies, and parapsychology, as well as a Doctor of Divinity. Credits are earned through a combination of correspondence coursework and life experience assessment. Claims accreditation from the World Organization of Institutes, Colleges, and Universities, an agency we've never heard of and could not locate.

Open International University for Alternative Medicines   B, D

80 Chowringhee Rd.
Calcutta 700 020, India
Fields offered: Alternative medicine
Phone: +91 (33) 247 0157
Fax: +91 (33) 240 2792
Email: info@altmeduniversity.com
Web site: www.altmeduniversity.com

Distance-learning bachelor and doctoral programs in alternative medicines, Indo allopathy, yoga & massage, bio-chemic, electro-homeopathy, naturopathy, Bach flower treatment, Reiki healing, accupressure, magnetotherapy, medicinal herbalism, gem-tele-chromo, hypnotherapy, aromatherapy, pyramid healing (in case you have a sick pyramid), and medical astrology. Accredited by the unrecognized and nonwonderful World Association of Universities and Colleges. Formerly the Indian Institute of Alternative Medicines.

Open University of Alternative Medicines   B, M, D

3 Canal St.
Calcutta 700 014, India
Fields offered: Alternative medicine, homeopathy, phylosophy [sic]
Phone: +91 (33) 471 8394
Fax: +91 (33) 471 2164
Web site: www.angelfire.com/ak/ouam

It would appear from its Web site as if this institution, accredited by the unrecognized and nonwonderful World Association of Universities and Colleges, awards degrees at all levels, including the M.D., following one or two years of distance learning, at a total cost of $300 to $450. They claim to have awarded more than 40,000 degrees and credentials. In a lengthy autobiography, Chancellor Biswas explains that he was "never bound by the limitations of established conventions. He is a man of imagination with the capacity to give his imagination a well-planned complete shape, a man always suffering from the pain of creating something new, and each one of his creations gives birth to the pain of creating something new again. Thus his life is a history of continuous search for the ultimate, and he leaves no stone unturned to achieve his goal." Also known as the Medical College of Alternative Medicines.

Open University of America   B, M, D
3916 Commander Dr.
Hyattsville, MD 20782
Fields offered: Many fields
Year founded: 1968
Phone: (301) 779 0220

Established in 1968 by Drs. Daniel and Mary Rodgers, this school grants degrees entirely on the basis of prior achievements. The catalog is large and, at first glance, impressive. But in response to a routine request for information, Chancellor Rodgers wrote back saying, "Your attempt to extort data from me by blackmail method [sic] is reprehensible . . . Be advised that you are not at liberty to criticize, extol, describe, interpret or represent knowledge about the Open University of America in any way." Years ago, John visited the "campus," a private home in a nice neighborhood. When he expressed interest in the university (he was not asked to identify himself), he was taken into the basement of the home, where Chancellor Rodger's elderly mother was at work stuffing envelopes. We can't determine whether they are still operating, but in 2000, the university number was still listed with the phone company, although the phone was answered merely, "Hello." Not approved by the Maryland Board for Higher Education. We shall say no more.

Orion College   B, M
P.O. Box 4000
Mandeville, LA 70470
Fields offered: Business administration, management, computer science, engineering technology, engineering management, criminal justice, general studies, paralegal studies, psychology
Year founded: 1997
Phone: (504) 626 3500 ▪ (800) 283 0017
Fax: (504) 674 2553
Email: inquire@distance.edu
Web site: www.distance.edu
Note: Formerly known as LaSalle University which, prior to mid-1997 and under different ownership, was a degree mill (see listing in chapter 27). The following listing pertains to the school

known as LaSalle University from mid-1997 to 2000 and Orion College thereafter.

Orion College has been operated since mid-1997 by the LaSalle Education Corporation, a Louisiana corporation run by a five-member Board of Trustees, all of them politically active Louisiana citizens. It is a nonprofit educational foundation. Orion offers bachelor's and master's degrees entirely by distance learning, in a wide variety of subjects. Doctoral degrees were dropped in 1999 preparatory to applying for accreditation from the Distance Education and Training Council. They were not successful in this application but plan to try again. It is still a real concern that their Web site continues to state that "LaSalle University was established in 1973 to meet the growing educational demands of adult students." The name LaSalle was not used publicly until the mid-1980s, and the school did not operate lawfully until 1997.

Oxford International University
See: Bircham International University

Pacific Southern University (California)   B, M, D
9581 W. Pico Blvd.
Los Angeles, CA 90035-1248
Fields offered: Business, management science, social science, engineering, education
Year founded: 1978
Phone: (310) 551 0304
Fax: (310) 277 5280

Degrees at all levels in the above fields by directed non-resident independent study. Approved to grant degrees by the state of California. Also registered in Hawaii at 7 Waterfront Plaza #400, Honolulu 96813 (a mail forwarding service).

Pacific University of Hawaii
See: International University of Professional Studies

Pacific Western University (California)   B, M, D
600 North Sepulveda Blvd.
Los Angeles, CA 90049
Fields offered: Business administration, public administration, management
Year founded: 1977
Phone: (310) 471 0306 ▪ (800) 423 3244
Fax: (310) 471 0306
Email: admissions@pwu.com
Web site: www.pwu-ca.edu

B.S. in business administration or public administration, an MBA, an M.S. in management, and a Ph.D. in business administration, with numerous areas of specialization (marketing, management, health service administration, criminal justice, etc.). Each course has a midterm and final examination, and a written research paper. The doctorate includes an oral defense of the dissertation. Same ownership as Pacific Western University (Hawaii), which is run by the same people from the same building.

Pacific Western University (Hawaii)   B, M, D

1210 Auahi St.
Honolulu, HI 96814-4922
Fields offered: Business, management, science, engineering, social science, education, helping professions
Year founded: 1977
Phone: (808) 597 1909 ▪ (800) 423 3244
Fax: (310) 587 8603
Email: admissions@pwu.com
Web site: www.pwu.com

The school's literature states that "all degree programs are primarily based on what the student has already learned. If the student is worthy, competent, and eminently qualified, the University will confer the appropriate degree." The program includes preparation of a resume/learning portfolio, a "warrant" (a 600-word essay on the student's career field), a bachelor's thesis (8 pages) or qualifying exercise (12 pages), a master's project or doctoral dissertation. In 1997, the State of Hawaii Department of Consumer Affairs sued Pacific Western, claiming violation of the state law relating to disclosure of non-accreditation, and demanding that all students and alumni wishing a refund be given one. Around the same time, the national television program *American Journal* did a segment on PWU, in which they showed an empty room in Hawaii as the "campus" there (the university is run from Los Angeles), and claimed one of their staff members was able to complete a master's degree in less than two weeks (a charge later disputed by PWU, but no legal action was taken).

Patriot University   B, M, D

2035 Church Ave.
Alamosa, CO 81101
Fields offered: Theology, business
Phone: (719) 587 9332

This fundamentalist Christian school apparently operates from a private home in Colorado, from which they award degrees in religious and secular subjects. (A person who is not a fan of theirs has posted an amusing annotated photograph on the Internet at *www.geocities.com/odonate/patriot.htm*.) Their accreditation is from the unrecognized American Accrediting Association of Theological Institutions, whose literature suggests that they accredit on payment of a $100 fee.

Permaculture Academy   B

P.O. Box 1
Tyalgum, NSW 2484, Australia
Fields offered: Education, media, community services, finance & business, technical & resource development, architecture & building, research, site design & development

Diplomas and bachelor's degrees in the above fields, using the principles of the open university, and specializing in educating people in poverty, those in remote locations, or others not served by traditional institutions. Courses can be convened anywhere a teacher (approved by the Academy) and a group of 15 or more students can be assembled. The programs are all based on the concept of permaculture, a human-centered ecological philosophy that seeks sustainable farming methods, community building, conservation, and other worthwhile things.

Pickering University   B, M, D

1155 Fort St. Mall
Honolulu, HI 96813
Fields offered: Many fields
Year founded: 1994
Phone: (808) 523 3338 ▪ (888) 871 5181
Fax: (808) 531 1270
Email: info@pickering.edu
Web site: www.pickering.edu

The "campus" is a mailbox service called Island Mail Service Centers. They identify themselves as "United Congregational Church Society of Friends Group." This school offers degrees at all levels by a combination of traditional correspondence, video, software, and Internet courses. Fields of study include theological studies, liberal arts, business management, computer science, environmental studies, and more. Accreditation is claimed from the unrecognized Association of Christian Schools and Colleges.

Portland College   B, M

1102 West Babcock St.
Bozeman, MT 59715
Fields offered: Business administration, global leadership, human resource management, knowledge management, marketing management, multimedia technology, psychology, teaching, instructional design, Internet strategies
Year founded: 2000
Fax: (801) 729 5904
Email: info@portlandcollege.edu
Web site: www.portlandcollege.edu

A completely virtual university owned by the Intelligent Learning Corporation, an educational software company and developer of proprietary online course delivery systems. Online master's and bachelor's degrees in the above fields.

Preston University   B, M, D

1204 Airport Parkway
Cheyenne, WY 82001
Fields offered: Business administration, computer science
Year founded: 1976
Phone: (307) 634 1440
Fax: (307) 634 3091
Email: admissions@preston.edu
Web site: www.wyoming.com/~preston

Offers degrees at all levels in business administration and computer science, through a range of distance-learning methods. There are affiliated campuses in many other countries. While this seems to be a sincere endeavor, a few questions remain, especially their accreditation claimed from the unrecognized and nonwonderful World

Association of Universities and Colleges, which they feature without mentioning that it is an unrecognized agency. Earlier literature said that the school was first established in Pakistan in the mid-1980s (the president is Dr. Abdul Basit) and came to the U.S. a decade later.

Robaco Global   M
8 Nesburn Rd.
High Barnes SR4 7LR, United Kingdom
Fields offered: Teaching English as a foreign language
Phone: +44 (410) 794 056
Fax: +44 (191) 551 9102
Email: admim@robaco.net
Web site: www.robaco.net

Offers certificates, diplomas, and a master's in teaching English as a foreign language. According to the Web site, the master's is "externally moderated" by Trinity College & University (U.K.), a highly suspect institution that backdates diplomas (see listing in this chapter).

Robert Kennedy University   B, M, D, Law
95 Leutschenbachstrasse
Zurich 8050, Switzerland
Fields offered: Business administration, law
Phone: +41 (1) 308 3908 ▪ (800) 966 8176
Fax: +41 (1) 308 3512
Email: admission@college.ch
Web site: www.kennedyuniversity.com

They call themselves a "Univerisity [*sic*] Without Walls." Perhaps a "univerisity" is something different from a university, but we can find nothing positive in the way they present themselves, offering distance degrees at all levels, including law, ostensibly from Switzerland (though all email comes from Italy). Further, the literature we have seen states that they are "the First Reality in Switzerland that gives you the possibility to continue your studies totally at home or in office, in your own peace" [*sic, sic,* and *sic*]. No names are mentioned in the badly written, badly spelled, and badly designed literature we have seen. Their "Castle Campus" turns out to be a city-owned historic building in which they rent rooms a few times a year. The small "world class faculty" has included Professor Emir Mohammed, identified as "an accomplished academic [and] recognized world-wide as an expert on distance education." Professor Mohammed is, in fact, a young Trinidadian (early 20s) living in Canada. When we asked Dean Costa if the university had permission from the Robert Kennedy family to use the name, he told us it was named after a "New York banker" of the same name, but declined to give us any further information.

Rockwell College of Arts and Sciences
See: Eurotechnical Research University

Romano Byzantine College   B, M, D
2123 West 5th St. # 2
Duluth, MN 55806
Fields offered: Christian liberal education, pastoral psychology, theology, canon law, holistic healing

Year founded: 1995
Phone: (218) 733 9676
Fax: (218) 733 0349

Part of the Romano Byzantine Orthodox Catholic Church. Offers distance-learning degree programs in Christian liberal education, pastoral psychology, theology, canon law, and a host of related disciplines. Claims accreditation from the unrecognized Universal Accrediting Commission for Schools, Colleges and Universities (Athens, Greece).

Rushmore University   B, M, D
370 Anchor Dr., #250
Dakota Dunes, SD 57049
Fields offered: Business administration
Year founded: 1995
Phone: (605) 232 6037
Fax: (508) 302 0558
Email: drcox@rushmore.edu
Web site: www.rushmore.edu

Owner Michael Cox is now up-front in the school materials about lack of accreditation, and about his credentials for the enterprise. The sell sheet that comes with the modest catalog is titled "How I raised myself from failure to success by using nontraditional, unaccredited, distance learning." The address is a business service that forwards the mail and calls to the owner in Georgia. Prior to the recent change in its accreditation statement, Rushmore had claimed accreditation from as many as five different unrecognized agencies, at least two of them apparently nonexistent. Now they have one of the longest explanations of "why we are not accredited" that we've ever seen. Nonetheless, we find statements like, "These degrees have the same legal validity as the degrees offered by any of the top programs in the United States" misleading. The words are true, but the implication is that the Rushmore degrees are just as useful, which they surely are not. Original name: MBA University.

Saint Clair University
4846 N. University Dr., #281
Lauderhill, FL 33351
Fields offered: Business
Email: info@stclairuniversity.org
Web site: www.stclairuniversity.org

The minimalist half-page Web site refers to business degrees at all levels offered online. The Florida address appears to be a convenience address. There is no listed telephone number there for the university, and the Web site is registered to an address in Sylvania, Ohio. There is also a post office box address in Nassau, Bahamas.

Saint Clements University   B, M, D
Churchill Building Front St.
Grand Turk, Turk & Caicos Islands
Fields offered: Professional studies, business administration
Year founded: 1995
Phone: +61 (8) 8342 0088
Fax: +61 (8) 8269 4931
Email: admin@stclements.edu

Web site: www.stclements.edu

Although the school is registered in the Turks and Caicos Islands (which has no government accreditation program), St. Clements' Web site is registered to Earls Tavern, a bar located in Adelaide, South Australia, run by "Prof. Dr." David LeCornu. LeCornu has admitted that his "Dr." title is for "internal purposes only"; however, in his role as vice president of the World Association of Universities and Colleges (an unrecognized and nonwonderful accrediting agency), he seems to brandish the "Dr." title quite freely. In its literature, St. Clements removed all mention of its Australian administration after it came under scrutiny by the South Australian Accreditation and Registration Council. Also claims a "diploma of recognition" from the Association Internationale des Educateurs pour la Paix Mondiale, which is generously awarded to anyone who believes in world peace and human rights. St. Clements appears to be aggressively marketed in Nigeria.

Saint George University International   A, B, M, D

Tokushima-Prefecture, Tokushima-City
Kawauchi-cho, Tsurushima 337-1-901, Japan
Fields offered: Many fields
Year founded: 1997
Email: japan@stgeorgeuniversity.edu
Web site: www.stgeorgeuniversity.edu

Degrees offered at all levels in a broad range of subjects from a school established to provide handicapped people with distance education; non-disabled people can enroll as well. Supposedly a residential campus in Oxford, England. We have concerns about some of the claims made in the school's prospectus, including its affiliation with other institutions in other countries. Accredited by the unrecognized International University Accreditation Foundation, whose domain name (*iuaf.org*) is owned by (you guessed it) St. George University. The school is not listed in any standard directory of schools.

Saint John's University of Practical Theology   B, M, D

31916 University Circle
Springfield, LA 70462-8243
Fields offered: Many fields
Year founded: 1969
Phone: (504) 294 2129
Fax: (504) 294 2157
Email: st.johns@i-55.com
Web site: www.i-55.com/~stjohn

St. John's University of Practical Theology offers degrees in religion and theology, metaphysics, psychology, addictionology, hypnotherapy, parapsychology, business, police science, social justice, security and private investigation, social services, education, and journalism. Hundreds of home-study classes, ranging from foot reflexology to "the confidence man" to "creating a succe$$ful hypnotherapy center." The only required attendance is at the graduation ceremonies, although this can be waived for incarcerated students, those in the military, or those suffering disabilities that limit their ability to travel. Accreditation is claimed from two unrecognized theological agencies. Dr. Winkler has complained about our listing the last

three words of the school name, but they appear prominently on the school sign on the highway just past the Crawgator Lounge. When John drove by in late 1997, he found a modest building on a one-lane country road called "Shelly Lane." It is presumably St. Johns' driveway that has been named "University Circle." No one was home that day. Formerly in Nebraska and Ponchatoula, Louisiana. Former names: Eastern Nebraska Christian College and Midwestern University. No relation to another unaccredited St. John's University that operated from New Orleans in the 1980s.

Saraydarian University

P.O. Box 7068
Cave Creek, AZ 85327
Year founded: 2000
Phone: (480) 502 1909
Email: info@tsg-publishing.com
Web site: www.saraydarianuniversity.org

Established to teach the "higher principles and values of ageless wisdom" through correspondence courses.

School of Natural Health Sciences

Hudson & James Ltd.
103 Queen St.
Newton Abbot TQ12 2BG, United Kingdom
Fields offered: Natural health
Phone: +44 (700) 900 0166
Email: info@learnbymail.com
Web site: www.learnbymail.com/main

Offers distance-learning courses in natural health fields. Bachelor's, master's, and doctorates awarded through the highly suspect Trinity College & University (U.K) (see listing in this chapter). Like Trinity, claims to be a division of "The United Interdenominational Church."

Senior University International   B, M, D

200-2900 Simpson Rd.
Richmond, BC V6X 2P9, Canada
Fields offered: Many fields
Year founded: 1993
Phone: +1 (604) 244 7754 ▩ (800) 939 7822
Fax: +1 (604) 244 9952
Email: registrar@senioru.bc.ca
Web site: www.senioru.edu

Based in British Columbia but without degree-granting authority there, SUI claims its authority to grant degrees by its license from the state of Wyoming's Department of Education. Offers wholly nonresident, individually tailored, self-paced degree programs in a wide range of fields, including consciousness studies, Middle Eastern studies, military studies, and women's studies. Co-established and partly owned by Dr. Les Carr, principal owner of Columbia Pacific University. Has claimed accreditation from the Academy for the Promotion of International Culture and Scientific Exchange (APICS), an unrecognized agency.

SERSI Freie und Private Universität   M, D

Degersheimerstrasse 29
Herisau AR 9102, Switzerland

Fields offered: Industrial sciences, industrial engineering, applied sciences, communication techniques, sociology
Year founded: 1982
Phone: +41 (71) 352 35 25
Fax: +41 (71) 352 25 60
Email: sersi@unihe.ch
Web site: www.unihe.ch

The university is not recognized by the Swiss Central Office for Higher Education, and the degrees are not recognized in Germany. Accreditation is claimed from the unrecognized and nonwonderful World Association of Universities and Colleges. Degrees offered in a wide range of subjects. Applicants must have worked "at a high professional level" for at least three years; in the past, students have been "offered the opportunity to turn their prior academic experience, expertise, and skills into a doctoral dissertation..." They also use the English (Private and Independent University), French (Université Libre et Privé), and Italian (Universita Libera e Privata) versions of their name.

SERSI Private and Independent University
See: SERSI Freie und Private Universität

Soka University of America   M
26800 W. Mulholland Highway
Calabasas, CA 91302
Fields offered: Education
Year founded: 1987
Phone: (818) 880 6400
Fax: (818) 880 9326
Web site: www.soka.edu

Soka currently offers an M.A. in second & foreign language education, and plans to gradually expand its curriculum, focusing on education, Pacific Rim studies, and liberal arts. Approved to operate in the state of California, the school is affiliated with the accredited Soka University based in Tokyo. While nonreligious, the school is founded on Buddhist principles.

South Atlantic University   B, M, D
Department 50, 10 College Terrace
Docklands, London E3 5AN, United Kingdom
Fields offered: Engineering & technology, business administration, management, sciences, liberal arts, tourism & hospitality
Year founded: 1998
Phone: +44 (181) 989 4122
Fax: +44 (181) 530 8065
Email: uk-office@southatlantic.demon.co.uk
Web site: sau.hypermart.net

Established in 1998 in Karachi, Pakistan, to offer nontraditional degrees in business, computer science, engineering, and other fields (but presumably not geography, since Pakistan is not exactly a south Atlantic nation). According to SAU's Web site, day-to-day management and administration takes place at an office in London. The school's U.S. office is a private residence in the state of Ohio. Claims accreditation from the unrecognized and dubious Council of Post Secondary Accreditation.

"Don't cry, Laughing Bear. Now Mommy can be a stay-at-home mom *and* a full-time student."

Southeastern Institute of Technology   M, D
200 Sparkman Dr.
Huntsville, AL 35807
Fields offered: Applied science, engineering, management, business administration
Year founded: 1976
Phone: (256) 837 9726
Web site: www.spie.org/web/oped/oped20a.html

They offer state-approved, though unaccredited, degrees in engineering and science, with a specialty in optics and a focus on defense and space matters. Courses are offered residentially or by "continuing education." The Web site is copyrighted by the International Society for Optical Engineering.

Southern California University for Professional Studies (SCUPS)   B, M, D, Law
1840 East 17th St.
Santa Ana, CA 92705-8605
Fields offered: Business administration, management of engineering, technology, liberal studies, psychology, criminal studies, law
Year founded: 1978
Phone: (714) 480 0800 ▪ (800) 477 2254
Fax: (714) 480 0834

Email: enroll@scups.edu

Web site: www.scups.edu

Approved to operate in the state of California, SCUPS offers distance-learning degrees at all levels in the above fields. The law school's J.D. program qualifies graduates to sit for the California bar. SCUPS advertises heavily in Asia, using the initials SCU which, our mail tells us, some people confuse with the prestigious USC. In April 1997, the *Chronicle of Higher Education* reported that SCUPS had been called a diploma mill by the Thai government and banned from Thailand. In the early 1990s, SCUPS distributed what they claimed was a reprint of their listing in this book, but they had changed it to make it more favorable to the school. Same ownership as Northcentral University in Arizona.

Southern Pacific University   B, M, D

8120 Loma Del Norte N.E.

Albuquerque, NM 87109

Year founded: 1998

Phone: (505) 292 9050

Fax: (505) 292 7466

Email: spuni@flash.net

Web site: www.spuni.edu

They began advertising their degree programs in Asia, despite lacking any licensing or approval in their own state of New Mexico, or anywhere else. When we questioned their operation, the response was quite hostile. However, subsequently, in the spring of 1998, proprietor Anil Verna decided we were not so dreadful, and politely communicated the fact that he was now seeking New Mexico licensing before marching onward. Two years later, SPU, whose campus is an answering service called Alternative Business Communications in Albuquerque, claims to have incorporated in Delaware and on the Caribbean island of Turks and Caicos. We find their accreditation statement disingenuous. In a section called "Accreditation/memberships" (the "/" was added later), they list their membership in a trade association (International Technology Education), which anyone can join. If the section were just called "Memberships," then no problem.

Southwest Graduate School

See: Southwest University

Southwest University   B, M

2200 Veterans Blvd.

Kenner, LA 70062

Fields offered: Business administration, criminal justice, administrative studies, health services administration, organizational management

Year founded: 1982

Phone: (504) 468 2900 ▦ (800) 433 5923

Fax: (504) 468 3213

Email: southwst@southwest.edu

Web site: www.southwest.edu

Southwest was established in 1982, in Phoenix, Arizona, by its president, Dr. Grayce Lee, and administrator Dr. Reg Sheldrick, and is now appropriately licensed in Louisiana. (The latter also established the school now called Newport University.) Southwest maintains a curriculum development office in Omaha, Nebraska. Offers credit for experiential learning, and through correspondence courses, research projects, and a thesis or dissertation. When John visited in late 1997, he found a ten-room suite of offices in a commercial building near the New Orleans airport. Southwest applied to the Distance Education and Training Council in 1997. That process was put "on hold" by mutual agreement.

Stanton University (Hawaii)   B, M, D

101 Kaahumanu Ave., Suite H

Kahului, HI 96732

Fields offered: Education, engineering, management, psychology, languages

Year founded: 1999

Phone: (830) 825 9404 ▦ (877) 988 2288

Fax: (830) 825 9405

Email: admission@stanton.edu

Web site: www.stanton.edu

The campus address is a mailbox service in Hawaii. The Web site is associated with Egbert Phipps of Vancouver, Canada (see also George Washington University, Inc.; chapter 31), and Jacqueline May, whose telephone is in New Braunfels, Texas. (The people in Texas deny that Phipps is involved.) The university address given for Internet registration is 8550 United Plaza Boulevard, Baton Rouge, Louisiana 70809. The "Student Service Center" is a mailbox rental service in Marble Falls, Texas. Accreditation is claimed from the dubious Accrediting Commission International and the Association Internationale des Educateurs pour la Paix Mondiale.

Stellar International Institute   M

7532 W. Indian School Rd., Suite B

Phoenix, AZ 85033

Fields offered: Leadership

Phone: (623) 873 5824

Email: info@sii.edu

Web site: www.sii.edu

Their 36-unit master's in leadership is available residentially or entirely online. Owned by the Arizona Institute of Business and Technology, an accredited two-year for-profit junior college.

Summit University   B, M, D

7508 Hayne Blvd.

New Orleans, LA 70126

Fields offered: Many fields

Year founded: 1988

Phone: (504) 241 0227

Fax: (504) 243 1243

Email: sul-info@summitunivofla.edu

Web site: www.summitunivofla.edu

Summit University is a religious institution, operating as an "assessment university," sharing a small house with American Coastline University. They have the stated mission of "critically assessing a person's lifelong learning." They award degrees at all levels in many fields. Learners are evaluated by a provost, who determines how many credits are needed to earn the desired degree and, with the learner, explores community resources that may be used to earn those credits. Several of the administrators have been involved with accredited nontraditional programs in the past. With regard to accreditation, they state that "Summit's international learning community aligns itself with all nations; avoiding a process, accreditation, that tends to be exclusive and restrictive." Following the death of administrator Ray Chasse in 2000, the telephone message said the university would be closed until later in the year.

Swiss Business School   M
Balz-Zimmermann-Strasse 34
8058 Zürich Flughafen, Switzerland
Fields offered: Business administration
Phone: +41 (1) 813 80 50
Fax: +41 (1) 274 27 65
Email: info@sbs.edu
Web site: www.sbs.edu

Offers an MBA by distance learning. Accredited by the unrecognized and nonwonderful World Association of Universities and Colleges. Misleadingly advertises itself as a "member" of the Association of Collegiate Business School Programs (ACBSP); though it may pay membership dues to this GAAP-recognized agency, it is *not* accredited by the ACBSP. The Internet site is registered to Michael Schmelczer at Taborstrasse 24A, Zurich.

Transworld University   M
3242 McKinley Dr.
Santa Clara, CA 95051
Fields offered: Business
Phone: (408) 241 4896
Web site: www.transworld.edu

The state-approved university offers an online MBA, in which students are matched with mentors who, they say, are typically senior executives of Silicon Valley companies. A close relationship with the ICFAIAN Foundation (Integrity, Character, Fearlessness, Achievement, Innovation, Adventure and Nobility) which also awards its credential to Transworld graduates.

Trinity College & Seminary   B, M, D
4233 Medwel Dr., Box 717
Newburgh, IN 47629-0717
Fields offered: Human resource management, theology, biblical studies, philosophy, history, women's studies, distance education, conflict management, counseling
Year founded: 1969
Phone: (812) 858 6415 ▪ (800) 473 0307
Fax: (812) 858 6419
Email: info@trinitysem.edu
Web site: www.trinitysem.edu

While strongly religious, Trinity does offer some more secular degrees, such as bachelor's and master's degrees in human relations management and women's studies. (Doctorates are all in theological fields, and beyond the scope of this book.) Accredited in the U.S. by the unrecognized National Association of Private Nontraditional Schools and Colleges (which temporarily put them on probation in 2000 when a student discovered that some course materials were "borrowed" from other, uncited textbooks). Trinity degrees have been accepted by the religion department of the traditional and legitimate University of Liverpool, which has used the word "accreditation" to describe their acceptance; however, this is not accreditation in the U.S. sense. Also known as Trinity College of the Bible and Trinity Theological Seminary. Originally established in Ohio as Toledo Bible College. The same people operate Master's Divinity School, a religious institution whose degrees seem absurdly easy to acquire.

Trinity College & University (U.K.)   B, M, D
54 Mason Rd.
Manor Park
Ilkeston, Derbyshire, DE7 9JP, United Kingdom
Fields offered: "any subject (except Traditional Medicine)"
Phone: +44 (115) 944 2007
Fax: +44 (115) 932 9493
Email: apl@ses-consultants.co.uk
Web site: www.trinitycollege.org.uk

Operating since at least the early '90s, this school, a division of the "The United Interdenominational Church," certainly has a cosmopolitan presence—they have a British address (more than one, in fact), claim to operate from Spain, and are incorporated in Delaware. They award degrees, based on assessment of life experience, at all levels in "any subject (except Traditional Medicine)." Accreditation is claimed from the Correspondence Accreditation Association, which appears to be an agency of Trinity's own creation. In their literature, they say they are willing to backdate a diploma—they call it "alternative dating of documentation"—at the student's request; we know of no legitimate school on the planet that engages in this practice.

More than one "agent" claims to represent TC&U and handle its affairs: SES Consultants (*www.ses-consultants.co.uk/trinity*) and Hudson & James, Ltd. (*www.learnbymail.com/trinity*). We note that these two agents quote different fee schedules for the degrees. (Hudson & James is more expensive.)

To add to the confusion, there is a Trinity College & University in the U.S. (see separate listing below), which, although once affiliated with its U.K. parent, appears to have broken all ties.

In 1997, a correspondent sent us a copy of a diploma he ordered from the British TC&U: a Ph.D. in "Alternative and Complimentary Heath [*sic*] Sciences." Although he called and faxed the school dozens of times, requesting a new diploma with the word "Health" spelled correctly, he says that TC&U never responded.

Much of TC&U's literature is identical to that of Earlscroft University. Any connection to the Trinity C & U in Panama (see: Global Money Consultants) is unknown.

Trinity College & University (U.S.)   B, M, D
Degree Consultants, Inc.
2601 South Minnesota Ave.
PMB: 105-103

Sioux Falls, SD 57105-4730
Fields offered: Many fields
Phone: (605) 339 0215
Email: admin@trinity-college.edu
Web site: www.trinity-college.edu

Offers degrees at all levels by assessment of life experience and learning. Prices range from $600 (for a bachelor's) to $1500 (for a doctorate). Began in the late '90s as an American outpost of Trinity C & U in the U.K. (see listing above). First incorporated in Louisiana; later moved its incorporation to South Dakota where it is registered as Degree Consultants, Inc. (*www.degreeconsultants.com*). At some point, there was a split with its British parent; now states that "We are not associated with any other college or university with the same or similar name anywhere in the world." Claims accreditation from the Association of Private Colleges and Universities (APCU), which TC&U had a hand in founding, as well as the Association for Online Academic Excellence, both unrecognized agencies.

United International Universities   B, M, D

Heyendlaan 20
Essen 2910, Belgium
Fields offered: Business administration, business communication & public relations, computer science
Fax: +32 (3) 677 2975
Email: kmc@skynet.be

Offers degrees in the above fields through a combination of correspondence coursework and life-experience credit. Applications and tuition payments are directed to an address in Belgium, but the prospectus also lists an address in Honolulu, Hawaii.

Universal Life Church & University   D

10001 E. Leila Dr.
Tuscon, AZ 85730
Fields offered: Divinity
Phone: (520) 721 2882
Email: ulc@ulc.org
Web site: www.ulc.org

The Universal Life Church was founded in the 1950s by Kirby J. Hensley of Modesto, CA. Mr. Hensley, who claimed to be illiterate, apparently believed that every man, woman, and child has the right to be an ordained clergy person. To this end, the Universal Life Church will ordain anybody, for no cost, and without examination. Ordination is free, but an honorary Doctor of Divinity (D.D.) degree will cost you $20. The Ph.D. in Religion is a bit pricier ($100) and requires that you read the ULC Bible and take a test answering 75% of the questions correctly. ULC comes with its very own accrediting agency: the International Accrediting Association.

Oh, and the ULC also sells a "press card" ($5) that you can put in your car window. Their sales pitch: "If you get stopped by a cop and are going too fast, tell him you are on your way to a meeting to get a news story. Chances are, 9 out of 10 times, he will let you go." And for five bucks more, they'll make you a Saint of their church.

Universitas Mons Calpe   M, D

Management Business Academy
1 Corral Rd., Suite 2A, P.O. Box 569, Gibraltar
Fields offered: Business administration, management
Phone: +41 (91) 610 2299
Email: puc@ticino.edu
Web site: www.umc-puc.edu/umc-puc/umc.htm

In 1998, they began offering master's and doctorates for $1,500 to $2,000. Headquartered in Gibraltar, they claim their campus is in Lugano, Switzerland. They claim accreditation from the Council for National Academic Accreditation, an unrecognized Wyoming-based agency that appears to be in a private home and has no listed telephone.

University City   B, M

P.O. Box 45226
Philadelphia, PA 19124-3032
Fields offered: Many fields
Email: info@vtu.edu
Web site: www.vtu.edu

When we made an inquiry to learn more about this university, specifically asking where they were located, under what authority they granted degrees, why no faculty or administrators were named on their Web site, why a list of Fortune 1000 companies that accepts their degrees had not been posted six months after they said it would be, what is the connection with something called "Professors Without Borders," how they expected, as they claim, to be directly accredited by "United States Congress," and a few others things, we received this response:

"Dear Mr. Bear:

It is incredible, how fast you checked the information from registering agency, and gave our site a superficial view, and formed an informed decision as you claim. As far as what you wish to put in your next book is entirely your business, you can use free speech in any form, after all you need to make money some how, and hocking books is as good a profession as any.

Had you actually been an objective reader, you may have seen an 'under construction sign' on the site for University City. Thus in trying to debunk schools, you ended up becoming a fool at your own game. How did you assume that faculty listing will not be provided before the site becomes functional?

I suggest that you learn to actually read the entire site and wait for the site to be completed, and information posted, before you go out with blazing guns. It perhaps would help if you actually read the entire site, rather than offering premature conclusions. I have read your books, they are supposed to be informative. Now I believe that your claim to fame is far from any real research and is principally based on pomposity and utter ignorance, when facts are not in evidence, yet you are able to provide conclusions. You want information about the site, then wait until it is completed. Next time you make a call, please

be decent enough to identify yourself and submit your query. There is no requirement for us to defend ourselves before you or anyone else. In regards to our site, you have proven to be an utter fool, who jumped to conclusions after a superficial and cursory view of a site. If you learned your great insightful research from Michigan State University, then its a shame that they did not teach you enough patience about relevant and exacting research as is required for most educators.
Sincerely
Haider Abbas"

What more can we say, except that they are also known as Virginia Theological University and as Free University.

University of Advanced Research B, M
P.O. Box 334
Papaikou, HI 96720
Fields offered: Business administration
Phone: (808) 883 3827
Fax: (808) 883 1155
Email: admissions@uarhawaii.com
Web site: www.uarhawaii.com
Offers MBAs and BBAs by CD-ROM. Tuition ranges from $500 to $1000. They claim that the degrees can be earned in six months.

University of America (LA, IA, TN) B, M, D
P.O. Box 381903
Germantown, TN 38183
Fields offered: Many fields
Year founded: 1987
Phone: (504) 561 6561 ▪ (800) 347 8659
Web site: www.universityofamerica.com
They have offered nonresident degrees in a wide range of fields, originally from a convenience address in Louisiana (although run at the time from Arkansas), then Iowa, and now, it seems, Tennessee, with a Hawaii registration thrown in for good measure. We say "it seems" because the Web site has been "under construction" throughout our writing process. In 1999, the U of A dropped its doctoral programs, ostensibly in order to apply for accreditation with the Distance Education and Training Council, but the Ph.D.'s have apparently been resumed. Accreditation has been claimed from the American Education Association for the Accreditation of Schools, Colleges, and Universities, an organization we've never been able to find. The president, Dr. James Benton, claims a Ph.D. from American University Without Walls, another organization we've never been able to find.

University of America (St. Kitts, Georgia) B, M, D
10 Central St., Box 175
Basseterre, St. Kitts, West Indies
Fields offered: All fields
Web site: www.universityamerica.edu
Although based in Georgia, they claim to operate under the law of St. Kitts and Nevis in the Caribbean, where there is no listed telephone. They claim accreditation from the unrecognized (and unfindable by us) International Association of Colleges and Universities. According to an applicant (who tells us he applied, was accepted, assigned student number 10,001, and "as Alek Trebek says, 'we know what that means'"), it seems to be run by two men from Lawrenceville and/or Dunwoody, Georgia. Amusingly, the Web site offers for sale various paraphernalia of the university (T-shirts, mugs), with or without the school mascot—but there is no mention of what the mascot might be.

University of Antioch
See: Ignatius University

University of Asia B, M, D
68 Cavenagh St.
P.O. Box 3875
Darwin, NT 0801, Australia
Fields offered: Business administration, law, computer science, hospitality & tourism, Islamic business studies
Year founded: 1998
Phone: +61 (8) 8941 7332
Email: uniasia@uniasia.edu
Web site: www.uniasia.edu
This institution appeared on the Internet in March, 1998. Offers distance-learning degrees at all levels in business, law, and computer science. Originally located in a leased room in a block of serviced offices in Adelaide, Australia, but fled to the Northern Territory after it was requested to comply with South Australian Accreditation and Registration guidelines. Also has a New York office, and is registered as a business in Delaware and Florida, but has no authority to grant degrees from these places. The claim is that the university is run by "highly qualified acedemics" [*sic*], but no names of faculty or administration are provided in any of the school's literature other than that of the president, "Prof Dr. Bilal Nasrullah (B.A., DIP.Ed., M.B.A., L.L.D., Phs.D.)." Nasrullah refuses to divulge where he earned his long list of degrees. The school has claimed accreditation from a string of unrecognized agencies, including the Commonwealth Universities Association (U.K.), the Association of World Universities and Colleges (Switzerland; unconnected to the WAUC), the Australian Universities Association, and Uniworld Association Incorporated. All of the Web sites promoting these agencies are registered to Bilal Nasrullah. When newsgroup posters have raised some legitimate questions about this school, Dr. Nasrullah has responded more than once with threats of legal action.

University of Berkley B, M, D
19785 Twelve Mile Rd. West, #324
Southfield, MI 48076
Year founded: 1993
Phone: (814) 825 6604
Fax: (814) 825 1104
Email: director@uofb.com
Web site: www.berkley-u.edu
The campus is a Mail Boxes Etc. store in a shopping mall. In early 1998, the FBI and the Postal Service began intercepting mail sent to the "campus" (identified by the FBI as a shack behind a garage in Erie, Pennsylvania). Degrees

are offered in virtually any subject, from parapsychology to dance, computer engineering to hypnosis. No faculty or staff are listed in the catalog. The university is part of the Society of God and Pantheistic Philosophy. The school's director, Dr. Victor Pancerev, did not respond to several letters asking about the faculty or the degree-granting authority, which would appear not to exist. However, a faithful reader in Erie tells us that Dr. Pancerev is a local actor and comedian, and wonders if the whole university thing is some kind of multi-media performance event. No connection with the University of California at Berkeley or to the University of Berkeley.

University of Ecoforum For Peace   B, M, D
Via Foletti 20
Lugano, Massagno 6900, Switzerland
Fields offered: Many fields
Phone: +41 (91) 967 66 66
Fax: +41 (91) 967 21 10
Email: info@uep.org
Web site: www.uep.org
Offers degrees at all levels by independent study, focusing on an ecological way of thinking in each field of science. Headquartered in Switzerland, where it shares an address, fax number, and Internet service provider with its non-GAAP and nonwonderful accreditor, the Academy for the Promotion of International Cultural and Scientific Exchange.

University of God's Logos System   B, M, D
11265 Redbird Lane
Baptist, LA 70401
Fields offered: Many fields
Year founded: 1986
The materials received from this school make it appear eccentric, to say the least. They have no phone or fax, and the letter, typed in all capitals, included the intriguing sentence, "I'm sure you have some grasp and with a name like 'Bear' and the Soviet Union state insignia: I thought this birthmark on my meron/front-leg [*sic*] (like the one on my mother Marilyn William's glutes) was bad, you have my 'empathy'." Dr. Durand claims to have "the only court-proven non-fraudulent curricula in the nation." The letter was on stationery for the Mesmer Institute, but the connection is unclear.

University of James   M, D
215 Lake Blvd., Suite #219
Redding, CA 96003-2506
Fields offered: Many fields
Year founded: 1998
Fax: (530) 244 6651
Email: scripture-ch-c@geocities.com
Web site: www.geocities.com/CollegePark/Center/2412
They offer external graduate degree programs from a Mail Boxes Etc. store in northern California. They are accredited by the unrecognized and nonwonderful World Association of Universities and Colleges. Named for William James.

University of Management and Technology   M, D
1925 N. Lynn St., Third Floor

Arlington, VA 22209
Fields offered: Management, business administration
Year founded: 1998
Phone: (703) 516 0035
Fax: (703) 516 0985
Email: info@umtweb.edu
Web site: www.umtweb.edu
Offers an MBA and an M.S. and Ph.D. in management. There is a short residency requirement for the Ph.D. program.

University of Melchizedek   B, M, D
c/o Office of the Ambassador of Melchizedek
611 East Fourth St.
Jacksonville, FL 32206
Fields offered: Many fields
Phone: (904) 463 1201 ▪ (800) 343 4737
Fax: (904) 642 3277
Email: unserv@aol.com
Web site: www.melchizedek.com/university.htm
This school has appeared on the Internet, offering degrees at all levels as, and we quote, "a non-profit governmental corporation for charitable and educational purposes . . . fostering academic scholarship in the arts and sciences of philosophy and religion as disciplines of knowledge given by GOD to the human race." What government? That would be the Dominion of Melchizedek, a country invented by a man calling himself Branch Vinedresser (a.k.a. Tzemach Ben Netzer and David Korem), claiming sovereignty in Jerusalem, but apparently existing in uncontested form only on two uninhabited Polynesian islands (Karitane and Taongi). There was an Embassy of Melchizedek listed in the Washington, DC, yellow pages, allegedly involved in selling international bank charters, a matter which has been the focus of several lengthy investigative reports in *The Economist* magazine, the *Washington Post*, and elsewhere. In 2000, they were also incorporated in Arizona. Once known as Dominion University of Melchizedek.

University of Metaphysics   B, M, D
11684 Ventura Blvd.
Studio City, CA 91604
Fields offered: Metaphysics, metaphysical counseling, new thought ministry
Phone: (818) 763 9343 ▪ (888) 866 4685
Fax: (818) 763 5415
Email: oksum@aol.com
Web site: www.metaphysics.com
This school is operated by the International Metaphysical Ministry, offering bachelor's, master's, and doctorates in metaphysics, metaphysical counseling, and new thought ministry. They say they are the "most advertised school of its type, and therefore most recognized." The campus address appears to be the Valley Mail and Telephone Service. Special one-year program allows students to earn degrees at all levels through self-paced correspondence courses (48 lessons for the bachelor's, an additional 18 lessons plus a 6,000-word thesis for the master's, and an additional 10,000-word dissertation for the doctorate).

The Web site is registered at 925 East Desert Inn Road, Las Vegas, NV 89109.

University of Natural Medicine B, M, D

P.O. Box 4069
Santa Fe, NM 87502
Fields offered: Natural medicine, naturopathy, holistic nursing,
Phone: (505) 424 7800 ▪ (800) 893 3367
Fax: (505) 424 7878
Email: natmedu@aol.com
Web site: www.unaturalmedicine.edu

Offers degrees at all levels in the above fields. Distance-learning students must locate a proctor in their local area to supervise exams. Students may also be required to do an "externship" at a local clinic of natural medicine.

University of Northern Washington B, M, D

7 Waterfront Plaza
500 Ala Moana Blvd, Suite 400
Honolulu, HI 96813
Fields offered: Many fields
Phone: (808) 599 5537
Fax: (808) 599 2869
Email: info@unw.edu
Web site: www.unw.edu

Offers degrees at all levels in many fields, with an emphasis on business, from their "campus" which is a mail receiving and forwarding service in Hawaii. When a Honolulu reporter attempted to learn more, she was rebuffed at every turn and featured University of Northern Washington in a major article in *Pacific Business News* (May 26, 2000) under the headline, "Inside Hawaii's 'Diploma Mills'."

University of Santa Barbara M, D

5266 Hollister Ave., Bldg. A-117
Santa Barbara, CA 93111
Fields offered: Education, business
Year founded: 1973
Phone: (805) 569 1024
Fax: (805) 967 6289
Email: usb.139@juno.com

M.A., Ed.D., and Ph.D. in education; MBA, M.S., and Ph.D. in business. Each field offers a number of related areas of emphasis. There used to be a three-week residency, but all degrees are now done entirely by distance learning. Originally established in Florida as Laurence University. At one time accredited by the legitimate but unrecognized Pacific Association of Schools and Colleges, which is no longer in business.

University of the Rockies B, M, D

3525 S. Tamarac Dr., #270
Denver, CO 80237
Fields offered: Education, ministry
Year founded: 1981
Phone: (800) 292 0555
Email: rockies@compuserve.com

Founded in 1981 as the Christian Learning Institute of Denver. The present name was adopted in 1987. All coursework is completed through supervised independent study. Most faculty are part-time working practitioners with professional degrees in their area of teaching. A tollfree phone allows students throughout the U.S. and Canada to be connected with their instructors as necessary. Final exams are mailed to approved proctors in the student's geographic area. Credit is granted for documented experiential learning and examination.

US Global University B

11825 SW Greenburg, Suite 1-C
Tigard, OR 97223-6460
Fields offered: Nursing, business
Phone: (503) 684 7524 ▪ (888) 874 5625
Fax: (503) 568 5209
Email: info@usglobaluniversity.edu
Web site: www.usglobaluniversity.edu

Offers bachelor's programs in nursing and business-related fields. According to its literature, US Global's mission "is to provide the finest distance learning education programs available through a fully recognized and accredited institution." Its accreditor, the Academy for the Promotion of International Culture and Scientific Exchange, is an unrecognized agency. Any connection to United States Global University, registered in Hawaii (see listing in chapter 31), is unknown.

Virginia Theological University

See: University City

Virtual Online University

See: Athena University

Wakefield International University B, M, D

266 Banbury Rd., Summertown, Suite 132
Oxford OX2 7DL, United Kingdom
Fields offered: Many fields
Phone: +44 (1962) 875 404
Fax: +44 (1865) 514 656
Email: info@wakefieldinternational.com
Web site: www.wakefieldinternational.com

They offer degrees at all levels based on evaluation of life and work experience. One correspondent said the process could be as fast as seven days. Although using an address in England, the institution is registered in St. Kitts and Nevis, West Indies. They claim that Wakefield's "by-laws provide the authority for the granting of undergraduate and post-graduate degrees worldwide." In other words, they have granted themselves permission to award degrees.

Warnborough College

See: Warnborough University

Warnborough International

See: Warnborough University

Warnborough University   B, M, D

Friars House
London SE1 8HB, United Kingdom
Fields offered: Many fields
Year founded: 1973
Phone: +44 (20) 7922 1200
Fax: +44 (20) 7922 1201
Email: admin@warnborough.edu
Web site: www.warnborough.edu

Formerly known as Warnborough College, this school offers residential and nonresidential degrees in liberal arts, scientific studies, and professional studies. In 1996, it was rocked by scandal for giving the impression that it was a degree-awarding part of Oxford University. Up to its ears in lawsuits, debts, fines, and bad press, Warnborough College disappeared from its home in Oxford, emerging in London as Warnborough University.

Until the mid 1990s, degree-granting authority, they say, came from an affiliation with Greenwich University in Hawaii. In 1997, they incorporated as Warnborough University in Ireland. The Irish government wrote to us that Warnborough is not empowered by the government to grant degrees. They grant degrees, it would seem, because of the authority they have given themselves.

John visited Warnborough in their former location in London in late 1997 and met with Mr. Julian Ng, the administrator in their large one-room office (four or five desks) in an elegant neighborhood. Mr. Ng assured John that the "troubles" in America (a lawsuit by the attorney general of Washington, claiming that students were misled into thinking Warnborough was a part of Oxford University) were brought about by an independent and renegade agent in America, no longer connected, and that the suit was against Warnborough College, not the new Warnborough University.

Washington International University (PA)   B, M, D

817 Summit Grove Ave.
Bryn Mawr, PA 19010
Fields offered: Business, engineering, health care management, computer systems management & information technology, liberal arts
Year founded: 1996
Phone: (610) 527 1757
Email: info@washint.edu
Web site: www.washint.edu

Formerly Washington University, until the legitimate Washington University in St. Louis got an injunction. Mr. Yil Karademir, owner of Washington International University, wrote to Mariah, "Regarding your father's comments to our present or prospective students is [sic] UNPROFESSIONAL at best, and EVIL at worst! Lets [sic] don't [sic] forget that he is a man who also tryed [sic] his luck with a Hawaii University [sic] but failed…. I do not wish to take legal action against your father based on a his [sic] email communication with [name of recipient] but if he continues to make negative remarks against Washington University instead of just stating the facts-and we catch again [sic], I shall have no choice to proceed! [sic]"

The fact is that this "university" is incorporated in South Dakota and the British Virgin Islands (two places that have no evaluation procedures whatsoever), but operates from a small office in Pennsylvania. The school picture in their catalog is of the building in which their answering service is located.

Mr. Karademir writes to us, "We list our faculty in our catalog. How many shady universities offer education via Doctorate degree holders from HARVARD, PERDUE [sic]….? " The "Faculty" section on the Web site had (as of 15 July 2000) absolutely nothing but two tiny and murky photographs captioned "Academic and Office Staff Dinner Party."

In lieu of any accreditation, "All Washington International University degrees are ATTESTED and SEALED for authenticity by a government NOTARY!" (In the U.S., anyone can get anything notarized on paying a $10 fee.)

The catalog is filled with skillfully written statements like this: "Highly trained staff is the KEY communication link between Washington International University professors and the students. The efficiency of the staff allows smooth and prompt passage of the information from one end to the other."

Washington School of Law   M, D, Law

Washington Institute for Graduate Studies
2268 East Newcastle Dr.
Sandy, UT 84093
Fields offered: Taxation
Year founded: 1976
Phone: (801) 943 2440
Fax: (801) 944 8586
Email: washingtoninstitute@earthlink.net
Web site: www.washingtonschooloflaw.com

Lawyers and CPAs may earn a master's in taxation (LL.M. for lawyers, M.S. for CPAs) after 360 hours of study, in residence or by videocassette. There is a Ph.D. in taxation for accountants and businesspeople, and a Doctor of Juridical Sciences (J.S.D. or S.J.D.) for attorneys. The college uses what it identifies as the most advanced integrated system of textbooks on taxation of any graduate tax program. The school is accepted for CPE credit by the Treasury, Internal Revenue Service for Enrolled Agents, the National Association of State Boards of Accountancy, and by the state boards of accountancy of virtually all states requiring such approval. Accreditation is claimed from the National Association of Private Nontraditional Schools and Colleges, an unrecognized but legitimate agency.

Weimar Institute   B

20601 W. Paoli Lane.
Weimar, CA 95736
Fields offered: Education, religion, health
Year founded: 1978
Phone: (916) 637 4111 ▪ (800) 525 9192
Fax: (530) 637 4722
Web site: www.weimar.org

The mission of Weimar is "to educate students for productive Christian leadership. This mission embraces the idea that the gospel of Jesus Christ restores and ennobles the mind, body, and spirit in a cohesive whole." We have been told that this conservative Seventh-Day Adventist school chooses not to seek accreditation, viewing it as too worldly. But they have sought and gained California state approval. Formerly Weimar College.

Westbrook University   B, M, D

University Plaza
120 Llano St.
Aztec, NM 87410
Fields offered: Naturopathy, psychology, world philosophies, alternative/holistic medicine
Year founded: 1988
Phone: (505) 334 1115 ▪ (877) 507 2065
Fax: (505) 334 7583
Email: admissions@cyberport.com
Web site: www.westbrooku.edu

Programs at all levels in the above fields, with a wide range of specializations. Licensed by the state of New Mexico. Claims accreditation from three unrecognized accreditors, two of which have written word-for-word identical letters granting "accreditation." The address for one of them, the National Board of Naturopathic Examiners, is the same as the address for Matts Health Foods, whose owner, Norbert Matts, is also a faculty member at Westbrook. The address for the other, the American Naturopathic Medical Certification and Accreditation Board, was shared with the home of another faculty member before changing to a mail receiving service. More than half the faculty have unaccredited degrees, a large portion from Westbrook. We note that in the growing number of states that regulate the practice of naturopathy (14 when we went to press), not one grants licensure to people with distance-learning credentials. Westbrook was formerly known as the International Institute of Theology.

Western Governors University   A, M

9136 East 10th Place
Denver, CO 80230
Year founded: 1997
Phone: (303) 365 7500 ▪ (877) 435 7948
Fax: (303) 739 2904
Email: helpme@wgu.edu
Web site: www.wgu.edu

In 1995, Governor Mike Leavitt of Utah proposed the development of a multistate program to deliver distance-learning courses and systems, with a special focus on competency-based education. Currently 18 western states are involved (Alaska, Arizona, Colorado, Guam, Hawaii, Idaho, Indiana, Montana, Nebraska, Nevada, New Mexico, North Dakota, Oklahoma, Oregon, Texas, Utah, Washington, and Wyoming) with more to join in the near future, and they plan to bring together not only established universities, but also corporate training programs. The initial degree offerings were a master's in learning & technology and three associate's programs (education, network administration, electronic marketing). Articles in the *Chonicle of Higher Education*, and elsewhere, have suggested that

WGU has enrolled many fewer students than expected. Indeed, one of the 111 students in the only master's program told us, in 2000, that 110 of the students were subsidized by the states of Utah and Washington, and he was the only "paying customer." In November, 2000, WGU was granted candidacy by a new entity, the Interregional Accrediting Committee, a joint venture of the four regional accrediting agencies that deal with states where WGU operates.

Western States University for
Professional Studies   B, M, D

P.O. Box 430
Doniphan, MO 63935
Fields offered: Many fields
Phone: (573) 996 7388
Fax: (573) 996 3187
Email: wsu@clnet.net
Web site: www.westernstates.edu

This school's attorneys have demanded that we not say anything about the school. Fair enough, but about the school's founder, Glenn Hudson, we will mention that his doctorate is from the University of England at Oxford, a diploma mill whose proprietors were sentenced to federal prison in 1987 for selling degrees for $200 each. Dr. Hudson's bachelor's and master's are from Metropolitan College Institute, another fake school that sells degrees for $100.

Westport University   B, M, D

181 North 200 West #3
Bountiful, UT 84010
Fields offered: Business, education, psychology
Email: registrar@westport.edu
Web site: www.westport.edu

Formed when Newport University sold off part of its assets; the buyer set up shop in Utah and called his new school Westport University. Degrees at all levels are offered through their schools of business, education, and psychology. Westport makes its lack of accreditation clear, but no faculty are listed in its catalog or on its Web site. In fact, a correspondent has reported that on an initial interview for acceptance as a student, he was offered instead a professorship, for which he felt he was quite unqualified. He declined.

William Carey International University   B, M, D

1539 E. Howard St.
Pasadena, CA 91104
Fields offered: International development
Phone: (626) 398 2141
Fax: (626) 398 2111
Email: admissions@wciu.edu
Web site: www.wciu.edu

Field-based degrees at all levels in the field of international development, primarily for Christian missionaries, focusing on "the work of voluntary organizations involved in cross-cultural service."

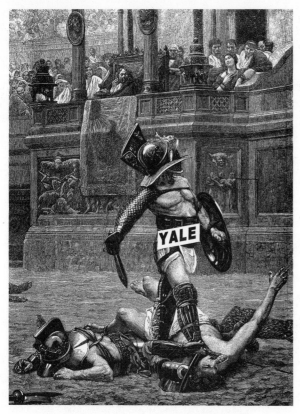

The Delinquent Student-Loan Enforcement
Officer turns to the Dean for the traditional
"Thumbs Up" or "Thumbs Down" verdict.

William Howard Taft University   M, D, Law

201 East Sandpointe Ave., #400
Santa Ana, CA 92707
Fields offered: Business, taxation, law, education
Year founded: 1976
Phone: (714) 850 4800 ▪ (800) 882 4555
Fax: (714) 708 2082
Email: admissions@taftu.edu
Web site: www.taftu.edu

MBA programs in entrepreneurship and healthcare
administration (through their Deming School of Business),
an M.S. in taxation (designed for accountants), a doctorate
in education (through their Boyer Graduate School of
Education), as well as a California Bar-qualifying J.D.
law program and an LL.M. in taxation, all entirely by distance
learning. At one time, we were concerned that Taft claimed
accreditation from the World Association of Universities
and Colleges. The evidence is now clear that Taft believed
certain claims made by the WAUC, and later came to
recognize they were not true, resulting in a successful legal
action by Taft against WAUC (see the sidebar on page 58).

Wittfield University   B, M, D

1750 Kalakaua Ave., Suite 3-773
Honolulu, HI 96826-3795
Fields offered: Many fields
Phone: (888) 316 9216
Fax: (808) 955 8889
Email: info@wittfielduniversity.org
Web site: www.wittfielduniversity.org

Wittfield grants bachelor's, master's, and doctoral degrees
based on previous learning and life/work experience.
The school is not seeking accreditation and the Web site
claims "the University's official by-laws provide authority
for the granting of graduate and postgraduate degrees in
a variety of fields and disciplines worldwide." In other
words, they have given themselves the authority to grant
degrees.

World University (Arizona)   D

P.O. Box 2470
Benson, AZ 85602
Fields offered: Spiritual science
Year founded: 1967
Phone: (520) 586 2985
Fax: (520) 586 4764
Email: desertsanctuary@theriver.com
Web site: www.worlduniversity.org

World University tells us that they are an association of
"schools and colleges throughout the world," with what
they call a "Desert Sanctuary Regional Campus" near
Benson, Arizona. No degrees are presently offered from
its world headquarters, but its parent institution, incorporated in Arizona and California as the World University
Roundtable, awards a "cultural doctorate as a professional honor for career excellence with an acceptable
biodata," for the price of $250.

Yorker International University   B, M, D

3213 West Main St., Suite 310
Rapid City, SD 57702
Fields offered: Marketing, business administration,
sociology, psychology, philosophy, alternative
healing, hypnosis
Phone: (212) 521 4139 ▪ (888) 718 1060
Fax: (605) 342 0554
Email: nyuniversity@mindspring.com
Web site: www.nyuniversity.net

Offers degrees at all levels in the above fields. Claims that
a degree can be earned in as little as six months. No faculty members other than Prof. Marco E. Grappeggia
(apparently the school's director) are mentioned on the
Web site. Literature is up-front about lack of accreditation.
The South Dakota address given for the school's "head
office" is a Mail Boxes Etc. store; Web site also lists
addresses for agents in New York City, Italy, Greece,
Argentina, and Ghana. Formerly known as New Yorker
University. The Web site is registered to New Yorker
University at 590 Madison Avenue, New York, NY 10022.

CHAPTER 22

Other Schools with Short Residency Programs

A log in the woods, with Mark Hopkins at one end and me at the other—that is a good enough university for me.

President James Garfield

The schools in this chapter do not meet the standards of GAAP, Generally Accepted Accreditation Principles (explained in detail on page 95). They are not necessarily bad, illegal, or fake, but they are unlikely to be accepted as accredited, despite the claims that many of them may make.

The degree programs listed in this chapter can be completed mostly through distance-learning methods; however, they do require some sort of campus attendance at some point in the program.

The basic format for each listing is as follows:

Name of School   Associate's, **B**achelor's, **M**aster's, **D**octorate, **Law**
Postal Address (United States if country not specified)
Fields of study **offered**
Year founded
Phone ▦ Tollfree phone (If a U.S. number, country code (+1) not included)
Fax
Email address
Web site URL
Description of programs

Information in this book, especially the listings, changes fast. Updates and corrections are posted on our Web site at *www.degree.net/updates/bearsguide14*.

And remember, our readers play a huge role in helping us keep this book up to date. Please, whether it's a defunct area code or a hot new distance-learning program, bring it to our attention at *johnandmariah@degree.net* or *Bears' Guide*, P.O. Box 7123, Berkeley, CA 94707.

Asia International Open University   B, M
P.O. Box 1266
Macau
Fields offered: Business administration

Year founded: 1992
Phone: +853 781 698
Fax: +853 781 691
Email: genoffice@aiou.edu
Web site: www.aiou.edu
Formed by the restructuring of the University of East Asia when it came under Macau's control. Offers MBA and BBA programs in English and Chinese. Also has a campus in Hong Kong. A member of the Asia Pacific International Educational Consortium. See: Asia Pacific International University

Asia Pacific International Graduate School of Management
See: Asia Pacific International University

Asia Pacific International University   B, M, D
155 Cyril Magnin St.
San Francisco, CA 94102-2129
Fields offered: Business fields
Year founded: 1991
Phone: (415) 834 2748 ▦ (800) 661 8788
Fax: (415) 834 2758
Email: info@apiu.edu
Web site: www.apiu.edu
Asia Pacific offers the following degrees: Bachelor of Business Administration in financial management, information technology, or marketing management; Bachelor of Science in manufacturing management; MBA in international management; Master of Information Systems; and Doctor of Business Administration in international management. The BBA degree completion program is available totally online. Classes are held during monthly weekend sessions. A member of the Asia Pacific International Educational Consortium, which includes Asia International Open University (Macau) and Asia Pacific International Graduate School of Management (Vancouver). Students can study at any member's campus, which includes New Zealand, Vancouver, Singapore, and Macau.

Berne University   D

35 Center St., Unit 18
Wolfeboro Falls, NH 03896
Fields offered: Many fields
Year founded: 1993
Phone: (603) 569 8648
Fax: (603) 569 4052
Email: berne@berne.edu
Web site: www.berne.edu

Berne's administrative office is in New Hampshire. Its degree-granting authority comes from the country of St. Kitts and Nevis in the Caribbean, which has also accredited Berne. The doctorate is earned through a one-month residency in St. Kitts, followed by two semesters of part-time work by distance learning with a faculty mentor. The doctorate is normally completed in one to two years of part-time study, but persons who have acceptable published work can complete the degree through the one-month residency plus one 5-month term of guided independent study. Applicants must have a bachelor's or master's degree or equivalent, with a minimum of one year of experience as a practicing professional. Degrees offered include a DBA, MBA, Ed.D., Ed.M., Th.D., Th.M., and Doctor and Master of Public Administration, as well as doctorates and master's in education, health services, international relations, psychology, social work, and religion. Berne has announced that they have been approved by the U.S. Department of Education for participation in student loan programs. According to the official we asked, the financial aid is restricted to "liberal arts" programs, and may only be used for the residential portion of the program. The Berne literature states that their "accreditation status ensures recognition of the programs of study in all countries in the world." A major survey of registrars suggests that unless a Caribbean school is accredited by the University of the West Indies, it is unlikely the degrees will be accepted. Berne is not accredited by UWI. Persons residing in countries other than St. Kitts and Nevis should satisfy themselves of recognition by their own area, of any school that does not meet GAAP, Generally Accepted Accreditation Principles. See, for instance, the "Oregon" section in chapter 7.

Bob Jones University   B

Office of Extended Education
1700 Wade Hampton Blvd.
Greenville, SC 29614
Fields offered: General studies, arts & sciences, religious fields, education
Year founded: 1927
Phone: (864) 242 5100 ▪ (888) 253 9833
Fax: (800) 232 9258
Email: extended@bju.edu
Web site: www.bju.edu

Degree-completion program leading to a Bachelor of General Studies, and other bachelor's degrees in which up to 30 credits can come by correspondence. The Bob Jones brochure says "Religiously, our testimony is, 'Whatever the Bible says is true.'" They have not sought accreditation, believing that secular accrediting agencies are not relevant for a school such as theirs.

California Graduate Institute   B, M, D

1100 Glendon Ave., #1119
Los Angeles, CA 90024
Fields offered: Psychology, psychotherapy, marriage & family therapy
Year founded: 1968
Phone: (310) 208 4240
Fax: (310) 208 0684
Email: cgi@ix.netcom.com
Web site: www.cgi.edu

Established to expand the scope of traditional graduate study in psychology, psychoanalysis, and marriage & family therapy. Faculty are practicing professionals in the field of mental health. Curriculum includes clinical psychology, behavioral medicine, psychoanalysis, and marriage, family, and child counseling, and courses can be taken in residence or through distance learning. Graduates are eligible to take California licensing exams.

Capital University of Integrative Medicine   M, D

1131 8th St. NE
Washington, DC 20002
Fields offered: Integrative health sciences
Phone: (202) 544 1500
Fax: (202) 544 1533
Email: admissn@cuim.org
Web site: www.cuim.org

Offers a master's and a doctorate in integrative medicine and health. Classes are held on the Washington, DC, campus during one extended weekend each month. Only considers applicants with accredited degrees in the health sciences.

EcoVersity   B, M

Route 1, Box 28-A
Santa Cruz, NM 87567
Fields offered: Agriculture, ecology, appropriate technology, environmental education, leadership skills, earth wisdom studies, community development
Phone: (505) 351 4492
Email: dean@ecoversity.org
Web site: www.ecoversity.org

Offers B.A. completion and M.A. programs in the arts and sciences of sustainable earth stewardship. The Roving Scholars Program begins with a week-long residency on the school's campus in northern New Mexico, followed by a student-designed itinerary linking existing training programs, internships, seminars, conferences, and workshops throughout the world. Students maintain contact with faculty mentors by email.

Institute for Advanced Study of Human Sexuality   M, D

1523 Franklin St.
San Francisco, CA 94109
Fields offered: Human sexuality
Year founded: 1976
Phone: (415) 928 1133
Email: iashs@iashs.edu
Web site: www.iashs.edu

Degrees offered are Master of Human Sexuality, Master of Public Health in Sexology, and Doctor of Human Sexuality. Minimum of nine weeks' residency for the master's (three weeks in each of three trimesters); 15 for the doctorate (five trimesters), although additional residency is encouraged. The school's founders, including such prominent sexologists as Kinsey's coauthor, Wardell Pomeroy, designed these programs to rectify what they believe is "a woeful lack of professionals who are academically prepared in the study of human sexuality." Many courses available on videocassette; comprehensive exams and a basic research project are expected of all students. The Institute is approved by the state of California. While most of the staff have degrees from other schools as well, 12 of the 14 also have an advanced degree from IASHS.

Institute of Imaginal Studies   M, D

47 Sixth St.
Petaluma, CA 94952
Fields offered: Psychology
Phone: (707) 765 1836
Fax: (707) 765 2351

Offers weekend master's and doctoral programs in psychology that qualify graduates to sit for the MFCC and Psychology License exams. Classes meet one weekend a month for nine months, and for one week during the summer. Students take three courses each quarter; the doctorate takes three years of coursework post-M.A., four years post-B.A.

International University of
Graduate Studies   M, D

161 West 54th St., Suite 203
New York, NY 10019-5322
Fields offered: Psychotherapy, cognitive behavior, psychoanalysis, addiction studies, forsenic mental health, marriage & family therapy
Year founded: 1979
Phone: (212) 386 3338 ▪ (888) 989 4723
Web site: www.iugrad.com

Offers doctoral and master's programs in the above fields; one week of residency on the island of St. Kitts required. The president of the school is Norma Ross, a New York-based psychoanalyst. When we placed a call to IUGS, it was fielded by a third-party answering service. The university claims accreditation from two unrecognized accreditors: the World Association of Universities and Colleges and the Global Accreditation Commission.

New Bridge International College

See: New Bridge University

New Bridge University

3337 Wilshire Blvd.
Los Angeles, CA 90019
Fields offered: Translation, clinical psychology, business, educational management
Phone: (213) 383 4461
Web site: www.nbu.edu

Approved by the state of California to offer bachelor's and master's in translation and interpretation (designed for Japanese and Koreans), the MBA, a master's in clinical psychology, and a Ph.D. in educational management. Formerly New Bridge International College.

Ola Grimsby Institute   M, D

4420 Hotel Circle Court, Suite 210
San Diego, CA 92108
Fields offered: Physical therapy, orthopedic manual therapy
Year founded: 1990
Phone: (619) 298 4116 ▪ (800) 646 6128
Fax: (619) 298 4225
Email: ogioffice@aol.com
Web site: www.olagrimsby.com

Founded by Ola Grimsby, an educator in Norwegian orthopedic manual therapy, this professional consortium offers postgraduate degrees in physcial therapy. Students take courses at a local clinic one day a week for two years, or they may elect to do coursework by distance learning followed by an intensive six weeks of clinical work under supervision. Orientation takes place in Salt Lake City, UT; after that all residential clinic work may be accomplished at centers in Alabama, Alaska, Arizona, California, Florida, Illinois, Kansas, Louisiana, Michigan, Tennessee, Texas, Utah, and Washington, as well as Belgium and Switzerland. Authorized to grant degrees by the Utah State Board of Regents System of Higher Education.

Oxford Graduate School   D

American Centre for Religion/Society Studies
500 Oxford Dr.
Dayton, TN 37321-6736
Fields offered: Sociological integration of religion and society
Year founded: 1982
Phone: (423) 775 6597 ▪ (800) 933 6188
Fax: (423) 775 6599
Email: oxnet@oxnet.com
Web site: www.oxnet.com

This school (no relation to the other, somewhat better known Oxford) offers an interdisciplinary program leading to a Ph.D. in sociological integration of religion and society. Residency is required but flexible. To quote from materials sent to us by the school, "A function of the program is to synthesize foundational studies into a working philosophy of service with a functional and research application to society. This interpretation is focused on the humanities and social sciences and a particular research application, and culminates in problem-solving research."

Pan-American School of
Bioenergetic Medicine   D

POB 553
Charlestown, Nevis, West Indies
Fields offered: Naturopathy
Phone: +869 469 9490
Email: panamint@caribsurf.com

Web site: www.panaminstitute.com
Doctorate in naturopathy (N.D.) can be earned through seven postgraduate home study courses plus a minimum of four weeks residency at the Nevis Naturopathic Clinic in the West Indies. Candidates must be actively licensed in the healing arts, e.g. nurse, massage therapist, acupuncturist, physical therapist, chiropractor, etc.

School of Natural Healing   M
P.O. Box 412
Springville, UT 84663
Fields offered: Herbology
Year founded: 1953
Phone: (801) 489 4254 ▪ (800) 372 8255
Fax: (801) 489 8341
Email: snh@qi3.com
Web site: www.schoolofnaturalhealing.com
A program offering the Master Herbalist (formerly Master of Herbology) degree, through home study courses, plus a six-day seminar by the heirs of the school's founder, Dr. John R. Christopher.

SMAE Institute
149 Bath Rd.
Maidenhead, Berkshire SL6 4LA, United Kingdom
Fields offered: Physiotherapy, surgical chiropody & podiatry, sports injury therapy
Year founded: 1919
Phone: +44 (1628) 621 100
Fax: +44 (1628) 674 483
Email: 106033.3541@compuserv.com
Diplomas in chiropody and podiatry are earned through distance-leaning courses, plus short residency in their London suburb. Physiotherapy program includes massage, joint manipulation, and medical electricity. It can be completed in three years, with several two- to three-day residential sessions each year in England. The chiropody program takes about two years; the final exam must be taken in England, followed by 100 hours of practical training in the school clinic. Their Web site reports that "people living everywhere are having more wrong with their feet than their teeth, yet there are more dentists than there are Chiropodists/Podiatrists and they are over worked."

Southern College of Naturopathy   D
P.O. Box 160
Boles, AR 72926
Fields offered: Naturopathy
Phone: (501) 637 4766 ▪ (888) 372 9555
Fax: (501) 637 5513
Offers an "accelerated" Doctor of Naturopathy degree program. Students come to Arkansas for two weeks of intensive clinical training; graduation ceremonies take place on the 14th day. According to the school's marketing literature, most states will soon have laws regulating the practice of naturopathy; "However, if you have a degree and are practicing before enactment of these laws, you may continue to practice under a grandfather clause!" This is certainly something a potential student would want to

'In this business simulation, we'll let
A = the company, B = the government regulator,
C = the balance of trade, and D = the tax collector.'

confirm in his or her area. Accredited by the unrecognized American Association of Drugless Practitioners.

Southern Eastern University
28 Concorde Dr.
London E6 4XL, United Kingdom
Phone: +44 (171) 473 6306
The proprietor, Mr. Grimaldi, assures us that the British newspaper article reporting that he offered to sell thousands of diplomas to an undercover reporter was in error. He also informs us that the university's plan to move to spacious quarters in London were changed following an IRA bomb attack. When John visited the campus in late 1997, he found the address to be a small unmarked home near the London docks. The email and Web addresses we were given were not operational in mid-2000.

Universidat di Aruba   B, M, D
z/n Dr. Schaepman St.
Sint Nicolaas, Aruba
Fields offered: Business, psychology, education, medicine
Phone: +297 (8) 45287
Fax: +297 (8) 47274
Email: arubauniversity@hotmail.com
Web site:
www.inc.com/users/UnivOfAruba.html?999
The Web site states that "pending final approvals, we will soon offer a WHO-recognized fully accredited M.D. program." However, when we communicated with the Ministry of Health in early 2000, the minister, Dr. Posner, said he was unaware of the plan. The Web site reports that the university has been offering bachelor's, master's and doctorates in business, psychology, and education for more than 30 years.

University for Metaphysical Studies   M, D
P.O. Box 5900
Santa Fe, NM 87502

Phone: (505) 992 0000
Fax: (505) 982 6292
Email: hstewart@umsonline.edu
Web site: www.umsonline.edu

Established in the late 1990s by professional psychic Helen Stewart, whose Ph.D. in sociology is from Brandeis. The literature states that "these are rigorous programs. They are not for the faint-hearted or the emotionally or mentally unprepared. There are reasons for that rigor. One is due to the subjective nature of metaphysical realities, and the strength and discipline required to develop a balanced, fulfilling life as a metaphysical practitioner. Second, the discipline is presenting itself to society in the full spectrum of its history and potential to serve individuals and humanity so it must, therefore, be an example of excellence. Third, since there is no 'licensed' or 'official' metaphysical profession, the credibility of the degree is based on the quality of the program, professionalism of the practitioner, and quality of UMS, as the granting institution." We applaud their honesty.

University of Berkeley   B, M
1911 Addison St.
Berkeley, CA 94704
Fields offered: Business, multimedia communications
Year founded: 2000
Phone: (510) 644 9700

No connection whatsoever with the University of California at Berkeley, two blocks away. Run from an Asian-student job-finding service. Their first advertisements appeared in the Berkeley newspapers in September, 2000. The small type does appropriately explain that they have received temporary interim approval from the state of California to operate for at least 90 days, or until there is a site visit. It is hard for us to imagine that they will be permitted to use this name. The university seal has the date 1974, which would seem to predate the establishing of the university by 26 years.

University of the Seven Rays   B, M, D
128 Manhattan Ave.
Jersey City Heights, NJ 07307
Fields offered: Esoteric arts and sciences

Year founded: 1985
Phone: (201) 798 7777
Fax: (201) 659 3263
Email: univ7rays@sevenray.com
Web site: www.sevenray.com

An alternative institute for students of Esotericism. Bachelor's, master's, and doctorates in various esoteric arts and sciences designed to strengthen the spiritual will, the spiritual love, and the practical spiritual intelligence of its students. Academic curricula derive "from the teachings of the Christ, the Buddha, and other members of the Spiritual Hierarchy of the Planet." While most of the work is done at a distance, there are necessary meetings of cohort groups several times a year, at almost any prearranged location worldwide. There is also a presence in Australia, in association with the Australian College of Trans-Himalayan Wisdom.

Western Institute for Social Research   B, M, D
3220 Sacramento St.
Berkeley, CA 94702
Fields offered: Psychology, education, social sciences, human services/community development
Year founded: 1975
Phone: (510) 655 2830
Fax: (510) 655 2831
Email: wisruniv@aol.com
Web site: www.california.com/wisr

Degrees at all levels, primarily for people concerned with educational innovation and/or community and social change, through a combination of residential and independent study. The typical student is enrolled for two to three years, which must include two months per year of residency or several days every couple of months. The approach involves intensive study with a faculty advisor and in small seminars, and projects combining practical and intellectual approaches to community and educational problems. WISR is state approved, and graduates may take state licensing exams. Formerly Western Regional Learning Center.

Western Regional Learning Center
See: Western Institute for Social Research

CHAPTER 23

Other Schools with Nontraditional Residential Programs

"Whom are you?" he asked, for he had been to night school.

George Ade

The schools in this chapter do not meet the standards of GAAP, Generally Accepted Accreditation Principles (explained in detail on page 95). They are not necessarily bad, illegal, or fake, but they are unlikely to be accepted as accredited, despite the claims that many of them may make.

The academic programs listed in this chapter are all, in some aspect, nontraditional, but they generally require class attendance at a school facility, often during evenings or on weekends.

The basic format for each listing is as follows:

> **Name of School** Associate's, **B**achelor's, **M**aster's, **D**octorate, **Law**
> Postal Address (United States if country not specified)
> **Fields** of study **offered**
> **Year founded**
> **Phone** ▦ Tollfree phone (If a U.S. number, country code (+1) not included)
> **Fax**
> **Email** address
> **Web site** URL
> Description of programs

Information in this book, especially the listings, changes fast. Updates and corrections are posted on our Web site at *www.degree.net/updates/bearsguide14*.

And remember, our readers play a huge role in helping us keep this book up to date. Please, whether it's a defunct area code or a hot new distance-learning program, bring it to our attention at *johnandmariah@degree.net* or *Bears' Guide*, P.O. Box 7123, Berkeley, CA 94707.

Academy of Oriental Heritage
See: International College of Traditional Chinese Medicine

American Academy of Tropical Medicine
16126 E. Warren
Detroit, MI 48224
Fields offered: Tropical medicine
Phone: (313) 882 0641
Fax: (313) 882 5110

Offers diplomas and certificates, not degrees. The Academy is incorporated in Ohio, but since their literature indicates the work is not transferable as college credit, they are not regulated by the Ohio Board of Regents. Also awards the designations of FAATH (Fellow of American Academy of Tropical Medicine) or FICTM (Fellow of International College of Tropical Medicine). Candidates must be licensed physicians, allied health practitioners, or other health-care providers, licensed in their area of specialty. The school does not accept laypersons.

American Graduate School of Business   B, M
Place des Anciens-Fosses
La Tour-de-Peilz 1814, Switzerland
Fields offered: Business
Phone: +41 (21) 944 95 01
Fax: +41 (21) 944 95 04
Email: agsb@vtx.ch
Web site: www.agsb.ch

Offers traditional residential courses in business, leading to bachelor's and master's degrees in international business. Accreditation is claimed from the unrecognized and nonwonderful World Association of Universities and Colleges. There is also a Web site in Chinese, based in Hong Kong (*www.liton.com.hk*). This school has asked not to be listed in the guide, and says they are not interested in receiving inquiries from our readers.

American Graduate School of International Relations and Diplomacy   M, D
6, rue de Lubeck
Paris 75116, France

Fields offered: International relations, diplomacy
Year founded: 1994
Phone: +33 (1) 39 73 13 40
Fax: +33 (1) 39 73 13 60
Email: info@agsird.edu
Web site: www.agsird.edu

Master of Arts in International Relations & Diplomacy and Ph.D. in International Relations & Diplomacy, in a residential program, run by Americans, in Paris. Their literature states that they are incorporated in the state of Minnesota, and are "authorized by the French Ministry of Interior as an Institution of Higher Learning." The faculty listed in the literature have impressive credentials, although the administrator is listed with the unusual credential of "Phd [*sic*] Honoris Causa."

American University of Asturias   B

Principado, 9
33007 Oviedo, Spain
Fields offered: Many fields
Phone: +34 (98) 520 1242
Fax: +34 (98) 520 8848
Email: aua@asturnet.es
Web site: www.asturnet.es/auna

Apparently a serious attempt to create an American-style semi-residential university, offering a range of courses that have at least some distance component. The university was incorporated in the state of Delaware; their U.S. telephone is in New York, and their fax is in California.

Anglo-American Institute of Drugless Therapy

30 Kinloch Rd.
Renfrew, Scotland, United Kingdom
Fields offered: Naturopathy, osteopathy
Year founded: 1911
Phone: +44 (1776) 703 346

At one time, they offered a doctorate in naturopathy; now it is a diploma. The naturopathy program involves completing about 50 lessons by correspondence, in subjects ranging from anatomy and physiology to chiropractic and spondylotherapy (which appears to involve emptying the stomach and appendix by means of concussion, with positive effect, according to the catalog, on heart trouble, bust development, syphilis, and impotence). The Institute, was established in Indiana in 1911, moved to Scotland in 1939, to England in 1948, and back to Scotland in 1977.

Association for Advanced Training in
the Behavioral Sciences   M, D

5126 Ralston St.
Ventura, CA 93003
Fields offered: Psychology
Year founded: 1982
Phone: (805) 676 3030 ▪ (800) 472 1931
Fax: (805) 676 3033
Email: info@aatbs.com
Web site: www.aatbs.com

State-approved weekend and evening classes for professionals already working in psychological service areas, with classes in Ventura, San Francisco, Irvine, Westlake, and Los Angeles. Former name: Cambridge Graduate School of Psychology.

Benjamin University   M, D

7342 Orangethorpe Ave., C-101
Buena Park, CA 90621
Fields offered: Religion
Phone: (714) 522 0111
Web site: www.benjaminuniversity.com

State-approved, unaccredited university, offering degrees in a variety of religious subjects, from divinity to church music, apparently with a large residential component.

British Institute of Homeopathy

520 Washington Blvd., #423
Marina del Rey, CA 90292
Fields offered: Homeopathy
Year founded: 1987
Phone: (310) 306 5408 ▪ (800) 498 6323
Fax: (800) 495 8277
Email: pattys@web.net
Web site: www.homeopathy.com

Offers diplomas in homeopathy (basic diploma, postgraduate course, veterinary, or homeopathic pharmacy) through home study courses; also, certificates in human sciences and in nutrition & herbology. They state that graduates are "entitled to use the initials DHM." While the "D" presumably stands for "Diploma," it could be mistaken for "Doctor." The California address is for applications only; lessons are sent to the school's U.K. address in Staines, Middlesex.

California Institute for Human Science   M, D

701 Garden View Court
Encinitas, CA 92024
Fields offered: Human science, psychology
Phone: (760) 634 1771
Fax: (760) 634 1772
Email: cihs@adnc.com
Web site: www.cihs.edu

Master's degrees and doctorates through evening programs. The degrees offered include an M.A. and Ph.D. in human science, with concentrations in either life physics or comparative religion, an M.A. in general psychology, and a Ph.D. in clinical counseling psychology, with concentrations in clinical and experimental biopsychology, integral psychology, or parapsychology. The school focuses on the study of emotional, mental, and spiritual energies.

California International University   B, M

2706 Wilshire Blvd.
Los Angeles, CA 90057
Fields offered: Business fields
Year founded: 1973
Phone: (213) 381 3719
Fax: (213) 381 6990
Email: jdmcinty@earthlink.net

Degrees in business management and international business, specially tailored for international students who use English as a second language. Evening classes.

California Yuin University   B, M, D

2007 East Compton Blvd.
Compton, CA 90221

"Honey, I found a whole cave full of bats for your zoology home-study project."

Fields offered: Acupuncture, Oriental medicine, Christian theology, business
Phone: (310) 609 2705
Fax: (310) 609 1415
Email: cyu@yuin.edu
Web site: www.yuin.edu
Offers California-approved degrees in the above fields through evening, weekend, and off-campus study. They also offer what they call a Korean doctorate in business administration that can be earned in 18 months. They claim their accreditation from the unrecognized and nonwonderful Academy for the Promotion of International Culture and Scientific Exchange in Germany.

Cambridge Graduate School of Psychology
See: Association for Advanced Training in the Behavioral Sciences

Center for Psychological Studies   D
1398 Solano Ave.
Albany, CA 94706
Fields offered: Clinical, developmental, and organizational psychology
Year founded: 1979
Phone: (510) 524 0291
Fax: (510) 524 4696
Web site: www.radioguide.com/cps/cps.htm
Ph.D. in clinical, developmental, or organizational psychology, meeting the educational requirements for the psychology license, through evening and weekend courses. Formerly the Graduate School of Human Behavior.

Chicago College of Naprapathy
See: Chicago National College of Naprapathy

Chicago National College of Naprapathy   D
3330 N. Milwaukee Ave.
Chicago, IL 60641

Fields offered: Naprapathy
Year founded: 1907
Phone: (773) 282 2686
Fax: (773) 282 2688
Email: naprapath@aol.com
Web site: www.naprapathy.org
Residential school offering an evening program leading to the Doctor of Naprapathy (a discipline concerned with evaluation and treatment of connective tissue disorders). Formerly operated under the name Oakley Smith School of Naprapathy; later changed to the Chicago College of Naprapathy. In 1971 this school merged with the National College of Naprapathy to form the present school.

College of Southeastern Europe   B, M
The American University of Athens
17 Patriarchou Ieremiou
Athens 114 75, Greece
Fields offered: Business
Phone: +30 (1) 725 9301
Fax: +30 (1) 725 9304
Email: info@southeastern.edu.gr
Web site: www.southeastern.edu.gr
An American-owned (incorporated in Delaware) residential school in Greece, offering residential study in business and other fields. While they are now accredited by the recognized ACICS agency, they have also been listed in the directory of the World Association of Universities and Colleges (an unrecognized and nonwonderful accrediting agency).

Dharma Realm Buddhist University   B, M
2001 Talmage Rd.
Talmage, CA 95481
Fields offered: Buddhist fields, Chinese studies
Year founded: 1976
Phone: (707) 462 0939
Fax: (707) 462 0949
Email: drbabtts@jps.net
Web site: www.drba.org/drbu.htm
This state-approved school (a division of the larger Dharma Realm Buddhist Association) offers bachelor's and master's degrees in Buddhist studies & practice and translation of Buddhist texts, a bachelor's in Chinese studies, and a master's in Buddhist education.

Dominion Herbal College
7525 Kingsway
Burnaby, BC V3N 3C1, Canada
Fields offered: Traditional herbalism
Year founded: 1926
Phone: +1 (604) 521 5822
Fax: +1 (604) 526 1561
Email: herbal@uniserve.com
Web site: www.dominionherbal.bc.ca
The title of "Chartered Herbalist" is awarded to students who complete a 63-lesson correspondence program in herbalism. A Master Herbalist program, one in clinical herbal therapy, and two clinical phytotherapy (one for physicians, the other for everybody else) are also offered. Summer seminars are not required, but are recommended.

English Institute of Alternative Medicine

2020 Babcock, #14
San Antonio, TX 78229
Fields offered: Naturopathic medicine, herbology, accupressure
Phone: (800) 778 6808
Fax: (210) 692 0879
Web site: www.txdirect.net/corp/english

This unaccredited school at one time offered health-related degrees at all levels. Now, due to changes in Texas law, those programs have become certificates at three levels in naturopathy and intermediate programs in herbology and accupressure. (It is the "English" institute because of founder Roy English, Jr.)

European University   B

Amerikalei 131
B-2000 Antwerp, Belgium
Fields offered: Many fields
Phone: +32 (3) 216 9896
Fax: +32 (3) 216 5868
Email: admission.office.antwerp@euruni.be
Web site: www.euruni.be

The full-color literature is impressive looking, but we remain confused, and correspondence with President Lambrechts has not cleared everything up. While the school is not listed in the authoritative International Handbook of Universities, it does claim affiliation agreements with Troy State and Central State universities (both accredited), in which those schools agree to accept EU's students into their MBA programs. Membership is claimed in the American Association of Collegiate Schools of Business, an organization we cannot locate. There is an American Assembly of Collegiate Schools of Business, but EU is not a member. The school's literature states that more than 1,500 students are enrolled in the residential bachelor's program in language, business, information systems, hotel administration, or public relations, and that the university operates its own radio station. Courses also given in Switzerland, France, Greece, Portugal, Germany, Spain, and the Netherlands.

Galien College of Natural Healing

See: Galien University Tutorial College

Galien University Tutorial College

BCM Forest
London WC1N 3XX, United Kingdom
Fields offered: Natural health sciences, business, religious studies, elementary teaching
Year founded: 1982
Phone: +44 (378) 267 318

Diploma programs in natural health sciences, business, religious studies, and elementary teaching. These credentials may offer some opportunity for misinterpretation. For instance, anyone who completes the "diploma in naturopathic medicine" course may use the letters "N.D." after their name. Formerly known as Galien College of Natural Healing, this school now incorporates the programs of the London College of Holistic Medicine. We did find some resumes, on the Internet, listing a Ph.D. from Galien.

Gestalt Institute of New Orleans

1539 Metairie Rd.
Metairie, LA 70005
Fields offered: Gestalt therapy, psychogenetics
Year founded: 1976
Phone: (504) 891 1212 ▓ (800) GESTALT
Email: ateach@gestalt-institute.com
Web site: www.gestalt-institute.com

Evening and weekend courses leading to two levels of diploma (not degree), and a correspondence program providing written assignment, audio-, and videotapes for students unable to attend in person at any of their three locations (New Orleans, New York, Santa Cruz). Registered with the Louisiana Board of Regents.

Graduate School of Human Behavior

See: Center for Psychological Studies

Hsi Lai University   B, M

1409 N. Walnut Grove Ave.
Rosemead, CA 91770
Fields offered: Business administration, languages, religious studies, English as a second language
Year founded: 1990
Phone: (626) 571 8811
Fax: (626) 571 1413
Email: info@hlu.edu
Web site: www.hlu.edu

This residential university offers courses in Chinese literature and culture, comparative religious studies, Buddhist studies, ESL, and other fields. It is approved to operate by the state of California.

Institut P-2000   B, M

P.O. Box 5211
Zurich 8022, Switzerland
Phone: +41 (1) 241 41 83
Fax: +41 (1) 241 30 33

At one time accredited by the World Association of Universities and Colleges (an unrecognized and non-wonderful accrediting agency). WAUC's directory said that Institut P-2000 "is a scholastic entity for therapy, psychological therapy and psychosomatic therapy at the levels of Practitioner, Bachelor's and Master's proficiency." Programs are residential.

International College of Traditional Chinese Medicine

1847 West Broadway, S#301
Vancouver, BC V6J 1Y6
Fields offered: Chinese medicine
Year founded: 1986
Phone: (604) 731 2926
Fax: (604) 731 2964
Email: ictcmv@direct.ca
Web site: mypage.direct.ca/i/ictcmv

A series of Chinese herbal medicine or astrology courses, leading to a certificate of completion in six months to a year, entirely by mail. At one time operated out of Washington State under the name Academy of Oriental Heritage, which still appears in the catalog.

International School of Management   M, D

World Trade Center
1250 6th Ave., 8th floor
San Diego, CA 92101
Fields offered: International management, business administration
Year founded: 1994
Phone: (619) 702 9400
Fax: (619) 702 9476
Email: ism@inetworld.net
Web site: www.ism.edu

The MBA can be completed in 5 quarters, the MIM in 3 quarters, and the DBA in 2–3 years through classes held primarily in the evenings on campus. ISM is approved to operate in the state of California, admits only U.S. nationals, and does not require GMAT and TOEFL scores.

International Technological University   B, M, D

1650 Warburton Ave.
Santa Clara, CA 95050
Fields offered: Technological fields, business
Phone: (408) 556 9010
Fax: (408) 556 9012
Email: registrar@itu.edu
Web site: www.itu.edu

This residential state-approved school offers degrees at all levels in technological fields, plus an MBA with a focus on U.S.-China matters.

Ivy University   M

100 S. Fremont Ave.
Building A12
Alhambra, CA 91803
Fields offered: Business
Fax: (626) 282 8362
Email: ivyuniv@earthlink.net

This state-approved school offers an MBA and an M.A. in management, with an emphasis on trade between North America and the Pacific Rim. The M.A. can often be completed in as little as 32 weeks, the MBA in less than 50. All instruction is offered in English and Chinese.

Keimyung Baylo University

See: South Baylo University

London College of Holistic Medicine

See: Galien University Tutorial College

National College of Naprapathy

See: Chicago National College of Naprapathy

Northern California Graduate University   D

1710 S. Amphlett Blvd., #124
San Mateo, CA 94402
Fields offered: Psychology, education
Year founded: 1989
Phone: (650) 341 6690
Fax: (650) 655 7665
Email: admin@ncgu.edu
Web site: www.ncgu.edu

Ph.D.'s in counseling psychology and higher education, as well as Psy.D. and Ed.D. geared to persons already practicing in the appropriate field, and a master's in marriage and family therapy, through evening and Saturday courses. Approved by the state of California.

Nyingma Institute

1815 Highland Place
Berkeley, CA 94709
Fields offered: Human development based on Tibetan Buddhism
Year founded: 1972
Phone: (510) 843 6812
Fax: (510) 486 1679
Email: nyingma-institute@nyingma.org
Web site: www.nyingma.org

Curriculum includes philosophy, psychology, language study, meditation practice, history, culture, and comparative studies.

Oakley Smith School of Naprapathy

See: Chicago National College of Naprapathy

Ryokan College   B, M, D

11965 Venice Blvd.
Los Angeles, CA 90066
Fields offered: Human behavior, counseling psychology, clinical psychology
Year founded: 1979
Phone: (310) 390 7560
Fax: (310) 391 7956
Web site: www.ryokan.edu

The state-approved degree programs are for mature, career-oriented people with at least two years of undergraduate college work. Classes are held in supportive small group settings; there are no exams and no grades.

Samra University of Oriental Medicine   M

3000 South Robertson Blvd., 4th Floor
Los Angeles, CA 90034
Fields offered: Oriental medicine, acupuncture, herbology
Year founded: 1965
Phone: (310) 202 6444
Fax: (310) 202 6007
Email: Info@samra.edu
Web site: www.samra.edu/

Clinical facilities established to serve the needs of the community. Classes are taught day, evening, and Saturday, in English, Chinese, and Korean. Minimum time required to earn a degree is 36 months; all students must complete 60 semester credits of general/technical education (some of this requirement can be met with military training).

South African College of Natural Medicine

Bergzicht Building
36 De Villiers St.
Strand, 7140, South Africa
Fields offered: Natural medicine, herbalism
Year founded: 1987
Phone: +27 (21) 854 3529

Fax: +27 (21) 853 1596
Email: natmed@ilink.nis.za
Diplomas in natural or herbal medicine, through distance learning. Coursework is delivered mainly via written assignments and readings, with close faculty contact maintained by telephone and/or audiotape. Affiliated to the British School of Phytotherapy.

South Baylo University   B, M, D

1126 N. Brookhurst St.
Anaheim, CA 92801
Fields offered: Oriental medicine, acupuncture
Year founded: 1978
Phone: (714) 533 1495 ▪ (888) 642 2956
Fax: (714) 533 6040
Email: siom@siteconnect.com
Web site: www.southbaylo.edu
Residential programs in Oriental medicine and acupuncture. Also known as Keimyung Baylo University. At one time, offered bachelor's, master's, and doctorates but now, apparently, only a Bachelor of Science in holistic science.

Southern California Psychoanalytic Institute   D

9024 Olympic Blvd.
Beverly Hills, CA 90211
Fields offered: Psychoanalysis
Year founded: 1950
Phone: (310) 276 2455
Email: scpilib@earthlink.net
Web site: www.socalpsa.org
The Southern California Psychoanalytic Institute offers the Ph.D. in psychoanalysis for psychiatrists, clinical psychologists, and psychiatric social workers. It also offers a small research program in psychoanalysis for which a Ph.D. degree in an academic field is required. Approved to operate by the state of California.

Tien Tao Chong Hua University   B, M, D

5440 Pomona Blvd.
Los Angeles, CA 90022
Fields offered: Tien tao
Year founded: 1990
Phone: (323) 722 6693
Fax: (323) 722 6178
Offers degrees at all levels in tien tao–oriented studies, which materials on the school describe as a Confucian pursuit of truth and knowledge.

University of Northern California   B, M, D

101 S. San Antonio Rd.
Petaluma, CA 94952
Fields offered: Biomedical engineering, languages, applied linguistics
Year founded: 1993
Phone: (707) 765 6400
Fax: (707) 769 8600
Email: admits@uncm.ed
Web site: www.uncm.edu
Offers the B.A. in engineering, applied linguistics, and languages, and B.E., M.S., and Ph.D. degrees in biomedical engineering, through evening and weekend courses. Approved to operate in the state of California.

University of Santa Monica   M

Center for the Study & Practice of Spiritual Psychology
2107 Wilshire Blvd.
Santa Monica, CA 90403
Fields offered: Applied psychology, counseling psychology
Year founded: 1976
Phone: (310) 829 7402
Email: info@gousm.edu
Web site: www.gousm.edu
M.A. in spiritual psychology, in which students earn the degree by demonstrating knowledge, skills, and qualities of efficiently relating with themselves and others. According to the school's materials, they are "guaranteed to positively transform your life while you earn a Master's degree! . . . dynamic graduate programs on the cutting edge where psychology interfaces with spirituality." Formerly called Koh-I-Noor University.

World University of America   B, M, D

107 N. Ventura St.
Ojai, CA 93023
Fields offered: Many fields
Year founded: 1974
Phone: (805) 646 1444
Fax: (805) 646 1217
Email: contact@worldu.edu
Web site: www.worldu.edu
Named by Indian holy man Sai Baba, they offer degrees and certificates offered in counseling psychology global studies, yoga, spiritual ministry, and hypnotherapy. The school's stated goal is "to promote spiritual growth within the framework of an academic curriculum." They are a member of the nonwonderful and unrecognized World Association of Universities and Colleges. Not affiliated with the formerly accredited World University of Puerto Rico.

Yuin University

See: California Yuin University

Grading homework assignments at the
Acme College of Bicycle Tire Repair.

CHAPTER 24

High School Diplomas

> Education is what remains when you have forgotten everything you learned in school.
>
> *Albert Einstein*
>
> *(also attributed to B.F. Skinner)*

The first thing to say is that, even if you have not completed high school, you probably will not need to do so in order to enroll in a nontraditional college degree program.

The high school diploma is the usual "ticket of admission" to a traditional university. However, many universities, both traditional and nontraditional, believe that anywhere from two to seven years of life or job experience is at least the equivalent of a high school diploma. So if you are over the age of 25, you should have no trouble finding schools that do not require a high school diploma. If you are between 18 and 25, you may have to shop around a little, or may find it necessary to complete high school (or its equivalent) first. And if you're under 18, it will be a bit more of a challenge, but we've heard from lots of people who succeeded (including two in our own family).

Here are six ways to complete high school (or its equivalent) and get a high school diploma by nontraditional means:

1. The High School Division of a University

While many universities offer high school–level correspondence courses, not many award high school diplomas entirely through correspondence study. These diplomas are the exact equivalent of a traditional high school diploma and are accepted everywhere.

Brigham Young University
Attn: High School Programs
P.O. Box 21514
Provo, UT 84602-1514
Phone: (801) 378 5078
Web site: ce.byu.edu/is
With an extensive catalog of online and correspondence high school courses, BYU has a program where students who are 19 or older can earn a high school diploma through cooperating school districts.

Indiana University High School
Owen Hall 001
790 E. Kirkwood Ave.
Bloomington, IN 47405-7101
Phone: (800) 334 1011
Email: scs@indiana.edu
Web site: scs.indiana.edu
Indiana University's School of Continuing Studies, provider of the university's distance-learning degrees, also offers a high school diploma program. Courses, developed and taught by certified high school teachers, are mostly print-based, though some employ the Internet, CD-ROMs, or other technologies.

Texas Tech University High School
Box 42191
Lubbock, TX 79409
Phone: (806) 742 2352 ▪ (800) 692 6877
Fax: (806) 742 2318
Email: distlearn@ttu.edu
Web site: www.dce.ttu.edu
Established in 1993, Texas Tech University High School is a public high school accredited by the Texas Education Agency to provide curriculum to self-motivated traditional and nontraditional students completely at a distance.

University of Missouri—Columbia High School
Center for Distance and Independent Study
136 Clark Hall
Columbia, MO 65211-4200
Phone: (573) 882 2491 ▪ (800) 609 3727
Fax: (573) 882 6808
Email: cdis@missouri.edu
Web site:
cdis.missouri.edu/MUHighSchool/HShome.htm
Provides a diploma program, with over 130 courses to choose from, for adults and other students with a need for an alternative to traditional high school attendance. Accredited by the North Central Association of Colleges and Schools.

University of Nebraska—Lincoln

Independent Study High School
Clifford Hardin Nebraska Center for Continuing
    Education, Room 255
33rd and Holdrege
Lincoln, NE 68583-9100
Phone: (402) 472 4321
Fax: (402) 472 1901
Email: unldde1@unl.edu
Web site: dcs.unl.edu/disted

Founded in 1929 to help small rural schools, and now serving 14,000 students from all 50 states and 135 countries. Accredited by the North Central Association and the Nebraska Department of Education and authorized to grant an accredited high school diploma.

2. State and Local Departments of Education

Several state and local school districts offer people throughout the United States, Canada, and worldwide the opportunity to earn a high school diploma by studying correspondence courses.

Florida High School

445 West Amelia St., 5th Floor
Orlando, FL 32801
Phone: (407) 317 3326
Web site: www.sbac.edu/~fhs

Begun in August, 1997, as a joint project between Alachua and Orange County Public Schools. Offers online courses to Florida residents and, in 2001, plans to round out its curriculum and issue its own diplomas.

Kentucky Virtual High School

Phone: (877) 740 4357
Email: kcvu@mail.state.ky.us
Web site: www.kvhs.org

Managed by the Kentucky Department of Education, KVHS offers a wide range of online courses, which count for credit toward a degree at the student's local high school.

Michigan Virtual High School

University Corporate Research Park
3101 Technology Parkway, Suite G
Lansing, MI 48910-8356
Phone: (517) 336 7733
Fax: (517) 336 7787
Email: mivu@mivu.org
Web site: www.mivu.org

Scheduled to open in 2001, with plans to serve homebound students as well as adult learners pursuing their G.E.D.'s.

Mindquest

Bloomington Public Schools
8900 Portland Ave. South
Bloomington, MN 55420
Phone: (952) 885 8450
Fax: (952) 885 8640
Email: coordinator@mindquest.bloomington.k12.mn.us
Web site: www.mindquest.org

Billed as "the world's first public high school diploma completely on the Internet," Mindquest is a part of the Bloomington public school district in Minnesota. Free for Minnesota residents, but students anywhere in the world may enroll for a fee.

North Dakota Department of Public Instruction

Division of Independent Study
Box 5036
1510 12th Ave. North
Fargo, ND 58105-5036
Phone: (701) 231 6000
Fax: (701) 231 6052
Web site: www.dis.dpi.state.nd.us

Vance-Granville Community College

P.O. Box 917
Henderson, NC 27536
Phone: (252) 492 2061
Fax: (252) 430 0460
Email: info@vgcc.cc.nc.us
Web site: www.vgcc.cc.nc.us

The Adult High School Diploma is available to anyone over the age of 18. Applicants take a diagnostic reading inventory to determine reading proficiency. They must have a high school reading proficiency before beginning other coursework.

Virtual High School

72 Victoria St. South, Suite 401
Kitchener, Ontario N2G 4Y9, Canada
Phone: +1 (519) 772 0325
Web site: www.virtualhighschool.com

Accredited coursework delivered via the Internet for earning the Ontario Secondary School Diploma. No textbooks to buy and no classes to attend. Electronic texts have been designed and developed for each course.

3. Accredited Private High Schools

Here are some. The DETC, Distance Education and Training Council, is a recognized accreditor, specializing in home study programs, including high school diploma programs.

American School

2200 East 170th St.
Lansing, IL 60438
Phone: (708) 418 2800 ▪ (800) 531 9268
Web site: www.americanschoolofcorr.com

Founded in 1897 and accredited by the North Central Association and DETC.

Cambridge Academy

3855 SE Lake Weir Ave.
Ocala, FL 34480
Phone: (352) 401 3688 ▪ (800) 252 3777
Fax: (352) 401 9013
Email: info@cambridgeacademy.com
Web site: www.cambridgeacademy.com
Founded in 1978 and accredited by the Southern Association of Colleges and Schools.

Christa McAuliffe Academy

3601 W. Washington Ave.
Yakima, WA 98903
Phone: (509) 575 4989
Fax: (509) 575 4976
Email: cma@cmacademy.org
Web site: www.cmacademy.org
Founded in 1985 and accredited by the Northwest Association of Schools and Colleges.

Citizens' High School

P.O. Box 1929
Orange Park, FL 32067
Phone: (904) 276 1700
Fax: (904) 272 6702
Email: citizenschool@schoolmail.com
Web site: www.citizenschool.com
Founded in 1981 and accredited by DETC.

Harcourt High School

925 Oak St.
Scranton, PA 18515
Phone: (570) 342 7701 ▪ (800) 275 4409
Email: info@harcourt-learning.com
Web site: www.harcourt-learning.com/programs/diploma
Founded in 1972. Accredited by DETC. A division of Harcourt Learning Direct. Formerly called ICS-Newport/Pacific High School.

Home Study International

P.O. Box 4437
Silver Spring, MD 20914
Phone: (301) 680-6570 ▪ (800) 782 4769
Fax: (301) 680 5157
Email: contact@hsi.edu
Web site: www.hsi.edu
Founded in 1909 and accredited by DETC.

James Madison High School

Professional Career Development Institute
430 Technology Parkway
Norcross, GA 30092
Phone: (770) 729 8400 ▪ (800) 223 4542
Fax: (770) 729 9296
Web site: www.pcdi-homestudy.com/courses/jm
Founded in 1987 and accredited by DETC.

When the Crabtree twins failed the G.E.D. for the 34th time, they decided to take matters into their own hands.

Keystone National High School

School House Station
420 West 5th St.
Bloomsburg, PA 17815-1564
Phone: (570) 784 5220 ▪ (800) 255 4937
Fax: (570) 784 2129
Email: info@keystonehighschool.com
Web site: www.keystonehighschool.com
Founded in 1972. A division of NLKK, Inc. Accredited by DETC.

Phoenix Special Programs and Academies

1717 West Northern Ave., Suite 104
Phoenix, AZ 85021-5469
Phone: (602) 674 5555 ▪ (800) 426 4952
Fax: (602) 943 9700
Email: e-mail@phoenixacademies.org
Web site: www.phoenixacademies.org
Founded in 1926 and accredited by the North Central Association.

Richard Milburn High School

14416 Jefferson Davis Highway, Suite 8
Woodbridge, VA 22191
Phone: (703) 494 0147
Fax: (703) 494 6093
Email: rmhsinfo@aol.com
Web site: www.rmhs.org
Founded in 1975 and accredited by the Southern Association of Schools and Colleges and DETC.

4. Unaccredited distance high schools

As in the world of higher education, unaccredited schools offer some interesting options, but before undertaking such a program, one must be very, very certain that the diploma will meet one's needs. Here are three options:

CALCampus

P.O. Box 734
East Rochester, New York 14445
Fax: (716) 381-6648
Email: director@calcampus.com
Web site: www.calcampus.com
Founded by the late Ray Chasse, who was also involved in the operation of several unaccredited universities in Louisiana and Alabama, this high school diploma program is run from New York, registered with the state of California, with records stored in Louisiana. The diploma is issued by the American Academy of the American Coastline Professional Development Institute of Studio City, California, affiliated with Chasse's American Coastline University in Louisiana.

Covenant Home Curriculum

N63 W23421 Main St.
Sussex, WI 53089
Phone: (262) 246 4760 ▪ (800) 578 2421
Email: educate@covenanthome.com
Web site: www.covenanthome.com
The school's literature says "A New Kind of Revival is in the Land," and that they offer a "complete, eclectic, classical approach" to K-12 education.

Dennison Academy

P.O. Box 29781
Los Angeles, CA 90029
Phone: (818) 371 2001
Email: principal@dennisononline.com
Web site: www.dennisononline.com
Registered with the Los Angeles County Office of Education and the California State Board of Education. Claims accreditation from the Accreditation Commission for International Internet Education, an unrecognized agency.

5. Home Schooling

There is a large and growing movement toward educating children at home. It isn't easy, but it can be richly rewarding. There are now quite a few local, regional, and national support organizations, both religious and secular. Here are two national organizations:

Holt Associates Book and Music Store

2380 Massachusetts Ave., Suite 104
Cambridge, MA 02140-1226
Phone: (617) 864 3100 ▪ (888) 925 9298
Fax: (617) 864 9235
Email: info@holtgws.com
Web site: www.holtgws.com
John Holt is the author of *How Children Fail* and other books on educational reform, and founded a magazine called *Growing Without Schooling*. His organization has a nice catalog of educational materials for the home schooler.

Home School Legal Defense Association

P.O. Box 3000
Purcellville, VA 20134
Phone: (540) 338 5600
Web site: www.hslda.org
This evangelical Christian organization offers advice and information for parents interested in—and/or having legal problems with—home schooling. They also sell a high school diploma, so that people who home school their children can still award those children an attractive certificate. This document may not be accepted in some situations, and their literature makes it clear that, "by sale of this diploma, Home School Legal Defense Association does not certify completion of any course of study."

6. State Equivalency Examinations

Each of the 50 states offers a high school equivalency examination, sometimes called the G.E.D., which is the equivalent of a high school diploma for virtually all purposes, including admission to college. Although each state's procedures differ, in general the examination takes from three to five hours, and covers the full range of high school subjects: mathematics, science, language, history, social studies, etc. It must be taken in person, not by mail. For the details in any given state, contact that state's Department of Education in the state capitol.

It is important to note that significant changes to the G.E.D. will be implemented in early 2002, so that if you prepare for the test with currently available materials, you will really not be ready for the new test, which has been redesigned to reflect changes in what experts feel a high school graduate should know. For instance, the math portion will include dealing with a calculator, and the science portion will require an understanding of experimental design. Details on the new G.E.D. can be found at *www.acenet.edu/calec/ged*. There are still no announced plans for an online version, although there are many who have talked about and recommended it.

CHAPTER 25

Law Schools

Laws are like spider's webs which, if anything small falls into them, they ensnare it, but large things break through and escape.

Solon (7th century B.C.E.)

The law is a curiosity of the academic world. On one hand, it is possible to graduate from a world-famous law school and not be able to practice law. And on the other hand, it is possible to practice law without ever having seen the inside of a law school.

What makes this unusual set of circumstances possible is, of course, the Bar exam. In all 50 states of the United States, the way most people are "admitted to the Bar" is by taking and passing this exam. Each state administers its own exam, and there is the Multi-State Bar exam, which is accepted by most states for some or all Bar exam credit.

Until the 20th century, most lawyers learned the law the way Abraham Lincoln, Andrew Jackson, and several other U.S. presidents did—either by apprenticing themselves to a lawyer or a judge or by studying on their own and, when they had learned enough, taking the Bar. A small handful of states still permit this practice, although it is little used.

Most of those who do study law nontraditionally deal in one way or another with the state of California, where the study of law is, in many aspects, different from the rest of the U.S. This is why California is considered separately in this chapter.

In a few states, if one graduates from a law school in that state, it is not necessary to take that state's Bar exam in order to practice law. In a few states, graduates of unaccredited law schools may be permitted to take the Bar exam. There are two problems we have in reporting these facts: one is that the situation keeps changing—states seem regularly to revise or reinterpret their regulations—and the other is that rules and regulations seem often to be rather flexible or at least inconsistent in the way they are interpreted (see chapter 29, "Bending the Rules").

The Bar Exam

The Bar exam has come under increasing criticism in recent years, on a number of grounds.

For one thing, there often seems to be little correlation between performance on the Bar and performance as a lawyer. Most Bar exams, for instance, do not test ability to do legal research, conduct interviews, or argue in court.

In addition, a test score that will pass in one state will fail in another. Consider the score required to pass, in several states, in one recent year:

California: 145	Pennsylvania: 129
New York: 135	Texas: 128
Florida: 130	Wisconsin: 125

One critic has pointed out that if California test takers had gone en masse to New York, their pass rate would have been 74% instead of California's rather dismal 42% that year.

In recent years, the Bar exam has undergone frequent and major changes. Gordon Schaber, former chairman of the ABA's section on legal education, points out that the California exam underwent "10 serious structural changes" over a ten-year period, during which time the pass rate dropped 12%. Following significant changes after that ten-year period, the pass rate dropped another 9%. The failure rate might have been higher, but nearly half the minority graduates at UCLA (which has the largest minority law student population in the state) chose not to take the California Bar exam. The pass rate for some minorities has been significantly lower than for other groups, although the majority of those who failed in California would have passed the New York or Pennsylvania exam with the same scores.

Although the quality of law education is generally felt to continue to improve, the percentage of people passing the Bar has steadily declined in recent years. As one example, Schaber cites an entering Stanford class which had the highest LSAT (Law School Admissions Test) scores ever, and a grade point average of 3.79 on a scale of 4. Yet when this class graduated four years later and took the Bar exam, only 75% passed—down 17% from a few years earlier.

Can it be, people are asking more and more, that there may be too many lawyers in the world, and the already established ones are trying to limit the new competition? In recent years, the number of lawyers has increased at more than double the rate of the population as a whole. There are more lawyers in Chicago than in all of Japan; more in New York than in all of England.

The Law Degree

Until the early 1960s, the law degree earned in America was the LL.B., or Bachelor of Laws. An LL.D., or Doctor of Laws, was available at some schools as an advanced law degree, earned after several years of study beyond the LL.B. Many lawyers didn't like the idea that lots of other professionals (optometrists, podiatrists, civil engineers, etc.) put in three years of study after college and got a doctorate, while lawyers put in the same time and got just another bachelor's. Law schools took heed, and almost universally converted the title of the law degree to a J.D., which can stand for Doctor of Jurisprudence or Juris Doctor. Most schools offered their alumni the opportunity to convert their old LL.B.'s into nice shiny J.D.'s. One survey reported that a large percentage accepted, but another report suggests that very few of these actually use the J.D. professionally, still listing the LL.B. in legal directories. In either event, very few lawyers refer to themselves as "Doctor," although those with the J.D. certainly have that option.

Unaccredited Residential Law Schools

Six states and the District of Columbia permit the operation of law schools not approved by the American Bar Association, but only in California can law study by correspondence also qualify one to take the Bar. The unaccredited residential schools—located in Alabama, California, Georgia, Massachusetts, Tennessee, Virginia, and D.C.— are not nontraditional, in the sense that one must attend classes, and then take the Bar. (California has more than 30 such non-ABA-approved residential schools, Alabama has two, and the other states mentioned have one each.)

In many situations, graduates of these schools can only take the Bar in the state where the school is located, or in a state in which one has permanent residence. Taking the Bar in a second state typically requires a certain number of years of practice in the first state (three to ten).

Correspondence Study

California is the only state that regularly permits graduates of correspondence law schools to take the state Bar. (We say "regularly" because, as indicated earlier, there are apparently special case exceptions in other states, from time to time.)

To be eligible to take the California Bar, a correspondence student must be a graduate of a school located in California, despite the claims made by certain correspondence law schools in Kansas, Louisiana, and elsewhere. (This was not always so; before 1990 there was no requirement that the correspondence school be located in California.)

The procedure works like this: After completing one year of law study, which must include a documented 864 hours of study (about 17 hours a week), the student must take the First Year Law Students' Qualifying Exam, known as the "Baby Bar." This is a consumer protection measure, to help students studying law nontraditionally determine whether or not they are making progress. The Baby Bar typically last for eight hours, and includes questions on contracts, torts, and criminal law.

Baby Bar pass rates have been low in recent years. The factors that come into play are

▶ the quality of the school's course materials and methods (since pass rates have ranged from under 10% to more than 50%);

▶ the first-year law students not giving this examination the respect it deserves; and

▶ the often-voiced suspicion that law graduates from ABA schools who grade non-ABA law students' exams may not be as objective as one may wish.

Once the Baby Bar is passed, the student then continues for three additional years of study, 864 hours a year. When at least four years have passed and at least 3,456 hours have been logged, the regular Bar exam may be taken.

Copies of recent years' versions of the Baby Bar, with answers, may be purchased from the State Bar of California, 180 Howard Street, San Francisco, CA 94105-1639; (415) 538 2000; *www.calbar.org*.

The Baby Bar is also required of all students in unaccredited residential law schools.

Until 1996, law students who took the Baby Bar were "on hold" until the results came in three or four months later; they could not continue their formal studies. A new and very sensible law allows courses completed within a year after the Baby Bar to count for credit.

California Exam Performance

One could spend days studying and analyzing the huge amounts of data made available by the State Bar of California, giving pass rates by school, by date, by kind of school, by ethnic background, by number of previous exam attempts, and so forth.

Rather than fill this chapter with endless charts and tables, we have elected to present only the following data:

▶ Complete summary of statistics for a recent Bar exam

▶ Pass rates for individual correspondence law schools, cumulative for four consecutive Bar exams

▶ Recent results for California's First Year Law Students' Exam ("Baby Bar") for correspondence law schools

Please bear in mind that these statistics will vary considerably from year to year and school to school. Also of significance are the statistics on the "parlay" from the Baby Bar to the main Bar. If, for instance, only 10% of a school's students pass the Baby Bar, and if only 10% of those pass the main Bar, then only 1% of the original class (10% of 10%) will actually become lawyers.

Critics of the nontraditional approach argue that the lower pass rates "prove" that the approach cannot work. They point out that one of the largest unaccredited schools had about a 10% pass rate on the Baby Bar, and then about 25% on the main Bar, suggesting that out of every 100 students who start this program, only two or three will become lawyers.

Supporters point out that truly dedicated and highly motivated students do pass, and that many of these people would never have been able to pursue the degree by traditional means. They also suggest that some people take the Bar exams as a matter of curiosity, with little expectation of passing.

It is clearly the case that for the would-be lawyer who cannot afford either the time or the money for traditional law study, or who cannot gain admission to an accredited law school, California approaches offer the best hope.

In addition to qualifying students for the California Bar, completion of unaccredited law programs may also qualify graduates to take the exams required for practice before U.S. tax and patent courts, workers compensation boards, the Interstate Commerce Commission, and various other federal courts and agencies. As with any degree program, potential students should satisfy themselves in advance that the degree will meet their personal needs.

Overall California Bar Data

February 2000

	Took	Passed	%
All takers, all schools	**4793**	**1959**	**41%**
First-time takers	1654	871	53%
Repeaters	3139	1088	35%
ABA-approved schools	**2696**	**1171**	**43%**
First timers	783	387	49%
Repeaters	1913	784	41%
California-Bar accredited but not ABA-approved	**678**	**179**	**26%**
First timers	122	37	30%
Repeaters	556	142	26%
Not ABA-approved and not California Bar-accredited	**213**	**36**	**17%**
First timers	42	8	19%
Repeaters	171	28	16%
Correspondence schools	**88**	**31**	**35%**
First timers	36	21	58%
Repeaters	52	10	19%
Private study with lawyer or judge	**5**	**0**	**0%**
First timers	1	0	0%
Repeaters	4	0	0%

Correspondence Law Schools, Baby Bar

October 1999

	Took	Passed	%
Abraham Lincoln U.	24	6	25%
Blackstone School of Law*	1	0	0%
British-American U.	4	1	25%
City U. Los Angeles*	2	0	0%
Concord U. School of Law	20	7	35%
Kensington U.*	1	0	0%
Newport U.	3	0	0%
Northwestern California U.	17	3	18%
Oak Brook College of Law	39	20	51%
Saratoga U.	3	2	67%
Southern California U.	5	1	20%
William H. Taft U.	40	10	25%

No longer qualifies students for California Bar

Correspondence Law Schools, Regular Bar—All Test Takers

for the four test sessions from July 1998 through February 2000

	Took	Passed	%
Abraham Lincoln	3	1	33%
Bernadean University	3	0	0%
British-American U.	1	0	0%
City University Los Angeles	7	0	0%
Kensington University	18	4	22%
Newport University	33	8	24%
Northwestern California U.	52	6	12%
Oak Brook College of Law	21	16	76%
Southern California U.	7	1	14%
Thomas Jefferson College	6	1	17%
William H. Taft University	124	22	18%

Correspondence Law Schools, Regular Bar—First-Time Takers

for the four test sessions from July 1998 through February 2000

	Took	Passed	%
Abraham Lincoln	2	1	50%
Bernadean University	0	0	0%
British-American U.	1	0	0%
City University Los Angeles	0	0	0%
Kensington University	2	1	50%
Newport University	13	3	23%
Northwestern California U.	17	3	18%
Oak Brook College of Law	21	16	76%
Southern California U.	3	1	33%
Thomas Jefferson College	0	0	0%
William H. Taft University	30	10	33%

Results for the main Bar exam can be found on the California Bar's Web site at www.calbar.org. "Baby Bar" results can be obtained by calling the California Committee of Bar Examiners at (415) 538 2303.

Becoming a Lawyer by Apprenticeship

There are still a few states left where it is possible to qualify for the Bar exam by studying law privately under the supervision of either a lawyer or a judge. Though it's not easy to set up an apprenticeship program on one's own, it can be, and has been, done.

All of the states where apprenticeship is possible—Alaska, California, Maine, New York, Vermont, Virginia, Washington, and Wyoming—require evidence of four continuous years of law study. Some of those—Alaska, Maine, New York, and Wyoming—require that one of those years be at an ABA-approved law school. California also requires one year at a law school, but it doesn't have to be ABA-approved. (These are general guidelines; be sure to contact the individual state's Bar for specific requirements.)

For those aspiring to become a lawyer by apprenticeship, one noteworthy resource is the Law School Apprenticeship Program, operated by Roger Agajanian, who also runs the British-American University School of Law (see listing later in this chapter). Its library of over 200 video lectures (available over the Web, on CD-ROM, or on tape) is designed to supplement the study of apprentice law students.

Law School Apprenticeship Program
2565 I-Rd.
Grand Junction, CO 81501
Phone: (800) 529 9383
Fax: (970) 256 0565
Email: info@lawprogram.com
Web site: www.lawprogram.com

Correspondence Law School in Other Countries

It is theoretically possible to study law either in person or by correspondence study from a country other than the United States, and then qualify for the Bar exam, or, in the case of some states, to petition for admission to the Bar without taking the exam (see list of states below). While the situation is different in every state, the common requirement is that the non-U.S. law school must be one in which the principles of English law are taught, and that the training come from an English-speaking common-law nation. (The lone U.S. exception is Louisiana, whose law is based on the Napoleonic code.)

The qualifying countries are pretty much limited to Australia, Canada, China (Hong Kong only), England, Ireland, Scotland, and Wales.

But in practice, the only school that offers appropriate correspondence courses leading to the law degree (the Bachelor of Law, or LL.B.) is the University of London.

The J.D. to LL.M. to Bar Exam "Parlay" Strategy

There is an intriguing strategy that has been devised for Americans who wish to study law by correspondence, and who do not live in one of the states that will accept or consider either an unaccredited California law degree or a degree from the University of London. The strategy is based on the fact that the Master of Law degree (LL.M.) is in fact a more advanced degree than the Doctor of Jurisprudence (J.D.).

It is theoretically possible for the holder of an unaccredited J.D. to gain admission to an ABA-approved LL.M. program and, on completion of that LL.M., to sit for the Bar exam in most states. Again, each state has its own rules and interpretations, and some (list follows) offer a more straightforward path than others.

There are three issues at work here:

1. Finding an LL.M.-offering ABA-approved law school that is willing to accept students with an unaccredited J.D. degree.

2. Making the necessary arrangement with a state, to be confident that one will be able to take the Bar exam under such circumstances.

3. Hoping that the American Bar Association doesn't change the rules, in order to prevent this strategy from working.

With regard to the first, there are at least two California correspondence schools—British-American University and Saratoga University—that state they have made arrangements for their J.D. graduates to be admitted to an ABA-approved LL.M. program.

With regard to the second, before undertaking five years of study (four for the J.D., one more for the LL.M.), one should be as certain as one can be that one will be permitted to sit for the Bar. There is no precedent here; no one has yet done this. The notion of getting a written guarantee does come to mind.

With regard to the third, it seems clear that the American Bar Association is not enthusiastic about the study of law other than in schools they have accredited. Many states that used to offer either the apprenticeship approach or allow unaccredited schools succumbed to ABA pressure, and have changed their laws. Lawyers such as John Adams, Thomas Jefferson, John Quincy Adams, Andrew Jackson and Abraham Lincoln would no longer be able to qualify in the way they originally did. There is simply no way of knowing if this J.D. to LL.M. to Bar exam parlay will attract the attention, the concern, or even the wrath of the ABA and, if so, what the effect will be on people who

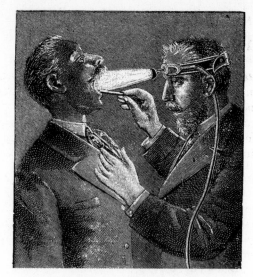

Darryl knew that there would be an oral examination at the end of his distance-learning course, but this was not what he had expected.

have completed, or are on the path to completion, of their degrees by this path.

The Nature of LL.M. Study

The Master of Laws is not a wildly popular degree option in the U.S., and as a result, there is rarely a waiting list for admission, except perhaps to the top-tier programs such as Harvard and Yale. It is typically regarded as an opportunity for law school graduates to specialize in a certain aspect of the law, such as taxation, international business, labor law, ocean and coastal law, etc., although there are a fair number of general programs as well.

While the LL.M. is generally regarded as a full-time residential program, it can be quite nontraditional, in that it is typically based on a one-to-one mentor-student relationship without classroom attendance. As a result, there is the possibility of negotiating, as with the British research degrees described in Appendix D, for a course of study involving occasional meetings, which conceivably could be done at least in part by Internet, telephone, or other distance means. Regent University School of Law (see listing below) offers its LL.M. in international taxation entirely over the Internet.

The bottom line here is that the "parlay" approach is intriguing, but until it has been tested and proven, must be considered at least a bit risky. We look forward to learning more as the pioneers move along this path.

Lists of States That Offer Various Law Options

States and jurisdictions where people with a non-ABA-approved law degree may be eligible to take the Bar examination

Specific rules vary widely, but often require a certain number of years (five is common) of prior active practice in another state. Consult the individual state's Bar.

Alabama	Kentucky
Alaska	Maine
Arizona	Nevada
California	New Mexico
Colorado	New York
Connecticut	Pennsylvania
District of Columbia	Texas
Hawaii	Wisconsin

States where people who have studied law by apprenticeship with a lawyer or judge may petition to take the Bar examination

Alaska	Vermont
California	Virginia
Maine	Washington
New York	Wyoming

States which allow foreign law graduates to petition to practice law without taking the Bar examination

District of Columbia	Ohio
New York	Washington
North Carolina	Wisconsin

States which may allow foreign law graduates to practice law after passing the Bar examination

Alabama	North Carolina
California	Ohio
Colorado	Oregon
Connecticut	Pennsylvania
District of Columbia	Rhode Island
Hawaii	Tennessee
Kentucky	Texas
Maine	Utah
Missouri	Vermont
Nevada	Virginia
New Mexico	Washington
New York	

States in which a person with an unaccredited J.D. and an ABA-approved LL.M. may petition to take the Bar exam

Arizona	Michigan
California	New York
Connecticut	Virginia
Kansas	West Virginia
Montana	

Since the rules and regulations on who can take the Bar not only vary from state to state but also change from time to time (and are subject to interpretation), it would make good sense to consult our source for this information, the American Bar Association, which publishes state-by-state charts and tables of Bar admission requirements, as well as supplementary remarks helping to define or explain the various rules. On the Web go to *www.abanet.org/legaled*, or call (800) 285 2221 and ask for the annually updated *Comprehensive Guide to Bar Admission Requirements*, $12.50.

Bar-Exam-Qualifying Correspondence Law Schools

At the time of writing, graduates of all schools in this section qualified to take the California Bar exam. Since the rules change from time to time, it would be appropriate to confirm the status with the California Committee of Bar Examiners (180 Howard Street, San Francisco, CA 94105-1639; (415) 538 2303; email: *info@calbar.org*; Web site: *www.calbar.org*) before embarking on any program. In the past, even when a school was disqualified, graduates were given a generous time period (typically seven years) in which to pass the Bar. But, as any lawyer would caution, that is no guarantee of future behavior. And, as suggested in an earlier section, the University of London may qualify one to sit for the Bar in various ways in eighteen states plus Puerto Rico and the District of Columbia.

Abraham Lincoln University
3000 South Robertson Blvd., Suite 420
Los Angeles, CA 90034
Phone: (310) 204 0222
Fax: (310) 204 7025
Email: info@alulaw.com
Web site: www.alulaw.com
It is possible to listen to sample lectures at the school's Web site.

British-American University School of Law
2026 Summer Wind
Santa Ana, CA 92704
Phone: (714) 850 1027 ▪ (888) 264 3261
Fax: (714) 850 4621
Email: info@lawprogram.com
Web site: www.british-american.edu
Established in 1998 by Roger Agajanian, who also established the Law School Apprenticeship Program described earlier. The law students have access to the more-than-200 video lectures that are also a part of the apprentice program.

Concord University School of Law
1133 Westwood Blvd., Suite 2000
Los Angeles, CA 90024
Phone: (310) 824 6980 ▪ (800) 439 4794
Fax: (888) 564 6745
Email: info@concordlawschool.com

Web site: www.concord.kaplan.edu

Owned and operated by the very large Kaplan test preparation company which is, itself, a part of the very much larger Washington Post company. When Concord opened its virtual doors in 1998, there was much hope and expectation that, with Washington Post money and Kaplan's expertise in test preparation, the school could not only attract many students but also improve significantly on the typically very low pass rates achieved by correspondence law students. Unfortunately, the Baby Bar results for Concord's first few classes suggest much room for improvement.

Newport University School of Law

20101 S.W. Birch Street, Suite 120
Newport Beach, CA 92660
Phone: (949) 757 1155 ▪ (800) 345 3272
Fax: (949) 757 1156
Email: info@newport.edu
Web site: www.newport.edu
See full listing in chapter 21.

Northwestern California University School of Law

1750 Howe Ave., Suite 535
Sacramento, CA 95825
Phone: (916) 922 9303
Fax: (916) 922 0418
Email: nculaw@aol.com
Web site: www.nwculaw.edu

The university divides its law studies into four parts. Students who complete the first two parts earn a Bachelor of Science in law. Those who complete three parts earn the J.D. degree but do not qualify to take the Bar exam. Completion of four parts qualifies students to take the California Bar.

Oak Brook College of Law and Government Policy

P. O. Box 26870
Fresno, CA 93729
(559) 650 7755 ▪ (888) 335 3425
Fax: (559) 650 7750
Email: info@obcl.edu
Web site: www.obcl.edu

Oak Brook has achieved impressive results on both the "Baby Bar" and the main Bar. The school is appropriate for students who support or are comfortable with their mission, as stated in their literature: "At Oak Brook College we believe that our nation has strayed from its Biblical moorings, and that its legal system is in need of reform. Oak Brook College is committed to training lawyers who understand the Biblical foundations of our legal institutions and who desire to practice law consistent with the Biblical principles of truth, justice, mercy and reconciliation." While the study is done totally by distance learning, mostly using the Internet, all new students must attend a one-week orientation conference held in Oklahoma City.

Saratoga University

780 Blairwood Court
San Jose, CA 95120.

Phone: (408) 927 6760 ▪ (800) 870 4246
Email: mhn@saratogau.edu
Web site: www.saratogau.edu

Offers a B.S. in law as well as the Juris Doctor (J.D.) wholly through correspondence. The programs are approved by the state of California and qualify graduates to sit for the Bar. (There is also a non-Bar program for those seeking professional development, etc.) The University states that it has made arrangements with several ABA-accredited law schools, whereby a student can complete either the 3-year (non-Bar) or 4-year (Bar-qualifying) J.D. at Saratoga, then go on to get a one-year LL.M. (Master of Law) at the other school, and thus qualify to take the Bar exam in virtually every state. Saratoga declines to name the ABA schools with which they have the arrangements, claiming that this is a "commercial secret," but says they will do so after a person enrolls and pays tuition, after signing an "indemnity" document, presumably preventing the student from disclosing the names. To our knowledge, no student has yet qualified to sit for a Bar exam by this method.

Southern California University for Professional Studies

1840 East 17th Street
Santa Ana, CA 92705-8605
Phone: (714) 480 0800 ▪ (800) 477 2254
Fax: (714) 480 0834
Email: enroll@scups.edu
Web site: www.scups.edu

The law school offers a number of degree programs, including a B.S., M.S., Bar-qualifying J.D., non-Bar-qualifying J.D., and LL.M., as well as a paralegal program. See full school listing in chapter 21.

University of Honolulu School of Law

1031 McHenry Ave., Suite #13
Modesto, CA 95350
Phone: (209) 523 4064
Fax: (209) 522 3312
Email: uhlaw@thevision.net
Web site: www.thevision.net/uhlaw
Originally from Hawaii.

University of London

The Information Centre, Malet St.
London WC1E 7HU United Kingdom
Phone: +44 (20) 7862 8360
Fax: +44 (20) 7862 8358
Email: enquiries@external.lon.ac.uk
Web site: www.lon.ac.uk/external
See full listing in chapter 18.

William Howard Taft University

201 East Sandpointe Ave., #400
Santa Ana, CA 92707-5703
Phone: (714) 850 4800 ▪ (800) 882 4555
Fax: (714) 708 2082
Email: admissions@taftu.edu
Web site: www.taftu.edu

In addition to the Bar-qualifying J.D. program, offers an LL.M. in taxation. See full listing in chapter 21.

Non-Bar-Exam-Qualifying Correspondence Law Schools

California law has changed several times with regard to Bar qualification. At one time, graduates of unaccredited law schools located anywhere in the U.S. could take the California Bar exam. Now, in order for its graduates to qualify to sit for the Bar, an unaccredited school must not only be located in California but also have state approval from the Bureau for Private, Postsecondary, and Vocational Education. (Students who graduated from unaccredited schools before the rules changed are still allowed to sit for the Bar; that is why we still sometimes see the name of a non-Bar-qualifying school in the Bar results.)

Thus there are two categories of non-Bar-exam-qualifying schools: those that once qualified students but don't any more, and those that never did.

American Barristers Academy

300 S. Capitol Ave.
Lansing, MI 48933
Email: tebrennan@aol.com
Web site: www.barristersacademy.com

Established by the former Chief Justice of the Michigan Supreme Court, T. E. Brennan, they claim to be the only law school in America which offers the degree of Legum Licentiatus (LL.L.), Licentiate of Laws, and the title Barrister at Law. The LL.B. and LL.M. is also offered. They say they prepare students to practice their profession in the most expeditious and effective manner, employing the most up-to-date electronic solutions in the service of their clients. All the work is done either online, or in a series of apprenticeships with practicing lawyers and judges, in one's own area. The charter class began in the fall of 2000, and it remains to be seen whether this degree will qualify one for the Michigan or other Bar exams.

Bernadean University

4842 Whitsett
North Hollywood, CA 91607
Phone: (818) 718 2447 ▪ (800) 542 3792
Email: bernadeanuniversity@mail.com
Web site: members.tripod.com/~bernadeanuniversity

At one time, graduates qualified to take the California Bar. A part of the Church of Universology, which in the past has offered to its graduates absolution from all sins.

City University Los Angeles

P.O. Box 4277
Inglewood, CA 90309-4277
Phone: (310) 671 0783 ▪ (800) 262 8388
Fax: (310) 671 0572
Email: info@cula.edu
Web site: www.cula.edu

Law programs were Bar-qualifying until the school lost its California approval in 1995. See full listing in chapter 21.

Columbia Pacific University

105 Digital Dr.
Novato, CA 94949
Phone: (415) 883 1400 ▪ (800) 552 5522

Offers a three-year non-Bar-qualifying law degree in international law. Graduates never qualified to take the Bar. Columbia Pacific's uncertain future is described in chapter 21.

Kensington University

520 East Broadway, Suite 400
Glendale, CA 91205
Phone: (818) 240 9166 ▪ (800) 423 2495
Fax: (818) 240 1707
Email: kensington@earthlink.net
Web site: www.kensington.edu

Lost its California approval in 1995. See full listing in chapter 21.

Regent University School of Law

1000 Regent University Dr.
Virginia Beach, VA 23464-9800
Phone: (757) 226 4613 ▪ (877) 850 8435
Fax: (757) 226 4654
Email: llm@regent.edu
Web site: www.regent.edu/acad/schlaw/llm

LL.M. (for lawyers) and general master's (for non-lawyers) in international taxation. See full listing in chapter 18.

Thomas Jefferson College of Law

3900 West Brown Deer Rd.
Suite A-288
Milwaukee, WI 53209-1220
Phone: (414) 297 9555 ▪ (800) 262 0175
Web site: www.heed.edu

A part of Heed University. No connection with Jefferson University or with Thomas Jefferson School of Law. See Heed's full listing in chapter 21.

Washington School of Law

2268 East Newcastle Dr.,
Salt Lake City, UT 84093
Phone: (801) 943 2440
Fax: (801) 944 8586
Email: washingtoninstitute@earthlink.net
Web site: www.washingtonschooloflaw.com

LL.M. and J.S.D. in taxation for lawyers.

Unaccredited Residential Law Schools

In previous editions, we also included a list of unaccredited but Bar-qualifying *residential* law schools in California. These schools all offer the standard law curriculum, mostly through evening and/or weekend courses. Their students, like those in correspondence law schools, must take the "Baby Bar" exam after their first year. The California Bar posts this list of schools, complete with contact information, on its Web site at *www.calbar.org/shared/2admsch.htm*.

Interstate Legal Strategies

Since the rules for becoming a lawyer vary so much from state to state, the question often arises: what about qualifying to practice law in one state (an "easier" one), and then moving to another state to practice?

It is possible, but quite impractical. Twenty-seven of the 50 states permit lawyers from another state to take the Bar in their state, but, in all but a few cases, only after they have practiced in their "home" state for a minimum number of years, and only if their degree is from an ABA-approved, accredited school. The minimum waiting time ranges from three years in Maine and Wisconsin to 20 years in Connecticut, but is four or five years in most states. Indiana and Iowa will, under certain conditions, permit lawyers admitted in other states to take their Bar with no waiting period.

Studying Law Nights or Weekends

In previous editions, we included a list of law schools that offered the law degree entirely through evening and/or weekend study. This practice, once relatively rare, has grown so rapidly that there are now a great many schools doing it. Simply check any standard school directory or the yellow pages of your telephone book for this information.

Paralegal Degrees

Many people who are intrigued by the law, and wish to be involved with the law, are unwilling or unable to pursue a law degree or to be admitted to the Bar. A fairly satisfactory solution for some of these people is to pursue an alternative degree, entirely by correspondence, or with short residency, in a law-related subject.

For instance, many people have earned nonresident master's or doctorate degrees in business law, law and society, import-export law, consumer law, and so forth. The titles of such degrees are things like M.A. in legal studies or Ph.D. in corporate law. Of course such degrees do not permit one to practice law. Many schools offering nonresident nontraditional degrees will consider such degree programs.

There are also many people who have never passed the Bar, but who are still working in the law. They have jobs with law firms, primarily doing research, preparing briefs, etc. They cannot meet with clients or appear in court, but they are most definitely lawyers working in the law.

Some of the schools offering paralegal studies by distance learning:

Blackstone School of Law
P.O. Box 701449
Dallas, TX 75370
Phone: (972) 418 5141 ▪ (800) 826 9228
Fax: (972) 418 1519
Email: blkstone@airmail.net
Web site: www.blackstonelaw.com

Harcourt Learning Direct
925 Oak Street
Scranton, PA 18515
Phone: (570) 342 7701 ▪ (800) 275 4409
Email: info@harcourt-learning.com
Web site: www.harcourt-learning.com

Kaplan College
1801 Clint Moore Road, Suite 215
Boca Raton, FL 33487
Phone: (561) 994 2522 ▪ (800) 669 2555
Fax: (561) 988 2223
Email: info@kaplancollege.com
Web site: www.kaplancollege.com

Paralegal Institute, Inc.
2933 West Indian School Road
Phoenix, AZ 85017
Phone: (602) 212 0501 ▪ (800) 354 1254
Fax: (602) 212 0502
Email: paralegalinst@mindspring.com
Web site: www.theparalegalinstitute.com

Professional Career Development Institute
430 Technology Parkway
Norcross, GA 30092
Phone: (770) 729 8400 ▪ (800) 223 4542
Fax: (770) 729 9296
Web site: www.pcdi.com

University of Maryland University College
3501 University Blvd. East
Adelphi, Maryland 20783
Phone: (301) 985 7000 ▪ (800) 283 6832
Fax: (301) 454 0399
Email: umucinfo@umuc.edu
Web site: www.umuc.edu

CHAPTER 26

Medical Schools

Five years after you finish medical school, everything you were taught will be wrong; but if you wait an additional five years it will be right again.

Traditional

Note: In early editions, this chapter was restricted to schools offering only the M.D. degree. Then, for a number of years, in response to many letters, we changed it to list "health-related" schools. Now we are changing back to "medical only," since we note that the line between "health-related" and general schools is increasingly difficult to draw, as in the case, for instance, of a degree in "running community health organizations" or "nursing management." Now all schools, except those offering the doctor of medicine, have been relocated to chapters 18 to 23, as relevant.

There are, of course, no legitimate correspondence medical schools, but there are some nontraditional approaches to earning a traditional medical degree.

The traditional approach in the U.S. consists of attending a regular college or university for four or more years to earn a bachelor's degree (in any field; it need not be scientific) and then going on to medical school for another four years, after which the Doctor of Medicine (M.D.) is awarded. Then one spends anywhere from two to eight years of internships, residency, and training in clinical specialties (surgery, psychiatry, etc.).

The problems caused by this huge expenditure of time and money (tuition of $30,000 a year is not uncommon) are compounded by the even greater problem of admission to a traditional medical school. The simple fact is that the great majority of applicants are not admitted. Many schools have anywhere from two to 50 applicants for each opening. Although schools are not allowed, by law, to have quotas by race or by sex, as they once did, they definitely have quotas based on age. Applicants over the age of 30 have a much harder time getting in, and those over 40 have almost no chance at all. The schools argue that their precious facilities should not be taken up by persons who will have fewer years to practice and to serve humanity.

Is There a Shortage of Doctors?

The reason it is so hard to get into medical school is that there are not enough openings available. And the reason there are not enough openings available is the subject of bitter debate between and among medical and political people.

The American Medical Association and the Association of American Medical Colleges both said throughout the 1980s that we would have too many doctors by the 1990s. But in 1988, a major study conducted by the RAND Corporation and the Tufts University School of Medicine strongly suggested that while there might be a surplus of general practitioners in some large and pleasant cities, there would be serious shortages by the early 2000s and thereafter, especially in major areas of specialty such as heart, chest, blood, kidney, gastrointestinal, blood disease, cancer, and infectious disease.

The AMA suggests that too many doctors, whether from medical schools or from other countries, may mean that U.S. doctors' skills could deteriorate because the physician "may not perform certain procedures frequently enough to maintain a high level of skill." But the RAND/Tufts study suggests that in the early years of the new millennium, many areas may not have anywhere near the specialists they need.

In this context, Andy Rooney writes that "the AMA sounds like a bricklayers' union. The bricklayers want to limit membership in the union so that there will always be more bricks that need to be laid than there are bricklayers to lay them. Doctors don't want a lot of young doctors offering their services for less so they can pay back the money they borrowed to get through medical school."

Accelerated Medical Programs

One slightly nontraditional approach to the M.D. is that of compressing the total elapsed time between high school and receiving the M.D. by two or three years. Many schools now offer a "3–4" program in which you enter medical school after the third year of a four-year bachelor's program, and receive the bachelor's degree after the first year of medical school. While most accelerated programs take seven years, some take six (Boston University, Lehigh University, Wilkes College, for instance), and one (Wofford College in South Carolina) takes five. The U.S. is, apparently, moving very slowly toward the British system, in which one enters medical school right after high school, and earns the Bachelor of Medicine in four or five years. (In England, the Doctor of Medicine is a less common advanced degree.)

Advanced placement in a medical school

This, annoyingly, is one of those "bending the rules" matters, where we simply cannot be specific. Several schools used to offer people with a Ph.D. a two-year M.D., based on the notion that the first two years of medical school are usually spent learning the relevant academic but non-medical subjects (anatomy, physiology, biology, etc.). On the assumption that a person who has already earned an accredited Ph.D. in certain scientific fields will have this knowledge, these schools used to offer the shorter M.D. to such people. They no longer do. But we still hear from people who have gained advanced placement in an M.D. program based on comparable scientific credentials. As always, there can be no harm in asking, but please don't ask us for school recommendations, since this seems always to be done on a case-by-case basis, if at all.

Foreign Medical Schools

In previous editions of this book, several pages were devoted to a discussion of the history, philosophy, and present practice of dealing with foreign medical schools: those in Mexico that cater to English-speaking students from the U.S. and elsewhere, and those throughout the Caribbean established to provide a medical education for Americans unable to get into an American medical school.

The situation is immensely complex, and almost impossible to evaluate for a nonmedical layman. Unfortunately, the book we turned to for advice on this subject is now out of print. Witty, information-packed, delightfully written, and heavily opinionated, *Foreign Medical Schools for U.S. Citizens*, written and self-published by Carlos Pestana, M.D., Ph.D., a professor at the University of Texas medical school, was by far and away the best reference in the field. Dr. Pestana is now retired and no longer updating his book. (At the time we went to press, he told us that he only has a few dozen copies left, and when they're gone, he's "closing that venture." So if you're looking outside the U.S. for a medical school, consider ordering one of the last available copies. It is worth far, far more than the $20 he charges for it by mail. See our bibliography for ordering information.)

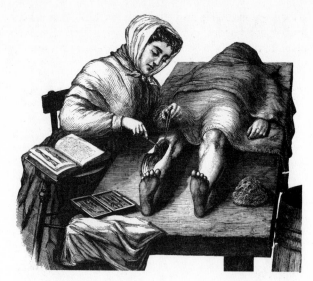

"The leg bone connected to the ankle bone. Yep."

In brief, Dr. Pestana's advice is not to even consider foreign school unless your MCAT exams scores are in the upper 20s or 30s. According to Dr. Pestana, most U.S. students who study abroad come back unable to pass the necessary examinations (currently the USMLE) to qualify for residency training and eventual licensure in the U.S.

Note: Another small book on the subject, *The Official Guide to Caribbean Medical Schools*, was published in 1997 by two graduates of the medical school on Saba. It describes the curriculum of six Caribbean schools in some detail, and offers reflections on the Caribbean lifestyle. Further detail is provided in our bibliography.

Using Exam Pass Rates to Judge Schools

People who attend a medical school outside the U.S. and wish to be licensed in the U.S. must pass a qualifying exam, administered by the Educational Commission for Foreign Medical Graduates (3624 Market Street, Fourth Floor, Philadelphia, PA 19104-2685; phone: (215) 386 5900; fax: (215) 387 9963; *www.ecfmg.org*). This United States Medical Licensure Examination (USMLE) has three parts. The first is basic science (anatomy, biochemistry, microbiology, etc.). The second is clinical sciences (medicine, surgery, obstetrics, gynecology, pediatrics, etc.). The third is a practice exam, given after graduation, during residency training.

The ECFMG used to publish pass rates for graduates of specific non-U.S. schools, and they ranged from nearly 100 percent (Sackler in Israel) to near zero. Now all that is available are pass rates by country where the medical schools are located, but that still provides a lot of useful information. Indeed, Dr. Pestana's very strong advice is seriously to consider only schools in Israel, Australia, the United Kingdom, and Grenada. Note that the first table is for everyone trained in a given country, U.S. citizens, locals, and others. The second table is just for U.S. citizens. Note, also, that Step Two is typically a harder exam than Step One, and it may be taken either before or after Step One.

Pass Rates for More Than 30,000 People Who Took the USMLE for the First Time in 1994–95 (the latest results available)

Country of Training	Step One	Step Two
Australia	91%	98%
Israel	86%	88%
Canada	82%	99%
United Kingdom	81%	90%
Germany	73%	73%
India	63%	56%
China	59%	39%
Romania	59%	43%
Nigeria	56%	53%
Syria	54%	42%
Poland	51%	46%
Egypt	45%	31%
Italy	40%	29%
Philippines	35%	31%
Russia/Soviet Union	31%	36%
Mexico	20%	20%
Dominican Republic	12%	13%

USMLE Exam Pass Rates for About 2,500 U.S. Citizens Trained in the Following Countries

Country	Step One		Step Two	
	1st try	All tries	1st try	All tries
Israel	89%	97%	78%	94%
Grenada	72%	83%	56%	88%
Dominica	48%	63%	46%	73%
Montserrat	42%	56%	37%	58%
India	42%	51%	53%	65%
Philippines	32%	39%	28%	41%
Italy	23%	30%	17%	42%
Mexico	14%	20%	18%	34%
Dominican Republic	8%	12%	15%	23%

There are dozens of foreign schools that welcome students from the U.S. and other countries. Here are the ones most highly recommended by Dr. Pestana:

Sackler School of Medicine

Tel Aviv University, Tel Aviv, Israel
U.S. office: 17 East 62nd St., New York, NY 10021
Phone: (212) 688 8811
Fax: (212) 223 0368
Email: sacklersch@internetmci.com
Web site: www.tau.ac.il/medicine
In Dr. Pestana's opinion, "this is without question the best foreign medical school that a U.S. citizen may attend."

Technion-Israel Institute of Technology

Haifa, Israel
U.S. office: Touro College School of Health Sciences, 1700 Union Blvd., Bay Shore, NY 11706
Phone: (631) 665 1600
Email: biomed@touro.edu
Web site: www.touro.edu/shs/biomed.html

Ben Gurion University of the Negev

Beer Sheva, Israel
U.S. office: 630 West 168th St., PH 15E-1512, New York, NY 10032
Phone: (212) 305 9587
Fax: (212) 305 3079
Email: bgcu-md@columbia.edu
Web site: cpmcnet.columbia.edu/dept/bgcu-md

Royal College of Surgeons in Ireland

123 St. Stephen's Green
Dublin 2, Ireland
Phone: +353 (1) 402 2100
Email: info@rcsi.ie
Web site: www.rcsi.ie

Here are the schools Dr. Pestana identifies as "the big players" in recruiting American students:

St. George's University

Grenada, West Indies
U.S. office: One East Main St., Bay Shore, NY 11706-8399
Phone: (631) 665 8500 ▪ (800) 899 6337
Fax: (631) 665 5590
Email: sgu_info@sgu.edu
Web site: www.stgeorgesuniv.edu

Ross University School of Medicine

Dominica, West Indies
U.S. office: 460 West 34th St., 12th Floor, New York, NY 10001
Phone: (212) 279 5500 ▪ (888) 404 7677
Fax: (212) 629 3147
Email: admissions@rossmed.edu
Web site: www.rossmed.edu

Universidad Autonoma de Guadalajara

Guadalajara, Mexico
U.S. office: 4715 Fredericksburg Rd., Suite 300, San Antonio, TX 78230
Phone: (210) 366 1611
Fax: (210) 377 2975
Email: uagsat@uag.edu
Web site: www.uag.edu/opciones/medicina/med.htm

Here are some other medical schools in the Caribbean that specifically cater to Americans. While they are not on Dr. Pestana's "recommended" list, they may well meet the needs of many. This particular section is difficult to keep current, since these schools tend to come and go. As many as twenty medical schools that once existed in the Dominican Republic and Puerto Rico are no longer there, for instance.

American University of the Caribbean

St. Maarten, Netherlands Antilles, West Indies
U.S. office: 901 Ponce de Leon Blvd., Suite 201, Coral Gables, FL 33134
Phone: (305) 446 0600
Web site: www.aucmed.edu
Formerly on Montserrat, which was destroyed by a volcano in 1995-96, one of the hazards of life in the Caribbean.

International University of the Health Sciences

St. Kitts, West Indies
U.S. office: 9200 Bonita Beach Road, Suite 209, Bonita Springs, FL 34135
Phone: (941) 949 6888 ▪ (888) 484 7338
Fax: (941) 949 6883
Email: info@iuhs.edu
Web site: www.iuhs.edu
Pre-clinical portion of the M.D. offered partly by distance learning.

Saba University School of Medicine

Saba, Netherlands Antilles, West Indies
U.S. office: P.O. Box 386, Gardner, MA 01440
Phone: (978) 630 5122 ▪ (800) 825 7754
Fax: (978) 632 2168
Email: saba@tiac.net
Web site: www.saba.org

Spartan Health Sciences University

St. Lucia, West Indies
U.S. office: P.O. Box 989, Santa Teresa, NM 88088
Phone: (505) 589 1372
Fax: (505) 589 1487
Web site: www.geocities.com/CollegePark/Grounds/5401

University of Health Sciences Antigua

Box 510, St. John's, Antigua, West Indies
Phone: +1 (268) 460 1391
Fax: +1 (268) 460 1477
Email: fmcp@uhsa.edu.ag
Web site: www.uhsa.ag

University of Sint Eustatius School of Medicine

Sint Eustatius, Netherlands Antilles, West Indies
U.S. office: 22 Cross St., Gardner, MA 01440
Phone: (978) 632 8877 ▪ (877) 878 2842
Fax: (978) 632 9977
Email: info@eustatiusmed.org
Web site: www.eustatiusmed.org

Windsor University School of Medicine

St. Kitts, West Indies
U.S. office: 6033 Capital Place, Virginia Beach, VA 23464
Phone: (757) 479 4703
Fax: (757) 479 8889
Email: windsoradm@hotmail.com
Web site: www.windsor.edu

Consulting Services

In earlier editions, we have listed various services that advertise heavily (the Sunday *New York Times* seems the most common place), offering to assist in the process of becoming admitted to medical school, whether in the U.S., the Caribbean, or elsewhere. These services come and go. Some are connected directly with one school (although not always openly). What we have read and been told suggests that it typically makes more sense to deal directly with the schools.

Illegal Medical Degrees

Very few fake school operators take the higher risk of offering fake medical degrees, although there are a handful of them sprinkled throughout chapter 27, "Degree Mills." And in 2000, John had the pleasure of testifying as an expert witness in the trial of a man who had been practicing for years with two degrees from fake medical schools: Metropolitan Collegiate Institute and the British West Indies School of Medicine. (He was found guilty on all counts.)

Two of the largest operations were closed down in 1984 as a result of the F.B.I. DipScam operation: the Johann Keppler School of Medicine (which had operated from various addresses in Canada, Switzerland, the U.S., and Mexico) and the United American Medical College (operating from Louisiana, Florida, and California). In both cases, the perpetrators went to prison. But the fake doctor who had been involved with both returned to the scene ten years later, apparently affiliated with a British school that purported to offer surgical training by correspondence study.

In the mid 1980s, it was discovered that two medical schools in the Dominican Republic, known as CETEC and CIFAS, were involved in selling M.D. credentials at a cost of $5,000 to $50,000. It has never been fully determined how many of the more than 5,000 M.D. degrees awarded by these two schools were genuinely earned and how many were sold to people who never attended the school.

More alarmingly, a major California university acknowledged that someone had tampered with their computer records, and had rigged the system to show that at least one unqualified person had a medical degree from them. Because the school did not retain any paper records whatsoever, they had no simple way to determine how many other fake medical alumni their computer claimed they had.

One man arrested and jailed as a medical-degree broker earned $1,500,000 in fees from his 165 clients, 44 of whom actually passed the foreign medical students' exam and were practicing medicine in the U.S.

Some of the fake schools listed in the chapter on diploma mills have sold medical degrees, most frighteningly sometimes under the name of legitimate schools. Recently, an Arkansas organization that advertised in *USA Today* was selling the M.D. of Stanford University, no questions asked, for under $400. And, as described in chapter 27, John has a very realistic diploma showing that he earned a medical degree from Harvard. It cost him $50 from a "lost diploma replacement service."

Results of the 2nd Cartoon Caption Contest

The winner is faithful reader John McAuley, who gets a free copy of this book, plus lunch with the authors, if we're ever in the same place at the same time. Thanks to all who entered. This edition's new contest is at the end of the book on page 420.

"All right, Mr. Levicoff, you get three credits for 'Nineteenth-Century Fashion Design,' three for 'Advanced Theatrical Costuming,' and three for 'Obscure Folk Dances'!"

CHAPTER 27

Degree Mills

Con man extraordinaire in the realms of the spiritual hustle ... was 'Dr.' Theodore White of Baltimore, who mulcted more than 20,000 suckers out of millions of dollars in the space of two years. [His] Correspondence College of Science offered charms, incantations, secret prayers, and talismans guaranteed to provide any kind of miracle desired.... Following White's conviction in Baltimore for fraud, in which he received a three-year prison term and a $1,500 fine, the 'doctor' turned to hundreds of the 'students' who had graduated from his wacky college, paying $15 each for a 'degree,' and who had flocked to see their private miracle worker. White, manacled, called out to them, "Do you all have your diplomas?" Dozens of rolled-up pieces of paper were waved majestically above the marks' heads. "Then you are free spirits," said White, nodding, "Full of eternal magic." A guard leading White away looked over his shoulder at the waving diplomas and said to the hustler, "Why don't you give those poor boobs a break. Tell 'em you're a fake." White shook his head knowledgeably. "They wouldn't believe me," he said.

Jay Robert Nash, Hustlers and Con Men

In most earlier editions of this book, the degree mill section began with the following sentence: "Degree mills have been around for hundreds of years, and they are still flourishing all over the world."

Then, for ten or more years, we were able to report that the number of currently operating phony schools significantly diminished as a result of the "DipScam" diploma-mill task force of the FBI, whose work helped secure indictments and, in most cases, convictions of a great many people who were responsible for the operation of scores of phony colleges and universities.

Unfortunately, the trend has reversed and things are getting worse again. With the winding down of DipScam in the early 1990s, and the advent of inexpensive laser printers, color copiers, overnight delivery services, toll-free telephone numbers, faxes, computer bulletin boards, and, most significantly, the growth of the Internet, diploma mills have made a real comeback, both in the U.S. and Europe.

There are, astonishingly, more than 400 diploma mills now listed in this chapter—and, we need to say, more than a few in the earlier "non-GAAP" chapters, that were a really difficult judgment call, as to whether they belonged there

or here. After adding only 5 or 10 fakes a year, on the average, now it is more like 40 or 50 a year, and the rate of growth seems to be increasing.

For an article in *University Business* magazine (March, 2000; *www.universitybusiness.com/0003/diploma.html*), John calculated that fake degree selling represented more than a $200 million a year business. In the light of new information—that the immense fraud known as Columbia State University apparently took in more than $70 million a year all by itself—it would seem appropriate to raise that estimate significantly.

There are now dozens of places where one can buy bachelor's, master's, doctorates, even law and medical degrees, with no questions asked, on payment of fees of anywhere from one dollar to several thousand. To demonstrate this, John purchased (for $53) an extremely authentic-looking law degree (Doctor of Jurisprudence) of Harvard University, from an outfit in Florida that has been advertising nationally, complete with an 800 phone number. Their ads have been running for at least four years now, and they even have a little retail establishment where they print diplomas while you wait. Transcripts are available as well. And no, we will not provide the address, or those of any other illegal schools. We have no wish to give them business. And our lawyer has advised us that we could be considered "accessories before the fact" should someone buy a fake degree and use it to defraud others. (We will, of course, cooperate with law enforcement officers and bona fide investigative reporters.)

One of the main reasons that fake schools continue to exist is that it is so very difficult to define legally exactly what is meant by the term "diploma mill" or "degree mill."

Surely any school that will send you a Ph.D. by return mail on payment of $100, no questions asked, is a fraud. But what about a school that requires a 5-page dissertation before awarding the doctorate? How about 20 pages? 50? 100? 200? Who is to say? One man's degree mill is another man's alternative university. And nobody seems to want the government stepping in to evaluate doctoral dissertations before permitting schools to grant degrees. Would you want [insert the name of your least-favorite politician] grading your thesis?

Another large gray area is the one dealing with religious schools. Because of constitutional safeguards in the U.S. guaranteeing separation of church and state, most states have been reluctant to pass any laws restricting the activities of churches—including their right to grant degrees to all who make an appropriately large donation. In many states, religious schools are not regulated, but are restricted to granting religious degrees. But in some, like Louisiana and Hawaii, if you established your own one-person church yesterday, you could start your university today, and award a Ph.D. in nuclear physics tomorrow.

Many states say that religious schools can only grant religious degrees. A diploma mill in Louisiana took that argument to new limits when they announced that because God created everything, no matter what you studied, it was the study of the work of God, and therefore a religious degree. Twice, the Louisiana courts upheld this argument!

Why Are Degree Mills Allowed to Operate?

The answer is that, as just indicated, it is almost impossible to write a law that will discriminate clearly between legitimate schools and mills. Any law that tries to define something that is subjective—obscenity, pornography, threatening behavior, or the quality of a school—is bound to be controversial. There can never be a quantitative means for, in effect, holding a meter up to a school and saying, "This one scores 83; it's legitimate. That one scores 62; it's a degree mill."

Also, degree mills that do not muddy their own local waters, but sell their products only in other states or other countries, are more likely to get away with it longer. A goodly number of degree mills have operated from England, selling their product only to people in other countries (primarily the U.S., Africa, and Asia). Many British authorities seem not to care as long as the only victims are foreigners, and authorities in the U.S. find it virtually impossible to take action against foreign businesses.

After decades of debating these matters (even Prince Charles made a speech about the diploma mill problem), Britain has taken two tiny steps. Step one is to forbid unrecognized schools to call themselves a "university." However, this law had been in effect for about three minutes when one of England's leading diploma mills, the Sussex College of Technology, found the loophole. The law declares that it pertains to everyone enrolling after April 1, 1989. Sussex immediately began offering to back-date applications to March 31, 1989, which appears not to be illegal. They are still getting away with this ploy. Step two is to require that unrecognized schools must say in their literature that they do not operate under a Royal Charter or an Act of Parliament (the two ways schools become legitimately recognized in Britain). This, however, is unlikely even to be noticed by degree-buyers in other lands.

Other states and jurisdictions have tried to craft laws that would permit legitimate nontraditional schools to operate while eliminating degree mills. For instance, for many years California had a law that stated that the main requirement for being authorized by the state to grant degrees was ownership of $50,000 worth of real property. That law was apparently passed to eliminate low-budget fly-by-night degree mills. But $50,000 ain't what it used to be, and from the 1960s through the early 1980s, dozens of shady operators declared that their home or their book collection was worth $50,000 and proceeded to sell degrees with wild abandon.

In 1978, John had the pleasure of advising the *60 Minutes* people from CBS on which California "universities" they might wish to send Mike Wallace in to expose. The proprietor of California Pacifica University was actually arrested while Wallace was interviewing him, and soon after pleaded guilty to multiple counts of mail fraud, and went off to federal prison. Two years later, California Pacifica was still listed in the state's official publication, the *Directory of California Educational Institutions*.

California, thankfully, has tightened things up considerably since then, by eliminating the "authorized" category, and adding requirements that there must be elements of instruction provided by state-*approved* schools. Once again, of course, we have a law trying to define subjective matters.

In 1990, John had the further pleasure of appearing on the nationally syndicated program *Inside Edition* to help expose yet another major degree mill, North American University. Its proprietor, Edward Reddeck, who had previously been to prison for running another fake school, was convicted on multiple counts of mail and wire (telephone) fraud, and sent to federal prison for a few years.

Another reason for the proliferation of degree mills in the past is that the wheels of justice ground very slowly, when they ground at all. Dallas State College was shut down by authorities in Texas in 1975. The same perpetrators almost immediately opened up as Jackson State University in California. When the post office shut off their mail there, they resurfaced with John Quincy Adams University in Oregon. It took 12 more years and a major effort by the FBI before the Dallas State perpetrators were finally brought to justice in a federal courtroom in North Carolina in late 1987, nearly two decades and millions of dollars in revenues after they sold their first doctorate. And when the FBI, the IRS, and the postal inspectors raided a diploma mill in Louisiana in 1995, where they recovered more than $10 million in cash, the front-page newspaper account at the time said that these agencies had spent more than five years preparing for their visitation.

It was the entry of the FBI into the diploma mill arena that changed the rules of the game.

DIPSCAM

In the late 1970s, the Federal Bureau of Investigation launched an operation called DipScam (for Diploma Scam), which methodically investigated degree-granting institutions from coast to coast and abroad, with some cooperation from Scotland Yard and other foreign authorities.

John consulted with the FBI on matters of degree mills from 1979 until 1992, when arch diploma mill-exposer Special Agent Allen Ezell retired, and DipScam wound down.

The FBI looked into hundreds of unaccredited schools. Some were found to be harmless, innocuous, even good, and no actions were taken. When there was evidence of chicanery, a search warrant was issued, and FBI vans hauled off tons of papers and records. In many cases, but not all, a federal grand jury handed down indictments. And when they did, in many, but not all, cases the indictees pleaded guilty to mail or wire (telephone) fraud, and received fines and sentences in federal prison. When this has happened, it is described in the listing for those schools later in this chapter.

The wording of the federal grand jury indictments is quite wonderful. Here is a sample, from one indictment. (This is just a small excerpt from a thick document.)

SCHEME AND ARTIFICE: Count One: That from some unknown time prior to, on, or about [date] and continuing through some unknown time after [date] within the Western District of North Carolina and elsewhere in the United States, [defendants] did knowingly, intentionally, and unlawfully combine, conspire, confederate and agree with each other and with others to the Grand Jurors both known and unknown, to commit offenses against the United States, that is, having devised and intending to devise a scheme and artifice to defraud and for obtaining money by false and fraudulent pretenses, representations and promises, for the purpose of executing said scheme and artifice to defraud and attempting to do so knowingly and intentionally placing and causing to be placed in a post office and an authorized depository for mail matter, and causing to be delivered by United States mail according to the direction thereon, matters and things to be sent and delivered by the United States Postal Service, in violation of Title 18, United States Code, Sections 1341 and 2, and knowingly and intentionally transmitting and causing to be transmitted by means of wire communication in interstate commerce, certain signs, signals and sounds, to wit, interstate telephone conversations, in violation of Title 18, United States Code, Section 1343.

In other words, they sent fake degrees by mail, and made interstate phone calls to their customers.

In its earlier days, DipScam went after the fake medical schools—the most dangerous degree-sellers of all. They were quickly able to shut down the two worst perpetrators, Johann Keppler School of Medicine and the United American Medical College, and send their respective founders to prison.

DipScam's largest case came to its grand finale in a federal courthouse in Charlotte, North Carolina, in October 1987, with John present as an expert witness and observer. On trial were the seven perpetrators of a long string of degree mills, most recently including Roosevelt University, Loyola University, Cromwell University, University of England at Oxford, Lafayette University, DePaul University, and Southern California University, as well as several fake accrediting agencies.

More than 100 witnesses were called over a two-and-a-half-week period, including many who established the substantial size and scope of bank deposits and investments made by the defendants. Witnesses from Europe testified to the mail forwarding services the defendants used in England, France, Belgium, Germany, Holland, and elsewhere.

The circuslike atmosphere was not helped by the fact that Jim and Tammy Faye Bakker, Jessica Hahn, and company, were appearing in the courtroom right next door, and so the grounds of the courthouse were covered by photographers and reporters, none of whom took much interest in the DipScam trial.

Two of the minor players were dismissed by the judge for lack of definitive evidence, but the five main defendants were found guilty by the jury on all 27 counts of mail fraud, aiding and abetting, and conspiracy. They were sentenced to prison terms ranging from two to seven years.

Even though the DipScam project is no longer active, the FBI, the postal inspectors, and some crusading state agencies are still actively working to keep fake schools from operating and phony degrees from being sold.

Why Degree Mills Prosper

The main reason—really the only reason—for the success of degree mills (and drug dealers, and pornographers) is, of course, that people keep on buying their product. They crave the degrees and somehow, despite much evidence to the contrary, they really believe that they are going to get away with it.

Unfortunately, many newspapers and magazines continue to permit the perpetrators to advertise. At this writing, for instance, some of the biggest phony schools advertise in nearly every issue of *The Economist, USA Today, Forbes, Psychology Today, Inc., Discover, Investors Business Daily,* the *International Herald Tribune,* regional editions of *Time* and *Newsweek*, and dozens of other publications that should know better.

Indeed they do know better. As a public service, we routinely write to such publications to suggest they are doing their readers a disservice by running these ads. With the exception of the *Wall Street Journal*, which promptly changed its policies, we have failed utterly. In 1997, *USA Today* told us they were going to change their policies, but they apparently changed their minds. *The Economist* even wrote to us to say that their readers were smart enough to make up their own minds. Then, when we tried to run a "Diploma Mill Alert" in *The Economist*, it was rejected, because "We don't run ads critical of our advertisers."

There have been occasions in the past when a class action suit filed on behalf of fraud victims also named the advertising medium where the fraud advertised. We can only hope that such a suit will attract the attention of the lawyers for other such publications.

An Emphatic Warning

We must warn you, as emphatically as we can, that it is taking a very big risk to buy a fake degree, or to claim to have a degree that you have not earned. It is like putting a time bomb in your resumé. It could go off at any time, with dire consequences. The people who sell fake degrees will probably never suffer at all, but the people who buy them often suffer mightily.

In part as a result of all the publicity the FBI activities have gotten, credentials are being checked out now as never before. *Time* magazine, in an article on fake degrees (February 5, 1979), said that "with the rate at which job candidates are now fibbing on resumes and faking sheepskins, graduate schools and companies face detective work almost every time they see an application. . . . Checking up on about 12,000 inquiries a year, UCLA finds two or three frauds a week. For its part, Yale has accumulated a file of 7,000 or so bogus Old Blues."

Often people get caught when something unexpectedly good happens in their lives, and they become the focus of the news media, which love stories involving fake degrees.

Degree Mills in the News

Here is just a small sampling of the stories from our over-flowing file on people who have gotten in trouble over degrees and credentials in recent years.

▶ The chairman of the board of a major Florida university resigned, after it became known that he had bought his degrees from an Oklahoma diploma mill. And when we put the name of the school in an earlier edition, the school's lawyers threatened to sue for "revealing" what had been page-one news in the papers. Talk about killing the messenger if you don't like the message!

▶ Two American presidential candidates had problems over credentials claims. Joseph Biden's campaign literature "misstated" the nature of his graduate degrees, and Pat Robertson's official biography had to be changed from saying that he did "graduate study, University of London" to "studied briefly at the University of London" after the revelation he had taken only a short undergraduate seminar on art for Americans.

▶ The superintendent of schools for California's second largest school district lost his job and faced serious legal consequences when the Stanford Ph.D. he had claimed for years turned out to be a phony one.

▶ A popular columnist for *Forbes* magazine, Srully Blotnick, was dropped from the magazine when his Ph.D. credentials (as well as his research methodology) came under close scrutiny.

▶ Arizona's Teacher of the Year (a major honor in that state) was found to be using a doctorate he had never earned. A $10,000 prize had to be returned.

▶ The biggest business scandal in Sweden in half a century, the Fermenta affair, was triggered when a former employee of a major industrialist, believed to be the richest man in Sweden, charged (correctly) that the industrialist had lied about possessing two doctorates. According to *The Economist* magazine, "Fermenta's share price halved as this charge about bogus qualifications spread." A billion-dollar deal with Volvo was canceled in the wake of the scandal.

▶ During the New York City parking meter scandals, one of the government's star witnesses, according to the *Daily News*, "admitted he has a bogus doctorate from Philathea College. . . ."

▶ In 1985, Congressman Claude Pepper convened a congressional panel, which asserted that more than 500,000 Americans have obtained false credentials or diplomas. (Pepper's staff got him a Ph.D. from Union University. All "Dr. Pepper" allegedly had to do was submit four book reports, which his staff wrote for him.)

▶ As a result of accumulating over 7,000 "client" names from its diploma mill raids, the FBI identified more than 200 federal employees, including 75 in the Defense Department, with bogus degrees.

▶ Congressman Ron Wyden of Oregon said that as many as 40,000 physicians who failed their qualifying exams may nonetheless be practicing medicine.

▶ According to *Sports Illustrated*, the owner of the Indianapolis Colts made the "frequent boast that he played Big Ten football at the University of Illinois, while getting a degree in electrical engineering." The magazine says he neither played football nor earned a degree.

▶ A fake degree scandal rocked Indonesia, with the revelation that a war hero turned businessman was bilked of huge sums of money by an executive of his shipping line, who had been hired because of his doctorate in economics from a U.S. degree mill, Thomas Edison College of Florida and Arkansas (not the legitimate one in New Jersey).

▶ And even in Russia … one Alexander Shavlokhov was arrested for selling at least 56 fake degrees of the Gorky Agricultural Institute, at 1,000 rubles each, to industrialists around the country. (Note: Russia once refused to allow us to advertise this book in that country, saying there is no need for it.)

Two Other Insidious Academic Frauds

In addition to those who sell fake degrees, there are two other "services" that undermine the academic establishment.

One is the so-called "lost diploma replacement service." If you tell them you had a legitimate degree but lost it, they will replace it for a modest fee. That's why John has a Harvard "Doctor of Neurosurgery" diploma hanging on his wall (next to his real Michigan State one). The Harvard phony sold for $49.95. When the FBI raided one such service, in Oregon (they had been advertising in national publications), they found thousands of blank diplomas from hundreds of schools—and records showing an alarmingly large number of clients.

The Oregon service no longer advertises, but others crop up from time to time, such as the one from which John bought his Harvard law degree. Since the services require their clients to sign a disclaimer saying they really had the original degree, and since the diplomas come with a "Novelty Item" sticker (easy to peel off), the services may well be operating legally. On one occasion, at least, the Justice Department was unable to get an indictment from a federal grand jury for these reasons.

The other is term paper and dissertation writing services. Several of them put out catalogues listing over a thousand already written term papers they will sell, and if they don't have what you want, they will write anything from a short paper to a major dissertation for you, for $7 to $10 a page.

How This Chapter Has Changed

Earlier editions used to include all those schools that John regarded as diploma mills, religious and otherwise. The problem with this approach was that many of the schools were, in fact, operating legally, either because they were church-run, or because they were in locations with few or no laws regulating schools. Until 1985, for instance, Arizona had no laws whatsoever regulating universities and degrees, and so a good many degree mills operated from that state. Now, every state has some form of law regulating or registering or approving or accrediting colleges and universities. Some states are very thorough in their licensing process; others have little or no evaluative process, but simply register any school that applies for registration.

Twenty years ago, this chapter also used to give the addresses of the degree mills. We've become convinced that this served no legitimate or useful purpose, so the detailed

addresses have been deleted, and we will not supply them if you write to us.

Finally, there are a handful of schools that we firmly believe are diploma mills, but we do not have sufficient proof to say so in print, and we do not enjoy being sued. These have been listed in the "Other Schools" chapters, generally with descriptions that are less than wonderful, but factual. (At one time, John thought about leaving behind a posthumous edition of this book, so that all the things he knew but dared not say would finally be aired. But now that John's daughter Mariah has joined the team, you may have to wait another half-century for this special edition!)

Again, we remind you that we rely on reader correspondence to keep these listings up to date. If you've picked up the trail of a degree mill not listed here, let us know about it. Email us at *johnandmariah@degree.net* or write to us at *Bears' Guide*, P.O. Box 7123, Berkeley, CA 94707. Updates and corrections to this and other chapters are posted on our Web site at *www.degree.net/updates/bearsguide14.*

The Diploma Mills

Here, then, are the many schools that have been publicly identified as diploma mills. From time to time, people have supplied us with information that has persuaded us that a certain school should not have been included here, and we have moved it to chapter 31, "Miscellaneous Schools," or at least provided additional information here.

Please note that more than a few diploma mills take names that are similar to, or identical to, legitimate schools. "E&T" stands for *Education & Training*, a British magazine that used to report regularly on European and other degree mills. "COE" stands for the Council of Europe, an intergovernmental agency based in Strasbourg, France, which keeps track of what they believe are degree mills in Europe and elsewhere. In addition to the findings from our own research, we report here those institutions which these two European entities have publicly called degree mills.

A+ Institute See: Advanced Education Institute

Academy College of Holy Studies Sheffield, England. Identified as a degree mill by E&T.

Academy of the Science of Man See: Sussex College of Technology

Accademia di Studi Superiori Minerva Milan, Italy. Identified as a degree mill by COE. However, the courts decided otherwise. In District Court of Fiorenzuola d'Arda in 1958, one Amorosa d'Aragona Francesco was brought to trial for using a degree from this school. The court apparently ruled that the school may not be great but it is legal. It moved from Bari to Milan a few years later, and then went out of business.

Accademia di Studi Superiori Phoenix Bari, Italy. Identified as a degree mill by COE. Very likely the same as the school listed above.

Accademia Universale de Governo Cosmo-Astrosofica-Libero de Psico-Biofisica Trieste, Yugoslavia. Identified as a degree mill by COE. Can you imagine what their school cheers sound like?

Accademia Universitaria Internazionale Rome, Italy. Identified as a degree mill by E&T.

Adams Institute of Technology See: National Certificate Company

Addison State University Ottawa, Canada. Bachelor's, master's, and doctorates in almost any field but medical or dental are sold for about $30.

Advanced Education Institute There is an apparent loophole in the state of Washington's education laws, which regulate instruction and the offering of higher education, but do not regulate the awarding of degrees. Something calling itself the Accelerated Peer Graduate Degree Program of the Advanced Education Institute Trust drove its bus through the loophole, arising on the Internet in 1999 to offer bachelor's, master's, and doctorates in any field, based entirely on resume evaluation, with the diplomas coming from a wide range of school names (all nonexistent): Concorda University, Concorda Graduate Institute, Audentes Technical Academy, Cathedra Institute, Primus Postgraduate College, Valorem Academy, Holy Acclaim Graduate Institute, Holy Acclaim University, and Holmes University. A reverse directory check showed that at the "university" location, one finds the A+ Real Estate Institute and the Home Boys Construction company. (Sorry, apparently no degrees from Home Boys University.)

Alabama Christian College See: R/G Enterprises. No connection with a legitimate school of this name in Montgomery, Alabama.

Albany Educational Services Northampton, England. Offers to act as an agent to obtain American bachelor's, master's, and doctorates for a fee of $150 to $250. Letters to the director, L. W. Carroll, asking which schools he represents, have not been answered.

Albert Einstein Institut Zurich, Switzerland. Sells the phony degrees of Oxford Collegiate Institute (of the International University). One of the many fake degree operations of Karl Xavier Bleisch.

Albert Switzer Institute This nonexistent school appeared briefly on the Internet in 1999–2000. The Web site was registered to a man in Plano, Texas.

Alexis de Toqueville University See: Monticello University

American College in Switzerland Berne, Switzerland. Totally phony doctorates are offered by yet another of "Professor Doctor" Karl Xavier Bleisch's degree mills. Affiliations with Georgetown University and with the University of Florida are falsely claimed in this school's literature.

American Extension College of Law Probably related to American Extension School of Law, below.

American Extension School of Law Chicago, Illinois. Identified as a degree mill by COE.

American Institute of Science Indianapolis, Indiana. Identified as a degree mill by COE.

American Institute of Technology See: Bureau for Degree Promotions

American International Academy New York and Washington. Identified as a degree mill by COE.

American International University (California) Established in California in the 1970s by Edward Reddeck (who was convicted of mail fraud for a previous diploma mill operation, and later went to prison for his University of North America using Missouri, Utah, and Hawaii addresses). His employee, Clarence Franklin, left to establish American National University, and was later indicted by a federal grand jury. Degrees of all kinds were sold for $1,600 to $2,500, whether or not the required eight-page dissertation was written. No longer in operation. American International resurfaced briefly in 1987, using a Kansas City, Missouri, address which was a mail forwarding service.

American Legion University U.S. location unknown. Identified as a degree mill by E&T.

American Management Institute See: International Universities Consortium

American Martial Art University Small magazine ads in the mid-1990s offered a "Doctor of Martial Art Philosophy" from this nonexistent school, ostensibly in Iowa, with the tagline "looks authentic and genuine," for $34.50. Bachelor's and master's degrees, the small print read, were available at the same price, presumably for fakes with lower self-esteem.

American Medical College (Burma) Rangoon, Burma. Identified as a degree mill by COE.

American Medical College (Idaho) Nampa. Doctor of Medicine degrees have been awarded by this apparently nonexistent school. A student there (with a phony undergraduate degree) provided what appears to be a letter from the Idaho superintendent of public instruction confirming that the school is appropriately registered with his office. There is no listed telephone for them in Nampa.

American National Educational Institute Phony awarder of fake degrees sold by International Awards Committee.

American National University (Arizona) Phoenix. The university was established by Clarence Franklin, a California chiropractor formerly associated with American International University who was subsequently indicted by a federal grand jury for operating this school. Degrees were offered on payment of fees in the vicinity of $2,000. Accreditation was claimed from the National Accreditation Association, which had been established by Franklin and a colleague in Maryland. Apparently stopped operations in 1983 or 1984. Franklin was convicted of violation of federal law a few years later. A new and unrelated American National University was authorized in California in 1987.

American School of Metaphysics Location unknown. Identified as a degree mill by COE.

American University (California) San Diego. Degrees of all kinds were offered on payment of a fee of $1,500 to $2,500. The claim was made that all degrees were "registered with the government" in Mexico, where the school was allegedly located. No longer in business.

American West University See: California Pacifica University. One of the many fake schools created and run by Ernest Sinclair in the 1970s.

American Western University Operated from a mail drop in Tulsa, Oklahoma, in the early 1980s by Anthony Geruntino of Columbus, Ohio, who later went to federal prison for this school and his next venture, Southwestern University. American Western's mail delivery was stopped in 1981 by the U.S. Postal Service, at which time a new address was utilized. Affiliated schools included the National College of Arts and Sciences, Northwestern College of Allied Science, Regency College, and Saint Paul's Seminary.

Amherst University A short-lived, mid-2000 diploma mill attempt by the infamous Les Snell. See: Monticello University

Amritsar University Amritsar, India. Identified as a degree mill by COE.

Anglain University This diploma mill, ostensibly based in Britain, sells people the degree of their choice for $100 or less. Their ugly little Web site, which appeared in 2000, says, "But is it really legal? Categorically yes!" We say, in contrast, "Categorically no!" Amusingly, they decline to say where they are located; one must email them in order to find out.

Anglo-American College of Medicine See: National College

Anglo-American Institute of Drugless Medicine See: National College

Anglo-American University This school's homegrown-looking catalog leads with what most students really care about—"Our diploma . . is printed on superior parchment paper with the University seal embossed in gold. This is a diploma you can be proud to display in your home or office as the proof of your achievement and competence." Their discussion of accreditation is a bit disinguous as well, although they are very upfront about their lack thereof, and like many unaccredited schools, they misquote the famous Sosdian & Sharp study on acceptance of nontraditional degrees.

Degrees are offered in many fields at all levels, with very generous awards for life-experience learning—indeed, the catalog states in large type "you may have already fulfilled your degree requirements." Almost certainly the product of Edward Reddeck, who has been to jail three times for degree fraud.

Aquinas University of Scholastic Philosophy New York. Identified as a degree mill by E&T.

Argus University Fairplay, Colorado. A fictitious university formed apparently just for fun in 1977. Its stated purpose is selling doctorates to dogs and their humans. The founder writes that Argus "will confer a degree to any dog whose owner sends a check for $5 to Argus University." Same fee for humans, apparently.

Armor University They offer all degrees "absolutely free." One only has to pay for the diploma. You are asked to take the Graduate Record Exam in the field of your choice. If you "pass the exam," you tell them (no verification required) and then you can buy your diploma. Note: the Graduate Record Exam is *not* a "pass-fail" exam. There is no clue on their Web site as to the location of the "university," but their Internet portal appears to be in Belgium.

Arya University Srinigar, India. Identified as a degree mill by COE.

Aspen Christian College Colorado. Following a local television feature on Denver station KUSA, in which a pet dog was awarded a degree, the attorney general's office took action to close this school, and it is no longer operating.

Aspen University Colorado. This school, as well as Darwin University, run by the same prankster, offers "honorary doctorates" that are clearly intended to be humorous (Doctor of Universal Confusion from "UCLA—the Ulcer Club of Los Angeles"). We list them only on the principle that however innocent the seller's intentions, one never knows what the purchaser might try to pull.

Atlanta Southern University Atlanta, Georgia. See: California Pacifica University. Another of Ernest Sinclair's degree mills. The president of a large respectable university used to tell people his degree was from Atlanta Southern; he doesn't anymore.

Atlantic Northeastern University Their address in New York was a mail forwarding service. They offered all degrees, using well-designed and printed promotional materials, almost identical to those used by Pacific Northwestern and Atlantic Southern universities. Fake (but realistic-looking) transcripts were available for an additional fee. Apparently no longer in business.

Atlantic Southern University Operated briefly from addresses in Atlanta, Georgia, and Seattle, Washington. The materials look identical to those of Pacific

Northwestern University. Newspaper publicity in 1980 apparently caused them to cease operations.

Audentes Technical Academy See: Advanced Education Institute

Australian Institute See: Bureau for Degree Promotions

Avatar Episcopal University London, England. Identified as a degree mill by E&T.

Avatar International University London, England. Identified as a degree mill by E&T.

Bantridge University See: Sussex College of Technology

Benchley State University See: LTD Documents

Benson University Same management as Laurence University of Hawaii.

Bettis Christian University In the mid-1980s, Ph.D.'s were sold for $800 by two inmates of the Arkansas State Prison. Another instance of a "University Behind Walls."

Beulah College Nigeria and Texas. In 1990, offered to award an honorary Doctor of Humanities to anyone sending them $500.

Bible University Ambuhr, North Arcot, India. Identified as a degree mill by COE.

Bonavista University Douglas, Wyoming. All degrees were sold for fees of $500 to $700. Other Bonavista literature had been mailed from Sandy, Utah, and Wilmington, Delaware. No longer in business, at least at those locations.

Bosdon Academy of Music See: ORB

Boston City College See: Regency Enterprises

Boswell Active Promotions This organization has been very active on the Web, offering "fully accredited," "honorary" degrees from "a respected Swiss institution." The degrees are, of course, none of those things and, refreshingly, the man behind them agrees, saying "I make no pretense that these degrees are worth the paper they are printed on. To a true academic, especially one who worked hard for his degree, they are nonsense. To a person from the Third World who needs a ticket to a better job, they are interesting." To an employer who hires that person and then discovers he has a phony degree, they may also be interesting.

Bradford University Same management as Laurence University of Hawaii. No connection with the chartered University of Bradford in England.

Brandenburg University This rather disturbing mill came into operation on the Internet in 2000, offering fake medical degrees (medical, dental, optometry, osteopathy, and chiropractic, to be exact), as well as any other degree at any level. They have been advertising over the Internet, soliciting people who post to distance-learning newsgroups.

Brantridge Forest School See: Sussex College of Technology

Brantridge University Started in the mid-1990s by Bruce Copen, the operator of the diploma mills called the Sussex College of Technology and the Brantridge Forest School in England. Copen registered this fake university in Louisiana, and then moved it to a convenience address in Hawaii. When we last checked, in late 2000, the school was still in operation, even though Copen died in 1999. Also known as Brantwood University and Brantwood Forest University.

Brentwick University See: University of San Moritz

Bretton Woods University New Hampshire. Diplomas of this alleged institution have been sold for $15 by a "collector of elite unit militaria" who says they were "obtained through various unknown third parties . . . Some are original unawarded certificates, while others could be reproductions."

British College of Soma-Therapy England. Identified as a degree mill by E&T.

British Collegiate Institute London, England. They used to sell degrees of all kinds for a fee of $100 to $300, through a London address, and an agent in Inman, Kansas. The provost was listed as Sir Bernard Waley, O.B.E., M.A., D.Litt. See also: College of Applied Science, London

British West Indies School of Medicine Ostensibly located on the islands of Turks and Caicos in the Caribbean, this apparently nonexistent institution was run by "Dr." Gregory Caplinger, a man with numerous fake medical credentials, whom John had the pleasure of testifying against in 2000. (Caplinger was found guilty on all counts.) The School of Medicine was apparently operated by Caplinger from an address in Gary, Indiana, at the same address of the equally spurious American Nutritional Medical Association.

Broadhurst University See: West London College of Technology

Brownell University Degrees of this "university that does not now exist" were sold for $10, both by Associated Enterprises of Jacksonville, Florida, and Universal Data Systems of Tustin, California. An extra $5 bought a "professional lettering kit" so you could add any name and date you wish. School rings, decals, and stationery were sold as well. Since the sellers in Tustin (apparently two schoolteachers) slammed the door on a *60 Minutes* crew some years ago, the degrees have apparently not been sold.

Brundage Forms Georgia. Brundage sells blank forms for all purposes. His college-degree form, which you can fill in yourself, costs less than a dollar. His motto: "No advice, just forms." Our motto: "You can get in just as much trouble with a phony 50¢ doctorate as with a phony $3,000 doctorate."

Buckner University Texas. All degrees, including some in medicine, were sold for $45 each. They claim there is a real Buckner in Texas. There isn't. The literature says, "We believe this modestly priced yet extremely impressive document will give you great enjoyment, prestige, and potential profitability." It is also likely to give you the opportunity to meet some nice people from your district attorney's office. The degrees were sold by University Press of Houston, and by Universal Data Systems of Tustin, California (which also sold Brownell and other fake diplomas).

Bureau for Degree Promotions Holland. Sells the fake degrees of Addison State University, Atlantic Southeastern University, the Australian Institute, American Institute of Technology, and International University of India for $50 to $100, and knighthoods at $500, all completely worthless.

Byron University Started when Rev. Salter, D.D., saw the outrageous prices that Trinity College & University charges for its degrees. He "felt that people should have a chance to earn an honorary degree, without paying big bucks." So he gave out his honorary degrees for free. Byron University died, along with its founder, in 2000.

Calgary College of Technology Calgary, Canada. One of Canada's most ambitious degree mills offered the bachelor's, master's, and doctorate for fees up to $275. The literature included a lengthy profile of the dean, Colonel R. Alan Munro, "Canada's premier Aeronaut." A book of heraldry lists "Colonel the Chevalier Raymond Allen Zebulon Leigh Munro, C.M., G.C.L.J., C.L., K.M.L.J., S.M.L.J., A.D.C., C.O.I., C.O.F., M.O.P., B.S.W., M.H.F., LL.B., M.A., LL.D., D.Sc.A., C.D.A.S., F.R.S.A., F.S.A. Scot, A.F.C.A.S.I., C.R.Ae.S., A.F.A.I.A.A., M.A.H.S., M.C.I.M., M.C.I.M.E." Could this be the same person? The Calgary catalog even included a telephone number. That phone was answered, "Spiro's Pizza Parlor." Truly. Could "Ph.D." stand for "Pizza, Home Delivery"?

California Central University A newspaper ad for this school touted "College Degrees! No Studies!" from a post office box in southern California, for the bargain basement price of $19.95.

California Christian College See: R/G Enterprises

California Institute of Behavior Sciences California. Humorous but well-designed doctorates were awarded, at least in the 1960s, with the title of Doctor of Image Dynamics, citing "mastery of Machiavellian Manipulations . . . discovery of the failsafe Success Mechanism, and the fail un-safe Failure Mechanism . . . ."

California Institute of Higher Learning See: London Institute for Applied Research

California Pacifica University Hollywood, California. Widely advertised degree mill operated by Ernest Sinclair. Degrees from California Pacifica or almost any other school one wanted were sold for $3,500. The slick catalog showed photos of faculty and staff, all fictitious. Sinclair was the main subject of a CBS *60 Minutes* exposé in April 1978. He pleaded guilty to 3 of the 36 counts on which he was arrested. While his trial was on, he opened yet another fake school, Hollywood Southern University. Sinclair's advertising was regularly accepted by the *New York Times* and other major publications. Two years after he was arrested, California Pacifica was still listed in the official California directory of authorized schools! Sinclair once sued John for $4 million for calling his degree mill a degree mill, but he went to prison before the scheduled trial. One report had it that he continued to sell degrees while in federal prison—if true, the first known instance of a "University Behind Walls" program.

Cambridge State University Run from southern California, this enterprise originally operated from a "campus" that was a mailbox store in Shreveport, Louisiana. At the time the Louisiana attorney general closed them down, in 1998, the New Orleans newspapers revealed that Cambridge State had been bankrolled for $1 million by the notorious fraud, Columbia State University (see listing in this chapter). After the Louisiana closure, the "campus" was moved to a mailbox rental store in Honolulu. Soon after, the Hawaii Department of Commerce and Consumer Affairs sued Cambridge State for fraud, but even though they won the suit, they seem unable to close this place down. Cambridge State literature sent out in mid-2000 shows full accreditation by the World Association of Universities and Colleges, "based on a thorough evaluation of . . . professional integrity." Degree programs cost between $2,500 and $5,300. Incorporated in Delaware.

Canadian Temple College of Life of the International Academy Burnaby, British Columbia, Canada. Identified as a degree mill by COE.

Capital College See: National Certificate Company

Cardinal Publishing Company Florida. They publish a variety of fake diploma forms and blanks.

Carlton University Same management as Laurence University in Hawaii.

Carnegie Institute of Engineering See: Regency Enterprises

Carolina Institute of Human Relations Sumter, South Carolina. Identified as a degree mill by COE.

Carroll Studios Illinois. Since 1988, they have been selling "College Diploma" forms for $2 each, in which the buyer must letter not only his or her own name but the name of the school and degree earned. Two dollars also buys you a marriage certificate, a birth certificate, a divorce

certificate, and, if devastated by all of the above, a last will and testament.

Cathedra Institute See: Advanced Education Institute

Central Board of Higher Education India. Identified as a degree mill by COE.

Central States Research Center Ontario, Canada. They sold well-printed fake diplomas "in memory of famous names." The samples they sent out included Christian College, the Ohio Psychological Association, and Sussex College of Technology. Another address in Columbus, Ohio.

Central University See: National Certificate Company

Chaparral Western University Ships degrees by Fed Ex within ten days of your order. Their online sales pitch doesn't give out the name of the university—"to protect the university name from being seen by mere casual browsers . . . thereby diminishing both the value of your diploma and the University name"—but the domain name, *yourdegreenow.com*, is owned by Chaparral [*sic*] Western University, located at the home address of a man named Robert Kerr. The school claims accreditation from the Inter-Collegiate Joint Committee on Academic Standards, an unrecognized accreditor whose domain name, *jointcommittee.org*, is also owned by Robert Kerr. We especially like the fact that "degree mill" is listed as a keyword in the Web site's source code.

Charitable University of Delaware Identified as a degree mill by E&T.

Chartered University of Huron Identified as a degree mill by COE.

Chicago Medical College Florida. Their literature says that "Your beautiful 11 x 15 graudate [*sic*] diploma is printed on the finest sturdy parchtone . . . . It will add prestige and beauty to your office." Or cell. The price of their medical degree is a mere $450.

Chillico, the Business College Ohio. Identified as a degree mill by E&T.

Chirological College of California Identified as a degree mill by COE.

Christian College See: Central States Research Center

Christian Fellowship Foundation See: Lawford State University

Church of Universal Confusion Nevada. This "school" offers an honorary doctorate in universal confusion for a very reasonable $15. It's clearly all in fun (the head of the school is listed as the Grand Poobaa, etc.), but still, we don't recommend listing it on your resume.

City Medical Correspondence College London, England. Identified as a degree mill by E&T.

Clayton Theological Institute California (the address appears to be a private home). Their doctorate was awarded on completion of a dissertation of at least 25 words and a fee of $3. When this was done (John's dissertation was 27 words; he worked extra hard), he got a nice letter saying that he had indeed been awarded their doctorate, but if he wanted the actual diploma, it would cost $50 more. Recent letters to the institute have been returned as undeliverable.

Clemson College See: R/G Enterprises

CliffPort University This nonexistent institution arose in 2000, claiming to be incorporated in New Jersey, but the only address we could find on the minimalist Web site is in Pakistan. Accreditation (or, as they call it, "accrediation") is claimed from the nonexistent (as best we can determine) International Accrediting Agency for Private and Post Secondary Institutes.

Clinton University Livonia, Michigan. For years, they sold fake degrees of all kinds for $25 and up, offering 'a masterpiece so perfect, it absolutely defies detection.' Mail to their address is now returned as undeliverable.

Coast University Another name for Gold Coast University; see them later in this chapter. While this probably was an Edward Reddeck venture, the name was reserved by Nancy Akamu.

Colgate College See: R/G Enterprises

College of Applied Science London England. The college exists on paper only, but, like Brigadoon, it was real (well, almost real) for one day. As reported by a German magazine, a wealthy German industrialist bought a fake doctorate from this place, and insisted that it be presented in person. The president, "Commander Sir" Sidney Lawrence enlisted the aid of his friend, "Archbishop" Charles Brearly, who ran several fake universities in Sheffield. They rented a fancy girls' school for the day, installed carpets and candelabra, and rented costumes for their friends, who dressed up as "counts hung around with medals, an abbess in a trailing robe . . . and the knights of the Holy Grail." The German arrived in a Rolls Royce, and received his degree in an impressive ceremony, which only cost him $15,000. Sir Sidney, incidentally, appends to his letters a rubber stamp saying "Hon. Attorney General U.S.A."

College of Divine Metaphysics England. Identified as a diploma mill by E&T.

College of Franklin and Marshall See: Regency Enterprises

College of Hard Knocks See: USSI

College of Hilton Head See: University of East Georgia

College of Homeopathy Missouri. Identified as a diploma mill by E&T.

College of Journalism West Virginia. Identified as a diploma mill by E&T.

College of Life Florida. Honorary doctorates were sold for $2, but the school has since gone away.

College of Naturatrics Missouri. Identified as a diploma mill by E&T.

College of Nonsense Nevada. "You can fool your friends and tell them you have a doctorate degree. If they don't believe you, you can show your friends your Doctor degree." John bought a Doctor of Politics for $2. A Doctor of Martyrism, Cheerleading, or Nose Blowing would have been 50¢ extra. Silly stuff, but a better-printed diploma than many legitimate schools provide.

College of Spiritual Sciences England. Identified as a diploma mill by E&T.

College of Universal Truth Chicago, Illinois. Identified as a diploma mill by E&T.

Collegii Romanii See: International Honorary Awards Committee

Collegium Technoologicum Sussexensis Britannia See: Sussex College of Technology

Colorado Christian University Subject of a landmark court case in which the state of New York successfully sued to prevent them from selling their degrees to New Yorkers, or to advertise in publications distributed from New York. No connection whatever with the accredited Rockmont College, which changed its name in 1989 to Colorado Christian University.

Columbia School Unknown U.S. location. Identified as a diploma mill by COE.

Columbia State University This is one of the biggest and most insidious diploma mills the world has ever known. Using a mail forwarding and telephone answering service in Louisiana, owner Ronald Pellar (using more than 40 aliases) ran his business from a warehouse in southern California (930 Calle Negrocio, Suite E, San Clemente, CA). Columbia State's ads (which ran regularly in major magazines) offered the bachelor's, master's, or Ph.D. in 27 days, "fully accredited" (by two non-existent agencies). Enough people fell for this that Columbia State was able to deposit more than $16 million in just one year into its bank account number 749-4023968 at California Federal, 570 Camino De Estrella, San Clemente. And it had been in operation for nine or ten years.

In late 1997, Pellar was convicted in Federal Court in Los Angeles on 11 criminal counts (including jury tampering) for one of his earlier degree mills. He escaped to Mexico just before the sentencing, and was a federal fugitive until his capture shortly after ABC's 20/20 gave his fraud its first major national exposure.

The Columbia State catalog has on its cover, as its alleged campus, a photograph of Lyndhurst, a stately home in upstate New York. It lists as president Austen Henry Leyard, a well-known archaeologist who died over 100 years ago. Pellar, using the name Herald Crenshaw, published a book that looks very much like an earlier edition of this one, and indeed is largely copied from ours, but which identifies Columbia State as the best university in the United States (and, for good measure, identifies the quite legitimate Greenwich University, with which John was once associated, as the worst university in the United States). In 1994, Pellar managed, by a clever ruse, to steal the mailing list of recent buyers of this book. Those people were sent a newsletter from "U.S. Official Publications," in which

Pellar, now using the alias Edward Connelly, spent eight pages attacking this book (which he called a "brochure") and John Bear. Needless to say there is no such organization as U.S. Official Publications.

Pellar used to be known as Doctor Dante, had a stint as a well-known television and stage hypnotist in the '60s, briefly married Lana Turner, and served a seven-year prison term for attempted murder. While he was on the run, the fake school was run by his wife, Elizabeth Dante, and his cousin, Lauri Gerald. They took hundreds of thousands of dollars from the bank account every Tuesday and Friday and brought it to Pellar in Mexico. More than 20 people worked at the San Clemente facility in sweatshop conditions (no payroll deductions, no workers compensation insurance, etc.) filling orders.

John is often asked why he did not sue Pellar. Even though two lawyers advised that this was the clearest case of libel they'd ever seen, the cost of mounting a proper suit could easily reach six figures, and the probability of collecting a dime from this 70-plus-year-old criminal following a courtroom victory is small.

As of late 2000, the Justice Department was still working on its case against Columbia State. If all goes well, there may be indictments in 2001.

Commercial University Delhi, India. Listed as a degree mill by COE. The Ministry of Education writes that it is a "coaching institution" whose degrees are "not recognised for any purpose." However, a reader insists that his B.Com. degree from this school was accepted by the Malaysian government.

Commonwealth School of Law Washington. Identified as a diploma mill by COE.

Commonwealth University California. Degrees of this nonexistent school were sold by mail for $40. Also sold by the same firm: Eastern State University.

Concorda Graduate Institute See: Advanced Education Institute

Concorda University See: Advanced Education Institute

Constantina University In 1989, a mailing went out to Italian businessmen, offering them the opportunity to earn a doctorate from this apparently nonexistent school, in association with the accredited Johnson & Wales University (which denied any knowledge of the scheme). For $3,000, they would spend a week in New York, see Niagara Falls, and go home with a doctorate. According to one source in Italy, more than 100 people signed up.

Continental University In 1990, a reader in Japan sent us a copy of a diploma (dated 1989) from the nonexistent school, allegedly in Los Angeles.

Conway College A correspondent writes that this "school" operates from a post office box in Conway, New Hampshire, but fraudulently claims to be a division of the University of New Hampshire.

Cosmopolitan University In 1998, this institution arose on the Internet, with a mostly German-language Web site, but claiming to be in Missouri, Miami Beach, and various other places from New Zealand to Belgium. In addition to selling degrees of all kinds, they sell honorary consular documents, and honorary doctorates, no questions asked. The Web site seems to suggest that they are actually operating from Chile. Alleged degree-holders range from German Chancellor Kohl to a minister in Dallas, a journalist in the Netherlands, an attorney in Miami Beach, and the chairman of Daimler Benz.

Cranmer Hall Theological College Identified as a diploma mill by E&T.

Creative University of Southeast London London, England. Identified as a diploma mill by E&T.

Cromwell University London, England. This diploma mill was one of many run for years by the Fowler family of Chicago, five of whom were sentenced to prison in 1987 for these activities. Cromwell sold degrees of all kinds for $730, through a mail forwarding service. Accreditation was claimed from the nonexistent Western European Accrediting Society of Liederbach, Germany.

Crown Institute, Inc. An ad in *The Economist* states that this institute offers an M.A. in astrology-alternative medicine. The "campus" in New York City is a mail receiving and forwarding service called New York Executive OFFC.

Dallas State College Dallas, Texas. One of the first heavily advertised diploma mills, Dallas State flourished in the early 1970s under the guidance of at least one of the Fowler family of Chicago. In 1975, the attorney general of Texas permanently enjoined Dallas State from operating in that state.

Damnation University From *www.damu.com*: "You can spend a bundle of money chasing down a degree from one of those fancy-schmancy four-year institutions and you still might be asking, 'Do you want fries with that?' as you pay off your student loans. Damnation University has the solution. For less than you'd pay for a single textbook in an Economics class, we'll deliver a gorgeous framed diploma (signed, sealed, and singed on the Damnation University campus in Hell, Michigan), a Dam U automobile window sticker, a Dam U license plate frame, and a selection of top-quality apparel, all emblazoned with the beloved Damnation University seal."

Darthmouth College See: Regency Enterprises

Darwin University See: Aspen University

Delaware Law School Identified as a diploma mill by E&T, and we're sorry the people at the genuine Delaware Law School, now a part of Widener University, are upset that we mention this, but don't blame us when diploma mill operators choose to use the same name as a legitimate school.

DePaul University (France) Paris. A diploma mill operated for years by the Fowler family, from a mail forwarding service in Paris. Operations ceased following five Fowlers' sentencing to prison in 1987. Degrees of all kinds were sold for $550, and accreditation was claimed from the Worldwide Accrediting Commission, allegedly of Cannes, France. Other addresses used in Clemson, South Carolina, and Santa Monica, California.

Diplomatic State University See: R/G Enterprises

Diplomatic University See: National Certificate Company

Earl James National University Toronto, Canada. Identified as a diploma mill by COE.

Eastern Missouri Business College The nonexistent school established by the attorney general of Missouri, in a sting operation. During its one day of existence, the head of the International Accrediting Commission for Schools, Colleges and Theological Seminaries visited the one-room office in St. Louis, overlooked the fact that the school had officers named Peelsburi Doobuoy and Wonarrmed Mann, overlooked the fact that the marine biology text was *The Little Golden Book of Fishes*, did not overlook the accreditation "fee" he was handed, and duly accredited the school, which disappeared forever the next day.

Eastern Orthodox University India. Identified as a diploma mill by COE.

Eastern State University See: Commonwealth University

Eastern University See: National Certificate Company

Ecclesiastical University of Sheffield See: University of Sheffield

Education Certificate Replacement Service According to a notice on the Internet, this service offers 'replacement' copies of any degree you might wish. They make the claim that this is not illegal because they state that these certificates are not original degrees.

Elysion College They used to offer degrees from various addresses in California, although the proprietor was in Mexico. Several book reports or essays and $500 were required to earn the degree. When the proprietor died, his daughter continued the operation from her home in San Francisco. She told authorities she was not operating the school, but an FBI analysis of her garbage revealed that she was, and after her indictment by a federal grand jury, and her guilty plea, Elysion College faded away.

Emerson University California. Identified as a diploma mill by COE.

Empire College of Ophthalmology Canada. Identified as a diploma mill by COE.

Episcopal University of London London, England. Identified as a diploma mill by E&T.

Episcopal University of Saint Peter Port Frankfurt, Germany. Identified as a diploma mill by E&T.

Études Universitaires Internationales Leichtenstein, Luxembourg. Identified as a diploma mill by COE.

Eugenia Institute of Metaphysics See: ORB

European College of Science and Man Sheffield, England. Identified as a diploma mill by E&T.

Evaluation and Management International Inglewood, California. These folks have sent out a three-page, unsigned letter saying that on receipt of $2,100 they will arrange for the degree of your choice to be issued to you. They require 50 percent down before they reveal the name of the school that is to be your alma mater. Can anyone ever have fallen for this? (The school, incidentally, seems to be City University Los Angeles.)

Faraday College England. Identified as a diploma mill by E&T.

Felix Adler Memorial University Charlotte, North Carolina. Identified as a diploma mill by E&T.

Florida State Christian College Fort Lauderdale, Florida. They used to advertise nationally the availability of bachelor's, master's, doctorates, and honorary doctorates, until both the postal service and the state of Florida acted to shut them down. They also operated Alpha Psi Omega, a professional society for psychological counselors.

Florida State Christian University This school presented an associate with a rather impressive-looking blank diploma as a gift—assumedly so the recipient could fill in the blanks with the title and field of his choice.

Forest Park University Chicago, Illinois. Identified as a diploma mill by COE.

Four States Cooperative University Texas. Identified as a diploma mill by COE.

Franklin University (Hawaii) Same management as Laurence University.

General Delivery University A rather charming and silly Internet endeavor, purporting to be "America's only Genuine Diploma Mill," and offering net surfers the opportunity to download diplomas from such worthy institutions as the Ponzi School of Business and the College of Rock Music, for an eminently reasonable $3.95. It's all quite funny and well done.

Geo-Metaphysical Institute New York. 'Here's a great way to get instant status,' said their national advertising, offering an ornate personalized and totally phony honorary doctorate in geo-metaphysics for $5.

Georgia Christian University Georgia. The first pyramid scheme diploma mill. When you 'graduate' (buy a degree), you become a professor and can sell degrees to others. When your students buy degrees and become professors, you become a dean and share in their profits, and so on, up the academic ladder.

German-American Dental College Chicago, Illinois. Identified as a diploma mill by COE.

Glamount University The Web site is identical to the equally phony CliffPort University. While the claim is made that it is incorporated in Texas, it appears, instead, to operate only from Pakistan.

Global Money Consultants This Greek-based organization, operating largely over the Internet, offers much more than no-questions-asked degrees—their services include similarly easy-to-obtain passports, driver's licenses, anonymous bank accounts, diplomatic appointments (!), and more. Ranging from $1,500 for a bachelor's degree to $2,000 for a doctorate, the degrees are awarded from either of two schools located in Panama City, Panama: the University of the Americas or Trinity College & University. (We don't know if there is any connection to the Trinity C & U's in the U.K. or the U.S.) Marketing literature for both of Global Money's schools is identical, including this puzzler: "The University does not have a campus or buildings, but is to compare more to a scientific entity." Of course.

Gold Coast University Hawaii. Opened by Edward Reddeck, previously imprisoned for operating other diploma mills. Later changed to Coast University. Although Hawaii authorities showed no interest, federal authorities closed the 'school' in 1992 after Reddeck was indicted on many counts of mail fraud and conspiracy. He was convicted on all 22 counts in early 1993, and returned to prison.

Golden State University Operated from California and Colorado in the 1950s and 1960s. Exposed as a degree mill on Paul Coates's television program in 1958. No connection with the state-approved school of the same name that opened in 1979.

Gordon Arlen College England. Identified as a diploma mill by E&T.

Gottbourg University of Switzerland See: ORB

Graduate University See: National Certificate Company

Great Lakes University Higgins Lake, Michigan. One of several degree mills operated by W. (for Wiley!) Gordon Bennett. Degrees were sold for $200. Also used addresses in Dearborn and Berkley, Michigan, and Chicago. Also involved was former major university administrator Achille Borque (see: Pacific Northwestern University).

Gulf Southern University Louisiana. The literature is identical to that used by several other mills, such as Pacific Northwestern and Atlantic Northeastern. Degrees were sold for $45 to anyone but Louisiana residents.

Hamilton State University Arizona. Sold degrees for $50 or less. The fake diploma says they are in Clinton, New York, home of the old and respectable Hamilton College. See also: Regency Enterprises and R/G Enterprises.

Hamilton University In mid 1998, we responded to an advertisement from the Academic Resource and Referral Center, offering to find us the perfect school. We submitted a short, fictitious name, and were informed by return mail (the letterhead said Kentucky, but the postmark was Rock Springs, Wyoming) that the perfect school was Hamilton University, and that we had already qualified for a degree from this fine institution. The official Web site for the State of Wyoming points out that Wyoming cannot regulate religious schools, which is what Hamilton claims to be, even though it happily awards degrees of any kind. Comes complete with its very own fake accrediting agency, the American Council of Private Colleges and Universities (ACPCU). There is a comparable pairing of a phony school-finding service (Higher Education Research Institute) and dreadful school (American State University), which is probably the same people, but may simply be one stealing from the other.

Hancock University Tennessee. Arose briefly in 1995, with ads in *USA Today*, selling honorary degrees of all kinds, but after a month or so, subsided for a while. Now, they appear to be active again.

Harley University London, England. John found the university in a tiny corner of the London College of Beauty Therapy. The salon receptionist was the university registrar. Ph.D. degrees were awarded on completion of a dissertation of less than 20 pages. The co-proprietor of Harley U. (who refused to tell us the source of his own Ph.D.) wrote that "the details in your booklet are totally untrue in every respect." The detailed questions then put to him in our reply to that letter were never answered. Harley University apparently is no more. Its proprietor later established Saint Giles University College and Somerset University.

Harrington University See: University of San Moritz

Hartford Technical Institute See: Regency Enterprises

Harvard University for External Studies They were registered as a business in Hawaii as of May, 2000, but it is certainly not that school in Massachusetts, although the registrants may wish that people thought so. Stated purpose: to offer "international home study course for the purposes of promoting educational access." Their address in London, England, is a mail forwarding service.

Hillcrest Farm Institute "A fully accredited institution of lower learning" offering a degree in farm management. Courses include litter box cleaning, dog yard scooping, and lawn mower driving. According to their Web site, graduates have gone on to exciting and rewarding careers in the fields of dog administration, cat-keeping, and horse maintenance. The diploma can be printed right off the Internet.

Hirshfeld College See: USSI

His Majesty's University of Polytechnics Sacramento, California. Used to sell honorary doctorates in all subjects (but "no profanities or obscenities") for all of $5. But the "university" closed down many years ago, so please stop trying to write to them, so the former proprietor won't have to write us any more annoyed letters.

Hollywood College California. Identified as a diploma mill by E&T.

Hollywood College of Naturopathy In the 1960s, a felon in southern California took a diploma from the legitimate Hollywood College of Chiropractic, covered up the last word with "Naturopathy," reprinted them, and sold them to anyone willing to pay the price.

Hollywood Southern University See: California Pacifica University

Holmes University See: Advanced Education Institute

Holy Acclaim Graduate Institute See: Advanced Education Institute

Holy Acclaim University See: Advanced Education Institute

Holy Toledo University American Educational Publishers has invented the delightful and humorous doctorates of Holy Toledo U., offering the Doctor of Philosophy in Adorableness, Defrosting, Worrying, and other fields. They are nicely designed (the gold seal says, in small type, 'My goodness how impressive!') and sold for $12 a dozen.

Honoré College See: ORB

Hoover University In the late 1990's, they apparently offered master's and doctorates by correspondence for a few hundred dollars each. The facilitator who handled their incorporation in South Dakota was "outraged" when he learned that Hoover (as well as Maxipoint University and Monticello University) was listing his address as the location of their campus. The founder, apparently an academician in Australia, explained/defended to us that Hoover "would appear to meet your criteria for the term 'degree mill' with the arguable difference of a genuine selective entry policy, full upfront disclosure of nature and purpose, and to have a function not dissimilar to your own London Institute for Applied Research [LIAR is described elsewhere in this chapter]. As far as I've been able to ascertain it's perfectly legal and plans to operate ethically." This person seems to have thought better of the idea, and it appears that Hoover U is no more. Now we'll never know if it was named after Herbert, J. Edgar, or the vacuum cleaner.

Humberman University College Identified as a diploma mill by E&T.

Idaho College of Commerce See: International Universities Consortium

Illinois State University See: Regency Enterprises

Imperial Philo-Byzantine University Madrid, Spain. Identified as a diploma mill by COE.

Independence University (Missouri) Flourished in the late 1970s, offering degrees by correspondence, until exposés in the Chronicle of Higher Education and a Chicago newspaper helped close them down. The *Chicago Tribune* reported that the headmaster of a prestigious Chicago private school resigned "after disclosures that he was using the office there as a center of activity for the diploma mill." A community college president in Chicago subsequently lost his job for using an Independence doctorate. There apparently is also a humorous and unrelated Independence University, offering realistic-looking diplomas from its School of Hard Knocks, and signed by "A. Harry World."

Independent Study Programs, Inc. Missouri. Degrees of all kinds sold in the late 1970s. No longer there.

Indiana State University See: Regency Enterprises

Institut Inter-Européen Switzerland. Offers degrees at all levels in a number of business-related fields.

Institut Patriarcal Saint Irenée Beziers, France. Granted honorary doctorates to the founder's American colleagues and perhaps others. See also: Inter-State College

Institute of Excellence Florida. All degrees, including medical and dental, at $10 each. The fake diplomas are very poorly printed, and say, in small type, 'for novelty purposes only.'

Inter-American University (Italy) Rome. Identified as a diploma mill by COE.

Inter-State College England, France. Established by Karl Josef Werres, granting honorary doctorates from England. One of the recipients claims that the college is 'legally chartered' to do this, but all that means is that in their corporate charter, they give themselves the right. See also: Institut Patriarcal Saint Irenée.

Intercollegiate University Incorporated in Kansas before World War II. As the *American Mercury* reported, 'Intercollegiate specialized in hanging its M.A. on some of England's minor men of God—for $50; and for a few dollars more, it was willing to bestow a dazzling D.C.L. Before the war this had grown into a roaring and profitable trade, but when wartime law prohibited sending money out of England, the Intercollegiate professors were obliged to suspend their work of international enlightenment.'

Internation University U.S. Identified as a diploma mill by E&T.

"…and so, if you enroll in Tonya's Institute of Ice Skate Sharpening right now, by providing your credit card number, you'll receive, at no additional charge …Sir? Sir? Are you listening to me?"

International Academy for Planetary Planning See: International Honorary Awards Committee

International American University (Italy) Rome. Identified as a diploma mill by COE.

International Awards Committee Washington, D.C. For $225, this organization will award an honorary doctorate based on a request for consideration, a copy of your resume, and an outline of your professional, academic, and public service accomplishments.

International College of Associates in Medicine Texas. Used to offer a Ph.D. and a Doctor of Medical Letters on payment of modest fees.

International Honorary Awards Committee California. They sold a wide range of doctorates and other awards, mostly for $100 or less. The well-designed doctoral diplomas came from Collegii Romanii, the International Academy for Planetary Planning, Two Dragon University, and the Siberian Institute. One could also buy diplomatic regalia including the Grand Cross of the Imperial Order of Constantine and the Sovereign Order of Leichtenstein, complete with rosettes, medals, and sashes. The late Francis X. Gordon, founder of all these establishments, had a delightful sense of humor about his work. His widow apparently carried it on for a while.

International Internet University OK, this was one of the strangest experiences in decades of checking out sleazy schools. The IIU Web site looks decent, at first glance, for what claims to be a large school based in Florida. The campus and the courses are described in some detail. But then the pieces start not to fit. The ZIP code does not match the address. There is no such street in Pensacola. And the accreditation is claimed from the North Central agency, which does not deal with Florida. And then . . . we phoned their toll-free number, and the phone was answered (we quote exactly), "Mmmmm, welcome, we're wet and ready for you right now. Come on baby, let's play." We are then invited to give our credit card number, for a "hot and nasty" experience. It would appear that the registrar is wearing no clothes.

International Open University (California) In 1997 and 1998, John received numerous emails from people in the Ukraine, who claimed to be operating branches of this alleged California university. When we explained to them there was no such place, they insisted that it was "fully registrated" by the State of California, and provided a corporate number and an address. That address turned out to be a private home. Presumably someone has formed a corporation with this name, and has sold franchises throughout the Ukraine, Russia, and Moldova. The people there may in fact be providing some educational services, but they are in complete denial regarding the nonexistence of the California "anchor."

International Protestant Birkbest College England. Identified as a diploma mill by E&T.

International School of Business and Legal Studies Mail to their London, England address returned as unforwardable. This unaccredited school had awarded degrees entirely on the basis of an applicant's credentials, under somewhat unusual circumstances. They'd solicited agents in other countries, and offered to award degrees on the basis of agents' recommendations. They required that these agents have doctorates, which they offered to provide for £450, £175 more for wig and gown.

International Universities Consortium Missouri. In 1989, help-wanted ads appeared in the academic press, soliciting faculty for a consortium of nontraditional schools. Being the suspicious sort, John fabricated a resume of the most outrageous sort, under an assumed name, and submitted it. Shortly thereafter, his nom de plume was appointed to the faculty of what was alleged to be a group of eight "universities"—one a long-established diploma mill (London School for Social Research), one a school we had been suspicious about for years (Northern Utah University), and six new ones, characterized by the common theme that they do not appear to exist (no listed phones). They are: Southwestern University (allegedly in New Mexico), St. Andrews University (allegedly in Baha [sic] California, Mexico), Northwestern Graduate Institute (allegedly Montana), University of the West (allegedly Wyoming), Idaho College of Commerce (allegedly Idaho), and American Management Institute (no location given). Northern Utah actually issued a catalog, complete with the "faculty" names of all those boobs who answered the ad and signed up to be on the staff, no questions asked. But the address and phone numbers in the catalog are not working. Consortium president Warren H. Green writes that the whole scheme, which he defends as completely legitimate, has been canceled.

International University (Greece) Athens. The literature claims that the doctorates are nonacademic, but nonetheless fully recognized as educational and professional degrees by the republic of Greece. The embassy of Greece has written to us that this is not a correct statement. The president is listed as a 'Right Reverend Bishop Doctor,' who later established a 'university' in Louisiana. There apparently was, at least at one time, an affiliation with International University of Missouri.

International University (India) Degrees of this institution are sold for $50 to $100 each by the Bureau for Degree Promotion in Holland.

International University (Louisiana) Opened in the early 1980s by relatives of James (Thomas) Kirk, later imprisoned for his role in LaSalle University. Offered degrees of all kinds. Accreditation was claimed from the North American Regional Accrediting Commission, which we have never been able to locate. Following a stern letter from the Louisiana Proprietary School Commission, International University apparently faded away.

International University (Switzerland) Zurich. One of the many diploma mill operations of Karl Xavier Bleisch, this one selling bachelor's, master's, and doctorates for $500 to $1,000. The literature has a photocopy of a San Jose State College diploma awarded to Celia Ann Bleisch in 1967. What can this mean?

Jackson State University Los Angeles, Nashville, Reno, Chicago. Sold degrees of all kinds for $200. The postal service issued 'false representation orders' and stopped their mail years ago, and the perpetrators finally were sentenced to federal prison in 1987. No connection whatsoever with the legitimate school of this name in Mississippi.

Janta Engineering College Karnal, India. Identified as a diploma mill by COE.

Japan Christian College Tokyo, Japan. Identified as a diploma mill by COE.

Jefferson and Madison School of Law See: Monticello University

Jerusalem University Tel Aviv, Israel. Degrees of all kinds are sold for $10 to $40 from this nonexistent university. Buyers must sign a statement that they will not use the degrees for any phony purpose.

Johann Keppler School of Medicine There are very few people daring or stupid enough to start a fake medical school. This was one of the most ambitious, complete with catalog, and an alleged faculty in Switzerland, Canada, and Mexico. The claim was made that the degrees were recognized in many countries. When John asked their representative (who telephoned to make sure he would put them in this book) which countries, he thought a while and then said, 'Well, Mauritius for one.' All addresses used were mail forwarding services. Accreditation was claimed from the American Coordinated Medical Society, a fake organization started by L. Mitchell Weinberg, who has been to prison several times for fake medical school operations, and who was involved with Keppler as well. Operations ceased in the wake of the FBI DipScam operation in 1983. Weinberg was indicted and sentenced to prison again.

John Hancock University See: Hancock University

John Quincy Adams College Portland, Oregon. A totally phony school, selling any degree for $250. Later used addresses in Illinois and Nevada. Operated by the Fowler family, five of whom were sentenced to prison in 1987.

Kennedy Honorary University A relatively new Colorado-based degree mill, offering phony degrees at all levels in a wide range of fields.

Kent College One of the alternative names used by La Salle University during its diploma mill days.

Kentucky Christian University Ashland, Kentucky. They offered degrees in everything from chemical engineering to law at all levels for a $300 fee. Same auspices as Ohio Christian and Florida State Christian, all now defunct.

Kentucky Military Institute See: Bretton Woods University

Kenwood Associates Long Green, Maryland. For $15 each or three for $30, they will sell bachelor's, master's, or doctorates in the name of any school, with any degree and any date. Then you can buy, for $12, a Jiu Jitsu master Instructor certificate to flash when the authorities come to take you away. Long Green, indeed.

Kingsley University See: Bradford University

Lafayette University (Netherlands) Amsterdam, through a mail forwarding service. One of many fake schools operated by the Fowler family, five of whom were sentenced to prison for operating diploma mills, in late 1987. Degrees of any sort, with any date, were sold for $725. Accreditation was claimed from an equally fake accrediting agency, the West European Accrediting Society of Liederbach, West Germany.

Lamp Beacon University See: California Pacifica University

LaSalle University (1986 to mid-1997) Note carefully: LaSalle operated as a degree mill until mid-1997, when it was sold to new and serious owners. In October 2000, the name was changed to Orion College, but the old LaSalle continues as well for those students who wish to finish a LaSalle degree for whatever reason. Here is the chronology, which may be helpful in evaluating a specific LaSalle degree:

▶ 1986 through 1997: LaSalle operates as a diploma mill (although there were some students who did real work, even though they didn't have to).

▶ 1997 through January 1999: Run legally by new owners, although some students still may be doing the less-demanding work of the old LaSalle.

▶ January 1999 through October 2000: All students doing courses designed to meet DETC standards; they all switch to Orion College. No new enrollments under the old LaSalle standards, or lack of same.

▶ October 2000: Orion College begins.

The "old" LaSalle University was established by James Kirk (also known as Thomas McPherson and Thomas Kirk), who had earlier operated Southland University and International University (Louisiana). Following ten years of operation in Missouri and Louisiana, the school was raided in July 1996 by a joint task force of the FBI, the Postal Inspection Service, and the Internal Revenue Service, after a five-year investigation. Kirk and several colleagues were subsequently indicted on 18 counts of mail fraud, tax fraud, money laundering, and other charges, and more than $10 million in cash was confiscated. The indictments claimed among other things that more than 15,000 students were being handled by fewer than five faculty, none of them with traditional academic credentials; that the university was run by a church Kirk had established for the purpose of tax evasion; and that the accreditation was from a nonexistent agency established by LaSalle. Kirk pleaded guilty, in a plea bargain, and was sentenced to five years in federal prison. He was ordered never to operate a school again. (Kirk married for the fifth or sixth time while in prison, and his new wife's name appears on the literature of Acton (originally Edison) University, which operates from a secretarial service in Hawaii, using literature almost identical to LaSalle's.) LaSalle students and graduates prior to mid-1997 were given the option of a full refund, but only if they turned in their diplomas, an option accepted by a relatively small number of alumni.

Laurence University Hawaii. All degrees in all fields except medicine and law, for a fee of $45. The literature says, 'We are confident you will find the benefits you can obtain with a degree from Laurence University are very valuable indeed.' The main benefit we can think of is a period of room and board at government expense. The same seller, Associated Enterprises, also issues the fake degrees of Benson University, Carlton University, Kingsley University, Buckner University, Franklin University, and Bradford University. There is, of course, no connection with the legitimate school formerly called Laurence University (now University of Santa Barbara) in California.

Lawford State University Maryland. They used to sell degrees of all kinds for $6.99 from a post office box in Baltimore, now closed. The other school names were Université de Commerce de [sic] Canada and the Christian Fellowship Foundation. The hard-to-decipher signatures on the quite-realistic-looking certificates were "Thoroughly Fake, Ph.D." and "Too Much Fun, Jr."

Leiland College of Arts and Sciences Arose in 1992, offering degrees to martial artists for under $100. Diploma identical to that of Eurotechnical Research University (see listing in chapter 21) whose president originally opened the post office box they used but later turned it over to a colleague, and denied any knowledge of Leiland.

Libera Universita di Psico-Biofisica Trieste, Yugoslavia. (That's what their literature says, even though Trieste is now in Italy and Yugoslavia, of course, no longer exists.) Identified as a diploma mill by E&T.

Life Science College California and Oklahoma. The proprietors were arrested in 1981 for an array of charges, including selling Doctor of Divinity degrees, and income tax evasion through the operation of the college and the associated Life Science Church.

Lincoln City University Ostensibly founded in the State of Delaware in 1997, its main purpose seems to be the selling of degrees to people in Hong Kong and elsewhere in Asia. There is an office in Hong Kong. The "registered office" (the only address in any of the literature) is a company-forming service. In the tradition of other such frauds, the well-designed literature has many photographs of academic buildings and scenes that have nothing whatever to do with Lincoln City University.

Lincoln-Jefferson University See: California Pacifica University

London College of Physiology England. Identified as a diploma mill by E&T.

London College of Theology England. Identified as a diploma mill by E&T.

London Educational College England. Identified as a diploma mill by E&T.

London Institute for Applied Research England. All right, he did it (as he's been saying in this book for more than 20 years now). In 1972, while living in England, John was involved in fund-raising for a legitimate school. He figured that since major universities were 'selling' their honorary degrees for millions, why not use the same approach on a small scale? He and his associates created L.I.A.R. and ran ads in the U.S. reading 'Phony honorary doctorates for sale, $25.' Several hundred were sold, but the whole thing seemed to have upset half the world's educational establishment. (The other half thought it was a good gag.) So L.I.A.R. was retired. Then an offer came from a Dutchman who lived in Ethiopia (you must believe us on this—who would make up such a story?) who wanted to trade 100 pounds of Ethiopian ear-pickers and Coptic crosses for the remaining L.I.A.R. certificates. Now he's selling them from Holland without the humorous disclaimer, and has added a bunch more fake school names. And if anyone would like some Ethiopian trinkets, have we got a deal for you!

London School for Social Research London, England. The well-prepared literature offers degrees of all kinds for fees of up to $2,000. The address is in a dingy little building off Leicester Square, where John climbed five flights of stairs so narrow that he had to go up sideways, and at the top found the little one-room office of Archangel Services, a mail-forwarding service that told him they forward the London School mail to Miami. Some literature has also been mailed from Phoenix. See also: International Universities Consortium

London Tottenham International Christian University England. Identified as a diploma mill by E&T.

Loyola State University Illinois. A new venture inspired by our old friend Dr. Dante, described in the write-up for Columbia State University in this chapter. It seems that one of Dante's victims was so angry at having been fooled, and then unable to get her money back, that she decided to start her own fake, so she could make good her losses. The requirements of this latest "school" appear no more rigorous—the catalog states that "all we see, touch, or do becomes a learning experience. Earth becomes our campus and life our instructor." She was only in business for a few weeks before the alert Illinois Attorney General's office struck them down. The name was also registered in Hawaii in 1996, but apparently not used there.

Loyola University (France) Paris. Through a mail-forwarding service, degrees of all kinds were sold for a payment of up to $650. The brochure claimed that "Many of our successful graduates have used their transcripts to transfer to other colleges and universities in the U.S.A." If this really did happen, it would have been only because of name confusion with the four legitimate Loyolas in the U.S. The perpetrators of this Loyola were sentenced to federal prison in 1987.

LTD Documents New York. Extremely well-done, and thus especially dangerous, fake diplomas with the name of any school and any degree printed on them for $69.50. Also, preprinted degrees from the nonexistent San Miguel College and Benchley State University for $49.50. They even explain how to 'age' a certificate to make it look older.

Lyne College England. Identified as a diploma mill by E&T.

Madison State University See: R/G Enterprises

Marcus Tullius Cicero University San Francisco, California. A Swiss company advertised in the International Herald Tribune that they could provide the 'registered legal degree' of the so-called university for a mere $3,000. The diploma indicates that the university is 'officially registered' with the secretary of state which, if true, simply means it is a California corporation. Checks are made payable to The Knights of Humanity. There is, of course, no such university in California or, presumably, anywhere else.

Marlowe University New Jersey and Florida. Active during the 1960s and 1970s, selling all kinds of degrees for $150 or less.

Marmaduke University California. Degrees of all kinds were sold for $1,000 and up. The literature reports that "usually the student qualifies for more advanced study than he initialy [sic] expected." Mention was made of a 30-day resident course in the use of lie detectors, but the voice on the phone (answering simply, "Hello") said it had been canceled "because of the building program." Marmaduke was actually once authorized by the state of California, back in the days (late 1970s) when such things were vastly easier.

Martin College Florida. They used to sell degrees of all kinds for $200. Graduates were required to pass some tough exams, as evidenced by this example given in the school's literature: 'True or false—the Declaration of Independence was signed on the 4th of July by British Royalty.'

Maxsell Corporation Florida. A "diploma replacement service," offering to "recreate any lost or stolen document to your specifications." They go on to assure that "documents are for the exclusive personal use and enjoyment of our clients, and any misuse is their sole responsibility." Glad we got that cleared up.

May Kong College Hong Kong. Also called itself May Kong Evening College of Business and Technology or May Kong Institute. A credentials evaluator from World Education Services forwards a sheaf of documentation on his investigation of this school, which he concludes is a diploma mill. There appears to have been some association with Sussex College of Technology, a notorious British degree mill.

Meta Collegiate Extension Nevada. Chartered in Nevada before World War II, they sold the Ph.D. for $50, with a 20 percent discount for cash.

Metropolitan Collegiate They sell all degrees, including medical and dental, for $100 or less. The address in the year 2000 was a mailbox service, which was also used for Sussex General Hospital, a nonexistent hospital where some Metropolitan Collegiate graduates claim to have worked. Over the previous 25 years, two other mail forwarding services have been used. We visited one, which told us that they forward the mail to Yorkshire, England. It is hard to imagine that such things can be tolerated, but this place has been going for years. It is hard to imagine that anyone could take this seriously, but in 2000, John was an expert witness in a Federal case involving a man who had bought his $100 MD and had been practicing for more than 20 years. (He was found guilty.) We have this little fantasy in which the prime minister of England becomes gravely ill on a trip abroad, and the doctor who is summoned to treat him 'earned' his M.D. from Metropolitan Collegiate.

Midwest Ohio College Their literature says that they are "an equal opportunity Internet-based college dedicated to providing a no cost college degree which represents a desire to pursue life long learning. We award credits for life activities just as many other colleges and universities. Our difference is we do not charge you tuition for education you acquired without our help." When one requests a doctorate; they will assume that you meet all of the qualifications and will email you a diploma for a Ph.D. in American Cultural Studies.

Millard Fillmore Institute In 1966, the year John earned his real doctorate (from Michigan State University), Bob Hope received one of his first honorary doctorates after making a large gift to Southern Methodist University. Aware that Millard Fillmore, our great 13th president, was the only president who routinely turned down offers of honorary doctorates (including one from Oxford), John was inspired to create the fictitious Institute, to poke fun at the way universities trade honorary degrees for money. The ornate diploma read, 'By virtue of powers which we have invented . . . the honorary and meretricious' title was awarded, 'magna cum grano salis' (with a big grain of salt). Many were given away, and some were sold, complete with a cheap plastic frame, for five bucks. Most people thought it was amusing, but a few saw it as a threat to civilization as we know it, and so, after a few years, the fictitious gates of the institute were closed, perhaps forever.

Miller University Philadelphia, Pennsylvania. Identified as a diploma mill by E&T.

Milton University Maryland and New York. Identified as a diploma mill by E&T.

Mindspring Enterprises New Hampshire. This organization offered "real-looking degrees and certificates" in any field but medical, via an ad on America Online, "for novelty purposes only."

Ministerial Training College Sheffield, England. Identified as a diploma mill by COE.

Monticello University Until 1999, Monticello University was a highly visible institution, advertising heavily in such publications as *The Economist* and *USA Today* while claiming a presence in Canada, the West Indies, Hawaii, China, and England. In reality, the only physical location of Monticello University—also known as Thomas Jefferson University, Monticello University International, Jefferson & Madison School of Law, Alexis de Tocqueville University, and Mars Hill University—was the back of the Snell Insurance Agency in Overland Park, Kansas. In 1999, the state of Kansas finally caught up with operator Les Snell, who has apparently gone under as many pseudonyms as his school, sued him for violating the state's Consumer Protection Act, and ordered Snell's Internet service provider to shut down Monticello's Web site. The states of Kansas and Hawaii each won judgments of well over $1 million against Snell. Snell dropped from sight, reappearing briefly in mid-2000 with a short-lived attempt at a new fake, Amherst University.

Montserrat University California. Degrees of all kinds were sold for $10 or $20 from a post office box in San Francisco in this name and those of the equally fake Stanton University and Rochfort College. Apparently now defunct.

Morston-Colwyn University England and Canada. Identified as a diploma mill by E&T.

Mount Sinai University Identified as a diploma mill by E&T.

Nassau State Teachers College See: Regency Enterprises

National Certificate Company New York. These people sold the degrees of eight nonexistent universities at $20 to $30 each, and also sold a 'make your own' kit consisting of a blank diploma and press-on letters. The eight fake schools are Diplomatic University, Central University, Capital College, Adams Institute of Technology, Eastern University, Western College, Graduate University, and the Southern Institute of Technology. Buyers must sign a statement saying they will not use them for any educational purpose. Suuuuure.

National College Kansas and Oklahoma. Doctorates of all kinds, including medical, were sold by 'Dr.' Charles E. Downs. Accreditation claimed from a bogus accrediting association established by 'Dr.' Weinberg, founder of several fake medical schools himself. See also: East Coast University (chapter 31).

National College of Arts and Sciences Once a very active mill, finally closed down by authorities in

Oklahoma in 1982. Same ownership as American Western, Northwestern College of Allied Science, and other fake schools. A quite wonderful event in the annals of degree mills occurred when a state official in New York innocently wrote to National College to verify a master's degree claimed by a job applicant. National College misinterpreted the letter, and sent a master's degree to the state official, in his own name, complete with a transcript listing all the courses taken and grades received!

National Ecclesiastical University Sheffield, England. Identified as a diploma mill by E&T.

National Stevens University California. Identified as a diploma mill by E&T.

National University (Canada) Toronto. Identified as a diploma mill by COE.

National University (India) Nagpur. Identified as a diploma mill by COE.

National University of Colorado Denver, Colorado. Identified as a diploma mill by COE.

National University of Dakota South Dakota. Identified as a diploma mill by E&T.

National University of Sheffield Sheffield, England. Identified as a diploma mill by COE and E&T. No connection, of course, with the legitimate University of Sheffield.

Nebraska College of Physical Medicine England. Degrees in chiropractic and osteopathy are sold to people who, according to newspaper articles, are said to use them to practice medicine.

New Christian Institute of New England See: ORB

New York State College See: R/G Enterprises

Newcastle University England. Not to be confused with the legitimate University of Newcastle. Identified as a diploma mill by E&T.

NIC Inc., Law Enforcement Supply Louisiana. This service has been offering about 100 phony degrees and certificates via the Internet.

North American College of the Artsy With the purchase of the Complete Conductor Kit, the Portable Maestro of St. Paul, Minnesota, awards a master's degree from the North American College of the Artsy and Somewhat Musically Inclined.

North American University (Utah, Hawaii, Missouri) Formerly University of North America. Degree mill, run by Edward Reddeck, who has gone to prison more than once for educational frauds. A great many people were defrauded by this "school," largely because national publications like *USA Today* kept accepting his advertising. Enjoined from operating by Utah in 1989, but the order was ignored. Reddeck was indicted by

a federal grand jury in 1992 for mail fraud and conspiracy, convicted in 1993, and imprisoned.

Northern Utah University (or Management Institute) They have been around for years, but now are apparently a part of the International Universities Consortium, described earlier in this chapter. The phone listed in Salt Lake City is not in service, and mail was returned as undeliverable in 1990.

Northwest London College of Applied Science London, England. Same location as the College of Applied Science, London. Also known as Northwest London University. Links with several medical degree mills, including Keppler and the Chicago Medical School. The signature of Karl Josef Werres, founder of Inter-State College and Institut Patriarcal Saint Irenée, and past officer of two large American nontraditional schools, appears on their diploma. Professor Werres wishes people to know that he has nothing to do with this school, and that his name has been forged. Done.

Northwest London University See: Northwest London College of Applied Science

Northwestern College of Allied Sciences Oklahoma City, Oklahoma. Authorities in Oklahoma closed this mill down in 1982. It had been under the same management as American Western, National College, and several other fake schools operated under the cloak of the Disciples of Truth by James Caffey of Springfield, Missouri. Caffey was indicted by a federal grand jury in 1985, pleaded guilty, and was sentenced to prison.

Northwestern Graduate School Allegedly in Montana. See also: International Universities Consortium

Notre Dame de Lafayette University Originally known as Lafayette University, and operating under a religious exemption in Aurora, Colorado, they were ordered by the state to stop offering secular degrees such as the MBA. Following an expose on ABC radio in Denver, in which the reporter's pet cat was awarded a degree in Christian Counseling, the Colorado Attorney General ordered them to close down. Just before leaving for Minnesota, they ordered $20,000 worth of computer equipment, and then reported it stolen. When they reopened as the Occidental Orthodox Catholic Church in Long Prairie, Minnesota, authorities found the "stolen" computers at the new offices.

Novastate University We have a photocopy of a degree, issued in 1977, from this apparently nonexistent university. And that's all we know.

Obura University London, England. Identified as a diploma mill by E&T.

Ohio Central College See: Regency Enterprises

Ohio Christian College One of the more active degree mills in the 1960s and 1970s, they sold degrees of all kinds for fees of $200 and up. Literature identical to that of Florida State Christian University, which was closed by authorities in that state. They claimed to be a part of Calvary Grace Christian Churches of Faith, Inc.

Ohio Saint Mathew University Columbus, Ohio. Identified as a diploma mill by E&T.

Open University (Switzerland) Zurich. One of the many diploma mills operated by Karl Xavier Bleisch.

ORB A supermarket of phony degrees that offered diplomas from eight nonexistent institutions at fees of $5 to $65 each. The more authentic-sounding ones were more expensive. The schools were: Bosdon Academy of Music, Eugenia Institute of Metaphysics, Gottbourg University of Switzerland, Honoré College of France, New Christian Institute of New England, Royal Academy of Science and Art, Taylor College of England, and Weinberg University of Germany. ORB (other literature reveals that it stands for Occult Research Bureau) has been operated by Raymond Buckland, author and former curator of the Buckland Museum of Magick.

Oriental University Washington, DC. Identified as a diploma mill by COE.

Oxford College of Applied Science Oxford, England. A diploma mill selling degrees of all kinds. Apparently operated from Switzerland by Karl Xavier Bleisch, who has been involved with many other degree mills.

Oxford College of Arts and Sciences Canada. Identified as a diploma mill by E&T.

Oxford Collegiate Institute Readers have told us about another Oxford-based mill, but we cannot locate any place with this name.

Oxford Institute for Applied Research London, England. Fake honorary doctorates sold for $250.

Oxford Open University This nonexistent institution was created by a man named Emir Mohammed, to show how easy it is to set up an attractive Web site for a totally phony school (*www.angelfire.com/mo/EmirMohammed/university.html*). As far as we know, no degrees were ever sold.

Pacific College Sold everything from high school diplomas to doctorates for $75 because they believed that "everyone has the right to live and experience life according to his or her own convictions." This presumably includes convictions for fraud.

Pacific Northwest University In 1996, we received a resume from a prison inmate, listing a B.S. from the phony Jackson State University and an MBA from this school, allegedly in Monterey, California (rather far south to qualify as the Pacific Northwest, and too elusive to qualify as legitimate).

Pacific Northwestern University This clever fraud operated from Seattle in the late 1970s. What made it unusual was that it was the product of a man who was a senior official at a traditional local university. Achille Bourque, Seattle University's Director of Planned Giving, operated Pacific Northwestern University as a sideline. His ads read, "A College Degree—No Studying, No Exams, No Classes." While Borque was not prosecuted—apparently selling degrees was not illegal in Washington at the time—he subsequently was sued by the state of Illinois for another of his ventures, the equally non-existent Great Lakes University.

Pacific Southern University (New Jersey, California) No connection whatsoever with the state-approved school of the same name in Los Angeles. This Pacific Southern has operated from various post office boxes and offers "degrees you can be pround [*sic*] of" at $250 each.

Pacific States College Degrees from this nonexistent school have recently been sold for $5 if blank; $15 if professionally lettered. The literature describes them as 'some of the finest, most authentic looking college degrees on the market. It is almost impossible to distinguish them from the real thing.'

Palm Beach Psychotherapy Training Centre See: Thomas A. Edison College

Peckham Polytechnic See: University of Bums on Seats

Pensacola Trade School See: Regency Enterprises

People's National University Identified as a diploma mill by E&T.

Philo-Byzantine University Madrid, Spain. Identified as a diploma mill by E&T.

Pigeon Hill University A good reference site on the Internet, with links to many other sites that can benefit the distance learner, and the tongue-in-cheek (we certainly hope) option of printing out a diploma stating that one has completed a "Master Degree in Educational Surfing" of PHU.

Poupon U The Mt. Horeb Mustard Museum in Wisconsin, which features the world's largest collection of prepared mustards, sells an M.D. (Doctor of Mustard) for $6. Also available is a D.D.S. (Doctor of Didley Squat).

Primus Postgraduate College See: Advanced Education Institute

Progressive California. Offered free Ph.D.'s through an ad in *Popular Mechanics* in the 1990s. Probably related to the Progressive Universal Life Church.

Progressive Universal Life Church This operation offers astonishingly inexpensive credentials in a number of fields, with little or no work required. Their certification program leads to such titles as Certified Tarot Advisor, Certified Clairvoyant, Certified Psychic, Certified Hypnotherapist, and so on. Their doctoral program awards professional and technical Ph.D.'s based entirely on life experience in such fields as psychic sciences, counseling, pastoral hypnotherapy, herbology, homeopathy, ministerial education, alternative therapy, motivation, theocentric humanities, and more. In a move that Harvard might want to look into, they offer an innovative "buy one get one free" incentive for purchasing doctorates. Probably related to the organization that has offered, through an ad in *Popular Mechanics*, free Ph.D.'s.

R/G Enterprises Florida. They sold degrees from 10 schools with almost-real names at prices up to $37.50. The schools were: Alabama Christian College, California Christian College, Clemson College, Colgate College, Diplomatic State University, Hamilton Institute of Technology, Hamilton State University, Madison State University, New York State College, and Tulsa College. The literature says, "This offer not valid in states where prohibited by law," which doubtless encompasses all 50 of them.

Raighlings University See: USSI

Regency College See: American Western University

Regency Enterprises Missouri. They used to sell degrees with the names of real schools, often slightly changed, such as Stamford (not Stanford) University, or Texas University (not the University of Texas). Others included Cormell University, Indiana State University, Boston City College, the University of Pittsburgh, Illinois State University, Rockford Community College, Hartford Technical Institute, Carnegie Institute of Engineering, Stetson College, Nassau State Teachers College, Darthmouth College, Ohio Central College, College of Franklin & Marshall, and Pensacola Trade School. A blank diploma with a lettering kit was sold for $20. Buyers were asked to sign a statement that they would not use these phony diplomas for any fraudulent purposes. Ha!

Regency University In late 2000, this phony appeared on the Internet and in magazine ads, apparently the new venture of a man previously in trouble for earlier fakes.

Rhode Island School of Law Identified as a diploma mill by E&T, which believed it to be in Wyoming.

Rochfort College See: Monserrat University

Rockford Community College See: Regency Enterprises

Roosevelt University (Belgium) Degrees of any kind were sold for a "tuition" of $400 to $600. Also used an address in Zurich, Switzerland. Five of the proprietors were sentenced to federal prison in 1987.

Royal Academy of Science and Art See: ORB

Royal College of Science Identified as a diploma mill by E&T. Apparently affiliated with, or the same as, Empire College of Opthalmology.

Rumson University A Web site for this nonexistent "university" was created as a hoax by an Internet prankster. We are confident that no degrees were ever awarded.

Saint Andrews Correspondence College Identified as a diploma mill by E&T.

Saint Andrews Ecumenical Foundation University Identified as a diploma mill by E&T.

Saint Andrews University Allegedly in Mexico. See also: International Universities Consortium

Saint James University This nonexistent school appeared briefly on the Internet in 1999-2000. The Web site was registered to a man in Plano, Texas.

Saint John Chrysostom College London, England. Identified as a diploma mill by E&T.

Saint John's University (India) India. Identified as a diploma mill by COE.

Saint Joseph College Degrees at all levels, all available for under $200. Operated by Vince Ballew of Troy, Michigan, who moved his campus from a Mail Plus box rental store in Detroit to a Mail Boxes Etc. in Sioux Falls, South Dakota, probably when he became hip to the fact that his school was illegal in Michigan.

Saint Joseph University New York. They offered bachelor's, master's, doctorates, and law degrees.

Some of the literature was well-done, some of it was ludicrous—the name "Saint Joseph," for instance, was often inserted in gaps where clearly some other school's name had once appeared. The location was variously given as New York, Louisiana, and Colorado, even in the same catalog. Degrees cost from $2,000 to $3,000.

Saint Paul's Seminary See: American Western University

San Francisco College of Music and Theater Arts In 1987, a San Francisco man began advertising this apparently nonexistent school in Chinese and African papers. Somehow, it was certified as legitimate by the Immigration and Naturalization Service. The *San Francisco Chronicle* reports that three Chinese dancers came to San Francisco to train at the school and ended up being forced to work as servants for its founder.

San Miguel College See: LTD Documents

Sanders International University On the Web site that appeared in 2000, there is no clue whatsoever as to where this fraud is located. The Web site is not traceable, and students are required to supply their credit card numbers online to buy their bachelor's and master's degrees, no questions asked, for $350 and up. The only mystery is why they don't also sell doctorates.

Sands University Yuma, Arizona. Sold degrees of all kinds in the mid 1980s. Proprietor Wiley Gordon Bennett, who operated from Tennessee, was convicted and sent to prison thanks to the FBI's DipScam operation.

School of Applied Sciences London and New York. Identified as a diploma mill by E&T.

School of Pyschology and Psychotherapy England. Identified as a diploma mill by E&T.

Seattle College A reader told us there is a diploma mill of this name, but we have been unable to find any school, good or bad, called Seattle College.

Self-Culture University India. Identified as a diploma mill by COE.

Shield College See: USSI

Siberian Institute See: International Honorary Awards Committee

Sir Edward Heyzer's Free Technical College Hong Kong. Associated with the National University of Canada, identified as a diploma mill by COE.

South China University Hong Kong and Macau. Identified as a diploma mill by E&T.

South Eastern Extension College Essex, England. All degrees but medicine or law, at £20 for one or £45 for three. "Our degrees are indistinguishable from degrees issued by other colleges in the traditional way," the sales letter says. Same ownership as Whitby Hall College.

Southern California University California. One of the many fake school names used by the Fowler family, five

of whom were sentenced to prison in 1987 for their part in running diploma mills worldwide. Degrees of all kinds were sold for $200 and up. No connection with Southern California University for Advanced Studies or the University of Southern California.

Southern Institute of Technology See: National Certificate Company

Southwestern University (Arizona, Utah) The university had its own impressive building in Tucson, with many of the trappings of a real school. But after they sold degrees to an FBI agent during the DipScam operation, several administrators were indicted by a federal grand jury. President Geruntino pleaded guilty, and served a term in federal prison. The names of more than a thousand Southwestern "alumni" were made public, and many jobs were lost as a result, including some in NASA and the Pentagon. Many students had enrolled following a glowing recommendation for the school from an educational guidance service in Columbus, Ohio, that was also run by Geruntino. When Arizona started to get tough, Geruntino went north to St. George, Utah, and announced that the small town was to become the center for distance learning in America. At a public hearing on whether to grant him a business license, many town leaders spoke up for him. When the chair asked if anyone else had anything to say, the FBI agent sitting in the back said, in effect, "Yes. I have a warrant for the arrest of Mr. Geruntino for running diploma mills."

Southwestern University (New Mexico) Allegedly in Albuquerque. See also: International Universities Consortium

Specialty Document Company California. In the late 1980s, they sold fake diplomas for a Doctor of Medicine, Doctor of Veterinary Medicine, bachelor's degrees, and Ph.D. certificates (no school specified) for $1 each, or 100 for $15. Imagine that! A medical degree for 15¢!

Spicer Memorial College India. Identified as a diploma mill by COE.

Stamford Private University Portugal. This school, claiming to be a U.S. institution, has offered degrees at all levels in any field (with the exception of medicine or dentistry) to Portuguese residents, based entirely on life experience. We have been unable to get more information.

Stanton University (California) See: Montserrat University

Staton University In the early 1980s, music teachers in North America received an invitation to join the American Guild of Teachers of Singing, upon which they would be awarded an honorary doctorate from this nonexistent school, which was supposed to be in Ohio.

Stetson College See: Regency Enterprises

Sussex College of Technology Sussex, England. Perhaps the oldest of Britain's degree mills, Sussex was run for more than 20 years by "Dr." Bruce Copen from his home, south of London. At the same address, but with different catalogs, are the Brantridge Forest School and the University of the Science of Man. Brantridge has also used a box rental service in Hawaii. Each offer "earned" degrees for which a few correspondence courses are required, and "extension awards" which are the same degrees and diplomas for no work at all. Honorary doctorates are offered free, but there is a $100 engraving charge. "Professor Emeritas" [*sic*] status costs another $100. One flyer admits Sussex is not "accrediated" [*sic*] but goes on to say that "No student who has taken our courses and awards have to date had problems." This statement would not be accepted by, among many others, a former high-level state official in Colorado who lost his job when the source of his doctorate was discovered. Sussex continues to advertise extensively in newspapers and magazines in the U.S. and worldwide. In 1988, a new British law came into effect, forbidding such "schools" to accept students who enrolled after May 1st. Sussex's solution to this minor annoyance was to offer to back-date all applications to April 30th, 1988—a creative response that British law apparently hasn't caught up with yet. Copen died in 1999, but his "schools" continue to operate.

Taurus International University California. The claim is that the Taurus International Society was established in 1764 by James Boswell. The Ph.D. is sold for all of $2, and the Doctor of Whimsey for $1.

Taylor College of England See: ORB

Taylor University of Bio-Psycho-Dynamic Sciences This school was established in Chattanooga, Tennessee, in the early 1920s by some of that city's "most respected citizens, including a philanthropic capitalist, merchant prince, a dentist . . . and a woman of high intelligence." The doctorate sold for $115, or $103.50 cash in advance.

Temple Bar College Identified as a diploma mill by E&T.

Tennessee Christian University Tennessee. Affiliated with Ohio and Florida State Christian in the sale of fake degrees.

Texas Christian Bible University Crowley, TX. Sells bachelor's for $300, master's for $400, and doctorates for $500. Likes to be confused with the regionally accredited Texas Christian University.

Texas Theological University Texas. Identified as a diploma mill by E&T.

Texas University See: Regency Enterprises

Thomas A. Edison College Florida and Arkansas. Totally fake school run by the Rt. Rev. Dr. George C. Lyon, M.D., Ph.D., LL.D., D.D. After twice being fined heavily and sentenced to prison for running fake schools in Florida, he moved to Arkansas, arriving with an entourage in a red Mercedes and a green Rolls Royce, and bought a vacant church for cash. But the FBI's DipScam operation caught up with him again, and Lyon, then in his 80s, went off to federal prison once again. Thomas A. Edison College managed to fool an awful lot of people over the years, and not just because it sounds like the legitimate nontraditional Edison in New Jersey. This Edison was listed in many otherwise reputable college guides (like Lovejoy's) as a real school for years. Lyon's other nefarious enterprises have included the Palm Beach Psychotherapy Training Center, the Florida Analytic Institute, and an involvement with two phony medical schools, United American Medical College and the Keppler School of Medicine.

Thomas Jefferson University (Kansas) See: Monticello University

Thomas Jefferson University (Missouri) In the early 1980s, catalogs were mailed from this school, allegedly in St. Louis (the address was a private home), but there was never a listed phone, and the postmark was Denver. Degrees at all levels were offered for $1,500 on up. The catalog was almost identical to that used by a legitimate California school. Letters were never answered. With the catalog came a Servicemen's Allotment Account form, for military people to have the "university" paid directly each month from their paycheck, into a bank account in New York.

Thomas Jefferson University School of Law See: Monticello University

Thomas University Pennsylvania. They used to sell fake degrees for up to $1,000. They claimed accreditation from the fake Middle States Accrediting Board.

Tremonte University See: USSI

Trinity College and University (Panama) See: Global Money Consultants

Trinity Collegiate Institute University England and Switzerland. The London mail service forwards the mail to Karl Bleisch, an operator of many diploma mills in Switzerland. According to an expose in *The Times* of London, Bleisch told the forwarding service that Trinity was a language school only, with "no question of awarding degrees." Within two months, he was handing out degrees in subjects from beer marketing to scientific massage. (One alumnus went on to start Inter-State College and Institut Patriarcal Saint Irenée.)

Tuit University Georgia. The doctorates, sold for $10, are amusing when you read the small print, which says, for instance, that the recipient "has not had the time to do the necessary work leading to the degree of Doctor of Philosophy . . . ."

Tulsa College See: R/G Enterprises

Two Dragon University See: International Honorary Awards Committee

United American Medical College A medical degree mill, operated from the apartment of its founder in Louisiana, and from a mail-forwarding service in Canada. The approach was almost identical to that of the Johann Keppler School of Medicine, described earlier. When owner L. Mitchell Weinberg was first arrested (1977) for violating Louisiana school laws, he maintained the school was fully accredited by the American Coordinated Medical Society in California. Indeed, said society wrote that "we of the accreditation committee feel that U.A.M.C. has the highest admission requirements of any medical college in the world . . . due to the great leadership of it's [sic] President, L. Mitchell Weinberg." The founder and proprietor of the American Coordinated Medical Society is L. Mitchell Weinberg. In 1982, Weinberg pleaded guilty to charges of selling medical degrees and was sentenced to three years in federal prison.

United Free University of England Identified as a diploma mill by E&T.

United States University of America Washington, Florida. The 11-page typewritten catalog actually listed names of some legitimate faculty who had been duped into doing some work for "Dr." Frank Pany and the school he ran from his Florida home, using a Washington, DC, mail-forwarding service. One of the faculty, the "Chairman of the Marriage Counseling Department," whose doctorate was from U.S.U.A. was more candid. "You're in California," he said on the phone. "Why not deal with a degree service closer to home?" In the wake of an FBI visit, and a grand jury indictment in February 1986, "Dr." Pany departed suddenly for Italy.

Universal Bible Institute Birmingham, Alabama. The state declared it was a diploma mill, and ordered it closed, because doctoral degrees could be acquired in less than two months on payment of appropriate fees, and the school was not affiliated with any religious organization. According to Alabama authorities, the institute's president moved to Florida, taking all the records with him, as the Alabama investigation began.

Universal Ecclesiastical University Their doctorates were offered in any field but law or medicine for a 10-page dissertation, and honorary doctorates to anyone with 'good moral character' plus $200 to spend. Our last letter to Professor Gilbert at the university's address in Manchester, England, was returned with the word 'Demolished' written in big blue crayon letters across the front. Let us hope they were referring to the building, not the professor.

Universal Light Church London. Doctor of Divinity, Metaphysics, or Philosophy offered for a hundred dollars or so; for another hundred bucks one can add priest's credentials, or for a big $500, become a bishop.

Universidad Brasileira Rio de Janeiro, Brazil. Identified as a diploma mill by COE.

Universidad Indigenista Moctezuma Andorra's only diploma mill—identified as such by COE.

Universidad Latino-Americana de la Habana Havana, Cuba. Identified as a diploma mill by COE.

Universidad Sintetica Latina y Americana El Salvador. Identified as a diploma mill by COE.

Universidad Tecnológica Nacional Havana, Cuba. Identified as a diploma mill by COE.

Universitaires Internationales Liechtenstein, India, Sudan, Morocco, Japan, etc., etc. Identified as a diploma mill by E&T.

Universitas Iltiensis England, Switzerland. Identified as a diploma mill by E&T.

Universitas Internationalis Studiorum Superiorium Pro Deo In 1989, they began offering 'honoris causa' doctorates from an address in New York, under the imprimatur of the Titular Archbishop of Ephesus.

Universitates Sheffieldensis See: University of Sheffield

Université de Commerce de Canada See: Lawford State University

Université des Science de l'Homme France. Same as University of the Science of Man. See also: Sussex College of Technology

Université Internationale de Paris Paris, France. Identified as a diploma mill by COE.

Université Nouvelle de Paris Paris, France. Identified as a diploma mill by COE.

Université Philotechnique Brussels, Belgium, and Paris, France. Identified as a diploma mill by COE.

Université Voltaire de France Marseilles, France. Identified as a diploma mill by COE.

University College of Nottingham See: Whitby Hall College

University del Puerto Monico Panama. Degrees from this nonexistent institution were sold by Neil Gibson & Company in England, who also represented University de la Romande. They say that 'the degree certificates are excellently presented and make a superb and unusual wall decoration. They are for self-esteem only but remain very popular indeed.' The same management later opened Knightsbridge University, but Knightsbridge is under new and more reputable management.

University in London Same as Obura University. Identified as a diploma mill by E&T.

University of Appenzell According to a correspondent, a diploma mill of this name operated from Switzerland in the 1990's.

University of Bums on Seats This clever joke arose on the Internet in 2000. Its "Fasttrack E-Degree" program allows potential students to graduate and get their diploma *before* actually commencing any studies.

Degrees available at all levels in management diagram construction, post-rational discourse, post-feminist needlework, and arse-elbow differentiation, among others. In the attempt to "revolutionise our educational paradigm to ensure a rich diversity of abilities are represented in our student body," no one is rejected on any grounds except nonpayment of fees. Vice Chancellor Alan Dubious (MAd, TOTP, DipSHiT) lists his Ph.D. as from the University of Oxford in Zimbabwe and is a leading light in the field of Academic Downsizing. We don't help you with Web sites for dangerous degree mills, but we'll trust you with this one: *www.cynicalbastards.com/ubs*. Formerly known as Peckham Polytechnic.

University of Cape Cod An iffy-sounding school of this name was promoted in eastern Massachusetts in the early 1980s.

University of Corpus Christi Reno, Nevada. Affiliated with the Society of Academic Recognition. Identified as a diploma mill by E&T. No connection with the legitimate school formerly known as University of Corpus Christi but now a part of Texas A & M University.

University of Coventry England. Identified as a diploma mill by E&T. There is a legitimate university with the same name.

University of Devonshire See: University of San Moritz

University of East Carolina See: University of East Georgia

University of East Georgia Georgia. Degrees in all fields, including medicine, psychiatry, surgery, and neurology sold for $500 and completion of a thesis on 'a subject and length of your own choosing.' Embarrassingly enough, John was duped by the first literature he received from proprietor John Blazer in 1975, but the game soon became clear. Blazer also operated the University of the Bahama Islands, the College of Hilton Head, the University of East Carolina, and the University of Middle Tennessee. In 1984, he was indicted by a federal grand jury as a result of the FBI's DipScam operation. He pleaded guilty to the charge of mail fraud and was sentenced to prison.

University of Eastern Florida Chicago, Illinois. Degrees of all kinds except medicine and law were sold for $40 each. The school claimed to be a 'state chartered university' in Florida (not true).

University of England London, England. Degrees of any kind were sold for about $200 by a school using both this name and the name University of England at Oxford. In 1987, the American proprietors were indicted by a federal grand jury. Five of them were found guilty and sentenced to prison. The founder of Western States University claims a degree from this institution (the school, not the prison).

University of England at Oxford See: University of England

University of Fishigan An online auction house has offered the rather attractive diploma of their College of Angling, with the degree of Master of Exaggeration. We have deduced that the dean, Dr. Rod N. Reel, may well be fictitious. The going price seems to be in the vicinity of $10.

University of Huntington This nonexistent university's "College of Pursuit" offered diplomas for sale on an Internet auction site, ostensibly as a gag gift for hunters, with the Master of Exaggeration as the degree awarded. Quite a well-designed diploma. When we checked, bids were up to $6.

University of Independence A realistic-looking diploma was given or sold as a promotional piece to independent businesspeople. The Ph.D. came from the School of Hard Knocks. A reader sent us a photo of a well-known author and lecturer, from a national magazine, showing the diploma prominently displayed on his wall. Only the school name, the man's name, and 'Doctor of Philosophy' are readable. This is one way that even 'gag' fake diplomas can be misused.

University of Man's Best Friend A lovely $2 Ph.D. in Love and Loyalty, with paw prints as signatures.

University of Middle Tennessee See: University of East Georgia

University of North America Diploma mill operated by Edward Reddeck from a mail-forwarding service in Missouri in the late 1980s. After he was fined $2,500,000 for this operation, he fled to Utah, changing the name of the school slightly, to North American University (see separate listing). He was indicted for mail fraud and conspiracy in the spring of 1992, found guilty on all 22 counts in 1993, and sent back to prison.

University of Palmers Green See: University of San Moritz

University of Pittsburg See: Regency Enterprises

University of Rarotonga Fictitious school whose paraphernalia is sold on this South Seas island.

University of Saint Bartholomew After John gave a talk on diploma mills on Australian radio, a number of people called or wrote to mention a school by this name in Oodnadatta, Australia that merrily sold its fake product to Europeans.

University of San Moritz This phony, also known as Harrington University, University of Palmers Green, Brentwick University, and University of Devonshire, may be the biggest degree mill operation ever, with reported revenues in the range of $2 million a month. In 1998, these nonexistent "schools" began sending unsolicited email messages saying "UNIVERSITY DIPLOMAS. Obtain a prosperous future, money earning power, and the admiration of all. Diplomas from prestigious non-accredited universities based on your present knowledge and life experience." They seem to operate only by Internet, where an insider reports they are sending out more than one million "spam" messages a week. People who phone (the area codes have been in New York City, Ohio, New Hampshire, and Texas) and leave a message are called back, and offered the opportunity to purchase the degrees of their choice, at prices between $600 and $3,500. The mailing address is a secretarial service in England. Customers are told to wire their payment by Western Union, and it ends up in a bank in Limassol, Cyprus. A former employee reports that diplomas are printed in Jerusalem, and shipped by overnight service to America and elsewhere. In addition to the fake diplomas, customers can buy transcripts, showing grades of their choice.

University of Sealand Identified as a diploma mill by E&T. Sealand is a self-declared country, located on Roughs Tower, an island fortress built by the British during World War II, nine miles from the Thames Estuary, and occupied by "Prince Roy" and his family in the 1960s.

University of Sheffield Sheffield, England. Also called Universitates Sheffieldensis, Ecclesiastical University of Sheffield. There is a legitimate, traditional University of Sheffield, and then there is this fake one, run (according to an article in The Times of London) by Charles Brearly, an auto mechanic who styles himself Ignatius Carelus, successor to Cardinal Barberini of Rheims. He is a sometime associate of 'Sir' Sidney Lawrence, proprietor of the College of Applied Science, London. We have received a stern letter from the academic registrar of the real University of Sheffield, suggesting that 'in order that our academic standing not be endangered, I would ask that your publication make it quite clear in the future that the college mentioned has no connection whatsoever with this institution.' Done, and thanks for thinking that our modest book could endanger your large, old, well-established university.

University of Sulgrave England. Identified as a diploma mill by E&T.

University of the American Republic Another name for the fraudulent Monticello University.

University of the Americas (Panama) An organization called Global Money Consultants claims to be the exclusive agent for this school. You send them a CV, a photocopy of your passport, three color photos, and between $1,500 and $2,000 and, within 30 days, they either send you a University of Americas degree of your choice or your money back. Many fields offered, including law, but no medical or dentistry. The school is allegedly located in Panama City, Panama. We have

been told, we think reliably, that the university is operated by the vice president of an unaccredited California-based Hawaii-registered school. Indeed, they were registered as a business in Hawaii as of May, 2000, but we could not find evidence of the school in that state, or anywhere else.

University of the Bahama Islands See: University of East Georgia

University of the Eastern United States Identified as a diploma mill by E&T.

University of the New World Arizona and Europe. Identified as a diploma mill by E&T.

University of the Old Catholic Church Sheffield, England. Identified as a diploma mill by E&T. Presumably the same management as the fake University of Sheffield.

University of the President Utah. They have sold honorary doctorates in iridology, psionics, macrobiotics, endogenous endocrinotherapy, and dozens more, in exchange for a $25 'donation.'

University of the Republic A fictitious school started by *Arizona Republic* newspaper reporters Jerry Seper and Rich Robertson as part of a series on degree mills, to show how easy it was to do such things in Arizona at the time. Public outrage led to a tough new school-regulating law being passed.

University of the Science of Man See: Sussex College of Technology

University of the ULC of Alabama Offers honorary paranormal and religious degrees, for "mostly amusement."

University of the West See: International Universities Consortium

University of Walla Walla California. Advertising in a national women's magazine offered a Doctor of anything ending in 'ologist' for $18.90.

University of Winchester London, England. Same address as the London School of Social Research. The $15 diplomas have been widely advertised as 'completely spurious, nonetheless as impressive as genuine.'

University of Wyoming (England) Of course there is a real University of Wyoming in Laramie, but there is also a fake one. A man named Cunning, using an address in London, England, and literature printed in German, has been selling Ph.D.'s, law degrees, and alarmingly, M.D.'s of the University of Wyoming for about $500. We wrote to the general counsel of the real University of Wyoming, thinking they might be interested, but there's been no reply. (Since there's a purveyor of fake degrees named Wiley Bennett, one can't help wondering if they might some day get together, to form a Wiley and Cunning partnership.)

USSI Florida. In late 1994, they began selling a range of documents ranging from the obviously silly (such as Super Mom or Total Airhead) to the highly deceptive. "Diplomas" are offered from Hirshfeld University, Shield College (U.K.), Tremonte University, Wellingsburg University, Raighlings University, or the College of Hard Knocks. Degrees include bachelor's, master's, doctorates, and law degrees, in a wide range of fields, for prices ranging form $59.50 to $101.50. A warning on the order form states "These novelty items (Certificates) are very realistic in appearance. In view, they may be mistaken as authentic certificates. USSI, it's [*sic*] staff and any hired agency or service are not liable for any representation by the purchaser of our products." More alarmingly, USSI also offers to produce diplomas from any university and for any degree. To test this, John ordered a medical degree from Harvard. Someone from USSI telephoned him and suggested that they would be willing to make a Harvard law degree instead, and that is what they did.

Valorem Academy See: Advanced Education Institute

Vocational University India. Identified as a diploma mill by COE.

Wallace University This non-existent institution, using a Colorado mail drop address, offers what they call, with commendable honesty, "diploma-appearing documents," and "vanity degrees," which they freely admit have no academic validity. They arose in 2000, entirely on the Internet, asking prices of $350 and up for their useless pieces of paper.

Washington International Academy New York. Identified as a diploma mill by E&T.

Webster University (Georgia) Identified as a diploma mill by E&T. (There is an accredited school of the same name in Missouri. No connection, of course.)

Weinberg University of West Germany See: ORB

Wellingsburg University See: USSI

Wellington University (Louisiana) Shreveport. Sells diplomas, including a Doctor of Medicine, that are, by its own admission, "non-academic and unaccredited and sold as novelties only."

Wellington University (New Jersey) Offered some correspondents the opportunity to earn an M.D. from a medical school in Sri Lanka, upon payment of $1,000. See chapter 31: Open International University for Complementary Medicine

West London College of Technology London, England. Advertisements appearing in African magazines offered a 12-month correspondence program leading to various qualifications, including the MBA, 'in association with Broadhurst University.' The address given is a mail

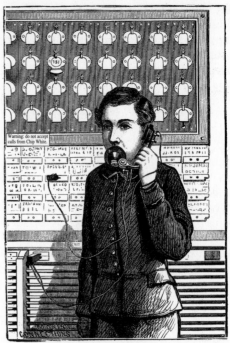

"Good morning. This is Monticello University's live faculty assistance center. I am the faculty. How may I help you?"

receiving and forwarding service in London, and there is no telephone. We can find no evidence of the existence of either the West London College or of Broadhurst University.

Western Cascade University California. Degrees of all sorts at $45 each. The address is a mail forwarding service. In an apparent effort to avoid prosecution, they will not sell their product to California residents.

Western College See: National Certificate Company

Western Orthodox University Glastonbury, England. Identified as a diploma mill by E&T.

Western Reserve Educational Services For years, they sold diplomas that they claimed to have "salvaged" from "genuine schools that have gone out of business" from an Ohio post office box. The proprietor, Robert Kim Walton, claimed to have been commended by the Sacred Congregation in Rome—not, one dares hope, for selling fake degrees.

Western University (San Diego) One of the early American degree mills, operating from southern California (San Diego and Jacumba) in the 1940s and 1950s. A Western University with addresses in Georgia, Montana, Colorado, and Delaware has been identified as a diploma mill by E&T; one in India has been identified as a diploma mill by COE.

Whitby Hall College Essex, England. M. Palmer offers degrees of almost any kind for about $100, earned for your resumé and a poem, a story, or a two-page book review. His other school names are the University College of Nottingham, and South Eastern University.

Williams College Idaho. When the late Lane Williams left New Mexico to move his 'college' to Mexico, he changed its name from Williams to Elysion. But Williams was apparently left in other hands, and continued to operate, selling bachelor's and law degrees for about $300 each. See also: Elysion College

Wordsworth Memorial University England and India. Identified as a diploma mill by E&T and by COE.

World University of Advanced Studies of Hawaii This San Diego-based phony charted new territory in 2000 by offering its doctorates on the eBay online auction site. Although the illustration shows a badly printed certificate, the bids actually reached as high as $20.

CHAPTER 28

Honorary Doctorates

Why anybody can have a brain. That's a very mediocre commodity. Back where I come from we have universities—seats of great learning—where men go to become great thinkers. And when they come out they think deep thoughts, and with no more brains than you have. But they have one thing you haven't got: a diploma! Therefore by virtue of the authority vested in me by the Universitatis Commititatum E Pluribus Unum, I hereby confer upon you the Honorary Degree of Th.D.

That's, uh, er, ah, Doctor of Thinkology.

L. Frank Baum, The Wizard of Oz

The probable origin of the honorary doctorate was discussed in chapter 3. The persistence of this "degree"—indeed, its usage has grown tremendously, with more than 50,000 being awarded by major universities in the last decade—is one of the mysteries of the academic world, for there is nothing whatever educational about the honorary doctorate. It is, purely and simply, a title that some institutions have chosen for a variety of reasons to bestow upon certain people (and a few animals).

That the title given is "Doctor"—the same word used for academic degrees—is what has caused all the confusion, not to mention most of the desirability of the honorary doctorate. It is exactly as if the government were to honor people by giving them the title of "Senator" or "Judge." Whatever the reason, honorary doctorates have become highly valuable, even negotiable, commodities.

Not everyone takes them seriously, however. When a German university handed its Doctor of Music diploma to the composer Handel, he rolled it into a dunce cap, placed it on the head of his servant, and said, "There! Now you're a doctor, too."

Poet Robert Frost expressed particular delight at the announcement of his 40th honorary doctorate (from Oxford), because he confessed that he had been having the decorative hoods given with each award made into a patchwork quilt, and now it would all come out even. He revealed this en route to England "to collect some more yardage."

When artist Thomas Hart Benton accepted an honorary degree from Rockhurst College, he gestured to the graduating class and said, "I know how those boys behind me feel. They're thinking 'I worked four years for this, and that bum gets it free.'"

One of the curiosities of the honorary doctorate is that the title given rarely has much relevance to the recipient's qualifications. Hence we have actor Fess Parker getting a Doctor of Letters (from Tennessee, after portraying Davey Crockett), Robert Redford a Doctor of Humane Letters (from Colorado; he said it is "as important to me as my Oscar"), Times Square restaurant owner Dario Toffenetti a Doctor of Laws (from Idaho, for promoting the baked potato), and the late industrialist Clarence Mackay a Doctor of Music (but there was a logical reason for this: his daughter had married Irving Berlin).

Perhaps Mark Twain said it best:

It pleased me beyond measure when Yale made me a Master of Arts, because I didn't know anything about art. I had another convulsion of pleasure when Harvard made me a Doctor of Literature, because I was not competent to doctor anybody's literature but my own. . . . I rejoiced again when Missouri University made me a Doctor of Laws because it was all clear profit, I not knowing anything about laws except how to evade them and not get caught. And now at Oxford I am to be made a Doctor of Letters—all clear profit, because what I don't know about letters would make me a millionaire if I could turn it into cash.

Not all titles have been inappropriate, of course. In 1987, Mister Rogers received a Doctor of Humanities (Bowling Green), and led the audience in singing "Won't you be my neighbor." Admiral Byrd received a Doctor of Faith and Fortitude. Charlie McCarthy, the impertinent ventriloquist's dummy, received a Master of Innuendo from Northwestern. Antioch University gave a Master of Communication to a campus switchboard operator, and Brooklyn College, which averages only one honorary degree every four years, gave a Doctor of Delectables to a longtime campus hot dog vendor.

And then there are the animals. A heroic seeing-eye dog named Bonzo received a Doctor of Canine Fidelity from Newark University. A mule named Elwood Blues got a doctorate from Yale. When Southampton College awarded a Doctor of Amphibious Letters to Kermit the Frog, many students expressed displeasure. A marine biology major named Samantha Chie said, "After five years of hard work, now we have a sock talking at our commencement. It's kind of upsetting." And so it goes.

Why Honorary Doctorates Are Given

1. To Attract Celebrities to Campus

These humorous (or, some say, ludicrous) examples illuminate one of the four major reasons that honorary doctorates are given: to bring publicity to the graduation ceremonies of the school. If a small college can lure a baseball star, a movie or television personality, or even the wife of a famous politician to the campus, the commencement is more likely to make the evening news and the next morning's papers, which may help student or faculty recruiting, fund-raising, or membership in the alumni association. It may even increase the chances that a top high school quarterback will come to the school next year. Indeed, when John Carroll University awarded an honorary doctorate to Miami Dolphins coach Don Shula, it almost certainly was not for his academic achievements.

And that is why we have Dr. Marlon Brando, Dr. Henry Fonda, Dr. Michael Bolton, Dr. Arnold Schwarzenegger, Dr. Bruce Willis, Dr. Robert DeNiro, Dr. Jane Fonda, Dr. Bob Hope (more than 40 times over), Dr. Captain Kangaroo, Dr. Michael Jackson, and thousands of others.

High tech came to the world of honorary degrees when Liverpool University awarded its honorary doctorate to Arthur C. Clarke via a satellite link to Sri Lanka.

Sometimes the publicity is not the kind the school had in mind. St. Joseph's College, a Catholic school, offered its honorary doctorate to columnist Ann Landers, then created a big flap by withdrawing it after Landers wrote a pro-abortion column. And as Louisiana Tech was presenting its honorary doctorate to former football quarterback Terry Bradshaw, outraged alumni flew over the ceremony and dropped a cascade of leaflets protesting the award.

There is nothing new going on here. During the Revolutionary War, Harvard gave an honorary degree to Lafayette. When he heard this, Baron von Steuben urged his troops, then approaching Cambridge, to ride through town "like the devil, for if they catch you, they make a doctor of you."

2. To Honor Distinguished Faculty and Administrators

Honorary degrees are often given to honor distinguished faculty at the donating school, or other schools. This is perhaps the most academically defensible reason. In American society, there is nothing equivalent to the national honors given in many European countries (e.g., the Queen's Honours List in Britain, at which hundreds of people each year become knights, ladies, Members of the British Empire, etc.) The honorary doctorate remains one of the few honors we have to bestow. And so, each June, from 40% to 60% of all honorary degrees go to unknown academics, often, it is said, in the hope that their school will honor someone from our school next year.

This practice has resulted in a new world record. In 1982, then-president of Notre Dame Father Theodore Hesburgh collected his 90th honorary title, eclipsing Herbert Hoover's record of 89. The good Father is now in a head-to-head sheepskin-to-sheepskin battle with the King of Thailand. In early 1998, the King vaulted into first place with honorary doctorate number 137, but Hesburgh surged into the lead in June with two honoraries, moving him up to 138.

3. For Political Reasons

American presidents, British prime ministers, and other statesmen are regularly so honored, and often take the opportunity to make major speeches. Winston Churchill used the occasion of receiving an honorary degree in Missouri to deliver his famous "iron curtain" speech, and General George Marshall announced the Marshall Plan while receiving an honorary doctorate.

Although every American president has collected some honorary doctorates (George Washington had seven), none caused quite the furor of Harvard's award of an honorary Doctor of Laws to President Andrew Jackson. The Sons of Harvard erupted in anger. John Quincy Adams wrote about how his alma mater had degraded herself, "conferring her highest literary honors on a barbarian who could not write a sentence of grammar and could hardly spell his own name." Harvard president Josiah Quincy responded, "As the people have twice decided that this man knows enough law to be their ruler, it is not for Harvard College to maintain they are mistaken."

The ceremony itself must have been quite extraordinary. After Jackson had been given the sheepskin and expressed his thanks in a few short remarks, an aide reminded him that he was expected to make a speech in Latin. Thereupon, according to biographer Robert Rayback, he bellowed out, in tones of thunder, all the Latin he knew: "E pluribus unum, sine qua non, multum in parvo, quid pro quo, ne plus ultra." So much for Dr. Jackson.

Haverford College made a rather dramatic political statement when they awarded honorary Doctor of Laws degrees to the 3,000 inhabitants of a French village that helped save the lives of 2,500 Jews during World War II.

Withholding of honorary doctorates has also been used to make political statements. In 1987, the governing body of Oxford University voted 738 to 319 to withhold an honorary doctorate from Prime Minister Thatcher because of her role in cutting university research funds. And the proposed awarding of degrees to Richard Nixon has caused controversies in more than a few places—including his alma mater, Duke University, which ultimately turned him down. Indeed, one report had it that during the final days of Watergate, someone in the Nixon administration had the idea that an honorary doctorate would give Nixon some favorable publicity for a change. The only school they could find that would agree to do it was General Beadle State College, and that is why Air Force One descended into South Dakota one day in the spring of 1974. (General Beadle subsequently changed its name to Dakota State, but denies there was any connection with the Nixon visitation.)

In 1988, it was revealed that the faculty of Dan Quayle's alma mater voted overwhelmingly to deny him an honorary doctorate, largely because of his poor academic record, but they were overruled by the administration. The same thing happened when predominantly black South Carolina State College offered an honorary degree to Strom Thurmond. "No South Carolinan has done more over the past 40 years to impede the advancement of black people," said a petition signed by most faculty and students. They were overruled by president Albert Smith, hence we have Dr. Senator Thurmond.

The decision of a Jesuit school, Fairfield University in Connecticut, to award an honorary degree to Billy Joel produced some major objections from people who contended that Joel's song "Only the Good Die Young" was insulting to Catholics. He got his degree.

But former Secretary of Transportation Drew Lewis stunned a commencement audience at his alma mater, Haverford College, when he removed his purple doctoral hood after the honorary degree had been bestowed on him. He said that Quakers are supposed to act by consensus, but he had learned that a third of the faculty opposed his award because of his role in breaking the air traffic controllers' strike. The audience gave him a standing ovation.

Not everyone who is offered an honorary degree accepts. While the noble 13th president of the United States, Millard Fillmore, was the only president with a firm policy of rejecting all honoraries (he said that he had not learned to read until he was nearly 20, and just didn't feel comfortable with academic awards), more than a few celebrities have taken the occasion of the offer to make a point or two. Pablo Neruda very publicly rejected an honorary degree from Harvard, because of America's involvement in Vietnam. And when George Bernard Shaw was asked if he would accept a Harvard Doctor of Letters, he replied,

> I cannot pretend that it would be fair for me to accept university degrees when every public reference of mine to our educational system, and especially to the influence of universities on it, is fiercely hostile. If Harvard would celebrate its 300th anniversary by burning itself to the ground and sowing its site with salt, the ceremony would give me the greatest satisfaction as an example to all the other famous old corrupters of youth, including Yale, Oxford, Cambridge, the Sorbonne, etc., etc., etc. Under the circumstances, I should let you down very heavily if you undertook to sponsor me.

4. For Money

Although schools sanctimoniously deny there is any connection whatsoever, they have regularly awarded doctorates to academically undistinguished folks who just happened to donate a bundle of money. How long has this been going on? Well, in *A Distant Mirror*, Barbara Tuchman writes that in the 14th century, the University of Paris "had taken to selling degrees in theology to candidates unwilling to undertake its long and difficult studies."

A few centuries later, George Baker gave Harvard millions for a new business school. Harvard gave George Baker a Doctor of Laws along with their hearty thanks. John Archbold contributed a new football field to Syracuse University. Soon after, he was doctored by Syracuse University. William Randolph Hearst "traded" $100,000 and 400 acres of land to Oglethorpe University for an honorary doctorate.

A few years ago, a British dry-goods merchant named Isaac Wolfson gave about £10 million to Cambridge University, and they not only gave him an honorary doctorate, they named a college of the university for him. Then he made the same gift to Oxford, and they too both doctored him and named a college for him. Thus, as one London paper wrote in a caustic editorial, only two men in all history have had a college named for them at both Oxford and Cambridge: Jesus Christ and Isaac Wolfson. (The price seems to be going up. The Kellogg people invested more than £12 million before Oxford renamed another college in favor of the inventor of corn flakes.)

The Shah of Iran made a $1 million gift to the University of Southern California, whose president then hand-carried an honorary doctorate to Iran. Around the same time, the University of Wisconsin exchanged an honorary doctorate for a $2.5 million gift from oil millionaire C. George Weeks.

John Hope Franklin of the National Humanities Center worries, as do many others, about "the delicate matter of honorary degrees. One cannot help wondering in how many ways some institutions sell their souls in conferring them. . . . Better that a university cease to exist altogether than sell its soul."

One solution to this matter is to award the honorary degree first, in the hopes that the recipient will give the school his thanks in the form of a check or other favors. This approach made headlines a while back when the *Washington Post* uncovered the "Koreagate" scandal, in which 11 U.S. congressmen had accepted, among other favors, honorary doctorates from South Korean universities, complete with all-expense luxury trips to Korea to collect them, in an apparent effort to win congressional approval of the Korean regime.

To their credit, three congressmen rejected the honorary doctorates. But it is rare indeed for an honorary doctorate to be turned down. Oxford University used to have a policy, before Richard Nixon came along, of offering an honorary doctorate to every outgoing U.S. president. Of all those to whom it was offered, only good old Millard Fillmore turned it down, saying that he felt he had done nothing to merit it, and besides, the diploma was in Latin and he never accepted anything he couldn't read.

How to Get an Honorary Doctorate

How, then, does the ordinary person, who is not a movie star, an athlete, or a millionaire, acquire an honorary doctorate? There is no simple way, other than buying one from a less-than-respectable institution, or having one printed to order at the neighborhood print shop. Nonetheless, here are five possibilities:

1. Donate Money

The question naturally arises, how little money does it take to buy an honorary doctorate from a major accredited university? If the school is in financial trouble, as little as $10,000 has been said to turn the trick. The cheapest case we personally know about is $50,000 from an Arab businessman to an accredited California university whose building fund was in trouble.

A Los Angeles businessman once ran a small ad in *The New Republic* magazine, offering to donate $10,000 to any accredited school that would give him an honorary degree. When we contacted him, he told John he had gotten the degree, but refused to name the school.

2. Perform a Valuable Service

Honorary doctorates have gone to heads of fund-raising committees, who never gave a dime themselves; to real estate brokers who put together a big deal to acquire more land or refinance a mortgage for the school; to friends of friends of celebrities who managed to get the Senator or the Star or the Second Baseman to speak at the commencement; to a nurseryman who wangled the donation of hundreds of trees and supervised their planting on campus; to a golf pro who donated his time to the college team; and so on.

Lawyers are sometimes rewarded too. When Cecil Rhodes died in 1902 he left money for scholarships for "white American boys from all 13 states." The lawyer who got this legal mess untangled, and persuaded Parliament to come up with funds for "white American boys" from all the other states, got a Doctor of Civil Law from Oxford for his efforts.

Perhaps the most valuable service one can perform is finding a cash donor. Remember that $50,000 honorary doctorate for an Arab businessman, just described? Well, the man who found that donor for the university in question also got an honorary doctorate, as a finder's fee.

3. Capitalize on Trends

Honorary doctorates seem to be rather trendy things, and those trends seem to run for three to five years. For instance, in the late 1950s, space science was in vogue, and people ranging from Wernher von Braun to the founder of a local rocketry society were being honored. In the 1960s, it was the Peace Corps. Sargent Shriver, its first director, set a record that stood for thirty years by accepting seven doctorates in one month (June, 1964), and a lot of other Peace Corps people and other youth workers were in demand on commencement platforms. (Nelson Mandela holds the current record, with nine in one day, all from British universities, in some sort of joint ceremony.)

The 1980s seemed heavy on jazz and classical musicians, medical researchers, people who work with the handicapped, the very elderly (several people over 100 got them for no apparent reason other than survival), Vietnam veterans, economists, and public interest lawyers.

In the 1990s, more than a few kudos have gone to authors of children's books, radio talk-show hosts, AIDS researchers or counselors, investigative reporters, coaches of nonmajor sports (lacrosse, rugby, field hockey, volleyball), and schoolteachers. Who knows what the 2000s will bring?

Some people have reported success by directly or, more often, indirectly contacting a school that has given a certain honorary degree this year, suggesting they may wish to consider a similar one next year.

4. Buy One

If all you really want is a fancy but meaningless document to hang on the wall (actually, all honorary doctorates fit that description, but some may be perceived as more meaningless than others), some of the unaccredited but legal schools are likely to oblige. A few years ago, *Spy* magazine had a reporter shop around to buy a degree, honorary or otherwise, and just about every unaccredited school he approached was willing to make the sale. (This caper was reported in their February 1995 edition.)

Of course any of the diploma mills would be more than pleased to dispense an honorary doctorate on payment of a fee that can range from 50¢ to over $1,000, but you're on your own for locating those; we don't give out addresses.

Another common source of honoraries are the Bible schools, some of which reward donors with honorary degrees.

But you'll do just as well at the local print shop, where you can have the type set for the diploma of your choice. Just don't get carried away and have a whole batch printed for sale to the public (or you may wind up in chapter 27 of this book).

5. Wait

A few years ago, we wrote that "We think it is inevitable that one or more well-known, respectable, fully accredited colleges, faced by the cash crunch that is upon so many worthy institutions, will face reality and openly put their honorary doctorates up for sale." A few years later, it happened. A small, accredited college took out a national ad, suggesting a donation of $25,000. The accrediting agency got quite upset at this, and the offer was withdrawn. But later, the well-respected Embry-Riddle Aeronautical University bought a *Wall Street Journal* ad offering a Trusteeship of the University in exchange for a $1 million donation (from an otherwise qualified donor). That, too, caused a furor.

So maybe we are still a bit premature in saying, "Wait." It may be that the deals will continue to go on just below the surface for a while longer.

The Etiquette of Soliciting Degrees

Here's one that Emily Post never had to deal with. How straightforward should one be in letting it be known that one would like an honorary doctorate? There is no way to know. Our feeling is that in the majority of situations, the direct approach is inappropriate. One must work through intermediaries—friends of school officials or trustees, who drop hints. But there are some schools and awards committees who seem to find the blunt approach refreshingly candid. These are people who realize and admit that what they are really doing is selling honorary degrees, so why not be up front? The president of a small eastern college told John that he was once approached by a second-rate actor who really wanted an honorary doctorate, "just like Marlon Brando and Henry Fonda." They negotiated terms, and the degree was awarded the following June—presumably after the check cleared the bank.

On the other hand, a high U.S. Air Force official in Europe got a lot of unfavorable publicity when *Stars and Stripes* revealed that he had solicited honorary doctorates for himself and some associates from universities that were doing contractual work for the air force. Two of the universities (Southern California and Maryland) turned him down. "It wasn't appropriate to ask for it, and it

---

Is There a Doctor in the House?

Here are some of the people who have been "doctored" by major universities in recent years:

Doctor Ella Fitzgerald	Doctor J. Edgar Hoover	Doctor Celia Cruz	Doctor Terry Bradshaw
Doctor Bonnie Raitt	Doctor Dan Rather	Doctor Gavin McLeod	Doctor Duke Ellington
Doctor Roger Maris	Doctor Charles Addams	Doctor Jane Pauley	Doctor Walter Cronkite
Doctor Isaac Stern	Doctor Candace Bergen	Doctor Ted Williams	Doctor James Earl Jones
Doctor Mister Rogers	Doctor Captain Kangaroo	Doctor John Wayne	Doctor Kirk Douglas
Doctor Billy Joel	Doctor Pinchas Zuckerman	Doctor Ozzie Nelson	Doctor Marcel Marceau
Doctor B. B. King	Doctor Robert Redford	Doctor Idi Amin	Doctor Sammy Davis Jr.
Doctor Dolores Hope	Doctor Marvin Hamlisch	Doctor Arthur Ashe	Doctor Mrs. Anwar Sadat
Doctor Stevie Wonder	Doctor Margot Fonteyn	Doctor Don King	Doctor Whoopi Goldberg
Doctor Doctor Seuss	Doctor Dave Winfield	Doctor Kermit the Frog	Doctor Steven Spielberg
Doctor Bing Crosby	Doctor Norman Mailer	Doctor Phil Rizzuto	Doctor Sidney Poitier
Doctor Helen Hayes	Doctor Aretha Franklin	Doctor Barbra Streisand	Doctor Maurice Sendak
Doctor Max Factor	Doctor Leontyne Price		

Some new doctors we've learned about since the last edition:

Doctor Bill Gates	Doctor J.K. Rowling	Doctor Wayne Gretzky	Doctor Ingar Bergman
Doctor Bob Dylan	Doctor Julia Butterfly Hill	Doctor Art Linkletter	Doctor Buffy Sainte-Marie
Doctor Sting	Doctor James Taylor	Doctor David Bowie	Doctor Placido Domingo
Doctor Desmond Tutu	Doctor Lennox Lewis	Doctor Yasser Arafat	Doctor Paul Lawrie
Doctor Miss Peggy Lee			

wasn't appropriate to give it," one school official said. But the third university gave it to him.

The army's counterpart in Europe, when asked if he would solicit honorary doctorates, replied, "You've got to be out of your tree."

One of the more awkward solicitations came from actor George Wendt, better known as the beer-guzzling Norm on the popular sitcom *Cheers*. Here is how the Miami *Herald* reported the event:

> Notre Dame Coach Lou Holtz looked toward a big Fighting Irish fan—a really big Fighting Irish fan—to motivate his team Friday night. George Wendt … burst into a frenzied pep rally unannounced as the 10,000-plus students chanted 'Norm!'
>
> Wendt proclaimed that the Fighting Irish had some unfinished business to attend to Saturday. As far as motivation speeches go, though, this wasn't much of one. Other than the unfinished-business line, Wendt did little more than yell unintelligibly at the top of his lungs until he was dragged away.
>
> Wendt, who failed out of Notre Dame after three years, asked for an honorary degree, but Holtz gave him an autographed football instead …

The Wonderful Wacky World of Honorary Degrees

Here are just a few of the recipients we learned about in recent years.

Recipient	School	What, why, etc.
Dr. Robin Williams	Juilliard	After lampooning Jesse Helms and Dan Quayle ("President Quayle, raise your right hand. No, your other right hand."), he said "I would like to do something from Hamlet. I just need a moment to prepare." As the crowd roared, he continued, "To be or … wait! I know this!"
Dr. Patrick Ewing	Shaw University	For his athletic abilities and his work with youth.
Dr. Sonny Bono	National Disaster Conference	The degree in disaster medicine was awarded after he helped carry stretchers following a bus accident in Palm Springs.
Dr. Bill Cosby	University of Maryland	"There are no courses in valet parking, waitressing, and grinding coffee. You people are not prepared. You are well-educated and you look cute, but that's not going to do it."
Dr. Mother Teresa	University of Scranton	The degree is in social sciences; as soon as it was awarded, she had a police escort back to the Wilkes-Barre airport.
Dr. Sun Myung Moon	Shaw Divinity School	Dr. Moon was in prison for tax evasion at the time.
Dr. Oprah Winfrey	Morehouse College	Doctor of Humane Letters. She gave $1 million for a scholarship fund at the all-male school.
Dr. Goober	U. of North Alabama	George Lindsey, Goober on the Andy Griffith Show, was a sterling fund raiser for his alma mater.
Dr. Frank Sinatra	Stevens Institute	A third of the graduating class signed a petition objecting, not to Sinatra but to the fact the degree was in engineering. Sinatra was born in Hoboken, site of the school.
Dr. Bryant Gumbel	Bates College	"I was not the hardworking 4.0 student….Life doesn't end when you graduate with less than a 3.0."

Recipient	School	What, why, etc.
Dr. Elwood Blues	Yale University	This mule received a Doctor of Portage Equus for carrying rocks for the Yale geology team. "We don't consider this a joke," said a National Park Service spokesman. "It's not likely an honorary doctorate has ever been given to a mule before from an Ivy League school."
Dr. Mike Tyson	Central State University	After the ceremony, he told a reporter, "I'm successful, I'm young, I'm single, I'm rich, I have God in my life . . . and may I be permitted to say, you are such an incredible-looking woman."
Dr. Victor Borge	University of Denver	"Now that I'm a doctor," he said, "I think I have to get some malpractice insurance."
Dr. Jim Evans	Central Missouri State	He invented Cheerios.
Dr. Cinderella	Miami-Dade College	For her efforts at literacy, as part of a book fair.
Dr. Chevy Chase	Bard College	Speaking to his alma mater, he said, "Never tell the truth. Embellish, patronize, pander, use hyperbole, braggadocio, mollify, but never actually tell the truth. Your job is to act. Keep the dream alive. Also, never call me."
Dr. Alexander Solzhenitsyn	Dartmouth College	Doctor of Letters. He speaks almost no English, refused to be interviewed, and did not speak to the graduating class.
Dr. Dolly Parton	Carson-Newman College	Doctor of Letters for "her personal commitment to the educational and economic vitality of East Tennessee . . ."
Dr. Prince Charles	Harvard University	Ronald Reagan was to deliver the keynote address, but declined when Harvard refused him an honorary degree because of the controversy over his academic deficiencies. The Prince of Wales accepted. His eagerly awaited first words on arrival at Logan Airport: "Hello, how are you?"
Dr. Soupy Sales	Marshall University	The newspaper story was headlined "Degree better than pie in face," when his alma mater presented the award.
Dr. Paul McCartney	University of Sussex	"Just call me Dr. Rock," he said. Since he didn't do too well at school, "it was great to get this degree without having to revise [study] for it."
Dr. Oliver North	Liberty University	Chancellor Jerry Falwell called him an American hero and compared his legal predicament to the suffering of Jesus.
Dr. Magic Johnson	Rust College	He said, "This is the greatest and biggest day of my life. This tops any championship, any MVP I've won. . . ."
Dr. Bob Hope	University of San Diego	On receiving his 44th honorary doctorate, he said, "I love commencement. I love the happy, ecstatic, joyous faces. But enough about the teachers."
Dr. Joe DiMaggio	Columbia University	When he was spotted in the procession, "applause grew and several people chanted 'Joe D., Joe D., Joe D.' He waved."

Recipient	School	What, why, etc.
Dr. Steve Wozniak	University of Colorado	The Apple founder was expelled for tampering with the school's computer system. Twenty-five years later, they gave him a doctorate.
Dr. Scott Hamilton	Bowling Green State Univ.	The gold medalist never attended the school, but he did learn to skate on the university's ice arena.
Dr. Jerry Lewis	South Central Tech College	He stuck a glass all the way into his mouth, hid behind a giant flower arrangement, then said, "I never know what's going to happen until I get to the podium. I'm guided by instinct."
Dr. Joseph Haydn	Oxford University	He wrote Symphony #92 to thank Oxford for awarding him the degree, but it wasn't done in time, so #91 was played at the ceremony.
Dr. Doctor J	University of Massachusetts	Julius Erving received the honorary doctorate at the same time as his earned bachelor's in leadership & management.
Dr. Prince Philip	Asian Institute of Technology	For his work in saving the environment and wildlife.
Dr. Milt Hinton	Skidmore College	The Judge, patriarch of jazz bass players, played two songs on his stand-up bass in lieu of making a speech.
Dr. Tony Bennett	Art Institute of Boston	He said, "When I get into the art zone, I forget about any pains that I have." He said he paints and sings every day.
Dr. Ed McMahon	Catholic University	Watch for a diploma in your mailbox.
Dr. Michael Jackson	Fisk University	For his support of the United Negro College Fund.
Dr. Alex Haley	Coast Guard Academy	The author of *Roots* received the academy's first honorary degree. While at sea during World War II, he penned letters for his shipmates' girlfriends at one dollar each.
Dr. Dustin Hoffman	Santa Monica College	He enrolled there to study music, but took an acting class and never looked back (and never graduated).
Dr. Stan Musial	Washington University	Stan the Man never went to college, but as the newspaper account said, "most college graduates can't hit a curve ball."
Dr. George Bush	University of Kuwait	For his "distinguished leadership, lofty stance, and honorable endeavors in . . . the triumphant restoration of Kuwait's independence and sovereignty."
Dr. George Wallace	Tuskeegee Institute	He said, "Very few people have one. You wouldn't have thought I'd have had that, would you? If I was a bad man, I wouldn't have gotten that. No way."
Dr. Nelson Mandela	Carabobo State University	He was offered hundreds; this one was from Venezuela.

CHAPTER 29

Bending the Rules

Any fool can make a rule, and every fool will mind it.

Henry David Thoreau

One of the most common complaints or admonishments we get from readers goes something like, "You said thus-and-so, but when I inquired of the school, they told me such-and-such." Often, a school claims that a program we have written about does not exist. Sometimes a student achieves something (such as completing a certain degree entirely by correspondence) that we had been told by a high official of the school was impossible.

One of the open secrets in the world of higher education is that the rules are constantly being bent. But, as with the Emperor's new clothes, no one dares point and say what is really going on, especially in print.

The purpose of this brief essay is to acknowledge that this sort of thing happens all the time. If you know that it happens regularly, then at least you are in the same boat with people who are already benefiting from those bent rules.

Unfortunately, we cannot provide specific examples of bent rules, naming names and all. This is for two good reasons:

1. Many situations where students profit from bent rules would disappear in an instant if anyone dared mention the situation publicly. There is, for instance, a major state university that is forbidden by its charter to grant degrees by correspondence study. But they regularly work out special arrangements whereby students are carried on the books as residential, even though all their work is done by mail. Indeed, some graduates of this school have never set foot on its campus. If this ever got out, the Board of Trustees, the accrediting agency, and all the other universities in that state would probably have conniptions, and the practice would be suspended at once.

2. These kinds of things can change so rapidly, with new personnel or new policies, that a listing of anomalies and curious practices would probably be obsolete before the ink dried.

Consider a few examples of the sort of thing that is going on in higher education every day, whether or not anyone will admit it, except perhaps behind closed doors or after several drinks:

► A friend of John's, at a major university, was unable to complete one required course for her doctorate before she had to leave for another state. This university does not offer correspondence courses, but she was able to convince a professor to enroll her in a regular course, which she would just happen never to visit in person.

► A man in graduate school needed to be enrolled in nine units of coursework each semester to keep his employer's tuition assistance plan going. But his job was too demanding one year, and he was unable to do so. The school enrolled him in nine units of "independent study" for which no work was asked or required, and for which a "pass" grade was given.

► A woman at a large school needed to complete a certain number of units before an inflexible deadline. When it became clear that she wasn't going to make it, a kindly professor turned in grades for her, and told her she could do the actual coursework later on.

► A major state university offers nonresident degrees for people living in that state only. When a reader wrote to say that he, living a thousand miles from that state, was able to complete his degree entirely by correspondence, John asked a contact at that school what was going on. "We will take students from anywhere in our correspondence degree program," she told him, "but for God's sake, don't print that in your book, or we'll be deluged with applicants."

► If we are to believe a book by a member of Dr. Bill Cosby's dissertation committee at the University of Massachusetts (*Education's Smoking Gun*, by

'I'll never tell them you're seven years old, Reginald, but don't you try to bribe your mentor with a hand-made beanbag.'

Reginald Damerell), the only class attendance on Cosby's transcript was one weekend seminar, and the only dissertation committee meeting was a dinner party, with spouses, at Cosby's house.

▶ Partway through John's supposedly definitive final doctoral oral exam, a key member of his committee had to leave for an emergency. He scrawled a note, and passed it to the dean who read it, then crumpled it up and threw it away. The grueling exam continued for several hours more. After it was over and the committee had congratulated John and departed, he retrieved the note from the wastebasket. It read, "Please give John my apologies for having to leave, and my congratulations for having passed."

▶ A man applied to a well-known school that has a rigid requirement that all graduate work (thesis or dissertation) must be begun after enrollment. He

started to tell an admissions officer about a major piece of independent research he had completed for his employer. "Stop," he was told, "don't tell me about that. Then you'll be able to use it for your master's thesis."

▶ We've heard from more than a few people who benefited from the bending of various tuition, scholarship, and financing rules. Working on the theory that an empty seat in a classroom is like an empty seat on an airplane—it can never be filled retroactively—some schools with declining tuition have been unusually generous and/or creative in finding ways to offer those seats to people who could not easily qualify for traditional scholarships, loans, or grants. There is never any harm in asking.

▶ Mariah was initially denied admission to the University of California at Berkeley because of some "irregularities" on her high school transcript. (It was a nontraditional high school.) The high school's records had been destroyed in a fire. The former principal checked with the University and discovered that the admissions people would be glad to admit her, once the computer said it was OK. He typed up a new transcript saying what the computer wanted said. The computer said OK, and three years later, she graduated Phi Beta Kappa. But how many other applicants accepted the initial "No," not knowing that rules can often be bent?

▶ The Heriot-Watt University MBA by distance learning, with which John was once involved as the U.S. agent, had a written policy stating that if a student failed an exam in a compulsory course twice, they could not continue in the program. Some students who had passed several courses, but then failed a course twice, were quietly offered another opportunity. Now, to its credit, the university has made this an official policy, and that particular rule no longer needs to be bent.

Please use this information prudently. It will do no good to pound on a table and say, "What do you mean I can't do this? John Bear says that rules don't mean anything, anyway."

But when faced with a problem, it surely can do no harm to remember that in many, many situations the rules have turned out to be far less rigid than a school's official literature would lead one to believe.

CHAPTER 30

Advice for People in Prison

In the midst of winter I discovered there was in me an invincible summer.

Albert Camus

Note: *More than a few readers and users of this book are institutionalized. We have invited a man who has completed his accredited bachelor's, master's, and doctorate while in prison, and who consults often with inmates and others around the country to offer his thoughts and recommendations. There is some very useful advice for noninstitutionalized persons as well. (The above quotation has been on Dr. Dean's bulletin board since he began his baccalaureate.)*

Arranging Academic Resources for the Institutionalized

by Douglas G. Dean, Ph.D.

One obstacle for any institutionalized person interested in pursuing a degree is limited resources: availability of community faculty, library facilities, phone access, and financial aid. To overcome these, it helps to streamline the matriculation process. Time spent in preparation prior to admission can help avoid wasted effort and time when in a program, thereby reducing operating expenses and cutting down the number of tuition periods.

A second obstacle is finding ways to ensure that a quality education can be documented. Because courses are generally not prepackaged, it is the student's responsibility to identify varied learning settings, use a range of learning methods, find and recruit community-based faculty, provide objective means to appraise what has been learned, and indeed design the study plan itself.

Finding a Flexible Degree Program

Most well-established degree programs grant credit for a variety of learning experiences. In terms of cost and arrangements required, equivalency examinations and independent study projects are the most expedient. Credit for life-experience learning is another option sometimes offered. If a degree program does not offer at least two of these options, it is unlikely that the program as a whole will be able to accommodate the needs of the institutionalized student.

Writing a Competency-Based Study Plan

The traditional method of acquiring credits is to take narrowly focused courses of two to four credits each. Since the nontraditional student must enlist his or her own instructors, find varied learning methods, and quantify the whole experience, the single-course approach creates much needless duplication of effort.

A better approach is to envision a subject area which is to be studied for 9 to 12 credits (e.g., statistics). As an independent-study project, the student identifies what topics are germane to the area (e.g., probability theory, descriptive statistics, inferential statistics); at what level of comprehension (e.g., introductory through intermediate or advanced); how the topic is to be studied (e.g., directed reading, programmed textbooks), and how the competencies acquired are to be demonstrated (e.g., oral examination, proctored examination including problem solving). This way, a single independent-study project can take the place of a series of successive courses in a given area (e.g., Statistics 101, 201, 301).

Designing the Curriculum

Every accredited degree program has graduation requirements. These requirements broadly define the breadth of subject areas that comprise a liberal arts education and the depth to which they are to be studied. It is the responsibility of the external student not only to identify a curriculum fulfilling these requirements but, in most cases, to design the course content that will comprise each study module.

But how does a student know what an area of study consists of before he or she has studied it? The answer lies in meticulous preparation.

Well in advance of formally applying for an off-campus degree program, the prospective student should obtain course catalogs from several colleges and universities. Look at what these schools consider the core curriculum and what is necessary to fulfill the graduation requirements. With this broad outline in mind, the student can begin to form clusters of courses fulfilling each criterion. This approach helps shape the study plan academically rather than touch it up later as an afterthought.

Next, decide which subjects are of interest within each criterion area. Compare topical areas within each subject as described in the course listings and commonalities will emerge. From there, it is simply a matter of writing to the various instructors for a copy of their course syllabi. These course outlines will provide more detailed information about the subject matter and identify the textbooks currently used at that level of study.

Means of Study

Having decided what is to be studied, the student must then propose various ways to study it.

Equivalency exams (such as CLEP) enable the student to acquire credits instantly, often in core or required areas of study. This helps reduce overall program costs by eliminating the need for textbooks and tuition fees. More importantly, it helps reduce the number of special learning arrangements that must otherwise be made.

"Testing out" of correspondence courses (taking only the examinations, without doing the homework assignments) is another excellent way to acquire credits quickly. This can, however, be an expensive method since full course fees are still assessed. Nonetheless, if a student studies on his or her own in advance according to the course syllabus, and if the instructor can then be convinced to waive prerequisite assignments, it can be an efficient and cost-effective method to use.

Independent study projects should form the balance of any study plan. With the topical areas, learning objectives, and learning materials identified, an independent study project allows the student to remain with the same instructor(s) from an introductory through an intermediate or advanced level of study. This eliminates the need for new arrangements to be made every two to four credits. An independent study project can take the form of simple directed reading, tutorial instruction, practicum work, or a combination of these methods, culminating in the final product.

Direct tutorial arrangements, similar to the European don system, commit a student to learn under a single instructor until he or she is convinced that the student has mastered a given subject at a predetermined level of competency. The tutoring itself may take the form of directed reading from both primary and secondary sources, writing and orally defending assigned topical papers, monitored practica, and supervised research projects. The caveat is that the tutor determines when a student has satisfied all study requirements, so the study plan should meticulously spell out the breadth and depth of what is to be studied.

One may also be able to use existing classroom courses as a setting in which to evaluate a student's mastery of a given subject. Some institutions periodically offer an on-site college or vocational course (e.g., communications skills). Instead of taking such a course for the standard two to three credits, the student could arrange for specific communication skills (composition, rhetoric) to be evaluated at a given level of mastery (beginning to advanced). In this single step, a student may be able to earn advanced credit and fulfill all the communication skills core requirements for graduation.

Various professions require practitioners to earn continuing education credits, usually through seminars and/or home study courses. These courses represent the latest knowledge in a given field, come prepackaged with an evaluation test, and are an excellent source of study material. The breadth and depth of specialization offered in such courses is especially useful to students with graduate or postgraduate aspirations.

Independent study projects require the aid of qualified persons to act as community faculty, and to oversee personally the progress of the work. Therefore, it is highly advantageous to line up faculty in advance of entering the degree program. It is equally important to have alternates available in the event an instructor is unable, for any reason, to fulfill his or her commitment. It is better to anticipate these needs at the preparatory stage than to be scrambling for a replacement while the tuition clock is running.

Multiple Treatments of Subject Matter

The external student is often without benefit of lecture halls, interactions with other students, or readily available academic counseling services. For the institutionalized student, picking up the phone or stopping in to see a faculty member for help with a study problem are not options. This is why alternate methods of study are so valuable.

One approach is to use several textbooks covering the same subject matter. If something does not make sense, there is a different treatment of the subject to turn to.

Programmed textbooks make especially good substitute tutors. A programmed text breaks the subject matter into small segments requiring a response from the reader with periodic tests to check progress. Such texts are now available in many subject areas, but are particularly useful for the sciences. Titles can be obtained from the *Books in Print* subject guide, or by writing directly to textbook publishers.

Audio-visual (A-V) materials can, to some extent, make up for college life without the typical lectures and classes. Writing to A-V departments at large universities often yields a catalog of materials available for rental. These materials frequently take the form of a comprehensive tape series, and may address even the most advanced subject matter. When using such materials, it is best to work through the school or social service department of the student's institution of residence.

Some large campuses have lecture note services, which employ advanced students to attend class lectures and take copious lecture notes, which are then sold to students. Aside from gaining insights into good note-taking, these published notes are an additional treatment of course content, and can indicate what topical areas are given special emphasis. Such notes are especially recommended for new students.

Documenting Study

The administrators of a degree program must be convinced that there are acceptable ways to document what has been learned, and what levels of subject mastery have been achieved, without taking the student's word for it. Community faculty members may be asked to provide written or oral examinations, but it does not hurt to make their jobs easier.

It is highly recommended that each study project be evaluated using a number of means (objective tests, essay exams, oral exams) and documented using a variety of methods (student narrative, faculty narrative, test results, final product, grade equivalent, etc.).

Self-evaluation, not unlike personal logs or journals, provides an excellent primary source from which to glean what a student truly knows, how they came to know it, and what new questions arise from the acquired knowledge. Any future employer or admissions counselor unfamiliar with nontraditional or off-campus degree programs can gain a fuller appreciation of the process through such narratives.

Likewise, a narrative evaluation written by the instructor provides a description of student competencies that ordinary assessment methods are unable to detect or reflect. Nuances of learning style, ability to converse in the field of study, and scholarly integrity are examples of such insights.

Depending on the subject at hand, the final product may take the form of a research monograph, video presentation, musical manuscript, senior thesis, etc.—whatever will best provide proof and record that the student has achieved the target level of competency in that field.

Most professions (accounting, psychology, law, medicine, etc.) have licensing and/or board certification examinations that must be taken. An industry has built up around this need, providing parallel or actual past examinations to help prepare students. By agreeing to take a relevant sample examination under proctored conditions, and negotiating cutoff scores in advance, the community faculty member is relieved of having to design his or her own objective examination for just one student. This approach adds validity to the assessment process, and provides a standardized score that has some universal meaning. This is an optional approach but may be worth the effort.

Recruiting Community Faculty

Just as it is easier for a student to organize a study plan into blocks of subject areas, a competency-based study plan of this sort makes it easier for a prospective instructor to visualize what is being asked of him or her.

A typical independent study project would define for the instructor what specific topics are to be studied, what levels of mastery will be expected of the student, what textbooks or other materials will be used, and what is expected of the instructor.

Many traditional academics are unfamiliar with external degree programs. Consequently, they tend to assume that their role as instructor will require greater effort and time on their part than for the average student, who may expect their services in many roles, from academic advisor to tutor. The more an institutionalized student can do up front to define clearly the role and expected duties of the community faculty member, the more successful a student will be in enlisting instructors for independent study projects.

Instructors may sometimes be found on the staff of the institution where the student resides. They may also be found through a canvassing letter sent to the appropriate department heads at area colleges, universities, and technical schools. The same approach may be used to canvass departments within area businesses, museums, art centers, hospitals, libraries, theaters, zoos, banks, and orchestras, to name but a few. People are often flattered to be asked, providing it is clear to them exactly what they are getting into.

The more a student can operate independently, and rely on community faculty for little more than assessment purposes, the more likely a student will be successful in recruiting help, and thereby broadening the range of study options.

Revealing Your Institutionalized Status

It is generally proper and appropriate to inform potential schools and potential faculty of one's institutionalized status. (Many institutions now have mailing addresses that do not indicate they are, in fact, institutions.) Some schools or individuals may be put off by this, but then you would not want to deal with them anyway. Others may be especially motivated to help.

A recommended approach is to first make a general inquiry about the prospective school or program. With this information in hand, information intended for the general student, one may better tailor inquiries to specific departments or faculty, addressing your specific needs.

Financing the Educational Process

Unfortunately, there are virtually no generalizations to be made here, whatsoever. Each institution seems to have its own policy with regard to the way finances are handled. Some institutionalized persons earn decent wages, and have access to the funds. Others have little or no ability to pay their own way. Some institutions permit financial gifts from relatives or friends; others do not. Some schools make special concessions or have some scholarship funds available for institutionalized persons; many do not. One should contact the financial aid office of the prospective school with any such questions.

Again, start with a general inquiry, as would any student, then ask about the applicability of specific programs to your own situation. Often a key element is to find someone on campus, perhaps in the financial aid office or your degree program, who is willing to do the actual legwork, walking your financial aid paperwork to various administrative offices. A financial aid package is of no use to anyone if that package cannot be processed.

America used to embrace the view that funding education for prisoners paid for itself, in a significant reduction in recidivism for better-educated inmates. In 1995, the Omnibus Crime Bill deleted the one-half of one percent of Pell Grants that went to prisoners. In 1998, in the debate over the reauthorization of the Higher Education Act, the party in control of the House and Senate resoundingly defeated attempts to fund educational opportunities for prisoners. This law will not be revisited until the year 2003 or 2004. And, as the icing on this bitter cake, the only foundation that regularly provided tuition money to prisoners, Davis-Putter, made so many grants from its endowment that it ran out of money and went out of business.

Is there any hope? Minimal. Students who are incarcerated in local correctional institutions may be eligible for Pell Grants. Students in state and federal institutions are definitely not eligible for Pell Grants or federal student loans, but they may qualify for Supplemental Educational Opportunity Grants (SEOG) or College Work Study, if the school participates in these so-called "campus-based" programs. Prison education officers should have details on these matters.

In Conclusion

Institutionalized students must be highly self-directed, and honest enough with themselves to recognize if they are not. Because the student lives where he or she works, it takes extra effort to set aside daily study time, not only to put the student in the right frame of mind, but also to accommodate institution schedules. It can mean working with a minimum number of books or tapes to comply with property rules. It can mean study periods that begin at 11 P.M., when the cell hall begins to quiet down. It means long periods of delayed gratification, in an environment where pursuing education is often suspect. And it is the greatest feeling in the world when it all comes together.

In 2000, we learned that the Helping Hands Association in Utah is willing to work with inmates in achieving their academic goals, and has disbursed scholarships and grants to qualifying inmates and their spouses. Direct inquiries to:

Helping Hands Association
Att: President Carol Farmer
P.O. Box 584
Clearfield, UT 84041
Phone: (801) 825 3877

We were also pleased to learn that the University of Southern Colorado offers a unique degree for prison inmates. Qualifying inmates can receive financial assistance in the form of grants and scholarships. Information is available from:

University of Southern Colorado
Office of Continuing Education
Att: Donald Spano
2200 Bonforte Blvd.
Pueblo, CO 81001
Phone: (877) 872 9653, select option #3
Email: orspano@rmi.net

CHAPTER 31

Miscellaneous Schools

There are more things in heaven and earth, Horatio,
than are dreamt of in your philosophy.

William Shakespeare

This chapter lists all of the schools that, for whatever reason, are not listed in any of the earlier chapters.

There are three main reasons why a school would be listed here rather than there:

1. They have been in earlier editions of this book, and are no longer in business (or findable by us, despite our best efforts).

2. They have been in earlier editions of this book, and, while they are still in business, they no longer offer the non-traditional program(s) earlier described.

3. They are schools which may offer (or have offered) certain degree programs nontraditionally, but about which we have not been able to learn enough information to give them a proper listing.

We hasten to add that a listing or mention in this chapter is not necessarily a negative thing.

We welcome help of (at least!) two kinds:

1. **Help in checking out schools in general:** Our research is often hindered by distance. One can often learn more from a brief in-person inspection than by hours of research or communication from afar (such as in the not-uncommon case, when a "campus" turns out to be a mail-forwarding service). Sometimes we are hindered by John's notoriety—some schools simply won't communicate with John Bear (or anyone named Bear) at all, or won't answer questions about their programs.

   We do have an informal array of pen pals in cities around the world who have been very helpful in checking out schools, either in person or by correspondence—but more are always needed. If you would be willing to do this from time to time, please drop us a note or email to let us know. If you frequently travel to a certain city and could check out schools there, let us know that too. Thank you. (John and Mariah Bear, P.O. Box 7123, Berkeley, CA 94707; *johnandmariah@degree.net*)

2. **Help in learning about specific schools:** We are regularly asked for information on certain schools, by law-enforcement officials, personnel officers, reporters, alumni, or other interested members of the public. Often we can help, but many times we cannot, especially when it comes to the schools listed in this chapter. If you know anything about the schools listed below, even if it is only a scrap of information or a bit of hearsay, please let us know. Thank you again. We won't use your name in any way—but if you'd prefer, anonymous letters are acceptable. (If you sent us a letter about any of these schools and see that your information was not incorporated, please don't be dismayed. In the past, updating was a much more haphazard affair. Our new database has made updating much more reliable although, of course, not perfect. We will keep striving for perfection ... maybe in the 15th edition ...)

Abilene Christian University Texas. At one time offered an accredited external M.S. in human relations or management.

Academic Credit University Started in Culver City, California, by the former president of Southland University and some Ethiopian colleagues; mail now returned as undeliverable.

Academy of Open Learning They used to offer a Bachelor of Arts in valuation sciences for appraisers, but now mail to their former address in Geneva, Illinois, is not answered and there is no listed phone.

Academy of Professional Studies They are claimed by the unaccredited Frederick Taylor International University of Hawaii (run from California) as a degree-granting affiliate, but, while they apparently operate legally in London, England, they do not seem to have permission to award degrees.

Academy of Technical Sciences See: Bedford University

Academy of Traditional Sciences They were established to provide distance-learning study in astrology, transpersonal psychology, esoteric philosophy, shamanic counseling, and sacred sciences. But in 2000 there was no listed telephone in Scarborough, Canada, and the Web site was inoperative.

Achievement University In 2000, they were listed as members of the unrecognized and nonwonderful accrediting agency called the World Association of Universities and Colleges, but WAUC does not provide any information on where in the world they are located, and we have been unable to find them.

Advanced School of Herbology They were in Sacramento, California, but we cannot locate them now.

Airola College See: North American Colleges of Natural Health Science

Aiwa Medical University The holistic healing program of this Japanese university is accredited by the unrecognized and nonwonderful World Association of Universities and Colleges. We have been unable to find this university on the Internet, and they have not responded to the faxes we sent. (The World Association does not make the addresses of many of its accreditees available.)

Akademie fur Internationale Kultur This school is apparently located in Muelheim, Germany; a letter from Denis Muhilly (who has been involved with many nonwonderful schools) says that the academy is a consortium of state colleges and universities throughout Europe, offering degrees at all levels. We can find no evidence of this.

Al-Manaf International Islamic University This university, established by Ray Chasse, has been operated as a department of American Coastline University (see listing in chapter 21). Shortly before his death in 2000, Dr. Chasse told us it will not have an address or telephone, but will operate entirely over the Internet. We have been unable to find a Web site. Indeed, a thorough Internet search yielded only one reference: a doctorate from this school on the resume of Dr. Tzemach David Ben Netzer Korem, vice president of the nonexistent country of Melchizidek (whose Dominion University also had a connection with Ray Chasse).

Allen Maxwell University See: Allen Mitchell School of Psychology

Allen Mitchell School of Psychology They appeared briefly on the Internet in 2000. The Web site gave a street address (Rock Creek Road) without saying what state it was in, and the telephone number was given with no area code. The Web site was registered to Allen Maxwell University of Madera, California (we can't find

that, either). Accredited by the International Association of Monotheistic Schools (ditto).

Aloha State University They were registered as a business in Hawaii as of May, 2000, but we could not find evidence of the school in that state, or anywhere else.

Aloha University They were registered as a business in Hawaii as of May, 2000, but we could not find evidence of the school in that state, or anywhere else.

Alternative Medicines Research Institute Awarded degrees at all levels, as well as diplomas, to practitioners of holistic and alternative medicine, apparently based entirely on work experience and research. In 1999 founder Egbert Phipps wrote us that the school had been "terminated." Dr. Phipps' medical degree is from the Open International University for Complementary Medicine, a school in Sri Lanka that has offered the M.D. by mail for $1,000 to people with some medical background. See also George Washington University, Inc., and Stanton University (Hawaii).

Ambassador College The school is still in existence in Big Sandy, Texas (it was formerly located in Pasadena, California), but no longer offers any nontraditional programs.

Amerasian University They were registered as a business in Hawaii as of May, 2000, but we could not find evidence of the school in that state, or anywhere else, other than two online resumes from acupuncturists who say they studied at this school in Wailuku, Hawaii.

America West University They were registered as a business in Hawaii as of May, 2000, but we could not find evidence of the school in that state, or anywhere else. Clearly not connected with the other America West from thirty years earlier. Thomas Lavin, founder, has been involved with many other schools, including Kensington, Pacific Western, and Bedford.

American College in Paris At one time offered bachelor's degrees through summer or year-round study in Paris.

American College of Finance Formerly a California-authorized school, but mail has been returned as undeliverable and there is no listed telephone in Sunnyvale, California.

American College of Health Science See: American Health Sciences Institute

American College of Nutripathy Arizona. This alternative healing school ceased operations in 1990; some of its programs (and all student records) are now maintained by North American University of Scottsdale, Arizona.

American Commonwealth University See: Huron International University

American Cornerstone University They were registered as a business in Hawaii as of May, 2000, but we could not find evidence of the school in that state, or anywhere else.

American Crescent University All we know is that in 2000, this name was registered with the state of Hawaii, as a name change from an earlier school name, but the listing didn't say which, or where the university may be located.

American Eastern Graduate University They were registered as a business in Hawaii as of May, 2000, but we could not find evidence of the school in that state, or anywhere else.

American Floating University In the 1930s they offered Bachelor and Master of World Affairs degrees to students who studied while traveling on ocean liners. Now they have sunk from view. Constantine Raises of San Francisco was in charge.

American Hawaii University They were registered as a business in Hawaii as of May, 2000, but we could not find evidence of the school in that state, or anywhere else. Apparently not the same school as American University of Hawaii.

American Health Sciences Institute Texas. At one time, offered a diploma in nutritional science and, in an earlier incarnation as the Life Science Institute, awarded doctoral degrees. Now they are apparently gone.

American Heritage University In 2000, we found a school of this name on a list of incorporated Arizona entities, but we cannot learn any more information.

American Institute of Hypnotherapy Offered degrees in hypnotherapy until California threatened to drop its state approval if AIH continued to offer its doctoral programs. The owner opened up a "sister school" in Hawaii where these degrees are now offered. See: American Pacific University

American Institute of Real Time Education Appeared on the Internet offering an MBA in just four to six weeks of study. No listed phone number; its address is a Mail Boxes Etc. store. Its Web site is "Temporarily out of order."

American Institute of Traditional Chinese Medicine State-approved residential school, formerly in San Francisco, now in Berkeley.

American Institute of Vedic Studies At one time, the school in Santa Fe, New Mexico (*www.vedanet.com*) offered a master's degree in ayurveda, a traditional Indian approach to health, but apparently no longer.

American International Graduate University They were registered as a business in Hawaii as an "educational institution which benefits the public," but we could not find evidence of the school in that state, or anywhere else, unless it is another name for American International University in Hawaii.

American International University (Indiana) The Web site says almost nothing about this institution, other than that it also seems to be known as Universidad Internacional de las Americas. No literature was ever sent in response to our requests.

American International University of Management and Technology They were registered as a business in Hawaii as of May, 2000 to offer "university teaching and training activities in higher education" but we could not find evidence of the school in that state, or anywhere else, unless it is the same as American International University in Hawaii. The registered address is a Mail Boxes Etc., which presumably is where the unrecognized and nonwonderful World Association for Universities and Colleges went to visit them, before granting them full accreditation.

American International University of Pastoral Counseling They were registered as a business in Hawaii as of May, 2000, apparently associated with the Universal Life Church, but we could not find evidence of the school in that state, or anywhere else.

American Management and Business Administration Institute AMBAI offers a diploma (not a degree) in business through an entirely free online course (*www.mbaii.org*).

American Medical Institute See: Pacific National University

American National University (California) They had been a California state-authorized school, but mail to their La Palma, California, address was returned as undeliverable and there is no listed telephone. Apparently there was no connection with a diploma mill of this name which operated from California and Arizona in the 1970s and early 1980s. There is a school of this name on the Internet, with its Web site in an Asian language.

American National University (Hawaii) They were registered as a business in Hawaii as of May, 2000, but we could not find evidence of the school in that state, or anywhere else. Presumably not connected with either the California or Arizona institution of the same name.

American Open University This was a well-funded effort by a consortium of traditional universities to establish a nontraditional university in Lincoln, Nebraska. Donald McNeil, a distance-learning visionary who had headed up the similar University of Mid-America, founded AOU. The project ended before any students were enrolled, although some of its programs still exist in limited scope at the New York Institute of Technology.

American Pacific Coast University They were incorporated as a business in Hawaii in 1997, but we could not find evidence of the school in that state, or anywhere else.

American Pacific University (California) This formerly state-authorized school in Costa Mesa, CA, is no longer operating. Apparently no connection with the American Pacific University in Honolulu, Hawaii.

American Pan Pacific University It was announced in 1994 as a planned school, hoping to raise $7 million to open in Alameda, California, but as of the fall of 2000, this had not yet come to pass.

American Schools California. Never responded to our requests for information about their nontraditional programs, and then one day the requests came back marked "forwarding order expired."

American States University They were registered as a business in Hawaii in 1991, but we could not find evidence of the school in that state, or anywhere else. Apparently unconnected with American State University, also associated with Hawaii. Nancy Akamu was the registered agent.

American University Colleges & Graduate Studies Scotts Valley, CA. By all indications, this school is no longer operating: phone is dead, links on its Web page (*www.americanuniversity.edu*) are all inactive, and we've gotten no response to our emails. Of course, we haven't been able to find anybody to confirm this.

American University for Foreign Students This unaccredited school was located in Kaneohe, Hawaii, but the corporation was involuntarily dissolved by the state in 1990.

American University Graduate School See: American University Colleges & Graduate Studies

American University Hawaii They were registered as a business in Wailuku, Hawaii as of May, 2000 as a post-secondary educatgional degree granting institution. Apparently unconnected with either American Hawaii University or American University of Hawaii.

American University of China Registered in Hawaii using an address in Longwood, Florida to offer educational products andservices. Founder Adam Starchild is a prominent author of books on investing, acquiring second passports, cooking, etc. Identical registrations for American University of Korea, of Japan, and of the Philippines.

American University of Japan See: American University of China

American University of Korea See: American University of China

American University of Oriental Studies Formerly a state-authorized school. Mail to their Los Angeles address returned as undeliverable, and there is no listed telephone number.

American University of Technical and Liberal Arts and Science They registered as a business in Kapaa, Hawaii, but we could not find evidence of them there.

American University of the Pacific They were registered as a business in Hawaii as of May, 2000, using a post office box address, but we could not find evidence of the school in that state, or anywhere else.

American University of the Philippines See: American University of China

American University Without Walls Dr. James Benton, president of University of America (see listing in chapter 21), claims a Ph.D. from this school. We can find no other evidence of its existence.

American Westpoint University They were registered as a business in Hawaii as of May, 2000, but we could not find evidence of the school in that state, or anywhere else.

Americas University Supposedly headquartered in the Bahamas, but they have a secretarial service "campus" in St. Petersburg, Florida. The information provided is quite short on specifics, other than the $11,000 required for a degree. They say they "will make application to the Crown for appropriate recognition within their purview [and] we anticipate no burden in meeting the required standards." We would anticipate a rather substantial burden. In mid-April 1998, the Florida State Board of Independent Colleges and Universities told us they had never heard of Americas University. In response to several questions, we received an email stating that "the Web site is being deactivated."

Americus University of Natural Health Clearwater, Florida. We've inquired about this school's programs, but letters sent to their last known address were returned as undeliverable.

Amwealth University In the early 1990s, they were registered with the Louisiana Board of Regents (then an automatic process), but mail to the New Orleans address was returned as undeliverable, and there is no listed telephone number.

Ana G. Mendez University System A limited number of distance programs are offered in Spanish from the campus in Puerto Rico.

Anasazi University While a university of this name was incorporated in Eagar, Arizona in 1996, there was no listed telephone number there in 2000, and we could not locate them on the Internet.

Andrew Jackson College Originally established as American Community College, then Andrew Jackson University and Andrew Jackson University College, in Louisiana by Dr. Jean-Maximillien De La Croix de Lafayette. Subsequently used an address that was apparently Dr. De La Croix de Lafayette's home in Maryland, but now apparently no longer in business.

Andrew Jackson University College See: Andrew Jackson College

Anthony University See: Susan B. Anthony University

Appalachian State University North Carolina. This accredited school used to offer a B.A. in which over 75% of the credits could come from life-experience learning.

Appraisal College Formerly registered with the Louisiana Board of Regents, then an automatic process. Mail to their Baton Rouge address is returned as undeliverable, and there is no listed telephone number.

Arizona International University A school of this name was developed by University of Arizona faculty in the mid-1990s, ostensibly to be a separate, freestanding campus. It was approved by the state Board of Regents, but only as a branch campus of the University of Arizona. Based on newspaper reports from Tucson, the project appears to have been quite controversial. ("Beam us up when this thing gets off the launch pad—we know some high school seniors we want to warn to steer clear of this sci-fi nightmare," wrote a Tucson newspaper.)

Arizona Open University They existed in Scottsdale at one time, but no more. We have no further information.

Army University In 2000, the Secretary of the Army announced that the army was to launch a $550 million distance learning effort, to make college-level courses available to military personnel. Details were very sketchy as to whether degrees would be involved, but current information should be available on the "eArmy" Web site, *www.earmyu.com*.

Arnould-Taylor Education Ltd. United Kingdom. No longer grants degrees because of changes in British higher education laws. Had offered both a bachelor's and master's in physiatrics entirely through correspondence. Their material emphasized that these were professional—not academic—degrees offered to persons already qualified in the field of physical therapy.

Arthur D. Little School of Management Cambridge, Massachusetts. Formerly the Management Education Institute, they once offered an M.S. in international management education. Now all they do is a residential M.S. in management.

Ashiya University They were registered as a business in Hawaii as of May, 2000, but we could not find evidence of the school in that state, but there is a large and traditional Ashiya University in Japan.

Asia Pacific University They were registered as a business in Hawaii as of May, 2000, but we could not find evidence of the school in that state, or anywhere else. No apparent connection with either Newport Asia Pacific University or Asia Pacific International University.

Asian American University Formerly authorized to grant degrees by the State of California. Letters to their San Diego address have not been answered, and there is no listed telephone number.

Atlanta Law School Georgia. Unaccredited, and now defunct, law school.

Atlantic Institute of Education An accredited Canadian program offering master's degrees and doctorates through distance learning. Closed after they lost their funding.

Atlantic University (New York) As a promotional gimmick, *Atlantic Monthly* magazine once offered an honorary doctorate from Atlantic University to new subscribers. A harmless gag, perhaps, but we have now seen two instances in which Atlantic University appeared on a job-application resumé.

August Vollmer University Approved by the State of California, but it seems there are not any distance or online programs.

Australasian Institute The school's Web site is a single-page apology for "misleading or deceptive Internet course delivery claims" made in advertisements published in various Australian newspapers and magazines: specifically, that it is "a body of high academic standing" and that its MBA program is delivered and/or approved by the University of Ballarat, University of Newcastle, or American International University. (We're certainly amused by the invocation of American International University as a marketing device.) This apology came at the "request" of the Australian Competition and Consumer Commission.

Avon University Several bible school administrators have listed degrees from this school, which one said was founded in Boston in 1897, but we have been unable to locate it.

Azusa Pacific College California. At one time offered master's degrees through evening study.

Babson College Wellesley, Massachusetts. Accredited evening MBA discontinued.

Baden-Powell University of Scouting We learned from an article in a December 1996 publication of the Boy Scouts of America that for years, it seems, the Scouts have awarded a bachelor's, a master's, and a doctorate to scout leaders who attend a one- to three-day training session. The degrees are in the name of Baden-Powell University, named after the founder of the Boy Scouts, Lord Baden-Powell, and alternately referred to as the University of Scouting. Obviously the Scouts are not running a diploma mill, but it could be considered unfortunate that they have chosen academic titles to award to their leaders. When this information was posted on an Internet news group, for instance, there were responses of the following sort: "I know one person with a 'Ph.D' from the Baden-Powell University who always insists that others call him 'Dr.,' and constantly brags about his 'academic' achievement."

Bahamas Institute of Alternate Studies This radio station in the Bahamas offers a Doctor of Arts in Sun Tanning. Diploma shipped on receipt of student's tuition. They're on the Web at *www.100jamz.com*.

Balance Therapy University This Japanese university is accredited by the unrecognized and nonwonderful World Association of Universities and Colleges. We have been unable to find the university on the Internet, and they have not responded to a fax we sent to +81 (3) 456 0428. (The World Association does not make the addresses of many of its accreditees available.) They also formed a company of this name in Hawaii, but did not provide its address to the state.

Bay Area Open College California. At one time offered undergraduate degrees through a range of nontraditional methods. Affiliated with the traditional Wright Institute.

Beacon College Established in Boston and later moved to Washington, DC, Beacon had probably the most flexible, most nontraditional master's degree ever to achieve traditional accreditation, which was granted in 1981. Accreditation was subsequently lost due to licensing difficulties, and the school went out of business. Former name: Campus-Free College.

Bedford University Operated briefly in Arizona, offering degrees at a time when that state had no laws regulating schools. Closed in 1983. Had offered degrees in conjunction with the Academy of Technical Sciences of Beirut, Lebanon. According to the Arizona Republic newspaper, clients of the Educom Counseling Service in California were referred to Bedford as "the school most suited" to their needs. Educom was run by Thomas Lavin, an officer of Kensington University, later Bedford's founder, later still an officer of Clayton University, and his daughter.

Belize Institute of Technology They had offered independent study programs leading to associate's and bachelor's degrees in business, computer science, electronics, engineering, and hospitality, and seemed to have the proper documentation from its government to operate. But in July 2000, the Web site was gone, and the telephone not answered. There had been an affiliation with the unaccredited American University of Hawaii.

Bell Isles College See: College of the Palm Beaches

Ben Franklin Academy and Institute for Advanced Studies Washington, D. C. They offered bachelor's, master's, and doctorates through correspondence study. "Deserving Americans" could request honorary doctorates, which required a donation. They claimed to be "not just another degree mill, but a fully accredited degree-granting institution." The accreditation was from the American Association of Accredited Colleges and Universities which we could never locate. The former address (P.O. Box 1776) and former phone number (USA-1776) were the best part; at least it shows they had influence somewhere in Washington.

Bentley Institute New Iberiia, Louisiana. At one time, registered with the Louisiana Board of Regents, but

"It's one thing for a new school to go belly up, but I think this is carrying the symbolism a bit too far."

apparently never accepted students, and no longer exists.

Berea School of Theology Letters to their address in Linton, Indiana returned as undeliverable.

Berean Christian College A correspondent writes that he sent money to this school at an address in Long Beach, California, but soon after his mail was returned and the phone was disconnected. No apparent connection with various other schools that start with the word "Berean."

Berkeley International University In 1993, advertisements in *The Economist* magazine described a distance-learning MBA, but a visit to this school's San Francisco office yielded only the information that their catalog was not yet ready, and some biographical information on members of "The Berkeley Group," many with degrees listed from various Russian universities. Less than a year later, the phones had been disconnected and they were gone.

Beta International University Apparently now out of business (letters to their Chicago address have been returned to sender), Beta was an evangelical Christian school that offered nonreligious degrees of all kinds, including law, by correspondence. Claimed accreditation from "Af Sep," an organization with which we are not familiar. No names were given in their newsprint catalog other than a "Dr. Ellis."

Beverly Law School California. Alternative law school, no longer around.

Bio Resonance University This university is accredited by the unrecognized and nonwonderful World Association of Universities and Colleges. We have been unable to find the university on the Internet, and they have not responded to the message we left three times on their answering machine in the Los Angeles area. (The World Association does not make the addresses of many of its accreditees available.)

Biscayne College See: Saint Thomas University

Blake College A reader asked for information on this school, which he said operated in both Mexico and Eugene, Oregon, but we have not been able to find a Blake College, other than the traditional one in London.

Board of Governors B.A. Degree Program Springfield, Illinois. This consortium plan offered nonresident B.A.'s through a number of Illinois schools; these schools are now offering the plans individually and the consortium apparently no longer exists.

Body Mind College Several letters to the Madisonville, Louisiana, address have been returned as undeliverable.

Borinquen University Medical School Mail to their last known address in Puerto Rico was returned as undeliverable; cannot locate.

Boulder Graduate School This unaccredited school in Boulder, Colorado, offered master's degrees in psychology and counseling and in health and wellness, emphasizing a balance between academic training and experiential learning. Formerly the Colorado Institute of Transpersonal Psychology. Now out of business.

Brentford University A school of this name was incorporated in Arizona in 2000. While we were able to find a Web site (*www.brentford-university.com*), none of the links on the site were operational.

Brighton University The "campus" was a mail box rental store called Mail Exchange, but in July 2000, they were gone, and the telephone was out of service. They had claimed to be a "Christian University of the United Congregational Church," with branch seminaries in China, Korea, and India. Brighton formerly used an address in Louisiana. Accreditation was claimed from the unrecognized Association of Christian Schools and Colleges. They claimed a sister-school relationship with Hong Kong Tak Ming College.

California Acupuncture College Letters to their address in Los Angeles were returned as undeliverable. They had been approved to grant degrees by the state of California.

California American University Formerly authorized by the State of California, but mail sent to their address in Escondido is returned as undeliverable and there is no listed telephone number. Had offered an M.S. in management involving a five-week summer session.

California Christian College of Los Angeles See: California Christian University

California Christian University Established in Los Angeles (later moved to Adelanto, California) by the Reverend Bishop Doctor Walter G. Rummersfield, B.S., Ms.D., Ps.D., GS-9, D.D., Ph.D.M., Ph.D., Ph.D., D.B.A., S.T.D., J.C.D., J.S.D. Formerly called California Christian College of Los Angeles. Honorary doctorates were awarded on payment of a donation of "$1,000 or less." Dr. Dr. Dr. Dr. Dr. Dr. Dr. Rummersfield apparently transferred control to new management in the 1980s. We found a telephone listing in Berkeley, California in 2000 but are not certain whether it is the same school.

California College of Commerce Letter to their Long Beach address returned marked "forwarding order expired."

California College of Law Formerly authorized by the State of California, but we have been unable to verify whether it's still in existence.

California College of the Natural Healing Arts See: Heartwood Institute, Ltd.

California Graduate School of Psychology See: American Schools of Professional Psychology, whom they became part of in 1998, moving from Corte Madera to Richmond, California.

California Institute of Electronics and Materials Science Hemet, Ca. This unaccredited school granted degrees at one time, but, as they put it "following some problems with the State of California," they stopped doing so.

California Institute of the Arts Valencia, California. This accredited school no longer offers its B.F.A. with up to 75% life-experience learning credit.

California Lakewood University While the name is charmingly American, this unrecognized Japanese institution apparently has no connection with America other than their membership in the unrecognized and nonwonderful World Association of Universities and Colleges. The Web site is registered to Hosoki Nobuyuki in Japan.

California Open University They were registered as a business in Hawaii as of May, 2000, but we could not find evidence of the school in California, Hawaii, or anywhere else.

California University for Advanced Studies In 1989 they lost their state authorization and closed their offices in Petaluma, California. The school maintained they were harassed out of existence. The state will not comment, other than to say that the school no longer met the requirements for authorization. Many enrolled students were allowed to complete degrees, but many others neither finished nor received refunds, and have been attempting unsuccessfully to locate University owner George Ryan. The "Roberta Bear" who was listed briefly as president is not known to either of us.

California University of Business and Technology Hacienda, California. All we know about this school at the moment is that they exist and are approved by the state of California. They seemed unwilling to provide more information by telephone, and do not have a Web site.

California University of Liberal Physicians A medical degree from this school was claimed by at least one practitioner who claimed to cure paralyzed people by rubbing them with a salve made from freshly-minced bull testicles. His pneumonia cure involved alcohol and red forest snails. We can find no record of this university ever having existed.

California Virtual University Began in 1998 by former governor Pete Wilson as California's answer to Western Governors University. The project lost steam when the venture's partners—California's three public college systems and the association of independent colleges—balked at the operating costs. The Web site, *www.california.edu*, still operates as a directory/search engine for online courses offered by California schools, but the university has gone out of business.

Cambridge University in America See: Thomas Jefferson Education Foundation

Campus-Free College See: Beacon College

Canarsie University Established in 1932 by the New York Mafia, for the sole purpose of fielding a football team, and making massive profits from gate receipts. Was there any truth to Joel Sayre's popular novel and movie Rackety Rax? Or was it all pure fiction?

Carthage College Kenosha, Wisconsin. Accredited school no longer offers its bachelor's with over 75% life-experience learning credit.

Central School of Religion This school, operating in England, the U.S., and Australia, has been identified as a degree mill by E&T. The school's dean, Mark Gretason, has written to express his unhappiness with this. However, we've also heard from the State of Indiana's Commission on Proprietary Education about their questions regarding the school (which has claimed a presence in Indiana). We remain curious about where, exactly, the school gets its degree-granting authority from, and welcome any information from readers that might help to clear this up.

Centro de Estudios Universitarios Xochicalco Cuernavaca, Mexico. There were actually two medical schools by this name: the original, which had recognized programs offered in conjunction with a school in Philadelphia, and the second, apparently an identical program started by a disgruntled faculty member of the first. Neither school is now in business.

Charles Dederich School of Law This unaccredited law school was operated by the Synanon Foundation. During the short time of their existence in Badger, California, they achieved an impressive success rate in bar exam passes, including 8 out of 9 one year.

Chase University Dr. Elmer P. Chase III sincerely attempted to start a university in various locations, most recently Kenner, Louisiana, but none of them got off the ground, and the effort has apparently been abandoned.

Chicago Conservatory College Offered accredited bachelor's and master's of music through evening study. Ceased operation in 1981.

Chirichua College We were asked about this school and asked for a catalog; they wrote back stating they had no printed brochures. The only contact for the school appears to be a P.O. Box. in Magdalena, New Mexico.

Christian Congregation, Inc. They used to issue honorary doctorates in divinity, in return for a donation. Donors were encouraged to be as generous as circumstances and conscience permitted. Mail to the last address we had, in Monroe, North Carolina, has been returned as undeliverable.

Christian University of Hawaii They were registered as a business in Kapaa, Hawaii, to "equip and/or instruct various education courses and endeavors [*sic*]." No listed telephone.

CIFAS School of Medicine Santo Domingo, Dominican Republic. This large Caribbean medical school, which primarily served Americans, was found to be offering a legitimate education through the front door and selling M.D. degrees for up to $27,000 out the back door. Several administrators went to prison for so doing.

Clayton Graduate School See: Clayton University

Clayton Institute of Technology See: Clayton University

Clayton Technical University See: Clayton University

Clayton University Operated for many years as a nonresident institution based in Clayton, Missouri. Shut down after the disappearance of its founder, Eugene Stone. American Coastline University has begun offering its degrees to students "left in the lurch" by Clayton's disappearance. For a few hundred dollars, these people can get either an ACU degree or one from the specially-created-for-this-occasion Clayton Graduate School, with a convenience address in Mobile, Alabama. According to the late Dr. Ray Chasse, who orchestrated the "new" Clayton, all board members earned their Ph.D.'s at Clayton (Missouri) and are part of a class action suit filed but not active because they cannot find founder Eugene Stone, who some readers have reported is still operating in Europe, Asia, and elsewhere. Original name: Open University, and later American International Open University.

Clinical Hypnosis Center Florida. Apparently once offered an alternative degree in hypnotherapy. Probably the same as the Gracie Institute of Hypnosis.

Clinical Psychotherapy Institute At one time, authorized by the state of California. Letters to their address in San Rafael, California are returned as undeliverable and there is no listed telephone number.

Colby-Sawyer College New London, New Hampshire. No longer offers its accredited evening-study B.S. for women.

Colegio Jacinto Trevino Mercedes, Texas. Offered a bilingual B.A. in interdisciplinary studies to Chicano students through evening programs and community service. Letters returned as undeliverable.

College for Human Services New York. A one-time unaccredited human services master's program, primarily for minority students.

College of Adaptive Education Sciences Inc. At one time registered with the Louisiana Board of Regents. Letters to their address in Baton Rouge were returned as undeliverable, and there is no listed telephone number. A reader informed us of a mailbox service address in Hawaii; another reader told us the school may be moving to Pompano, FL. But at presstime, we had not located it.

College of Clinical Hypnosis This Honolulu school used to offer a degree in clinical hypnosis through a $350 correspondence course. The founder and president "earned" his degree from Thomas A. Edison College, a notorious degree mill. They apparently closed in 1988.

College of Life Science See: American Health Sciences Institute

College of Oriental Studies This Los Angeles school used to offer bachelor's, master's, and doctorates in philosophy and religion, but they appear to have moved on.

College of Professional Studies The College of Professional Studies of the University of San Francisco apparently took on the international business programs that European University of America had run.

College of Racine Wisconsin. At one time offered a university without walls program.

College of the Palm Beaches West Palm Beach, Florida. Offered a B.A. and MBA through residential study, with a great deal of credit possible for prior experience. Unaccredited but licensed by the state. Declined to provide recent information. Formerly Bell Isles College, then University of Palm Beach. No listed telephone in late 2000.

Colorado Institute of Transpersonal Psychology See: Boulder Graduate School

Colorado Technical College Colorado Springs, Colorado. Used to offer a program through The Source, a computer correspondence system, but it was discontinued.

Commenius International University A 1981 article in Monato, an Esperanto-language magazine, featured an interview with the founder of this school, apparently located in San Diego. Mail addressed to the address given was neither answered nor returned as undeliverable, and there is no listed phone. The claim in the article that the university is "officially approved" by the state of California is not correct.

Common Wealth Institute See: Commonwealth International University

Commonwealth International University San Diego, CA. Purchased, in 1999, by the university consortium, Education America, Inc. (see listing in this chapter), which turned the school into its San Diego campus, renamed it Education America University, and discontinued any distance-learning degree programs. The same thing apparently happened with the Denver Business College, and Common Wealth Institute in Arizona.

Concordia International University This new university, located in Haabneeme, Estonia, offers the bachelor's degree and the MBA through residential study, in the English language, and is listed here only as a matter of reference, given their similarity in name to other schools, and the possibility that an online degree may be in their future. See also: Wisconsin International University.

Concoria Institute La Verne, California. They offered a B.A. in business administration, and claimed an affiliation with Nova College in Canada. The director's doctorate is from Elysion College, a now-closed California diploma mill.

Cooperating University of America Wilson, North Carolina. A retired professor at one time announced plans to establish a university by this name. The idea was to offer European students the opportunity to study in the U.S., in order "to prevent them from studying in Communist countries." We don't know if it ever happened, but it does not seem to be happening now, perhaps due to the lack of Communist countries to worry about. In October, 1993, a major Swiss news magazine, *Beobachter,* reported that a Swiss psychological school, the E.R. Schwank Institut, was offering the credentials of the C.U.A. of North Carolina.

Cornerstone University and Seminary of Hawaii The corporation was involuntarily dissolved in Hawaii in 1992. We are not certain whether there is a connection with American Cornerstone University, with a Hawaii name registration.

Coronado College of Financial Services The late Ray Chasse applied for California state approval for a school by this name. It appears that the project did not get off the ground before Chasse died.

Creative Development Institute Manila, Philippines. An American reader reports that he was awarded a Ph.D. by this Filipino school, based entirely on his career experience and writings, without having to go to the Philippines. He says many other such degrees have been awarded but we have not been able to locate the school.

Crestmont College At one time registered with the Louisiana Board of Regents, but letters to their address in Baton Rouge have been returned as undeliverable, and there is no listed telephone.

CSM Institute of Graduate Studies TASMAC, an unrecognized entity in Puna, India, which claims membership in the equally unrecognized and nonwonderful World Association of Universities and Colleges, states that they offer the bachelor's and master's degree programs of this institution, which quite possibly is the Canadian School of Management, which does hold recognized accreditation.

Cyberam University Also known as Universidad Medico Naturalista Hispano-America. Had offered degrees of all kinds, from psychology to music to astrology, for fees of $150 to $300. Apparently no longer in business.

Dartmoor University See: Thomas Jefferson Education Foundation

DeHostos School of Medicine Puerto Rico. Questionable medical school. Letters returned as undeliverable.

Denver Business College See: Commonwealth International University

Distance Learning University Ever since we learned of their existence, in 2000, as an accreditee of the unrecognized and nonwonderful World Association of Universities and Colleges, we have been trying to learn more about them, but we could no evidence of them on the Internet, and WAUC does not provide the addresses of many of their members, only their fax numbers. They have not responded to the fax we sent to Indonesia.

Doctor Yoshiro Nakamats World University of Advanced Studies They were registered as a business in Hawaii as of May, 2000, using an address in San Diego, California, but we could not find evidence of the school in Hawaii or California.

Donsbach University See: International University for Nutrition Education

Douglas University According to an ad we saw in the back of *Mother Jones* magazine, this school offers a Master's of Environmental Advocacy. However, the listed toll-free number is not in service, and our further attempts to track this school down have proved fruitless.

Duarte Costa University Years ago, this school was in business, operated by the Servants of the Good Shepherd. While the Servants were in Altoona, PA, the school was apparently in Missouri, but they declined to provide an address or telephone number. Bishop Duarte Costa left the Catholic church in 1945, in Brazil, to form his own church, in protest over the number of Nazis entering Brazil with Vatican passports.

East Coast University They offered master's and doctorates in many subjects, with literature identical to that of the National Graduate School, National College (see "Degree Mills" chapter), Roger Williams College, and National University. Their address was a residential hotel in St. Louis. When John asked for them there, the man at the desk acknowledged they got their mail there, but would say no more. They have used addresses in Mobile, Alabama; Tampa, Brooksville, and Dade City, Florida (also called Roger Williams College there), and Sweet Springs, Missouri. Recent mail to their various addresses has been returned as undeliverable. They claimed accreditation from the International Accredited Commission for Schools, Colleges, and Theological Seminaries, an unrecognized agency that was enjoined from operating by the state of Missouri.

Eastern Caribbean University They arose briefly in 1997 from their owner's town of Smithville, Texas although claiming to be on the island nation of St. Kitts. Their Web site featured master's and doctorates in an odd array of topics, including a James Bond-oriented master's, with courses like "The economic geography of Bond films." Even though they seemed never actually to exist other than their bizarre Internet site (now gone), they achieved full accreditation from the government of St. Kitts.

Ecumenical Institute of Seminary Studies Norwalk, California. This organization once sent John an honorary doctorate, and that's about all we know about them.

Eden University They were registered as a business in Hawaii (no address provided) as of May, 2000, but we could not find evidence of the school in that state, or anywhere else.

Edison University See: Acton Liberty University

Education America A large, for-profit consortium that has been buying up small schools all over the country, including Commonwealth International University, Remington College, and Denver Business College. Although some of the purchased schools had offered distance learning, Education America does not. However, at the time we went to press, their Web site—*www.educationamerica.com*—announced plans to introduce online programs in the future.

Eire International University On the literature of a new international accrediting association, Denis Muhilly, who has been involved with a number of nonwonderful (in our opinion) institutions, is listed as the President of Eire International University, allegedly located in Hawaii. There is no listed telephone number in the state of Hawaii. Dr. Muhilly has written us letters that we regard as extremely insulting.

Emmanuel College Oxford Oxford, England. The claim is made that degrees will be awarded solely on completion of a master's thesis (about 100 pages) or doctoral dissertation (about 400 pages) and payment of about $1,800. They have not responded to our inquiries, and we are concerned about the lack of telephone, the absence of names on any of the literature we have seen, and the spelling, several times, of "Ph.D." as P.hD." Somewhat reassuring is their policy of not asking for any money until a proposal has been approved and a faculty advisor assigned, as well as the note, typed onto their flyer, that they are not part of the University of Oxford, and have no Royal Charter.

Empire University They were registered as a business in Hawaii as of May, 2000, but we could not find evidence of the school in that state, or anywhere else. (No connection with an "Empire University" that provides wine information for a distributor named "Empire.")

E-School! International While we were researching this school, which offered high school–level distance-learning programs but was expanding into higher education, its Web site disappeared from the Internet and its phone number went out of service.

Escuela de Medicina Benito Juarez-Abraham Lincoln See: Escuela de Medicina Dr. Evaristo Cruz Escobedo

Escuela de Medicina de Saltillo Apparently defunct Mexican medical school.

Escuela de Medicina Dr. Evaristo Cruz Escobedo Saltillo, Mexico. Also known as Universidad Interamericana and Escuela de Medicina Benito Juarez–Abraham Lincoln, they were one of the more controversial Mexican medical schools, and, as such, received a lot of bad press. Now, they are gone.

Essenes Research Foundation San Diego, California. They have awarded Ph.D.'s through the Graduate School Consortium for the Religious Arts and Sciences. We have never been able to find an address or phone number for them.

Eubanks Conservatory of Music and Arts Los Angeles, California. This state-approved school offered bachelor's and master's programs in performance (classical or jazz) theory and composition, accompaniment, church music, and music history. In 1998, they informed us that they were no longer granting degrees.

Eula Wesley University Arizona, Louisiana. Unaccredited school was originally established in Arizona in founder Samuel Wesley's home, later moved to Louisiana. Wesley told an *Arizona Republic* reporter that his own doctorate has been earned from Eula Wesley, "After his thesis . . . was reviewed by members of the . . . board of directors," whom he identified as two local educators. Both denied ever being on the board, or conferring the degree. "They're lying," Wesley told the reporter. Then, according to the article, "Wesley later admitted . . . his degree was an honorary one, and had been awarded by . . . James Jenkins, an unemployed janitor, and Eula Wesley, Wesley's mother."

Eureka Foundation In 1996, a correspondent reported that "an open university known as the Eureka Foundation has commenced advertising in Australia." We have never been able to learn more about them.

Euro American International University They were registered as a business in Hawaii as of May, 2000, but we could not find evidence of the school in that state, or anywhere else.

European University of America They had offered a 10- to 14-month master's program in San Francisco, California, based around a major independent study project centering on international business, but that program is no longer offered, and none of their other offerings are nontraditional.

European University of Chinese Medicine They offer correspondence studies in Chinese medical philosophy and principles of diagnosis through the North American College of Acupuncture. At press time, the OnLine University portion of their Web site was "under construction," so we do not have information on the programs. The Web site is at *members.home.net/eucm2/statistics*, but the phone number given in Surrey, British Columbia, was not functioning in 2000.

Everett University They were registered as a business in Hawaii as of May, 2000 (no address provided), but we could not find evidence of the school in that state, or anywhere else.

Evergreen University At one time, they advertised heavily in southern California, offering a B.S. and M.S. in human services through courses that met once a month, on one full weekend day. According to a correspondent, the school was housed in a building calling itself the Alternative Education Learning Center, with no mention of the name Evergreen on it. In 2000, there was no listed telephone, and we could not find an Internet presence.

Excelsior University They were registered as a business in Hawaii as of May, 2000 (no address provided), but we could not find evidence of the school in that state, or anywhere else. Presumably unrelated to Excelsior College, the new name of Regents College, New York.

Faculté Libre de Médecine Lille, France. At one time, offered the first two years of medical school through the Catholic University of Lille, after which the student transferred to a school in his or her own country.

Federal State University They were registered as a business in Hawaii (no address provided) as of May, 2000, but we could not find evidence of the school in that state, or anywhere else. No connection, we assume, with a school of this name in Brazil.

Flaming Rainbow University Stilwell, Oklahoma. Flaming Rainbow University, an accredited Oklahoma university, officially closed its doors on February 18, 1992, thereby removing one of the more delightful university names from the arena.

Florida Green University In 1998 we received a fax announcing Florida Green University, incorporated in Delaware, with an office in Miami and its main campus in Karachi, Pakistan. We faxed back asking for more information but never got a response. Florida Green is listed as an accredited member on the Web site of the unrecognized and nonwonderful World Association of Universities and Colleges.

Florida Institute of Remote Sensing Offered correspondence programs and, apparently, a degree in this field, involving interpretation of aerial photos, and other technology. No longer in existence in Marianna, Florida as best we can determine.

Franconia College New Hampshire. At one time offered many experimental and innovative programs.

Frank Ross Stewart University System This Centre, Alabama university has offered some courses from time to time, all taught by Mrs. Stewart. Honorary doctorates have been offered to people who inquired about courses. Mrs. Stewart writes that "we do not find it attractive nor necessary" to be in this book. Well la-de-da.

Franklin and Marshall College Lancaster, Pennsylvania. This accredited school at one time offered an M.S. in physics entirely through evening study.

Free University John once saw a diploma—a huge, spectacular diploma—on a wall. It awarded the "Academic degree of Bachelor of Dentistry" of the Free University for the recipient's exploits on a geographical expedition. We have never been able to locate the university, which was part of the International Federation of Scientific Research Societies. Possibly the same Free U. identified as a diploma mill by E&T magazine.

Freedom College Colorado Springs, Colorado and Santa Ana, California. Established in 1957 by Robert LeFevre, a well-known libertarian author. Later renamed Rampart College. Destroyed by heavy rains (was this a message?) in 1965, reopened in 1968, and closed for good in 1975. Later, LeFevre became president of Southwestern University, an Arizona degree mill that was closed following an FBI investigation.

Freedom University Originally established in Florida, then moved to Albuquerque, New Mexico, this now-defunct school was, according to a correspondent, "put together by the local pagan/artist/martial arts/dancer types quite a number of years ago." No connection with the Freedom College in Colorado.

Freeman University Las Vegas, Nevada. We found them in a Las Vegas phone book, but can't find them in any school directory, nor have our letters to 4440 S. Maryland Parkway been answered.

Fremont College Officers of another university list doctorates from this school, which they say was or is in Los Angeles, but we can find no evidence of it. According to one correspondent, it may be the same as a defunct school founded in New Mexico some time in the 1940s, which went out of business following a dust-up with the state department of education.

Galatia University A correspondent saw an advertisement for this school, which he thinks was in Salem, Oregon, and wrote for a catalog. He received a postcard saying they were temporarily out, and would send one soon. Nothing more was heard, and he has lost the address.

George Washington University, Inc. Offered degrees at all levels, with little or no coursework, from a mailing service in St . Louis, MO. (Not to be confused, though perhaps that was intended, with the regionally accredited Washington University in St. Louis.) According to founder Egbert Phipps (see also Alternative Medicines Research Institute), George Washington University "was terminated in November of 1998." Phipps is now involved with Stanton University (Hawaii).

Gil Boyne Graduate School of Inspirational Healing See: University of Analytic Counseling

Girne American University The former University College of Northern Cyprus is now affiliated with the accredited Southeastern University in Washington, D.C., and indeed advertises itself as the "Girne Campus of Southeastern University," according to a reader in the area.

Global Citizen University A school of this name was incorporated in Arizona in 2000, and was "unveiled" as a "dream of the Divine Mother" in a ceremony at Sedona, Arizona in that year.

Global Crown University All we know about GCU is that they are members of the unrecognized and non-wonderful World Association of Schools and Colleges. WAUC does not provide the locations of many of their members, generally only fax numbers, but in this instance, we could not send a fax because their country was not identified, and a search of the Internet and our reference library proved fruitless.

Global Extension University An ad in *The Economist* stated GEU offers a unique modular MBA including interactive software with no entry requirements. But when we checked a few months later, neither the telephone in Mukilteo, Washington, nor the Web site was operating.

Global Focus University Unsolicited messages were posted on various newsgroups in 2000, announcing the establishment of this university. No information was provided, not even its location, other than that degrees at all levels in many fields were available by distance learning. These postings originated in Hungary. The Web site is only accessible by password, and we were not given one. The claim of being in the DETC accreditation process does not seem to be supported by the facts.

Global Virtual University They were registered as a business in Hawaii as of May, 2000, but we could not find evidence of the school in that state. We did find a school of this name on the Internet (*www.gvu.ac.nz*), ostensibly coming from New Zealand, but the information on founding faculty and teaching faculty was not available.

Gracie Institute of Hypnosis See: Clinical Hypnosis Center

Graduate School for Community Development At one time, authorized by the state of California. Letters to the address in San Diego have been returned as undeliverable, and there is no listed phone.

Graduate School of Patent Resources Washington, D.C. This unaccredited but legitimate school offered advanced study in patent-related matters for lawyers, engineers, and businesspeople, but has no active programs at this time.

Graduate School of the Suggestive Sciences El Cajon, California. They offered master's degrees and doctorates in what they called "Hypnoalysis," but letters have been returned as undeliverable.

Great Desert University A school of this name was incorporated in Arizona in 2000, but we could find no evidence of their existence, either on the Internet or in the real world.

Great Lakes Bible College No longer offers correspondence courses leading to a degree.

Green Field University A school of this name appears on the membership list of the World Association of Universities and Colleges, an unrecognized and non-wonderful accrediting agency, but with no contact information, and no clue as to where in the world they may be located.

Gulf States University Established in 1977 in South Carolina as Southeastern University. Moved to Louisiana a few years later. Offered doctoral programs requiring several weeks of summer residency in New Orleans. Following financial problems, the university closed in 1987. Many students who had not finished their degrees at the time transferred to the subsequently accredited University of Sarasota (or Argosy University).

Hallmark University An advertisement once ran in the Los Angeles Times offering a "University for sale" called Hallmark University. We could never find any evidence of its existence.

Hamburger University This is the training school for McDonald's. They have awarded the Doctor of Hamburgerology to graduates. Of course it's not a diploma mill; in fact, it has even been licensed to grant real associate's degrees. But we are mentioning it here because we are convinced that anything that can be misused will be misused (see Atlantic University, above, for instance).

Hanoi National University Hanoi National University (Dai Hoc Ngoai Ngu) is part of Vietnam National University and is accredited by the Ministry of Education. It was previously known as the Hanoi University for Teachers of Foreign Languages. They offer an M.A. in English and an M.A. in TESOL both through distance learning programs.

Harvard University (Hawaii) This clever name was reserved as a business name in Hawaii in 1995, but apparently not used.

Hassayampa University In 2000, we found them on a list of incorporated entities in Arizona, but we could not otherwise locate them.

Hawaii American University They were registered as a business in Hawaii as of May, 2000, but we could not find evidence of the school in that state, or anywhere else. Apparently not connected with American Hawaii University or American University of Hawaii.

Hawaii International University Honolulu. Apparently originated in California as American International University, then operated briefly from Hawaii, and administrator Diana Barrymore told us they would be moving to Iuka, Mississippi, but there is no listed telephone number there.

The Plumley Sisters, practicing for their final examination in the Sugar Ray Binkley Home Study Institute of Pugilism.

Hawaii Picpes University They were registered as a business in Hawaii as of May, 2000, but we could not find evidence of the school in that state, or anywhere else, nor do we know what a Picpes is.

Hawaii State University They were registered as a business in Hawaii as of May, 2000, but we could not find evidence of the school in that state, or anywhere else. Whatever it may be, it is certainly not a state university.

Hawaii University Established by William Onopolis of Ohio to award degrees to clients of his credit evaluation service, this school offered degrees at all levels, in a vast number of fields. Their "campus" was a Mail Boxes Etc. store in Honolulu, but they are no longer getting mail there.

Hawaii University of Linguistics They were registered as a business in Hawaii as of May, 2000, but we could not find evidence of the school in that state, or anywhere else.

Hawaii Yuin University They were registered as a business in Hawaii as of May, 2000, but we could not find evidence of the school in that state, although there is a Yuin University in California.

Hawthorne University (California) Hawthorne opened in the fall of 1982, offering degrees at all levels in general studies, with an emphasis at the master's level in humanistic computer studies. The school evolved from a formerly state-approved school named Paideia, now apparently alive but dormant in Berkeley. Indeed, seven of Hawthorne's 10 faculty members have their highest degree from Paideia. A letter sent to their last

known address in mid 1997 was returned "addressee unknown."

Headlands University Mendocino, California. At one time, they offered both residential and nonresidential programs, but they faded away.

Heartwood Institute, Ltd. Formerly awarded bachelor's and master's in health-related fields when it was known as California College of the Natural Healing Arts. Now offers certificate programs in massage therapy and alternative health fields, ranging from one-week intensives to year-long residencies. Accredited by the GAAP-recognized Accrediting Council for Continuing Education and Training.

Higher Education Research Institute Offered degrees at all levels in nutrition, health sciences, and other fields through home study from a "prestigious, chartered university." That school turned out to be the less-than-wonderful, unaccredited American State University, which typically offered applicants its degrees by return mail.

Highland University Athens, Tennessee. Once offered a 25-month Ed.D. program involving three four-week summer sessions with independent study in between. Now mail has been returned and there is no listed phone number in Athens. Originally chartered in North Carolina, moved to Sweetwater, Tennessee, then Athens.

Holistic Life University Flourished in San Francisco in the late 1970s and early '80s, but is no longer findable there. They offered coursework that they claimed could be applied to degree programs at Antioch, Redlands, and Sonoma State University.

Holy Cross Junior College Merrill, Wisconsin. When the original school of this name went bankrupt, others began offering a Ph.D. program in psychology or education, from the Institute of Learning of Holy Cross Junior College. After a newspaper exposé, holders of the degree (most of them school administrators and psychologists) maintained that they had done substantial work and truly earned their degrees. Critics disagreed, and the school faded away.

Horizon University (Canada) Established in Shelburne, Ontario, to offer off-campus degrees based on independent study, with credit for prior learning. Apparently a victim of a 1984 provincial law strictly regulating universities. At least, we cannot locate them now.

Horizon University (Utah) Provo. Here is a case where a large corporation takes a university name for its training programs, and awards what they call degrees on completion of certain courses. Ameritech is a very large company, and they offer what are undoubtedly useful courses in dealing with their Horizon system for library services. But the degrees are awarded on completion of one or more two-day courses. There is nothing wrong with this, other than the unfortunate nomenclature, since it offers the opportunity for people to say, "I have my degree from Horizon University," which is true but easily misinterpreted.

Horizon University of Theology They were registered as a business in Hawaii as of May, 2000, with a P.O. box address, to offer independent courses of studies through a Christian university.

Houston International University Houston, Texas. They sent a letter saying "Sorry, we are no longer a university." They had specialized in social work and public administration education for Hispanics and other international students for whom English was a second language. Original name was Hispanic International University.

Howard University International One of two schools that were listed on the Web site of the International University Accreditation Foundation, a phony accreditor invented by St. George University International (the other listed school). Howard University International's URL address (*www.howarduniversity.edu*) is defunct, and we can find no other evidence of the school's existence.

Huron International University At one time, they offered degrees at all levels, based on a very short residency and a learning contract approach. But in 2000, their phones had been disconnected and their Web site was no longer operational. Originally known as William Lyon University, then as American Commonwealth University. They had been accredited by ACICS (Accrediting Council for Independent Schools and Colleges), a recognized accreditor, but no longer. No apparent connection with the regionally accredited Huron in South Dakota.

Independence University (Missouri) In the mid-1950s, the National Association for Applied Arts and Sciences (an organization we'd never heard of) apparently established a credit bank similar to that of Excelsior College. From this evolved Independence, a degree-granting entity. But it is no more.

Independent University of Australia Morwell, Victoria. Identified as a diploma mill by E&T. However, we are persuaded by material sent by persons familiar with the school that it may have been a sincere attempt to establish an alternative university over the constant objections of the educational establishment. It survived from its founding in 1972 until the death of founder Ivan Maddern. Name changed to Independent Universal Academy after the government forbade use of the word "university."

Indiana Northern Graduate School of Professional Management Run from a small dairy farm in Gas City, Indiana, they once offered a Master of Professional Management degree, primarily through independent study, with some class meetings in various northern Indiana cities. Ceased operations in 1985. Originally called Indiana Northern University, but the "university" and the doctoral programs were dropped by agreement with the state of Indiana, which accredited the school. Run by the Most Reverend Bishop Dr. Gordon Da Costa, Ph.D., Ed.D., D.Sc., D.C., whose only earned degrees were from Indiana Northern, and who established several accrediting agencies which, in turn, accredited Indiana Northern. The school faded away following the Most Reverend's death.

Indiana Northern University See: Indiana Northern Graduate School of Professional Management

Inner City Institute for Performing and Visual Art The Institute, which awarded some degrees, is apparently temporarily closed, but they say they expect to reopen.

Institute for European Business Administration At one time, this Belgian school offered American students an MBA with emphasis on European business, through distance learning, with a five-week intensive residential program offered through the accredited George Mason University in Virginia. But we could not find IEBA on the Internet or on published lists of Belgian schools.

Institute for Information Management At one time, authorized to grant degrees by the state of California, but there is no longer a listed telephone number in Sunnyvale, California.

Institute for Management Competency San Francisco, California. An unaccredited but state authorized master's program has been discontinued.

Institute of Business Administration and Information Systems All we know about IBAIS is that they are members of the unrecognized and nonwonderful World Association of Schools and Colleges. WAUC does not provide the locations of many of their members, generally only fax numbers, but in this instance, we could not send a fax because their country was not identified, and a search of the Internet and our reference library proved fruitless.

Institute of Global Education Oregon. Offers peace- and spirituality-oriented courses broadcast by shortwave radio, but no degrees. Formerly University of the Air.

Institute of Human-Potential Psychology Palo Alto, California. Offered an external Ph.D. program for a while. Name then changed to Psychological Studies Institute but that, too, seems to have faded away.

Institute of Nutritional Science According to a correspondent, this school offered master's degrees and doctorates in nutrition through nontraditional programs, but a letter to their last known address in San Diego, California, came back stamped "attempted, not known."

Institute of Open Education Massachusetts. Once offered a fully accredited M.Ed. through two summer sessions and independent study for working teachers.

Institute of Paranormal Science Fremont, California. Announced the intention of offering a degree program in the early 1980s, but there is no evidence of them now.

Institute of Professional and Academic Equivalence
See: William Bradford University

Institute of Psychorientology This institution, a part of the Silva Mind Control organization, apparently has awarded degrees in the past. The only Web site we could find was in Swedish.

Institute of Science and Mathematics They have not responded to several requests for information about the nontraditional programs they have advertised, and there is no listed telephone in West Monroe, Louisiana.

Instituto de Estudios Iberamericanos Saltillo, Mexico. Offered bachelor's, master's, and doctorates, mostly to Americans, with a five-week summer session in Mexico plus independent study. No longer in operation.

Inter-American University (New York) While the Web site says mostly reasonable things, there is no mention of faculty, nor an explanation of why the telephone number is in New York but the fax number is in California. And there are phrases like: "Before an applicant for a Ph.D. degree is submitted to the Admissions Committee, he or she would have been found qualified to make such application by a Doctoral Committee, whose second function, if called upon, is to exam the candidate at the end of his or her studies to confirm the quality of the matriculation . . . " Accreditation is claimed from the International Council on Education and Development, an agency we cannot locate. A school of this name was registered in Hawaii in 2000.

International Academy of Philosophy Liechtenstein. Has not responded to several requests for information about their nontraditional programs. We could not locate them on the Internet, or in directories of European schools.

International American University (Turkey) North Cyprus. The Web site has been "under construction" for a very long time, and no literature was ever sent in response to our requests.

International College (California) Los Angeles. Alas, this intriguing idea did not survive. In ancient times, when John listed his favorite schools in this book, International College regularly made the top ten. They offered bachelor's, master's, and doctorates through private study with tutors worldwide, sometimes even in the tutors' homes. Apparently many of the well-known tutors (Lawrence Durrell, Yehudi Menuhin, Ravi Shankar, Judy Chicago, etc.) had very few (or no) students. After its demise, many of the students transferred to William Lyon University. No connection with the International College operating in Hollywood in 2000, apparently a language school that does not grant degrees.

International College of Arts and Sciences The college in Athens, Greece apparently has a connection with the University of Indianapolis, but they have not responded to several requests for information about their

nontraditional programs, and we cannot find them on the Internet.

International College of Natural Health Sciences United Kingdom. A recent letter to this organization, whose legality we'd never been entirely sure of, was returned marked "addressee has gone away."

International Commercial Management Institute A correspondent forwarded a transcript suggesting that this British school offered nonresident business degrees, but a letter to their address in Jersey was returned marked "gone away."

International East-West University They were registered as a business in Hawaii as of May, 2000, but no address was provided. The Web site (*www.iewu.edu*) suggests that it was established in Asia, and "is now in the process of applying for membership at regional accreditation." (The relevant regional accreditor, Western Association, reports that they have never heard of IE-WU.)

International Eastern Web University See: International East-West University

International Entrepreneurial Culture University They were registered as a business in Hawaii as of May, 2000, but we could not find evidence of the school in that state, or anywhere else.

International Free Protestant Episcopal University See: Saint Andrew's Collegiate Seminary

International Graduate School Established in St. Louis in 1980 as the doctoral-level affiliate of the then-accredited World University (Puerto Rico), offering the doctorate in business or education. They received candidacy for accreditation with the North Central Association in the remarkably short time of one year. However, the candidacy was withdrawn in late 1987, and in 1988 the school told the state of Missouri that it would be closing down.

International Graduate University They offered Ph.D. degrees in clinical psychology and behavioral science, through an affiliation first with American College of Switzerland and later with Florida Institute of technology, but no longer.

International Institutes of Science and Technology At one time registered with the Louisiana Board of Regents, but letters to them are returned as undeliverable, and there is no listed telephone number in Monroe, Louisiana.

International Japan University At one time, authorized by the state of California, but letters are undeliverable, and there is no listed telephone number in Orange, California.

International Open University (Louisiana) Baton Rouge. Has not responded to several requests for information about their nontraditional programs. The "campus" is a mailbox service called The Mailbox Incorporated.

International Pacific University They were registered as a business in Hawaii as of May, 2000, but we could not find evidence of the school in that state, or anywhere else. No apparent connection with either Pacific International University (Missouri and California), but possibly associated with Pacific International University, also a Hawaii-registered name.

International Studies in Humanistic Psychology In the 1970s they offered a nonresident Ph.D. in their field, from Cotati, California.

International University (California) Pasadena. A now-dormant unaccredited school that may or may not have had some ties to Southland University and/or its founder, James Kirk.

International University (Hawaii) In 1997, this clever name was reserved in Hawaii, no address provided, as the intended name of a "milti-national [sic] consortium." In 2000, we could not locate it.

International University at Torrey Pines San Diego, CA. Renamed Commonwealth International University before it was purchased, in 1999, by the university consortium, Education America, Inc., which turned the school into its San Diego campus, renamed it Education America University, and discontinued any distance-learning degree programs.

International University for Nutrition Education They operated for years under this name and, earlier, Donsbach University. In July 2000, we were unable to find the university, either at its most recent location in Chula Vista, California, or anywhere else. (It had previously operated from Huntington Beach and Concord, California, and registered as a corporation in Hawaii at 4917 Ali Ali Road, Kapaa 96746.) At one time, they were authorized to operate by the state of California.

International University "Nicholas Doubrowa" All we know about this school (not listed in the International Handbook of Universities or other standard directories) is that it is located in Santiago, Chile. A letter sent to the last known address was returned as undelivcerable.

International University of America Had offered degrees at all levels in business administration. Offered programs in Hong Kong and Paris as well. Admitted a large number of students from overseas, particularly from France, where its advertising stressed its California state approval. Returning to France, graduates from IUA had problems finding jobs; their complaints led to an expose in *Le Figaro* (a French newsweekly). The school could no longer be found at its San Francisco address or telephone number in 1998.

International University of America School of Management We have been unable to locate this university, which has been accredited by the World Association of Universities and Colleges, an unrecognized and nonwonderful agency. WAUC only provides the fax numbers for many of its accreditees, not their locations. Our fax to this school (presumably in France) was never answered, and we could not locate IUASM on the Internet.

International University of Applied Arts & Sciences At one time registered with the Board of Regents of Louisiana, but letters are returned as undeliverable, and there is no listed telephone in New Orleans.

International University of Kyrgyzstan The IUK is a member of the unrecognized and nonwonderful World Association of Universities and Colleges. Despite many attempts, we were unable to open their Web site at *www.iuk.kg*, and we received no response to a fax we sent.

International University of the Americas (Costa Rica) We have read about this new institution, offering podiatrists the opportunity to earn an M.D. with ten months in Costa Rica and another year of study in the U.S., but have been unable to find an address or telephone.

International University of the Americas (Hawaii) They had been registered as a business in Hawaii using a mailbox service address, but the corporation was involuntarily dissolved in 1996. No apparent connection with any of the dozens of other International Universities.

International University of Vienna This evangelical Christian school was apparently founded in 1980 in Nashville, Tennessee, as European Christian College, and then opened in Austria by its founder, Christian missionary Otis Gatewood. It apparently operates as an American-style bible school in Europe, with additional sites in Spain and in the Ukraine.

Internet University Another school from the late Ray Chasse of American Coastline University. According to him, the Internet University is a "place," not an entity as such. But whatever it may have been, it appears to be no more.

Iowa Commonwealth College The Iowa State Coordinating Committee for Continuing Education at one time hoped to develop an external degree program by this name, but it never came to pass.

Irvine College of Business This unaccredited school never responded to requests for information about their nontraditional programs, and in 1998 a letter sent to their last known address—not surprisingly, in Irvine, California—was returned as undeliverable.

Jakarta Institute of Management Studies JIMS claims its accreditation from the unrecognized and nonwonderful World Association of Universities and Colleges. We were unable to learn about them through the Internet, and our fax to (506) 652 4281 was not answered.

James Tyler Kent College of Homeopathic Medicine Offered a five-year program in homeopathic medicine, from Phoenix, Arizona, but mail was returned and there is no listed phone in Phoenix. A correspondent wrote to us that they might have relocated to Argentina.

Jamilian University Full-page advertisements in *Omni* magazine (and that ain't cheap) in 1987 and 1988 heralded the arrival of Jamilian University of Reno, Nevada, in which a "much-talked-about but little known group of mystics is offering to share" the "age old secrets for prolonging life and expanding intelligence." We chose not to invest $25 in the admissions package and they chose not to send us a catalog, so you will have to learn the secrets for yourself, if you can find them.

Japan Aeronautical University of America They were registered as a business in Hawaii as of May, 2000, to operate an "educational business at college level," but we found no evidence of them at their registered address of 212 Merchant St., #303, Honolulu, HI 96813. Alternative address in Sacramento, California, under the name of Parasec, Inc.

Jean Ray University A reader inquired about this school, allegedly in Namus, Belgium, from which a prominent person in his community had claimed a doctorate, but we can find out nothing about it.

Jefferson College of Legal Studies At one time registered with the Board of Regents of Louisiana, but letters to their address are returned as undeliverable, and there is no listed telephone in Gretna, Louisiana.

Jefferson United University They were registered as a business in Hawaii as of May, 2000, but we could not find evidence of the school at the Honolulu address.

John Rennie University At one time, authorized by the state of California, but letters are returned as undeliverable, and there is no listed telephone in Irvine, California.

Johnson University They were registered as a business in Hawaii as of May, 2000, but we could not find evidence of the school in that state, or anywhere else.

Joseph E. Spot University They were registered as a business in Hawaii as of May, 2000, but we could not find evidence of the school in that state, or anywhere else.

Juarez-Lincoln Bilingual University Letters to the address we had in Austin, Texas were returned as undeliverable.

Julius Caesar University The Internet site is not very informative, although it is possible to enroll online (on payment of a $5 fee) for their only degree, a master's in leadership. JCU identifies itself as "the premier institution providing a classical education. Julius Caesar University is dedicated to molding today's slackers into tomorrow's leaders." We are not sure where they are located, but the Web site is registered to the same Fremont, CA, address as that of the Association of Virtual Universities, Colleges, and Schools, an unrecognized accrediting agency.

Justice University Justice University was begun by a former professor from Lincoln Law School in Sacramento named S.L. Roullier and had a part time law school. A letter sent to their last known address in Roseville, California was returned in 1998, and the phone has been disconnected.

Kairos College New Mexico. Never responded to several requests for information about their nontraditional programs; the latest letter to their last-known address was returned "attempted, not known."

Kansai Gadai University They were registered as a business in Hawaii as of May, 2000 with the local address of 5257 Kalanianaole Hwy., Honolulu, HI 96821.

Keichu Technological Institute Registered with the Louisiana Board of Regents in 1988, but mail to the registered address is returned as undeliverable, and there is no listed phone. President Karl Marx was affiliated with Andrew Jackson University, formerly of Baton Rouge.

Keltic University A reader in England inquires about Keltic University, but letters to 3 Vicarage Close, Kirby Muxloe, Leicestershire have not been answered. There is certainly no recognized school by this name in England.

Kensington College A state-approved business college in Santa Ana, California, apparently not degree-granting, not to be confused with Kensington University (which operates from California despite a Montana address) or Kensington College in London.

Kernel University They were registered as a business in Hawaii as of May, 2000, for the purposes of offering degrees through the doctoral level, but their listed phone was not in service.

Kobe Womens University They were registered as a business in Hawaii as of May, 2000, but we could not find evidence of the school in that state. There is such a school in Japan.

Korey International University They were registered as a business in Hawaii as of May, 2000 (no address provided), but we could not find evidence of the school in that state, or anywhere else, although there is apparently a connection with Edward Korey, founder of the Canadian School of Business, Northland Open University, and several other schools.

Kripalu Institute Summitt Station, Pennsylvania. They offered a master's in humanistic studies. There was a connection with an International University in Kayavorahan, India but the phone is disconnected and mail is returned as undeliverable.

Krisspy University We have been sent a transcript showing a master's degree from Krisspy University of Bayamon, Puerto Rico, but cannot locate such a school. (Is it possible they merged with Rice University?)

LA International University Louisiana. This school offered unaccredited nonresidential doctorates in many fields, but a letter sent to their last known address (a secretarial service in New Orleans) was returned marked "forwarding order expired."

La Jolla University At one time offered unaccredited student-directed degrees at all levels. The academic model was changed from time to time, sometimes involving a short residency, sometimes not. There once arose a La Jolla University with a New Orleans address that was associated with Denis Muhilly, who has been involved with more than a few nonwonderful schools. Also involved was Waldo Bernasconi, later to establish the unrecognized APICS accrediting agency in Europe. At the time, various parties maintained that the Louisiana La Jolla was the one true school while others suggested it was a renegade effort to transfer California students to another entity without their permission. Before we could sort it all out, all the La Jollas had faded from the scene.

LaSalle Extension University This huge correspondence university, owned by the Macmillan Publishing Company of New York, discontinued operations in 1982, not long after losing their accreditation from the National Home Study Council (now the Distance Education and Training Council). The Federal Trade Commission took them to task for overly aggressive selling techniques. No connection with LaSalle University, in either Philadelphia or Louisiana.

Lawyer's University In late 1987, a law officer was trying to locate a school of this name, possibly in Florida or Los Altos, California. We could find no trace.

Leadership Institute of Seattle Offers a B.S. completion program and a master's in applied behavioral science, with a focus on leadership, training, and organization management, through an association with the accredited Bastyr University.

Leland Stanford University Baton Rouge, Lousiana. Established by friends of a Louisiana state official, who hadn't believed him, when he told them how easy it was to become a legal Louisiana institution. It apparently never accepted students or awarded degrees, but the point was clearly made.

Life Science Institute See: American Health Sciences Institute

Lincoln Graduate School See: Lincoln University of the U.S.A.

Lincoln International University They were registered as a business in Hawaii as of May, 2000 (no address provided), but we could not find evidence of the school in that state, or anywhere else, nor any connection with the dozen-or-so other schools with "Lincoln" in the name.

Lincoln University (New Guinea) The degrees were based on writing up to 10 papers in a given field. Established in Arizona when that state had no school laws, it later moved to London, England, in 1987, where the address was a mail-forwarding service, and then to New Guinea. The university's founder seems to be a sincere scholar and, indeed, Lincoln may have achieved some level of acceptance. Claimed alumni included the head of government for the kingdom of Lesotho, and the former minister for education and culture in Ghana.

Lincoln University Graduate School See: Lincoln University of the U.S.A.

Lincoln University of the U.S.A. Des Moines, IA. When we last checked in (June 2000), we were told that Lincoln University is no longer accepting students to its unaccredited MBA program while the owners reassess the future of the school. Had been operating from the same address as Barrington University, but there is apparently no connection other than using the same secretarial service address.

Linfield College Oregon. At one time, this accredited school offered bachelor's programs in which up to 80% of the necessary units could come form a combination of assessment of prior learning and equivalency exams; this option apparently no longer exists.

London International College This British entity had offered degrees in cooperation with the unaccredited Andrew Jackson University College of Louisiana and, later, Maryland.

"The best part of doing my degree by distance learning is that no one complains when I smoke in class!"

Lone Mountain College At one time this then-regionally-accredited college offered an external master's in psychology. The college was absorbed into the University of San Francisco, but the external degree did not survive.

Los Angeles College of Law See: Van Norman University

Los Angeles Institute and Society for Psychoanalytical Studies California. At one time, this unaccredited organization offered graduate degrees in psychoanalytic fields to licensed mental health professionals via resident programs. A letter to their last known address, in 1997, was returned stamped "unable to forward."

Los Angeles Psychosocial Center A letter requesting information was returned to sender, and there is no listed telephone in Los Angeles.

Los Angeles University In an earlier edition, we noted that the University had not responded to three requests for information on their programs. Finally, Director D. E. Brimm did respond, by demanding that we say nothing about his university. Since we know nothing about it, other than that it is unaccredited and the address is an unmarked home in a residential neighborhood at 6862 Vanscoy, Los Angeles 91605, there is nothing we can say.

Louisiade International University They were registered as a business in Hawaii as of May, 2000 (no address provided), but we could not find evidence of the school in that state, or anywhere else.

Louisiana Central University At one time they were registered with the Louisiana Board of Regents, but letters have been returned as undeliverable, and there is no listed telephone in Metairie, Louisiana.

Louisiana Christian University They never responded to our requests for information about their nontraditional programs and, in 1997, a letter sent to their last known address in Lake Charles, was returned stamped "forwarding order expired."

Louisiana International University Inc. At one time they were registered with the Louisiana Board of Regents, but letters have been returned as undeliverable, and there is no listed telephone in New Orleans, Louisiana.

Louisiana Pacific University Louisiana Pacific was established in Louisiana in 1989, then had an Iowa address, then Hawaii, and now, it seems, oblivion. The phone number on the quarter-page Web site was not operational. They also claimed affiliations with several business colleges in Barcelona, Spain, whose graduates earned the Louisiana Pacific degree following residential study in Spain.

Louisiana University of Medical Sciences This unaccredited school never responded to requests for information about their nontraditional programs, and in early 1998 a letter sent to their last known address in Baton Rouge, Louisiana was returned as undeliverable.

Loyola College This regionally accredited school once offered a B.S. in nursing for RNs with only two days on campus; this program has been discontinued, and while the school exists, they offer only more traditional weekend and evening programs.

Loyola Southwestern University A caller insisted that there is a school by this name in Baton Rouge, Louisiana, but neither we nor the authorities in Louisiana have heard of it or can find it.

Lyle University Operated for a while in the mid-1980s from New Orleans and Metairie, Louisiana, offering bachelor's, master's, and doctorates at $750 for a complete program. Started by a Columbia Pacific University graduate, and quite similar in approach to Columbia Pacific's early model. No longer registered with the Louisiana Board of Regents, and not findable on the Internet, therefore presumably no longer in business.

Magna Carta University At one time, an alternative California law school, no longer around.

Manoa University of Hawaii They were registered with the state of Hawaii in May, 2000, but there was no listed phone or findable Internet site. While the University of Hawaii's main campus is at Manoa, there would appear to be no connection.

Manx University In 1987, there was an announcement that a university by this name was to open on the Isle of Man in 1992. A multimillion-pound fundraising appeal was said to have begun, and anyone making a donation, however small, was to become a trustee of the university, at least for a while. The people behind the endeavor chose to remain anonymous, and we can find no evidence that the school ever opened.

Marquis Guiseppe Scicluna International University Foundation In an earlier edition, John wrote that in 1987 the Universal Intelligence Data Bank (of Independence, Missouri) had written to businessmen in Asia offering them an honorary doctorate from this institution, on receipt of a $500 payment. Baron Marcel Dingli-Attard, of the Foundation (who also has had a connection with International University in Missouri), has assured us that the offer was only made to a limited number of people, not necessarily in Asia (an Internet search found several, including President Maumoon Gayoom of the Maldives) and, in any event, is no longer being made. Our apologies for the incorrect statements made earlier.

Mashdots College This state-approved school had offered undergraduate liberal-arts programs centering on Armenian language and culture. However, a letter sent to their last-known address, in Pasadena, California, came back as undeliverable, and when we phoned in mid-2000, the phone was answered, "Hello."

Maxipoint University This school appeared on the scene in 1999, apparently connected to Australia. The agent who handled their incorporation in South Dakota was "outraged" when he learned that Maxipoint (as well as Hoover University and Monticello University) was listing his address as the location of their campus. He tells us Maxipoint is run from Croatia by Goran Pinjusic, who is also involved with a number of other, um, unusual Internet activities. Maxipoint's responding email to our May 2000 inquiry was "We are not in the active status."

McDonough 35 Prep/Bernadean University At one time registered with the Louisiana Board of Regents, but letters have been returned as undeliverable and there is no listed telephone number in New Orleans. We don't know what the name means. Bernadean University is described elsewhere.

Medicina Alternativa Institute See: Open International University for Complementary Medicine

Mellen Research University Apparently a predecessor of Mellen University (described elsewhere), it operated from San Francisco, but never granted degrees. Mail to their address is returned as undeliverable, and there is no listed telephone.

Mensa University A correspondent reports that Mensa, the international organization for people with high IQs, was at one time associated very briefly with a Maryland university.

Meridian University A private, nonprofit religious institution affiliated with the Buddhist Theosophical Society, Meridian at one time offered degrees at all levels, based on prior coursework, credit for "documented personal achievement," examinations, and the school's own upper-division courses. They are apparently out of business, as mail has been returned and the phone in Lafayette, Louisiana, has been disconnected.

Metropolitan University Operated in Glendale, California in the 1950s, apparently quite legitimately, offering degrees with substantial life-experience credit. Long gone.

Mid-Valley College of Law Van Nuys, California. An unaccredited, and now defunct, law school.

Midway Baptist College The San Diego, California–based Midway Baptist Church at one time operated an unaccredited college, but no longer does so.

Millikin University This accredited school no longer offers degrees through its Evening Division.

Mirus University An offshoot of The Teaching Company, which produces and markets the "Superstar Teachers" tapes that are advertised in many magazines, Mirus University was formed to offer bachelor's and master's degree programs in liberal studies, built around these taped lectures from famous professors at universities such as Harvard, Yale, etc. It was an interesting experiment, but one that failed. Student enrollment lagged, and the parent company folded the business before the university got the DETC accreditation it had been seeking.

Miskatonic University A fake diploma, purportedly from this nonexistent school, appeared in *Masskerade,* a humor magazine published in 1983 by the Massey University Students' Association in New Zealand. Once again, though it was clearly a joke, you never know when these things will pop up. Probably the same general geneaology as Myskatonic University.

Mission Institute of Distance Education Distance-learning degree programs designed for students living in China. Before it was taken down, their Web site (*www.mission-institute.org*) claimed that every accepted student would have the chance to study abroad at the school's campus on the island of Cyprus and that "once you obtain a degree, you possess good qualifications for applying for Canadian permanent residence." When we called to request a catalog for more information, we were told that their brochures are out of date and that any inquiries should be directed to their email address, *mission@asiavsat.com*. They have asked not to have a regular listing in this book, and we are glad to oblige.

Missouri Central College Letters are returned and there is no listed telephone number in Clayton, Missouri. This unaccredited school's 10-page catalog had dedicated two pages to a misrepresentation of the Sosdian-Sharp study. There were no listed faculty and no listed telephone.

Modern American University They were registered as a business in Hawaii as of May, 2000, but we could not find evidence of the school in that state, or anywhere else. (We did, however, locate an interesting contrarian book called *The Modern American University,* by Malvolio Ruttledge.)

Mole Ltd. University Louisiana. Created as a joke, and to prove how easy it is to start a university, by entrepreneur C. Denver Mullican, this school granted exactly two degrees (doctorates, to Mullican's two dogs—whose characters, he claims, were greatly improved by the credentials). Still, he tells us that he received numerous letters from people offering money for the degrees, including $200 from a man in Malaysia who offered to sell the degrees and cut Mullican in for $100 each. He sent the money back. Thus, if you run into anyone claiming a degree from this university, and they're not a dog, something fishy is almost certainly going on.

More University California. Once offered unaccredited degree programs. Now, the descendant of this organization offers "personal enrichment" programs in sensuality, communication, and lifestyle under its original name, Lafayette Morehouse.

Morgan State College At one time, they offered a nontraditional degree program for urban African Americans, focusing on "black perspective and minority group problems," but no longer does so.

Mount Saint Joseph's College At one time, they offered accredited bachelor's degrees in which over 50% of credit could come from prior learning.

Mundelein College This independent, traditional school, in operation since 1929, had offered a bachelor's in which up to 75% of credits could be earned through assessment. However, in 1993, their programs were absorbed by Loyola University of Chicago.

Mundi Causa Global University In 1996, we received an email from Eberhard Weber, president of the Mundi Causa Society of Fresno, California, and a self-styled "pragmatic aspirationalist," proclaiming the establishment of a new campus-based university that is intended to differ from traditional universities in that "personal and principled initiative and commitment [will replace] organizational and procedural rigor." Four years later, we could find no evidence of the university.

Myskatonic University Chaosium Publishing, which comes out with role-playing games based on H.P. Lovecraft's Cthulu mythos stories, has offered bachelor's, master's and doctoral degrees in medieval metaphysics from Myskatonic University in Arkham, Mass. These are provided as novelties, and have never been suggested as real degrees.

Naif Arab Academy for Security Sciences NAASS is one of the largest Arab security and police academies, occupying a $250 million campus near Riyadh, Saudi Arabia, and the Chairman of their board is HRH Prince Naif ibn Abdulazin al-Saud, the Saudi Minister of the Interior. However, they are members of the non-wonderful and unrecognized World Association of Universities and Colleges.

Nasson University In mid-2000, we could no longer locate this institution. Their phone had been disconnected, their campus (a secretarial service called Answering-Mobile in Alabama) was gone, and their Web site was gone. Nasson had had the same address as the University of the United States (also gone). The mail that we and others got in the late 90s was postmarked Rhode Island, where Chancellor Edward Mattar lived. Nasson College was a regionally accredited school in Maine, which went out of business some years ago. Edward Mattar, who had no connection to Nasson College, opened up Nasson University shortly thereafter. The Nasson College alumni have officially expressed concern over having to deal with Nasson University to get their transcripts. Nasson College offered nonresident degrees at all levels in fields ranging from dance to astronomy.

National Christian University There was once one located in Richardson, Texas and another in Dallas. Then some ads appeared for the National Christian University of Missouri, but one was to write to the dean of theology in Oklahoma City. A National Christian also appears on the Council of Europe's list of degree mills. An Internet search found no evidenceof them.

National College for the Natural Healing Arts Birchdale, Minnesota. Offered programs leading to bachelor's, master's, and doctorates in naprapathy, reflexology, iridology, homeopathy, acupuncture, cancer research, and so forth, possibly through nonresidential study. Mail has been returned and there is no listed phone number in Birchdale.

National College of Education At one time, they offered an accredited bachelor's degrees in which up to 75% of credit could come from prior learning.

National Graduate School See: East Coast University

National Radio Institute A reader tells us they once offered nonresident degrees in business management and accounting from a Washington, DC, location and had accreditation, but we can find no evidence of them.

National University (Missouri) See: East Coast University

National University of America This unaccredited school apparently offered degrees at all levels in business-related fields, from a Missouri "campus" address that is a secretarial service used by a number of other "universities." In 2000, the telephone was out of service, and we could find no Internet presence.

New World College They once offered unaccredited degrees at all levels; mail to their last known address was returned marked "not for this address." As the school never had a listed phone, we couldn't call to follow up.

NewAmerica University Their Web site (now apparently defunct) talked of the development of not-yet-existing technologies which can be found in "futuristic literature." Through a method of "condensed learning," degrees can be earned in greatly reduced time. Apparently some kind of connection to the Principality of New Utopia. See: International University of Advanced Studies

Nobel University They registered as a business in Hawaii in the early 1990s, but the corporation was involuntarily dissolved (or, possibly, blown up) in 1995. We don't know if they ever awarded degrees. Founder Franklin Burroughs had been involved in the founding of the dreadful World Association of Universities and Colleges.

Nomad University Based in Seattle, they pesented public classes for groups of 500 or more in cities worldwide, but did not seek accreditation or grant degrees because "education should be for discovery, not for approval." The first three courses were $25 each, and you were not told what they will be; you'd simply pay and then go. It was all rather charming, but they seem to have folded their tents and moved on.

Norfolk State University They apparently once offered an external master's degree in communication.

North American College of Law Apparently this school once offered nontraditional law programs, but that's all we know, as a letter sent to their last known address was returned as undeliverable, and there is no listed telephone in La Mirada, California.

North American College of Naprapathic Medicine A reader told us of this school, apparently operating out of the founder's home in Waldron, Arkansas while waiting for state approval. There is no listed telephone in Waldron.

North American Colleges of Natural Health Science San Rafael, California. Offered professional career education in holistic natural health sciences. Mail has been returned; no listed telephone. Formerly called Airola College.

North American University (Hawaii) They were registered as a business in Hawaii as of May, 2000, but we could not find evidence of that school at the given address.

North Continental University They have used a P.O. box in Santa Rosa, California, and at one time they put on demonstrations of sacred dance, but they were not state-approved and our inquiries have never been answered.

Northwest University of Metaphysics A school of this name was listed as the source of a degree for a faculty member at a traditional school, but we have not been able to locate it.

Nova Land University A correspondent reported an encounter with someone claiming a Ph.D. from this institution, but we haven't been able to find any other trace of its existence.

Occidental Institute of Chinese Studies A quote from their Web site says it all: "The Occidental Institute of Chinese Studies (O.I.C.S.) was an acupuncture school started in 1972 in Toronto, Ontario, and a few years later in Montreal, Quebec, Canada. At one time the O.I.C.S. had an enrollment of some two thousand students through out the English speaking world via a unique Extension Training (Home Study) Program. The Institute was eventually branded by the authorities as an 'illegal medical school' (even though acupuncture itself had not been defined as the practice of medicine), and the O.I.C.S. along with its staff relocated to Miami, Florida.... After three years in Miami, the Board of Directors decided to relocate the Alumni Association to California, because of a healthier climate for acupuncture and the licensing of acupuncture schools. Ironically, while loading the moving vans, the State of Florida served them with a 'duces tecum' subpoena demanding (among other things) all of the membership records, and contending that they were in actuality an acupuncture school....Fortunately, all those membership records were already on their way to California, and Florida later dropped the matter..." In California, they operated through an affiliation with the Universal Life Church, and then, in 1984, moved to Canada, where they carry on the same work.

Ocean University At one time they were authorized to grant law and other degrees in California, but no longer. Operated from addresses in Lancaster and Santa Monica. Apparently unconnected with a school of the same name in Taiwan.

Ohana Honua University This Hawaii-registered school was involuntarily dissolved in 1991.

Oklahoma Baptist University Shawnee, Oklahoma. At one time, they offered a Bachelor of Arts in Christian studies through a wholly nonresident program, but that has apparently been discontinued.

Old Pueblo University In 2000, we found them on a list of Arizona incorporations, but could not locate the university.

One Institute of Homophile Studies See: One Institute of Human Relations

One Institute of Human Relations At one time, they offered study in many aspects of male and female homosexuality and a state-approved graduate degree in homophile studies, but in 2000, there was no listed telephone in Los Angeles, and we could not locate them on the Internet.

Open International University for Complementary Medicine Columbo, Sri Lanka. We can't seem to find out much about this institution, but what we do know is troubling: 1) It is not an accredited medical school in Sri Lanka, and 2) in the '90s a New Jersey school called Wellington University was offering to sell OIU's M.D. degree for $1,000. Although many people and institutions in the world of natural medicine claim degrees and/or affiliations with OIU, we have been unable to reach the school itself for comment. Also known as Medicina Alternativa Institute.

Open University (Florida) They offered a bachelor's and a master's degree in entrepreneurship that can be completed either in residency or at a distance, but in 2000, they were no longer at the phone number in Orlando, Florida, and the Web site was inoperative.

Orange University of Medical Sciences A major article in the *Los Angeles Times* in 1982 announced the highly controversial impending opening of this investor-owned for-profit medical school. We've often wondered what happened, but haven't been able to find out.

Oregon Institute of Technology This accredited school no longer offers any sort of nontraditional program.

Osaka University of Economics and Law USA This large and traditional Japanese university was registered as a business in Hawaii in 2000, using a convenience address but not, as best we could tell, actually operating there.

Oxford College of Pharmacy In 2000, the Web site (*www.delmarapply.com*) of this Del Mar, California, organization reported that the educational programs of OCP were being "restructured" and were not currently available. They continue, however, to sell their surfboards and skateboards on the Internet.

Oxford Oriental Medical Mission University of Hawaii They were registered as a business in Hawaii as of May, 2000 "for training of individuals to improve and develop their capabilities..." Their address is an apartment house; we found no evidence of a university there.

Pacific Baptist University They had been a state-approved school, but in 2000, there was no listed telephone number in Norwalk, California, and we could not locate them on the Internet.

Pacific Coast University Registered with the Louisiana Board of Regents at one point, but mail to them is returned as undeliverable, and there is no listed telephone in Baton Rouge. Mark Zeltser was the man behind it. Also registered in Hawaii (where the campus is a mail forwarding service) at 415 Dairy Road E247, Hahului, HI 96732.

Pacific College of Oriental Medicine Approved by the state of California to award degrees, but they appear to do nothing in the way of nontraditional degrees; rather, a four-year on-campus master's, in San Diego, and in Illinois.

Pacific Institute for Advanced Studies At one time they were authorized by the state of California, but letters have been returned as undeliverable and there is no listed telephone in Studio City.

Pacific International University (California) At one time, they were authorized to grant degrees by the state of California. They did not respond to three requests for information about their programs. Almost certainly unrelated to the Pacific International University that operated from Hollywood, California, at least through 1964, offering correspondence and residential degrees in science and engineering.

Pacific International University (Hawaii) They were registered as a business in Hawaii as of May, 2000, but we could not find evidence of an operating school. May or may not be connected with the International Pacific University, also a Hawaii-registered name. The address is the same as that used by Greenwich University in Hilo, Hawaii.

Pacific National University Formerly located in Hollywood, California. Originally called American Medical Institute, this school trained doctors in traditional Chinese medicine, but went dormant after the founder, David Chiu, returned to mainland China. For a while, transcripts were obtained from Ray Chasse's University Services in Mobile, Alabama, but since Chasse's death in 2000, it is uncertain what has happened to the service.

Pacific Rim University They were registered as a business in Hawaii as of May, 2000, but we could not find evidence of the school in that state, or anywhere else.

Pacific School of Nutrition They offered correspondence programs leading to certification as a nutritionist and/or herbologist, through written tutorial. Mail to their last-known address is returned as undeliverable, and there is no listed telephone in Ashland, Oregon.

Pacific States University Los Angeles, California. Offered state-approved degrees in a number of fields, but has discontinued its correspondence program.

Pacific University of Hawaii Registered in Kihei, Hawaii. In the fall of 2000, the man who answered the phone ("Hello") said that the university is not currently operating, but will do so after conversion to a non-profit entity.

Pacifica University They were once registered as a business in Hawaii , but we could not find evidence of the school in that state, or anywhere else.

Palladium International College The unrecognized Distance Graduation Accrediting Association claims this school as one of its members, but we have found no other evidence of its existence.

Palo Alto School of Professional Psychology See: Western Graduate School of Psychology

Pan American University We heard a report of this school operating somewhere in Europe, but we've been unable to confirm anything beyond that.

Pan Pacific University (California) In 2000, plans were announced to begin a school by this name on a decommissioned former naval base in Alameda, California.

Pan Pacific University (Hawaii) Registered in Hawaii, but we have not been able to find the actual university at the registered address in Honolulu. No connection with the Pan Pacific University which, in 2000, was hoping to open in Alameda, California.

Pan Pacific University (Hawaii) Registered in Hawaii, but involuntarily dissolved by the state in 1993.

Pan-African University Washington, D.C. Created by poet and former schoolteacher Abena Walker, this unaccredited school was the center of a controversy in 1993 when the *Washington Post* ran a series of articles questioning (and, in the case of some columnists, supporting) Walker's credentials, after she came to prominence in developing the D.C. area's first Afro-centric education program for the public schools. She was criticized for holding a self-awarded master's degree.

Patent University of America They were registered as a business in Hawaii as of May, 2000, by the Paracorp Corp., using the address in Marina del Rey, California, which is an office building for lawyers and accountants. Accreditation is claimed from the unrecognized and

"My good man, if you sign up now, I am authorized to give you an additional kilogram of genetically modified soybean seeds."

nonwonderful World Association of Universities and Colleges. The fax number appears to be in Japan.

Pearblossom School In the last edition, we asked for information on this school, which we could not locate. Now we have a Web site (*www.av.qnet.com/~privatesch*) which was supposed to open for business in 1998. Still hasn't.

Pennsylvania Military College At one time, offered a B.A. and MBA through evening study; its programs were, according to a correspondent, absorbed by Widener University some years ago.

People's University of the Americas A correspondent has reported that such a university exists, with an address at a post office box in Solna, Sweden, from which no response has been heard. More recently, a second correspondent reports that they are operating from an address in Spain, and managed by the Christian Orthodox Church of Puerto Rico. At press time, we're not entirely sure it's the same organization or, in fact, what the Spanish school's status is. All we can say for (fairly) certain is that there is no connection with an orthodox Christian naturopathic medical school of the identical name in Puerto Rico (*www.pua.edu*).

Permaculture University We were told that a Texan named Inger Myhre was in the process of putting together a New Mexico–based school to award under- and post-graduate degrees in the field of permaculture, based on the work being done by Australia's Permaculture Academy. We have found reference on the Internet to a Permaculture Academy, apparently in Pojoaque, New Mexico, where the listed phone number turns out to be a fax machine. We're still looking.

Phoenix Medical School Phoenix, Arizona. Incorporated and began recruiting students even though the university existed, as an article in the *Arizona Republic* noted, only "on a few pieces of paper stacked on a rented credenza under a rented scenic picture in a small office [in] Mesa." President Gloria Coates announced an opening date for the university, but apparently it never came to pass.

Phoenix University The president of a bible school lists among his credentials a Ph.D. from the Bari Research Center of Phoenix University for archeological research, bestowed by its president, His Serene Highness Prince Francisco D'Aragona. We are unfamiliar with this institution but see (we suspect) Accademia di Studi Superiori Phoenix in chapter 27, "Degree Mills." Certainly not related to the accredited University of Phoenix in Arizona.

Pitzer College At one time, they offered an external B.A. from their regionally accredited California campus.

Plantation University A hoax perpetrated by a prankster on an Internet news group, the claim was made that this "venerable" Kentucky institution was accredited by the Southern Commission for Schools and Colleges.

Point Park College Pittsburgh, Pennsylvania. At one time, they offered accredited bachelor's degrees through weekend classes.

Presidential American University See: Thomas Jefferson Education Foundation

Presidents University They were registered as a business in Hawaii but the corporation was involuntarily dissolved by the state in 1996.

Prestige Graduate Degrees Some school or service advertised in *The Economist* under this heading, offering "Prestige Graduate Degrees by research, residential or distance learning" under the guidance of "eminent mentors." They never responded to our inquiries, so we do not know which "prestigious" school's degrees were being peddled.

Professional School for Humanistic Studies Listed as the source of a faculty member at a traditional school's degree. We have not been able to locate the institution.

Professional School of Psychological Studies San Diego, California. At one time, authorized by the state of California. No response to three letters asking for information, and the person who answers the listed telephone says the school no longer exists, and good-bye.

Professional Studies Institute Phoenix, Arizona. Offered unaccredited bachelor's, master's, and doctorates in physical and mental health fields, but can no longer be located.

Prometheus College Tacoma, Washington. Arose in the mid 1970s and rather quickly became a candidate for accreditation. Then suddenly they were gone—perhaps back to Olympus.

Protea Valley University Dr. Bernard Leeman established this school in Toowoomba, Australia in 1991, and registered it in Louisiana, with the intention of providing education for black South African exiles. He gained Archbishop Desmond Tutu's backing for the idea, but abandoned it in the planning stages when it became clear that majority rule was going to become a reality in South Africa.

Psychological Studies Institute See: Institute of Human-Potential Psychology

Quimby College Alamagordo, New Mexico. Offered a B.A. in life arts and an M.A. in spiritual studies and counseling. Locally controversial, perhaps in part because of the focus on aura balancing, and the assertion that the college had its start when the thoughts of Phineas P. Quimby, a New England watchmaker who died in 1866, were transmitted to an Alamagordo woman. No longer findable.

Radvis University A correspondent asks about this school, which she believed is or was located in Canada, but we can find no information.

Rampart College See: Freedom College

Rand Graduate Institute Santa Monica, California. In the past, they have offered an accredited apprenticeship-based Ph.D. in policy analysis.

Regents University Searcy, Arkansas. An unaccredited religious school now known as World Ministries Association. Not to be confused with the regionally accredited Excelsior University (formerly Regents College) or Regent University (Virginia).

Reid College of Detection of Deception Chicago, Illinois. The college began as a school held in the laboratories of John Reid, a prominent polygraph specialist, then went on to offer a state-authorized M.S. in detection of deception. While Reid's company still exists, it appears that the degree program is no longer.

Rem University A reader has inquired about nontraditional doctorates in psychology issued by this establishment, possibly in South Euclid, Ohio, but we could find no evidence of it.

Remington College See: Education America

Republic State University They were registered as a business in Hawaii as of May, 2000, but we could not find evidence of the school in that state, or anywhere else. The registered address (9229 Kaufman Place, Brooklyn, NY 11236) appears to be a term paper writing service.

Reykjavik Institute of Education Claims to be a university registered in Reykjavik, Iceland, offering degrees at all levels over the Internet. Repeated attempts to confirm any of this information have been unsuccessful. The Web site at *www.rvik.edu*, truly an exercise in minimalism, offers no contact information other than an email address to which we have sent many unanswered inquiries. The Web domain name is registered to a residential address in Austin, Texas, which we hear has a very different climate than Iceland's.

Richfield University They were registered as a business in Hawaii as of May, 2000, but we could not find evidence of the school in that state, or anywhere else. Apparently established by the Richfield Technology Corporation.

Ripon College Wisconsin. At one time, they offered accredited bachelor's degrees in which up to 75% of credit could come from prior learning.

Roanoke College At one time, they offered a variety of accredited master's degrees through evening courses.

Rochdale College This legitimate, if unorthodox, institution in Toronto, Canada used to "award" honorary degrees as a fundraising tool for the college to anyone who made a modest donation. The honorary Ph.D. had a watermark; when you held the diploma up to the light, you saw "Caveat Emptor."

Rockwell University Scottsdale, Arizona. They offered degrees of all kinds by correspondence study. The only requirement was the writing of a thesis. A former president of Loyola University in Louisiana was claimed to be one of the five founders. "An education for the 1980s" was their slogan, but they didn't make it through the '80s themselves.

Roger Williams College See: East Coast University. Not to be confused with the fully accredited school by the same name in Rhode Island.

Rosebridge Graduate School of Integrative Psychology See: American Schools of Professional Psychology, whom they apparently became a part of in 1998.

Royal Orleans University At one time, they were registered with the Board of Regents of Louisiana, but mail is returned as undeliverable and there is no listed telephone number in Lake Charles, Louisiana.

Russell Sage College At one time, they offered their accredited bachelor's and master's degrees in education through evening courses.

Sacred Heart College A program offering a very short residency bachelor's in management and criminal justice has been canceled, at least for the time being.

Saint Andreas University Our first fault with St. Andreas University is that they are members of the unrecognized and nonwonderful World Association of Universities and Colleges. Fault #2 is that we could not find them on the Internet. And fault #3 is that they did not respond to the fax we sent to the number provided on the WAUC site, apparently in Japan.

Saint Andrew's Collegiate Seminary In the late 1950s, Saint Andrew's was a small and apparently sincere and legitimate seminary in London, England offering master's and doctoral work in theology and counseling. Later, to raise funds, the seminary offered honorary doctorates to clergy and others who made donations. This evolved into awarding nonresidential degrees for life experience in the name of the Saint Andrew's Ecumenical Church Foundation Intercollegiate. This further evolved into a worldwide enterprise, again offering degrees entirely based on resumes, called the International Free Protestant Episcopal University. None of these entities survive today.

Saint Andrew's Ecumenical Church Foundation Intercollegiate See: Saint Andrew's Collegiate Seminary

Saint Bonaventure University Degrees through evening study are no longer available.

Saint Charles University DeQuincy, Louisiana. In the spring of 1998, they began advertising in Singapore. We are not familiar with them, and can find no reference to them in standard books or lists of accredited schools. We have left telephone messages several times over the last two years, but none has been returned. We do not have a catalog, and we cannot find a Web site, so we are unable to describe their programs.

Saint Claire College and University In 2000, we received an inquiry from a university registrar about an applicant claiming a degree from this institution, using a post office box in Buffalo, New York, with, they say, a learning center in Qatar in the Middle East. We have yet been unable to find any evidence of this institution; there is no listed telephone. We don't know if there is any connection with the equally elusive "St. Clair University" listed in chapter 21.

Saint Cloud State University Minnesota. At one time, they offered accredited bachelor's degrees in which virtually all credit could come from prior learning experiences.

Saint Columbia University They were registered as a business in Hawaii as of May, 2000, but we could not find evidence of the school in that state. They are, however, accredited by the unrecognized and nonwonderful World Association of Universities and Colleges, which will not give out their "real" address or telephone, but does offer a Japanese fax number. Incidentally, there is no St. Columbia. Perhaps they meant to honor St. Columba.

Saint George Center for Training At one time, they were authorized to grant master's degrees by the state of California. There was no response to three requests for information on their programs, and there is no listed telephone number in Berkeley.

Saint Giles University College This England-based school offered nonresident bachelor's, master's, doctorates, and certificates in psychology, physiatrics, teacher training, and science. The Doctor of Science program consisted consisted of three lessons: (1) factors influencing children's sweet eating, (2) psychiatry and psychology, and (3) radiation and human health. Raymond Young was the moving force behind Saint Giles, Harley University, and Somerset University.

Saint Ignatius University They were registered as a business in Hawaii as of May, 2000, but we could not find evidence of the school in that state or anywhere else.

Saint John's College (England) This London-based school, a division of City Commercial College, did not offer their own degrees, but conducted the coursework leading to a bachelor's or an MBA from an unspecified-in-their-literature nontraditional school in California. They apparently closed down in the wake of student protests.

Saint Johns University (California) Registered in Hawaii at P.O. Box 4488, Hilo 96720. The corporation, apparently based in Walnut Creek, California, was involuntarily dissolved by the state in 1990.

Saint John's University (Louisiana) A very small school established in Edgard, Louisiana, by District Court Judge Thomas Malik, they used to offer nonresident degrees, but that program was discontinued. No connection with Saint John's University of Practical Theology (also in Louisiana) or the regionally accredited Saint John's University in New York.

Saint Louis University Missouri. At one time, they offered a number of degrees through evening study.

Saint Maria Frontier University They were registered as a business in Hawaii as of May, 2000, but we could not find evidence of the school in that state, or anywhere else.

Saint Martin's College and Seminary This unaccredited school offered nonresidential graduate degrees in business, divinity, and ministry, as well as state-approved programs in alcohol and substance abuse. In 2000, there was no listed telephone in Milwaukee, Wisconsin, and our written request for information had not been responded to after six months.

Saint Paul College and Seminary A reader asks about an honorary doctorate that a co-worker claims from this institution, apparently in Rome, but we have not found it.

Saint Paulos International University SPIU is a member of the unrecognized and nonwonderful World Association of Universities and Colleges. The fax number listed on the WAUC Web site did not include a country code, so we do not know where this school is located. An Internet search proved fruitless.

Saint Thomas University Miami, Florida. At one time, they offered B.A., B.S., and master's degrees through evening, weekend, and summer programs in the School of Continuing and Adult Education. Formerly called Biscayne College.

Samuel Benjamin Thomas University A grand plan by King Theophilus I of the Ashanti Kingdom to establish a distance learning university in Sierra Leone apparently has not yet come to pass.

San Diego State University At one time they offered external bachelor's and master's degrees.

San Francisco College of Acupuncture At one time, authorized to grant degrees by the state of California, but letters are returned as undeliverable and there is no listed telephone in San Francisco.

San Francisco School of Psychology At one time, they offered flexible evening programs leading to a state-approved M.A. or a Psy.D. In 2000, the phone had been disconnected, and the Internet site was no longer operational.

San Francisco Theological Seminary San Anselmo, California. They have discontinued their Doctor of Science in theology once offered through summer sessions.

Santa Barbara University Goleta, California. They appeared in the 1986 directory of schools put out by the state of California, offering master's and doctorates in business but by 1988 there was no telephone listing. Presumably not the same as University of Santa Barbara (formerly Laurence University).

Santa Fe College of Natural Medicine Offered nonresidential bachelor's, master's, and Ph.D. programs as well as residential studies. Now there is no response to letters, and the phone in Santa Fe, New Mexico, is no longer in service. No connection to University of Natural Medicine, also in Santa Fe.

School of Botany A reader has inquired about an honorary degree a colleague of his was using. Possibly in Spain, but we could not locate it.

School of Real Estate Center for Architecture and Urban Studies SRECAUS is a member of the unrecognized and nonwonderful World Association of Universities and Colleges. We could not locate them on the Internet, and our fax to the number in Indonesia given on the WAUC Web site was not answered.

Scuba University of Hawaii They were registered as a business in Hawaii as of May, 2000, but we could not find evidence of the school in that state, or anywhere else.

Searchers World University They were registered as a business in Hawaii , but were listed as inactive when we checked in late 2000.

Seattle International University Letters to the school have been returned as undeliverable, and there is no listed telephone number in Seattle or Federal Way, Washington. This unaccredited school had offered the BBA and MBA entirely through evening and weekend study.

Sedona College/Sedona University Sedona, Arizona. According to an article in the *Arizona Republic,* an application to operate this school was made in Arizona by two men, one a former employee of Southwestern University (whose owner was imprisoned for selling degrees), the other the police chief of Sedona, whose doctorate was from De Paul University, a degree mill whose owners were sentenced to prison in 1987. According to a spirited defense of Sedona College in the *Sedona Times* newspaper (September 19, 1984), James H. Smith of California "purchased Sedona College from its founder, Ted Dalton" (president of Newport University). We are uncertain as to whether Sedona ever accepted students, but there is no listed phone for them in Sedona now. We have been told that there were actually two schools—Sedona College and Sedona University—perhaps quite independent of each other. In 2000, Sedona University was still a legal Arizona corporation.

Sequoia University In 1984 a Los Angeles judge issued a permanent injunction against Sequoia University, which had operated from California and Oklahoma, and its president to cease operation until the school could comply with state education laws. The university had offered degrees in osteopathic medicine, religious studies, hydrotherapy, and physical sciences.

Shelton College This college, founded by fundamentalist radio preacher Carl McIntire, challenged New Jersey's school licensing law, claiming that it should be exempt from licensing under freedom of religion and speech precedents. New Jersey maintained that any exceptions to its right to license would diminish the value and integrity of degrees awarded in the state. Now there is no listed telephone in Cape May, New Jersey.

Sierra University Orange, California. This school closed in 1994; prior to that, they had offered nonresident state-approved degrees at all levels in business, religion, psychology, health administration, public administration, communications, education, and human behavior.

Sino-American International University They were registered as a business in Hawaii in 1995 to develop an American style university which would provide degrees (B, M, D) to students living in China and other far Eastern countries. The campus address seems to be a mailbox service.

Somerset University In July 2000, the Somerset Education Department in Taunton reported that Somerset University had recently ceased to exist. Degrees at all levels were earned through correspondence study. In the past, correspondence went to a convenience address in New Orleans or Metairie, Louisiana, but more recently directly to England. The school's catalog lists a number of officers and faculty with traditional British credentials. The doctorates in law, science, and divinity were awarded entirely based on prior work. Founder Raymond Young previously operated Harley University from his hair salon in London. There has been an affiliation with Villarreal University of Peru. See also: International College of Higher Education, which may be their new name.

Sonoma Institute They offered training for an M.A. in humanistic and transpersonal psychology through a cooperative relationship with the University of Redlands. Now there is no listed telephone in Bodega, California.

South Pacific University Registered in Hawaii. At one time, shared its address (a mail forwarding service) with Honolulu University of Arts, Sciences, and Humanities (see listing in chapter 21).

Southeast Asia Interdisciplinary Development Institute They offered the M.A., M.A./Ph.D., and Ph.D. in organizational development and planning, in an independent study program, including Socratic and practicum conferences. In 2000, the telephone was not in service, and we could not locate them on the Internet.

Southeastern College of the Assemblies of God Florida. This school at one time offered totally nonresident B.A.'s in religious fields through correspondence courses in combination with a number of other alternative methods, such as supervised fieldwork and independent study. In mid 1996, however, following an investigation by the NCAA into whether coaches at the school had obtained bogus eligibility for student athletes through these programs, the distance education program was shut down.

Southeastern Graduate School At one time they advertised, from South Carolina, that doctorates were available in 100 fields, with a one-month residency. The literature made troublesome statements about accreditation eligibility. We have been unable to locate them.

Southeastern University (South Carolina, Louisiana) See: Gulf States University

Southern International University New Orleans. A letter sent to their last known address was returned as undeliverable. This unaccredited school had offered degrees at all levels in psychology, human behavior, fine arts, and business through wholly nonresident programs. In other matters concerning other schools we've had

questions about, founder Dr. Denis Muhilly has been less than pleasant. In May, 2000, the *Pacific Business News* determined that the name was registered in Hawaii.

Southern States University They have offered state approved degrees, but in 2000, their telephone in Huntington Beach, California rang but was never answered, and we could not locate them on the Internet.

Southland University Southland University operated from Pasadena, California and later from Arizona in the 1980s. Following a visit from the FBI's "DipScam" diploma mill team, which carried off four truckloads of records, Southland closed. No indictments were handed down. La Salle University in St. Louis (later to move to Louisiana) subsequently opened under the same management with similar programs, including some law materials bearing the name Southland. This time the FBI raid bore fruit, and the founder of Southland and La Salle was indicted on 18 counts of mail fraud and related offenses, and sent to federal prison in 1997.

Southwest Acupuncture College In the last edition, we mentioned this school, thinking it might be out of business. They have simply moved, in New Mexico, but do not have distance or online degree programs.

Southwestern Polytechnic University They were registered as a business in Hawaii as of May, 2000, but we could not find evidence of the school in that state, or anywhere else.

Southwestern University Law School California. Alternative law school, no longer around.

Spectrum Virtual University In 1995, word on the Internet was of this organization, offering free or virtually free classes in fields ranging from spirituality to Internet issues to creative writing. However, it appears to exist no more.

Stamford University "In The Mould Of A Modern University," according to its motto. Its Web site, *www.stamford-university.net*, appears to be quite unfinished: All links on the home page are dead and there is little text other than the claim that the school was established in 1841 and has 160 campuses in 42 countries. The only other evidence of this school's existence can be found on the Web site for the London Institute of Technology & Research, which claims to be a partner institution. According to LITR, Stamford offers degrees at all levels and is accredited by the New York State Education Department (not true), the National Council for Private School Accreditation (not a higher education accreditor), and the International Association for Continuing Education and Training (not an accreditor of degree programs). Stamford's Internet site is registered to Stamford Group USA, Inc., at an address in Jackson Heights, NY. The man who answered our call to the Stamford Group claimed no knowledge of the university and told us that they are a "placement service" for international students. Hmmmm . . .

State University of Nebraska Used to offer a largely correspondence degree.

Steelframe University They were registered as a business in Hawaii as of May, 2000, but we could not find evidence of the school in that state, or anywhere else.

Stetson University Our research indicates that the school no longer offers Bachelor of Arts and Bachelor of Science degrees through evening study. It no longer seems to offer a Bachelor of Science in medical technology.

Steward University The Web site for this university provides little information, but the site is registered to Ben Maxedon of Zebulon, Georgia. We're not listing the telephone, since it was answered "Hello" by a woman who sounded quite annoyed when we asked for the university. Degrees of all kinds are offered, based on life experience, for the price of $299 and up.

Stewart University System See: Frank Ross Stewart University System

Stratton College Navan, Ireland. An external degree program was announced by the college. Then the college was taken over by the Institute of Maintenance Engineering and the degree program was canceled.

Sun Moon University Choongnam, Korea. In the last edition, we said we were looking into it. Our review of the Web site (*www.sunmoon.ac.kr*) suggests that there are no distance-learning programs.

Sun University Singapore. The founder corresponded with us in 1998 when he was first putting this school together. Last we heard, the operation folded due to lack of enrollment.

Sunshine University Probably (but we've never been sure) a gag or promotional diploma. The Ph.D. they sent John is quite attractive and appears to be signed by the mayors of three Florida cities and the chairman of the Pinellas County Commission.

Susan B. Anthony University Pennsylvania. Established in the mid-1970s, this now-defunct school was an honest attempt to create a good alternative university, offering degrees at all levels in education, environmental studies, naturopathy, and peace & freedom studies. According to founder Dr. Albert Schatz (the inventor of streptomycin), it never got off the ground due to limited funding. Formerly known as Anthony University.

Synthesis Graduate School for the Study of Man An ambitious-seeming endeavor that offered the M.A. and Ph.D. in psychology and medical synthesis. Buckminster Fuller and a Nobel laureate in medicine were on the board of advisors. Most faculty were disciples of Roberto Assagioli. But now the school seems to be gone; we have been unable to locate it in San Francisco, or elsewhere.

Taiken University See: Taiken Wilmington University

Taiken Wilmington University This school was advertised in *USA Today* in mid-1997; when we called to request literature, the woman answering the phone said that she didn't know where the university was located, although the Web site appears to be in Taiwan. They were registered as a business in Hawaii in 2000, and the Web site (*www.taikenwu.edu*) lists an address in Anaheim, California. Apparently the same as, or affiliated with, Taiken University. There has also been a connection either with Kensington University or former Kensington personnel, which we continue to look into.

TASMAC TASMAC (Training and Advanced Studies in Management and Communication) appears to be a well-established residential education provider in Pune, India, which, for whatever reason, claims a whole litany of accreditations and affiliations with unrecognized and generally nonwonderful American universities and accreditors, including the World Association of Universities and Colleges, Barrington University, Adam Smith University, Global University, Frederick Taylor University, the Global Accreditation Commission, and the International Accrediting Commission for Post Secondary Educational Institutitons. Rarely have we seen as many nonwonderful affiliations with a single entity, which can be found at *www.tasmac.ac.in*.

Teachers University A reader asks about this school, which she believes used to exist in Miami, but we can find no evidence of it.

Technion Institute Our research suggests that the Master of Science in industrial management (which required one day a week on the campus in Haifa) is no longer being offered.

Temple University Philadelphia. At one time, they offered accredited degrees at all levels through evening study.

Tennessee Southern University and School of Religion Established in late 1981 for the purpose, according to founder Dr. O. Charles Nix, of "developing students with a special sense of social responsibility, who can organize and apply knowledge for human betterment." Mail to several Tennessee addresses was returned as undeliverable.

Texas Graduate School of International Management Corpus Christi, Texas. This unaccredited school never responded to requests for information about their non-traditional programs, and in 1998 a letter sent to their last known address was returned as undeliverable.

Theseus International Management Institute This residential business school on the French Riviera was listed in the last edition as a place we were trying to learn more about. Now we have the Web site (*www.theseus.fr*), and it seems clear that they do not offer distance degree programs.

Thomas Jefferson Education Foundation Answering a 1998 ad appearing in *USA Today*, we were faxed a 20-page catalog from the Thomas Jefferson Education Foundation, claiming to be some kind of umbrella organization for the following schools: Thomas Jefferson University of Virginia, University of Williamsburg, Dartmoor University, Presidential American University, and Cambridge University in America. No distinction was made between these schools other than their names. Offered degrees at all levels by "professional assessment of career achievements." Accreditation claimed from the College for Professional Assessment, an agency we've never otherwise come across. We have been unable to confirm if TJED is still operating: Web site is down; phone and fax numbers are defunct. The address given in the catalog is that for a lawyer in Sioux Falls, South Dakota, who has expressed "outrage" that many of the unaccredited schools he has filed incorporation for have given his office address as the location of their campuses. One of these was Les Snell's Monticello University (see listing in the "Degree Mills" chapter), which has also gone by the name Thomas Jefferson University. We don't know if there is a connection (but we're certainly suspicious).

Thomas Jefferson University of Virginia See: Thomas Jefferson Education Foundation

Townsend Hawaii University They were registered as a business in Hawaii as of May, 2000, but we could not find evidence of the school in that state, or anywhere else. There is, however, a Townsend Harris University that is a member of the nonwonderful and unrecognized World Association of Universities and Colleges. There was no response to the fax we sent to the fax number listed on the WAUC Web site. (The man named Townsend Harris was the first American envoy in Japan, sent by President Buchanan in the 1850s.)

Towson State University Our research seems to indicate that the school no longer offers bachelor's degrees through evening classes.

Tri-State College and University Several readers have asked about this institution, but letters to Dr. J. Roy Stewart at the Oxon Hill, Maryland address provided were never answered, and there was no listed telephone.

Tucson University At one time, they operated in Tucscon, Arizona, but they are no longer in business.

Unification Theological Seminary Offers accredited master's degrees through residential programs in Barrytown, New York. We had reported on some long-past accreditation problems, but never noted when those problems were favorably resolved. For this oversight, we apologize.

Union College A school of this name was listed in another directory of alternative education as having a correspondence degree program, based in South Africa, but we have not been able to find them.

Union University Los Angeles. Unaccredited and somewhat questionable school once offered master's degrees and doctorates though nonresidential study. No connection with schools of the same name in Tennessee or New York.

United Pacific University They were registered as a business in Hawaii as of May, 2000, but we could not find evidence of the school in that state, or anywhere else.

United State Open University Hawaii. This school was once located in Louisiana, then relocated to Hawaii. Now it appears to be totally defunct.

United States Global University They were registered as a business in Hawaii as of May, 2000, but we could not find evidence of the school in that state. We did, however, locate a school of this name incorporated in Arizona in 2000 (2042 E. Yale, Phoenix 85008) but our mail to incorporator Lincoln Salem was not answered, and there is no listed phone.

United States International University—Europe Offered bachelor's and master's degrees in residence on the campus near London, in association with the accredited United States International University in San Diego. No longer operating.

Universidad Boricua District of Columbia. A university without walls program developed primarily for Puerto Ricans, by Puerto Rican scholar Antonia Pantoja. It no longer appears to exist.

Universidad Iberoamericano The bachelor's degree in sociology or theology is based largely on individual study, with study guides, required weekly group sessions on the university's campus, and individualized tutorial with the faculty, as requested by the student. The time commitment involved is one of at least five years.

Universidad Interamericana See: Escuela de Medicina Dr. Evaristo Cruz Escobedo

Universidad Medico-Naturalista Hispano-America See: Cyberam University

Universidad Nordestana Dominican Republic. This medical school is apparently no longer accepting American students.

Universitas Sancti Martin We have some questions about this school, apparently based in Reynosa, Mexico. All correspondence goes through Oklahoma (a mailbox service called Postal Plus), and directory assistance in Reynosa has no listing for such a university. A correspondent was told that he could receive a doctorate under the school's "challenge" program, wherein "all independent course study requirements will be waived in lieu of a scholarly paper." Claims accreditation from the apparently nonexistent InterAmerican Association of Postsecondary Colleges and Schools, and recognition from the similarly elusive National Diet and Nutrition Association. Chairman Dr. A. Mason James has never responded to our letters requesting clarification of these and other issues.

Université de Paris VII—Vincennes The Vincennes campus of the University of Paris is known as the "university of second chance." The more than 30,000 students come from more than 100 countries, but primarily (or perhaps entirely) by residential study.

University Associates Graduate School San Diego, California. At one time authorized in California, the school closed in 1987.

University College Academy Christians International In 1987, John was sent a document submitted by a clergyman in Puerto Rico in support of a degree claimed from this entity. The document, purporting to be a certification by the state of New York that "University College" is legitimate and accredited, is clearly a fake. It has a number of misspellings, and is simply not true.

University College of Northern Cyprus See: Girne American University

University de la Romande Pay attention, this is complex. UDLR was established in Sudbury, England, by Neil Gibson & Company. The spokesman for Neil Gibson was John Courage. Then a book was published on nontraditional degrees, by a William Ebbs, calling UDLR the best nontraditional school in the world. John Courage and William Ebbs do not, in fact, exist. They were both pseudonyms for one man, Raymond Seldis, of Neil Gibson & Company. Early advertising identified UDLR as a private and fully accredited Swiss university. The claimed accredited agency turned out not to exist. The university later advertised from a post office box on the Isle of Man, clearly stating that it is not accredited—but the mail went to Sudbury. Degrees were earned by writing a thesis, which could be quite short. Neil Gibson & Company also used to sell degrees that even they admitted were fake, from the University del Puerto Monico, Panama. No longer operating. (The UDLR operators also started Knightsbridge University, which is now under entirely unrelated management.)

University for Humanistic Studies They have offered a state-approved Bachelor of Arts in humanistic studies; Master of Arts in psychology, leadership development, sports counseling, and marriage, family, & child counseling; Ph.D. in psychology; and Psy.D. But in 2000, there was no listed phone number in Solana Beach, California, and their Web site was not operational.

University of America (Massachusetts) In 2000, a correspondent told us about an apparently new school of this name, but neither he nor we were ever able to open the Web site at *www.universityofamerica.org* (which is registered to an address in Cambridge, Massachusetts, and an email address associated with Boston University). No apparent connection with the University of America in Iowa/Arkansas/Louisiana/Tennessee/etc.

University of Analytic Counseling They were registered as a business in Hawaii as of May, 2000, but no address was listed, and we could not find evidence of the school operating in that state, or anywhere else. The Gil Boyne Graduate School may be a part of this.

University of Applied Studies This school was approved by the state of California to operate, but when we wrote to the Hacienda, California address in 1998, the letter was returned as undeliverable.

University of Azania The name was registered in England by Dr. Bernard Leeman (see Lincoln University [New Guinea]), in the hope and expectation of establishing a school that would ultimately be located in a "free South Africa." (Azania is a name that some black South Africans have used for their country.)

University of Beverly Hills The University thrived as an unaccredited school in the 1970s and two of its officers went on to start comparable schools, Century and Kennedy-Western. While UBH ostensibly closed in the mid 1980s, advertising (mostly in Asia) in its name went on for an additional four or five years, using an address in Council Bluffs, Iowa. A visitor to the Council Bluffs address found no University of Beverly Hills, but did find an educational service company whose manager became hostile when asked about the University.

University of California—Riverside Their off-campus Master of Administration program has been discontinued.

University of California—San Diego Their nonresidential Bachelor of Arts program has been discontinued.

University of California—Santa Cruz Their B.A. in community studies through evening study has been discontinued.

University of Canterbury Established by two psychologists in Los Angeles, California in the late 1970s. They offered graduate degrees in psychology and other fields with a four-week residency requirement in either California or England, but within a few years they were gone.

University of Central Arizona Tempe, Arizona. Operated in the late 1970s, offering Doctor of Art in education and Doctor of Business Management, based on readings, examinations, and a dissertation. The two founders agreed to a consent judgment and stopped awarding doctorates.

University of Central California Sacramento, California. Once offered degrees of all kinds by correspondence, typically after a student responded to 100 to 200 multiple-choice, true-or-false, and essay questions to demonstrate competency, followed by independent study, a thesis, and an examination. They were authorized by the state of California, but both the "authorized" status and the university are no more.

University of Dona Ana We left numerous messages on the answering machine at the number provided by the World Association of Universities and colleges, the unrecognized and nonwonderful organization of which they are a member, but none was ever returned. The phone is apparently in Las Cruces, New Mexico, which is in Dona Ana County.

University of East Asia See: University of Macau; Asia International Open University

University of East London Essex, United Kingsom. This school offers flexible undergraduate and graduate programs, but not, it would seem from their Web site (*www.uel.ac.uk*), by distance learning.

University of Eclectic Study A school of this name was incorporated in Phoenix, Arizona, as of 2000, but we could find no evidence of its existence.

University of Generous Knowledge Reston, Virginia. A correspondent forwards some press materials from this decidedly unconventional business school, which claims to use movies instead of books as its primary teaching tools—*Gone with the Wind*, *Rocky*, *Top Gun*, and *The Color of Money*, among others. We're not sure whether this is a joke or not; the university has never responded to our inquiries.

University of Global Religious Studies We have been unable to find them on the Internet, and our fax to the number found on the Web site of their accreditor, the unrecognized and nonwonderful World Association of Universities and College, was not answered.

University of Health Science They are registered as a business in Hawaii, and claim their accreditation from the unrecognized and nonwonderful World Association of Universities and Colleges. Our call to their phone number was answered, "Hello." When we asked for the university, we were told to call another time.

University of Lawsonomy Sturtevant, WI. Founded by Alfred William Lawson (1869-1954), who was also the father of Lawsonomy, defined in the school's literature as "the knowledge of life and everything pertaining thereto." We have been unable to determine if this is a currently operating, degree-granting institution: The response to our inquiry for more information was a pamphlet of Mr. Lawson's essays and an order form for his books.

University of Linguistics at Hawaii They were registered as a business in Hawaii as of May, 2000, but we could not find evidence of the school in that state, or anywhere else.

University of Llano, California They were registered as a business in Hawaii as of May, 2000, but we could not find evidence of the school in that state, California, or anywhere else.

University of Los Angeles At presstime, was not yet operating awaiting state approval. The plan is to offer an MBA and an M.S. in international commerce and trade. Located in Rowland Heights, California.

University of Macau Macau. At one time offered wholly nonresident external programs in the English language at bachelor's and master's level. A letter sent in 1997 was returned marked "gone away." This school was created when the University of East Asia split its programs into two schools; the other is the Asia International Open University.

University of Malaya In the past, they apparently had offered an M.A. TESOL and an M.Ed. TESOL through distance learning programs, but we did not find one anymore on their Web site (*www.cc.um.edu.my*).

University of Mid-America A consortium of 11 midwestern universities, which was to establish the American Open University, spent $14 million from the National Institute of Education in organizing, and then went out of business in 1982 when the NIE shut its purse.

University of Mid-America (Iowa) Council Bluffs. In the mid-1980s, when Southwest University agreed with the state of Louisiana to stop granting distance-learning doctorates and to apply for DETC accreditation, the school began an association with some persons who had formerly been involved in the much more serious earlier school by the same name, to serve their current and prospective doctoral candidates. This lasted for a couple of years, but the school is no longer in existence.

University of Mississippi External degree programs are not available from the department. Some online courses are offered.

University of Missouri at Columbia They once offered a bachelor's degree in general agriculture through nontraditional methods. The program has been discontinued, although individuals can still take correspondence courses.

University of Naturopathy A reader inquires about a school of this name that he believed might be operating in East Orange, New Jersey, but there is no listed phone number there.

University of North Carolina at Chapel Hill Master's programs in health-related fields now require a minimum of two semesters of residency.

University of Northern California Arts and Sciences They existed for a while on the Internet in 1999–2000, claiming to exist only in virtual space, but referring to alumni from the 1960s. The site was registered to a man in Pleasanton, California, but no longer seems to exist.

University of Orlando In 1999, the unaccredited University of Orlando was purchased by the regionally accredited Barry University, which made it their Orlando campus, for law and education programs. There is no more distance learning.

University of Palm Beach See: College of the Palm Beaches

University of Psychic Sciences Someone sent John a business card for this school, located in National City, California, but we have not been sent any information on what they do. Perhaps they haven't picked up the message we've been beaming them.

University of Puget Sound At one time, offered accredited bachelor's and master's degrees through evening study.

University of Quartzsite A school of this name was incorporated in Arizona in 2000, but we could find no evidence of its existence.

University of Rochester No longer offers evening study degrees.

University of Saint Andrews St. Andrews, United Kingdom. No longer offers distance-learning programs.

University of Saint Lucia School of Medicine This medical school was started on the Caribbean island of Saint Lucia by self-styled "Crazy Eddie" Antar, New York electronics magnate, but closed abruptly a year later, in early 1984, stranding students and faculty alike. Saint George's University in Grenada agreed to take qualified students, but only 37 of Saint Lucia's 127 were accepted there. No connection with Saint Lucia Health Sciences University.

University of Science and Philosophy This Virginia-based school offers seminars (but not degrees, we believe) in such topics as transformational breathwork, transformation through joyful body movement, and searching for God. Their slogan is "Learn how the universe works."

University of Sciences in America Louisiana. Did not respond to several requests for information about their nontraditional programs and then, in mid 1997, a letter sent to their last known address, in Baton Rouge, was returned "attempted, not known."

University of Scouting See: Baden-Powell University of Scouting

University of South Wales No longer offers nontraditional degrees.

University of Taurus Feces A school of this name was incorporated in Arizona in 2000, but we could not find it. It is hard to imagine using a degree from such an institution, but it is entirely possible that the name would 'play' better in another country. As a public service, then, thanks to the excellent Lycos online translation site, we offer: La Universidad del Excremento Macho (Spanish); Universitat von Bulle Exkremente (German); Université de Faciès du Taureau (French), and l'Universita de Feci di Toro (Portuguese).

University of the Air (Oregon) See: Institute of Global Education

University of the Americas (Louisiana) Metairie. At one time, registered with the Board of Regents of Louisiana, but according to Thomas Lavin, who has also been affiliated with Kensington and Bedford Universities, the UOTA never opened for business, and no longer exists.

University of the Healing Arts They were registered as a business in Hawaii as of May, 2000, but we could not find evidence of the school in that state, or anywhere else. We did find evidence of a school of this name apparently opened by Dr. Harry Alsleben, who seems to have been a colleague of the later-imprisoned Kurt Donsbach of Donsbach University. UHA was said to be in Bonita, California, but there is no listed telephone there.

University of the Islands They were registered as a business in Hawaii as of May, 2000, but we could not find evidence of the school in that state, or anywhere else.

University of the Pacific At one time, offered accredited bachelor's degree in which over 80% of credit could come from prior learning.

University of the United States In 2000, we discovered that the campus (a secretarial service in Mobile, Alabama) had closed, and neither the phone nor the Web site was operational. It had the same owner and address as Nasson University, also apparently defunct. Mail was postmarked in Rhode Island, where Chancellor Mattar lived. Accreditation was claimed from two unrecognized agencies: the World Association of Universities and Colleges and the International Accreditation Commission for Post Secondary Educational Institutions.

University of the Western Pacific They were registered as a business in Hawaii as of May, 2000, but we could not find evidence of the school in that state, or anywhere else.

University of the World A reader told us that in 1988 it existed in La Jolla California, but we could not find any evidence.

University of Utopia San Francisco, California. Letter asking for information was returned, and the phone number we'd been given was someone's personal answering machine.

University of Vernon Woolf The minimal Internet site for World University (location unknown) suggests an affiliation with the University of Vernon Woolf (Moscow, Russia), which, it is claimed, operates throughout Russia. Education from kindergarten through doctorate degrees is apparently offered. Some information available at *www.astar-usa.com/II/wu_overviewF.html*.

University of Williamsburg See: Thomas Jefferson Education Foundation

University Without Walls/New Orleans Louisiana. Offered bachelor's degrees. Now mail is returned, and there is no listed phone.

University Without Walls/Project Success North Hollywood, California. In the mid-1980s their literature described bachelor's, master's, and doctorates in evolutionary systems design, but they are no longer there.

Upsala College New Jersey. Offered evening and weekend courses leading to accredited B.A. and B.S. degrees, but is no longer in business.

U.S. College of Music Boston, Massachusetts. In the past, the U.S. College of Music offered degrees in conjunction with Greenwich University. When that affiliation ended, the school briefly offered "decrees" in music and business. Currently, they offer a diplomas in a number of music-related fields.

Valley Christian University Fresno, then Clovis, California. Degrees in many fields at all levels by correspondence. Letters neither answered nor returned; no listed telephone.

Van Norman University Los Angeles, California. Unaccredited, and now defunct, law school (degrees were offered through its Los Angeles College of Law).

Vancouver University/Worldwide University Examines and consolidates work done at other schools, and awards its own degrees. They are neither licensed by nor registered with the British Columbia Private Post-Secondary Education Commission. The politics of post-secondary education in Canada is discussed at

length on their Web site (*www.vcn.bc.ca/wunicols*). Former name: New Summits University College.

Video University Jackson, Mississippi. In the early 1980s a major marketing effort was launched for Video U., which intended to offer many training courses. Now the phone has been disconnected.

Villarreal National University In 1988, this large Peruvian university (30,000 residential students) appeared to begin offering completely nonresident master's and doctoral programs, in English at a cost of nearly $10,000 to people living in the U.S. These programs existed for three or four years. But evidence emerged that suggested the degrees were not offered by the real Villarreal (a completely legitimate school) but rather by a Villarreal administrator, working with a less-than-wonderful unaccredited British institution, Somerset University. We were told at the time that the American Council on Education in Washington, the U.S. Information Agency in Lima, the Council of Europe in France, and the FBI were looking into these matters, but we were never able to learn anything more, and the whole matter seems to have just faded away. One victim told us that he understood that more than 1,000 Americans had signed up for the program.

Washington International College Washington, D.C. They offered a B.A. with two weeks' residency, achieved accreditation candidacy status, and then went out of business in 1982.

Washington International University (Virginia) In the late 1990s, former Japanese labor minister was arrested on charges of swindling over a million dollars from the Kunamoto Institute of Technology, ostensibly to open a school of this name in Virginia, which never happened. No connection, as far as we know, with the nonwonderful school of the same name in Pennsylvania (see listing in chapter 21).

Waters of Life University The Web site (*home.freei.com/watersoflife*) reports that they offer doctorates in nutrition, herbal studies, and energy medicine. No address is provided, but the founder is apparently in Keeau, Hawaii.

Wellsgrey College Greeley, Colorado. Advertisements appeared in business publications offering the MBA by computer, but mail was not answered and now there is no phone listing.

West Coast University Los Angeles, California. Offered certificate programs and degrees through evening and weekend study at locations in Southern California. As of 1998, the phone had been disconnected, and Internet links were no longer active.

West London University United Kingdom. A letter sent to them was returned with the notation "gone away."

West State University They were registered as a business in Hawaii as of May, 2000, but we could not find evidence of the school in that state, or anywhere else.

Western American University Our mail to the San Diego address was returned as undeliverable, and in 2000, we found that the telephone had been disconnected.

Western Australia Institute of Technology No longer offers external degrees.

Western Colorado University Grand Junction, Colorado. Offered nonresident degrees in many fields at all levels. Accredited by the unrecognized National Association for Private Nontraditional Schools and Colleges, with whom they shared staff and office space. Financial problems set in, and the doors were closed in the mid-1980s.

Western Graduate College Pakistan. The unaccredited school has offered bachelor's and master's degrees in business fields, and had an affiliation with American University in London, an unaccredited, Iowa-registered school located in England. A letter sent to their last known address in 1997 was returned as undeliverable.

Western Graduate School of Psychology At one time, they offered a Ph.D. in clinical psychology, approved by the state of California, but in 2000, they stopped accepting new students, and will be closing. Formerly Palo Alto School of Professional Psychology.

Western Pacific University They were registered as a business in Hawaii as of May, 2000, but we could not find evidence of the school in that state, or anywhere else, other than in the resume of one Japanese professor who claimed his doctorate from WPU.

Western Scientific University Opened in southern California in the early 1980s as a "Christian internal, external alternate degree program," offering M.D. (homeopathic) and various bachelor's, master's, and doctorates. Original name: Western University. No longer there.

Western Sierra Law School California. Apparently this school once offered nontraditional law programs, but a letter sent to their last known address, in San Diego, in 1997, was returned as undeliverable.

Western States Business University Wilmington, Delaware. We have written for more information to 1013 Centre Road, Wilmington DE 19805, but have never gotten any. May be associated with, or the same as, the unaccredited and nonwonderful Western States University in Missouri.

Western University (California) See: Western Scientific University

Western Washington University All nontraditional progams have been discontinued.

Westminster College (Missouri) This old established school for men started a nontraditional campus in Berkeley, California, then closed same in 1977 when it became apparent that the California branch was not upholding the parent school's high academic standards.

Westminster University They were registered as a business in Hawaii as of May, 2000, but we could not find evidence of the school in that state, or anywhere else. (There are other schools with this name, but none seems to have a Hawaii connection.)

Weston University They were registered as a business in Hawaii as of May, 2000, but we could not find evidence of the school in that state, or anywhere else.

Whitman University Michoacan, Mexico. Years ago, John received a "prototype" 1985–1986 bulletin, offering bachelor's, master's, and doctorates through guided independent study. Accreditation was claimed from the International Association of Non-Traditional Schools, England, an association we have not been able to locate. Students were asked to pay tuition in cash ($200 for the Ph.D., $600 for the B.A.), and to send it wrapped in carbon paper, in a thick envelope. Our letters asking for more information went unanswered, and recently have been returned by the post office.

Wichita State University At one time offered an accredited bachelor's degree in which over 80% of credits could come from prior learning.

Wild Rose College of Natural Healing Canada. Offered a correspondence program leading to a Wholistic Healing Degree (WHD) or Master Herbalist certificate. In 1997, a letter sent to their last known address, in Calgary, was returned as undeliverable.

William Bradford University Shreveport, LA. On its Web site (*expage.com/page/williambradforduniversity*), this school claims to offer its students master's and doctorate degrees "consisting of material and study of their own choosing for their personal fulfilment." We have been unable to verify this: no response to our emails or the message we left on their answering service (whose greeting, we might add, made no mention of any university). When we checked the Web site again a few weeks later, we noticed that the Lousiana mailing address (a mailbox rental service) and phone number had been removed.

William Darren University A correspondent asked for information on this school, apparently in or formerly in Phoenix, but we could find no record of them.

William James University They were registered as a business in Hawaii as of May, 2000, but we could not find evidence of the school in that state, or anywhere else.

William Lyon University See: Huron International University

Windsor University One of California's first nontraditional schools, Windsor opened in Los Angeles in 1972, soon became a candidate for accreditation, and had an affiliation with Antioch. But things fell apart in the wake of claims of misleading statements and falsified credentials, and Windsor is no more.

Wisconsin International University When we tried to find the campus in 1998, the address turned out to be a private home in a Milwaukee suburb. They are accredited by the unrecognized and dreadful Accrediting Commission International. On the several occasions we have telephoned the campus (most recently in mid 2000), the phone was answered "Hello," apparently by a child. We have never received the literature we asked for. The Web site suggests that the University's main clientele is in the Ukraine, Estonia (under the name Concordia International University), China, Brazil, and Ghana.

Woodrow Wilson College of Law Georgia. Unaccredited, and now defunct, law school.

World College West This innovative school in Petaluma, California offered a variety of weekend programs leading to degrees, but ran out of money and closed in 1993.

World Open University South Dakota. Once a part of the Li Institution of Science and Technology (LIST) founded by the late Dr. Shu-Tien Li (Ph.D., Cornell, 1926), who, according to the school's literature, had served as president of nine colleges and universities in China. Offered master's and doctorate degrees through programs guided by their adjunct (part-time) faculty. A letter sent to them in mid 1997 was returned marked "World Open Univ. was closed."

World University (Dominican Republic) Santo Domingo. It was a medical school incorporated in Puerto Rico, affiliated with the then-accredited International Institute of the Americas, and recognized by the World Health Organization. But the phone has been disconnected and mail has been returned.

World University (Hawaii) They were registered as a business in Hawaii as of May, 2000, but we could not find evidence of the school in that state, or anywhere else, unless it is the "mysterious" World University with a minimal Internet presence and a connection with the University of Vernon Woolf in Moscow. The statement is made that degrees at all levels, through doctorate, are offered.

As a family project, Rodney and his Uncle Ezra took a correspondence geography course together.

World University (Puerto Rico) There used to be a fully accredited World University with headquarters in Hato Rey, Puerto Rico, and various branches or alliances in places around the U.S., including the International Graduate School in St. Louis and World University of Florida. But the school is no longer accredited if, indeed, they are there at all.

Wyoming College of Advanced Studies This school was proposed as a nontraditional program offering non-residential MBAs, but after some problems with the Board of Education in Wyoming (primarily having their bond increased fivefold in1996), president Richard Crews (also president of Columbia Pacific University) decided, regretfully, that he couldn't afford to invest any more time or money into it.

Yaacov College International We heard that this school offered innovative programs, but when we wrote for information to the address provided (at Y.C.I. World Trade Center in Rotterdam), the letters were returned.

APPENDIX A

Glossary of Important Terms

When ideas fail, words come in very handy.

J. W. Goethe

AACRAO: The American Association of Collegiate Registrars and Admissions Officers.

academic year: The period of formal academic instruction, usually from September or October to May or June. Divided into semesters, quarters, or trimesters.

accreditation: Recognition of a school by an independent private organization. Not a governmental function in the U.S. There are more than 100 accrediting agencies, some recognized by the Department of Education and/or *CHEA*, some unrecognized, and some phony or fraudulent.

ACE: The American Council on Education, an influential nongovernment association in Washington.

ACT: American College Testing program, administrators of aptitude and achievement tests.

adjunct faculty: Part-time faculty member, often at a *nontraditional* school, often with a full-time teaching job elsewhere. More and more traditional schools are hiring adjunct faculty, because they don't have to pay them as much or provide health care and other benefits.

advanced placement: Admission to a school at a higher level than one would normally enter, because of getting credit for prior learning experience or passing advanced-placement exams.

alma mater: The school from which one has graduated, as in "My alma mater is Michigan State University."

alternative: Offering an alternate or different means of pursuing learning or degrees or both. Often used interchangeably with *external* or *nontraditional*.

alumni: Graduates of a school, as in "This school has some distinguished alumni." Technically for males only; females are *alumnae*. The singular is *alumnus* (male) or *alumna* (female), although none of these terms are in common use.

alumni association: A confederation of alumni and alumnae who have joined together to support their alma mater in various ways, generally by donating money.

approved: In California, a level of state recognition of a school, generally regarded as one step below *accredited*.

arbitration: A means of settling disputes, as between a student and a school, in which one or more independent arbitrators or judges listen to both sides, and make a decision. A means of avoiding a courtroom trial. Many learning contracts have an arbitration clause. See *binding arbitration*.

assistantship: A means of assisting students (usually graduate students) financially by offering them part-time academic employment, usually in the form of a teaching assistantship or a research assistantship.

associate's degree: A degree traditionally awarded by community or junior colleges after two years of residential study, or completion of 60 to 64 semester hours.

asynchronous: Not at the same time, as in an asynchronous online course, in which the faculty leaves messages for students, who read them later. Opposite of *synchronous*.

auditing: Sitting in on a class without earning credit for that class.

authorized: Until recently, a form of state recognition of schools in California. This category was phased out beginning in 1990, and now all schools must be *approved* or accredited to operate. Many formerly authorized schools are now billing themselves as candidates for approval.

bachelor's degree: Awarded in the U.S. after four years of full-time residential study (two to five years in other countries), or, typically, the earning of 120 to 128 semester units by any means.

binding arbitration: Arbitration in which both parties have agreed in advance that they will abide by the result and take no further legal action.

branch campus: A satellite facility, run by officers of the main campus of a college or university, at another location. Can range from a small office to a full-fledged university center.

campus: The main facility of a college or university, usually comprising buildings, grounds, dormitories, cafeterias and dining halls, sports stadiums, etc. The campus of a *nontraditional* school may consist solely of offices.

CEU: Continuing Education Unit, typically given in training courses at the rate of one for each ten hours of contact time. While standards are maintained by the International Association for Continuing Education and Training, the awarding of CEUs is not regulated, and they are rarely considered as equivalent to academic credit.

chancellor: Often the highest official of a university. Also a new degree title, proposed by some schools to be a higher degree than the *doctorate*, requiring three to five years of additional study.

CHEA: The Council on Higher Education Accreditation, successor to *COPA* and *CORPA* as the agency that recognizes accrediting agencies in the U.S.

CLEP: The College-Level Examination Program, a series of equivalency examinations that can be taken for college credit.

coeducational: Education of men and women on the same campus or in the same program. This is why female students are called coeds.

college: In the U.S., an institution offering programs leading to the *associate's* and/or *bachelor's*, and sometimes higher degrees. Often used interchangeably with *university*, although traditionally a university is a collection of colleges. In England and elsewhere, college may denote part of a university (Kings College, Cambridge) or a private high school (Eton College).

colloquium: A gathering of scholars to discuss a given topic over a period of a few hours to a few days. ("The university is sponsoring a colloquium on marine biology.")

community college: A two-year traditional school, offering programs leading to the *associate's degree* and, typically, many noncredit courses in arts, crafts, and vocational fields for community members not interested in a degree. Also called *junior college*.

competency: The philosophy and practice of awarding credit or degrees based on learning skills, rather than time spent in courses.

continuing education credit: See *CEU*.

COPA: The Council on Postsecondary Accreditation, a now defunct private nongovernmental organization that recognized accrediting agencies.

CORPA: The Commission on Recognition of Postsecondary Accreditation, a nationwide nonprofit corporation, formed in 1994, that took over the role of *COPA* (see above) in evaluating accrediting agencies and awarding recognition to those found worthy, and then relinquished it to *CHEA* a couple of years later.

correspondence course: A course offered by mail and completed entirely by home study, often with one or two proctored, or supervised, examinations.

course: A specific unit of instruction, such as a course in microeconomics, or a course in abnormal psychology. Residential courses last for one or more semesters or quarters; correspondence or distance-learning courses often have no rigid time requirements.

cramming: Intensive preparation for an examination. Most testing agencies now admit that cramming can improve scores on exams.

credit: A unit used to record courses taken. Each credit typically represents the number of hours spent in class each week. Hence a three-credit or three-unit *course* would commonly be a class that met three hours each week for one semester or quarter.

curriculum: A program of courses to be taken in pursuit of a *degree* or other objective.

DANTES: The Defense Activity for Non-Traditional Education Support, which regulates financial aid programs for active military, and administers equivalency exams for military and civilians.

degree: A title conferred by a school to show that a certain course of study has been completed.

Department of Education: In the U.S., the federal agency concerned with all educational matters in the nation that are not handled by the departments of education in the 50 states. In other countries, similar functions are commonly the province of a ministry of education.

DETC: The Distance Education and Training Council (formerly the National Home Study Council) is the recognized accreditor for schools offering degrees and diplomas largely or entirely by distance learning.

diploma: The certificate that shows that a certain course of study has been completed. Diplomas are awarded for completing a *degree* or other, shorter course of study.

dissertation: The major research project normally required as part of the work for a *doctorate*. Dissertations are expected to make a new and creative contribution to the field of study, or to demonstrate one's excellence in the field. See also *thesis*.

doctorate: The highest degree one can earn (but see *chancellor*). Includes Doctor of Philosophy (Ph.D.), Education (Ed.D.), and many other titles.

dormitory: Student living quarters on residential campuses. May include dining halls and classrooms.

early decision: Making a decision on whether to admit a student sooner than decisions are usually made. Offered by some schools primarily as a service either to students applying to several schools, or to those who are especially anxious to know the outcome of their application.

ECFMG: The Education Commission for Foreign Medical Graduates, which administers an examination to physicians who have gone to medical school outside the U.S. and wish to practice in the U.S.

electives: Courses one does not have to take, but may elect to take as part of a degree program.

essay test: An examination in which the student writes narrative sentences as answers to questions, instead of the short answers required by a *multiple-choice* test. Also called a *subjective test*.

equivalency examination: An examination designed to demonstrate knowledge in a subject where the learning was acquired outside a traditional classroom. A person who learned nursing skills while working in a hospital, for instance, could take an equivalency exam to earn credit in, say, obstetrical nursing.

external: Away from the main campus or offices of a school. An external degree may be earned by home study or at locations other than on the school's campus.

FAQ: Frequently asked questions. Increasingly, on the Internet and in print, information sources provide a list of FAQs to assist "newbies" (newcomers) in learning more about a given subject without having to bother people.

fees: Money paid to a school for purposes other than academic *tuition*. Fees might pay for parking, library services, use of the gymnasium, binding of dissertations, etc.

fellowship: A study grant, usually awarded to a graduate student, and usually requiring no work other than usual academic assignments (as contrasted with an *assistantship*).

financial aid: A catch-all term, including scholarships, loans, fellowships, assistantships, tuition reductions, etc. Many schools have a financial aid officer, whose job it is to deal with all funding questions and problems.

fraternity: A social organization, usually all-male, often identified by Greek letters, such as Zeta Beta Tau. There are also professional and scholastic fraternities open to men and women, such as Beta Alpha Psi, the national fraternity for students of accounting. See *sorority*.

freshman: The name for a student in the first of his or her four years of traditional study for a *bachelor's degree*. ("She is a freshman, and thus is a member of the freshman class.")

G.P.A.: See *grade-point average*.

grade-point average: The average score a student has made in all his or her classes, weighted by the number of credits or units for each class. Also called *G.P.A.*

grades: Evaluative scores provided for each course, and often for individual examinations or papers written for that course. There are letter grades (usually A, B, C, D, F) and number grades (usually percentages from 0% to 100%, or on a decimal scale of 0 to 3, 0 to 4, or 0 to 5). Some schools use a pass/fail system with no grades.

graduate: One who has earned a *degree* from a school. Also, in the U.S., used to describe programs offered beyond the *bachelor's* level. ("He is a graduate of Yale University, and is now doing graduate work at Princeton.") In the U.K. and elsewhere, the word used for upper-level work is *postgraduate*.

graduate school: A school or a division of a university offering work at the *master's degree* or *doctorate* level.

graduate student: One attending *graduate school*.

GRE: The Graduate Record Examination, which many traditional schools and a few *nontraditional* ones require for admission to *graduate* programs, and which can earn credit in some *bachelor's* programs.

honor societies: Organizations for persons with a high *grade-point average* or other evidence of outstanding performance. There are local societies on some campuses, and several national organizations, the most prestigious of which is called Phi Beta Kappa.

honor system: A system in which students are trusted not to cheat on examinations, and to obey other rules, without proctors or others monitoring their behavior.

honorary doctorate: A nonacademic award, given regularly by more than 1,000 colleges and universities to honor distinguished scholars, celebrities, and donors of large sums of money. Holders of this award may, and often do, call themselves "Doctor."

junior: The name for a student in his or her third year of a traditional four-year U.S. *bachelor's degree* program, or for a class of third-year students. ("He is a junior this year, and thus a member of the junior class.")

junior college: See *community college*.

language laboratory: A special room in which students can listen to foreign-language tapes over headphones, allowing many students to be learning different languages at different skill levels at the same time.

learning contract: A formal agreement between a student and a school, specifying independent work to be done by the student, and the amount of credit the school will award on successful completion of the work.

lecture class: A course in which a faculty member lectures to anywhere from a few dozen to many hundreds of students. Often lecture classes are followed by small group discussion sessions led by student assistants or junior faculty.

liberal arts: A term with many complex meanings, but generally referring to the nonscientific curriculum of a university: humanities, arts, social sciences, history, and so forth.

liberal education: Commonly taken to be the opposite of a specialized education; one in which students are required to take courses in a wide range of fields, as well as courses in their *major*.

licensed: Holding a permit to operate. This can range from a difficult-to-obtain state school license to a simple local business license.

life-experience portfolio: A comprehensive presentation listing and describing all learning experiences in a person's life, with appropriate documentation. The basic document used in assigning academic credit for life-experience learning.

LSAT: The Law School Admission Test, required by most U.S. law schools of all applicants.

maintenance costs: The expenses incurred while attending school, other than *tuition* and *fees*. Includes room and board (food), clothing, laundry, postage, travel, etc.

major: The subject or academic department in which a student takes concentrated coursework, leading to a specialty. ("His major is in English literature; she is majoring in chemistry.")

mentor: Faculty member assigned to supervise independent study at a *nontraditional* school; comparable to *adjunct faculty*.

minor: The secondary subject or academic department in which a student takes concentrated coursework. ("She has a major in art and a minor in biology.") Optional at most schools.

modem: The device that allows a computer to send and receive messages over a telephone line.

MCAT: The Medical College Admission Test, required by most U.S. medical schools of all applicants.

multiple-choice test: An examination in which the student chooses the best of several alternative answers provided for each question; also called an *objective test*. ("The capital city of England is (a) Zurich, (b) Ostrogotz-Plakatz, (c) Tokyo, or (d) none of the above.")

multiversity: A university system with two or more separate campuses, each a major university in its own right, such as the University of California or the University of Wisconsin.

narrative transcript: A transcript issued by a *nontraditional* school in which, instead of simply listing the courses completed and grades received, there is a narrative description of the work done and the school's rationale for awarding credit for that work.

nontraditional: Something done in other than the usual or traditional way. In education, refers to learning and degrees completed by methods other than spending many hours in classrooms and lecture halls.

nonresident: (1) A means of instruction in which the student does not need to visit the school; all work is done by correspondence, Internet, telephone, or exchange of audiotapes or videotapes; (2) a person who does not meet residency requirements of a given school and, as a result, often has to pay a higher *tuition* or *fees*.

objective test: An examination in which questions requiring a very short answer are posed. It can be multiple choice, true-false, fill-in-the-blank, etc. The questions are related to facts (thus objective) rather than to opinions (or subjective).

online: Connected, via computer, to another party, whether the Internet, a school, or an individual.

on the job: In the U.S., experience or training gained through employment, which may be converted to academic credit. In England, slang for having sex, which either confuses or amuses English people who read about "credit for on-the-job experience."

open admissions: An admissions policy in which everyone who applies is admitted, on the theory that the ones who are unable to do university work will drop out before long.

out-of-state student: One from a state other than that in which the school is located. Because most state colleges and universities have much higher *tuition* rates for out-of-state students, many people attempt to establish legal residence in the same state as their school.

parallel instruction: A method in which *nonresident* students do exactly the same work as residential students, during the same general time period, except they do it at home.

pass/fail option: Instead of getting a letter or number grade in a course, the student may elect, at the start of the course, a pass/fail option in which the only grades are either "pass" or "fail." Some schools permit students to elect this option on one or two of their courses each semester.

Phi Beta Kappa: A national honors society that recognizes students with outstanding grades.

plan of study: A detailed description of the program an applicant to a school plans to pursue. Many traditional schools ask for this as part of the admissions procedure. The plan of study should be designed to meet the objectives of the *statement of purpose.*

PONSI: The Program on Non-Collegiate Instruction; they evaluate educational training programs.

portfolio: See *life-experience portfolio.*

postgraduate: The British word for a person or a program more advanced than the *bachelor's* level. "She is working on a postgraduate certificate." Equivalent to *graduate* in the US.

prerequisites: Courses that must be taken before certain other courses may be taken. For instance, a course in algebra is often a prerequisite for a course in geometry.

private school: A school that is privately owned, rather than operated by a governmental department.

proctor: A person who supervises the taking of an examination to be certain there is no cheating, and that other rules are followed. Many *nontraditional* schools permit unproctored examinations.

professional school: School in which one studies for the various professions, including medicine, dentistry, law, nursing, veterinary, optometry, ministry, etc.

PSAT: Preliminary Scholastic Aptitude Test, given annually to high school juniors.

public school: In the U.S., a school operated by the government of a city, county, district, state, or the federal government. In England, a privately owned or run school.

quarter: An academic term at a school on the "quarter system," in which the calendar year is divided into four equal quarters. New courses begin each quarter.

quarter hour: An amount of credit earned for each classroom hour spent in a given course during a given quarter. A course that meets four hours each week for a quarter would probably be worth four quarter hours, or quarter units.

recognized: A term used by some schools to indicate approval from some other organization or governmental body. The term usually does not have a precise meaning, so it may mean different things in different places.

registrar: The official at most colleges and universities who is responsible for maintaining student records and, in many cases, for verifying and validating applications for admission.

rolling admissions: A year-round admissions procedure. Many schools only admit students once or twice a year. A school with rolling admissions considers each

application at the time it is received. Many *nontraditional* schools, especially ones with *nonresident* programs, have rolling admissions.

SAT: Scholastic Aptitude Test, one of the standard tests given to qualify for admission to colleges and universities.

scholarship: A study grant, either in cash or in the form of *tuition* or fee reduction.

score: Numerical rating of performance on a test. ("His score on the Graduate Record Exam was not so good.")

semester: A school term, generally four to five months. Schools on the semester system usually have two semesters a year, with a shorter summer session.

semester hour: An amount of credit earned in a course representing one classroom hour per week for a semester. A class that meets three days a week for one hour, or one day a week for three hours, would be worth three semester hours, or semester units.

seminar: A form of instruction combining independent research with meetings of small groups of students and a faculty member, generally to report on reading or research the students have done.

senior: The name for a student in his or her fourth year of a traditional four-year U.S. *bachelor's degree* program, or for a class of fourth-year students. ("Linnea is a senior this year, and is president of the senior class.")

sophomore: The second year of study in a four-year U.S. *bachelor's degree* program, or a member of that class.

sorority: A women's social organization, often with its own living quarters on or near a campus, and usually identified with two or three Greek letters, such as Sigma Chi. The male version is called a *fraternity.*

special education: Education of the physically or mentally handicapped, or, often, of the gifted.

special student: A student who is not studying for a degree because he or she either is ineligible or does not wish the degree.

statement of purpose: A detailed description of the career the applicant intends to pursue after graduation. A statement of purpose is often requested as part of the admissions procedure at a university.

subject: An area of study or learning covering a single topic, such as the subject of chemistry, or economics, or French literature.

subjective test: An examination in which the answers are in the form of narrative sentences or long or short essays, often expressing opinions rather than reporting facts.

syllabus: A detailed description of a course of study, often including the books to be read, papers to be written, and examinations to be given.

synchronous: At the same time. In a synchronous online or satellite course, the faculty and students can interact with one another. Opposite of *asynchronous*.

thesis: The major piece of research that is completed by many *master's degree* candidates. A thesis is expected to show a detailed knowledge of one's field and ability to do research and integrate knowledge of the field.

TOEFL: Test of English as a Foreign Language, required by many schools of persons for whom English is not the native language.

traditional education: Education at a residential school in which the *bachelor's degree* is completed through four years of classroom study, the *master's* in one or two years, and the *doctorate* in three to five years.

transcript: A certified copy of the student's academic record, showing courses taken, examinations passed, credits awarded, and grades or scores received.

transfer student: A student who has earned credit in one school, and then transfers to another school.

trimester: A term consisting of one third of an academic year. A school on the trimester system has three equal trimesters each year.

tuition: In the U.S., the money charged for formal instruction. In some schools, tuition is the only expense other than postage. In other schools, there may be *fees* as well as tuition. In England, tuition refers to the instruction or teaching at a school, such as the tuition offered in history.

tuition waiver: A form of financial assistance in which the school charges little or no *tuition*.

tutor: See *mentor*. A tutor can also be a hired assistant who helps a student prepare for a given class or examination.

undergraduate: Pertaining to the period of study from the end of high school to the earning of a *bachelor's degree*; also to a person in such a course of study. ("Alexis is an undergraduate at Reed College, one of the leading undergraduate schools.")

university: An institution that usually comprises one or more undergraduate colleges, one or more graduate schools, and, often, one or more professional schools.

USMLE: The U.S. Medical Licensing Exam, required of everyone who graduates from a non-U.S. medical school and wishes to be licensed in the U.S.

APPENDIX B

Bibliography

"What! Another of those damned, fat, square, thick books! Always scribble, scribble, scribble, eh, Mr. Gibbon?"

The Duke of Gloucester, Gibbon's patron, on being presented with Vol. III of his Decline and Fall of the Roman Empire

Most of these books are available in bookstores and libraries, on the Internet through services like www.amazon.com, and from a large service that specializes in providing books to distance-education students: Specialty Books, 5833 Industrial Drive, Athens, OH 45701; phone: (800) 466 1365 or (740) 594 2274; fax: (740) 593 3045; www.specialty-books.com. Some, however, are sold only or primarily by mail. In those cases we have given ordering information. In addition, some highly recommended books are now out of print. If you feel from the description that they would be useful in your situation, try your local library or a good second-hand bookstore. Where we have prices and other information, we've given it, though of course these things are always subject to change.

General Reference Books

The Ones We Use Every Day

Higher Education Directory (Higher Education Publications, 6400 Arlington Blvd., Suite 648, Falls Church, VA 22042; (703) 532 2300; *www.hepinc.com*). We list this first because it is the one we use the most. Until 1983, the U.S. Department of Education published a comprehensive directory of information on colleges and universities. When President Reagan announced his intention to shut down the Department of Education, their publication was discontinued and H.E.P. began publishing an almost identical directory. A new edition emerges toward the end of each year and gives detailed factual information (no opinions or ratings) on all accredited schools. They used to list California-approved schools as well, but stopped in 1988. More than 800 pages, $64.

International Handbook of Universities (Groves Dictionaries). 1,500 pages and an amazing $250 price tag. Gives detailed information on virtually every college, university, technical institute, and training school in the world. This book is widely used by collegiate registrars and admissions officers to evaluate schools.

Commonwealth Universities Yearbook (Association of Commonwealth Universities, London; distributed in the U.S. by Stockton Press, New York). This standard reference work covers what it refers to as all schools "in good standing" in 36 countries or areas. Many admissions departments use this book in making admissions or acceptance decisions. More than 600 institutions are described in great detail. More than 2,500 pages, $265.

The Others

Accredited Institutions of Postsecondary Education (Oryx Press). Issued around the middle of each year, this book lists every accredited institution and candidate for accreditation. This is the book many people use to determine conclusively whether or not a given American school is accredited. 735 pages, $70.

Barron's Profiles of American Colleges (Barron's Educational Series). A massive 1,300-page volume that describes every accredited college and university in America, with lists of majors offered by each school.

Bears' Guide to the Best Computer Degrees by Distance Learning by John Bear, Mariah Bear, and Larry McQueary (Ten Speed Press). We zero in on 100 of the best, accredited degree programs, both undergraduate and graduate, in such fields as telecom, computer science, MIS, and information technology. Lots of good information on which degrees will prepare you for which high-tech careers.

Bears' Guide to the Best MBAs by Distance Learning by John and Mariah Bear (Ten Speed Press). Full-page profiles on 100 distance-learning MBA programs, complete with advice on how to choose an MBA program that meets your needs.

Best's External Degree Directory by Thomas J. Lavin. More detail than this book but includes many fewer schools, and now quite out of date.

Campus-Free College Degrees by Marcie K. Thorson (Thorson Guides). This well-done book covers much of the same territory as this one, but accredited schools only, with considerably longer descriptions of each. Marcie does not include schools outside the U.S., even when they have U.S. accreditation.

College Degrees by Mail and Internet by John and Mariah Bear (Ten Speed Press). The publisher asked for a smaller and less comprehensive book on the topic, and this is it. We select 100 accredited schools with the best distance-degree programs, and write them up in more detail than this guide. Roughly ⅓ the size of this book for about half the price.

Degrees by Post by Cornelius A. Gillick (Moderne, Manchester, England). A 72-page book that lumps together completely fraudulent schools, major universities, and a bunch in between. Mr. Gillick seems sincere, but even when published in 1990, many of his listings were extremely out-of-date. (His reference to this book lists an address we left in 1979.)

Distance Degrees by Mark Wilson (Umpqua Education Research Alliance). Accredited schools only. A considerable improvement over the first edition, called *Campus Free Degrees*, and quite reminiscent of Marcie Thorson's book of similar title. While the geographical index lists only U.S. schools, the book also covers a few Canadian and British institutions.

Earn a College Degree at Home by Dennis L. Vinson (Crow Moon Books). Vinson does a decent job in this book that is somewhat reminiscent of ours. Quite a few of the listings were a bit dated even when the book came out in 1995. Still, it is written in a jolly style, has a lot of inspirational passages, and clearly separates the properly accredited schools from the others.

External Degrees in the Information Age: Legitimate Choices by Eugene Sullivan, David Stewart and Henry Spille (Onyx Press). Now why would they arrange a book on external degrees geographically, not alphabetically. A decent book, but many fewer listings than Thorson, Peterson, Wilson, or us. Nearly 10% of the text is devoted to one school. A very helpful chart comparing school-licensing laws in all the states.

How to Earn a College Degree Without Going to College by James P. Duffy (John Wiley & Sons). Much along the lines of our guide, but describes only bachelor's programs at accredited schools (fewer than 100 of them) and only wholly nonresident programs. Hasn't been updated since 1994.

How to Earn an Advanced Degree Without Going to Graduate School by James P. Duffy (John Wiley & Sons). The graduate-school version of the above book lists 140 accredited nonresidential master's and doctoral programs. Also not updated since 1994.

The Independent Study Catalog (Peterson's Guides). A master catalog listing 13,000 correspondence courses offered by more than 140 U.S. and Canadian institutions. Was updated regularly through 1998 but is now out of print.

The Internet University by Dan Corrigan (Cape Software). A comprehensive guide both to the entire practice of online education and courses and to more than 2,700 actual courses available.

Lovejoy's College Guide by Charles T. Straughn and Barbarasue Straughn (IDG Books Worldwide). Briefer descriptions than other guides, but still a huge book: 1,200 pages. The usefulness of *Lovejoy's* has been marred by the listing of some real clinkers, particularly totally phony diploma mills that somehow managed to get past the editors. Hasn't been updated since 1998.

Options: A Guide to Selected Opportunities in Non-Traditional Education by David Jones-Delcorde. Our former colleague has published his own book, the first two-thirds are reminiscent of ours; the final third has helpful information on various professional designations, and advice for distance-learning students.

Oryx Guide to Distance Learning (Oryx Press). 528 pages for a whopping $116.50. Lists more than 100 accredited U.S. institutions, focusing on audio, video, and online instruction. Not updated since 1997.

Peterson's Guide to Distance Learning Programs (Peterson's Guides). Probably the main competitor to our book, this is quite a comprehensive collection of information. Covers associate's and nondegree programs (which we don't); does *not* cover unaccredited schools or schools outside North America (which we do). Our real annoyance with this book is that more than one quarter of it, 200 pages, is taken up with paid advertising for schools, which until 2000 (when the practice finally came under some scrutiny from the press) was never identified as paid advertising, but simply as "in-depth descriptions." "It never occurred to us this is something we should highlight," explained Cristopher Maloney, Peterson's senior vice president for marketing.

Peterson's Guide to Graduate and Professional Programs (Peterson's Guides). Five large books, each describing in detail opportunities for residential graduate study in the U.S. Volumes cover social science and humanities, biological and agricultural sciences, physical sciences, and engineering. There is also a summary volume. The series is updated annually.

Peterson's Guide to Four-Year Colleges (Peterson's Guides). Another massive annual directory covering traditional accredited schools only.

World-Wide Inventory of Non-Traditional Degree Programs (UNESCO, c/o Unipub, 4611-F Assembly Dr., Lanham, MD 20706-4391; (800) 274 4447; *www.bernan.com*). A generally useful United Nations report on what many of the world's nations are doing in the way of nontraditional education. Some helpful school descriptions, and lots of detailed descriptions of evening courses offered by workers' cooperatives in Bulgaria and suchlike.

World Guide to Higher Education (Bowker Publishing Co.). A comprehensive survey, by the United Nations, of educational systems, degrees, and qualifications, from Afghanistan to Zambia.

Credit for Life-Experience Learning

Earn College Credit for What You Know by Lois Lamdin (Kendall/Hunt Publishing Company). How to put together a life-experience portfolio: how to gather the necessary information, document it, and assemble it, $25.

National Guide to Educational Credit for Training Programs (Oryx Press). Many nontraditional programs use this large volume, based on American Council on Education recommendations, to assign credit for more than 5,000 business, trade union, association, and government agency training programs. 1,200 pages, $85.

Guide to the Evaluation of Educational Experiences in the Armed Forces (Oryx Press). Many schools use this 2,000-page 3-volume set (one for each service) to assess credit for nonschool learning. Describes and makes credit recommendations for more than 8,000 military training programs.

Portfolio Development and Adult Learning: Purposes and Strategies by Alan Mandell and Elana Michelson (Council for Adult and Experiential Learning). Explores the eight approaches to portfolio development courses most typically used at colleges and universities, providing examples of each through a closer examination of prior learning assessment programs offered at 11 institutions of higher learning.

Prior Learning Assessment: The Portfolio by Marthe Sansregret (Hurtubise HMH, LaSalle, Quebec). A well-respected head of assessment for a major university told us that this is the book he asks his students to use to create their portfolios. It comes with software (Mac or DOS) to make the process more efficient. No longer in print, and the publisher appears to have gone out of business, so it may take some sleuthing to find a copy.

The Value of Personal Learning Outside College by Peter Smith (Acropolis Books). Dr. Smith, the founder of Vermont Community College and later the lieutenant governor of Vermont, has written a charming and very useful book on matters related to earning credit for non-school learning (which, he points out, accounts for 90% of what an adult knows). Many inspiring case histories of adults who pursued this path, plus appendices that help one identify and describe out-of-school learning. (Formerly titled *Your Hidden Credentials*.)

Medical Schools

Foreign Medical Schools for U.S. Citizens by Carlos Pestana, M.D., Ph.D. (P.O. Box 790617, San Antonio, TX 78279-0617). This wonderful book, unfortunately now out of print, gives anecdotal, well-written, and very informative write-ups on the good and less-good foreign schools for American medical school applicants, as well as application tips and other survival advice. Dr. Pestana, author and publisher, only had a couple dozen copies left when we went to press. Well worth the $20 (includes shipping by two-day priority mail).

The Medical School Applicant: Advice for Premedical Students by Carlos Pestana, M.D., Ph.D. (see immediately above). Another wonderful book by Dr. Pestana, also out of print, bringing his unique perspective to all the usual matters that books on medical schools have, and a great deal more, including a remarkable chapter on "Special angles: the dirty tricks department—a frank analysis of unconventional pathways to a medical education."

The Official Guide to Caribbean Medical Schools by S. K. Sarin and R. K. Yalamanchi (CaribMed, Inc., 4N 212 8th Avenue, Addison, IL 60101; *www.caribmed.com*). Well it's not "official" but it is a helpful little guide (104 pages, $18) describing what it is like to do a Caribbean M.D. (both the authors did so), with detailed descriptions of the major Caribbean medical schools.

Religious Schools

For a long time *Bears' Guide* included a chapter on unaccredited Bible and religious schools, but a few years back we made the decision to drop it. From a survey of our readers, it became clear that this chapter was of interest only to a tiny percentage, yet it accounted for a third of our mail and two thirds of our complaint letters. Whatever we said seemed to annoy or anger someone. Also, the majority of the hundreds of nonresident degree programs in religious fields are offered by small "Bible" schools specifically to members of their church or congregation. Many of these require little or no work, other than some Bible lessons, and thus cannot be compared to an academic program.

We acknowledge that there is need for information on these schools. At the moment, it is available from three Christian authors who disagree with each other vigorously on the merit of many schools.

Baker's Guide to Christian Distance Education by Jason D. Baker (Baker Book House). A professor of communication studies at Regent University profiles over 150 accredited Christian distance-learning programs, ranging from kindergarten to Ph.D.'s. A condensed version of these listings, complete with hyperlinks, can be found on the Web at *www.bakersguide.com*.

Name It and Frame It: New Opportunities in Adult Education and How to Avoid Being Ripped Off by "Christian" Degree Mills by Steve Levicoff (Institute on Religion and Law). A funny, informative, helpful, abrasive, and in some respects, quite outrageous book, which invites the dozens of schools called "degree mills" to sue the author if they don't like their listing. According to the author, none ever has. After publishing four editions,

Dr. Levicoff stopped selling his book, and now gives it away free on the Internet at *levicoff.tripod.com/nifi.htm*.

Walston's Guide to Earning Religious Degrees Nontraditionally by Rick Walston (Persuasion Press). "Josh" Walston and John Bear once collaborated on what they called *Walston & Bear's Guide to Earning Religious Degrees Nontraditionally*. As they had planned, by the 3rd edition, John bowed out, leaving the book entirely in Dr. Walston's hands. Walston is much more accepting than Levicoff of legal unaccredited schools, but takes a strong stand ("Shame," he says) against the many that improperly claim accreditation.

Financial Aid

Finding Money for College by John Bear and Mariah Bear (Ten Speed Press). We collected all the information we could find about the nontraditional and unorthodox approaches to getting a share in the billions of dollars that go unclaimed each year, including barter, real estate and tax gambits, negotiation, creative payment plans, obscure scholarships, foundations that make grants to individuals, etc. Any bookseller can supply or order this book.

The Scholarship Book by Daniel Cassidy (Prentice-Hall), **Dan Cassidy's Worldwide College Scholarship Directory** and **Dan Cassidy's Worldwide Graduate Scholarship Directory** (Career Press). These three books are, in effect,

a complete printout of the data banks of information used by Cassidy's National Scholarship Research Service, described in chapter 10. Tens of thousands of sources are listed for undergraduate and graduate students, for study in the U.S. and overseas.

The A's and B's of Academic Scholarships by Anna Leider (Octameron Associates). Lists more than 100,000 scholarships plus advice on earning them.

Don't Miss Out: The Ambitious Student's Guide to Financial Aid by Anna and Robert Leider (Octameron Associates). A complement to our *Finding Money* book, this one gives excellent advice (in 144 pages for $10) in pursuing the traditional route to financial aid.

Miscellany

Killing the Spirit: Higher Education in America by Page Smith (Viking Penguin). In 1990, one of John's writer-heroes issued this extraordinary book about everything that is wrong in higher education. From page 1: "The major themes might be characterized as the impoverishment of the spirit by 'academic fundamentalism,' the flight from teaching, the meretriciousness of most academic research, the disintegration of the disciplines, the alliance of the universities with the Department of Defense . . . etc., and last but not least, the corruptions incident to 'big time' collegiate sports." Read this wonderful book. Or listen to it: Page Smith reads it on 8 cassettes available from audio book sources.

College on Your Own by Gene R. Hawes and Gail Parker (Bantam Books). This remarkable book, now out of print, serves as a syllabus for a great many fields, for people who want to do college-level work at home, with or without the guidance of a college. A brief overview of each field (anthropology, biology, chemistry, history, etc.) and a detailed reading list for learning more about the field. Quite valuable in preparing learning contracts. Why doesn't some shrewd publisher put this fine volume back in print?

Diploma Mills: Degrees of Fraud by David W. Stewart and Henry A. Spille (Oryx). Originally this book was to provide details on specific operating diploma mills, but sadly, the authors either lost courage or were dissuaded by their attorneys, and it turned out to be only a moderately interesting survey of the history of the problem, with a once useful but now quite dated summary and evaluation of the current school laws in all 50 states.

The External Degree as a Credential: Graduates' Experiences in Employment and Further Study by Carol Sosdian and Laure Sharp (National Institute of Education). This 1978 report is probably the most often misquoted and misinterpreted educational survey ever published. Many schools (some good, some not) cite the findings (a high satisfaction level of external students and a high acceptance level of external degrees) without mentioning it related only to fully accredited undergraduate degrees, and has little or no relevance to unaccredited undergraduate or graduate degrees.

External Degrees in the Information Age by Eugene Sullivan, David W. Stewart, and Henry A. Spille (Oryx Press, 1997). In a sense, this is a successor to Stewart and Spille's *Diploma Mills*. It discusses principles of good practice in this field, along with guidelines for identifying bad schools. (We wish the authors didn't write such unkind things about John and about our book elsewhere.)

Getting a College Degree Fast by Joanne Aber (Prometheus Books, 1996). A decent enough book, focusing primarily on following the same path the author did: taking examinations to earn credit. Excellent information is provided on this topic, but not so useful for school and accreditation information (more than a few errors here).

Getting What You Came For: The Smart Student's Guide to Earning a Master's or Ph.D. by Robert L. Peters, Ph.D. (Noonday Press, 1997). Another wonderful and extremely helpful book. Quoting from the first chapter, "Graduate students run into problems because they do not understand how graduate school works, nor do most undergraduate counselors and graduate departments provide enough realistic guidance. . . . This book tells you what graduate school is really like. . . . I tell you how to create a comprehensive strategy that blends politics, psychology, and planning to ensure that your hard work pays off with a degree and a job." And he does, eloquently.

The Ph.D. Trap Revisited by Wilfred Cude (Dundurn Press). The author was treated very badly in his own graduate program, which turned him into a reformer. Farley Mowat writes that he is "the kind of reformer this

world needs. Humane, literate, reasonable, and utterly implacable, he has just unmasked the gruesome goings on in the academic morgue that deals in doctoral degrees. Any student contemplating the pursuit of a doctorate had better read *The Ph.D. Trap* as a matter of basic self-preservation. . . ."

Proving You're Qualified: Strategies for Competent People without College Degrees by Charles D. Hayes (Autodidactic Press). The author makes a strong case for competence being more important than credentials in life—but, since many gatekeepers disagree, Hayes goes on to show how to, well, how to do what the title says. Ronald Gross, who writes splendid books on education himself, says that "this is the wisest and most useful book I have ever read on this subject."

This Way Out: A Guide to Alternatives to Traditional College Education in the U.S. by John Coyne and Tom Hebert (E. P. Dutton). A delightful, if out-of-date and now out-of-print book that describes a small number of alternatives in detail, with inspirational interviews with participants. Includes an intriguing essay on self-education by hiring tutors, and sections as diverse as how to study, how to hitchhike successfully, what to do when revolution breaks out in the country in which you are studying, and how to deal with large universities worldwide.

Virtual College by Pam Dixon (Peterson's, 1996). A charming and very helpful little book (and she says nice things about ours, too), focusing on many of the issues the distance learner may face, including transfer of credits, employer acceptance, listing distance degrees on a resume, choosing technology, what it is like to be a distance student, and so on. $10.

Winning the Ph.D. Game by Dr. Richard W. Moore (Dodd, Mead & Co.). Now out of print, this is a lighthearted, extremely useful guidebook for current and prospective doctoral students. Covers the entire process, from selecting schools to career planning. Moore's aim is to "describe the folk wisdom passed from one generation of graduate students to the next [in order to] make the whole process less traumatic." He succeeds admirably.

Internet Resources

It is not surprising that what is fast becoming the primary medium *of* distance learning is exploding into the primary resource for information *about* distance learning. In previous editions we listed some of those Internet resources here—Web sites, newsgroups, listservs, etc.—but in a book covering a topic where things change fast, this list always seemed to go out of date the fastest.

So we've decided that the best place for keeping up with what's on the Net is on the Net itself. Start your search for online resources at the Bears' Guide Web site—*www.degree.net*—where we'll keep fresh and up-to-date our list of the best discussion groups, school directories, listservs, and Web-posted news items in the world of distance learning.

Journals

The academic journals typically address research aspects of the field (e.g., "The Effectiveness of Synchronous vs. Asynchronous Lectures on Exam Performance"). The main one in the U.S. is the **American Journal of Distance Education**, Pennsylvania State University, College of Education, 110 Rackley Building, University Park, PA 16802-3202; *www.ed.psu.edu/acsde*.

The main one in Canada is the **Journal of Distance Education**, published by the Canadian Association for Distance Education, 205-1 Stewart Street, Ottawa, ON K1N 6H7, Canada, and searchable on the Internet at *ultratext.hil.unb.ca/Texts/JDE/homepgENG.html*.

The **Chronicle of Distance Education and Communication** is published by Nova Southeastern University and is available free on the Internet at *www.fcae.nova.edu/disted*.

In Australia, the journal is **Distance Education**, published at the University of Southern Queensland, Distance Education Centre, Toowoomba Queensland 4350, Australia. It is searchable on the Internet at *www.usq.edu.au/dec/decjourn/demain.htm*.

Self-Serving Books

Every so often, the owners of less-than-wonderful schools have published entire books solely to be able to give themselves a splendid write-up in the midst of many other reasonably accurate school listings, and, occasionally, to "get even" on us for daring to criticize their "schools."

Directory of United States Traditional and Alternative Colleges and Universities by Dr. Jean-Maximillien De La Croix de Lafayette. This large $30 volume contains much useful information on schools. Universities are rated by number of stars. Among the small number of top-rated schools in the U.S. is Andrew Jackson University, established by Dr. De La Croix de Lafayette (no connection with the currently operating school of this name in Mississippi).

Guide to Alternative Education by Educational Research Associates. This $35 waste of time claims to be "continuously updated," but the so-called 1996 version we bought not only had hundreds of errors, but it listed schools that went out of business ten or more years ago. We learned about this book when a fictitious name we used in a communication with Century University received a solicitation to buy it. Not surprisingly, the longest and most favorable listing in the entire book is the one for Century University.

Guide to Education Abroad by I. B. Chaudhary. Published from a now-closed P.O. Box in Bombay, this is an illegal pirated copy of our book. If anyone ever sees an ad for this dreadful product, please let us know, so we can commence proper legal action. Thank you.

How to Earn a University Degree Without Ever Leaving Home by William Ebbs. A 54-page book selling for $20, with an astonishing number of errors of fact. Identifies the University de la Romande as the most outstanding nontraditional school in the world. William Ebbs is the pseudonym of Raymond Seldis, administrator, at the time, of the University de la Romande. What an amazing coincidence! The now-defunct California University for Advanced Studies is identified as the second best school in the world.

How to Obtain a College Degree by Mail by Edward P. Reddeck. Reddeck has been imprisoned at least twice for running phony schools, and once published this entire large book solely to be able to include a section extolling his phony American International University as one of the world's best.

Legal University Degrees by Mail (also called **University Degrees by Mail** and **Accredited College Degrees by Correspondence**) by "Jacques Canburry" or, in another printing, "Herald Crenshaw." Written and published by Ronald Pellar, the man who ran the diploma mill called Columbia State University from a mail forwarding service in Louisiana. Not surprisingly, the book chooses the fake Columbia State as the best university in America and refers to our book as a "phony guide," and a "brochure." Despite a cover price of $49.95, the book has been sent free to those who request it.

The Web Guide to Non-Traditional and Distance Learning University Degree Programs by The Commission on Distance Education. The book is sold by the unrecognized accrediting agency called World Association of Universities and Colleges, and, amazingly, of the forty-eight schools briefly described, half are accredited only by the World Association. All of the introductory essays are written by people associated with the World Association. School descriptions total about 24 pages of text in this slender and expensive volume.

• • • • •

Finally, a word or two about this book, *Bears' Guide*, from John: "Over the years, some critics have accused me of writing a self-serving book, because kind words were said about schools with which I had some connection or affiliation. This sort of criticism is, I believe, quite unwarranted. Of course I have said positive things about those schools with which I have had some connection over the past 23 years; I wouldn't have become involved with them if I didn't think they were good. But in this book, I have been careful to make clear my connections (there are none at this time), and I have always treated hundreds of other schools, some of them fierce competitors, very favorably."

APPENDIX C

About the Personal Counseling Services

If you would like personal advice and recommendations, based on your own specific situation, a personal counseling service is available, by mail. John started this service in 1977, at the request of many readers. While John remains a consultant, since 1981, the actual personal evaluations and consulting are done by two colleagues of his, who are leading experts in the field of nontraditional education.

For a modest fee, these things are done:

1. You will get a long personal letter evaluating your academic needs, recommending the best distance learning degree programs for you, and discussing how these programs work.

2. You will get answers to any questions you may have, and guidance in choosing a degree program and getting started on your studies.

3. You will get detailed, up-to-the-minute information on institutions and programs (also catalogue excerpts) and discussion (as needed) of portfolio assessment, equivalency exams, correspondence courses, online courses, sources of financial aid, and more.

4. You will be entitled to the service for a full year of extended personal advice, and updates on new programs and changes in your distance learning options.

If you are interested in personal counseling, please contact the service with your mailing address and you will be sent descriptive literature and a counseling questionnaire, without cost or obligation.

Once you have these materials, if you wish counseling, simply fill out the questionnaire and return it, with a letter and resumé if you like, along with the fee, and your personal reply and counseling materials will be prepared and airmailed to you.

For free information about this service, write, telephone, fax, or email:

Degree Consulting Services
P.O. Box 3533
Santa Rosa, California 95402
Phone: (707) 539 6466
Fax: (707) 538 3577
Email: degrees@sonic.net
Web site: www.degreeconsult.com

NOTE: Use the above address (etc.) only for matters related to the counseling service. For all other matters, write to us at P.O. Box 7123, Berkeley, CA 94707, or email *johnandmariah@degree.net*.

Thank you.

—John and Mariah Bear

APPENDIX D

Research Doctorates

Make your friends your teachers and mingle the pleasures of conversation with the advantages of instruction.

Baltasar Gracian, The Art of Worldly Wisdom

We appreciate the assistance of Dick Adams in preparing this section.

The research doctorate offers an interesting opportunity to earn the degree from a major British, Australian, or South African university, with the possibility of little, or even no residency, and at relatively modest cost. Unfortunately, there is no single simple and straightforward procedure to follow, even within departments at the same university, and even from one day to the next. Things are decided very much on a case-by-case basis.

This situation has proven difficult or annoying for Americans who are used to cookbook procedures for dealing with universities.

The research doctorate is typically available to people who already have a master's. There is no coursework involved, only the designing and executing of a research project, and then writing it up as a dissertation.

At the doctoral level, admissions rules and decisions are typically made, both formally and informally, in a school's individual departments, rather than by the university admissions or registrar's office. Different departments within a university may well have quite different programs, rules, and procedures.

It is the existence of these "informal" situations that makes things complicated and nonuniform. As far as we know, all doctoral programs ostensibly have some residential requirement; however, there are situations in which a department (or even a specific professor within the department) will agree that the residency can be done by telephone, fax, or email, or even by having the professor visit the student at the student's location and expense. Experience suggests that initial contact by old-fashioned mail is the most effective way to begin such a process.

The real problem here is that it is often not possible to determine the residency requirements until after the admissions process is complete, and sometimes not until the occasion of an actual face-to-face meeting. The feed-back we have gotten is extremely mixed. Some people are actually doing 100 percent nonresident degrees, and are very happy. But when we make contact with the university, and ask questions, we inevitably are told, "Oh that was a special circumstance." Other people went through the whole admissions process, went to a first meeting in Britain or Australia, and were told, "Now we expect you to return every month" (or every quarter), and were, as a result, quite unhappy.

The only way in which clear advance information has been available, it seems, is when the potential student establishes a relationship (by mail, email, fax, or phone, or even in person) with a specific faculty member within the department, who then becomes, so to speak, his or her sponsor or advocate (the term "promoter" is sometimes used), and helps persuade the school's decision-makers that this particular student should be allowed to do the degree nonresidentially (or with minimal residency).

Clearly a lot of research is required by the student, both in choosing the university (or universities) to apply to, and, if appropriate, learning about the faculty within the department and establishing communication with them. Here are a few guidelines:

1. Determine if the university has a department offering the topic(s) you wish to study. Almost all of these universities have a presence on the Internet. If the Net turns up nothing, then library research is called for. Some foreign universities' catalogs (or calendars, as they are often called) are available on microfiche cards, along with those of U.S. universities.

2. Determine whether research doctorates are possible in that topic. This will almost certainly mean reading the catalogs—some will be available on the Internet, others you may need to have sent to you. Some universities have combined catalogs with all departments listed; others issue a separate catalog, or prospectus, for each separate department or school.

3. Open communication with the department, or perhaps with a specific faculty member within the department. Some people have said that the approach that worked for them was to learn the names of the faculty, do some research to see what they had written (articles, books), or otherwise learn their special interests (sometimes catalogs give this information); then begin an academic correspondence, asking questions or commenting on their work. Only then, after the exchange of a few communications, did they bring up the notion of doing a research doctorate under the supervision of that person.

Dick Adams, a helpful reader, suggests sending a request for information to the "Office of Postgraduate Studies" at every university you can identify as having a department in your field. Then identify the research areas of the faculty. Read some of their published research. Formulate some research questions. Eliminate the parochial research questions. Prepare two or three research proposals and send them to the postgraduate office. Then wait for the responses.

A search in British and Australian bookstores yielded two books that offer some guidance, although neither is quite as simple and straightforward as we might have wished. They are:

How to Get a Ph.D. by Estelle M. Phillips and D. S. Pugh (Buckingham and Philadelphia: Open University Press, 1996). It is identified as "a handbook and survival manual for Ph.D. students, providing a practical, realistic understanding of the processes of doing research for a doctorate." It specifically addresses the particular problems of overseas students.

Working for a Doctorate: A Guide for the Humanities and Social Sciences by Norman Graves and Ved Varmna (London and New York: Routledge, 1997). Addresses the problems of the research process, finance, and time management. It is identified as "a vital guide and companion to anyone studying for, supervising or contemplating a doctoral degree in the humanities or social sciences."

Some of the schools

Here are the names and locations of *some* universities where readers have told us they are doing nonresident or very-short-residency research doctorates. But please remember, it may do no good simply to write or call and say, "I want to do a research doctorate." It might work, or it might cause annoyance and frustration on both ends.

Pursuit of a doctorate is a major investment of time, energy, and money. We strongly suggest treating it seriously by doing your own research and due diligence first. And do let us know what you learn, perhaps to help smooth the path for those who follow you.

The United Kingdom

Aston University
Aston Triangle, Birmingham B4 7ET, England
www.aston.ac.uk

Coventry University
Priory St., Coventry CV1 5FB, England
www.coventry.ac.uk

De Montfort University
The Gateway, Leicester LE1 9BH, England
www.dmu.ac.uk

Heriot-Watt University
Edinburgh EH14 4AS, Scotland
www.hw.ac.uk

Keele University
Keele, Staffordshire ST5 5BG, England
www.keele.ac.uk

Manchester Metropolitan University
All Saints, Manchester M15 6BH, England
www.mmu.ac.uk

Oxford Brookes University
Gipsy Lane, Headington, Oxford OX3 0BP, England
www.brookes.ac.uk

South Bank University
103 Borough Road, London SE1 0AA, England
www.southbank-university.ac.uk

Thames Valley University
St. Mary's Road, Ealing, London W5 5RF, England
www.tvu.ac.uk

University of Aberdeen
King's College, Aberdeen AB24 3FX, Scotland
www.abdn.ac.uk

University of Bradford
Bradford, West Yorkshire BD7 1DP, England
www.brad.ac.uk

University of Brighton
Mithras House, Brighton BN2 4AT, England
www.bton.ac.uk

University of Dundee
Nethergate, Dundee DD1 4HN, Scotland
www.dundee.ac.uk

University of Durham
Old Shire Hall, Durham DH1 3HP, England
www.dur.ac.uk

University of Edinburgh
South Bridge, Edinburgh EH8 9YL, Scotland
www.ed.ac.uk

University of Glasgow
Glasgow G12 8QQ, Scotland
www.gla.ac.uk

University of Kent at Canterbury
Canterbury, Kent CT2 7NZ, England
www.ukc.ac.uk

University of London
Senate House, Malet Street, London WC1E 7HU,
England
www.lon.ac.uk

University of Luton
Park Square, Luton LU1 3JU, England
www.luton.ac.uk

University of Manchester
Oxford Road, Manchester M13 9PL, England
www.man.ac.uk

University of Newcastle upon Tyne
Newcastle upon Tyne NE1 7RU, England
www.ncl.ac.uk

University of Northumbria at Newcastle
Ellison Place, Newcastle upon Tyne NE1 8ST,
England
www.unn.ac.uk

University of Sheffield
Western Bank, Sheffield S10 2TN, England
www.shef.ac.uk

University of Stirling
Stirling FK9 4LA, Scotland
www.stir.ac.uk

University of Strathclyde
16 Richmond St., Glasgow G1 1XQ, Scotland
www.strath.ac.uk

University of Wales—Aberystwyth
King Street, Aberystwyth, Ceredigion SY23 2AX,
Wales
www.aber.ac.uk

University of Wales—Bangor
Bangor, Gwynedd LL57 2DG, Wales
www.bangor.ac.uk

University of Wales—Cardiff
50 Park Place, Cardiff CF10 3UA, Wales
www.cf.ac.uk

University of Wales—Lampeter
Ceredigion SA48 7ED, Wales
www.lamp.ac.uk

University of Warwick
Coventry CV4 7AL, England
www.warwick.ac.uk

University of the West of England
Coldharbour Lane, Bristol BS16 1QY, England
www.uwe.ac.uk

University of Westminster
309 Regent St., London W1R 8AL, England
www.westminster.ac.uk

Australia

Australian Catholic University
P.O. Box 247, Everton Park, Queensland 4053
www.acu.edu.au

Central Queensland University
Bruce Highway, Rockhampton, Queensland 4702
www.cqu.edu.au

Charles Sturt University
Panorama Ave., Bathurst, New South Wales 2795
www.csu.edu.au

Curtin University of Technology
GPO Box U 1987, Perth, Western Australia 6845
www.curtin.edu.au

Deakin University
221 Burwood Highway, Burwood, Victoria 3125
www.deakin.edu.au

Edith Cowan University
Pearson St., Churchlands, Western Australia 6018
www.cowan.edu.au

James Cook University
Townsville, Queensland 4811
www.jcu.edu.au

Monash University
Clayton Campus, Victoria 3800
www.monash.edu.au

Southern Cross University
P.O. Box 157, Lismore, New South Wales 2480
www.scu.edu.au

University of Melbourne
Victoria 3010
www.unimelb.edu.au

University of New England
Armidale, New South Wales 2351
www.une.edu.au

University of South Australia
GPO Box 2471, Adelaide, SA 5001
www.unisa.edu.au

University of Southern Queensland
Toowoomba, Queensland 4350
www.usq.edu.au

South Africa

Potchefstroom University for Christian Higher Education
Private Bag X6001, Potchefstroom 2520
www.puk.ac.za

University of Pretoria
Pretoria 0002
www.up.ac.za

University of South Africa
P.O. Box 392, Unisa 0003
www.unisa.ac.za

Vista University
Private Bag X634, Pretoria 0001
www.vista.ac.za

India

Central Institute of English and Foreign Languages
Hyderabad 500 007, Andra Pradesh

Japan

Rikkyo University
3-34-1 Nishi-Ikebukuro, Toshima-ku, Tokyo 171-8501
www.rikkyo.ac.jp

Pakistan

Allama Iqbal Open University
Sector H-8, Islamabad
www.aiou.edu.pk

Accredited Foreign Schools That Don't Accept U.S. Students

A wise man's country is the world.

Aristippus of Cyrene (ca. 400 B.C.)

In previous editions of this book, we included in our listings many non-U.S. distance-learning schools that do not accept U.S. citizens (or, more specifically, only accept their own citizens). This has led to some obvious benefits (a Swedish reader living abroad could learn about Uppsala University and finish his degree from outside Sweden) and drawbacks (non-Swedish readers would have to sift through, and perhaps experience dashed hopes over, a program they're not eligible for).

As our database has expanded over the years, the lack of discrimination between foreign schools that do and do not accept U.S. students has become increasingly non-user-friendly. The best solution for everyone would be a separate detailed section outlining, country by country, international schools that don't accept U.S. students. Unfortunately, a truly detailed section would take up half of our fairly general guide; we may as well (and, one day, very well might) write a second book designed specifically for international students.

In the meantime, we have removed from earlier chapters the accredited schools that don't accept U.S. citizens and placed them in the list that follows, organized by country. Remember, this is *not* a list of all foreign distance-learning schools; those foreign schools that *do* accept U.S. students are covered in the earlier chapters.

And we remind you of the thoughts expressed in chapter 29, "Bending the Rules." We've heard from readers who have managed to negotiate their way through the "national students only" policy by establishing that they fluently speak the relevant national language, setting up a convenience address in the university's country of residence, handling examination requirements through the country's U.S. embassy, or similar means. If you would like to boldly proceed in this direction in your search for a B.A. in Japanese literature or an M.Phil. in Islamic studies, we wish you the best of luck. And let us know how things go; perhaps you can even establish a new university policy on U.S. students.

Africa and the Middle East

Algeria
Centre National d'Enseignement Generalise

Botswana
University of Botswana

Central African Republic
Ecole National d'Administration

Ghana
University of Ghana

Iran
Payama Noor University

Ivory Coast
Centre Ivoirien de Formation Permanente a Distance

Kenya

University of Nairobi

Lesotho

National University of Lesotho

Mali

Institut Pedagogique National du Mali

Mauritius

Mauritius Institute of Education
Ministry of Education, Science, and Technology
University of Mauritius

Nigeria

National Educational Technology Centre
University of Abuja
University of Ibadan
University of Lagos

Palestine

Al-Quds Open University

South Africa

AFM Theological College
Allenby In-Home Power Learning
Azaliah College
Christian Academy for Tertiary and Secondary
    Education
Rand Afrikaans University
SA Theological Seminary
South African College for Teacher Education
University of Natal
University of Port Elizabeth
University of the Orange Free State

Tanzania

Open University of Tanzania

Zambia

University of Zambia

Zimbabwe

Zimbabwe Open University

The (Other) Americas

Argentina

Instituto Universitario Auronautico
Universidad Nacional de la Patagonia San Juan Bosco

Bolivia

Universidad NUR

Canada

Atlantic School of Theology
College Mathieu
Contact North
Mount Allison University
Saint Stephen's College
Université de Moncton
Université de Sherbrooke
University of Windsor
Wilfrid Laurier University

Chile

Universidad Austral de Chile

Colombia

Universidad del Tolima
Universidad Mariana
Universidad Pontificia Bolivariana

Cuba

Universidad de la Habana

Honduras

Universidad Nacional Autonoma de Honduras

Mexico

Universidad del Valle de Atemajac
Universidad Nacional Autonoma de Mexico
Universidad Pedagogica Nacional

Panama

Universidad Interamericana de Educacion a Distancia
    de Panama

Peru

Pontificia Universidad Catolica del Peru

Universidad Nacional de Educacion "Enrique Guzman Y Valle"

Venezuela

Universidad Nacional Abierta

Asia

Bangladesh

Bangladesh Open University

China

China Central Radio and Television University

East China Normal University

Hong Kong Baptist University

Tongji University

University of Hong Kong

India

Alagappa University

Andhra University

Annamalai University

Bangalore University

Barkatullah University

Birla Institute of Technology and Science

Centre for Economic and Social Studies

Christian Medical College

Dr. B.R. Ambedkar Open University

Gujarat Vidyapith

Himachal Pradesh University

Indira Gandhi National Open University

International Institute for Population Sciences

Jain Vishva Bharati Institute

Jawaharlal Nehru Technological University

Kakatiya University

Kota Open University

Kurukshetra University

Maharshi Dayanand University

Meerut University

Mother Teresa Women's University

Osmania University

Panjab University

India, continued

Patna University

Punjabi University

SNDT Women's University

Sri Venkateshvara University

Tilak Maharashtra Vidyapith

University of Allahabad

University of Calicut

University of Delhi

University of Jammu

University of Kashmir

University of Kerala

University of Madras

University of Mumbai

University of Mysore

University of Pune

Utkal University

Yashwantrao Chavan Maharashtra Open University

Indonesia

Universitas Terbuka

Japan

Bukkyo University

Chuo University

Hosei University

Kawasaki College of Allied Health Professions

Keio University

Kinki University

University of the Air

Korea

Korea National Open University

Malaysia

Universiti Kebangsaan Malaysia

Universiti Sains Malaysia

Myanmar

University of Distance Education

The Philippines

University of Mindanao

University of the Philippines Open University

Singapore

Singapore Institute of Management
University of Hull

Sri Lanka

Open University of Sri Lanka

Taiwan

National Open University

Thailand

Ramkhamhaeng University
Sukhothai Thammathirat Open University

Australasia

Australia

Australian Graduate School of Management
Coolamon College
Open Learning Australia
Queensland University of Technology
RMIT University
St. John's Center of Ministry
Tabor College

Fiji

University of the South Pacific

New Zealand

Massey University
University of Waikato

Europe and the Former Soviet Union

Austria

Zentrum fuer Fernstudien Universitaet Linz

Bulgaria

New Bulgarian University

The Czech Republic

Technical University of Liberec

Denmark

Jutland Open University

England

Loughborough University
Middlesex University
Trinity College of Music
Westminster College

France

Federation Interuniversitaire de l'Enseignement a
    Distance

Ireland

Institute of Public Administration
University of Ulster

Italy

Consorzio per l'Universita a Distanza

Lithuania

Kaunas University of Technology
Law Academy of Lithuania
Siauliai University

Norway

Norwegian School of Management

Romania

Centre for Open Distance Education for the Civil
    Society (CODECS)

Russia

International Institute of Management
University of the Russia's Academy of Education (URAE)

Slovak Republic

University of Zilina

Sweden

Uppsala University

Turkey

Anadolu Universitesi

Subject Index

For years, our readers have been telling us how nice it would be if Bears' Guide had a complete index to the subjects offered by the many degree programs described. We are delighted that after 25 years, thanks to the excellent work of Tom Head, what lies before you is indeed a comprehensive subject index. For each field of study, we list the offering schools, the degrees offered (B, M, D), and whether or not they are entirely nonresident (NR) or require short residency (SR). To save space, we do not list the page numbers. The schools are easy enough to find, since all those listed are either in chapter 18 (nonresident) or chapter 19 (short residency). Unaccredited schools are not included in the subject index.

There are three more things to say about subject areas:

1. Many subject areas are so broad ("general studies") or all-inclusive ("social science") that a wide range of things can be done in them.

2. There are "side door" approaches to various fields. If a school offers only "history" and a student wishes to study "technology," it may be possible to do a degree in the "history of technology." The field of education is another commonly used side door.

3. There are a great many courses available by distance learning that do not result in a degree, but which may be applied to another school's degree. For instance, although there is no listing here for botanical sciences, there are individual courses available. A student could, for instance, take courses from any of a dozen universities, and apply those courses to the B.S. degree of schools such as Excelsior College, Thomas Edison State College, and Charter Oak State College. How does one find these courses? Many are offered by the schools listed in chapter 13. Others can be found on searchable Web sites, such as *www.dlcoursefinder.com* or *www.lifelonglearning.com*. Unfortunately, some of these online course directories, such as WorldWideLearn and the one on Yahoo, list quite a few fake and bad schools among the good ones. If you are considering the transfer strategy, confirm in advance that the target school (Excelsior, etc.) will accept credits from the school offering the course you'd like to take.

Accounting

Auburn U. (M, SR)
Caldwell C. (B, SR)
Capital U. (B, SR)
Central Queensland U. (B-M, NR)
Champlain C. (B, NR)
Charles Sturt U. (B-M-D, NR)
City U. (B, NR)
Connecticut State U. (M, NR)
Curtin U. of Technology (B-M, NR)
Deakin U. (M, NR)
Edith Cowan U. (B-M, NR)
Empire State C. (B, NR)
Excelsior C. (A-B, NR)
Golden Gate U. (M, NR)
Harcourt Learning Direct (A, NR)

Keller Graduate School of Management (M, NR)
Marywood U. (B, SR)
Monash U. (B, NR)
National Distance Education Centre (M, NR)
Nova Southeastern U. (M, SR)
Old Dominion U. (B, NR)
Purdue U. (M, SR)
Southern Cross U. (M, SR)
St. Mary-of-the-Woods C. (B, SR)
Strayer U. (B, NR)
State University of New York Institute of Technology at Utica/Rome (M, NR)

Technikon of Southern Africa (B-M-D, NR)
Thomas Edison State C. (B, NR)
Universidad Estatal a Distancia (B-M, NR)
U. of Kent at Canterbury (M-D, SR)
U. of London (B, NR)
U. of Maryland (B, NR)
U. of Melbourne (M-D, NR)
U. of New England (M, NR)
U. of Phoenix (B-M, NR)
U. of Pretoria (B, NR)
U. of South Africa (B-M-D, NR)
U. of South Australia (B, NR)
U. of Southern Queensland (B-M, NR)

B=Bachelor's · M=Master's · D=Doctorate · NR=Nonresident · SR=Short Residency

U. of Tasmania (M-D, NR)
U. of Technology, Sydney (D, NR)
U. of Teesside (M-D, SR)
U. of Wales-Aberystwyth
   (M-D, SR)
Upper Iowa U. (B, NR)
See also **Finance**
See also **Taxation**

Acquisition Management and Procurement

American Graduate U. (M, NR)
Capitol C. (M, NR)
Strathclyde Graduate Business
   School (M, NR)
Thomas Edison State C. (B, NR)

Acoustics

Pennsylvania State U. (M, SR)

Addiction Counseling and Intervention

Edith Cowan U. (B, NR)
Monterrey Institute for Graduate
   Studies (M-D, NR)
U. of London (M, NR)

Adult and Continuing Education

Brock U. (B, NR)
Central Queensland U. (B, NR)
Columbia U. (D, SR)
Edith Cowan U. (M-D, NR)
Griffith U. (B, NR)
Indiana U. (M, NR)
International Management Centres
   (B-M, SR)
National-Louis U. (M-D, NR)
Pennsylvania State U. (M, NR)
Royal Roads U. (M, SR)
St. Joseph's C. (M, SR)
Southern Cross U. (M, SR)
U. of Calgary (M, SR)
U. of Saskatchewan (B, NR) .
U. of Southern Queensland
   (B-M, NR)
U. of Wyoming (M, SR)

Adventure Education

Prescott C. (M, SR)

Aerospace Engineering

Auburn U. (M, SR)
U. of Colorado at Boulder (M, NR)

Virginia Polytechnic Institute and
   State U. (M, NR)
See also **Space Studies**

African Languages and Literature

U. of Pretoria (B-M, NR)
U. of South Africa (B-M-D, NR)
See also **Afrikaans Language and Literature**

African Politics

U. of South Africa (B-M-D, NR)

Afrikaans Language and Literature

U. of Pretoria (B, NR)
U. of South Africa (B-M-D, NR)

Agribusiness

See **Agriculture and Agriculture Management**

Agricultural Engineering

Colorado State U. (M, NR)
U. of Idaho (M, NR)
U. of Southern Queensland
   (B-M, NR)

Agriculture and Agriculture Management

Charles Sturt U. (B-M-D, NR)
Colorado State U. (M, NR)
Iowa State U. (B-M, SR)
Kansas State U. (M, NR)
Purdue U. (M, SR)
Universidad Estatal a Distancia
   (B-M, NR)
U. of Guelph (M, SR)
U. of London (M, NR)
U. of Saskatchewan (B, NR)
U. of Wales-Aberystwyth
   (M-D, SR)
Washington State U. (B-M, NR)

Agriculture Law

De Montfort U. (M, NR)

Air Warfare

American Military U. (M, NR)

American Studies

U. of Kent at Canterbury (M-D, SR)
U. of Melbourne (M-D, NR)
U. of New England (M, NR)

Ancient History

Macquarie U. (B-M, NR)
U. of Melbourne (M-D, NR)
U. of New England (B-M, NR)
U. of South Africa (B-M-D, NR)

Ancient Languages and Cultures

U. of South Africa (M, NR)

Animal Science

See **Veterinary Science**

Anthropology

California Institute of Integral
   Studies (M-D, SR)
Central Queensland U. (M, NR)
Charter Oak State C. (B, NR)
Edith Cowan U. (B, NR)
Thomas Edison State C. (B, NR)
U. of Kent at Canterbury (M-D, SR)
U. of Melbourne (M-D, NR)
U. of Saskatchewan (B, NR)
U. of South Africa (B-M-D, NR)
U. of Southern Colorado (B, NR)
U. of Southern Queensland (B, NR)
U. of Teesside (M-D, SR)
U. of Wales-Lampeter (M-D, NR)

Applied and Professional Studies

Antioch U. (D, SR)
California State U.-Dominguez
   Hills (B, NR)
Elizabethtown C. (B, SR)
Murdoch U. (B, NR)
Nova Southeastern U. (B, SR)
Southwest Missouri State U.
   (M, NR)
Thomas Edison State C. (M, NR)
Troy State U. (B, NR)

Applied Economics

U. of Southern Queensland (B, NR)
See also **Economics**

Applied Linguistics

Edith Cowan U. (M-D, NR)

Macquarie U. (M, NR)
Monash U. (M, NR)
U. of Kent at Canterbury (M-D, SR)
U. of Leicester (M, NR)
U. of Melbourne (M-D, NR)
U. of Southern Queensland
    (M, NR)
See also **Linguistics**

Applied Mathematics

Mary Baldwin C. (B, SR)
U. of Kent at Canterbury (M-D, SR)
U. of South Africa (B-M-D, NR)
U. of Southern Queensland (B, NR)
U. of Technology, Sydney (D, NR)
See also **Mathematics**

Applied Science

Technical U. of British Columbia
    (M, SR)

Applied Social Studies

See **Social Sciences**
See **Social Work**
See **Sociology**

Aquaculture

Curtin U. of Technology (B, SR)
Deakin U. (M, NR)
U. of Tasmania (M-D, NR)

Arabic Language and Literature

U. of Melbourne (M-D, NR)
U. of South Africa (B-M-D, NR)

Archaeology

U. of Kent at Canterbury (M-D, SR)
U. of Leicester (M, NR)
U. of Melbourne (M-D, NR)
U. of New England (B-M, NR)
U. of Saskatchewan (B, NR)
U. of South Africa (M, NR)
U. of Wales-Lampeter (M-D, NR)

Architecture

U. of Luton (M-D, NR)
U. of Melbourne (M-D, NR)
U. of Tasmania (M-D, NR)
U. of Technology, Sydney (D, NR)
See also **Contracting and Building**

Art

Atlantic Union C. (B, SR)
Atlantic U. (M, NR)
Bennington C. (M, SR)
Burlington C. (B, SR)
Caldwell C. (B, SR)
California State U.-Dominguez
    Hills (M, NR)
De Montfort U. (M-D, SR)
Maine C. of Art (M, SR)
Mary Baldwin C. (B, SR)
Norwich U. (M, SR)
Thomas Edison State C. (B, NR)
U. of Kent at Canterbury (M-D, SR)
U. of Melbourne (M-D, NR)
U. of South Africa (B-M-D, NR)
U. of Teesside (M-D, SR)
U. of Wales-Aberystwyth
    (M-D, SR)
See also **Cartooning**

Art Education

Edith Cowan U. (M-D, NR)

Art History

Charter Oak State C. (B, NR)
U. of Kent at Canterbury (M-D, SR)
U. of Melbourne (M-D, NR)
U. of South Africa (B-M-D, NR)
U. of Wales-Lampeter (M, NR)

Art Therapy

Norwich U. (M, SR)

Asian Studies

California Institute of Integral
    Studies (M-D, SR)
Central Queensland U. (B, NR)
Curtin U. of Technology (B, SR)
Mary Baldwin C. (B, SR)
Murdoch U. (B-M, NR)
U. of Melbourne (M-D, NR)
U. of New England (B-M, NR)
U. of Southern Queensland (B, NR)

Asthma Education

Charles Sturt U. (M, NR)

Astronomy

U. of South Africa (B-M-D, NR)
See also **Space Studies**

Audiology

Central Michigan U. (D, NR)
U. of Florida (D, NR)
U. of Melbourne (M-D, NR)
See also **Communication Disorders**

Auditing

U. of South Africa (B, NR)

Australian Studies

Central Queensland U. (B, NR)
Charles Sturt U. (M-D, NR)
Monash U. (B, NR)
U. of Melbourne (M-D, NR)

Automotive Science and Engineering

Kettering U. (M, NR)

Aviation Safety

Central Missouri State U. (M, NR)

Banking

See **Finance**

Biblical Studies

American Bible C. and Seminary
    (B-M, NR)
Global U. of the Assemblies of God
    (B-M, NR)
Greenwich School of Theology
    (B-M-D, NR)
Regent U. (M, SR)
Southern Christian U. (M, NR)
Taylor U. (A, SR)
U. of Pretoria (B-M-D, NR)
U. of South Africa (B-M-D, NR)

Biochemistry

Mary Baldwin C. (B, SR)
U. of Kent at Canterbury (M-D, SR)
U. of Melbourne (M-D, NR)

Bioethics

Monash U. (M, NR)
U. of South Africa (M, NR)
U. of Technology, Sydney (D, NR)
U. of Wales-Lampeter (M, NR)

Biology

Acadia U. (B, SR)

Central Queensland U. (B, NR)
Charter Oak State C. (B, NR)
Excelsior C. (B, NR)
Lehigh U. (M, NR)
Macquarie U. (B-M-D, NR)
Mary Baldwin C. (B, SR)
Monash U. (B, NR)
Thomas Edison State C. (B, NR)
U. of Luton (M-D, NR)
U. of Melbourne (M-D, NR)
U. of New England (B-M-D, NR)
U. of Saskatchewan (B, NR)
U. of Technology, Sydney (D, NR)
U. of Wales-Aberystwyth
   (M-D, SR)

Biophysics

Georgia Institute of Technology
   (M, NR)
Illinois Institute of Technology
   (M, SR)

British and Commonwealth Studies

Sheffield Hallam U. (M, SR)
U. of Wales-Lampeter (M, NR)

Building Services

See **Contracting and Building**

Bulk Solids Handling Technology

Glasgow Caledonian U. (M, NR)

Business and Commerce (General)

Acadia U. (B, SR)
Andrew Jackson U. (B, NR)
Athabasca U. (B, NR)
California C. for Health Sciences
   (B, NR)
Canadian School of Management
   (B-M, NR)
Central Queensland U. (B-M-D, NR)
Charles Sturt U. (B-M-D, NR)
Charter Oak State C. (B, NR)
City U. (B, NR)
C. of West Virginia (B, NR)
Dalhousie U. (M, SR)
Dallas Baptist U. (B, NR)
De Montfort U. (B, NR)
Eastern Oregon U. (B, NR)
Edith Cowan U. (B-M-D, NR)
Empire State C. (B-M, NR)
Excelsior C. (B, NR)
FernUniversität (B-M-D, NR)

Hampton U. (B, NR)
Iowa State U. (B, SR)
Judson C. (B, NR)
Kansas State U. (B, NR)
Liberty U. (B, SR)
Madurai Kamaraj U. (B-M, NR)
Memorial U. of Newfoundland
   (B, NR)
Mercy C. (B, NR)
Monash U. (B-M, NR)
Monterrey Institute for Graduate
   Studies (M-D, NR)
National U. [California] (B, NR)
Open U. [England] (B-M-D, NR)
Open U. of Hong Kong (B-M-D, NR)
St. Joseph's C. (B, SR)
Salve Regina U. (B, SR)
South Bank U. (M-D, SR)
Southern Cross U. (M, NR)
Southern Oregon U. (B, SR)
Strayer U. (B, NR)
Technikon of Southern Africa
   (B-M-D, NR)
U. of Luton (M-D, NR)
U. of Maryland (B, NR)
U. of Melbourne (M-D, NR)
U. of New England (B-M, NR)
U. of Phoenix (B-M, NR)
U. of Pretoria (B-M, NR)
U. of South Africa (B-M-D, NR)
U. of South Australia (B, NR)
U. of Southern Queensland
   (B-M, NR)
U. of Sunderland (B, NR)
U. of Surrey (M, NR)
U. of Technology, Sydney (D, NR)
U. of Teesside (M-D, SR)
Upper Iowa U. (B, NR)
See also **Business Administration**
See also **Finance**
See also **Management**

Business Administration (BBA/MBA/DBA)

Andrew Jackson U. (M, NR)
Athabasca U. (M, SR)
Auburn U. (M, SR)
Australian Graduate School of
   Business (M, SR)
Baker C. (B-M, NR)
Bellevue U. (M, NR)
California C. for Health Sciences
   (M, NR)
California National U. for
   Advanced Studies (M, NR)
California State U.-Dominguez
   Hills (M, NR)
Capella U. (M, SR)
Central Queensland U. (B-M, NR)
Charles Sturt U. (M-D, NR)

Cheltenham Tutorial C. (M, NR)
City U. (M, NR)
C. of Estate Management (M, NR)
Colorado State U. (M, NR)
Dalhousie U. (M, SR)
Dallas Baptist U. (M, NR)
Drexel U. (M, SR)
Duke U. (M, SR)
Eastern New Mexico U. (B-M, SR)
Edith Cowan U. (M, NR)
Empire State C. (M, SR)
Excelsior C. (B-M, NR)
Florida Gulf Coast U. (M, NR)
Florida Institute of Technology
   (M, NR)
Franklin U. (M, NR)
Golden Gate U. (M, NR)
Henley Management C. (M-D, NR)
Heriot-Watt U. (M, NR)
Hope International U. (B, NR)
Howard U. (M, NR)
International Management Centres
   (B-M, SR)
Iowa State U. (M, SR)
ISIM U. (M, NR)
Jones International U. (M, NR)
Keele U. (M, NR)
Keller Graduate School of
   Management (M, NR)
Lehigh U. (M, NR)
Liberty U. (M, SR)
Madurai Kamaraj U. (B-M, NR)
Maharishi U. of Management
   (M, NR)
Manchester Business School (M, SR)
Marist C. (M, NR)
Mercy C. (M, NR)
Mississippi State U. (M, NR)
Morehead State U. (M, NR)
Napier U. (M, NR)
National Technological U. (M, NR)
National U. [California] (M, NR)
New York Institute of Technology
   (B-M, NR)
Northeastern Illinois U. (M, SR)
Nova Southeastern U. (M, SR)
Open U. of the Netherlands (M, SR)
Oxford Brookes U. (M, SR)
Pace U. (M, SR)
Pfeiffer U. (M, NR)
Potchefstroom U. for Christian
   Higher Education (B-M, NR)
Purdue U. (M, SR)
Regent U. (M, SR)
Regis U. (M, NR)
Rensselaer Polytechnic Institute
   (M, NR)
Royal Roads U. (M, SR)
Salve Regina U. (M, SR)
Sheffield Hallam U. (M, SR)
Southern Cross U. (M-D, NR)

Southern Methodist U. (M, SR)
Strathclyde Graduate Business
    School (M, NR)
Strayer U. (M, NR)
Suffolk U. (M, NR)
Syracuse U. (M, SR)
Texas A&M U.-Commerce (M, NR)
Touro U. International (B-M-D, NR)
United States Open U. (M, NR)
U. of Baltimore (M, NR)
U. of California-Irvine (M, SR)
U. of Colorado at Colorado Springs
    (M, NR)
U. of Colorado at Denver (M, SR)
U. of Dallas (M, NR)
U. of Durham (M-D, SR)
U. of Florida (M, SR)
U. of Glasgow (M-D, NR)
U. of Guelph (M, SR)
U. of Leicester (M, NR)
U. of London (M, NR)
U. of Maryland (M, NR)
U. of New England (M, NR)
U. of Northumbria at Newcastle
    (M, NR)
U. of Phoenix (B-M, NR)
U. of Pittsburgh (M, SR)
U. of St. Francis [Illinois] (M, NR)
U. of St. Thomas (M, SR)
U. of Sarasota (M-D, SR)
U. of South Alabama (M, NR)
U. of South Australia (B-M-D, NR)
U. of Southern Queensland
    (B-M-D, NR)
U. of Stirling (M, SR)
U. of Surrey (M, NR)
U. of Tennessee-Knoxville (M, SR)
U. of Texas (M, NR)
U. of Texas at Dallas (M, SR)
U. of Warwick (M, SR)
U. of Westminster (M, SR)
U. of Wisconsin-Whitewater (M, NR)
U. of Wyoming (B, SR)
Virginia Polytechnic Institute and
    State U. (M, NR)
Worcester Polytechnic Institute
    (M, NR)

Business Administration (Other)

Athabasca U. (B, NR)
Caldwell C. (B, SR)
California National U. for
    Advanced Studies (B, NR)
California State U.-Fresno (B, NR)
Central Michigan U. (B-M, NR)
City U. (B, NR)
Clarkson C. (B, NR)
Columbia Union C. (B, NR)
Dallas Baptist U. (B, NR)

Elizabethtown C. (B, SR)
Franklin U. [Ohio] (B, NR)
Judson C. (B, NR)
Mary Baldwin C. (B, SR)
Marywood U. (B, SR)
Memorial U. of Newfoundland
    (B, NR)
New York Institute of Technology
    (B, NR)
Old Dominion U. (B, NR)
Oral Roberts U. (B, NR)
Pennsylvania State U. (A, NR)
Roger Williams U. (B, NR)
St. Mary-of-the-Woods C. (B, SR)
Southwest Missouri State U. (M, NR)
Southwestern Adventist U. (B, SR)
Stephens C. (B, SR)
United States Open U. (B, NR)
Universidad Estatal a Distancia
    (B-M, NR)
Universidad Nacional de
    Educacion a Distancia (D, SR)
U. of Sarasota (B, SR)
U. of South Africa (B-M-D, NR)
U. of South Australia (D, NR)
U. of Southern Queensland (B, NR)
U. of Wisconsin-Platteville (B, NR)
Washington State U. (B, NR)
See also **Business and Commerce
    (General)**
See also **Management**

Business Communication

Jones International U. (B-M, NR)
Old Dominion U. (B, NR)
See also **Communication**

Business Information Systems

Bellevue U. (B, NR)
Strathclyde Graduate Business
    School (M, NR)
U. of Southern Queensland (M, NR)
U. of Sunderland (B, NR)
See also **Management Information
    Systems**

Business Law

Central Queensland U. (M-D, NR)
De Montfort U. (M, NR)
Kaplan C. (D, NR)
Macquarie U. (M, NR)
Monash U. (B, NR)
U. of London (B, NR)
U. of South Africa (M, NR)
U. of Southern Queensland (M, NR)

Business Management

See **Business Administration**
See **Management**

Canadian Studies

U. of Manitoba (B, NR)
U. of Waterloo (B, NR)

Cancer Research

See **Oncology**

Cartooning

U. of Kent at Canterbury (M-D, SR)

Catalan Language and Literature

U. of Melbourne (M-D, NR)

Celtic Christianity

U. of Wales-Lampeter (M, NR)

Chemical Engineering

Auburn U. (M, SR)
Excelsior C. (B, NR)
Illinois Institute of Technology (M, NR)
Kansas State U. (M, NR)
Lehigh U. (M, NR)
Mississippi State U. (M, SR)
National Technological U. (M, NR)
Oklahoma State U. (M, NR)
South Bank U. (M-D, SR)
U. of Bradford (M-D, NR)
U. of Melbourne (M-D, NR)
U. of North Dakota (B, SR)
U. of South Carolina (M, SR)

Chemistry

Acadia U. (B, SR)
Central Queensland U. (B, NR)
Charles Sturt U. (B, NR)
Charter Oak State C. (B, NR)
De Montfort U. (M, NR)
Excelsior C. (B, NR)
Illinois Institute of Technology (M, NR)
Lehigh U. (M, NR)
Mary Baldwin C. (B, SR)
Monash U. (B, NR)
Murdoch U. (B, NR)
Open U. and Open C. (B, NR)
Thomas Edison State C. (B, NR)
U. of Bradford (M-D, NR)
U. of Kent at Canterbury (M-D, SR)
U. of Melbourne (M-D, NR)

U. of South Africa (B-M-D, NR)
U. of Technology, Sydney (D, NR)

Chemistry Education

U. of South Africa (M, NR)
See also **Science Education**

Children's Literature

U. of Southern Queensland (M, NR)

Chinese Language and Literature

U. of Melbourne (M-D, NR)
U. of New England (B-M, NR)

Church History

Macquarie U. (M, NR)
U. of South Africa (B-M-D, NR)
U. of Wales-Lampeter (M, NR)

Church Management

Griggs U. (B, NR)
North Central U. [Minnesota] (B, NR)
Oral Roberts U. (B, NR)

Civil Engineering

Auburn U. (M, SR)
Colorado State U. (M, NR)
Harcourt Learning Direct (A, NR)
Kansas State U. (M, NR)
Mississippi State U. (M, SR)
Monash U. (B, NR)
Old Dominion U. (B-M, NR)
Thomas Edison State C. (B, NR)
U. of Idaho (M, NR)
U. of Melbourne (M-D, NR)
U. of South Carolina (M, SR)
U. of Southern Queensland (B-M, NR)
U. of Technology, Sydney (D, NR)
Virginia Polytechnic Institute and State U. (M, NR)

Civil War Studies

American Military U. (M, NR)

Classics

U. of Kent at Canterbury (M-D, SR)
U. of Melbourne (M-D, NR)
U. of New England (B-M-D, NR)
U. of South Africa (B-M-D, NR)
U. of Wales-Lampeter (M-D, NR)

U. of Waterloo (B, NR)
See also **Ancient History**
See also **Greek**
See also **Latin**

Clinical Psychology

California Institute of Integral Studies (M-D, SR)
Fielding Institute (D, SR)
Union Institute (D, SR)
Universidad Nacional de Educacion a Distancia (M, SR)
U. of Pretoria (D, SR)
U. of South Africa (M, NR)
See also **Counseling**
See also **Psychology and Behavioral Science**

Commerce

See **Business and Commerce (General)**

Communication

Andrew Jackson U. (B, NR)
Atlantic Union C. (B, SR)
Caldwell C. (B, SR)
Capital U. (B, SR)
Central Queensland U. (B-M-D, NR)
Charles Sturt U. (M-D, NR)
Charter Oak State C. (B, NR)
Curtin U. of Technology (B-D, NR)
Edith Cowan U. (B, NR)
Elizabethtown C. (B, SR)
Excelsior C. (B, NR)
Jones International U. (M, NR)
Madurai Kamaraj U. (M, NR)
Mary Baldwin C. (B, SR)
Monash U. (B, NR)
Montana State U.-Billings (B, NR)
Murdoch U. (B, NR)
New York Institute of Technology (B, NR)
Old Dominion U. (B, NR)
Regent U. (M-D, NR)
Rensselaer Polytechnic Institute (M, NR)
Seton Hall U. (M, SR)
South Bank U. (M-D, SR)
Technikon of Southern Africa (B-M-D, NR)
Télé-université (B, NR)
Texas Tech U. (M, NR)
Thomas Edison State C. (B, NR)
U. of Bradford (M-D, NR)
U. of Kent at Canterbury (M-D, SR)
U. of Leicester (M, NR)
U. of Maryland (B, NR)
U. of Melbourne (M-D, NR)

U. of New England (B-M-D, NR)
U. of Northern Iowa (M, NR)
U. of Pretoria (B-M-D, NR)
U. of South Africa (B-M-D, NR)
U. of South Australia (B, NR)
U. of Southern Queensland (B-M, NR)
U. of Teesside (M-D, SR)
Victoria U. (M, NR)
Western Baptist C. (B, SR)

Communication Disorders

Eastern New Mexico U. (M, SR)
Kentucky Commonwealth Virtual U. (M, NR)
Macquarie U. (M, NR)
U. of Northern Colorado (M, NR)
See also **Audiology**
See also **Speech Pathology**

Communication Management

U. of Pretoria (B, NR)
U. of South Australia (B-M, NR)
See also **Telecommunications and Telecommunications Management**

Communication Systems

Brunel U. (M, NR)
See also **Mass Communications and Media Studies**
See also **Telecommunications and Telecommunications Management**

Community Studies

Brunel U. (B-M, NR)
Central Michigan U. (B, NR)
De Montfort U. (M, NR)
Deakin U. (M, NR)
Institute for Educational Studies (M, NR)
James Cook U. (D, NR)
Monash U. (B, NR)
Thomas Edison State C. (B, NR)
U. of Otago (M, NR)

Comparative Literature

California State U.-Dominguez Hills (M, NR)
Charter Oak State C. (B, NR)
Excelsior C. (B, NR)
U. of Kent at Canterbury (M-D, SR)
U. of South Africa (B-M-D, NR)

Comparative Religion

See **Religious Studies**

Complementary Health

Charles Sturt U. (B, NR)

Computer-Aided Design (CAD)

See **Industrial Computing**

Computer Engineering and Computer Engineering Technology

California National U. for
    Advanced Studies (M, NR)
Excelsior C. (B, NR)
Georgia Institute of Technology
    (M, NR)
Mississippi State U. (M, SR)
National Technological U. (M, NR)
Naval Postgraduate School (M, NR)
Old Dominion U. (M, NR)
U. of Colorado at Boulder (M, NR)
U. of Idaho (M, NR)
U. of Massachusetts at Amherst
    (M, NR)
U. of Pretoria (B-M, SR)
U. of South Carolina (M, SR)
U. of Southern Queensland
    (B-M, NR)
U. of Wisconsin-Madison (M, SR)
See also **Electrical Engineering**
See also **Software Engineering**
See also **Systems Engineering**

Computer Information Systems

American Institute for Computer
    Sciences (B, NR)
Athabasca U. (B-M, NR)
Baker C. (M, NR)
Caldwell C. (B, SR)
Capella U. (M-D, NR)
Capitol C. (B-M, NR)
Central Queensland U. (B-M-D, NR)
Champlain C. (B, NR)
Charles Sturt U. (B-M-D, NR)
Charter Oak State C. (B, NR)
City U. (B-M, NR)
Columbia Union C. (B, NR)
Deakin U. (M, NR)
Drexel U. (M, NR)
Edith Cowan U. (B-M, NR)
Excelsior C. (B, NR)
Florida State U. (B, NR)
Franklin U. (B, NR)

Harvard U. (B-M, SR)
ISIM U. (M, NR)
Monash U. (B-M, NR)
Napier U. (M, SR)
National Distance Education
    Centre (B, NR)
National Technological U. (M, NR)
New Jersey Institute of Technology
    (B-M, NR)
Nova Southeastern U. (M-D, SR)
Old Dominion U. (B, NR)
Open U. [England] (B-M-D, NR)
Park C. (B, SR)
Regis U. (M, NR)
Rensselaer Polytechnic Institute
    (M, NR)
Rochester Institute of Technology
    (M, SR)
St. Mary-of-the-Woods C. (B, SR)
Sheffield Hallam U. (M, SR)
South Bank U. (M-D, SR)
Southwest Missouri State U. (M, SR)
Strayer U. (A-B, NR)
Technical U. of British Columbia
    (M, SR)
Technikon of Southern Africa
    (B-M-D, NR)
Thomas Edison State C. (B, NR)
United States Open U. (B-M, NR)
U. of Bradford (M-D, NR)
U. of Dallas (M, NR)
U. of London (B, NR)
U. of Luton (M-D, NR)
U. of Maryland (B, NR)
U. of Massachusetts at Lowell
    (B, NR)
U. of Melbourne (M-D, NR)
U. of Phoenix (B-M, NR)
U. of South Africa (B-M, NR)
U. of South Australia (B, NR)
U. of Southern Queensland (M, NR)
U. of Sunderland (M, NR)
U. of Tasmania (M-D, NR)
U. of Technology, Sydney (D, NR)
U. of Teesside (M-D, SR)
U. of Tennessee-Knoxville (M, SR)
See also **Computer Science**

Computer-Mediated Communication

Regent U. (M, NR)
Texas Tech U. (M, NR)
See also **Internet Studies**

Computer Networking

City U. (B, NR)
U. of Southern Queensland (B, NR)
See also **Computer-Mediated
    Communication**

See also **Internet Studies**
See also **Telecommunications and
    Telecommunications
    Management**

Computer Programming

See **Software Engineering**

Computer Science

Acadia U. (B, SR)
American Institute for Computer
    Sciences (B-M, NR)
Auburn U. (M, SR)
California National U. for
    Advanced Studies (B-M, NR)
California State U.-Chico (B-M, NR)
Capital U. (B, SR)
Charter Oak State C. (B, NR)
Colorado State U. (M, NR)
Columbia U. (M, NR)
Columbus State U. (M, NR)
FernUniversität (B-M-D, NR)
Florida State U. (B, NR)
Franklin U. (B, NR)
Grantham C. of Engineering (B, NR)
Harcourt Learning Direct (A, NR)
Madurai Kamaraj U. (B, NR)
Maharishi U. of Management
    (M, NR)
Mary Baldwin C. (B, SR)
Mercy C. (B, NR)
Mississippi State U. (M, SR)
Murdoch U. (B, NR)
National Technological U. (M, NR)
New Jersey Institute of Technology
    (B-M, NR)
Northwood U. (B, SR)
Nova Southeastern U. (M-D, SR)
Oklahoma State U. (M, NR)
Open U. of Hong Kong (B-M-D, SR)
Open U. of Israel (B, NR)
Rensselaer Polytechnic Institute
    (M, NR)
Southern Methodist U. (M, SR)
Stanford U. (M, NR)
Thomas Edison State C. (B, NR)
U. of Colorado at Boulder (M, NR)
U. of Houston (M, NR)
U. of Illinois at Urbana-Champaign
    (M, NR)
U. of Kent at Canterbury (M-D, SR)
U. of Luton (M-D, NR)
U. of Maryland (B, NR)
U. of Massachusetts-Amherst
    (M, NR)
U. of Melbourne (M-D, NR)
U. of New England (B-M-D, NR)
U. of Saskatchewan (B, NR)
U. of South Africa (B-M-D, NR)

U. of Southern Queensland (B, NR)
U. of Technology, Sydney (D, NR)
U. of Texas (M, NR)
U. of Wales-Aberystwyth (M-D, SR)

Conflict Resolution and Peace Studies

Antioch University (M, SR)
California State U.-Dominguez
    Hills (M, NR)
Monash U. (M, NR)
Nova Southeastern U. (M-D, SR)
Royal Roads U. (M, SR)
U. of Bradford (M-D, NR)
U. of New England (M, NR)
U. of Pretoria (M, NR)
See also **Gandhian Thought**

Construction

Central Queensland U. (B, NR)
C. of Estate Management (M, NR)
South Bank U. (M-D, SR)
Thomas Edison State C. (B, NR)
U. of Bath (M, SR)
U. of Luton (M-D, NR)
U. of Melbourne (M-D, NR)
U. of Southern Queensland (B, NR)
See also **Contracting and Building**

Continuing Education

See **Adult and Continuing
    Education**

Contracting and Building

Brunel U. (M, NR)
Central Queensland U. (B, NR)
U. of Luton (M-D, NR)
U. of Southern Queensland (B, NR)
U. of Technology, Sydney (D, NR)
See also **Architecture**
See also **Construction**

Copyright Law

See **Intellectual Property Law**

Counseling

Antioch University (M, SR)
Athabasca U. (M, NR)
California Institute of Integral
    Studies (M-D, SR)
Charles Sturt U. (M, NR)
City U. (M, NR)
Global U. of the Assemblies of God
    (B-M, NR)
Liberty U. (M, SR)

Monash U. (M, NR)
Oral Roberts U. (B, NR)
Prescott C. (B-M, SR)
Seton Hall U. (M, SR)
Southern Christian U. (M, NR)
U. of Melbourne (M-D, NR)
U. of Sarasota (M-D, SR)
U. of South Africa (M, NR)
U. of South Australia (M, NR)
U. of Southern Queensland (M, NR)
See also **Clinical Psychology**
See also **Pastoral Counseling**
See also **Psychology and
    Behavioral Science**

Creative Writing

See **Writing**

Criminal Justice and Law Enforcement

American Military U. (B, NR)
Andrew Jackson U. (B-M, NR)
Bellevue U. (B, NR)
Bemidji State U. (B, NR)
Caldwell C. (B, SR)
California State U.-Fresno (B, NR)
Central Missouri State U. (M, NR)
Charles Sturt U. (B-M-D, NR)
Charter Oak State C. (B, NR)
C. of West Virginia (B, NR)
Concordia U. [Minnesota] (B-M, SR)
Crown C. (A, NR)
David N. Myers C. (B, NR)
Edith Cowan U. (B, NR)
Elizabethtown C. (B, SR)
Empire State C. (B, NR)
Florida Gulf Coast U. (B, NR)
Florida State U. (M, NR)
Griffith U. (B, NR)
Indiana State U. (M, NR)
Judson C. (B, NR)
Kaplan C. (B, NR)
Loyola U. [Louisiana] (M, NR)
Monterrey Institute for Graduate
    Studies (M-D, NR)
New York Institute of Technology
    (B, NR)
Park C. (B, SR)
Roger Williams U. (B, NR)
St. Joseph's C. (B, SR)
Seton Hall U. (M, SR)
Southern Oregon U. (B, SR)
Taylor U. (A, SR)
U. of Leicester (M, NR)
U. of Luton (M-D, NR)
U. of Melbourne (M-D, NR)
U. of South Africa (B-M-D, NR)
U. of Teesside (M-D, SR)
U. of Wisconsin-Platteville (M, NR)

Upper Iowa U. (B, NR)
Washington State U. (B, NR)
See also **Criminology, Forensic
    Psychology, and Criminal
    Intelligence**
See also **Forensics**

Criminal Law

U. of South Africa (M, NR)

Criminology, Forensic Psychology, and Criminal Intelligence

Capital U. (B, SR)
Charles Sturt U. (M, NR)
Indiana State U. (M, NR)
Simon Fraser U. (B, NR)
U. of Kent at Canterbury (M-D, SR)
U. of Leicester (M, NR)
U. of South Africa (B-M-D, NR)
U. of Teesside (M-D, SR)
See also **Criminal Justice**

Crisis Management

Charles Sturt U. (B, NR)
Empire State C. (B, NR)
Thomas Edison State C. (B, NR)
U. of Leicester (M, NR)

Cross-Cultural Ministry

Hope International U. (M, NR)

Cultural Studies

See **Anthropology**

Curriculum Design

Atlantic Union C. (M, SR)
City U. (M, NR)
Deakin U. (M, NR)
Florida Gulf Coast U. (M, NR)
Nova Southeastern U. (M, SR)
U. of Houston (M, NR)
U. of Nebraska, Lincoln (D, SR)
U. of Sarasota (M-D, SR)
U. of Southern Queensland (M, NR)
See also **Education**

Death Studies

See **Thanatology**

Defense Management

American Military U. (M, NR)

U. of New England (M, NR)

Dental Radiology

U. of London (M, NR)
See also **Dentristry and Dental Health**
See also **Orthodontics and Prosthodontics**

Dentristy and Dental Health

U. of London (M, NR)
Weber State U. (B, SR)
See also **Dental Radiology**
See also **Orthodontics and Prosthodontics**

Development Studies and Sustainable Agriculture

De Montfort U. (M, NR)
Deakin U. (M, NR)
Keele U. (M, NR)
Murdoch U. (M, NR)
South Bank U. (M-D, SR)
U. of Alaska (B, NR)
U. of Bradford (M-D, NR)
U. of London (M, NR)
U. of Melbourne (M-D, NR)
U. of New England (B-M, NR)
U. of South Africa (B-M-D, NR)
U. of Southern Queensland (M, NR)
U. of Waterloo (B, NR)
See also **Rural Development**

Developmental Psychology

Edith Cowan U. (B-M-D, NR)
Fielding Institute (D, SR)
Hope International U. (B, NR)
Macquarie U. (B-M-D, NR)
Salve Regina U. (M, SR)

Diaconology

See **Divinity**
See **Ministry**

Dietetics

See **Nutrition**

Digital Preservation

U. of Glasgow (M, NR)

Diplomacy

See **Conflict Resolution and Peace Studies**
See **Intelligence Science**
See **International Relations**

Direct Marketing

See **Marketing**

Disability Studies

Edith Cowan U. (B, NR)
U. of Kent at Canterbury (M-D, SR)

Distance Education

Athabasca U. (M, NR)
Deakin U. (M, NR)
Florida State U. (M, NR)
Marlboro C. (M, NR)
Nova Southeastern U. (M-D, SR)
Royal Roads U. (M, SR)
U. of London (M, NR)
U. of Maryland (M, NR)
U. of Southern Queensland (M, NR)

Divinity (B.D., M.Div.)

American Bible C. and Seminary (M, NR)
Southern Christian U. (M, NR)
U. of London (B, NR)
U. of Pretoria (M, NR)

Drama and Theater Studies

Central Queensland U. (B, NR)
Charles Sturt U. (M-D, NR)
Mary Baldwin C. (B, SR)
Thomas Edison State C. (B, NR)
U. of Kent at Canterbury (M-D, SR)
U. of Melbourne (M-D, NR)
U. of New England (B-M-D, NR)
U. of Wales-Aberystwyth (M-D, SR)

E-Business

See **E-Commerce**

E-Commerce

Bellevue U. (B, NR)
Capitol C (M, NR)
Drexel U. (M, NR)
Mercy C. (M, NR)
Monash U. (B, NR)
Monterrey Institute for Graduate Studies (M, NR)
National U. [California] (M, NR)

National-Louis U. (M, SR)
U. of Dallas (M, NR)
U. of Maryland (M, NR)
U. of Phoenix (B-M, NR)
U. of Southern Queensland (M, NR)

Economics

Acadia U. (B, SR)
Capital U. (B, SR)
Charter Oak State C. (B, NR)
Curtin U. of Technology (B, NR)
Deakin U. (M, NR)
Eastern Oregon U. (B, NR)
Excelsior C. (B, NR)
FernUniversität (B-M-D, NR)
Madurai Kamaraj U. (B-M, NR)
Mary Baldwin C. (B, SR)
Monash U. (B, NR)
Murdoch U. (B, NR)
Open U. of Hong Kong (B-M-D, NR)
Strayer U. (B, NR)
Thomas Edison State C. (B, NR)
Universidad Nacional de Educacion a Distancia (D, SR)
U. of Kent at Canterbury (M-D, SR)
U. of London (B-M, NR)
U. of Manitoba (B, NR)
U. of Melbourne (M-D, NR)
U. of New England (B-M-D, NR)
U. of Pittsburgh (B, SR)
U. of South Africa (B-M-D, NR)
U. of Southern Colorado (B, NR)
U. of Tasmania (M-D, NR)
U. of Technology, Sydney (D, NR)
U. of Wales-Aberystwyth (B-M-D, SR)
U. of Waterloo (B, NR)

Editing and Publishing

U. of Southern Queensland (M, NR)

Education

Acadia U. (B, SR)
Antioch University (M, SR)
Atlantic Union C. (B-M, SR)
Australian Catholic U. (B, NR)
California State U.-Fresno (M, NR)
California State U.-Hayward (M, NR)
Capella U. (M-D, NR)
Central Queensland U. (B-M-D, NR)
Charles Sturt U. (B-M-D, NR)
City U. (M, NR)
C. of Saint Scholastica (M, SR)
Curtin U. of Technology (B-M, NR)
De Montfort U. (M, NR)
Deakin U. (B-M, NR)
East Carolina U. (M, SR)
Eastern New Mexico U. (B-M, SR)

Eastern Oregon U. (M, SR)
Edith Cowan U. (B-M-D, NR)
FernUniversität (B-M-D, NR)
Flinders U. (D, NR)
Florida Gulf Coast U. (M, NR)
George Washington U. (M, NR)
Global U. of the Assemblies of God
    (B-M, NR)
Griffith U. (B, NR)
Iowa State U. (B, SR)
Judson C. (B, NR)
Keele U. (M, NR)
Lakehead U. (B-M, NR)
Lesley U. (M, NR)
Liberty U. (M, SR)
Loyola U. [Louisiana] (M, NR)
Macquarie U. (M-D, NR)
Monash U. (B-M, NR)
Montana State U.-Bozeman (M, SR)
Monterrey Institute for Graduate
    Studies (M-D, NR)
Murdoch U. (B-M, NR)
New Mexico State U. (M, SR)
Northern Territory U. (B-M, NR)
Norwich U. (M, SR)
Nova Southeastern U. (B-M-D, SR)
Open U. [England] (B-M-D, NR)
Open U. of Hong Kong (B-M-D, NR)
Open U. of Israel (B, NR)
Oral Roberts U. (B, NR)
Prescott C. (M, SR)
Regent U. (M, NR)
St. Francis Xavier U. (M, SR)
St. Joseph's C. (B-M, SR)
Seton Hall U. (M, SR)
South Bank U. (M-D, SR)
Southern Cross U. (B, NR)
Southern Oregon U. (M, SR)
Spertus C. (M, SR)
Stephens C. (B, SR)
Technikon of Southern Africa
    (B-M-D, NR)
Texas Wesleyan U. (M, NR)
Thomas Edison State C. (B, NR)
Universidad Nacional de
    Educacion a Distancia (D, SR)
U. of Alaska (B-M, NR)
U. of Bradford (M-D, NR)
U. of Calgary (M, SR)
U. of Houston (M, NR)
U. of Illinois at Urbana-Champaign
    (M, NR)
U. of Melbourne (M-D, NR)
U. of Nebraska-Lincoln (M-D, SR)
U. of New England (B-M-D, NR)
U. of Northern Iowa (M, NR)
U. of Phoenix (M, NR)
U. of Pretoria (B-M, NR)
U. of Sarasota (M-D, SR)
U. of South Africa (B-M-D, NR)
U. of South Alabama (M, NR)

U. of South Australia (B-D, NR)
U. of Southern Queensland
    (B-M-D, NR)
U. of Sunderland (B, NR)
U. of Tasmania (M-D, NR)
U. of Technology, Sydney (D, NR)
U. of Texas (M, NR)
U. of Wales-Aberystwyth (M-D, SR)
Walden U. (M-D, NR)

Educational Leadership and Administration

Atlantic Union C. (M, SR)
Central Queensland U. (M, NR)
City U. (M, NR)
Curtin U. of Technology (M, NR)
Edith Cowan U. (M-D, NR)
Fielding Institute (D, SR)
Keele U. (M, NR)
Liberty U. (D, SR)
Montana State U.-Bozeman (M, SR)
Monterrey Institute for Graduate
    Studies (M-D, NR)
Nova Southeastern U. (M-D, SR)
Purdue U. (D, SR)
Regent U. (M, SR)
Seton Hall U. (M, SR)
Southern Baptist Theological
    Seminary (D, SR)
Universidad Estatal a Distancia
    (B-M, NR)
U. of Calgary (M, SR)
U. of Montana (D, SR)
U. of Nebraska-Lincoln (D, SR)
U. of Northern Iowa (M, NR)
U. of Sarasota (M-D, SR)
U. of South Africa (B-M-D, NR)
U. of South Alabama (M, NR)
U. of Southern Queensland
    (M-D, NR)

Educational Psychology

Monterrey Institute for Graduate
    Studies (M-D, NR)
Texas A&M U.-Commerce (D, SR)
U. of Northern Colorado (M, NR)
U. of South Africa (B-M-D, NR)

Educational Technology

Boise State U. (M, NR)
City U. (M, NR)
Columbia U. (M, SR)
Edith Cowan U. (M-D, NR)
Florida Gulf Coast U. (M, NR)
George Washington U. [D.C.]
    (M, NR)
Marlboro C. (M, NR)
Nova Southeastern U. (M-D, SR)

Pepperdine U. (M-D, SR)
U. of Calgary (M, SR)
U. of Northern Iowa (M, NR)
U. of Pretoria (M, NR)
U. of South Alabama (M, NR)
U. of Southern Queensland (M, NR)
U. of Texas (M, NR)
Walden U. (M, NR)

Electrical Engineering

California National U. for
    Advanced Studies (B-M, NR)
Colorado State U. (M-D, NR)
Columbia U. (M, NR)
Harcourt Learning Direct (A, NR)
Kansas State U. (M, NR)
Mississippi State U. (M, SR)
Monash U. (B, NR)
National Technological U. (M, NR)
Naval Postgraduate School (M, NR)
Old Dominion U. (B-M, NR)
Rensselaer Polytechnic Institute
    (M, NR)
Rochester Institute of Technology
    (B, SR)
Southern Methodist U. (M, SR)
Stanford U. (M, NR)
U. of Bath (M, SR)
U. of Bradford (M-D, NR)
U. of Colorado at Boulder (M, NR)
U. of Houston (M, NR)
U. of Idaho (M, NR)
U. of Illinois at Urbana-Champaign
    (M, NR)
U. of Massachusetts-Amherst
    (M, NR)
U. of North Dakota (B, SR)
U. of Pretoria (B-M-D, NR)
U. of South Carolina (M, SR)
U. of Southern Queensland
    (B-M, NR)
U. of Technology, Sydney (D, NR)
U. of Texas (M, NR)
U. of Wisconsin-Madison (M, SR)
Virginia Polytechnic Institute and
    State U. (M, NR)
See also **Computer Engineering**
See also **Electronics**

Electromechanical Engineering

See **Robotics**

Electronic Commerce

See **E-Commerce**

Electronics

Excelsior C. (B, NR)
Harcourt Learning Direct (A, NR)
Open U. of Hong Kong (B-M-D, NR)
Thomas Edison State C. (B, NR)
U. of Kent at Canterbury (M-D, SR)
U. of Luton (M-D, NR)
U. of New England (B, NR)
U. of Pretoria (B-M-D, NR)
U. of Southern Queensland
    (B-M, NR)
World C. (B, NR)
See also **Electrical Engineering**

Elementary Education

See **Primary Education**

Emergency Management

See **Crisis Management**

Emergency Medical Services

American C. of Prehospital
    Medicine (B, NR)
Charles Sturt U. (B, NR)

Energy Management

New York Institute of Technology
    (M, NR)

Engineering (General)

Arizona State U. (M, NR)
Auburn U. (M, SR)
California National U. for
    Advanced Studies (B-M, NR)
Central Queensland U. (M-D, NR)
FernUniversität (B-M-D, NR)
Florida State U. (M, SR)
Iowa State U. (B, SR)
Kansas State U. (M, NR)
Kettering U. (M, NR)
Massachusetts Institute of
    Technology (M, SR)
Monash U. (B-M, NR)
New Mexico State U. (M, NR)
Open U. of Hong Kong (B-M-D, NR)
Potchefstroom U. for Christian
    Higher Education (B, NR)
Purdue U. (M, SR)
South Bank U. (M-D, SR)
Stanford U. (M, NR)
Technikon of Southern Africa
    (B-M-D, NR)
Texas Tech U. (M, NR)
U. of Illinois at Chicago (M, SR)

U. of Illinois at Urbana-Champaign
    (M, NR)
U. of Melbourne (M-D, NR)
U. of North Dakota (B, SR)
U. of South Carolina (M, SR)
U. of Southern Queensland
    (B-M, NR)
U. of Sunderland (B, SR)
U. of Tasmania (M-D, NR)
U. of Wisconsin-Madison (M, NR)
U. of Wisconsin-Platteville (M, NR)

Engineering Management

American Military U. (M, NR)
Columbia U. (M, NR)
National Technological U. (M, NR)
New Jersey Institute of Technology
    (M, NR)
Old Dominion U. (M, NR)
Southern Methodist U. (M, SR)
Syracuse U. (M, SR)
Texas Tech U. (M, NR)
U. of Colorado at Boulder (M, NR)
U. of Idaho (M, NR)
U. of Massachusetts-Amherst
    (M, NR)
U. of Pretoria (M, NR)
U. of Wisconsin-Madison (M, SR)
Washington State U. (M, NR)

Engineering Science

Murdoch U. (B, NR)
Open U. and Open C. (B, NR)
Rensselaer Polytechnic Institute
    (M, NR)
U. of Illinois at Urbana-Champaign
    (M, NR)

English Language and Literature

Acadia U. (B, SR)
Atlantic Union C. (B, SR)
Burlington C. (B, SR)
Caldwell C. (B, SR)
Capital U. (B, SR)
Eastern New Mexico U. (M, SR)
Excelsior C. (B, NR)
Judson C. (B, NR)
Macquarie U. (B, NR)
Madurai Kamaraj U. (B-M, NR)
Mary Baldwin C. (B, SR)
Murdoch U. (B, NR)
St. Mary-of-the-Woods C. (B, SR)
Stephens C. (B, SR)
Thomas Edison State C. (B, NR)
United States Open U. (B, NR)
U. of Houston (B, NR)
U. of Kent at Canterbury (M-D, SR)

U. of London (B, NR)
U. of Maryland (B, NR)
U. of Melbourne (M-D, NR)
U. of New England (B-M-D, NR)
U. of Northern Iowa (M, NR)
U. of Pretoria (B, NR)
U. of Saskatchewan (B, NR)
U. of South Africa (B-M-D, NR)
U. of Southern Queensland (B, NR)
U. of Teesside (M-D, SR)
U. of Wales-Aberystwyth (M-D, SR)
U. of Wales-Lampeter (M-D, NR)
U. of Waterloo (B, NR)

Entomology

U. of Nebraska-Lincoln (M, NR)

Environmental Economics, Engineering, and Management

Auburn U. (M, SR)
California National U. for
    Advanced Studies (B-M, NR)
Central Queensland U. (B, NR)
Charles Sturt U. (B-M-D, NR)
Colorado State U. (M, NR)
De Montfort U. (B-M, NR)
Deakin U. (M, NR)
Georgia Institute of Technology
    (M, NR)
Howard U. (M, NR)
Lehigh U. (M, NR)
Monash U. (B-M, NR)
Old Dominion U. (B-M, NR)
Rochester Institute of Technology
    (B-M, SR)
Royal Roads U. (M, SR)
South Bank U. (M-D, SR)
Southern Methodist U. (M, SR)
Universidad Nacional de
    Educacion a Distancia (M, SR)
U. of Bath (M, SR)
U. of Denver (M, NR)
U. of Kent at Canterbury (M-D, SR)
U. of London (M, NR)
U. of Luton (M-D, NR)
U. of Maryland (B-M, NR)
U. of South Africa (M, NR)
U. of South Carolina (M, SR)
U. of Southern Queensland
    (B-M, NR)
U. of Wales-Aberystwyth (M-D, SR)
Worcester Polytechnic Institute
    (M, NR)
See also **Environmental Law**
See also **Environmental Studies**
See also **Public Health**

Environmental Law

De Montfort U. (M, NR)
Macquarie U. (M, NR)
U. of Kent at Canterbury (M-D, SR)
U. of Wales-Aberystwyth (M, SR)

Environmental Studies

Antioch University (M, SR)
Central Queensland U. (B, NR)
C. of West Virginia (B, NR)
Macquarie U. (B-M-D, NR)
Open U. of Hong Kong (B-M-D, NR)
Prescott C. (M, SR)
Thomas Edison State C. (B, NR)
U. of Kent at Canterbury (M-D, SR)
U. of London (M, NR)
U. of Melbourne (M-D, NR)
U. of Tasmania (M-D, NR)
U. of Waterloo (B, NR)
See also **Environmental Economics, Engineering, and Management**

Epidemiology

Curtin U. of Technology (M, SR)
U. of London (M, NR)

Estate Management

C. of Estate Management (B, NR)

Ethics

Charles Sturt U. (M-D, NR)
U. of South Africa (B-M-D, NR)
See also **Bioethics**
See also **Moral Theology**

Ethnomusicology

U. of New England (B-M, NR)

European Studies

United States Open U. (B, NR)
U. of Bradford (M-D, NR)
U. of Kent at Canterbury (M-D, SR)
U. of Melbourne (M-D, NR)
U. of New England (B-M, NR)

Evangelism

Global U. of the Assemblies of God (B-M, NR)
Hope International U. (M, NR)
U. of South Africa (B-M-D, NR)
See also **Cross-Cultural Ministry**

Family Studies

Concordia U. [Minnesota] (B-M, SR)
Edith Cowan U. (B, NR)
Iowa State U. (B, SR)
Laurentian U. (B, NR)
Monterrey Institute for Graduate Studies (M-D, NR)
Pennsylvania State U. (A, NR)
South Bank U. (M-D, SR)
Southern Christian U. (M, NR)
U. of Otago (M, NR)
Western Baptist C. (B, SR)

Fashion

Manchester Metropolitan U. (B, NR)

Feminist Law

U. of Kent at Canterbury (M, SR)

Film Studies

Burlington C. (B, SR)
Central Queensland U. (B, NR)
U. of Kent at Canterbury (M-D, SR)
U. of Melbourne (M-D, NR)
U. of Wales-Aberystwyth (M-D, SR)

Finance

American C. (M, SR)
Central Queensland U. (M, NR)
Charles Sturt U. (M-D, NR)
City U. (M, NR)
Curtin U. of Technology (B, NR)
Dalhousie U. (M, SR)
Golden Gate U. (M, NR)
Keller Graduate School of Management (M, NR)
Macquarie U. (M, NR)
Manchester Business School (M, SR)
Marywood U. (B, SR)
Mercy C. (M, NR)
Monash U. (B, NR)
Monterrey Institute for Graduate Studies (M-D, NR)
Nova Southeastern U. (M, SR)
Old Dominion U. (B, NR)
Sheffield Hallam U. (M, SR)
Thomas Edison State C. (B, NR)
Universidad Estatal a Distancia (B-M, NR)
U. of Leicester (M, NR)
U. of London (B-M, NR)
U. of Melbourne (M-D, NR)
U. of New England (B-M, NR)
U. of Pretoria (M, NR)
U. of Sarasota (M, SR)
U. of South Australia (B, NR)

U. of Southern Queensland (B-M, NR)
U. of Tasmania (M-D, NR)
U. of Technology, Sydney (D, NR)
U. of Wales-Aberystwyth (M-D, SR)
U. of Wisconsin-Whitewater (M, NR)
See also **Accounting**
See also **Taxation**

Finance Law

Macquarie U. (M, NR)

Fine Arts

See **Art**
See **Humanities**
See **Music**
See **Writing**

Fire Science Service, Management, and Training

California State U.-Los Angeles (B, NR)
Charter Oak State C. (B, NR)
Colorado State U. (B, NR)
National Fire Academy (B, NR)
Eastern Oregon U. (B, NR)
Empire State C. (B, NR)
Grand Canyon U. (M, NR)
Thomas Edison State C. (B, NR)
U. of Maryland (B, NR)
Upper Iowa U. (B, NR)
Worcester Polytechnic Institute (M, NR)

Food Industry and Restaurant Management

See **Food Science**
See **Hospitality, Food Industry, and Restaurant Management**

Food Law

De Montfort U. (M, NR)

Food Science

Charles Sturt U. (B-D, NR)
U. of Melbourne (M-D, NR)

Foreign Languages and Literature (General)

Macquarie U. (B, NR)
Murdoch U. (B, NR)
Open U. [England] (B-M-D, NR)
Open U. of Hong Kong (B-M-D, NR)
U. of Bradford (M-D, NR)

U. of Luton (M-D, NR)
U. of Melbourne (M-D, NR)
U. of Pretoria (B, NR)
U. of South Africa (B-M-D, NR)
U. of Southern Queensland (B, NR)
See also **[Language] Language and
   Literature
   (e.g., English Language and
   Literature)**
See also **Applied Linguistics**
See also **Comparative Literature**

Forensic Psychology

See **Criminology, Forensic
   Psychology, and Criminal
   Intelligence**

Forensics

U. of Technology, Sydney (D, NR)
See also **Criminal Justice and Law
   Enforcement**
See also **Criminal Law**

Forestry

Lakehead U. (M, NR)
Thomas Edison State C. (B, NR)
U. of Melbourne (M-D, NR)

French Language and Literature

Charter Oak State C. (B, NR)
Mary Baldwin C. (B, SR)
U. of London (B, NR)
U. of Melbourne (M-D, NR)
U. of New England (B-M, NR)
U. of Saskatchewan (B, NR)
U. of South Africa (B-M-D, NR)
U. of Waterloo (B, NR)

Gandhian Thought

Madurai Kamaraj U. (M, NR)
See also **Conflict Resolution and
   Peace Studies**

Gender and Women's Studies

Antioch University (M, SR)
Atlantic Union C. (B, SR)
Edith Cowan U. (B, NR)
Laurentian U. (B, NR)
Monash U. (B, NR)
Murdoch U. (B, NR)
South Bank U. (M-D, SR)
U. of Bradford (M-D, NR)
U. of Kent at Canterbury (M-D, SR)

U. of Melbourne (M-D, NR)
U. of New England (B-M, NR)
U. of South Africa (B, NR)
See also **Feminist Law**
See also **Sexuality**

General Studies

Advance Learning Network (B, NR)
Andrews U. (A-B, SR)
Athabasca U. (B, NR)
Brigham Young U. (B, SR)
Capital U. (B, SR)
Charter Oak State C. (B, NR)
City U. (B, NR)
C. of West Virginia (B, NR)
Columbia Union C. (B, NR)
Fort Hays State U. (B, NR)
Hampton U. (B, NR)
Indiana U. (B, NR)
Indiana U. Southeast (B, NR)
Lakehead U. (B, NR)
Montana State U. College of
   Technology (B, NR)
Murdoch U. (B, NR)
Murray State U. (B, SR)
Open U. and Open C. (B, NR)
Simon Fraser U. (B, NR)
Strayer U. (A-B, NR)
Texas Tech U. (B, NR)
U. of Pretoria (B, NR)
U. of South Florida (B, SR)
U. of Southern Queensland (B, NR)

Genetic Counseling

Charles Sturt U. (M, NR)

Genetics

U. of Melbourne (M-D, NR)

Geographic Information Systems

Charles Sturt U. (B, NR)
Manchester Metropolitan U. (M, SR)
U. of Huddersfield (M, NR)
U. of Melbourne (M-D, NR)
U. of Southern Queensland
   (B-M, NR)

Geography

Central Queensland U. (B, NR)
Charter Oak State C. (B, NR)
Macquarie U. (B, NR)
Universidad Nacional de
   Educacion a Distancia (D, SR)
U. of London (B-M, NR)
U. of Luton (M-D, NR)

U. of Manitoba (B, NR)
U. of Melbourne (M-D, NR)
U. of New England (B-M, NR)
U. of Saskatchewan (B, NR)
U. of South Africa (B-M-D, NR)
U. of Wales-Aberystwyth (M-D, SR)
U. of Wales-Lampeter (M-D, NR)
U. of Waterloo (B, NR)

Geological Engineering

U. of Idaho (M, NR)

Geology

Acadia U. (B, SR)
Charter Oak State C. (B, NR)
Excelsior C. (B, NR)
Macquarie U. (B-M, NR)
U. of Luton (M-D, NR)
U. of Melbourne (M-D, NR)
U. of Saskatchewan (B, NR)

Geomatics

See **Geographic Information
   Systems**

German Language and Literature

Charter Oak State C. (B, NR)
Mary Baldwin C. (B, SR)
Queens U. (B, NR)
U. of Kent at Canterbury (M-D, SR)
U. of London (B, NR)
U. of Melbourne (M-D, NR)
U. of New England (B-M, NR)
U. of South Africa (B-M-D, NR)

Gerontology

Charles Sturt U. (B-M, NR)
Edith Cowan U. (B, NR)
Laurentian U. (B, NR)
The Robert Gordon U. (B, SR)
St. Mary-of-the-Woods C. (B, SR)
Thomas Edison State C. (B, NR)
U. of South Alabama (M, NR)
U. of Southern California (M, NR)

Gifted Education

U. of South Africa (B-M-D, NR)
U. of South Alabama (M, NR)
See also **Special Education**

Greek Language and Literature

U. of Melbourne (M-D, NR)
U. of New England (B-M, NR)
U. of South Africa (B-M-D, NR)

Guidance Counseling

City U. (M, NR)
U. of Sarasota (M, SR)
U. of South Africa (M, NR)
U. of Southern Queensland (M, NR)

Health Care

Baker C. (M, NR)
California C. for Health Sciences (B-M, NR)
Central Queensland U. (M, NR)
Clarkson C. (B, NR)
Empire State C. (B, NR)
Flinders U. (M, NR)
Florida Institute of Technology (M, NR)
Franklin U. [Ohio] (B, NR)
Golden Gate U. (M, NR)
Keele U. (M, NR)
Manchester Metropolitan U. (B, SR)
Monterrey Institute for Graduate Studies (M, NR)
Rochester Institute of Technology (M, SR)
St. Joseph's C. (B-M, SR)
Seton Hall U. (M, SR)
Thomas Edison State C. (B, NR)
Trinity U. [Texas] (M, SR)
Tulane U. (D, SR)
Universidad Estatal a Distancia (B-M, NR)
U. of California-Irvine (M, SR)
U. of Central Florida (B, NR)
U. of Colorado at Denver (M, SR)
U. of Dundee (M, NR)
U. of London (M, NR)
U. of Sarasota (M, SR)
U. of St. Francis [Illinois] (B-M, NR)
U. of St. Thomas (M, SR)
U. of South Africa (M, NR)
U. of Southern Queensland (M, NR)
Walden U. (D, SR)

Health Care Law

Kaplan C. (D, NR)

Health Communication Systems

Central Queensland U. (M, NR)
Curtin U. of Technology (M, NR)
Stephens C. (B, SR)

U. of Southern Queensland (M, NR)
U. of Wales-Aberystwyth (M, SR)

Health Education

U. of Dundee (M, NR)
U. of Illinois at Chicago (M, SR)
U. of South Africa (M, NR)
U. of Wyoming (M, SR)

Health Law

See **Medical Law**

Health Psychology

Monterrey Institute for Graduate Studies (M-D, NR)
U. of Kent at Canterbury (M-D, SR)

Health Science

Anglia Polytechnic U. (B, NR)
Athabasca U. (M, NR)
Central Michigan U. (B, NR)
Central Queensland U. (M-D, NR)
Charles Sturt U. (B-M-D, NR)
Curtin U. of Technology (B, SR)
Deakin U. (M-D, NR)
Edith Cowan U. (M, NR)
Florida Gulf Coast U. (B-M, NR)
George Washington U. [D.C.] (B, NR)
Indiana State U. (M, NR)
Nova Southeastern U. (M, SR)
Open U. and Open C. (B, NR)
Ottawa U. (B, SR)
South Bank U. (M-D, SR)
Southern Cross U. (M, SR)
Touro U. International (B-M-D, NR)
U. of Kent at Canterbury (M-D, SR)
U. of Luton (M-D, NR)
U. of St. Augustine for the Health Sciences (M-D, NR)
U. of St. Francis [Illinois] (B, NR)
U. of South Africa (B-M-D, NR)
U. of Technology, Sydney (D, NR)
U. of Teesside (M-D, SR)
Virginia Polytechnic Institute and State U. (M, SR)
Weber State U. (B, SR)

Hebrew Bible

U. of London (B, NR)
U. of Pretoria (B-M-D, NR)
U. of South Africa (B-M-D, NR)

Hebrew Language and Literature

Open U. of Israel (B, NR)

U. of Melbourne (M-D, NR)
U. of South Africa (B-M-D, NR)

History

Acadia U. (B, SR)
American Military U. (M, NR)
Arizona State U. (B, SR)
Atlantic Union C. (B, SR)
Bemidji State U. (B, NR)
Caldwell C. (B, SR)
California State U.-Dominguez Hills (M, NR)
Central Queensland U. (B-M, NR)
Charles Sturt U. (M-D, NR)
Charter Oak State C. (B, NR)
Excelsior C. (B, NR)
Judson C. (B, NR)
Macquarie U. (B-M, NR)
Madurai Kamaraj U. (B-M, NR)
Mary Baldwin C. (B, SR)
Monash U. (B, NR)
Murdoch U. (B, NR)
Open U. and Open C. (B, NR)
Queens U. (B, NR)
Thomas Edison State C. (B, NR)
Universidad Nacional de Educacion a Distancia (D, SR)
U. of Houston (B, NR)
U. of Kent at Canterbury (M-D, SR)
U. of London (B, NR)
U. of Luton (M-D, NR)
U. of Manitoba (B, NR)
U. of Maryland (B, NR)
U. of Melbourne (M-D, NR)
U. of New England (B-M-D, NR)
U. of Pittsburgh (B, SR)
U. of Saskatchewan (B, NR)
U. of South Africa (B-M-D, NR)
U. of Southern Colorado (B, NR)
U. of Teesside (M-D, SR)
U. of Wales-Aberystwyth (M-D, SR)
U. of Wales-Lampeter (M-D, NR)
U. of Waterloo (B, NR)

Hospitality, Food Industry, and Restaurant Management

Charles Sturt U. (B, NR)
Harcourt Learning Direct (A, NR)
New York Institute of Technology (B, NR)
Sheffield Hallam U. (B, SR)
U. of Delaware (B, SR)
U. of Houston (B-M, NR)
U. of London (M, NR)
U. of Wisconsin-Stout (M, NR)
See also **Food Science**
See also **Travel and Tourism**

Human Development

See Developmental Psychology

Human Factors Psychology

U. of Idaho (M, NR)

Human Resource Management

Baker C. (B-M, NR)
Bellevue U. (B, NR)
California National U. for
    Advanced Studies (M, NR)
Central Queensland U. (B-M, NR)
Charles Sturt U. (M, NR)
Colorado State U. (M, NR)
David N. Myers C. (B, NR)
Florida Institute of Technology (M, NR)
Indiana State U. (M, NR)
Keele U. (M, NR)
Keller Graduate School of
    Management (M, NR)
Monash U. (B, NR)
Monterrey Institute for Graduate
    Studies (M, NR)
Ottawa U. (M, SR)
St. Mary-of-the-Woods C. (B, SR)
Seton Hall U. (M, SR)
Sheffield Hallam U. (M, SR)
Sir Joseph Banks C. (NR)
Technikon of Southern Africa
    (B-M-D, NR)
Thomas Edison State C. (B, NR)
U. of Illinois at Urbana-Champaign
    (M, NR)
U. of Leicester (M, NR)
U. of Luton (M-D, NR)
U. of Sarasota (M, SR)
U. of Southern Queensland
    (B-M, NR)
Upper Iowa U. (B, NR)

Human Science

Saybrook Graduate School (M-D, SR)

Human Services

Capella U. (M-D, SR)
Charles Sturt U. (B, NR)
Charter Oak State C. (B, NR)
Concordia U. [Minnesota] (B-M, SR)
Elizabethtown C. (B, SR)
Empire State C. (B, NR)
Prescott C. (B, SR)
St. Mary-of-the-Woods C. (B, SR)
Southern Oregon U. (B, SR)
Upper Iowa U. (B, NR)
Walden U. (D, SR)

Humanities

California State U.-Dominguez
    Hills (M, NR)
Central Queensland U. (M-D, NR)
City U. (B, NR)
National Distance Education
    Centre (B, NR)
Open U. of Hong Kong (B-M-D, NR)
Open U. of Israel (B, NR)
Prescott C. (M, SR)
St. Mary-of-the-Woods C. (B, SR)
Thomas Edison State C. (B, NR)
United States Open U. (B, NR)
U. of Maryland (B, NR)
U. of Melbourne (M-D, NR)
U. of Pittsburgh (B, SR)
U. of Tasmania (M-D, NR)
See also **Liberal Arts**

Individualized Major

Antioch U. (M, SR)
Burlington C. (B, SR)
Capital U. (B, SR)
Charter Oak State C. (B, NR)
Eastern Illinois U. (B, NR)
Empire State C. (B, NR)
Goddard C. (B-M, SR)
Governors State U. (B, NR)
Judson C. (B, NR)
Lesley U. (M, NR)
National Technological U. (M, NR)
Norwich U. (M, SR)
Oklahoma City U. (B, SR)
Rensselaer Polytechnic Institute
    (M, NR)
Rochester Institute of Technology
    (M, SR)
Skidmore C. (B, SR)
Stephens C. (B, SR)
Southwestern Adventist U. (B, SR)
Southwestern Assemblies of God
    U. (B, SR)
Union Institute (B-D, SR)
U. of Wisconsin-Superior (B, SR)
Western Illinois U. (B, NR)
See also **Interdisciplinary Studies**

Indonesian Language and Literature

Monash U. (B, NR)
U. of Melbourne (M-D, NR)
U. of New England (B-M, NR)
U. of Southern Queensland (B, NR)

Industrial Administration

See **Industrial Management**

Industrial Computing

East Carolina U. (M, SR)
U. of Melbourne (M-D, NR)
U. of Southern Queensland (B, NR)

Industrial Engineering

Auburn U. (M, SR)
Colorado State U. (M-D, NR)
East Carolina U. (M, NR)
Georgia Institute of Technology
    (M, NR)
Harcourt Learning Direct (A, NR)
Mississippi State U. (M, SR)
Roger Williams U. (B, NR)
Universidad Nacional de
    Educacion a Distancia (D, SR)
U. of Houston (M, NR)
U. of Northern Iowa (B-M, NR)
Virginia Polytechnic Institute and
    State U. (M, NR)

Industrial Hygiene

Colorado State U. (M, NR)
See also **Occupational Health**

Industrial Management

Baker C. (M, NR)
Central Michigan U. (B, NR)

Industrial Psychology

U. of South Africa (B-M-D, NR)

Industrial Relations

See **Labor Studies and Industrial
    Relations**

Infectious Diseases

U. of London (M, NR)

Information Science

See **Library and Information
    Science**

Information Technology

See **Computer Information
    Systems**
See **Library and Information
    Science**

Instructional Technology

See **Educational Technology**

Instrumentation

Excelsior C. (B, NR)
U. of Southern Queensland
 (B-M, NR)

Insurance and Insurance Law

Regis U. (B, NR)
See also **Risk Management**

Intellectual Property Law

U. of South Africa (M, NR)

Intelligence Studies

American Military U. (M, NR)
Charles Sturt U. (M, NR)
See also **International Relations**

Interdisciplinary Studies

Athabasca U. (M, NR)
California State U.-Chico (M, SR)
C. of West Virginia (B, NR)
Edith Cowan U. (D, NR)
Empire State C. (B, NR)
Florida State U. (B, NR)
New York Institute of Technology
 (B, NR)
U. of Alabama, New C. (B, SR)
U. of Wisconsin-Green Bay (B, SR)
See also **General Studies**
See also **Humanities**
See also **Liberal Studies**

Interior Design

Atlantic Union C. (B, SR)
Rhodec International (B, NR)

International Business

Baker C. (M, NR)
Caldwell C. (B, SR)
Charles Sturt U. (M, NR)
Duke U. (M, SR)
Hope International U. (M, NR)
Monterrey Institute for Graduate
 Studies (M-D, NR)
National Technological U. (M, NR)
Old Dominion U. (B, NR)
Open U. of the Netherlands (M, SR)
Purdue U. (M, SR)
Sheffield Hallam U. (M, SR)
Thomas Edison State C. (B, NR)
U. of London (M, NR)
U. of Luton (M-D, NR)
U. of Maryland (M, NR)

U. of New England (M, NR)
U. of Phoenix (M, NR)
U. of Sarasota (M, SR)
U. of Southern Queensland (M, NR)
U. of Texas at Dallas (M, SR)
U. of Westminster (M, SR)

International Communication

U. of South Africa (B-M-D, NR)

International Law

De Montfort U. (M, NR)
Deakin U. (M, NR)
Regent U. (M, SR)
U. of Leicester (M, NR)
U. of South Africa (M, NR)
U. of Technology, Sydney (D, NR)

International Relations

Mary Baldwin C. (B, SR)
Salve Regina U. (M, SR)
Troy State U. (M, NR)
U. of Kent at Canterbury (M-D, SR)
U. of London (B, NR)
U. of South Africa (B-M-D, NR)
U. of Southern Queensland (B, NR)
U. of Wales-Aberystwyth (M-D, SR)
U. of Wales-Lampeter (M, NR)
See also **Conflict Resolution and
 Peace Studies**
See also **Intelligence Studies**

Internet Engineering

Capitol C. (B, NR)
East Carolina U. (M, NR)
Marlboro C. (M, NR)
Sheffield Hallam U. (M, SR)

Internet Law

U. of Strathclyde (M, NR)

Internet Studies

City U. (B, NR)
Curtin U. of Technology (M-D, NR)
Marlboro C. (M, NR)

Investment Law

Deakin U. (M, NR)

Islamic Studies

U. of Melbourne (M-D, NR)

U. of New England (M, NR)
U. of South Africa (B, NR)
U. of Wales-Lampeter (M-D, NR)

Italian Language and Literature

U. of Kent at Canterbury (M-D, SR)
U. of London (B, NR)
U. of Melbourne (M-D, NR)
U. of New England (B-M, NR)
U. of South Africa (B-M-D, NR)

Japanese Language and Literature

Central Queensland U. (B, NR)
U. of Melbourne (M-D, NR)
U. of New England (B-M, NR)
U. of Wisconsin-Madison (M, NR)

Jewish Education

Spertus C. (M, SR)
See also **Jewish Studies**
See also **Religious Education**

Jewish Studies

Macquarie U. (M, NR)
Open U. of Israel (B, NR)
Spertus C. (M-D, NR)
U. of London (B, NR)
U. of Melbourne (M-D, NR)
U. of South Africa (B-M-D, NR)

Journalism

Central Queensland U. (M-D, NR)
Charles Sturt U. (M, NR)
Deakin U. (B, NR)
Madurai Kamaraj U. (M, NR)
Monash U. (B, NR)
Regent U. (M, NR)
St. Mary-of-the-Woods C. (B, SR)
Thomas Edison State C. (B, NR)
U. of Memphis (M, NR)
U. of Southern Queensland (B, NR)

Kinesiology

Central Queensland U. (B, NR)
U. of Texas (M, NR)
See also **Physical Education**

Labor Studies and Industrial Relations

Charles Sturt U. (M, NR)
Empire State C. (B, NR)

Indiana U. (B, NR)
Keele U. (M, NR)
Thomas Edison State C. (B, NR)
U. of Kent at Canterbury (M-D, SR)
U. of Leicester (M, NR)

Land Warfare

American Military U. (M, NR)

Latin American Studies

U. of London (B, NR)

Latin Language and Literature

Acadia U. (B, SR)
U. of Melbourne (M-D, NR)
U. of New England (B-M, NR)
U. of South Africa (B-M-D, NR)
See also **Classics**

Law

Central Queensland U. (M-D, NR)
Charles Sturt U. (M, NR)
De Montfort U. (M, NR)
Deakin U. (B-M, NR)
FernUniversität (B-M-D, NR)
Holborn C. (B-M, NR)
Kaplan C. (D, NR)
Macquarie U. (B-M, NR)
Madurai Kamaraj U. (B, NR)
Open U. (B-M-D, NR)
Potchefstroom U. for Christian
    Higher Education (B, NR)
Regent U. (M, NR)
Southern Cross U. (M, NR)
Stephens C. (B, SR)
Technikon of Southern Africa
    (B-M-D, NR)
Universidad Nacional de
    Educacion a Distancia (D, SR)
U. of Glasgow (M, NR)
U. of Kent at Canterbury (M-D, SR)
U. of Leicester (M, NR)
U. of London (B-M, NR)
U. of Luton (D, NR)
U. of Melbourne (M-D, NR)
U. of New England (B-M-D, NR)
U. of Pretoria (B, NR)
U. of South Africa (B-M-D, NR)
U. of Southern Queensland (M, NR)
U. of Strathclyde (M, NR)
U. of Tasmania (M-D, NR)
U. of Technology, Sydney (D, NR)
U. of Teesside (M-D, SR)
U. of Wales-Aberystwyth (M-D, SR)
See also **Agriculture Law**
See also **Business Law**

See also **Criminal Justice and Law
    Enforcement**
See also **Criminal Law**
See also **Environmental Law**
See also **Feminist Law**
See also **Finance Law**
See also **Food Law**
See also **Health Care Law**
See also **Insurance and Insurance
    Law**
See also **Intellectual Property Law**
See also **International Law**
See also **Internet Law**
See also **Investment Law**
See also **Legal Psychology**
See also **Medical Law**
See also **Philosophy of Law**
See also **Taxation and Tax Law**
See also **Trade Law**

Law Enforcement

See **Criminal Justice and Law
    Enforcement**

Leadership

Antioch U. (D, SR)
Baker C. (M, NR)
Bellevue U. (B-M, NR)
Duquesne U. (M, NR)
George Fox U. (B, NR)
Global U. of the Assemblies of God
    (M, NR)
Regent U. (M-D, NR)
Royal Roads U. (M, SR)
Southern Christian U. (M, NR)
Strathclyde Graduate Business
    School (M, NR)
U. of Luton (M-D, NR)
U. of Pretoria (M, NR)
U. of Sarasota (D, SR)
U. of South Africa (M-D, NR)
U. of Southern Queensland
    (M-D, NR)
Upper Iowa U. (M, NR)
See also **Educational Leadership
    and Administration**
See also **Management**

Legal Psychology

U. of Leicester (M, NR)

Leisure Studies

Charles Sturt U. (B, NR)
Edith Cowan U. (M, NR)
U. of Luton (M-D, NR)
U. of Technology, Sydney (D, NR)
U. of Teesside (M-D, SR)

Liberal Arts

Excelsior C. (A-B, NR)
Harvard U. (B-M, SR)
Northeastern Illinois U. (B, SR)
Norwich U. (B, SR)
Prescott C. (B, SR)
Syracuse U. (A-B, SR)
Taylor U. (A, SR)
Texas Christian U. (M, NR)
United States Open U. (B, NR)

Liberal Studies

California Institute of Integral
    Studies (B, SR)
California State U.-Fresno (B, NR)
Charter Oak State C. (B, NR)
Duquesne U. (M, NR)
Empire State C. (M, SR)
Excelsior C. (M, NR)
Fort Hays State U. (M, NR)
Framingham State C. (B, SR)
Graceland C. (B, SR)
Iowa State U. (B, SR)
Montana State U.-Billings (B, NR)
New School University (B, NR)
Oral Roberts U. (B, NR)
Pennsylvania State U. (B, NR)
St. Joseph's C. (B, SR)
Salve Regina U. (B, SR)
Skidmore C. (M, SR)
Teikyo Loretto Heights C. (B, SR)
Thomas Edison State C. (B, NR)
U. of Central Florida (B, NR)
U. of Illinois at Springfield (B, NR)
U. of Iowa (B, NR)
U. of Northern Iowa (B, NR)

Library and Information Science

Central Queensland U. (M, NR)
Charles Sturt U. (M-D, NR)
Connecticut State U. (M, NR)
Curtin U. of Technology (M, NR)
Drexel U. (M, NR)
Edith Cowan U. (M, NR)
Florida State U. (B-M, NR)
Madurai Kamaraj U. (B-M, NR)
Monash U. (M, NR)
Nova Southeastern U. (M-D, SR)
San Jose State U. (M, SR)
Syracuse U. (M, SR)
U. of Arizona (M-D, SR)
U. of Illinois at Urbana-Champaign
    (M, SR)
U. of Northern Iowa (M, NR)
U. of Pretoria (B, NR)
U. of South Africa (B-M-D, NR)
U. of Wales-Aberystwyth
    (B-M-D, SR)

U. of Wisconsin-Milwaukee (M, NR)

Linguistics

Edith Cowan U. (M, NR)
Macquarie U. (M, NR)
Monash U. (M, NR)
U. of Luton (M-D, NR)
U. of Melbourne (M-D, NR)
U. of New England (B-M-D, NR)
U. of Pretoria (M, NR)
U. of South Africa (B-M-D, NR)
See also **Applied Linguistics**

Literacy Education

City U. (M, NR)
Edith Cowan U. (M-D, NR)
Indiana U. (M, NR)
Macquarie U. (M, NR)
U. of Technology, Sydney (D, NR)
U. of Texas (M, NR)

Literary Theory

Central Queensland U. (B, NR)
U. of Luton (M-D, NR)
U. of South Africa (B-M-D, NR)
See also **Comparative Literature**

Logistics, Decision Sciences, and Operations Management

Charles Sturt U. (M, NR)
Kettering U. (M, NR)
Monash U. (M, NR)
National Distance Education
  Centre (M, NR)
Thomas Edison State C. (B, NR)
U. of Southern Queensland (B, NR)
Walden U. (D, SR)
See also **Project Management**

Management

American Military U. (B-M, NR)
Bellevue U. (B, NR)
Caldwell C. (B, SR)
Canadian School of Management
  (B-M, NR)
Capital U. (B, SR)
Central Queensland U. (B, NR)
Champlain C. (B, NR)
Charles Sturt U. (B-M-D, NR)
Cheltenham Tutorial C. (M, NR)
City U. (B-M, NR)
Colorado State U. (M, NR)
David N. Myers C. (B, NR)
Edith Cowan U. (B, NR)
Empire State C. (B, NR)

Florida Institute of Technology
  (M, NR)
International Management Centres
  (B-M, SR)
Kaplan C. (B, NR)
Malone C. (B, SR)
Marywood U. (B, SR)
Monterrey Institute for Graduate
  Studies (M-D, NR)
National-Louis U. (B, NR)
Northwood U. (B, SR)
Old Dominion U. (B, NR)
Open U. of Israel (B, NR)
Park C. (B, SR)
Prescott C. (B, SR)
Purdue U. (M, SR)
Regent U. (M, SR)
Regis U. (B, NR)
Rensselaer Polytechnic Institute
  (M, NR)
Salve Regina U. (M, SR)
Southern Oregon U. (B, SR)
Technikon of Southern Africa
  (B-M-D, NR)
Thomas Edison State C. (M, SR)
Universidad Estatal a Distancia
  (B-M, NR)
U. of Action Learning (B- M, NR)
U. of Bradford (M-D, NR)
U. of Dallas (M, NR)
U. of Kent at Canterbury (M-D, SR)
U. of London (B-M, NR)
U. of Luton (M-D, NR)
U. of Maryland (B-M, NR)
U. of Melbourne (M-D, NR)
U. of Phoenix (B-M, NR)
U. of St. Francis [Illinois] (M, NR)
U. of Sarasota (B, SR)
U. of South Africa (B-M-D, NR)
U. of South Australia (D, NR)
U. of Southern Queensland
  (B-M, NR)
U. of Tasmania (M-D, NR)
U. of Technology, Sydney (D, NR)
U. of Wisconsin-Whitewater (M, NR)
Upper Iowa U. (B, NR)
Walden U. (D, SR)
Western Baptist C. (B, SR)
See also **Business Administration**

Management Information Systems

Bellevue U. (B, NR)
Deakin U. (M, NR)
Franklin U. [Ohio] (B, NR)
Judson C. (B, NR)
Keller Graduate School of
  Management (M, NR)
Nova Southeastern U. (M, SR)
U. of Illinois at Springfield (M, NR)

U. of London (B, NR)
U. of Maryland (B-M, NR)
See also **Business Information Systems**
See also **Technology Management**

Manufacturing and Manufacturing Engineering

Brunel U. (M, NR)
East Carolina U. (M, SR)
Excelsior C. (B, NR)
Kettering U. (M, NR)
National Technological U. (M, NR)
Rensselaer Polytechnic Institute
  (M, NR)
Southern Methodist U. (M, SR)
Thomas Edison State C. (B, NR)
U. of Luton (M-D, NR)
U. of Melbourne (M-D, NR)
U. of South Australia (M, NR)
U. of Technology, Sydney (D, NR)
Washington State U. (B, NR)

Manufacturing Management

Kettering U. (M, NR)
Southern Methodist U. (M, SR)
U. of South Australia (M, NR)

Maritime Management

Cheltenham Tutorial C. (M, NR)

Marketing

American Military U. (B, NR)
Baker C. (M, NR)
Caldwell C. (B, SR)
Central Queensland U. (B, NR)
Charles Sturt U. (B-M, NR)
City U. (B-M, NR)
Curtin U. of Technology (B, SR)
David N. Myers C. (B, NR)
Deakin U. (M, NR)
Edith Cowan U. (B, NR)
Golden Gate U. (M, NR)
Mary Baldwin C. (B, SR)
Marywood U. (B, SR)
Mercy C. (M, NR)
Monash U. (B, NR)
Monterrey Institute for Graduate
  Studies (M-D, NR)
Northwood U. (B, SR)
Nova Southeastern U. (M, SR)
Old Dominion U. (B, NR)
St. Mary-of-the-Woods C. (B, SR)
Sheffield Hallam U. (M, SR)
Strayer U. (A-B-M, NR)
Syracuse U. (M, SR)

Technikon of Southern Africa
(B-M, NR)
Thomas Edison State C. (A-B, NR)
U. of Leicester (M, NR)
U. of Luton (M-D, NR)
U. of Melbourne (M-D, NR)
U. of New England (M, NR)
U. of Phoenix (B, NR)
U. of Pretoria (M, NR)
U. of Sarasota (M, SR)
U. of Southern Queensland
(B-M, NR)
U. of Technology, Sydney (D, NR)
U. of Teesside (M-D, SR)
U. of Wisconsin-Whitewater (M, NR)
Upper Iowa U. (B, NR)

Mass Communication and Media Studies

Curtin U. of Technology (B-M-D, NR)
Madurai Kamaraj U. (M, NR)
Monash U. (B, NR)
New School University (M, NR)
U. of Bradford (M-D, NR)
U. of Leicester (M, NR)
U. of Luton (M-D, NR)
U. of Melbourne (M-D, NR)
U. of Southern Queensland
(B-M, NR)
U. of Technology, Sydney (D, NR)
U. of Teesside (M-D, SR)
See also **Communication**
See also **Internet Studies**

Materials Engineering

Auburn U. (M, SR)
Columbia U. (M, NR)
Illinois Institute of Technology (M, NR)
National Technological U. (M, NR)
Southern Methodist U. (M, SR)
Thomas Edison State C. (B, NR)
U. of London (M, NR)
U. of Technology, Sydney (D, NR)

Mathematics

Acadia U. (B, SR)
Central Queensland U. (B-M-D, NR)
Charles Sturt U. (B, NR)
Charter Oak State C. (B, NR)
Excelsior C. (B, NR)
FernUniversität (B-M-D, NR)
Madurai Kamaraj U. (B-M, NR)
Mary Baldwin C. (B, SR)
Monash U. (B, NR)
Montana State U.-Bozeman (M, SR)
Murdoch U. (B, NR)
Open U. and Open C. (B, NR)
Open U. of Hong Kong (B-M-D, NR)

Open U. of Israel (B, NR)
St. Mary-of-the-Woods C. (B, SR)
Thomas Edison State C. (B, NR)
U. of Bradford (M-D, NR)
U. of Kent at Canterbury (M-D, SR)
U. of London (B, NR)
U. of Melbourne (M-D, NR)
U. of New England (B-M-D, NR)
U. of Saskatchewan (B, NR)
U. of South Africa (B-M-D, NR)
U. of Southern Queensland (B, NR)
U. of Technology, Sydney (D, NR)
U. of Wales-Aberystwyth (M-D, SR)

Mathematics Education

Edith Cowan U. (M-D, NR)
U. of Idaho (M, NR)
U. of Melbourne (M-D, NR)
U. of Northern Iowa (M, NR)
U. of South Africa (M, NR)

Mechanical Engineering

Auburn U. (M, SR)
California National U. for
Advanced Studies (B-M, NR)
Colorado State U. (M-D, NR)
Columbia U. (M, NR)
Excelsior C. (B, NR)
Florida State U. (M, NR)
Georgia Institute of Technology
(M, NR)
Harcourt Learning Direct (A, NR)
Kettering U. (M, NR)
Michigan Technological U. (D, SR)
Mississippi State U. (M, SR)
Monash U. (B, NR)
National Technological U. (M, NR)
Naval Postgraduate School (M, NR)
Old Dominion U. (M, NR)
Rensselaer Polytechnic Institute
(M, NR)
Rochester Institute of Technology
(B, SR)
Southern Methodist U. (M, SR)
Thomas Edison State C. (B, NR)
U. of Bradford (M-D, NR)
U. of Colorado at Boulder (M, NR)
U. of Delaware (M, SR)
U. of Idaho (M, NR)
U. of Illinois at Urbana-Champaign
(M, NR)
U. of Melbourne (M-D, NR)
U. of North Dakota (B, SR)
U. of South Carolina (M, SR)
U. of Southern Queensland
(B-M, NR)
U. of Technology, Sydney (D, NR)
U. of Wisconsin-Madison (M, SR)

Virginia Polytechnic Institute and
State U. (M, NR)

Media Arts

U. of Luton (M-D, NR)
U. of Melbourne (M-D, NR)
U. of Technology, Sydney (D, NR)
See also **Mass Communication and
Media Studies**

Medical Ethics

See **Bioethics**

Medical Imaging

Anglia Polytechnic U. (M, NR)
Charles Sturt U. (B-M, NR)
Clarkson C. (B, NR)
See also **Dental Radiology**
See also **Radiology**

Medical Law

U. of Glasgow (M, NR)

Medieval Studies

U. of Kent at Canterbury (M-D, SR)
U. of Melbourne (M-D, NR)
U. of Waterloo (B, NR)

Mental Health

Charles Sturt U. (B, NR)
New York Institute of Technology
(B, NR)
Thomas Edison State C. (B, NR)
U. of Kent at Canterbury (M-D, SR)
U. of Sarasota (M, SR)
U. of South Africa (M, NR)

Metallurgical Engineering

Murdoch U. (B, NR)
U. of Idaho (M, NR)

Meteorology

Mississippi State U. (M, SR)
U. of Melbourne (M-D, NR)

Microbiology and Molecular Biology

Lehigh U. (M, NR)
U. of Kent at Canterbury (M-D, SR)
U. of Melbourne (M-D, NR)
U. of New England (B-M, NR)

U. of Saskatchewan (B, NR)
U. of Technology, Sydney (D, NR)

Microelectronics

Rensselaer Polytechnic Institute
(M, NR)
U. of Pretoria (B-M, SR)

Midwifery

Flinders U. (B-M, NR)
The Robert Gordon U. (B, SR)
U. of Dundee (B, SR)
U. of Southern Queensland (M, NR)
U. of Technology, Sydney (D, NR)

Military History

American Military U. (B-M, NR)

Mining

U. of Idaho (M, NR)
U. of Southern Queensland (B, NR)

Ministry

American Bible C. and Seminary
(D, NR)
Atlantic Union C. (B, SR)
Charles Sturt U. (M, NR)
Drew U. (D, SR)
Franciscan U. of Steubenville (M, SR)
Global U. of the Assemblies of God
(B-M, NR)
Hope International U. (M, NR)
Lee U. (B, NR)
St. Joseph's C. (M, SR)
St. Mary-of-the-Woods C. (M, SR)
Southern Christian U. (M-D, NR)
Spurgeon's C. (M, SR)
U. of Otago (M, NR)
See also **Cross-Cultural Ministry**
See also **Divinity**
See also **Evangelism**
See also **Pastoral Counseling**
See also **Religious Education**

Molecular Biology

See **Microbiology and Molecular
Biology**

Moral Theology

U. of South Africa (B-M-D, NR)

Museum Studies

U. of Leicester (M, NR)

Music

California State U.-Dominguez
Hills (M, NR)
Duquesne U. (M, SR)
Excelsior C. (B, NR)
Judson C. (B, NR)
Mary Baldwin C. (B, SR)
Norwich U. (M, SR)
Open U. and Open C. (B, NR)
U. of New England (B-M-D, NR)
U. of Saskatchewan (B, NR)
U. of South Africa (B-M-D, NR)

Music Education

Duquesne U. (M, SR)
Edith Cowan U. (M-D, NR)
Judson C. (B, NR)
U. of Northern Iowa (M, NR)
U. of Pretoria (M, NR)

Mythology

Pacifica Graduate Institute (M-D, SR)

Naval Warfare

American Military U. (M, NR)

New Testament Studies

Global U. of the Assemblies of God
(M, NR)
U. of London (B, NR)
U. of South Africa (B-M-D, NR)

Nonprofit Management

Hope International U. (M, NR)
Regis U. (M, NR)
See also **Organizational
Management**

Nuclear Engineering

Excelsior C. (B, NR)
Thomas Edison State C. (B, NR)

Nursing

Athabasca U. (B, NR)
California State U.-Dominguez
Hills (B-M, NR)
Capital U. (B, SR)
Case Western Reserve U. (M-D, SR)
Central Queensland U. (M-D, NR)

Charles Sturt U. (B, NR)
Clarkson C. (B-M, NR)
C. of West Virginia (B, NR)
Curtin U. of Technology (B-M, NR)
Deakin U. (M-D, NR)
Duquesne U. (B-D, NR)
Eastern New Mexico U. (B, SR)
Eastern Oregon U. (B, SR)
Edith Cowan U. (B-M-D, NR)
Excelsior C. (A-B-M, NR)
Flinders U. (B-M, NR)
Graceland C. (B-M, SR)
Indiana State U. (M, SR)
Indiana U. (M, NR)
Kaplan C. (B, NR)
Kentucky Commonwealth Virtual
U. (B, NR)
Lakehead U. (B, SR)
Laurentian U. (B, NR)
Liverpool John Moores U. (B, SR)
Loyola U. [Louisiana] (B, SR)
Memorial U. of Newfoundland (B, NR)
Mississippi U. for Women (B, SR)
Monash U. (B-M, NR)
Montana State U.-Bozeman
(B-M, SR)
Montana State U.-Northern (B, NR)
National Distance Education
Centre (B, NR)
National U. [California] (B-M, NR)
Northern Territory U. (B, NR)
Old Dominion U. (B-M, NR)
Open U. and Open C. (B, NR)
Open U. of Hong Kong (B-M-D, NR)
Potchefstroom U. for Christian
Higher Education (B, NR)
The Robert Gordon U. (B-M, SR)
St. Francis Xavier U. (B, SR)
St. Joseph's C. (B-M, SR)
Salve Regina U. (B, SR)
San Jose State U. (M, SR)
Southern Cross U. (B, SR)
Southern Oregon U. (B, SR)
Syracuse U. (M, SR)
Texas Christian U. (M, NR)
Thomas Edison State C. (B, NR)
U. of Central Florida (B, NR)
U. of Delaware (B-M, SR)
U. of Dundee (B, SR)
U. of Manitoba (B, NR)
U. of Melbourne (M-D, NR)
U. of Northern Colorado (B, NR)
U. of Phoenix (B-M, NR)
U. of Pretoria (B, NR)
U. of Saskatchewan (B, NR)
U. of South Africa (M, NR)
U. of South Alabama (B-M, NR)
U. of South Australia (B, NR)
U. of Southern Queensland
(B-M, NR)
U. of Technology, Sydney (D, NR)

U. of Teesside (M-D, SR)
U. of Victoria (B, NR)
U. of Wyoming (B-M, SR)

Nutrition

Acadia U. (B, SR)
American Health Science U.
  (Cert, NR)
Central Michigan U. (M, NR)
Deakin U. (M-D, NR)
Keele U. (M, NR)
Pennsylvania State U. (B, NR)
South Bank U. (M-D, SR)
Thomas Edison State C. (B, NR)
U. of Bridgeport (M, NR)

Occupational Health

Curtin U. of Technology (M, NR)
Edith Cowan U. (M-D, NR)
McGill U. (M, SR)
Nova Southeastern U. (M-D, SR)
Robert Gordon U. (B, SR)
San Jose State U. (M, SR)
Tulane U. (M, NR)
U. of London (M, NR)
U. of Southern Queensland (M, NR)
See also **Industrial Hygiene**
See also **Occupational Safety**

Occupational Psychology

See **Industrial Psychology**

Occupational Safety

Central Missouri State U. (M, NR)
Curtin U. of Technology (M, NR)
East Carolina U. (M, SR)
Edith Cowan U. (M-D, NR)
U. of Southern Queensland (M, NR)
See also **Industrial Hygiene**
See also **Occupational Health**

Ocean Engineering

Virginia Polytechnic Institute and
  State U. (M, NR)

Old Testament

See **Hebrew Bible**

Oncology

Robert Gordon U. (B, SR)
U. of Bradford (M-D, NR)
U. of Glasgow (M, NR)

Open and Distance Education

See **Distance Education**

Optical Engineering

Excelsior C. (B, NR)
National Technological U. (M, NR)

Organizational Development

Fielding Institute (M-D, SR)
Saybrook Graduate School (M-D, SR)
U. of Leicester (M, NR)

Organizational Management

Advance Learning Network (B, NR)
Charter Oak State C. (B, NR)
Hope International U. (B, NR)
Pfeiffer U. (M, NR)
Regent U. (M, NR)
Southern Cross U. (M, NR)
Thomas Edison State C. (B, NR)
U. of Phoenix (M-D, NR)
See also **Management**
See also **Nonprofit Management**

Organizational Psychology

Kansas State U. (M, NR)
U. of London (M, NR)

Orthodontics and Prosthodontics

U. of London (M, NR)
U. of Pretoria (M, NR)

Packaging Technology

Brunel U. (M, NR)
See also **Manufacturing**

Pain Management

U. of Glasgow (M, NR)

Palliative Care

Edith Cowan U. (M, NR)
U. of Dundee (M, NR)

Paralegal Studies

Crown C. (A, NR)
St. Mary-of-the-Woods C. (B, SR)
U. of Maryland (B, NR)

Pareschatology

U. of Wales-Lampeter (M, NR)

Pastoral Counseling

Atlantic U. (M, NR)
Global U. of the Assemblies of God
  (B-M, NR)
Oral Roberts U. (B, NR)
Southern Christian U. (M, NR)
U. of Sarasota (D, SR)
U. of South Africa (M-D, NR)

Peace Studies

See **Conflict Resolution and Peace
  Studies**
See **Gandhian Thought**

Penology

U. of South Africa (B-M-D, NR)

Petroleum Engineering

Texas Tech U. (M, NR)

Pharmaceutical Chemistry

Lehigh U. (M, NR)
U. of Manchester (M, SR)

Pharmacy

De Montfort U. (M, NR)
Duquesne U. (D, NR)
Keele U. (M, NR)
Potchefstroom U. for Christian
  Higher Education (B, NR)
Purdue U. (D, SR)
Queen's U. of Belfast (M, NR)
Robert Gordon U. (M, SR)
U. of Bradford (M-D, NR)
U. of Florida (D, NR)
U. of Manchester (M, NR)
U. of Melbourne (M-D, NR)
U. of Montana (D, SR)
U. of South Australia (B, NR)
U. of Tasmania (M-D, NR)
U. of Wisconsin-Madison (D, SR)
Washington State U. (D, SR)

Philosophy

Capital U. (B, SR)
California Institute of Integral
  Studies (M-D, SR)
California State U.-Dominguez
  Hills (M, NR)
Charter Oak State C. (B, NR)

Christopher Newport U. (B, NR)
Eastern Oregon U. (B, NR)
Excelsior C. (B, NR)
International Catholic U. (M, NR)
Madurai Kamaraj U. (M, NR)
Mary Baldwin C. (B, SR)
Murdoch U. (B, NR)
St. Mary-of-the-Woods C. (B, SR)
Stephens C. (B, SR)
Thomas Edison State C. (B, NR)
Universidad Nacional de
  Educacion a Distancia (D, SR)
U. of Glasgow (M, NR)
U. of Kent at Canterbury (M-D, SR)
U. of London (B, NR)
U. of Manitoba (B, NR)
U. of Melbourne (M-D, NR)
U. of New England (B, NR)
U. of Saskatchewan (B, NR)
U. of South Africa (B-M-D, NR)
U. of Wales-Lampeter (M-D, NR)
U. of Waterloo (B, NR)

Philosophy of Education

U. of South Africa (M-D, NR)

Philosophy of Law

South Bank U. (M-D, SR)
U. of Kent at Canterbury (M-D, SR)
U. of South Africa (M, NR)

Physical Education

Atlantic Union C. (B, SR)
Eastern Oregon U. (B, NR)
Edith Cowan U. (M-D, NR)
Emporia State U. (M, NR)
South Bank U. (M-D, SR)
U. of Melbourne (M-D, NR)
Virginia Polytechnic Institute and
  State U. (M, SR)
See also **Kinesiology**

Physical Therapy

Indiana U. (M, NR)
Nova Southeastern U. (M-D, SR)
U. of Melbourne (M-D, NR)
U. of St. Augustine for Health
  Sciences (D, SR)
See also **Therapeutic Recreation**

Physics

Acadia U. (B, SR)
Central Queensland U. (B-M-D, NR)
Charter Oak State C. (B, NR)
Excelsior C. (B, NR)

Georgia Institute of Technology
  (M, NR)
Illinois Institute of Technology (M, SR)
Mary Baldwin C. (B, SR)
Murdoch U. (B, NR)
Thomas Edison State C. (B, NR)
U. of Kent at Canterbury (M-D, SR)
U. of Melbourne (M-D, NR)
U. of South Africa (B-M-D, NR)
U. of Technology, Sydney (D, NR)
U. of Wales-Aberystwyth (M-D, SR)

Polish Language and Literature

U. of Melbourne (M-D, NR)

Political Science, Public Policy, and Social Policy

Acadia U. (B, SR)
Caldwell C. (B, SR)
Capital U. (B, SR)
Charles Sturt U. (B-M-D, NR)
Charter Oak State C. (B, NR)
Christopher Newport U. (B, NR)
Eastern Oregon U. (B, NR)
Empire State C. (B, NR)
Excelsior C. (B, NR)
Macquarie U. (B, NR)
Madurai Kamaraj U. (B-M, NR)
Mary Baldwin C. (B, SR)
Monash U. (M, NR)
Murdoch U. (B, NR)
Queens U. (B, NR)
Regent U. (M, SR)
South Bank U. (M-D, SR)
Thomas Edison State C. (B, NR)
Universidad Nacional de
  Educacion a Distancia (D, SR)
U. of Kent at Canterbury (M-D, SR)
U. of London (B, NR)
U. of Luton (M-D, NR)
U. of Manitoba (B, NR)
U. of Melbourne (M-D, NR)
U. of New England (B-M-D, NR)
U. of Pretoria (M-D, NR)
U. of South Africa (B-M-D, NR)
U. of Southern Colorado (B, NR)
U. of Wales-Lampeter (M-D, NR)
Virginia Polytechnic Institute and
  State U. (M, NR)

Polymer Science and Engineering

De Montfort U. (M, NR)
Lehigh U. (M, NR)

Portuguese Language and Literature

U. of Melbourne (M-D, NR)
U. of South Africa (B-M-D, NR)

Post-Colonial Literature

South Bank U. (M-D, SR)

Practical Theology

Regent U. (M, SR)
St. Mary-of-the-Woods C. (M, SR)
U. of South Africa (B-M-D, NR)

Preprimary Education

Atlantic Union C. (B, SR)
Charles Sturt U. (B, NR)
Edith Cowan U. (M-D, NR)
Elizabethtown C. (B, SR)
Macquarie U. (B-M-D, NR)
Nova Southeastern U. (B, SR)
St. Mary-of-the-Woods C. (B, SR)
U. of South Africa (B, NR)
U. of South Australia (B, NR)

Primary Education

Atlantic Union C. (B, SR)
Central Queensland U. (B, NR)
Charles Sturt U. (B, NR)
Judson C. (B, NR)
Murdoch U. (B-M, NR)
Nova Southeastern U. (B, SR)
Oral Roberts U. (B, NR)
Pennsylvania State U. (M, SR)
St. Mary-of-the-Woods C. (B, SR)
Universidad Estatal a Distancia
  (B-M, NR)
U. of Leicester (M, NR)
U. of Northern Iowa (B, NR)
U. of South Africa (B, NR)

Professional Studies

See **Applied and Professional Studies**

Project Management

American Graduate U. (M, NR)
Capitol C. (M, NR)
City U. (M, NR)
George Washington U. [D.C.] (M, SR)
Henley Management C. (M, NR)
Keller Graduate School of
  Management (M, NR)
Kettering U. (M, NR)
Mississippi State U. (M, NR)

National Technological U. (M, NR)
U. of Bradford (M-D, NR)
U. of Melbourne (M-D, NR)
U. of Pretoria (M, NR)
U. of South Africa (M, NR)
U. of South Australia (M, NR)
U. of Southern Queensland (M, NR)
U. of Wisconsin-Platteville (M, NR)

Prosthodontics

See **Orthodontics and
Prosthodontics**

Psychology and Behavioral Science

Acadia U. (B, SR)
Antioch University (M, SR)
Atlantic Union C. (B, SR)
Burlington C. (B, SR)
Caldwell C. (B, SR)
California Institute of Integral
Studies (M-D, SR)
California State U.-Chico (M, NR)
California State U.-Dominguez
Hills (M, NR)
Capella U. (M-D, SR)
Capital U. (B, SR)
Charles Sturt U. (B-M-D, NR)
Charter Oak State C. (B, NR)
City U. (M, NR)
Columbia Union C. (B, NR)
Curtin U. of Technology (B, SR)
Edith Cowan U. (B. NR)
Excelsior C. (B, NR)
Institute of Transpersonal
Psychology (M, NR)
Judson C. (B, NR)
Kansas State U. (M, NR)
Laurentian U. (B, NR)
Liberty U. (B, SR)
Mary Baldwin C. (B, SR)
Mercy C. (B, NR)
Monash U. (B, NR)
Monterrey Institute for Graduate
Studies (M-D, NR)
New York Institute of Technology
(B, NR)
Open U. and Open C. (B, NR)
Pacifica Graduate Institute (M-D, SR)
Prescott C. (M, SR)
Queens U. (B, NR)
St. Mary-of-the-Woods C. (B, SR)
Saybrook Graduate School (M-D, SR)
Stephens C. (B, SR)
Thomas Edison State C. (B, NR)
U. of Houston (B, NR)
U. of Idaho (M, NR)
U. of Kent at Canterbury (M-D, SR)
U. of Leicester (M, NR)

U. of Luton (M-D, NR)
U. of Manitoba (B, NR)
U. of Maryland (B, NR)
U. of Melbourne (M-D, NR)
U. of New England (B, NR)
U. of Pittsburgh (B, SR)
U. of Pretoria (M, NR)
U. of Saskatchewan (B, NR)
U. of Sheffield (M, SR)
U. of South Africa (B-M-D, NR)
U. of Southern Colorado (B, NR)
U. of Southern Queensland (B, NR)
U. of Tasmania (M-D, NR)
U. of Teesside (M-D, SR)
U. of Waterloo (B, NR)
Walden U. (M-D, SR)
See also **Clinical Psychology**
See also **Counseling**

Psychology of Religion

Monterrey Institute for Graduate
Studies (D, NR)

Public Administration

Andrew Jackson U. (M, NR)
California State U.-Northridge
(M, NR)
Central Michigan U. (B-M, NR)
Christopher Newport U. (B, NR)
Elizabethtown C. (B, SR)
Florida Institute of Technology (M, NR)
Golden Gate U. (B-M, NR)
Madurai Kamaraj U. (M, NR)
Potchefstroom U. for Christian
Higher Education (M, NR)
Regent U. (M, SR)
Roger Williams U. (B, NR)
Thomas Edison State C. (B, NR)
U. of London (M, NR)
U. of Luton (M-D, NR)
U. of South Africa (B-M-D, NR)
Upper Iowa U. (B, NR)
Valdosta State U. (M, NR)

Public Health

Charles Sturt U. (B, NR)
Curtin U. of Technology (M, NR)
Edith Cowan U. (M, NR)
Loma Linda U. (M, NR)
Murdoch U. (M, NR)
Tulane U. (M, NR)
U. of Glasgow (M, NR)
U. of London (M, NR)
U. of Melbourne (M-D, NR)
U. of Pretoria (M, NR)

Public Order

U. of Leicester (M, NR)
See also **Criminal Justice and Law
Enforcement**

Public Relations

Capital U. (B, SR)
Curtin U. of Technology (B, SR)
Deakin U. (B, SR)
Madurai Kamaraj U. (M, NR)
U. of Memphis (M, NR)
U. of Northern Iowa (M, NR)
U. of Southern Queensland
(B-M, NR)
U. of Teesside (M-D, SR)

Quality Assurance and Engineering

California National U. for
Advanced Studies (B-M, NR)
California State U.-Dominguez
Hills (B-M, NR)
Lehigh U. (M, NR)
Liverpool John Moores U. (B, SR)
Rensselaer Polytechnic Institute
(M, NR)
Sheffield Hallam U. (M, SR)

Race Relations

South Bank U. (M-D, SR)

Radiology

Anglia Polytechnic U. (B-M, NR)
Georgia Institute of Technology
(M, NR)
Medical C. of Georgia (B, NR)
Thomas Edison State C. (B, NR)
U. of London (M, NR)
Weber State U. (B, SR)
See also **Dental Radiology**
See also **Medical Imaging**

Real Estate

C. of Estate Management (M, NR)
Thomas Edison State C. (B, NR)
U. of Pretoria (M, NR)

Religion and International Relations

U. of Wales-Lampeter (M, NR)

Religious Education

Australian Catholic U. (B, NR)

Concordia U. (B-M, SR)
Edith Cowan U. (M-D, NR)
Global U. of the Assemblies of God
  (B-M, NR)
Griggs U. (B, NR)
Judson C. (B, NR)
Loyola U. (M, NR)
Maryvale Institute (B-M-D, SR)
Regent U. (M, SR)
Spertus C. (M, NR)
U. of Glasgow (M, NR)

Religious Studies

Andrews U. (B, SR)
Atlantic Union C. (B, SR)
Caldwell C. (B, SR)
California Institute of Integral
  Studies (M-D, SR)
Capital U. (B, SR)
Catholic Distance U. (M, NR)
Charter Oak State C. (B, NR)
Christopher Newport U. (B, NR)
Columbia Union C. (B, NR)
Griggs U. (B, NR)
Judson C. (B, NR)
Laurentian U. (B, NR)
Liberty U. (B-M, SR)
Loyola U. (M, NR)
Madurai Kamaraj U. (M, NR)
Mary Baldwin C. (B, SR)
Thomas Edison State C. (B, NR)
U. of Kent at Canterbury (M-D, SR)
U. of New England (B-M-D, NR)
U. of Saskatchewan (B, NR)
U. of South Africa (B-M-D, NR)
U. of Wales-Lampeter (M-D, NR)
U. of Waterloo (B, NR)

Respiratory Care

California C. for Health Sciences
  (B, NR)
Charles Sturt U. (M, NR)
Columbia Union C. (B, NR)
Open U. and Open C. (B, NR)
Weber State U. (B, SR)

Rheumatology

U. of Bath (M, SR)

Risk Management

U. of Leicester (M, NR)
See also **Insurance and Insurance
  Law**

Robotics

Excelsior C. (B, NR)

Monash U. (B, NR)
U. of Pretoria (B, NR)
U. of Southern Queensland
  (B-M, NR)

Rural Development

Charles Sturt U. (M, NR)
U. of London (M, NR)
U. of Melbourne (M-D, NR)
U. of New England (B, NR)
U. of South Africa (B, NR)
See also **Development Studies and
  Sustainable Agriculture**

Rural Health

Monash U. (M, NR)
U. of Southern Queensland (M, NR)

Russian Language and Literature

U. of Melbourne (M-D, NR)
U. of South Africa (B-M-D, NR)

Science Education

Curtin U. of Technology (M, NR)
Edith Cowan U. (M-D, NR)
Montana State U.-Bozeman (M, SR)
Nova Southeastern U. (B, SR)
U. of Melbourne (M-D, NR)
U. of South Africa (M, NR)

Scottish Literature

U. of Glasgow (M, NR)

Secondary Education

Central Queensland U. (B, NR)
Judson C. (B, NR)
Murdoch U. (M, NR)
Nova Southeastern U. (B, SR)
U. of South Africa (B, NR)

Secretarial Science

C. of West Virginia (B, NR)

Security Management

U. of Leicester (M, NR)
U. of Pretoria (M, NR)

Semitic Languages and Literature

U. of South Africa (B-M-D, NR)

See also **Arabic Language and
  Literature**
See also **Hebrew Language and
  Literature**

Sexuality

Laurentian U. (Cert., NR)
South Bank U. (M-D, SR)
Universidad Nacional de
  Educacion a Distancia (M, SR)

Social Sciences

Bemidji State U. (B, NR)
Caldwell C. (B, SR)
Charles Sturt U. (B-M, NR)
City U. (B, NR)
Curtin U. of Technology (B, NR)
Edith Cowan U. (M, NR)
Florida State U. (B, NR)
Kansas State U. (B, NR)
Madurai Kamaraj U. (M, NR)
Open U. of Israel (B, NR)
Southern Cross U. (B, NR)
Syracuse U. (M, SR)
United States Open U. (B, NR)
Universidad Nacional de
  Educacion a Distancia (D, SR)
U. of Luton (M-D, NR)
U. of Maryland (B, NR)
U. of New England (B, NR)
U. of Otago (M, NR)
U. of Pittsburgh (B, SR)
U. of Pretoria (B, NR)
U. of South Africa (B-M-D, NR)
U. of South Australia (M, NR)
U. of Southern Colorado (B, NR)
U. of Teesside (M-D, SR)
Upper Iowa U. (B, NR)
Washington State U. (B, NR)

Social Work

Capital U. (B, SR)
Charles Sturt U. (B-M-D, NR)
Curtin U. of Technology (B, SR)
James Cook U. (M-D, NR)
Lakehead U. (B, NR)
Laurentian U. (B, NR)
Memorial U. of Newfoundland (B, NR)
Monash U. (B, NR)
Universidad Estatal a Distancia
  (B-M, NR)
U. of Alaska (B, NR)
U. of Kent at Canterbury (M-D, SR)
U. of Manitoba (B, NR)
U. of Melbourne (M-D, NR)
U. of South Africa (B-M-D, NR)
U. of Victoria (B, NR)

Sociolinguistics

U. of South Africa (M, NR)

Sociology

Acadia U. (B, SR)
Caldwell C. (B, SR)
Capital U. (B, SR)
Central Queensland U. (B, NR)
Charter Oak State C. (B, NR)
Edith Cowan U. (B, NR)
Excelsior C. (B, NR)
Laurentian U. (B, NR)
Madurai Kamaraj U. (M, NR)
Mary Baldwin C. (B, SR)
Monash U. (B, NR)
Murdoch U. (B, NR)
New York Institute of Technology
   (B, NR)
Open U. and Open C. (B, NR)
South Bank U. (M-D, SR)
Thomas Edison State C. (B, NR)
U. of Kent at Canterbury (M-D, SR)
U. of Leicester (M, NR)
U. of London (B, NR)
U. of Luton (M-D, NR)
U. of Manitoba (B, NR)
U. of Melbourne (M-D, NR)
U. of New England (B-M, NR)
U. of Saskatchewan (B, NR)
U. of South Africa (B-M-D, NR)
U. of Southern Colorado (B, NR)
U. of Waterloo (B, NR)

Software Engineering

Capitol C. (B, NR)
Carnegie Mellon U. (M, NR)
Florida State U. (B, NR)
Kansas State U. (M, NR)
Murdoch U. (B-M, NR)
National Technological U. (M, NR)
Naval Postgraduate School (M, NR)
Rochester Institute of Technology
   (M, SR)
Southern Methodist U. (M, SR)
Technical U. of British Columbia
   (M, SR)
Texas Tech U. (M, NR)
U. of Maryland (M, NR)
U. of Melbourne (M-D, NR)
U. of Southern Queensland (B, NR)

Space Studies

U. of North Dakota (M, SR)
See also **Aerospace Engineering**
See also **Astronomy**

Spanish Language and Literature

Charter Oak State C. (B, NR)
Mary Baldwin C. (B, SR)
U. of Kent at Canterbury (M-D, SR)
U. of London (B, NR)
U. of Melbourne (M-D, NR)
U. of South Africa (B-M-D, NR)
See also **Catalan Language and
   Literature**
See also **Latin American Studies**

Special Education

Charles Sturt U. (M, NR)
Edith Cowan U. (B-M-D, NR)
Flinders U. (B-M-D, NR)
Griffith U. (M, NR)
Nova Southeastern U. (B, SR)
St. Mary-of-the-Woods C. (B, SR)
U. of Birmingham (B-M, NR)
U. of Northern Colorado (M, NR)
U. of Northern Iowa (M, NR)
U. of South Africa (B-M-D, NR)
U. of South Alabama (M, NR)
U. of Southern Queensland (M, NR)

Speech Pathology

California State U.-Northridge
   (M, NR)
Macquarie U. (M, NR)
See also **Communication Disorders**

Spirituality

U. of South Africa (M-D, NR)

Sport, Sport Sociology, and Sport Management

Edith Cowan U. (M, NR)
South Bank U. (M-D, SR)
United States Sports Academy
   (M, SR)
U. of Dallas (M, NR)
U. of Leicester (M, NR)
U. of Pretoria (B, NR)
U. of Technology, Sydney (D, NR)
U. of Teesside (M-D, SR)

Sports Medicine

U. of Bath (M, SR)

Statistics

Colorado State U. (M, NR)
Macquarie U. (M, NR)
Monash U. (B, NR)

Murdoch U. (B, NR)
Rochester Institute of Technology
   (M, SR)
Sheffield Hallam U. (M, SR)
U. of Kent at Canterbury (M-D, SR)
U. of London (B, NR)
U. of Melbourne (M-D, NR)
U. of New England (M, NR)
U. of South Africa (B-M-D, NR)
U. of Southern Queensland (B, NR)
U. of Technology, Sydney (D, NR)

Surveying

Central Queensland U. (B, NR)
Michigan Technological U. (B, SR)
Thomas Edison State C. (B, NR)
U. of Southern Queensland (B, NR)
U. of Tasmania (M-D, NR)

Systematic Theology

U. of South Africa (B-M-D, NR)

Systems Engineering

Colorado State U. (M-D, SR)
National Technological U. (M, NR)
Rensselaer Polytechnic Institute
   (M, NR)
Southern Methodist U. (M, SR)
U. of Southern Queensland
   (B-M, NR)
U. of Technology, Sydney (D, NR)
Virginia Polytechnic Institute and
   State U. (M, NR)

Systems Management

Florida Institute of Technology (M, NR)
Hampton U. (B, NR)
National Technological U. (M, NR)
Naval Postgraduate School (M, NR)
Texas Tech U. (M, NR)
U. of Maryland (M, NR)

Taxation and Tax Law

Golden Gate U. (M, NR)
Regent U. (M, NR)
U. of Pretoria (M, NR)
U. of South Africa (M, NR)

Teaching

Charles Sturt U. (B, NR)
De Montfort U. (M, NR)
Edith Cowan U. (B-M-D, NR)
Grand Canyon U. (M, NR)
U. of Saskatchewan (B, NR)
U. of South Africa (B-M-D, NR)

U. of Southern Queensland (M, NR)
See also **Education**

Teaching English as a Second or Foreign Language

Aston U. (M, NR)
Deakin U. (M, NR)
Macquarie U. (M, NR)
U. of Birmingham (M, NR)
U. of Southern Queensland (M, NR)
U. of Texas (M, NR)

Technical Writing

Sheffield Hallam U. (M, SR)
Utah State U. (M, NR)
See also **Writing**

Technology Management

Colorado State U. (M, NR)
Drexel U. (M, NR)
Griffith U. (M, NR)
Indiana State U. (D, SR)
Kaplan C. (B, NR)
Keller Graduate School of
    Management (M, NR)
Lehigh U. (M, NR)
Massachusetts Institute of
    Technology (M, SR)
Monash U. (M, NR)
Technical U. of British Columbia
    (M, SR)
U. of Maryland (M, NR)
U. of Phoenix (M, NR)
U. of Southern Queensland (B, NR)
U. of Waterloo (M, NR)
See also **Engineering Management**
See also **Systems Management**
See also **Telecommunications and**
    Telecommunications
    Management

Telecommunications and Telecommunications Management

California State U.-Chico (M, SR)
Capitol C. (M, NR)
Champlain C. (B, NR)
City U. (B, NR)
Golden Gate U. (M, NR)
Keller Graduate School of
    Management (M, NR)
Murdoch U. (M, NR)
Southern Methodist U. (M, SR)
Syracuse U. (M, SR)
U. of Colorado at Boulder (M, NR)
U. of Dallas (M, NR)
U. of Denver (M, NR)

U. of Maryland (M, NR)
U. of Technology, Sydney (D, NR)

Thanatology

U. of Wales-Lampeter (M, NR)

Theater Studies

See **Drama and Theater Studies**

Theology and Theological Studies

Atlantic Union C. (B, SR)
Charles Sturt U. (B-M, NR)
Columbia Union C. (B, NR)
Franciscan U. of Steubenville (M, SR)
Global U. of the Assemblies of God
    (B, NR)
Greenwich School of Theology
    (B-M-D, NR)
Griggs U. (B, NR)
International Catholic U. (M, NR)
Maryvale Institute (B-M-D, SR)
Murdoch U. (B, NR)
Potchefstroom U. for Christian
    Higher Education (B, NR)
Regent U. (M, SR)
St. Mary-of-the-Woods C. (B-M, SR)
Spurgeon's C. (M, SR)
U. of Kent at Canterbury (M-D, SR)
U. of Otago (B, NR)
U. of South Africa (B-M-D, NR)
U. of Wales-Lampeter (M-D, NR)

Therapeutic Recreation

Indiana U. (M, NR)
See also **Leisure Studies**
See also **Physical Therapy**

Therapeutics

Keele U. (M, NR)

Third World Studies

South Bank U. (M-D, SR)

Tourism

See **Travel and Tourism**

Trade Law

Deakin U. (M, NR)

Transpersonal Studies

Atlantic U. (M, NR)
Burlington C. (B, SR)
Naropa U. (M, SR)

Transportation Management

American Military U. (M, NR)
Monash U. (M, NR)
San Jose State U. (M, SR)
South Bank U. (M-D, SR)
Thomas Edison State C. (B, NR)
U. of South Africa (B, NR)

Travel and Tourism

Canadian School of Management
    (B-M, NR)
Central Queensland U. (B, NR)
C. of West Virginia (B, NR)
Monash U. (B, NR)
Sheffield Hallam U. (M, SR)
Southern Cross U. (B-M, NR)
U. of Luton (M-D, NR)
U. of Technology, Sydney (D, NR)
U. of Teesside (M-D, SR)
U. of Wisconsin-Stout (M, NR)

Travel Medicine

U. of Glasgow (M, NR)

Ukrainian Language and Literature

U. of Melbourne (M-D, NR)

Unconventional Warfare

American Military U. (M, NR)

Urban Ministry

U. of South Africa (M-D, NR)
See also **Cross-Cultural Ministry**
See also **Evangelism**

Veterinary Science

Charles Sturt U. (B, NR)
Kansas State U. (B, NR)
Murdoch U. (M, NR)
Purdue U. (A, SR)
U. of London (M, NR)
U. of Melbourne (M-D, NR)

Vocational Rehabilitation/Education

U. of Central Florida (B-M, NR)

Utah State U. (M, SR)

Web Site Development

Champlain C. (B, NR)
See also **Internet Engineering**

Welsh Language and Literature

U. of Wales-Aberystwyth (M-D, SR)

Women's Studies

See **Gender and Women's Studies**

Writing

Antioch U. (M, SR)

Burlington C. (B, SR)
California State U.-Chico (M, SR)
Goddard C. (M, SR)
Goucher C. (M, SR)
Monash U. (B, NR)
Norwich U. (M, SR)
U. of Melbourne (M-D, NR)
Utah State U. (M, NR)

Xhosa Language and Literature

U. of South Africa (B-M-D, NR)

Youth Studies and Youth Work

Brunel U. (B-M, NR)
Concordia U. (B-M, SR)

De Montfort U. (M, NR)
Edith Cowan U. (B, NR)
Nova Southeastern U. (M-D, SR)
U. of Victoria (B, NR)
U. of Wyoming (B, SR)

Zoology

U. of Melbourne (M-D, NR)
U. of New England (M, NR)

Zulu Language and Literature

U. of Pretoria (B-M, NR)
U. of South Africa (B-M-D, NR)

Coming Soon: The Bear Index of the Acceptability of Schools

One of the most common questions we get relates to the acceptability of a given school or degree program: "Will I be able to use it to transfer credits, or get into graduate school, or get a better job," etc. For years, all we could do was warn people to satisfy themselves of a degree's usability before they plunged into the program; meanwhile, we wished and waited for someone to do some comprehensive research on the acceptability of degrees from different kinds of schools.

Well, we got tired of waiting, and decided to take the, um, bear by the horns and do it ourselves. A major research project is underway, in which we are collecting data from a large number of university registrars and admissions officers, and from company human resource managers, regarding the acceptability of a wide range of schools, from regionally accredited to DETC-accredited to California-approved to Caribbean-registered, and many others. By the next edition, we hope and plan to have a zero-to-100 acceptance score for each school:

	Acceptance in academic world	Acceptance in in business world
American Plugmore University	**53%**	**81%**

These data may also be made available on our Web site, *www.degree.net*, before the next edition is published.

School Index

This is an index to all the schools listed in chapters 13, 18–27, and 31, as well as Appendixes D and E. Schools mentioned incidentally in other chapters are not indexed.

Q

R

Our Third Cartoon Caption Contest

The rules: Write a caption for this cartoon, preferably something related to distance learning. The best one wins a free copy of the 15th edition of Bears' Guide (in which it will be printed, with byline) plus a free lunch with the authors, in the event everyone happens to be in the same city at the same time. Send entries to Cartoon Contest, Bears' Guide, Ten Speed Press, P.O. Box 7123, Berkeley CA 94707, or email to *johnandmariah@degree.net*. Decision of judges is final. See the winner of the last contest on page 269.

More career and job-hunting guides from Ten Speed Press

What Color Is Your Parachute?
by Richard Nelson Bolles

With over six million copies in print, *What Color Is Your Parachute?* is the best-selling job-hunting book in the world. Richard Nelson Bolles helps you identify what your skills are, where your skills can best be used, and how you can find jobs that use those skills. In the end, you won't just have a job; you'll be engaged in work you love.
$16.95, ISBN 1-58008-242-4

The Career Guide for Creative and Unconventional People
by Carol Eikleberry, Ph.D.

Career expert Carol Eikleberry escorts readers through a proven step-by-step program aimed at locating and securing one of those artistically oriented jobs that many fantasize about but few actually pursue.
$11.95, ISBN 1-58008-075-8

High-Tech Careers for Low-Tech People
by William A. Schaffer

Author Bill Schaffer, a manager at Sun Microsystems, demystifies the high-tech industry, discusses the jobs that are available to those without a background in technology, and details successful strategies for getting hired. A one-of-a-kind resource for anyone eager to take advantage of the limitless opportunities in technology.
$14.95, ISBN 1-58008-039-1

Games Companies Play
by Dr. Pierre Mornell

Following up on his critically acclaimed *Hiring Smart*, business guru Pierre Mornell jumps to the other side of the interview table to share his knowledge of the hiring process with job-hunters of all levels. This indispensable guide is packed with street-smart advice on taking the plunge into a new career, readying the necessary resumes, cover letters, and recommendations, shining in the toughest of interview situations, and closing the deal on a dream job.
$24.95, ISBN 1-58008-183-5

Major in Success
by Patrick Combs

Whatever the dream, whatever the major, whatever the age, *Major in Success* has the answers. With cool job and internship ideas, smart strategies for overcoming fears, hot tips on interviewing, and directions to the best job-hunting Web sites, this savvy and inspiring guide will help job hunters discover their passions and excel in life.
$11.95, ISBN 1-58008-209-2

A Foot in the Door
by Katharine Hansen

Career counselors hype "networking" as the most effective means of uncovering hidden career opportunities, but for job hunters who are new to an industry, this advice begs the question: "Where to begin?" Career expert Katharine Hansen explains networking in a detailed, step-by-step fashion, showing job seekers the ins and outs of getting that foot in the door—and kicking it wide open!
$14.95, ISBN 1-58008-140-1

Damn Good Resume Guide
by Yana Parker

A longtime best-seller widely regarded as the best in the field, this crash course in resume writing addresses the two major types of resumes (functional and chronological) and shows how to tailor-make either one to your specific situation.
$7.95, ISBN 0-89815-672-6

Rewrite Right!
by Jan Venolia

Everyone knows that writing can be improved by the simple process of reviewing, editing, and rewriting, but many struggle with how to go about critiquing their own work. This practical guide describes in clear, direct language how to effectively rewrite whatever you've written, whether it's an admissions essay, master's thesis, or cover letter.
$12.95, ISBN 1-58008-239-4

Available at your local bookstore, on our Web site at *www.degree.net*, or direct from the publisher.

 Ten Speed Press
P.O. Box 7123 • Berkeley, CA 94707 • (800) 841-BOOK

More books on distance learning and alternative education from Degree.net and Ten Speed Press

Bears' Guide to the Best Computer Degrees by Distance Learning
by John Bear, Ph.D., Mariah Bear, M.A., and Larry McQueary

It's a sizzling job market for the high-tech elite. Companies everywhere are begging for software designers, database programmers, Web site builders, network administrators, and IT professionals. *Best Computer Degrees* maps the most direct route to those top dollar salaries, showing you how to earn a fully accredited undergraduate or graduate high-tech degree without setting foot on a college campus.
$17.95, ISBN 1-58008-221-1

Bears' Guide to the Best MBAs by Distance Learning
by John Bear, Ph.D., and Mariah Bear, M.A.

In this booming economy, fast-growing companies are paying top dollar for the business savvy of MBA holders. But who wants to carve out the two years and fork over the $60,000 it typically takes to get one? In this book, John and Mariah show you how to earn a fully accredited and widely respected MBA in as little as a year and for under $10,000—and you can do it while remaining fully employed.
$17.95, ISBN 1-58008-220-3

College Degrees by Mail and Internet
by John Bear, Ph.D., and Mariah Bear, M.A.

The Bears narrow down the field to 100 of the best accredited distance-learning programs in the world. Opinionated and conversational, *College Degrees by Mail and Internet* covers bachelor's, master's, doctoral, and law degrees that can be earned almost entirely by correspondence or over the Internet.
$14.95, ISBN 1-58008-217-3

Cool Colleges
by Donald Asher

This unprecedented guide to the "coolest" colleges profiles 40 of the most innovative and unusual schools in the country. From studying on a cattle ranch to spending winters snowed in with classmates on a mountain in Vermont, *Cool Colleges* is the place for students to find education opportunities as unorthodox as they are.
$19.95, ISBN 1-58008-150-9

Available at your local bookstore, on our Web site at *www.degree.net*, or direct from the publisher.

 Ten Speed Press
P.O. Box 7123 • Berkeley, CA 94707 • (800) 841-BOOK

Free update to Bears' Guide ...
on the Internet, or in your mailbox.

The world of distance learning changes fast: new schools, both good and bad; changed addresses and phones and Web sites; new accreditation information; and so on. You can get up-to-date information either from the Internet on a continuing basis, or from a free update we will mail you at the end of the year 2001.

Online: Go to http://www.degree.net/updates and register. Then return to the site for updates as often as you want.

By mail: Mail us this postcard, and we'll be in touch in late 2001.

Name _____

Address _____
<small>Street / Apartment</small>

_____
<small>City   State   Zip   Country</small>

Email _____

Degree.net
Ten Speed Press
P.O. Box 7123
Berkeley, CA 94707
USA